Fodor's

WALT DISNEY WORLD

Welcome to Walt Disney World

Little did we realize that the emergence of a novel coronavirus in early 2020 would abruptly bring almost all travel to a halt. Although our Fodor's writers around the world have continued working to bring you the best of the destinations they cover, we still anticipate that more than the usual number of businesses will close permanently in the coming months, perhaps with little advance notice. We don't expect things to return to "normal" for some time. As you plan your upcoming travels to Walt Disney World and Orlando, please confirm that places are still open and let us know when we need to make updates by writing to us at this address: editors@fodors.com.

TOP REASONS TO GO

★ **Walt Disney World:** Quite simply, the magic of the Disney parks touches all who visit.

★ **Universal Orlando:** Islands of Adventure and Universal Studios are high-energy fun.

★ **Resorts:** Elaborately themed resorts offer visitors fun and memorable experiences.

★ **International Drive:** Bustling strip with attractions like Fun Spot and Aquatica.

★ **Downtown Orlando:** Top restaurants, theater, and music create a thriving scene.

★ **LEGOLAND Florida:** A unique family-friendly theme park with fun rides, shows, and attractions.

Contents

Fodor's Features

MAPS

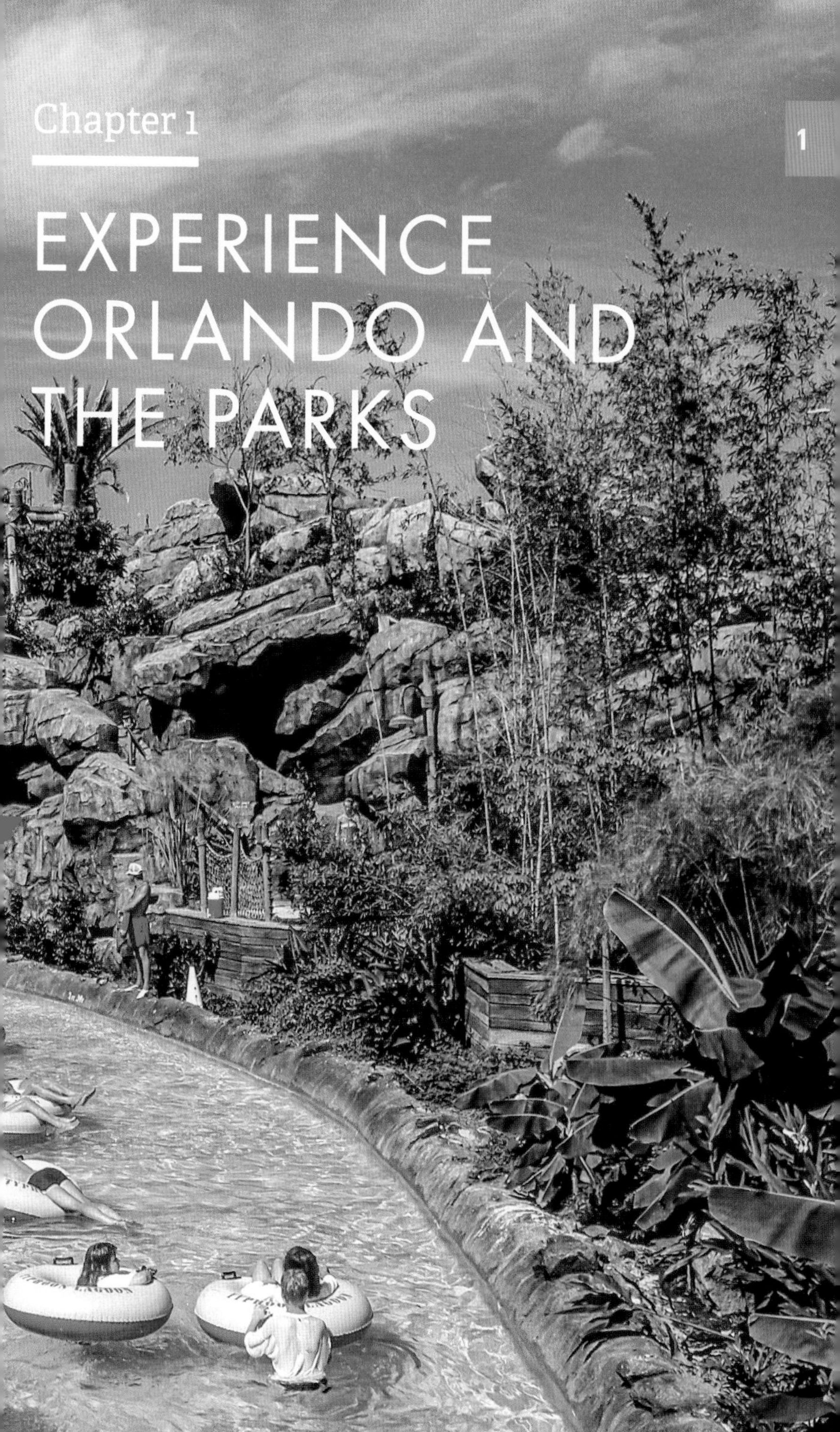

Chapter 1

EXPERIENCE ORLANDO AND THE PARKS

25 ULTIMATE EXPERIENCES

Walt Disney World offers terrific experiences that should be on every traveler's list. Here are Fodor's top picks for a memorable trip.

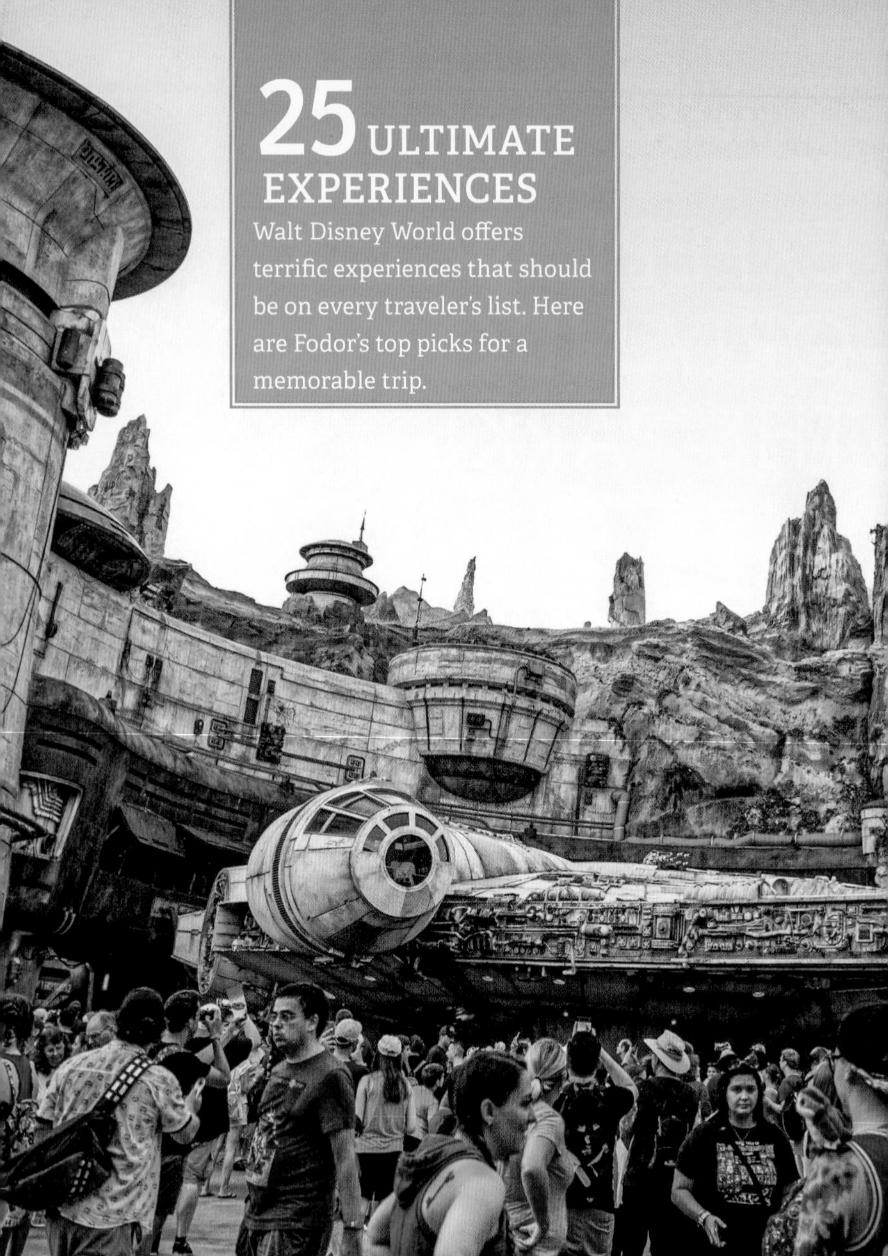

1 Galaxy's Edge

Walt Disney World's newest land is devoted to a galaxy far far away and features two of the park's most impressive and technologically advanced rides. *(Ch. 5.)*

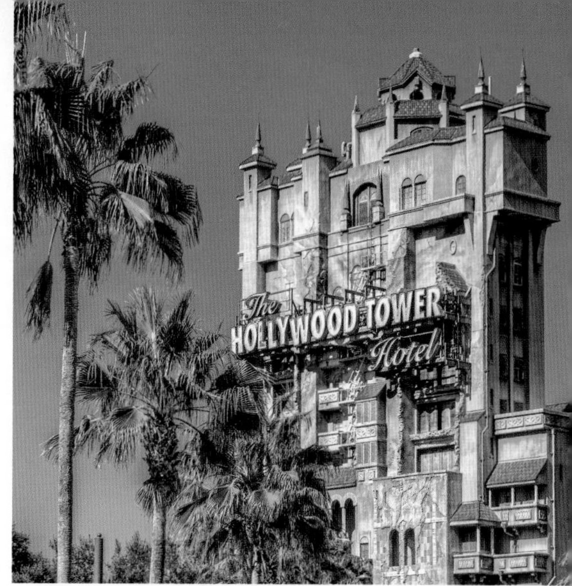

2 Ride the Tower of Terror

This classic takes you on a stomach-flipping elevator ride into the Twilight Zone. The best part? It's different every single time you ride it. *(Ch. 5)*

3 Channel your Inner Child

Dedicated to your favorite building blocks, the sprawling LEGOLAND theme park, 45 minutes from Orlando, is a great non- Disney option if you have younger kids. *(Ch. 11)*

4 Let It Go

After you've ridden Frozen Ever After, you can meet Anna and Elsa at Royal Summerhus just next door in EPCOT's Norway pavilion. *(Ch. 4)*

5 Rivers of Light

If you're looking for a seated and more understated way to end your day, Animal Kingdom's Rivers of Light offers beautiful music and visuals. *(Ch. 6)*

6 Experience Pandora

Animal Kingdom's newest section includes Avatar Flight of Passage, in addition to the otherworldly beauty of Pandora's bioluminescent flora and fauna. *(Ch. 6)*

7 Visit Winter Park

The lovely small town of Winter Park is one of the region's hidden gems, a great place to spend some quality family time and take a scenic boat ride across the town lake. *(Ch. 11)*

8 Ride Jurassic Park

At Universal Islands of Adventure, you can ride on a river past dinosaurs both gentle and scary, ending your journey with an 85-foot plunge. You will get wet. *(Ch. 9)*

9 A Night at CityWalk

Like Disney Springs, Universal's outdoor mall is full of shops, restaurants, and entertainment, but the experience feels more Las Vegas than Orlando. *(Ch. 9)*

10 Kayak the Wekiwa River

Wekiwa Springs State Park, an hour from Orlando, gives you a break from the go-go-go vibe in all the parks, with plenty of space to enjoy a quiet river adventure. *(Ch. 11)*

11 Stroll Down a Garden Path

If theme parks aren't your thing, you can relax in more than 50 acres of lush greenery at the Harry P. Leu Gardens, which offer flora and fauna from all over the world. *(Ch. 10)*

12 Get Spooked

No matter the time of year, the Haunted Mansion is a classic that can't be missed. It's more fun than spooky and definitely good for the whole family. *(Ch. 3)*

13 Stay at a Disney Resort

Staying at a Disney-owned resort gives you free transportation, early access to reservations, extra time at the parks, and a free Magic Band regardless of the price point. *(Ch. 3, 4, 6, 7)*

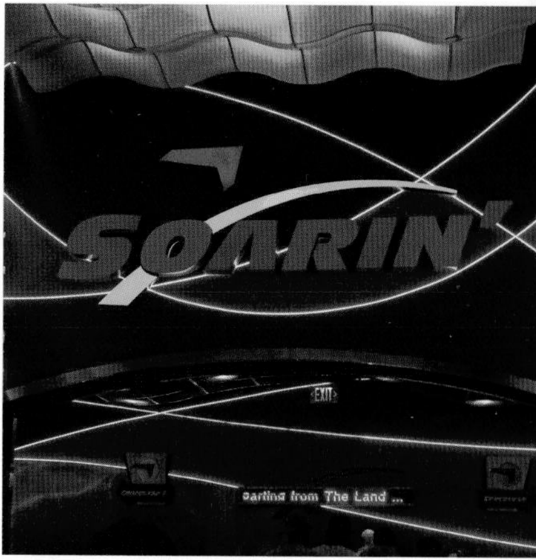

14 Soar Over the World

Soarin' lets you travel around the world on a simulated hang-glider, offering 180-degree panoramas and other special effects. You'll feel like you're really flying. *(Ch. 4)*

15 Ride the Waves

If you'd rather cool your heels and the rest of you in the waves, try one of Disney's two water parks or the new Volcano Bay at Universal. *(Ch. 5, 7, 9)*

16 Get Happily Ever After

For the quintessential Disney fireworks experience, the Magic Kingdom has a new animated spectacular that provides a fitting end to a fun day. *(Ch. 3)*

17 Be Their Guest

The Magic Kingdom's most popular restaurant is worth the time and trouble for a great prix-fixe breakfast, lunch, or dinner. Try the grey stuff—it's delicious! *(Ch. 3)*

18 A Night at Disney Springs

Disney's expanded and reinvigorated dining and shopping megacomplex is a fitting way to end your day with a meal, a movie, or a stroll. *(Ch. 7)*

19 Explore Everest

Journey to the summit of the world's highest peak at Animal Kingdom's exciting thrill ride, which moves both backward and forward. *(Ch. 6)*

20 Dine (or Drink) Around the World

With 8 restaurants in Future World and more than 25 in World Showcase, EPCOT allows you to eat a wide variety of cuisines, from American to Mexican to Moroccan. *(Ch. 4)*

21 Toy Story Land

Explore Andy's backyard and ride Slinky Dog Dash or the Alien Flying Saucers as you enjoy Pixar's movieland. *(Ch. 5)*

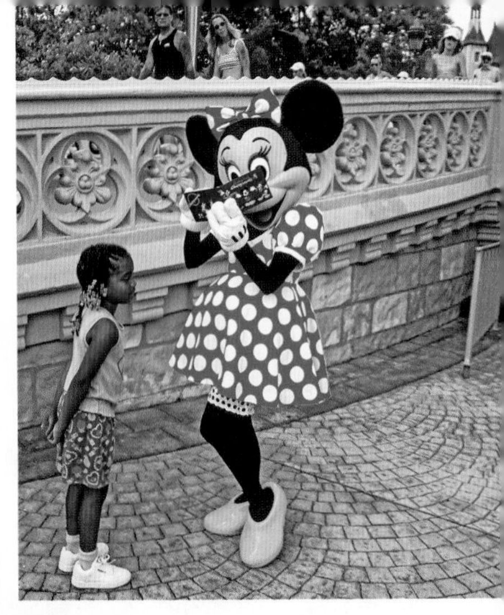

22 Meet the Characters

One of the best parts of going to Disney? Meeting beloved characters—from Minnie and Mickey to your favorite princess—and getting a hug and an autograph. *(Ch. 3, 4, 5, 6)*

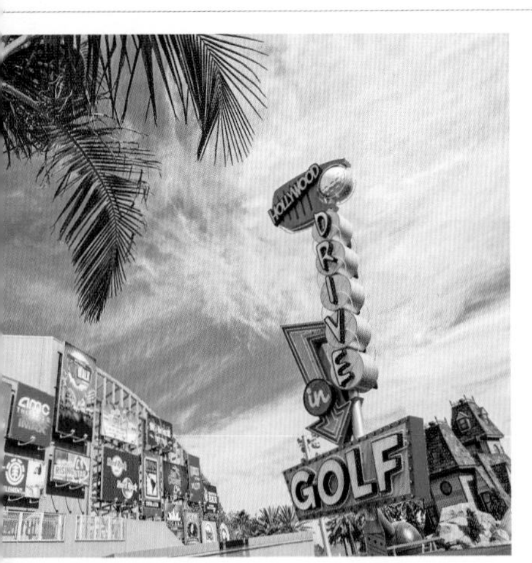

23 Putt Putt Your Way to Victory

If you're looking to hit the links but limit yourself to a putter, Orlando has you covered—from Walt Disney World to International Drive—with more than a dozen courses. *(Ch. 4, 5, 8, 9, 10)*

24 Ride the Mega Coasters

Universal Orlando is home to two of the country's biggest and most exciting rollercoasters: The Incredible Hulk Coaster and the Hollywood Rip Ride Rockit. *(Ch. 9)*

25 Get the Harry Potter Experience

Harry is the biggest draw at Universal Orlando Resort, whether you're going to Hogsmeade at Islands of Adventure or Diagon Alley at Universal Studios. *(Ch. 9)*

What's New in Orlando and the Parks

Prior to 1971, Orlando was a quiet town whose main industry was citrus. There was a new interstate highway and a nature park where you could see alligators, but that was about it. But then came Walt Disney World. The boom in tourism meant the city needed a more modern airport and new hotels. That, of course, meant Orlando would need more workers, which meant more housing and successively more theme parks, malls, as well as arts, culture, and industry to keep things going. Change is a constant in Orlando, and the city you see in the 2020s will transform gradually and constantly every year as the pace of growth increases. By 2021, a modern new terminal at Florida's busiest airport, Orlando International, will make its premiere to increase its capacity by 10 million more travelers each year.

And there are always new shows, events, and attractions at the theme parks as creative teams at Disney and Universal try to out-tech and out-dazzle each other—as evidenced in their open rivalry. When Universal was creating its Wizarding Worlds, Disney responded with the world of Pandora. As Universal continues to enhance all things Potter with new attractions like Hagrid's Magical Creatures Motorbike Adventure, Disney counters by applying its distinctive creativity to Marvel, *Star Wars*, and Disney film–theme experiences.

UNEXPECTED CLOSURES

The Covid-19 pandemic put the Magic Kingdom and all the other theme parks, attractions, restaurants, and many hotels in Orlando under lockdown during the spring of 2020. It was the biggest blow to tourism in Orlando since 9/11, and the ultimate effects are still being felt.

WALT DISNEY WORLD

Just as Universal holds a monopoly on the highly creative (and lucrative) Harry Potter lands, Disney now has the wildly popular Pandora–The World of Avatar at Animal Kingdom as well an ever-increasing number of attractions devoted to Marvel and Star Wars, in addition to its already impressive heritage of classic Disney characters.

In 2019 it premiered Star Wars: Galaxy's Edge at Disney's Hollywood Studios, where the signature attractions are Star Wars: Rise of the Resistance and Millennium Falcon: Smugglers Run. Also at the center of Disney's Hollywood Studios, Mickey & Minnie's Runaway Railroad opened in Spring 2020 to become the first-ever Disney attraction to star Mickey and his best girl. Each evening at the Studios, the Wonderful World of Animation is a tribute to nearly 100 years of Disney and Pixar animation from Sleeping Beauty to the Incredibles. In early 2020, Cirque du Soleil (whose level of creativity and innovation rivals Disney's) launched the new show, Drawn to Life, at its iconic theater at the Disney Springs entertainment complex.

For its anniversary in 2021, Disney will complete a major EPCOT reconstruction project that has involved transforming half of the park once known as Future World into three distinct new neighborhoods: World Discovery, World Nature, and World Celebration, whose focal point, Spaceship Earth, is being given a new guide and all-new narration that focuses on bringing people together through storytelling. At Mission: SPACE, the Space 220 restaurant offers a culinary experience that's out of this world—literally, as it appears as if you're dining 220 miles above the Earth. A Beauty and the Beast Sing-Along show was added to the France pavilion along with the new attraction Remy's Ratatouille Adventure and new restaurant, La Crêperie de Paris. The Canada pavilion premiered a new Circle-Vision-360 film, while down the street in the United Kingdom a Mary Poppins Attraction is being developed on Cherry Tree Lane. Halfway around the World Showcase, Wondrous China is a visually stunning 70-mm film that carries you on a breathtaking journey across the country.

Outside the theme parks, another high-flying attraction is the Disney Skyliner, a scenic gondola ride that opened in 2019 to connect Disney's Hollywood Studios and the International Gateway at EPCOT to Disney's Caribbean Beach Resort, Disney's Art of Animation Resort, Disney's Pop Century Resort, and the new Disney's Riviera Resort.

And, in a bit of retro-futuristic nostalgia, guests in the Magic Kingdom will soon be able to board a line of two-wheeled Lightcycles and speed off into the high-tech universe at the TRON Lightcycle Run, a ride first developed at Shanghai Disneyland. What's next? Who knows? Disney never stops dreaming.

UNIVERSAL ORLANDO

Working to keep pace with Disney (just as Disney works to keep pace with it), Universal Orlando completed several large-scale projects and announced several others, which will be taking shape into the early 2020s, most notably the addition of a fourth theme park—Epic Universe—which is set to open in 2023 with new attractions, shops, entertainment, and restaurants.

In Islands of Adventure, Hagrid's Magical Creatures Motorbike Adventure became the latest epic attraction to enhance The Wizarding World of Harry Potter with a trip beyond the grounds of Hogwarts castle and into the Forbidden Forest. Next door at Universal Studios, the Bourne Stuntacular is a live-action stunt show based on the blockbuster Bourne film franchise. In addition, a Velocicoaster is under construction in Jurassic Park. With new parks and attractions comes a need for more accommodations, which Universal accomplished by razing the landmark Wet n' Wild water park and replacing it with Endless Summer, whose two distinct resort hotels—Surfside and Dockside—combine to offer 2,800 rooms for relatively reasonable rates.

BEYOND THE THEME PARKS

Not all the local developments are happening at the city's two largest theme parks. Music legend Jimmy Buffett turned his songs about Key West into an empire, and at his highly themed, 175-room Margaritaville Orlando Resort, the new, 14-acre Island H2O Live! Water park features waterslides, a lazy river, and live entertainment. On International Drive, you won't miss the Orlando StarFlyer, which, incredibly, towers over the nearby 400-foot-tall Wheel at ICON Park. At 450-feet, the world's tallest swing ride carries you to the top of the tower whereyou're spun out into space at speeds up to 60 miles per hour—a thrill that competes with its ICON Park neighbor, the Orlando Slingshot that'll propel you 450 feet straight up. These compete with a *third* attraction here, the 400-foot Orlando Gyro Drop Tower, which is billed as the world's tallest free-standing drop tower, allowing you to experience free fall at speeds up to 75 mph.

WHAT'S WHERE

1 Magic Kingdom Park and Resort Area. The centerpiece of Walt Disney World's most popular park is Cinderella Castle. Nearby are several of Walt Disney World's premier hotels.

2 EPCOT Park and Resort Area. EPCOT is made up of four distinct worlds: World Discovery, World Nature, World Celebration, and World Showcase, which celebrates the cuisine and cultures of Canada, the United Kingdom, France, Japan, Morocco, America, Italy, Germany, China, Norway, and Mexico.

3 Disney's Hollywood Studios Park. Paying tribute to the movies, especially Disney movies, this park offers stunt shows, thrill rides, characters, and plenty of *Star Wars*.

4 Disney's Animal Kingdom Park and Resort Area. This is much more than a zoo. Attractions like Expedition Everest and It's Tough to Be a Bug combine Disney's trademark blend of thrills and laughs. Pandora is one of the most imaginative sections.

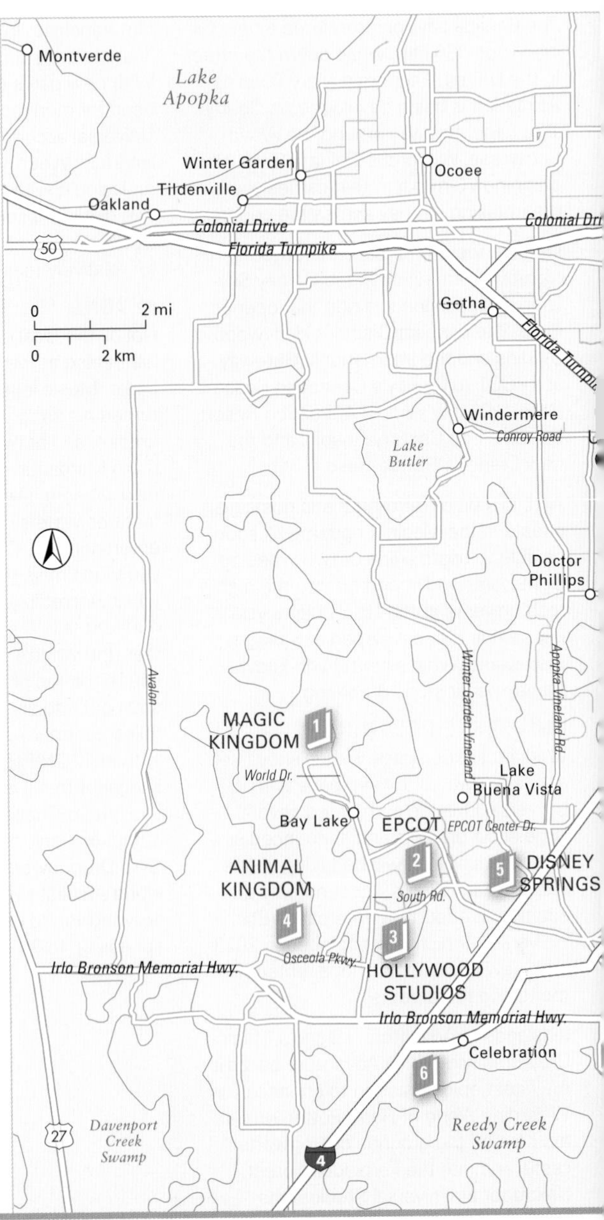

5 Disney Springs and Resort Area. Disney's popular shopping, dining, and nightlife area welcomes both resort guests and locals, who come to eat, bowl, go to the movies, and just hang out.

6 Kissimmee, Lake Buena Vista, and Celebration. Immediately adjacent to Walt Disney World are two communities, Lake Buena Vista and Disney's planned community of Celebration. Nearby is Kissimmee, which retains its small-town feel.

7 Universal Orlando. In addition to two theme parks (Universal Studios and Islands of Adventure) and its water theme park (Volcano Bay), it has several resort hotels and will be expanding to offer even more.

8 Orlando. The sleepy citrus town was completely transformed by Walt Disney World, but its busy downtown district and historic residential districts from the 1920s now give tourists a reason to go beyond the theme parks.

9 Excursions from Orlando. In the vicinity are several worthy trips: Winter Park, Maitland, Wekiwa Springs, Sanford, Mount Dora, LEGOLAND, and Bok Tower Garden.

Ways to Save Money in Orlando

TRAVEL OFF SEASON

The off-season in Orlando, times when the parks are less crowded, is growing smaller and smaller each year. That being said, those who can travel in January, February, May, and September will still see significant savings over those traveling at other times of the year.

FAMILY SUITES

Orlando has more hotel rooms than any other American city other than Las Vegas. One key feature in Orlando is the high number of hotels offering family suites—rooms that can sleep five or six people and can include an extra bathroom or a kitchenette where you can make simple meals.

SPLIT MEALS

Disney seems to cater to hefty eaters. If you have smaller kids (or if you prefer to snack throughout the day) consider splitting meals. Especially at counter-service locations, there is no charge to ask for an extra plate, and most entrées are big enough for an adult and a child to share.

BRING YOUR OWN BREAKFAST

Even those staying in a room without a kitchenette will find it easy to bring their own breakfast to the parks. Packing breakfast bars and a couple of bottles of apple juice is a hands-down easy way for a family of four to save up to $75 a day on a vacation. Pair that with the in-room coffeemaker for adults, and you're ready to start the day. Ambitious travelers can even make sandwiches and snacks to bring into the park.

RIDESHARE TO THE PARKS

Visitors staying at hotels not on Disney property can find themselves with the dilemma of how to get to the parks. While most hotels offer shuttles, they are usually slow and inconvenient. Instead of paying for a costly rental car and parking, plan to Uber or Lyft around Orlando. Most trips are much less than the cost of a day's parking.

DISNEY DINING PLANS

If you're staying at a Disney resort and have a large group and/or big eaters in your family, the Disney Dining Plan can be a great way to save money. Be aware that the plan does require some coordination since sit-down meals have to be booked in advance. Even cheaper is the Quick-Service Disney Dining Plan, which provides two counter-service meals per day (as well as two snacks and a refillable mug).

Free Locations to Visit

FLY INTO SANFORD
Flying into Orlando? Instead of heading to the big Orlando International Airport, check out flights into the Orlando Sanford Airport (SFB). Though it is farther from Disney World and Universal, flights there can be significantly cheaper on Allegiant Air. Be aware that it's an hour from the airport to most hotels.

EAT OFF-SITE
When you're able, look into eating at restaurants just beyond Disney's property boundary, something easier to do if you're staying at an off-site hotel as well. While it isn't worth it to leave a theme park to drive to any of these off-site restaurants—since theme-park tickets are so expensive—considereating at one on your first night in town, on a day off, or on the way back to your hotel.

BUY SOUVENIRS BEFORE YOU LEAVE
Souvenirs in the theme parks are one of the biggest unplanned expenses most families encounter. Consider buying some items at home before you travel. Even the Disney Store is cheaper than in the parks. If you have space, pack a few gifts for the last day.

LOOK INTO FREE ACTIVITIES
If you have an extra day and don't want to purchase a ticket, look around Orlando for free alternatives. Disney Springs and Universal's CityWalk are free to enter, though both have tempting wares to buy. Disney's BoardWalk Inn has an active boardwalk, with street performers, midway games, and music. Though not free, putt-putt courses are much cheaper than the theme-park options that line International Drive.

Best Orlando Thrill Rides

THE INCREDIBLE HULK COASTER
Roller coaster enthusiasts regularly list this as not only the smoothest roller coaster in Orlando, but also one of the most intense. Impossible to miss from the gates of Islands of Adventure, the Incredible Hulk Coaster is so extreme that you are required to empty your pockets before riding.

MAKO
Mako launched at SeaWorld in 2016 as the tallest, fastest, and longest roller coaster in Orlando. Some of the turns are sharp enough to make you feel like you've gotten some airtime.

HARRY POTTER AND THE FORBIDDEN JOURNEY
On this very nontraditional thrill ride, the main attraction in Hogsmeade, a "flying bench" takes you around Hogwarts with screens and technology to make the ride more intense.

HOLLYWOOD RIP RIDE ROCKIT
Hollywood Rip Ride Rockit is Universal Studio's most intense ride. You begin with a completely vertical takeoff at a 90-degree angle. And you get to choose your own soundtrack for the experience.

HARRY POTTER AND THE ESCAPE FROM GRINGOTT'S
The signature ride in Diagon Alley is an indoor, steel-track coaster that is more atmospherically thrilling than traditional attractions: 3-D projections that include original *Harry Potter* cast members make the effects seem more real.

MANTA
This flying roller coaster at SeaWorld simulates the feeling of—you guessed it—a manta in the water. You'll board Manta sitting upright and then be lowered down onto your stomach before departure, with safety bars, a vest harness, and flaps on your feet keeping you in place.

STAR WARS: RISE OF THE RESISTANCE
Star Wars: Galaxy's Edge, the most immersive area in any of the Orlando theme parks, is where you'll find this multipart attraction. It drops you right into the action of a *Star Wars* film. While at no point do you board a roller coaster, this ride is a wild one.

Expedition Everest

ROCK 'N' ROLLER COASTER STARRING AEROSMITH
Disney World's only roller coaster with inversions also features the sounds of the classic band Aerosmith. The takeoff is especially intense, as you travel directly into two inversions, but the ride itself is smooth, and most older kids can handle it. Plus, the soundtrack is fun.

EXPEDITION EVEREST
Located deep in Disney's Animal Kingdom, this coaster tries to take you up Mount Everest but is run off its rails by a ferocious yeti. Hands-down the most exciting part of Expedition Everest is when you find the yeti has torn up your track. This forces the car to careen backward in a circle so tight and so dark that those in the front will feel like they're being flipped upside-down.

ICE BREAKER
SeaWorld is taking things to the next level with its newest coaster. On the Ice Breaker, your car will undergo four different launches, as you travel forward and backward along the track. The final reverse launch is the steepest in all of Florida. You'll fall back 93 feet at a 100-degree angle. This is the culmination of SeaWorld's quest to become known for its roller coasters, so expect sharp thrills and long lines here.

The Best Non-Theme Park Restaurants in Orlando

THE RAVENOUS PIG
This popular gastropub has been making waves in the Orlando food scene since its opening in 2007, and owners James and Julie Petrakis have launched spin-offs such as the Cask & Larder, Swine & Son Provisions, and the Polite Pig at Disney Springs.

SOCO
At this downtown restaurant in the trendy Thornton Park neighborhood, the menu is inspired by selections normally found at diners across the South. Some of the best dishes are deviled eggs (with horseradish, smoked bacon, and pickled mustard seeds), chicken and dumplings (with lobster dumplings, local mushrooms, edamame, and soy butter), and meat loaf (with a three-meat blend, crispy onion rings, smoked Vidalia and andouille sausage gravy). Desserts are souped-up Southern sweets.

CAFÉ TU TU TANGO
An inviting atmosphere that looks like a Parisian artist's loft features hundreds of works of art (all for sale) on the walls. On the tapas-style menu are small plates like alforno-roasted pears and jalapeño mac and cheese. Larger dishes include Argentinean red shrimp with olive oil, butter, sliced chilies, and herbs; savory plates of Moroccan lamb meatballs; and spiced alligator bites,a Florida favorite.

CHEF'S TABLE AT THE EDGEWATER
Part of the resurgence of Winter Garden was the arrival of excellent restaurants like this one, where a three-course prix-fixe menu (which might include an appetizer of roasted beet salad or seared scallops, an entrée of pan-seared spiced duck breast or char-grilled filet mignon, and a dessert of sweet potato bread pudding or caramel cheesecake) changes regularly to ensure the freshest ingredients are served.

SEITO SUSHI
Located on Orlando's Restaurant Row, a contemporary setting complements award-winning sushi and pan-Asian cuisine. Sushi selections cover a wide of range of choices including The Trilogy (three pieces each of tuna, yellowtail, and salmon), and the Tuna Set (the chef's daily selection of tuna tastings). Noodle dishes and classic and signature rolls complement larger coal-fired entrées such as Dengaku sea bass, Korean-style short ribs, and a Kurabota pork tomahawk.

SAVION'S PLACE
In historic downtown Kissimmee, a cultural confluence of cuisine was sparked by Haiti-born/Florida-raised Pouchon Savion, who graduated through a series of noted restaurants before launching his own establishment. It has earned rave reviews, awards, television coverage, and a dedicated clientele for a menu that mixes Caribbean island influences with traditional American dishes.

Yellow Dog Eats (Windermere)

YELLOW DOG EATS
In an area of Orlando seldom visited by tourists, this unassuming spot draws locals, who drop by for a simple but extensive menu of sandwiches, salads, barbecue, and daily specials. The proprietors use more than a dozen varieties of locally grown baby greens; serve home-baked pastries and breads; smoke their own bacon and pork over natural woods; and carry an assortment of jams, jellies, condiments, and sauces. Try the Florida Cracker: pulled pork topped with tangy coleslaw, Gouda cheese, and pecan-smoked bacon served on thick-cut jalapeño cheddar bread.

BRIARPATCH
Upscale Park Avenue is always a popular destination for window shopping, people-watching, and casual dining. With its intimate sidewalk tables as well as seating in a charming indoor dining area, Briarpatch has been a traditional favorite since opening in 1980. Dinner is not served, but you can get creative spins on breakfasts of waffles, pancakes, omelets, scrambles, and equally creative and appetizing lunches featuring soups, salads, burgers, and sandwiches.

PISCES RISING
This contemporary restaurant in a converted home overlooking 4,500-acre Lake Dora is equally popular with locals and the town's steady stream of visitors. The bright, airy interior is enhanced by high ceilings, excellent service, and a diverse menu that features farm-to-table ingredients and selections such as fried green tomatoes, mushroom ravioli, peel-and-eat shrimp, herbed rib eye, and Cuban snapper—all of which can be enjoyed on the outdoor deck where a crowd gathers each evening for live music and dancing.

ENZO'S ON THE LAKE
Roughly 30 miles north of downtown, this family-owned lakeside restaurant has been Orlando's leading choice for upscale Italian food since 1980. Credit the family-style atmosphere of its individual dining rooms, its picturesque gardens, the natural beauty of its Lake Fairy setting, and, especially, its hand-crafted pastas—the foundation for dishes such as spaghetti alla carbonara, pappardelle alla farnese (with mushrooms and arugula), and fettucine al'aragosta e gamberi (with lobster and shrimp in a light saffron and green onion sauce).

Best Hotels in Orlando

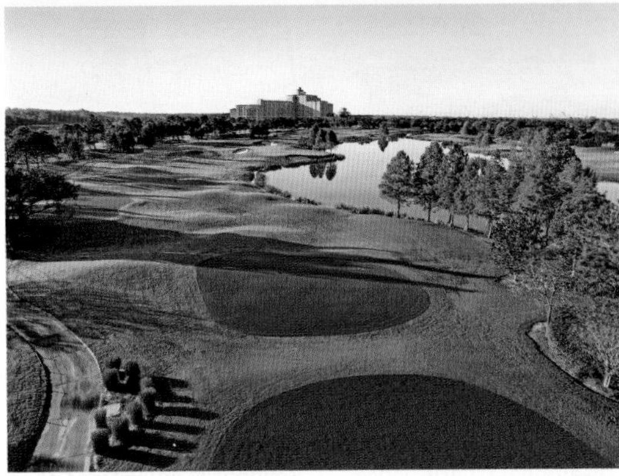

ROSEN SHINGLE CREEK

Shingle Creek is equidistant to the Orange County Convention Center and Orlando International Airport, but more than placement sets this resort apart. The tropical setting merges with the Florida landscape and the rolling greens of the Arnold Palmer–inspired golf course.

DISNEY'S ANIMAL KINGDOM LODGE

No one matches Disney's ability to dazzle, and that's exactly what this resort hotel does best, from the soaring lobby to the signature restaurants to the wildlife-inspired pool area to the animals grazing in the savanna just outside your window.

HILTON ORLANDO BUENA VISTA PALACE

While this family-friendly resort isn't owned by Disney, as a partner hotel it offers special perks such as Disney stores, character breakfasts, complimentary park shuttles, and early admission to Disney parks. And it's a short walk from Disney Springs.

DISNEY'S CONTEMPORARY RESORT

This treasured Disney classic is also the closest resort hotel to the Magic Kingdom, resting between natural Bay Lake and the man-made Seven Seas Lagoon. Its timeless A-frame design is still sleek and stylish, as is the iconic visual of monorails slipping through the hotel via the Grand Canyon concourse. At night, guests love dining at the rooftop California Grill.

HYATT REGENCY GRAND CYPRESS

There's a lot that goes into a 1,500-acre resort including nearly 800 rooms and suites, six dining establishments (highlighted by its signature restaurant, Hemingway's), a private lake, tennis courts, an 800,000-gallon lagoon-style pool, a rock-climbing wall, the Hollywood-inspired Marilyn Monroe spa, and an 18-hole Jack Nicklaus Signature golf course.

GRAND BOHEMIAN

Located in the heart of downtown Orlando at the epicenter of class and elegance, the Grand Bohemian has a style that is naturally appealing to overnight guests, yet it is also a favorite of day guests, who have made dining at the Boheme Restaurant or having drinks at the famed Bösendorfer Lounge a pre- and postshow ritual when attending performances at the adjacent Dr. Phillips Center for the Performing Arts.

Disney's Contemporary Resort

RITZ-CARLTON ORLANDO

This 582-room resort inspired by the grand palazzos of Italy promises elegance in every way, from the meticulously groomed Greg Norman–designed golf course to the array of personalized indulgences found in its 40,000 square-foot spa and salon. Culinary extravagances can be discovered in nearly a dozen dining establishments. From check-in to departure, the total experience affirms Ritz as the synonym for luxury.

UNIVERSAL'S HARD ROCK HOTEL

The "Hotel California" style of this premier Universal Orlando resort puts guests in a musical state of mind, and that feeling is enhanced by an eye-popping collection memorabilia, as well as by a sun-sparkled free-form pool that seems inspired by a rock 'n' roll fantasy. A short walk to Universal theme parks and CityWalk, its other perks include Velvet Session concerts and front-of-line access when you flash your Hard Rock room key at any Universal attraction.

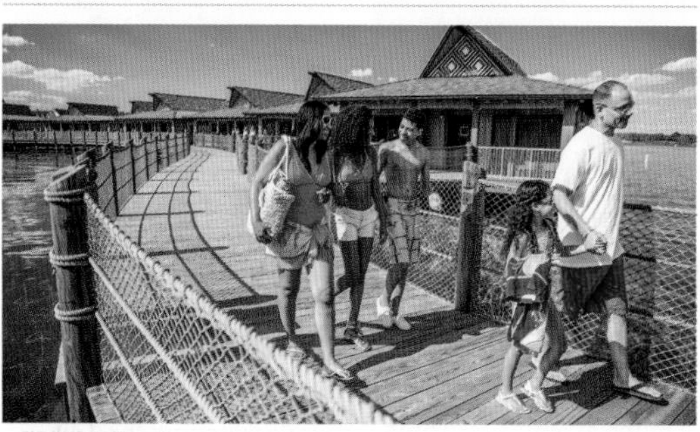

DISNEY'S POLYNESIAN RESORT

With a tranquil setting on the shores of the Seven Seas Lagoon, one of the original Disney resort hotels is beloved by guests who long to escape to a South Seas wonderland.

GAYLORD PALMS RESORT

This Kissimmee resort pays tribute to the Everglades in the flora and vegetation found in a soaring glass atrium; to St. Augustine with its cobblestone streets; and to Key West through vibrant, tropical colors that create a thoroughly comfortable feeling of Florida. Add to that a high level of hospitality found in free shuttle service to the theme parks, and a full-service spa.

Best Theme Park Foods in Orlando

EARL GREY AND LAVENDER ICE CREAM
Finish off your time in The Wizarding World of Harry Potter by braving the lines at Florean Fortescue's Ice Cream Parlour. Here you'll find a short but tempting list of unique flavors, but the most unusual and tasty one is the Earl Grey and lavender ice cream (yes, better than butterbeer).

TIRAMISU
This classic Italian dessert can be found at Mama Melrose's Ristorante Italiano in Disney's Hollywood Studios. It might be hard to save room when the menu has such delicious options like chicken alla parmigiana and seafood fra diavolo, but make sure to split the tiramisu at the end (or just make a reservation for dessert).

PINEAPPLE DOLE WHIP
While there are many great theme-park foods, only a few are so popular that they have spawned their own merchandise. The Pineapple Dole Whip Float at the Magic Kingdom is that good. Fresh pineapple juice is topped with either vanilla or pineapple-flavored ice cream to make this much sought-after treat. Use Disney's Mobile ordering app to skip the lines.

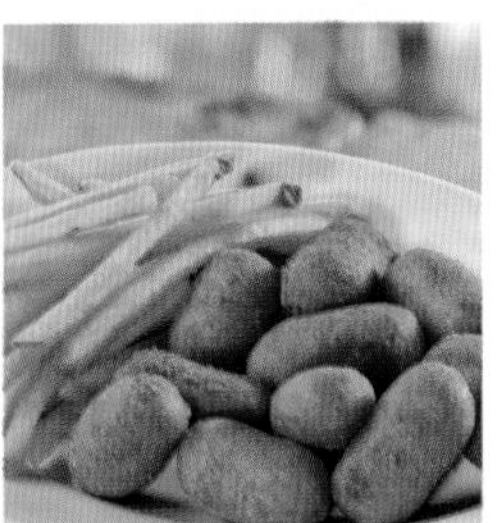

CASEY'S CORN DOG NUGGETS
A twist on the traditional corn dog, these little bites still thrill kids and adults alike. Since Casey's Corner at the Magic Kingdom is always popular for lunch, plan on grabbing a pick-me-up snack to chow down while watching the 3 pm parade. For a sharper bite, add jalapeños and chili-lime seasoning.

PLOUGHMAN'S LUNCH

The Ploughman's Lunch at the Leaky Cauldron is one of the best things on the menu. This meal is made to serve two, and includes Scotch eggs, apple beat salad, two large pieces of bread, three English cheeses, tomatoes, and salad. Add a couple of other items for a real feast.

BUTTERBEER

How can anyone miss Harry Potter's favorite drink? In the Wizarding World of Harry Potter, you'll find butterbeer available at every cart and restaurant you turn to. This butterscotch-esque sweet treat is also available as an ice-cream flavor!

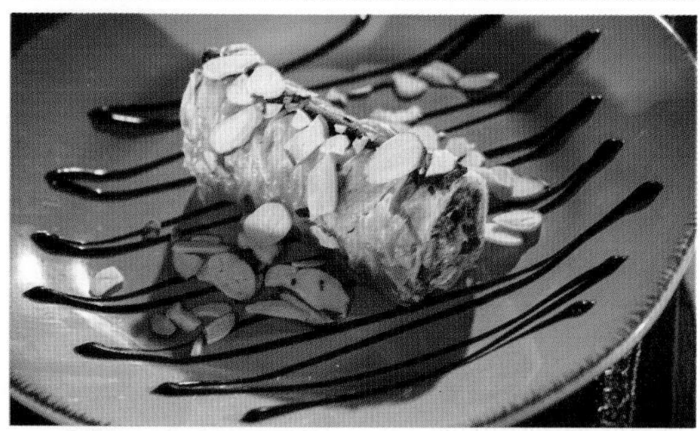

BAKLAVA

You cannot beat the baklava found in the Morocco pavilion at EPCOT's World Showcase. Make sure to grab some at Tangierine Café along with your hummus and tabbouleh, or find a piece at a stand next to Souk-al-Magreb on World Showcase Lagoon.

Braised lamb shank

PEANUT BUTTER AND JELLY MILK SHAKE

This is a specialty at 50's Prime Time Café in Disney's Hollywood Studios; if you can't get reservations,though, the milk shake is also offered at the neighboring Tune-In Lounge.

CARCIOFI PIZZA

Via Napoli Ristorante e Pizzeria in the Italy pavilion in EPCOT offers hand-tossed pizzas. The best is the family-sized carciofi, a white pizza with artichoke, fontina, mozzarella, and truffle oil.

BRAISED LAMB SHANK

Among the many excellent dishes at Tiffins, in the Animal Kingdom, the braised lamb shank might be the best. It's served with couscous, piquillo peppers, kottu (a stew of eggplant and chickpeas), and pan-roasted vegetables.

POTATO AND ONION WEB

A long-time Universal Studios favorite is Finnegan's Bar and Grill. Wise diners start with the potato and onion web, a beer-battered mixture of thinly sliced potatoes and onions that will satisfy the entire table.

Best Theme Park Souvenirs

EMBROIDERED MICKEY MOUSE EARS

The gold standard of Orlando souvenirs, these iconic chapeaus first appeared in the 1950s on the *Mickey Mouse Club* and continue to be a favorite for guests from around the world. The ubiquitous black beanie with the half-dome ears wouldn't be complete without your name.

PLUSH MICKEY OR MINNIE MOUSE

Nearly every character appearing in a Disney film is stamped, printed, stuffed, or otherwise memorialized in nearly every form and on every surface. But of hundreds of characters, none rivals the stature of Mickey and Minnie, whose plush doppelgangers are a comforting and cuddly memento of your Orlando visit (and they pack well, too).

GOOFY BASEBALL CAP

The age-old question "Is Goofy a dog?" doesn't detract from his popularity among Disney guests. The combination of his big feet, baggy pants, turtleneck sweater, tall hat, and exclamations of "Oh, gawrsh!" have placed him among Disney's Fab Five with Mickey, Minnie, Donald, and Pluto. A Goofy cap captures his unique personality with dangling ears hanging on the sides and Goofy eyes peering down the length of his outstretched nose.

BANSHEE

Animal Kingdom is filled with hundreds of unusual and eye-catching sights. One head-turner is the colorful banshee found perched on the shoulders of many park guests. Found at the shop at Pandora's–Avatar Flight of Passage, the multihued mechanical minidragons flap their wings, crane their necks, make sounds, and turn their heads (with a little bit of magic from you).

DROID

When you enter the Droid Depot at Galaxy's Edge and see a line of parts and pieces speeding along a conveyor belt, it's easy to cast costs aside and get busy building your personalized BB or R unit. With hundreds of possible combinations, it's easy to get creative—and those are the droids you're looking for. Working from blueprints, once you've assembled your personality-rich droid they're ready to roll via remote control. These souvenirs are priced on the high side but for the aficionado, it's a price worth paying.

HARRY POTTER WAND

As if by magic there happens to be several Orlando locations where Harry Potter fans can buy wands worthy of a wizard, including two branches of Ollivander's. Whether you're at Islands of Adventure or Universal Studios, you'll have access to multiple styles of wonderfully packaged wands either straightforward or, for a slight upcharge, "interactive." The latter version comes with a map and instructional chart that reveals how, with precise movements and the right incantation, you can cast a spell on objects throughout Hogsmeade and Diagon Alley.

Banshee

THING 1 (OR THING 2) T-SHIRT

Although it might be reaching the point where it's an old joke, couples (or kids or families) wearing Dr. Seuss–inspired Thing 1 and Thing 2 T-shirts is still a pretty funny joke. Visible at a hundred yards, the bright red shirt with the cartoonish lettering within a white circle is always good for a smile. More folks in the family? Things 3 and 4 are also available, as are Thing 1 and Thing 2 onesies.

GATORLAND T-SHIRT

One of Florida's original tourist attractions, Kissimmee's Gatorland has remained a popular destination since opening in 1949. Its appealing kitsch factor (you enter through the gaping mouth of a concrete alligator) has no doubt contributed to its longevity. An impressive souvenir shop featuring all things alligator includes T-shirts in a variety of fonts, colors, and styles. Those featuring "1949" and/or the legend "Alligator Capital of the World," are perennial favorites.

FACE PAINTING

It's rare for a child to leave a theme park unchanged in some way. The most visible sign are kids whose faces are primed and painted with the likeness of their favorite Marvel superheroes at Universal or their favorite characters or specialty designs at Disney. Relatively inexpensive (and easy to wash off), the colors can get a free touch-up until you leave the park.

SHAMU

It's impossible to watch SeaWorld's star performer splash and swim without a nagging desire to take him home, yet getting a life-size Shamu doll through airport security is an impossibility. The next best solution is a 20-inch supersoft version, which happens to be SeaWorld's most popular plush toy. It makes a perfect snuggling partner and is a touchingly tangible black-and-white snapshot of your vacation.

PICTURE WITH WALT AND MICKEY

Although no one changed the entertainment world more than Walt Disney, he was too gracious to accept all the credit. Instead, Walt maintained "It all started with a mouse. …" Today the pair are inseparable in show business and in the statue *Partners*, which stands in the hub of the Magic Kingdom in front of Cinderella Castle. At one of Orlando's most popular photo ops, guests from around the world line up for a souvenir picture with Walt and Mickey.

Orlando Weddings and Honeymoons

Thanks to the diversity of botanical garden backdrops and fantastical theme park settings, Orlando is a popular destination for showers, weddings, and honeymoons. Starry-eyed young couples and, more and more, older couples who are marrying for the second time or are renewing their vows in the wedding-vacation-reunion of a lifetime travel from across America and around the world to mark their memorable moment here.

More than anyone else, Disney has created a cottage industry from weddings. Just visit 🌐 *www.disneyweddings.com*, and you can begin designing the nuptials of your dreams, picking and choosing among hundreds of locations and enhancements until your imagination (or bank account) runs dry. One bride made an entrance in Cinderella's glass coach; her groom rode in on a white horse. A thrill-seeking couple took the free-fall plunge on the Tower of Terror at Disney's Hollywood Studios. Two couples, on separate occasions, tied the knot in the middle of their Walt Disney World Marathon run, exchanging vows in front of Cinderella Castle at the Magic Kingdom. Moonlight on the Ritz-Carlton lawn set the scene for another couple's romantic vow exchange, and a rooftop Orlando wedding wowed yet another couple's guests with a 360-degree view of the downtown skyline and scenic Lake Eola Park.

PREWEDDING EVENTS

Showers and bachelor and bachelorette parties are easy to arrange in a city where there's so much to do—provided you have a lot of money to spend. At Disney, the Mad Hatter can show up for a bridesmaids' tea event at the Grand Floridian. Parties can begin with dinner and a wine tasting at Hannibal's wine cellar in Winter Park before moving on to a local nightclub. Grooms who stay at Portofino Bay like to party at Universal CityWalk because no driving is required—a ferry will shuttle them back to the hotel.

For rehearsal dinners (or wedding receptions or honeymoons), Disney pulls out the stops to stage events ranging from an after-hours reception in one of the theme parks to an internationally themed event at one of the World Showcase countries in EPCOT.

WEDDINGS

You can opt for a traditional ceremony at Disney's Wedding Pavilion on the Seven Seas Lagoon by the Grand Floridian Resort & Spa. Designed with the charming features of a Victorian summerhouse, the pavilion is an airy room with a view of Cinderella Castle just across the lagoon. Alternatively you can plan an informal beachside vow exchange at a lakeside Disney resort; a garden or gazebo ceremony; an over-the-top, Cinderella-style wedding; or a Broadway-theme blowout.

Downtown Orlando and historic Winter Park are popular wedding destinations as well. Elegant, yet affordable, lakefront ceremonies are popular, with a variety of waterfront pavilions and gardens available in picturesque city and county parks and botanical gardens.

Other top wedding spots are downtown's Orange County Regional History Center; the Mennello Museum of American Art in the city's Loch Haven area; and Casa Feliz, a historic Spanish home–museum in Winter Park.

Another factor that makes Orlando the perfect choice for a wedding is the city's wealth of entertainment and resort hotels. Theme-park musicians and other performers often hire out for receptions at reasonable prices, and there's a lot of diversity, from zydeco and salsa bands to groups that specialize in swing music. Resort hotels like the Four Seasons, the

Ritz-Carlton, Waldorf Astoria, and Portofino Bay at Universal feature romantic backdrops for the ceremony plus smaller ballrooms ideal for receptions. The hotels can also support activities ranging from spa parties to golf outings for those in the wedding party.

HONEYMOONS

Central Florida resorts cater to honeymooners with special packages. Honeymoon suites with whirlpools and other amenities create the backdrop for romance that's enhanced with extras like champagne and chocolate-covered strawberries. Resort pools with cabanas, beaches, waterfalls, swaying palms, and poolside margarita delivery make the subtropical setting seem as exotic as a tropical island.

Disney's Fairy Tale Honeymoons division helps you customize a vacation package and even offers a Honeymoon Registry if your guests wish to contribute to your postwedding getaway rather than give a traditional gift. There are package deals to be had at Walt Disney World resorts and at Disney's Vero Beach Resort. Some couples make their wedding dreams or vow renewals come true at sea, where the honeymoon follows immediately.

PLANNING TIPS

If you're dreaming about a Central Florida wedding, keep these tips from the experts in mind:

- If your budget can handle the expense, hire a reputable planner long before the big date. Though you'll pay a fee for your planner, he or she will be an advocate with barter power when dealing with vendors.

- For a destination wedding, build in plenty of time to book travel arrangements and accommodations for all who plan to attend.

- If your budget is tight, plan your Orlando wedding between Monday and Thursday during nonpeak season for the lowest hotel rates.

- Split the wedding-planning tasks with your partner. If the groom is focused more on the reception's music, food, and beverages, the bride can focus on, say, wedding flowers and photography.

- Let your wedding planner arrange romantic escapes from your guests, especially if you plan to wed and honeymoon in Orlando. If everyone's staying at the Gaylord Palms Resort or the Hard Rock Hotel, have your wedding planner book you a spa package at the Waldorf Astoria or Ritz-Carlton.

- Start your research by visiting several Orlando-area wedding-planner websites: Visit Orlando at https://www.visitorlando.com/en/things-to-do/discover-orlando/weddings, and Disney's Fairy Tale Weddings & Honeymoons at 🌐 www.disneyweddings.com, 🌐 www.disneyweddings.disney.go.com.

Disney Cruises

When Disney first went to sea in 1998, some assumed their single ship—the *Disney Magic*—would be the lone vessel in its fleet. But the *Disney Wonder* made its debut the following year. Very quickly, Disney's level of style, class, characters, and theming proved so popular that Disney Cruise Line (DCL) leaped to the top of cruise passenger favorites. As a result, two more ships joined the fleet—the *Disney Dream* in 2011 and the *Disney Fantasy* in 2014, with three more ships starting with the *Disney Wish* scheduled to launch in 2022.

Disney Cruise Line
To book any Disney cruise or to check into vessels, staterooms, shore excursions, and more, contact the Disney Cruise Line. ☎ *800/370–0097* 🌐 *www.disneycruise.com.*

FOR GUESTS WITH DISABILITIES

Accessible staterooms for people with disabilities have ramps, handrails, fold-down shower seats, and handheld showerheads. Special communications kits are available with phone alerts, amplifiers, and text typewriters. Assisted-listening systems are offered in the ships' main theaters, and sign-language interpretation is offered for live performances on specified cruise dates.

ADULT ACTIVITIES

Poolside games, wine tastings, and behind-the-scenes seminars are among the adults-only diversions. Each ship's spa is a don't-miss for those who need some pampering—book early!

For a romantic dinner, the intimate, adults-only **Palo** (*all ships*) offers sweeping ocean views. Expect a fantastic wine list and dishes such as grilled salmon with creamy risotto and grilled filet mignon with a port-wine reduction and Gorgonzola cheese sauce. Reserve early for this hot ticket. The champagne brunch is another great Palo dining event.

The decor in the *Dream*'s and *Fantasy*'s exclusive, 80-seat restaurant, **Remy,** is a nod to the movie *Ratatouille,* and, of course, the cuisine is French inspired. The eight or nine tasting dishes served each night might include Kurobata pork tenderloin and belly with corn ragout and wild turbot with lemon, capers, and spinach. Wine pairings are amazing; so are the pastries. Remy also has a champagne brunch. Book as far ahead of your trip as possible.

CHILDREN'S ACTIVITIES

More than a few prospective passengers have passed on DCL, assuming the decks would be cluttered with kids. On the contrary—on all four ships, there's nearly an entire deck reserved for kids and you might enjoy a complete voyage without ever noticing them. Making it better for parents—and even better for the kids—are activity centers divided by age groups, for kids 10 and younger, for "tweens" 11–14, and for older teens ages 14–17. Counselors keep them focused with a wide-ranging assortment of activities including playrooms, rope bridges, scavenger hunts, science experiments, sports challenges, karaoke games, video games, trivia contests, and evening dance parties. While you're having fun with other adults, kids are literally having a ball on their own level. To help stay in touch, an onboard mobile phone service keeps you connected with activities counselors.

RESTAURANTS

Dining is one of the most anticipated experiences aboard the Disney ships, and the **Animator's Palate** is a favorite. Scenes featuring Disney characters change from black-and-white to Technicolor as the meal progresses on the *Magic* and *Wonder*; on the *Dream* and

Fantasy, diners are surrounded by an artist's studio where famous film scenes line the walls and fiber-optic "brush pillars" paint oversize ceiling "palettes" in vibrant colors. Dining is slightly more formal at **Lumiere's,** on the *Magic,* where beef tenderloin, lamb shank, and other entrées are served French style in a classic ocean-liner-style dining room.

At **Triton's,** on the *Wonder,* seafood, roast duck, pasta, and other selections are served in an elegant, art deco, under-the-sea-theme dining room. The *Dream*'s **Royal Palace** and the *Fantasy*'s **Royal Court** are inspired by Disney's princess films, with menus that might include crowned rack of lamb, beef Wellington, and other regal dishes. At the Caribbean-theme **Parrot Cay** restaurant (*Wonder*) and the new Rio de Janeiro–theme **Carioca's** (*Magic*), the mood is casual and festive. On the *Fantasy* and *Dream,* **Enchanted Garden** is the whimsical, more informal rotation restaurant. Character breakfasts are offered one morning on most seven-nights-or-longer sailings.

AFTER-DARK ENTERTAINMENT

Few can out-do Disney entertainment, and the level of stage shows, on-deck performances, and character greetings—Disney, Star Wars, and Marvel superheroes among them—is spectacular. **Lavish shows** and variety acts entertain families every night of every cruise. The over-the-top theatricals with Broadway-quality sets and staging are often musicals based on Disney's biggest blockbuster hits. You might see a *Toy Story* musical or an extravaganza based on *Frozen, Tangled, The Little Mermaid, Aladdin,* or *Beauty and the Beast.* Whatever is playing, prepare to be dazzled. The Golden Mickeys on the *Wonder* is a high-tech salute to the animation of Walt Disney in the form of a Hollywood-style awards ceremony. Twice Charmed: An Original Twist on the Cinderella Story is a Broadway-style production on the *Magic* that begins where the original Cinderella story ended.

Each ship also has a **cinema** screening classic Disney films, and every guest has the opportunity to experience a show or film featuring digital 3-D enhancements.

In addition to shows and shore excursions, a wide assortment of bars, lounges, dance clubs, piano bars, Irish pubs, sports bars, and nightclubs across the four ships appeals to adults. The best way to find one you prefer is to spend a few hours exploring the ship, checking the maps, and circling the decks to get your bearings and find the places that are perfect for you and the mood you're in. Everyone, it seems, is in the mood for the **Pirate Night event**, when swashbuckling servers dish up Caribbean and Bahamian taste treats, a cup of grog, and (on seven-night cruises) a pirate bandanna for every dinner guest. After dinner, you head off to a deck party where Captain Hook, Mr. Smee, and others appear for some high-spirited action, dancing, and fireworks.

CASTAWAY CAY

Disney's own private Bahamian island, Castaway Cay, is paradise found. When the ship docks, you go ashore into a land of white-sand beaches, towering palms, swaying hammocks, and abundant food. You can relax on the beach or join a snorkeling or parasailing excursion.

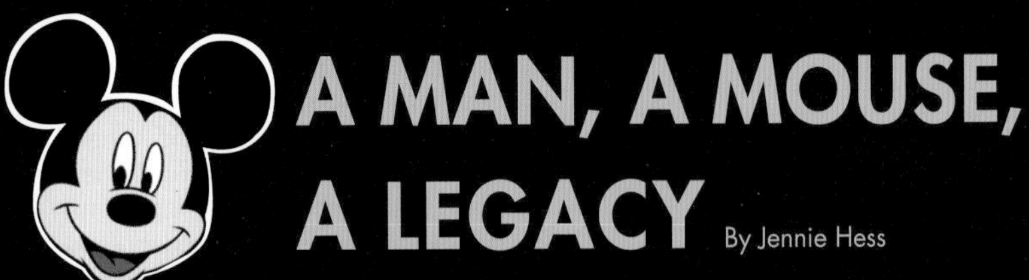

A MAN, A MOUSE, A LEGACY

By Jennie Hess

Walt Disney once said, "I only hope that we never lose sight of one thing—that it was all started by a mouse." His legendary mouse, Mickey, took the world by storm in 1928 in the theatrical debut of the animated short film Steamboat Willie. Today, Walt is Mickey, Mickey is Walt, and their legacy is legendary.

Above: Walt Disney; below: Mickey from Fantasia, 1940; right: Pinocchio, 1940

There's a tale still told (and disputed) that Walt imagined Mickey while on a train from New York to California, after a disastrous meeting where he lost the rights to a character called Oswald the Lucky Rabbit. Walt's friend and colleague, gifted Dutch cartoonist Ub Iwerks, first drew Mickey, but it was Walt who gave him a voice and personality.

He planned to name the mouse Mortimer, but his wife, Lilian, insisted the name didn't fit the cheerful little rodent.

The man behind the mouse, Walter Elias Disney, was born December 5, 1901, in Chicago. His early Midwestern years were spent nurturing his love of drawing. After driving an ambulance for the Red Cross in France during World War I, Walt returned to the States and worked for an ad company, where he met Ub.

Though Mickey appeared in the silent short *Plane Crazy* in May of 1928, the amiable mouse didn't really take a bow until the November debut of Steamboat Willie. Walt's use of synchronized sound made all the difference. By 1937, Walt and company had released their first animated feature-length film, *Snow White and the Seven Dwarfs*.

The many films that followed formed the creative and financial bedrock for a legacy of one theme park after another. But perhaps the greatest legacy of Walt and his mouse is that they both make memories for generation upon generation.

Hollywood studio opens	*Steamboat Willie* released	*Snow White* wins special Oscar
	1930	

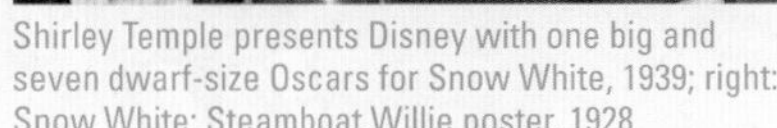

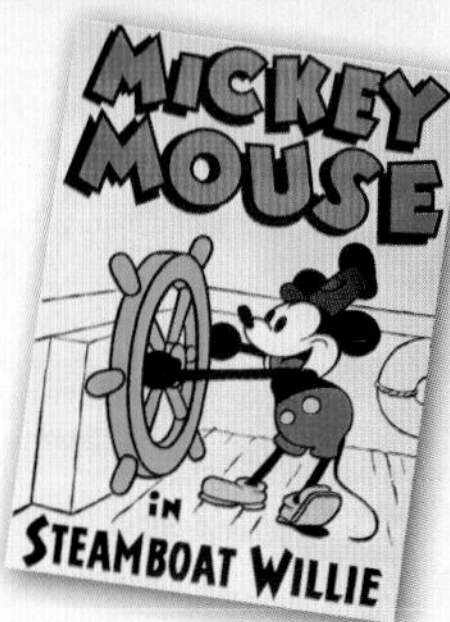

Shirley Temple presents Disney with one big and seven dwarf-size Oscars for Snow White, 1939; right: Snow White; Steamboat Willie poster, 1928

1920s–30s

A Mouse Is Born

Walt and his brother, Roy, establish a Hollywood studio in 1923. Animated shorts *Plane Crazy* and *Steamboat Willie*, starring both Mickey and Minnie, are released in 1928. Thereafter, Walt and his artists create dozens of Mickey shorts like 1930's *The Chain Gang*, when an orange pup named Pluto first appears.

Two years later, good-natured Goofy debuts as an audience extra in *Mickey's Revue*. His spasmodic laugh earns him a series of his own animated short films. Hot-tempered Donald Duck and his loyal girlfriend, Daisy, follow.

In 1937, America's first full-length animated feature, *Snow White and the Seven Dwarfs*, becomes the highest-grossing feature of its time. *Gone with the Wind* doesn't blow by that record until 1939, the same year that Disney's groundbreaking feature earns a special Academy Award: one full-size Oscar and seven dwarf Oscars presented by Shirley Temple.

■ **Visit:** Walt Disney: One Man's Dream, at Disney's Hollywood Studios

Goofy

1940s–50s

Characters Come to Life

Fans of all ages flock to see successive hits, from *Pinocchio* and *Fantasia* (both 1940) to *Dumbo* (1941) and *Bambi* (1942). Though *Fantasia* is panned by some, it earns Academy Awards kudos for innovating in the area of visualized music—specifically, animation set to music by composers such as Bach, Tchaikovsky, and Beethoven and recorded under the direction of conductor Leopold Stokowski.

During World War II, the Disney studio springs to patriotic action with a series of military training and propaganda films. After the war, the animation

First Disney theme park opens in California

1950 1960 1970

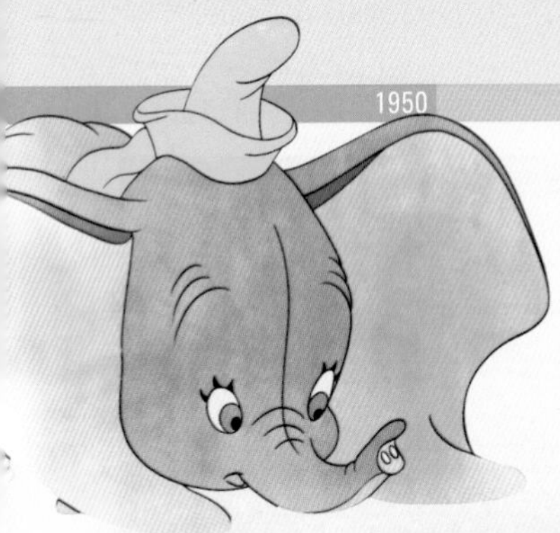

Left: Dumbo and Lady and the Tramp; right: entrance to Sleeping Beauty's Enchanted Castle, Disneyland, late 1960s

wizards cast a spell over the country with *Cinderella* (1950), *Alice in Wonderland* (1951), *Peter Pan* (1953), *Lady and the Tramp* (1955), *Sleeping Beauty* (1959), and others.

Walt's love for nature leads him to produce 13 True-Life Adventure films, eight of which win Oscars. Walt also brings his first live-action adventure film, Treasure Island, to the screen. He and his brother, Roy, begin dreaming up a new adventure altogether—Disneyland.

The first Disney theme park opens on July 17, 1955, in Anaheim, California. Many attractions and rides have Disney film themes. Drawing on his lifelong train infatuation, Walt encircles the park with the Disneyland Railroad.

- **Visit:** Cinderella Castle
- **Ride:** Prince Charming Regal Carrousel, Peter Pan's Flight, Dumbo the Flying Elephant, and Walt Disney World Railroad
- **See:** Mickey's PhilharMagic, all at Magic Kingdom

Cinderella Castle today

1960s–70s

A Magical New Frontier

In the early 1960s, Walt purchases 27,500 Orlando acres—an area twice the size of Manhattan. Sadly, he dies (December 1966) before Walt Disney World opens.

On October 1, 1971, the Magic Kingdom gates swing open, and a sleek monorail glides to the Contemporary and the Polynesian resort hotels. In November, a 640-acre western-style camping resort, Fort Wilderness, opens.

- **Visit:** Magic Kingdom
- **Ride:** The Monorail

Tokyo Disneyland opens

Disneyland Paris opens

1990

2000

Above: Disneyland Paris; Mickey hat; right: EPCOT's iconic Spaceship Earth

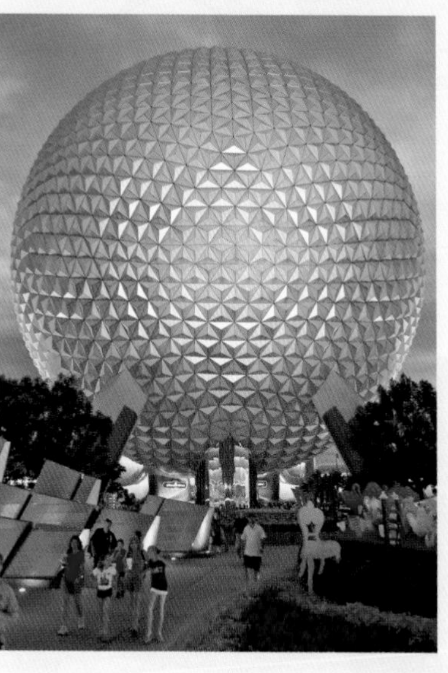

1980s–90s

A Worldlier Walt

Prior to his death, Walt begins work on what he hopes will be an ideal city. He names the project Experimental Prototype Community of Tomorrow. After the Magic Kingdom opens, Disney executives use some of Walt's ideas to create EPCOT Center. What opens in 1982 is the second Florida theme park—celebrating the world's cultures, the past, and the future—rather than an experimental community.

The 1980s are banner years for Disney Parks and Resorts. In 1983, the company's first international park—Tokyo Disneyland—opens. In 1989, Florida's third park, Disney-MGM Studios (later Disney's Hollywood Studios) premiers with celebrity fanfare. Not far from it, a new nightlife district, Pleasure Island, pumps up the volume, and Typhoon Lagoon crashes onto the scene with 6-foot waves and thrill-slide appeal.

The decade that follows is no less ambitious. In 1992 Euro Disney Resort (now Disneyland Paris) becomes the Mouse's second international destination; the first Disney cruise ships are launched from Port Canaveral, Florida; and the fourth Florida park, Disney's Animal Kingdom, earns raves for its authentic habitats. The icing on the Magic Kingdom's 20th anniversary cake? The animation studio is once again making big-screen hits with *Beauty and the Beast* (1991), *Aladdin* (1992), and *The Lion King* (1994)

Visit: Spaceship Earth at EPCOT; Beauty and the Beast—Live on Stage at the Studios; Kilimanjaro Safaris at Animal Kingdom; Typhoon Lagoon

Aladdin

Hong Kong Disneyland opens

Disney Dream cruise ship makes its maiden voyage

2010

2020

Finding Nemo's, Dory and Nemo

New Millennium

To Infinity and Beyond!

The new millennium sends the Mouse into overdrive. Hong Kong Disneyland opens (2005), as do several World attractions, among them one with a *Toy Story* theme, and two with a *Nemo* theme. Disney World also adds to its accommodations, bringing the total to 30,000 rooms, 3,200 Disney Vacation Club villas, and 800 campsites. New eateries like the Trattoria al Forno at Disney's Boardwalk open, as do luxurious on-Disney property resorts including Four Seasons Resort Orlando.

Looking ahead, it seems as if pixie dust will permeate the World for years to come. The Magic Kingdom's Fantasyland is complete with everyone's newest favorite ride, the Seven Dwarfs Mine Train family coaster. Disney Cruise Line now sails with four ships including the newer *Disney Fantasy* and *Disney Dream.* The multimillion-dollar makeover of Downtown Disney to Disney Springs has brought new shops, restaurants, and entertainment, and parking. In 2017, Pandora–The World of Avatar opened to acclaim. A new Toy Story Land opened in 2018, and Star Wars: Galaxy Edge opened in 2019.

Toy Story's Buzz Lightyear

FINDING MICKEY

A Hidden Mickey at Epcot

Hidden Mickeys began as an inside joke among Disney Imagineers, the creative folks behind the theme parks. When finishing an attraction, they'd slip a Mickey into the motif to see who might notice. You can get a list of Hidden Mickeys at any Guest Relations location, at www.allears.net, or at www.hiddenmickeys.org. Here are just a few to get you started, though:

Big Thunder Mountain Railroad (Magic Kingdom). As your train nears the station, look to your right for three rusty gears on the ground.

DINOSAUR (Animal Kingdom). Stare at the bark of the painted tree in the far left background of the wall mural at the entrance.

Haunted Mansion (Magic Kingdom). As you move through the ballroom, notice the Mouse-eared place setting on the table.

Spaceship Earth (EPCOT). Mickey smiles down from a constellation behind the loading area.

Twilight Zone Tower of Terror (Hollywood Studios). In the boiler room, look for a water stain on the wall after the queue splits.

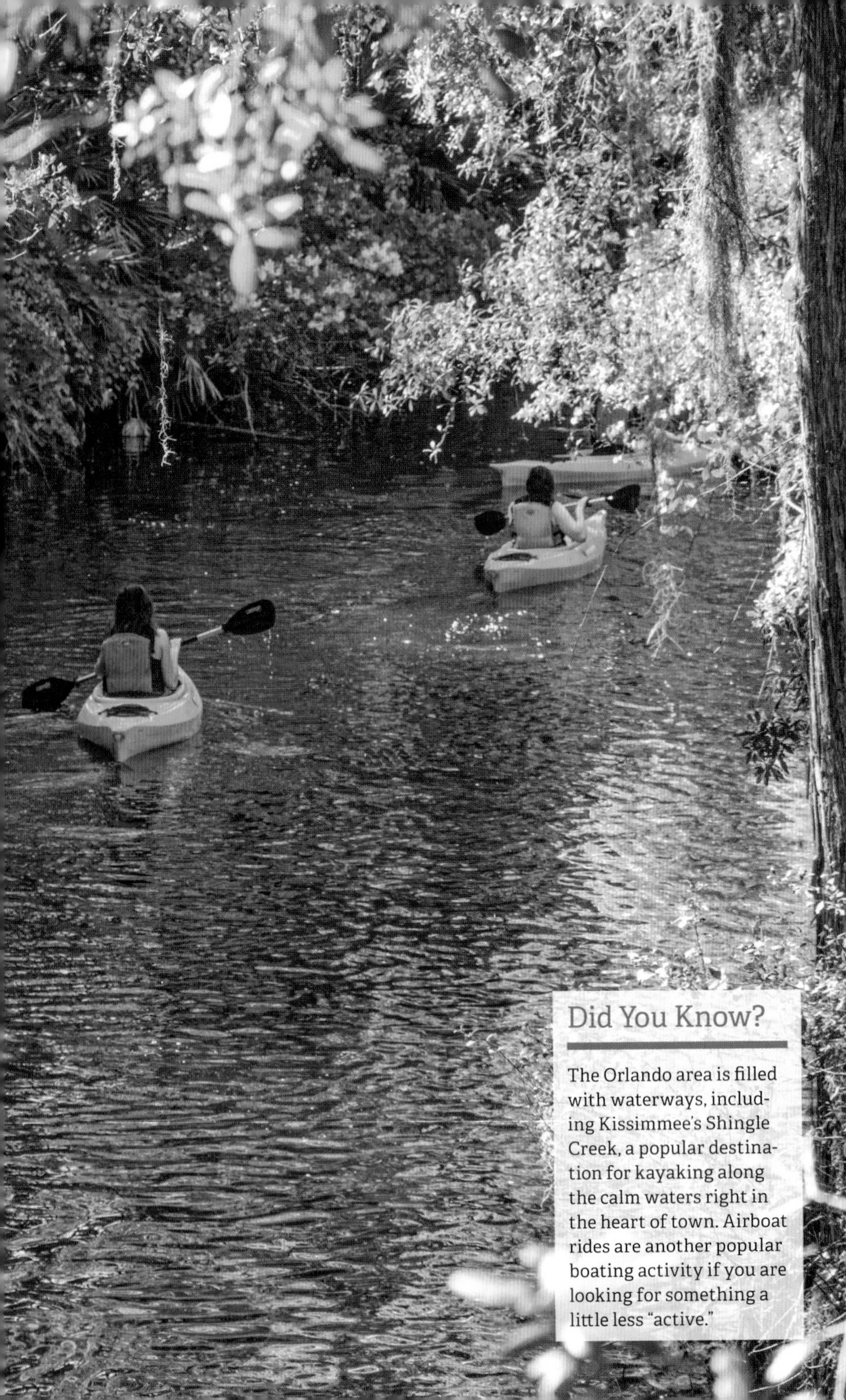

Did You Know?

The Orlando area is filled with waterways, including Kissimmee's Shingle Creek, a popular destination for kayaking along the calm waters right in the heart of town. Airboat rides are another popular boating activity if you are looking for something a little less "active."

Chapter 2

TRAVEL SMART

Updated by
Gary McKechnie

★ **STATE CAPITAL**
Tallahassee

POPULATION
290,000 (Orlando)

LANGUAGE
English

$ **CURRENCY**
U.S. dollar

AREA CODE
321, 407

⚠ **EMERGENCIES**
911

DRIVING
On the right side

ELECTRICITY
120–240 v/60 cycles; plugs have two or three rectangular prongs

TIME
Eastern Standard Time (same as New York); 3 hours ahead of Los Angeles

WEB RESOURCES
www.visitflorida.com
www.visitorlando.com

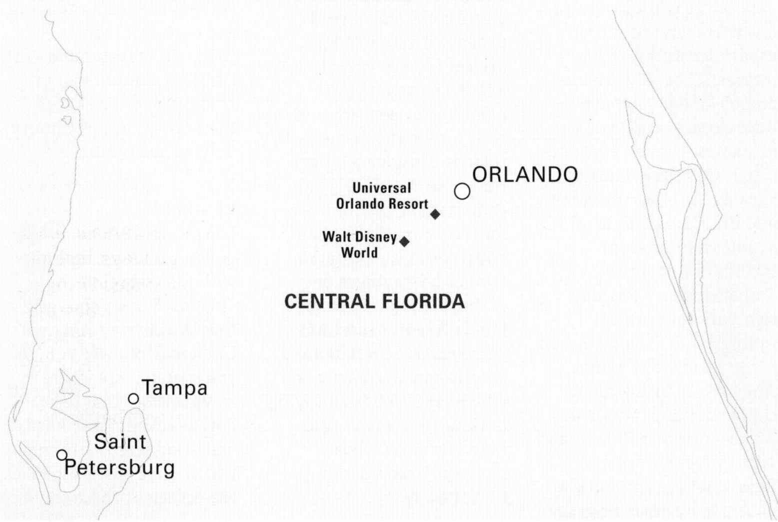

Know Before You Go

ROAD TRIP!

Within 30 minutes of the theme park attractions you'll find airboat rides that can take you into natural Florida; crystal-clear Wekiwa Springs, and small towns like Mount Dora, Winter Garden, and Winter Park. In these authentic towns, the theme is Old Florida.

THEME PARKS

Orlando is home to seven of the world's Top 10 theme parks, including Walt Disney World's Magic Kingdom, EPCOT, Hollywood Studios, and Animal Kingdom; Universal Orlando's Universal Studios and Islands of Adventure; and SeaWorld. Even on a generous five-day vacation, you'll have to leave some parks on hold until your next Orlando trip. For first-time visitors, seeing the Magic Kingdom, Universal Studios, and SeaWorld can give you a great overall experience while leaving a few extra days to add the others according to your interests. For a little more money (and if you have a little extra energy) you can buy a pass that will get you into *two* parks in one day, such as the Magic Kingdom and EPCOT or Universal Studios and adjacent Islands of Adventure. Embarking on a one-day, two-park tour can be taxing, but it's a good option if you have limited time. And be sure to download the Disney app (My Disney Experience) and Universal app (Universal Orlando Resort) where you can plan your trip by prearranging ride times and checking restaurant menus, show times, and more.

DRIVE TIME

When Walt Disney World opened in 1971 it attracted millions of happy guests—as well as millions of new motorists, millions of new residents, and hundreds of thousands new employees that now travel an ever-expanding network of roads and highways. Orlando never seems to get ahead of the curve when it comes to traffic, so before you head out be sure to know where you're going and be ready to deal with stop-and-go drivers, road construction, and toll plazas. If you're planning to spend most of your time at the theme parks, though, consider skipping the rental car entirely and calling a taxi, Lyft, or Uber for those rare times when you'll need transportation. If you'll be staying at one of the theme park's resort hotels, free transportation is provided to the parks and entertainment complexes, which saves you from paying parking fees or having to take a tram, ferryboat, or monorail from a parking lot far, far away.

AFTER HOURS

After a full day inside the theme parks, not every visitor is ready to handle a full evening of entertainment, but if you can, there are a few ways to do it. At Walt Disney World the entertainment complex known as Disney Springs is an always-active collection of shops, restaurants, attractions, nightclubs, and activities that span four districts. Highlights include Cirque du Soleil, a House of Blues, and the largest Disney store in the world. At Universal Studios, the CityWalk entertainment complex follows a similar approach with the world's largest Hard Rock Cafe, the Blue Man Group, and a host of iconic nightclubs and restaurants. Each is fabulously packed every evening, and each offers a tremendous diversity that pleases visitors of all ages. In addition, International Drive's dinner shows, movie theaters, theme restaurants, comedy clubs, hotel restaurants, towering Ferris wheel, and shopping and entertainment complexes are popular with the thousands of visitors attending conferences at the nearby Orange County Convention Center.

RESORTS

Long, long ago hotels were built without a theme and without a storyline. In Orlando, Disney changed that in a big way and then Universal followed suit. As you contemplate where to stay, consider that resort hotels—even those billed as "value lodging"—still come with a tinge of sticker shock. Nevertheless, these could be a bargain when you factor in the theme entertainment that's woven into every aspect of architectural design, as well as into each restaurant, game room, pool area, and bedroom. Whether you're staying in a resort hotel that evokes New Orleans, Saratoga Springs, Miami Beach, a South Seas island, a pop culture cartoon, or anything a designer can imagine, as a resort guest you're often given early admission to the theme parks and are provided with free transportation to the parks and entertainment complexes.

DOWNTOWN
Long before the theme parks, downtown Orlando had a theme based on the 1920s "City Beautiful" movement. This approach is still reflected in moss-draped Spanish oaks, pristine lakes, charming neighborhoods that mix Arts and Crafts bungalows with Spanish-Mediterranean mansions, and picturesque Lake Eola, which was (and remains) the centerpiece of the city and subject of hundreds of postcards and photographs. Although time and traffic have surrounded downtown, the essence of the City Beautiful remains, with the added attractions of the Amway Center (home of the NBA's Orlando Magic and touring concerts), the Dr. Phillips Center (which presents A-list performers and stage shows), Orange Avenue (with its string of nightclubs and restaurants), and the Thornton Park district (with its bohemian urban vibe).

AFFORDABLE FAMILY FUN
A vacation in Orlando doesn't mean you have to break the bank. Near the attractions are affordable family activities like miniature golf, water parks, and dinner shows. And don't forget that splashing around the hotel pool can give kids an outlet for their excess energy while providing parents with a much-needed physical and fiscal respite. And when it comes to dining, many restaurants offer free meals for kids 12 and under, and buffet restaurants are usually a great value, with an impressive range of appetizers, entrées, and desserts that have dazzled diners from around the world.

THE SPACE COAST IS NEARBY
Roughly an hour from Orlando is Cocoa Beach, the self-titled "Small Wave Capital of the World" and home to Ron Jon's, the world's largest surf shop (open 24 hours a day for your shopping and surfing convenience). For some, the beach alone is enough to make the drive over to the coast, but there's another even more spectacular reason: Kennedy Space Center. At America's primary portal into space, you can relive the glory days of the Mercury, Gemini, and Apollo missions at the Visitor Complex; look forward to the exciting new missions of SpaceX, Blue Origins, and the United Launch Alliance; and see the actual space shuttle *Atlantis* as well as an authentic Saturn V in two of the most impressive presentations anywhere.

JUST GIVE ME THE TICKET
Don't think your wallet will cool off after spending money on flights, hotels, and transportation. Now that you're here, you'll still be on the hook for meals, entertainment, and theme-park tickets. Priced at well over $100 per day—and with rates increasing with suspicious frequency—almost any of Orlando's theme parks can cost a family close to $1,000 for two days in the parks. One method of taking the pinch out of the price is going online and ordering your tickets well in advance. In addition to giving you far more time to decide exactly what kind of ticket package you really want (something nearly impossible to do when at a ticket kiosk with a line of anxious visitors behind you), online prices are always a few dollars less and will lock in your price.

PACKING
More than a few travelers have found that when they're ready to head home, their suitcases are no longer sufficient. Instead of buying new bags at an upscale mall (or even at an outlet store), look for a nearby thrift store where you can find perfectly suitable suitcases for about 10 bucks.

Getting Here and Around

 Air

All the major and most discount airlines fly into **Orlando International Airport** (**MCO**), which is among America's to 12 busiest airports. About 30 minutes north of town, the **Orlando-Sanford Airport** (**SFB**) is a far smaller but far more manageable option.

AIRLINES

Major U.S. airlines—including Alaskan Airlines, American, Delta, Frontier, JetBlue, Silver, Southwest, Spirit, Sun Country, and United—and several international airlines—including British Airways, Aer Lingus, Air Canada, Air Transat, and WestJet—(more than 40 total) fly in and out of MCO (the initials referencing its original name as McCoy Air Force Base), with more than 50 million passengers arriving and departing each year. Not only is this a busy airport with 850 daily flights that travel to 135 domestic and international destinations, it's a full-service one as well with more than 120 dining options; an in-terminal hotel; a fleet of taxis, shuttles, and buses; every rental car company you've heard of (and many you haven't); and, to accommodate the city's growing popularity, a completely new terminal scheduled to be open by 2021.

FLYING TIME

You can fly nonstop to Orlando from most major cities in the United States and from several international cities. It's 60 minutes from Miami, 90 minutes from Atlanta, 2 hours and 30 minutes from Washington, D.C. or Dallas, 2 hours and 50 minutes from Chicago or Detroit, 3 hours from New York City, 3 hours 30 minutes from Denver, 4 hours and 45 minutes from Los Angeles, 5 hours and 15 minutes from San Francisco, and 5 hours and 25 minutes from Seattle. Internationally, a nonstop flight from London takes 9 hours and 40 minutes.

DRIVING FROM THE AIRPORT

From the airport, the Beachline Expressway, aka State Road 528, is the toll road that leads west from the airport to the area attractions or east, to the Space Coast, which encompasses the Kennedy Space Center, Cocoa, Cocoa Beach, Titusville, and Melbourne. South of the airport, an access road leads to the southern perimeter of SR 417, which is the nearly completed beltway around Orlando, while SR 436 heads due north to take you closer to downtown Orlando and the suburbs of Winter Park, Maitland, and Altamonte Springs. If you need to pay cash for tolls, make sure you follow the signs and stay in the correct lane, or you'll be surprised to receive a bill for the tolls you skipped.

MAGICAL EXPRESS

If you're staying at a Disney hotel and flying on a participating airline, this free service will deliver your luggage from your home airport to your hotel (and back again) *and* shuttle you to and from your resort, albeit sometimes very slowly. You must book before departure by calling ☎ *407/939–1936*. Likewise, if you're tagging a Disney Cruise onto your vacation, call ☎ *800/951–3532* to arrange bus transportation to and from the ship at Port Canaveral. The $39 service is available on embarkation and disembarkation days only.

TAXIS AND SHUTTLES

Many non-Disney hotels offer free airport shuttles. If yours doesn't, taxis from the airport to the Disney area run $55–$75 and are available as you exit baggage claim. The Mears Transportation Group offers shuttle and charter services throughout the Orlando area (its shuttles can be booked in advance or at the airport after you arrive); a shuttle to a non-Disney hotel costs $23–$25 one-way.

Airport to:	By Shuttle (per person)	By Taxi/Car
Magic Kingdom	30–45 mins; $37 round-trip (RT); $23 one-way (OW)	35 mins; approx. $70 (taxi fare for up to 7 people, including tolls and tip)
Disney Springs	30–45 mins; $39 RT; $25 OW	25–30 mins; approx. $55
Animal Kingdom/ Hollywood Studios	30–45 mins; $35 RT; $23 OW	35 mins; approx. $58
Universal Orlando	30–40 mins; $35 RT; $23 OW	20 mins; approx. $48
Kissimmee	30–45 mins; $39 RT; $25 OW	30 mins; approx. $59
I-Drive (midway)	30–40 mins; $35 RT; $23 OW	20 mins; approx. $36
Downtown Orlando	30 mins; $35 RT; $23 OW	20 mins; approx. $34

Car

Depending on how much time you'll spend in Orlando, you may or may not need a rental car. If you're staying for a few days and plan to spend them at a Disney or Universal resort hotel visiting the theme parks, just catch a lift from the airport, and then rely on one of the resorts' complimentary transportation (buses or boats) that can take you straight to the parks and entertainment complexes. If you're staying off property but still want to avoid rental car expenses, calling a taxi or ride share will also help you avoid paying for theme-park parking, which can cost $20 to $25 per day.

If you'll be staying a little longer and plan to explore the surrounding areas (or if you are staying in a condo or other rental), then you will probably want to rent a car. Just be prepared to deal with the possibility of paying for valet parking if you are staying at a hotel and facing highway traffic that is often stop-and-go, especially on Interstate 4 in the 10-mile stretch between Walt Disney World and Universal Orlando. Another factor that affects driving is that Orlando, like Los Angeles, spills out in all directions, which generally makes reaching neighboring communities an epic journey.

SUNPASS

To save time and money while on the road, you might want to purchase a SunPass for your personal or rental vehicle. It provides a discount on most tolls, and you'll be able to sail past collection booths without stopping. If you'll be renting a car, rental car companies often offer a transponder to use during your stay. You also can use SunPass to pay for parking at Orlando, Tampa, Palm Beach, Miami, and Fort Lauderdale airports. (In addition, SunPass now interfaces with North Carolina's Quick Pass and Georgia's Peach Pass.) SunPass transponders can be purchased for $4.99 to $25 at drugstores, supermarkets, or tourism welcome centers, and you can charge them up with a credit card and reload as needed. For more info, check out *www.sunpass.com.*

ORLANDO DRIVING ROUTES

Beachline Expressway: Toll road from the airport to I-Drive and Disney ($2.25). Also good for Universal, SeaWorld, and Space Coast.

Interstate 4: Main east–west highway between Tampa and Daytona; it follows a north–south track through Orlando, making for a little confusion. **TIP→ Think north when Interstate 4 signs say east**

(toward Daytona, say), and south when they say west (toward Tampa).

Key exits:

–Exit 64B: Magic Kingdom/U.S. 192; *heavy* peak-season traffic near this exit

–Exit 65: Animal Kingdom, ESPN Wide World of Sports

–Exit 67: EPCOT/Disney Springs, Typhoon Lagoon, Universal; less-congested exit

–Exit 68: Disney Springs, Typhoon Lagoon

–Exits 71 and 72: SeaWorld

–Exits 72, 74A, and 75A: I-Drive

–Exits 74B and 75A: Universal Orlando Resort

Semoran Boulevard: One of the main roads north to Orlando and Winter Park from the airport, Semoran Boulevard (aka SR 436) is heavily traveled but moves well and has plenty of restaurants and gas stations.

Spacecoast Parkway or Irlo Bronson Memorial Highway (U.S. 192): Runs east–west to Kissimmee. Continues east to the coast at Melbourne. Crosses Interstate 4 at Exits 64A and 64B.

ROAD SERVICE

Walt Disney World's **Car Care Center** near the Magic Kingdom provides emergency services, including free towing on Disney property, even for non-AAA members. It's open daily, but hours vary. In a pinch, dial 511.

CAR RENTALS

Rates vary seasonally and can begin as low as $30 a day or $149 a week for an economy car (excluding 6.5% rental-car tax).

■ TIP→ **If you're returning a car to MCO, definitely fill up several miles from MCO. Some stations near the airport rip off unsuspecting travelers by doubling the price of a gallon.**

 Cruise

For some families, a definite plus to an Orlando vacation is the chance to double their pleasure by taking a cruise before or after their theme-park visits. Less than an hour from the attractions, Port Canaveral is the "berth-place" of four cruise lines—Disney, Carnival, Norwegian, and Royal Caribbean—whose range of excursions can take you to the eastern or western Caribbean or, with more time, to Mexico's Yucatàn peninsula, the Panama Canal, or South America. If you're traveling a distance to reach Florida (or if you're simply a fan of cruising), it might be worth extending your vacation with a few extra days at sea.

If you book a voyage with Disney Cruise Line, you can prearrange ground transportation from MCO or Walt Disney World. Other shuttle services between Orlando and the coast are Port Canaveral Shuttle and GoPort, each charging $15 one-way or $30 round-trip. Each will whisk you directly from MCO to the port in a little more than an hour, though when you book a private shuttle service, you will usually have to wait for the shuttle to fill before it departs.

 Public Transportation

The **I-RIDE Trolley** serves most attractions in the I-Drive area. It won't get you to Disney, but it does have a stop about a half-mile from Universal. A one-way trip is $2, but an all-day pass costs just $5, $7 for three days, and $9 for five days. This super-convenient option can take you as far south as the Orlando Vineland Premium Outlets south of SeaWorld (and to SeaWorld itself) and as far north as the Florida Turnpike and the Orlando International Premium Outlets and multiple stops in between.

Magic Kingdom to:	By Shuttle	By Taxi/Car
Disney Springs	N/A (use Disney transportation)	10–15 mins; approx. $18
Animal Kingdom/ Hollywood Studios	N/A (use Disney transportation)	15 mins; approx. $24
Universal Orlando	25 mins; $22 RT	25 mins; approx. $44
Kissimmee	N/A	25–30 mins; approx. $35
I-Drive (midway)	N/A	30 mins; approx. $44
Downtown Orlando	N/A	40 mins; approx. $64

Universal CityWalk to:	By Shuttle	By Taxi/Car
Magic Kingdom	N/A	25 mins; approx. $40
Disney Springs	N/A	20 mins; approx. $28
Animal Kingdom/ Hollywood Studios	N/A	30 mins; approx. $45
Kissimmee	30 mins; $37 RT; $23 OW	25 mins; approx. $36
I-Drive (midway)	25 mins; $18 RT; $10 OW	5–10 mins; approx. $10
Downtown Orlando	N/A	10 mins; approx. $31

The **LYNX** bus system provides service in Orlando, but it's geared toward the needs of commuters, not tourists.

Similarly, **Sunrail** provides quick and convenient commuter train service on weekdays all the way from Kissimmee to Winter Park, but it doesn't run on weekends and probaby won't meet the needs of most travelers.

Taxi

Taxis are widely available at the airport, at hotels, and even at theme parks. If you are at a Walt Disney World Resort hotel, the concierge can call a cab for you, but they are usually available at taxi stands at most other hotels in Orlando or can be called quickly. However, rates can be expensive due to distances and traffic. A rideshare is usually less expensive.

RIDESHARE

Both Uber and Lyft operate in Orlando and Walt Disney World, and you can save significantly by using rideshares over taxis. They are also allowed to do pick-ups and drop-offs at MCO in designated areas near baggage claim. Most of the larger hotels (especially those at the theme parks) also have designated areas for pick-ups and drop-offs. Getting from CityWalk to and from any of the hotels is easy. Just note that although Universal Orlando Resort offers free bus transportation between its hotels, , the waits can be fairly lengthy, so a rideshare is your best bet to get from one hotel to, say, a restaurant at another.

Essentials

Dining

The dining scene in Orlando was at one time epitomized by a plethora of fast-food fare, but there's been such an explosion of restaurants offering artisanal and locally sourced fare over the past five years that the city now has seven local chefs and nine international celebrity chefs with James Beard Award nominations. Some of the best restaurants in town can be found in resort hotels and theme-park complexes such as Disney Springs and the premium resort hotels of Universal Orlando, but if you have the time, explore the local treasures beyond the resorts.

The signs of Orlando's dining progress is most evident in the last place one would look: Disney's fast-food outlets. Every eatery on Disney property offers a tempting vegetarian option, and kiddie meals come with healthful sides and drinks unless you specifically request otherwise. Chefs at Disney's table-service restaurants consult face-to-face with guests about food allergies.

Around town, locals flock to the Ravenous Pig, Kres Chophouse, Artisan's Table, and other gastropubs where the menu changes regularly; Luma on Park, a suave home of thoughtfully created cutting-edge meals; and any number of dining establishments competing to serve the very finest steak. Orlando's culinary blossoming began in 1995, when Disney's signature California Grill debuted, featuring farm-to-table cuisine and wonderful wines by the glass. Soon after, celebrity chefs started opening up shop.

Orlando's destination restaurants can be found in the theme parks, as well as in the outlying towns. Sand Lake Road is known by foodies as Restaurant Row for its eclectic collection of worthwhile tables. Here you'll find fashionable outlets for sushi and seafood, Italian and chops, Hawaiian fusion and upscale Lebanese. Heading into the residential areas, the neighborhoods of Winter Park (actually its own city), Thornton Park, and downtown Orlando are prime locales for chow. Scattered throughout Central Florida, low-key ethnic restaurants specialize in the fare of Turkey, India, Peru, Thailand, Vietnam—you name it. When you think about it, with its abundance of international travelers, Orlando is a natural for international cuisine. Prices in these family-owned finds are usually delightfully low.

Restaurant reviews have been shortened. For full reviews, visit Fodors.com.

CONSIDERATIONS FOR DIFFERENT TYPES OF TRAVELERS

FAMILIES WITH YOUNG KIDS

Except for two, the ultraformal Victoria & Albert's and Christini's, most restaurants in and near the theme parks welcome children. Crayons, games, and kiddie menus are standard. If you're traveling with small children, they'll be over the moon if you set aside at least one outing for a character meal. At each of its four parks as well as at some of its resort hotels, Walt Disney World offers breakfast, lunch, and dinner with characters including Mickey, Donald, Goofy, Chip 'n' Dale, Cinderella, and other favorites who show up to sign autographs and pose for snapshots. Some dining events are buffets. Others are family-style or à la carte. All are fabulously entertaining.

At Universal, character meals are not as plentiful but are still offered. Year-round there's the Despicable Me Character Breakfast at the Loews Royal Pacific Resort and the Marvel Character Dinner at Islands of Adventure's Cafe 4. During the winter holidays, the Grinch & Friends Character Breakfast is held at Islands of Adventure, and, in the fall, the Halloween

Horror Nights Scareactor Dining Experience takes place at Universal Studios' Classic Monsters Cafe.

When possible, reserve your spot at these character meals far in advance. They are in high demand, especially at Walt Disney World.

TIP→ If your young children are theme-park newbies, have your character meal near the end of a visit, so they'll be used to seeing the large and sometimes frightening figures.

FAMILIES WITH TWEENS

Tweens who have outgrown character meals might be more impressed by highly themed restaurants like the 50's Prime Time Café in Disney's Hollywood Studios, a kitschy 1950s-theme space where "Mom," the waitress, might make parents finish their vegetables. At the Sci-Fi Dine-In Theater nearby, guests eat in top-down convertible cars that face a big screen airing 1950s and '60s sci-fi and monster trailers; there are even tasty vegetarian offerings.

Universal's Islands of Adventure also has theme eateries based on superheroes or other classic characters. The Three Broomsticks at Islands of Adventure and Leaky Cauldron at Universal Studios offer British pub food, and both are boons for Harry Potter fans.

FAMILIES WITH TEENS

CityWalk is filled with high-energy themed eateries that teens love. In fact, local high schoolers tend to congregate in the CityWalk common areas on weekend evenings. The lively Hard Rock Cafe is a consistent favorite.

At Disney's BoardWalk, the ESPN Club is a great choice for teen sports fans. Even its bathrooms are equipped with video monitors, so you don't have to miss a second of a great game.

COUPLES

Truly, you'd be hard-pressed to find more romantic restaurants than the ones on Disney property. Jiko, at the Animal Kingdom Lodge, pairs superb African-accented cuisine with an exceptional South African wine list and dramatic decor.
If you really want to go all out, there's absolutely nothing like Victoria & Albert's in the Grand Floridian. Treat yourself to a gourmet, seven-course, prix-fixe meal to live harp music in one of only 26 restaurants in America to hold both the AAA Five Diamond and Forbes Travel Guide Five-Star Awards.

Outside the theme parks, Norman's, at the Ritz-Carlton, has a sophisticated dining room and impressive New World cuisine.

SINGLES OR GROUPS OF FRIENDS

Singles often dine at the bars of upscale-casual favorites, including Seasons 52, Prato, and downtown Orlando's Ceviche, a tapas restaurant. Groups enjoy the festive antics of International Drive's Taverna Opa, where visitors often find themselves dancing around the dining room, and the Cafe Tu Tu Tango, a tapas restaurant modeled after a Parisian artist's loft. Every piece of artwork that adorns the walls is for sale, including the pieces being created by visiting artists.

LARGE GROUPS

Restaurants in theme-park hotels, in nearby convention hotels, on Sand Lake Road, and on International Drive have private party rooms for large groups more often than not. For an alternative, consider dinner shows. The food is plentiful, and the entertainment keeps younger family members engaged. The luaus at Disney and Universal hotels are good for all ages, as is the wonderfully hokey Hoop-Dee-Doo Musical Revue at Disney's Fort Wilderness Resort. One of the longest-running shows in the world, it premiered at Pioneer Hall in June 1974 and is still one of the most popular shows at Disney.

Many off-park venues also offer theme dining with shows. The concepts range from medieval jousting on horseback to pirates to comedic murder mysteries.

THEME-PARK MEALPLANS

Disney Dining Plans allow you to prepay for meals and choose the level of dining you'd like. The Quick Service Dining Plan is available for counter service locations that serve casual meals. The Disney Dining Plan offers meals at 50 table-service restaurants (reservations required). The comprehensive Disney Deluxe Dining Plan lets you take "an epicurean journey from appetizers to desserts." This option not only offers the most meals and delicious appetizers but also delectable snacks. Each plan includes nonalcoholic specialty beverages and, for guests 21 and older, beer, wine, and cocktails. Used wisely, Disney dining plans are a steal, but be careful to buy only the number of meals you'll want to eat. Moderate eaters can end up turning away appetizers and desserts to which they're entitled. Plan ahead, and use "extra" meals to your advantage by swapping two table-service meals for a Disney dinner show, say, or an evening at a high-end restaurant like California Grill.

Universal Dining Plans include options for sit-down or quick-service meals at participating walk-up eateries inside Universal Studios and Islands of Adventure, plus a snack and a soft drink. Daily prices are $35 for a quick-service option (which includes an all-you-can-drink souvenir mug) or, if you'd like to upgrade to a full-service meal at a sit-down restaurant, $64—although this can only be purchased with a Universal vacation plan.

RESERVATIONS

Reservations are strongly recommended throughout the theme parks. Indeed, you can make reservations for Disney restaurants and character meals at both Universal and Disney at least 90 (and up to 180) days out. And be sure to ask about the cancellation policy—at all table service Disney restaurants, for instance, you will be charged $10 per guest if you don't give 24 hours' notice.

For restaurant reservations within Walt Disney World, call or book online (☎ *407/939–3463* 🌐 *www.disneyworld.com/dining*). You can also get plenty of information on the Disney website, including the meal periods served, price ranges, and specialties of all Disney eateries. Menus for all restaurants are posted online and tend to be up to date. Call for Universal Orlando reservations (☎ *407/224–9255 theme parks and CityWalk, 407/503–3463 hotels*). You can also learn about the complex's 50-plus restaurants at the Universal website (🌐 *www.universalorlando.com/dining*).

In our reviews, reservations are mentioned only when they're essential or not accepted. Unless otherwise noted, the restaurants listed are open daily for lunch and dinner.

SMOKING

The Florida Clean Indoor Air Act bans smoking in all restaurants. You can smoke in some bars, provided less than 10% of their business comes from food sales. In other words: *Smoking is discouraged.*

TIPPING AND TAXES

In most restaurants, tip the waiter 15%–20% of the food and beverage charges before tax. Tip at least $1 per drink at the bar, and $2 for valet parking.

WHAT TO WEAR

Because tourism is king around Orlando, casual dress is the rule. Flip-flops and cutoffs are acceptable in just about all fast-food and mid-price restaurants. Although it's best to dress up for the ritzier restaurants, don't be shocked to find diners beside you in Levi's and polo shirts. Men need jackets only in the most exclusive establishments; however, such establishments are strict about enforcing dress code. If you plan to eat at a nicer place, check on dress codes so you aren't caught unprepared and turned away at the door.

What it Costs

$	$$	$$$	$$$$
AT DINNER			
under $15	$15–$21	$22–$30	over $30

Health and Safety

Recent health scares such as Zika, the West Nile virus, and coronavirus (COVID-19) can spark more than a little anxiety in travelers. For the latest updates on health issues being monitored by Florida health officials, visit the website of the Florida Department of Health (🌐 *www.floridahealth.gov*) and search for "current hazards."

Stepped-up policing against thieves preying on tourists in rental cars has helped address what was once a serious issue in Florida. Still, visitors should be wary when driving in unfamiliar neighborhoods and leaving the airport. Don't leave valuables unattended while you walk the beach or go for a dip. And never leave handbags, cameras, and so on, visible in your vehicle. Try to use ATMs only during the day or in brightly lighted, well-traveled locales. Even better, just use your debit card when picking up snacks, souvenirs, or sundries at a Walgreens or CVS and then ask for cash back from your purchase. It's much safer, and you won't have to pay a bank's ATM service fee.

If you're visiting Florida during the June through November hurricane season and a storm is imminent, be sure to follow safety orders and evacuation instructions—which most often consist of heading inland, which, often, is Orlando.

COVID-19

A new novel coronavirus brought all travel to a virtual standstill in the first half of 2020. Although the illness is mild in most people, some experience severe and even life-threatening complications. Once travel started up again, albeit slowly and cautiously, travelers were asked to be particularly careful about hygiene and to avoid any unnecessary travel, especially if they are sick.

Older adults, especially those over 65, have a greater chance of having severe complications from COVID-19. The same is true for people with weaker immune systems or those living with some types of medical conditions, including diabetes, asthma, heart disease, cancer, HIV/AIDS, kidney disease, and liver disease. Starting two weeks before a trip, anyone planning to travel should be on the lookout for some of the following symptoms: cough, fever, chills, trouble breathing, muscle pain, sore throat, new loss of smell or taste. If you experience any of these symptoms, you should not travel at all.

And to protect yourself during travel, do your best to avoid contact with people showing symptoms. Wash your hands often with soap and water. Limit your time in public places, and, when you are out and about, wear a cloth face mask

Essentials

that covers your nose and mouth. Indeed, a mask may be required in some places, such as on an airplane or in a confined space like a theater, where you share the space with a lot of people. You may wish to bring extra supplies, such as disenfecting wipes, hand sanitizer (12-ounce bottles were allowed in carry-on luggage at this writing), and a first-aid kit with a thermometer.

Given how abruptly travel was curtailed in March 2020, it is wise to consider protecting yourself by purchasing a travel insurance policy that will reimburse you for any costs related to COVID-19 related cancellations. Not all travel insurance policies protect against pandemic-related cancellations, so always read the fine print.

Lodging

With tens of thousands of lodging choices available in the Orlando area, from tents to deluxe villas, there is no lack of variety in price or amenities. Actually, narrowing down the possibilities is part of the fun.

More than 75 million visitors come to the Orlando area each year, making it the most popular tourism destination on the planet. More upscale hotels are opening as visitors demand more luxurious surroundings, such as luxe linens, tasteful and refined decor, organic toiletries, or ergonomic chairs and work desks. But no matter what your budget or desires, lodging comes in such a wide range of prices, themes, color schemes, brands, and guest-room amenities, you will have no problem finding something that fits.

Resorts on and off Disney properties combine function with fantasy, as befits visitor expectations. Characters in costume perform for the kids, pools are pirates' caves with waterfalls, and some, like the Gaylord Palms, go so far as to re-create Florida landmarks under a gargantuan glass roof, giving visitors the illusion of having visited more of the state than they expected.

International Drive's expanding attractions, including the Wheel at ICON Park (a 400-foot tall Ferris—or "observation"— wheel), Madame Tussauds, and a widening array of eateries are drawing more savvy conventioneers who bring their families along for the fun.

Many hotels have joined the trend toward green lodging, bringing recycling, water conservation, and other environmentally conscious practices to the table. Best of all, the sheer number and variety of hotel rooms means you can still find relative bargains throughout the Orlando area, even on Disney property, by researching your trip well, calling the lodgings directly, negotiating packages and prices, and shopping wisely.

FACILITIES AND AMENITIES

All hotels and resorts in Central Florida have air-conditioning, and most have cable or satellite TV, coffeemakers, mini-refrigerators, in-room irons, and ironing boards (except at Walt Disney World, where almost no rooms have coffeemakers). Those in the moderate and expensive price ranges often have bathrobes and hair dryers. High-speed wireless access (Wi-Fi) is now common even at budget properties, but some hotels still charge a daily fee for Internet service. If being connected is important, it's best to ask. Most hotels, even the budget ones, have a pool, and many have fitness facilities and business centers. Also, to avoid disconcerting surprises on your final bill, be sure to ask about resort fees. These can be in excess of $20 per night, and, sadly, most Orlando hotels now charge them.

If a particular amenity is important to you, ask for it; many hotels will provide extras upon request. Naturally, you'll want to double-check your bill at checkout and if a charge seems unreasonable, this is the time to have it remedied. If you're traveling with pets, note the hotel's pet policies. Some hotels require substantial cleaning fees. A big note to smokers: most of the hotels and resorts in Central Florida are entirely smoke-free, meaning even smoking outdoors on hotel property is frowned upon or prohibited. And don't try to sneak a smoke in your room—you'll pay a fee for the hotelier to clear you room of residual smoke.

PARKING

Driving at Walt Disney World can be a challenge, as the property is vast, and you are dealing with fellow drivers who are unfamiliar with the area. But each park entrance is clearly marked, and once through the tollbooth you benefit from a mastery of the "queuing experience" as you are guided through the sprawling, open-air parking lots to a specific spot and told to remember the location by the signs on light posts. It's easier to take a picture of the signs closest to your car before boarding a tram to reach the park entrance. At Universal, use the same snapshot technique to capture your parking area in the multilevel garage. If your hotel provides a shuttle, or if you use public transportation to get to the parks, you can avoid the hassle of parking, and driving, altogether, which isn't a bad idea considering you'll have to pay $25 just to park a far distance from the entrance. Note that Disney now charges all guests with cars a nightly parking charge of $15 to $25, depending on the hotel, though resort guests are then allowed to drive to and park at the Disney theme parks for no additional cost.

APARTMENT AND HOUSE RENTALS

The state's allure for visiting snowbirds (Northerners "flocking" to Florida in winter) has caused private home and condo rentals to boom in popularity, at times affording better options for vacationers, particularly families who want to have some extra space and cooking facilities. In some destinations, home and condo rentals are more readily available than hotels—and the surplus of AirBnBs provides travelers with additional options while providing hoteliers and innkeepers with competition that doesn't play by the same rules.

Although you can check out websites like 🌐 *VRBO.com* and 🌐 *AirBnB.com*, finding a great rental agency can help you weed out the risky options. Target offices that specialize in the area you want to visit, and have a personal conversation with a representative as soon as possible. Be honest about your budget and expectations. For example, ask the rental agent if having the living room couch pull double-duty as a bed is not OK. Although websites listing rentals directly from homeowners are growing in popularity, there's a higher chance of coming across Pinocchios advertising "gourmet" kitchens that have one or two nice gadgets but fixtures or appliances from 1982. To protect yourself, talk extensively with owners in advance, see if there's a system in place for accountability should something go wrong, and make sure there's a 24-hour phone number for emergencies.

ROOM RATES

In the Orlando area there's an inverse relationship between temperature and room rates. The hot and humid weather in late summer and fall brings lower prices and possibly hurricanes. Conversely, the balmy days of late February,

Essentials

March, and April attract lots of visitors for Spring Break; hotel owners charge accordingly. One note about hurricane season—it officially begins in June, but a hurricane in Florida before August is rare. Rates are often low from early January to mid-February, from late April to mid-June, and from mid-August to the third week in November.

Always call several places—availability and special deals can drive room rates at a $$$$ hotel down into the $$ range—and don't forget to ask whether you're eligible for a discount, perhaps AAA, AARP, or military. You can always save by preparing a few meals in a room, suite, or villa with a kitchenette or kitchen. Websites will often offer a better room rate; so compare the prices offered on the Web and through the hotel's local or toll-free number (if one is available). Always ask about special packages or corporate rates. Don't be shy. Polite assertiveness can save you money.

The Disney Dining Plan: On-site Walt Disney World hotels don't offer meal plans in their rates, but you can choose a Disney Dining Plan. It can be added to any on-site package, and many families swear by it. The plan saves you from having to carry around cash and—at least on the surface—masks the sting of coughing up nine bucks for a cheeseburger. To see if a Disney Dining Plan is right for your family, go to 🌐 *www.disneyworld.disney.go.com/dining* for more information.

What It Costs

$	$$	$$$	$$$$
FOR TWO PEOPLE			
under $175	$175–$249	$250–$350	over $350

WHERE SHOULD WE STAY?

When it comes to Orlando lodging, no matter who you are and where you decide to stay, you should book months in advance (at least six months for hotels at Disney). This is particularly important for travel when rates are lowest, specifically early January to mid-February, late April to mid-June, and mid-August to early December.

HOTELS ON DISNEY AND UNIVERSAL PROPERTY

If you're interested solely in attractions at Disney or Universal, **in-park hotels are best.** For starters, they offer such convenient transportation options that you probably won't need a rental car—a huge cost savings.

Walt Disney World's massive campus is tied together by a dizzying array of complimentary monorails, buses, ferries, and water taxis. All get you anywhere on the property you want to go. Universal provides complimentary shuttles and water taxis between its two theme parks, the Volcano Bay water park, and its six on-site hotels, with shuttle buses ferrying guests staying at its two Endless Summer off-site hotels to the parks.

Staying at a resort on Disney property, or at a Disney Good Neighbor hotel, brings a variety of benefits that other hotels don't offer—some designed to save money, some designed to save time. Among the perks: early park entry; extended park hours; and, if a round of golf is on the itinerary, guests receive reduced rates when playing at three Disney courses, along with priority tee times and complimentary transportation to and from the course.

HOTELS OFF THEME-PARK PROPERTY

If you plan to visit several parks or go sightseeing elsewhere in Central Florida, consider off-site hotels. Those closest to Disney are clustered in a few areas:

Where Should We Stay?

	Vibe	Pros	Cons
Disney	Thousands of rooms at every price; convenient to Disney parks; free transportation all over WDW complex.	Perks like early park entry, complimentary MagicBands or cards, and Magical Express, which lets you circumvent airport bag checks.	Without a rental car, you likely won't leave Disney. On-site buses, although free, can take a big bite of time out of your entertainment day.
Universal	On-site hotels offer luxury, convenience, and value. There are less expensive options just outside the gates.	Central to Disney, Universal, SeaWorld, malls, and I–4; free water taxis to parks from on-site hotels.	Most on-site hotels are pricey; expect heavy rush-hour traffic during drives to and from other parks.
I-Drive	A hotel, convention center, and activities bonanza. A trolley runs from one end to the other.	Outlet malls provide bargains; world-class restaurants; the Coca-Cola Orlando Eye lifts visitors up for a bird's-eye view; many hotels offer free park shuttles.	Transportation can be pricey, in cash and in time, as traffic is often heavy. After a rise in car burglaries and tourist-related crimes, security was increased.
Kissimmee	It offers mom-and-pop motels and upscale choices, restaurants, and places to buy saltwater taffy.	It's just outside Disney, very close to Magic Kingdom. The town has Old Florida charm and the lodgings offer low prices.	Some of the older motels here are a little seedy. Petty crime in which tourists are victims is rare—but not unheard of.
Lake Buena Vista	Many hotel and restaurant chains here. Adjacent to WDW, which is where almost every guest in your hotel is headed.	Really close to WDW; plenty of dining and shopping options; easy access to I–4.	Heavy peak-hour traffic. As in all neighborhoods near Disney, a gallon of gas will cost 10%–15% more than elsewhere.
Central Orlando	Parts of town have the modern high-rises you'd expect. Other areas have oak tree–lined brick streets winding among small, cypress-ringed lakes.	Locally owned restaurants, trendy hotels, vibrant nightlife, and some quaint B&Bs. City buses serve the parks. There's good access to I–4.	You'll need to rent a car. And you will be part of the traffic headed to WDW. Expect the 25-mile drive to take at least 45 minutes.
Orlando International Airport	Mostly business and flight-crew hotels and car-rental outlets.	Great if you have an early flight or just want to shop in a mall. There's even a Hyatt on-site.	Watching planes, buses, taxis, and cars arrive and depart is all the entertainment you'll get.

Essentials

along I-Drive; in the U.S. 192 area and Kissimmee; and in the Disney Springs–Lake Buena Vista Area, just off Interstate 4 Exit 68. I-Drive hotels such as the Holiday Inn & Suites, Best Western Plus Universal Inn, Hyatt House, and Clarion Inn & Suites are closest to Universal.

Nearly every hotel in these areas provides frequent (sometimes free) transportation to and from Disney or even Universal. In addition, there are some noteworthy and money-saving, if far-flung, options in the greater Orlando area. One suburban caveat: traffic on Interstate 4 in Orlando experiences typical freeway gridlock during morning (7–9) and evening (4–6) rush hours and often into the evening as guests head out of the theme parks and locals head into the entertainment complexes of Disney and Universal.

TIP→ Anyone can visit Disney hotels. To save money and still have on-site resort experiences, stay at a moderately priced hotel off-site and then visit the animals at the Animal Kingdom Lodge, say, or rent a boat at the Grand Floridian.

CONSIDERATIONS FOR DIFFERENT TYPES OF TRAVELERS

Whether you stay on theme-park property or off, prioritize your needs. A great spa is wonderful, but if you're running around with three young kids, will you actually use it? Do you want luxury or rustic simplicity? A splurge or a supersaver?

In addition, weigh what you get for the money. Sure, you might spend more on a room at a Disney or Universal resort than at an off-site property. But if staying at a cheaper off-site hotel means renting a car or spending a lot of money and time on cab rides, you might not ultimately be saving that much. Conversely, if you're planning to split your time between, say, Disney, Universal, and SeaWorld, you probably won't make full use of all the Disney or Universal perks and might be better off shopping for a good-value, centrally located, off-site hotel with free theme-park shuttle service.

Finally, if you're traveling with children, be sure to mention their ages when you make reservations. Sometimes hotels have special features, such as rooms with bunk beds, just for families. Such things aren't necessarily offered up front, so be sure to ask.

TIP→ Regardless of whether you stay at hotels near the theme parks or at on-site resorts, it can take between 20 minutes and an hour to get to and from park entrances.

FAMILIES WITH YOUNG KIDS

If this is a Disney trip, stick with Disney hotels or Hotel Plaza Boulevard properties: the transportation system makes it simple to scoot back for a nap or some downtime at the pool.

Many Disney properties are designed to appeal to kids, some with great children's facilities and supervised programs. There's the Cub's Den at Disney's Wilderness Lodge, Lilo's Playhouse at the Polynesian Village Resort, the Sandcastle Club at the Beach Club Resort, Simba's Cubhouse at Disney's Animal Kingdom Lodge, and Camp Dolphin at the Dolphin Hotel. What's more, most of these clubs are open from late afternoon until midnight, so parents can slip out for a romantic meal while the kids play games, do art projects, and enjoy a snack or dinner. For a full range of special kids activities (and they are legion) visit 🌐 *wdwnews.com/releases/extra-special-kid-stuff-at-walt-disney-world-resort*.

TIP→ Surprise kids with a wake-up call from Mickey while staying at a Disney resort.

Babysitting in Orlando

If you're staying in a room, suite, or condo and need to rent baby equipment, such as a stroller, bassinet, high chair, or even wheelchairs and scooters, call **K&M Rentals** (☎ *407/363–7388* 🌐 *www.orlandocribrental.com*) located near the attractions.

If you want to plan an adults-only evening, consider the **Kid's Nite Out** (☎ *407/828–0920, 800/696–8105* 🌐 *www.kidsniteout.com*) program, which works with hotels throughout Orlando. It provides in-room babysitting for children ages 6 weeks to 12 years. Fees start at $20 an hour for one child, and increase by $3 for each additional child. There's a four-hour minimum, plus a transportation fee of $12 for the sitter to travel to your hotel room. The service also rents baby equipment, such as strollers and jogging carriages, and will babysit your pet, too.

When you make a reservation, you must provide a credit-card number. There's a 24-hour cancellation policy; if you cancel with less than 24 hours' notice, your credit card is charged the four-hour minimum fee ($72 for one child, higher rates for multiple children booked). The service recommends booking from two weeks to 90 days in advance.

If you do stay off-site, book a hotel geared to small children. The Holiday Inn Resort Orlando—Waterpark, in Lake Buena Vista, offers brightly colored suites with bunk beds. The resort has a huge waterpark, and tons of kids' activities, including 4-D movies and an arcade.

East of International Drive, the connected JW Marriott and Ritz-Carlton Orlando, Grande Lakes resorts have rooms with adjoining kids' suites, complete with miniature furniture and toys. The Ritz also has a Kids Club with an engaging play area and daily scheduled activities.

FAMILIES WITH TWEENS

With tweens you don't really need a hotel that's super close to a theme park, so your selection is greater. Even properties that seem adult-oriented have offerings that tweens love. The "lazy-river" pools at hotels including the Omni Orlando Resort at ChampionsGate and the JW Marriott, for instance, are generally big hits.

Many hotels also have supervised camp-style programs, with trained counselors and fun, active, outdoorsy things to do. These are great for arrival and departure days, when you probably don't want to schlep to a park, but you also don't want to hear the dreaded "I'm so bored."

Standouts are at the Ritz-Carlton's Ritz Kids program, and in room camping and the Camp Hyatt program at the Hyatt Regency Grand Cypress, near Disney Springs. The latter is a top-class resort with sprawling grounds that abut Walt Disney World property, so it's perfect for families who want to be near the Mouse but prefer to take a break from Disney each night.

FAMILIES WITH TEENS

A great hotel pool is a major boon for teens, who might not want to spend all their time in the theme parks. Stormalong Bay, the pool complex shared by the Yacht Club and Beach Club, has it all: a lazy river, waterslide, sandy-bottom

Disney and Universal Resort Perks 

Disney Perks

Extra Magic Hours. You get special early and late-night admission to certain Disney parks on specified days. Call ahead for details so you can plan your early- and late-visit strategies.

Free Theme-Park Parking. Parking is no longer free for Disney hotel guests, but they do not have to pay the parking fee if they drive to and park in the theme-park lots.

Magical Express. If you're staying at a select Disney hotel, this free airport service means you don't need to rent a car or think about finding a shuttle or taxi or worry about baggage handling.

At your hometown airport, you check your bags in, and they will be delivered directly to your Disney hotel. Special coaches take you to your hotel from the Orlando airport. Your luggage is delivered to your room an hour or two after you arrive. If your flight arrives before 5 am or after 10 pm, you will have to collect your luggage and deliver it to the coach.

On departure, the process works in reverse (though only on some participating airlines, so check in advance). You get your boarding pass and check your bags at the hotel. At the airport you go directly to your gate and collect your bags when you get home. Participating airlines include American, Delta, JetBlue, Southwest, and United.

Charging Privileges. You can charge most meals and purchases throughout Disney to your hotel room, using your MagicBands or cards.

Package Delivery. Anything you purchase at Disney—at a park, a hotel, or in Disney Springs—can be delivered to the gift shop of your Disney hotel for free.

Priority Reservations. Disney hotel guests get priority reservations for rides in the parks through the My Disney Experience app, and at Disney restaurants, and choice tee times at Disney golf courses up to 30 days in advance, using MagicBands or cards and Fastpass+.

Guaranteed Entry. Disney theme parks sometimes reach capacity, but on-site guests can always enter.

Universal Perks

Head-of-the-Line Access. When staying at one of Universal's premium resort hotels (Hard Rock Hotel, Loews Royal Pacific, and Loews Portofino Bay) your room key is your special pass that lets you go directly to the head of the line at most Universal Orlando attractions. Unlike Disney's Fastpass+ program, you don't need to use this at a specific time; it's always good. A perk for all guests staying at any Universal hotel is early admission (usually an hour) to select parks.

Priority Seating. Many of Universal's restaurants offer priority seating to those staying at on-site hotels.

Charging Privileges. You can charge most meals and purchases throughout Universal to your hotel room.

Delivery Services. If you buy something in the theme parks, you can have it sent directly to your room, so you don't have to carry it around.

pool, and elevated tanning deck. This location is also surrounded by the shops, restaurants, and leisure activities of Disney's BoardWalk, a great place for teens to explore on their own.

Teens are usually partial to Universal's thrills, so the 1950s beach-party theme Cabana Bay Beach Resort on Universal property is also an excellent choice. It has a swimming pool with a sandy beach and volleyball court; "dive-in" movies on select nights; and even a bowling alley. The rock-and-roll-theme Hard Rock Hotel is also a great (although expensive) Universal option, with underwater speakers piping rock music into the pool.

TIP→ **If at all possible, book more than one room. As they say, the family that sleeps together .. hates each other in the morning.** Teens are used to having their own space; crabby moods stemming from cramped conditions can put a damper on the vacation. When booking, request connecting rooms—with a door linking your room to that of your teen—as opposed to adjoining rooms, which means only that your rooms are next to each other.

If booking more than one room is too pricey, look into accommodations at all-suites hotels or family suites at off-site hotels. These larger quarters are often reasonably priced and might include a kitchenette, which, on longer stays, can defray the expense of dining out. Just be sure to check on the hotel's definition of *suite*. Sometimes it's merely an L-shape room with a sitting area (i.e., there's no door separating you from your teen). The key question is, "Do your suites have two separate rooms with a door in between?"

SINGLES OR GROUPS OF FRIENDS

If you're traveling solo, you'll never feel lonely at a theme-park hotel. Consider one in Disney's BoardWalk area—perhaps the BoardWalk Inn and Villas, Disney's Yacht Club, or Disney's Beach Club. From here, you're just steps from shopping, dining, and nightlife. Similarly, Universal hotels like the elegant Loews Portofino Bay Hotel are just a blink away from the shopping and the hopping nightlife of CityWalk. Plus, Portofino has a spa.

If theme parks aren't your only interest, you can get your wow factor by staying at a hotel like the Gaylord Palms Resort. The interior of this place is like a Hollywood spectacular movie—about Florida. Just walking around in the 4-acre atrium is an adventure, with indoor gardens evoking the Everglades and old St. Augustine. There's also a lot to do on-site, including dining, shopping, swimming, pampering yourself at the spa, or working out in the large fitness center.

For more adventurous solo travelers (or couples), yet another option is staying outside of the attractions area and finding a cabin or cottage at a fish camp. At these lakeside or riverside Old Florida lodges, you'll be surrounded by the beauty and tranquillity of nature and worlds away from the traffic, crowds, and congestion of the attractions areas.

COUPLES

Luxury properties such as the Ritz-Carlton Orlando, Grande Lakes, or the Four Seasons spell romance. Ultraluxurious rooms, restaurants, and spa programs, plus championship golf courses, make these resorts among the best in the Orlando area. Another romantic option is downtown's Grand Bohemian, with a rooftop pool, jazz in the Bösendorfer Lounge, and short-walk access to the Dr. Phillips Center for the Performing Arts and the Amway Center's NBA games and world-class concerts.

Essentials

If you and your sweetie are Disneyphiles, Disney's five-star Grand Floridian absolutely drips with Victorian romance, and the Animal Kingdom Lodge offers the delights of sunsets over the savanna and giraffes and zebras munching leaves just below your balcony. The Port Orleans Resort–French Quarter, near Disney Springs, is a great, more affordable romantic choice for couples.

LARGE GROUPS

All-suites properties are the logical choice. If you're coming mainly for the theme parks, stay on Disney or Universal grounds, as the many perks—especially those involving transportation—definitely make life easier. Some Disney properties with suites include the cabins at Fort Wilderness Resort, the Beach Club Villas, the BoardWalk Inn and Villas, the Bay Lake Tower at the Contemporary Resort, the bungalows at the Polynesian Village Resort, the cabins at Wilderness Lodge, and the villas at Animal Kingdom. At the Universal properties, Cabana Bay has 1,800 rooms, half of them suites. But rest assured, area hotel reps are very familiar with group travel and are happy to discuss options.

If you plan to spend time away from the parks or will be shuttling between Universal and Disney, consider reserving an apartment or condo. This works best for families who can handle communal living for an extended period.

If your family members tend to get in each other's hair, you're better off reserving a block of hotel rooms. Add a courtesy suite, and you have all the benefits of togetherness, plus a place to retreat to when you need it. Talk to a hotel agent to figure out how many people each room can accommodate comfortably, and how many rooms you'll need.

RESERVATIONS

When booking by phone, expect a robot first, followed by a sometimes protracted wait before a real person—who will hopefully be polite and helpful.

Walt Disney Travel Co
Packages can be arranged through the Walt Disney Travel Co., a service set up for U.K. and European travelers. Guests can find planning tools on the website that allow them to customize vacation itineraries based on interests as well as age, height restrictions, and medical needs. ✉ *3 Queen Caroline St.* ☎ *800/2006–0809 toll-free in U.K., 203/666–9911 paid call in U.K.* 🌐 *www.disneyholidays.com.*

WDW Central Reservations Office
You can book many accommodations—Disney-owned hotels and some non-Disney-owned hotels—through the WDW Central Reservations Office. The website allows you to compare prices at the various on-site resorts.

People with disabilities can also use this number, as the representatives are all knowledgeable about services available at resorts and parks for guests with disabilities. All representatives have TTY ability. The website is also a valuable source for specific needs. Go to Guest Services and search the word *Disabilities.* ☎ *407/939–4357* 🌐 *disneyworld.disney.go.com.*

Packing

In general, Florida has a temperate climate although first-time visitors are usually astounded by the humidity, which can make a summer day absolutely unbearable. So when packing for a summer vacation, consider packing a cooling towel to wrap around your neck—and perhaps adding cooling shirts that wick the moisture and heat from your body.

Also during the summertime, expect afternoon thunderstorms, which go along with Orlando's status as the lightning capital of the world and help explain why savvy travelers often pack a handful of inexpensive ponchos. Bathing suits are a natural anytime of the year, but sweaters, fleeces, and jackets are usually needed only between December and February. If you forget apparel items, rest assured you can find them inside the parks, at souvenir stores near the attractions, and at Walmarts, Walgreens, and CVS markets near the airport.

Finally, it's rare that a family will leave Orlando without a treasure chest of souvenirs and apparel. Assuming you arrived with luggage bursting at the seams, just head to a local thrift store where you'll find a surplus of used but fully functional suitcases to carry home your extra swag.

Passport

American travelers never need a passport to travel domestically. Non-American travelers always need a valid passport to visit Florida. Passengers on cruises that depart from and return to the same U.S. port aren't currently required to carry a passport, but it's always a good idea to bring one if your ship travels through Caribbean waters in the unlikely event that you must fly out of a Caribbean airport during your trip.

Tipping

Tip in Orlando as you would in any big U.S. city. Servers in high-end and tourist-related restaurants depend on these tips to live and expect at least 20%, as do bartenders. Bellhops, hotel doorstaff, and valet parking attendants are usually given tips each time you use their services ($1 to $5 depending on the service). Hotel maids are usually tipped $1 or $2 per night (left each morning).

Visa

For international travelers, a tourism visa is required for traveling to Florida and the rest of the United States. If you're cruising from Florida to Cuba, you must have a passport and visa.

When to Go

Low Season: Orlando is the most visited place in the world, so you'll always have to deal with a lot of folks who, like you, wanted to come here on vacation. But you'll deal with a lot fewer of them if you visit in the slowest times of the year, which are traditionally mid-January through February (postholiday/pre-Spring Break; May (presummer vacation); October (kids back in school), and the weeks between Thanksgiving and December 20.

Shoulder Season: If you look at Orlando tourism like a Bell Curve, you'll find the attractions gearing up for, or winding down from, the peak seasons in early March, early May, early June, late August, and mid-December.

High Season: During Spring Break, summer vacation, and the holidays, plan on long waits for parking, dining, admission, and nearly every attraction. You can offset that by applying some of the tips listed earlier, such as downloaded park apps and reserving dining and attractions times.

Universal Orlando Ticket Price Chart

TICKET OPTIONS				
TICKET	**1-DAY**	**2-DAY**	**3-DAY**	**4-DAY**
BASE TICKET				
Ages 10–up	$119	$234.99	$309.99	$329.99
Ages 3–9	$114	$224.99	$299.99	$319.99
Base Ticket admits guest to one park per day, either Universal Studios or Islands of Adventure.				
PARK-TO-PARK				
Ages 10–up	$174	$294.99	$314.99	$329.99
Ages 3–9	$169	$284.99	$304.99	$319.99
Park-to-Park Ticket allows guest to go back and forth between Universal Studios and Islands of Adventure; 7-day ticket available.				
ADD: Quick Service Dining Plan	$25.99			
Blue Man Group	From $60			
City Walk Party Pass	$11.99			
City Walk Meal with a Movie	$28.12			
CityWalk Party Pass gives guest one-night access to CityWalk clubs and venues (some of which require you to be at least 21). CityWalk Meal with a Movie includes a free movie at the AMC Universal Cineplex 20.				
ADD: Volcano Bay to Universal Orlando Part-to-Park Ticket (2-day)	From $40			
One-day Volcano Bay Ticket	$80 for adults, $75 for kids.			
ADD: Universal Express Pass	From $74.99. Prices vary greatly by options and season; check website for details.			
Gives guest access to much shorter lines at Universal Studios and Islands of Adventure rides. (Note that this pass is included in the room rate at Universal Resort hotels.)				
All prices are subject to Florida sales tax				

Disney Theme Park Ticket Price Chart

TICKET OPTIONS (PRICES ARE BEFORE SALES TAX)							
TICKET	1-DAY	2-DAY	3-DAY	4-DAY	5-DAY	6-DAY	7-DAY
BASE TICKET							
Ages 10–up	\$116.09–\$169.34	\$209	\$305	\$380	\$395	\$405	\$415
Ages 3–9	\$110.76–\$164.01	\$197	\$287	\$360	\$375	\$385	\$395
Base Ticket admits guest to one of the four major theme parks per day's use. The price of every ticket varies seasonally. Park choices are: Magic Kingdom, EPCOT, Disney's Hollywood Studios, Disney's Animal Kingdom. 8-through-10-day tickets are also available. Prices per ticket are \$21.30 less when purchased in advanced. Applies to tickets for 3 or more days.							
ADD: Park Hopper	\$69.23	\$79.88	\$79.88	\$90.53	\$90.53	\$90.53	\$90.53
Park Hopper option entitles guest to visit more than one theme park per day's use. Park choices are any combination of Magic Kingdom, Epcot, Disney's Hollywood Studios, Disney's Animal Kingdom.							
ADD: Park Hopper Plus	\$21.30						
Park Hopper Plus option entitles guest to visit a choice of entertainment and recreation venues. Choices are Blizzard Beach, Typhoon Lagoon, Disney's Oak Trail golf course, Fantasia Gardens, Winter Summerland and Wide World of Sports. Guests get 1 visit for each day of their ticket.							
ADD: Water Parks & Sports	\$74.55						
Water Parks & Sports option allows 1 visit to any Disney water park or sports facility for each day of your ticket.							

MINOR PARKS AND ATTRACTIONS		
TICKET	AGES 10–UP	AGES 3–9
Typhoon Lagoon or Blizzard Beach 1-Day 1-Park	\$68.16–\$73.49	\$61.77–67.10
Disney's Oak Trail Golf Loure 1-Day	\$41.54	\$20.24
Disney's ESPN Wide World of Sports	\$20.24	\$14.91
Disney's Fantasia Gardens or Winter Summerland	\$14.91	\$12.78
NBA Experience	\$36.21	\$30.89
*All prices include 6.5% Florida sales tax		

Walt Disney World Great Itineraries

Walt Disney World can be overwhelming. Take a breath, relax, and consider one of these approaches.

If You Have One Day

If you have only one day to experience the essence of Disney, there's only one way to do it: visit the Magic Kingdom. Walt Disney's genius is on full display in this park adapted from his original at California's Disneyland, and you'll feel the pixie dust as soon as you step through the turnstiles.

Main Street, U.S.A. is a step into the past with horse-drawn streetcars rolling past, a barbershop quartet, and turn-of-the-20th-century buildings.

Ahead, the draw is Cinderella Castle, the focal point of the park. On your left Adventureland features two must-sees: the Jungle Cruise and its wisecracking skippers and Pirates of the Caribbean, an entertaining boat ride that inspired the movie franchise.

Continue your clockwise walk and enter Frontierland where the standouts are the Big Thunder Mountain Railroad, a roller coaster mine train; Splash Mountain, a water flume ride through scenes from *Song of the South*; and the Country Bear Jamboree, the classic attraction featuring a band of hillbilly bears. Liberty Square adjoins Frontierland with two more Disney classics: spooky Haunted Mansion and the inspiring Hall of Presidents.

A new and improved Fantasyland is next, highlighted by the Beast's Castle, Princess Fairytale Hall, and the Seven Dwarfs Mine Train along with it's a small world, Dumbo the Flying Elephant, the Under the Sea–Voyage of the Little Mermaid, and Prince Charming Regal Carousel.

Tomorrowland offers a retro-futuristic look in favorites like the Speedway, Buzz Lightyear's Space Station Spin, Astro Orbiters, and Space Mountain. Your round-trip complete, be sure to include time to watch a parade or circle the park via an authentic steam train.

If You Have Four Days

If you have the good fortune to spend four days at Disney, you have to see each of its four theme parks. After visiting the Magic Kingdom on Day 1, you can slow down the pace at EPCOT—but be prepared for a lot of walking. The park is divided into two sections: Future World and the World Showcase, with the former—at the entrance to the park—opening an hour earlier than its neighbor. Although it lacks the magic of the Magic Kingdom, Future World can be entertaining with high-tech demonstrations in the Innoventions areas and the virtual hang-gliding adventure at Soarin'.

But what most EPCOT visitors talk about is exploring the World Showcase. If travel abroad is out of your budget, you can test drive visits to exotic locations. At nearly every international pavilion—Canada, Great Britain, France, Morocco, Japan, United States, Italy, Germany, China, Norway, Mexico—there is usually entertainment (a movie, live show, street theater), a restaurant, art gallery, and a variety of gift shops. That evening, stick around for the grand finale. IllumiNations: Reflections of Earth is an over-the-top fireworks and laser show that wraps up the day with a dazzling finish.

On Day 3, plan a day at Disney's Hollywood Studios. Inspired by the movies (both Disney and otherwise), the park ushers you in past a few classic Tinseltown landmarks before sending you off to a galaxy far far away (or a small world in Andy's backyard). Must-sees here include the Muppet*Vision 3D, Star Tours: The Adventure Continues, Indiana Jones Epic Stunt Spectacular!, and the mind-blowing Twilight Zone Tower of Terror. Opened in 2019, Star Wars: Galaxy's Edge includes Millenium Falcon: Smuggler's Run and Star Wars: Rise of the Resistance. After dark, thousands of park guests flood into Hollywood to watch the final show of the evening, Fantasmic!, a celebration of classic Disney films and characters accompanied by music, water effects, and fireworks.

Day 4 brings you to Disney's Animal Kingdom, one of the most interesting parks you'll find. Two continents—and a new world—create the park. Just off the Oasis (the junglelike area just past the turnstiles), is Pandora–The World of Avatar, which opened in 2017 and turned the two-dimensional film blockbuster into a three-dimensional world with upside-down trees and a chance to fly on the back of a mountain banshee. In the center of the park, the Tree of Life conceals the don't miss 4-D film *It's Tough to Be a Bug!*, a comedy that shows how insects affect our lives and includes sensations that'll make you shiver—and laugh.

Farther inside the park, you'll enter Africa, where the Kilimanjaro Safari is extremely popular, since it offers a chance to see hippos, lions, giraffes, baboons, and more. But get here early because the wildlife is more active in the morning before the day gets too hot. Asia is filled with photo ops—and one incredible coaster. Expedition Everest takes you high into the Himalayas in search of the fabled yeti, and, at the very peak of the mountain, a surprise twist finds the entire coaster racing backward through the hills. Nearby, the Kali River Rapids offers similar thrills but via a whitewater raft ride. Look for shows, animal encounters, street performers, and the retro amusement park thrills of DinoLand U.S.A., and you'll easily pack in a full day.

If You Have Seven Days

If you can spend a full week at Walt Disney World, you'll enjoy a vacation that few have had the privilege to experience.

Follow the Day 4 suggestions (above), then take the fifth to recharge and relax. Although that might seem like a waste of a vacation day, after four straight days of theme-park hiking, you'll appreciate the chance to stretch out by the pool or perhaps head out for some souvenir shopping. That evening, head to Disney Springs, take in a movie, go bowling at Splitsville, watch a live concert at the House of Blues, or catch the new in 2020 Cirque du Soleil show, Drawn from Life.

Wherever you place your "free day," you're now up to Day 6—and this is a good time to pay a return visit to your favorite theme park, especially if you purchased a multiple-day "all-parks" pass. Since you have a full day to explore, consider splitting up your time between two parks—perhaps Animal Kingdom for an early morning safari and EPCOT or the Magic Kingdom to see that evening's fireworks display.

On Day 7, start to wind things down. Theme parks are still an option, but it's also a good time to review the list of souvenirs you need to take home. That evening, make a reservation for dinner at the California Grill atop the Contemporary Resort (which is also a wonderful vantage point to watch fireworks over the Magic Kingdom), or go all out and dine at Victoria & Albert's at the Grand Floridian—one of the rare AAA Five Diamond restaurants in Florida.

What a week! Thanks, Walt!

Orlando Great Itineraries

Away from the Theme Parks

If you need a break from theme parks, if you have people in your group who aren't interested in them, or if have an extra day or week, it's easy to get out and explore Central Florida. You'll find plenty of things to do and see outside the parks, particularly since Orlando is just one hour from the Atlantic Ocean and 90 minutes from the Gulf of Mexico.

IF YOU HAVE ONE DAY

If you head east from Orlando via SR528 (the Beachline Expressway, a toll road), you can be at the Kennedy Space Center in about an hour. It's an easy drive if you have a car, but you can also take an organized tour for about $100 per person. The exhibitions on American space travel and the pioneer astronauts who were launched into space from the Cape have enthralled visitors from around the world. The IMAX 3-D films and Shuttle Launch Experience are highlights, but the two most impressive sights are the space shuttle Atlantis, which takes center stage at the wonderfully educational and entertaining Atlantis Exhibit, which is enhanced by movies, simulators, and hands-on experiments. A bus tour will take you to the Saturn V Center, where there's an actual Saturn V built for an Apollo mission that was never launched, as well as early spacesuit protoypes, the Apollo XIV capsule, and even a moon rock you can touch. With the right timing, you might even see an actual SpaceX or Delta rocket rising from the nearby launch pads. On an overnight stay, you can lounge on the blissful beaches of Canaveral National Seashore, catch a wave like surfing legend (and local hero) Kelly Slater, or explore the adjacent 140,000-acre Merritt Island National Wildlife Refuge. There are also opportunities for horseback riding, hiking, bird-watching, and fishing. Cape Canaveral and Cocoa Beach make great bases if you want to explore the region further.

If it's Saturday and you're looking for a quieter alternative, head out early so you can start your spree at the Winter Park Farmers' Market, where there's free valet parking. Stalls sell locally sourced foods—including breakfast—and crafts. Regardless of the day, Park Avenue's boutiques and galleries line the east side of the street, opposite an inviting oak-shaded park. An alfresco lunch will carry you through an afternoon of still more shopping. In the evening, head to Orlando's Sand Lake Road for a plethora of multicultural cuisines—from Italian and Mediterranean to Thai, Mexican, Indian, and Hawaiian fusion.

IF YOU HAVE FOUR DAYS

Spend a day at Kennedy Space Center, but then explore Orlando itself. Among the highlights here are the Mennello Museum of Folk Art in Loch Haven Park. If you have kids, the Orlando Science Center, across the street, is a great alternative, and you can check to see what's playing at the adjoining Orlando Shakespeare Theater. If it's a nice day, explore the 50-acre Harry P. Leu Gardens, home to subtropical flora and a huge Floral Clock from Scotland. Arrive for one of the day's first guided tours (they start at 10) of the Leu House Museum.

Before returning to your hotel, a stroll around downtown's tranquil and beautiful Lake Eola Park brings views of the resident swans and waterbirds, along with the centerpiece fountain. Have a snack in the park's Relax Grill or at one of the many eateries in trendy Thornton Park. Afterward there are many happy hours at the bars or clubs of Orange Avenue. The

Dr. Phillips Center for the Performing Arts showcases A-list musicians, bands, and stage shows.

On your remaining three days, you can continue your exploration of the museums at the Orlando Museum of Art in Loch Haven Park, with its stunning permanent collection of pre-Columbian artifacts from South and Central America. Downtown's Orange County Regional History Museum offers several floors of family-friendly and gently educational local history. Winter Park's crowning jewel, the Charles Hosmer Morse Museum of American Art, houses the world's most complete collection of Tiffany windows, art glass, and ceramics. If you need some time outdoors, take a picnic on Winter Park's historic scenic boat tour, which offers a pleasant two-hour voyage through lakes and canals, past luxurious homes and the campus of Rollins College, the Southeast's oldest hall of academe. Central Florida's subtropical ecosystem contains lush natural greenery and wildlife that can be observed at several nearby state and local parks. The Audubon Center for Birds of Prey in Maitland houses injured eagles, hawks, owls, vultures, and more who cannot return safely to the wild. Just to the north is Wekiwa Springs State Park, where you can swim in crystal clear waters that power up from the Florida Aquifer, or rent a canoe to slip silently along the river, to glimpse alligators, turtles, herons, eagles, cranes, deer, and even bears. Blue Spring State Park, about 30 miles north near DeLand, is winter home to hundreds of manatees. A raised boardwalk meanders along the river to the springhead so you can observe the manatees without disturbing them.

IF YOU HAVE SEVEN DAYS

Expanding your range, one of Florida's most charming towns is Mount Dora, about 40 minutes northwest of Walt Disney World. The New England–style community rests on the shores of 4,500-acre Lake Dora and is centered on a historic shopping village filled with boutiques, gift shops, bakeries, bookstores, sidewalk cafés, and quiet parks. You could also spend a day shopping at one of Orlando's many outlet malls, explore the old-time Florida attraction Gatorland in nearby Kissimmee, drive out to Lake Wales to see beautiful Bok Tower Gardens, or head to Sanford along the St. John River, where you can visit the Central Florida Zoo & Botanical Gardens.

On the Calendar

If you've been to Orlando and its parks and enjoyed the top attractions at least once, consider a special trip around one of the many festivals and events, especially around the year-end holiday season, which is particular festive.

Winter

Candlelight Processional. Each holiday season between Thanksgiving and New Year's, a succession of celebrity narrators visit Disney to retell the story of Christmas before a full orchestra and large choir comprised of guest singers from local schools and churches. Presented at EPCOT's American Gardens Theatre, the show is truly a spectacle with singalong carols and a stirring performance of the Hallelujah Chorus from Handel's *Messiah*. A Candlelight lunch or dinner package includes a meal at one of EPCOT's pavilions as well as VIP early-access seating. ✉ *World Showcase, America Gardens Theatre, EPCOT* ☎ *407/939–3463.*

Christmas in The Wizarding World of Harry Potter. Already steeped in magic, Universal's dual Wizarding Worlds take on a winter veneer during the holidays; transformed with lights and festooned with Christmas decor and ornaments. In Universal Studios' Diagon Alley, buskers sing holiday songs at King's Cross Station, and Celestina Warbeck and the Banshees change up their set with holiday favorites. At Islands of Adventure, Hogsmeade takes on even more the look of a traditional English village, with Hogwarts Castle lit for the season and each shop decorated in a garland. In the evening the castle becomes a towering screen for The Magic of Christmas at Hogwarts, an elaborate special-effects projection show. ✉ *Islands of Adventure* ☎ *407/363–8000* 🌐 *www.universalorlando.com.*

Grinchmas Who-liday Spectacular. The holiday season takes a curmudgeonly turn at Seuss Landing during Grinchmas, an Islands of Adventure stage show based on the Dr. Seuss classic *How the Grinch Stole Christmas*. An original Mannheim Steamroller musical score backs up a half-dozen songs by an energetic and colorful cast including the Grinch and the Whos from Whoville. Stick around and this festive "Whobiliation" and the Grinch (as well as several Whos) will be out to say hello and pose for souvenir snapshots. ✉ *Islands of Adventure.*

Mickey's Jingle Bell, Jingle BAM! Held at Disney's Hollywood Studios, the park's buildings and rooftops come alive with scenes from *Mickey's Christmas Carol, Beauty and the Beast, Pluto's Christmas Tree*, and Tim Burton's *The Nightmare Before Christmas*. The seasonal show also features scenes from animated Disney classics, special effects, holiday songs, a little snow, and fiery display of fireworks (hence, the BAM!). ✉ *Disney's Hollywood Studios.*

Mickey's Very Merry Christmas Party. Come here during scheduled evenings in November and December, and you'll discover Mickey's Very Merry Christmas Party. On these evenings, the park's twinkling lights, fantasy architecture, and grand Cinderella Castle are made even more festive with a holiday parade, seasonal stage shows, fireworks, "snow" on Main Street, U.S.A., and platters of hot cocoa and cookies. It's the perfect setting for some wonderful photographs as well as lifelong memories. Since this is an evening event only, it's priced lower than a single day's park admission. Guests inside the park without the requisite Christmas Party wristband will be asked to exit, leaving the park clear for the guests arriving for the holiday event. ✉ *Magic Kingdom.*

Universal's Holiday Parade featuring Macy's. When Macy's NYC location has finished with its Thanksgiving Day balloons, several of them are shipped to the Sunshine State to be displayed in a festive recreation of the iconic parade, joining other inflatables specifically designed for this popular holiday season event. Minions, Shrek, and other Universal film characters are part of a fun-filled parade that includes incredibly detailed floats adorned with elaborate lighting displays, sound systems, and animation. The grand finale, of course, is Santa Claus. ✉ *Universal Studios, International Drive* 🌐 *www.universalorlando.com/web/en/us/things-to-do/events/holidays-at-universal.*

Walt Disney World Marathon. Walt Disney World Marathon Weekend attracts nearly 50,000 athletes from around the globe who compete in several races over several days in January. The most popular race of all is Sunday's 26.2-mile marathon, which takes runners through four theme parks and the ESPN Wide World of Sports Complex. Saturday is reserved for the 13.1-mile half marathon (through the Magic Kingdom and EPCOT). Goofy's Race and a Half is a two-day (weekends), 39.3-mile race through four theme parks. A 10K race on Friday and a 5K race on Thursday complete the calendar. Other running events include the Princess Half-Marathon Weekend in February, Star Wars Rival Run Weekend in April, and the Wine & Dine Half-Marathon Weekend in November. ✉ *Walt Disney World* 🌐 *www.rundisney.com.*

Spring

Mardi Gras at Universal Studios. One of the year's most popular events, Mardi Gras at Universal Studios is held on select evenings between February and April and brings the spirit of New Orleans to Orlando in a family-friendly festival. In addition to colorful floats, stilt walkers, New Orleans–style food and drinks, zydeco bands, and the distribution of nearly 2 million beads, there is a full calendar of concerts with performers like The Roots, Diana Ross, REO Speedwagon, Kool & The Gang, the B52s, and Kelly Clarkson. Best of all, all of it is free with park admission. ✉ *Universal Studios* 🌐 *www.universalorlando.com/Events/Mardi-Gras.*

Winter Park Sidewalk Art Festival. Far from the theme parks, this highly popular low-key community event captures the hearts of locals. Since 1960, the juried Winter Park Sidewalk Art Festival has found posh Park Avenue and oak-shaded Central Park filled with paintings, sculptures, and myriad works of art displayed by more than 225 artists and exhibitors. Consistently ranked among the nation's best arts festivals, when it's held during the third weekend of March, an estimated 350,000 visitors peruse this outdoor gallery, enhanced by food vendors, art workshops for children and adults, and the upscale shops of peaceful Park Avenue. If you're in the neighborhood, this art festival is a must. ✉ *Park Ave. and Central Park, Winter Park* 🌐 *www.wpsaf.org.*

Summer

City of Kissimmee July 4th Celebration. Starting at 5 pm on the shores of Kissimmee's Lake Tohopekaliga (aka Lake Toho), the city makes the most of the Fourth of July and its Lakefront Park with live music by artists you would recognize, entertainment, food, and children's events and activities. Just after 9 pm, the sky explodes with thunderous and colorful fireworks that rattle this still slow-paced cattle community on the doorstep of Disney. ✉ *Kissimmee.*

On the Calendar

Fireworks at the Fountain. The focal point of downtown Orlando is the Rainbow Fountain at Lake Eola, a nod to the city's origins as "The City Beautiful." The fountain is so beloved by residents that it's used as part of Orlando's official logo. On all other nights of the year, the fountain is illuminated with a choreographed six-minute show set to music, with the colors and songs changing with the season. But on July 4, the main event is a free celebration that begins in the afternoon with games, food, and live entertainment. Encircling the picturesque lake is a 1-mile promenade that, just after 9 pm, gives everyone a perfect vantage point to watch fireworks burst high above Lake Eola Park. ✉ *Lake Eola Park, Downtown Orlando* 🌐 *www.cityoforlando.net/fireworks.*

Gay Days Orlando. In early June, Gay Days Orlando brings more than 150,000 members of the LGBTQ community to Orlando, primarily arriving to visit theme parks—although Disney makes a point to say they don't "officially sponsor or promote" the event. Started in 1991 as a single day when participants wore red shoes as an identifier, it gathered steam and is now the largest such gathering in the world. The weeklong Gay Days celebration includes DJ parties, pool parties, music, and events at multiple theme parks, resort hotels, and locations throughout the metro area. ✉ *Orlando* ☎ *407/896–8431* 🌐 *www.gaydays.com.*

Fall

Epcot International Food & Wine Festival. A must for foodies, for six weeks (late September through mid-November) the EPCOT International Food & Wine Festival transforms the park into a food-and-wine wonderland with tasting seminars, culinary demonstrations, and a constant stream of celebrity chefs. Dine around the world at international marketplaces selling tasty bites, or splurge on wine schools and signature dinner events. Adding to the epicurean event is the Eat to the Beat concert series, featuring popular hit makers such as The Commodores, Pointer Sisters, Christopher Cross, and Squeeze. ✉ *World Showcase, EPCOT* 🌐 *https://disneyworld.disney.go.com/events-tours/epcot/epcot-international-food-and-wine-festival.*

Halloween Horror Nights. This extremely popular event incorporates all the special effects and movie make-up skills you'd expect from one of the leaders in the horror genre. Each evening, Universal Studios opens about a dozen chill-inducing haunted houses as well as scare zones populated by characters from your worst nightmares. A new theme is introduced each year, but, at heart, this terror-rific event has a simple purpose: to attract teens and young adults who can't get enough of its heart-pounding horrors. Admission for this after-park-hours event is separate but less than the price of regular park admission. ✉ *Universal Studios* 🌐 *www.halloweenhorrornights.com.*

Mickey's Not-So-Scary Halloween Party. As a marked contrast to Universal's super-intense Halloween Horror Nights, at Disney's Magic Kingdom kids in costumes own the streets during their quest for treats (no tricks!) at Mickey's Not-So-Scary Halloween Party. The gently spooky celebration takes place on scheduled evenings throughout September and October. Party tickets are priced below regular park admission, and it's easier to meet the characters and avoid ride queues. ✉ *Magic Kingdom.*

Contacts

Air

AIRPORTS Orlando International Airport. (*MCO*). ✉ *1 Jeff Fuqua Blvd., Orlando* ☎ *407/825–2001* 🌐 *www.orlandoairports.net*. **Orlando Sanford International Airport.** ✉ *1200 Red Cleveland Blvd., Sanford* ☎ *407/585–4000* 🌐 *flysfb.com*.

AIRPORT TRANSFERS Disney Cruise Line. ☎ *800/951–3532* 🌐 *disneycruise.disney.go.com*. **Disney's Magical Express.** ☎ *866/599–0951 for advance booking* 🌐 *www.disneysmagicalexpress.com*. **Mears Transportation Group.** ☎ *407/423–5566* 🌐 *www.mearstransportation.com*.

Car

CAR RENTALS Avis. ☎ *800/352–7900* 🌐 *www.avis.com*. **Budget.** ✉ *6 Sylvan Way* ☎ *800/214–6094* 🌐 *www.budget.com*. **Enterprise.** ☎ *800/736–8222* 🌐 *www.enterprise.com*. **Hertz.** ☎ *800/654–3131* 🌐 *www.hertz.com*.

ROAD SERVICE Car Care Center. ✉ *1000 W. Car Care Dr., Walt Disney World* ☎ *407/824–0976*.

Cruise

PORT CANAVERAL TRANSFERS GoPort. ☎ *321/735–8833* 🌐 *www.goport.com*. **Port Canaveral Shuttle.** ☎ *888/320–8497* 🌐 *www.portcanaveralquickshuttle.com*.

Public Transportation

I-RIDE Trolley
✉ *Orlando* ☎ *407/248–9590* 🌐 *iridetrolley.com*.

LYNX
✉ *Orlando* ☎ *407/841–5969* 🌐 *www.golynx.com*.

Sunrail
✉ *Orlando* 🌐 *sunrail.com*.

Taxi

CONTACTS Star Taxi. ☎ *407/857–9999*. **Town & Country Transportation.** ☎ *407/828–3035*. **Yellow Cab.** ☎ *407/422–2222*.

Did You Know?

Mickey Mouse was the inspiration for the Disney ships' colors—black hull, white superstructure, yellow trim and lifeboats, and giant red funnels (a color scheme that took some conversation with the government agencies who had rules in place regarding lifeboat colors). The ships recall classic ocean liners of the 1930s, and when the captain hits the horn, it plays the first seven notes of "When You Wish Upon a Star."

DOING ORLANDO AND THE PARKS RIGHT

by Jennie Hess

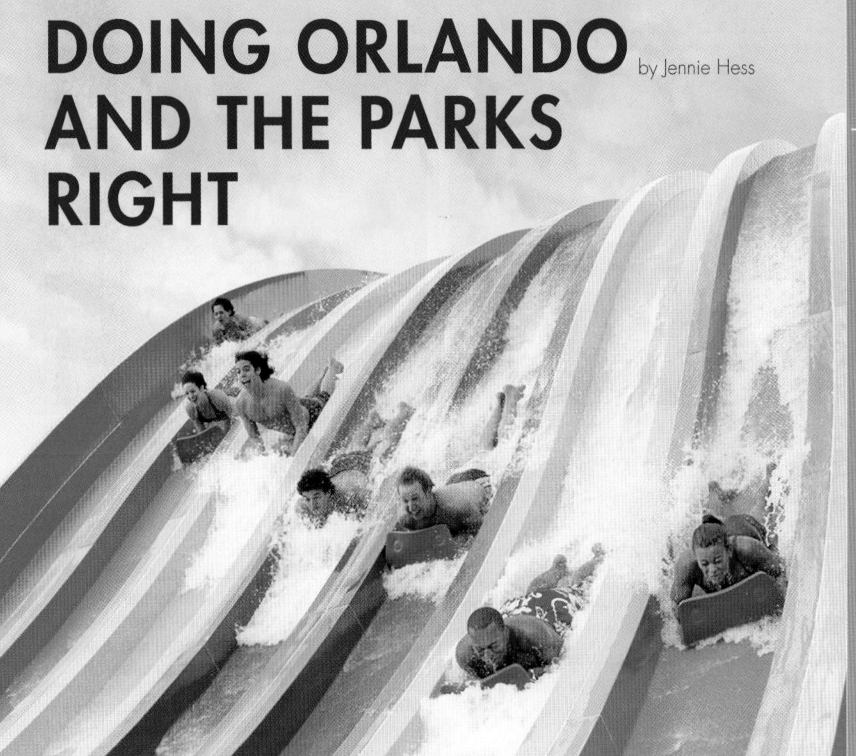

You don't have to wish upon a star to make all your Orlando vacation dreams come true. Your trip will be memorable, whether you're traveling with small children, tweens, teens, or the whole gang of friends or family; whether you're on your honeymoon or flying solo.

Gather (or cyber-gather) all your travel companions together to create a wish list. Then, as you create your itinerary, consider everyone's needs and plan accordingly.

Got small children? Know their theme-park limits to prevent meltdowns, and factor in time away from crowded parks for a laid-back visit to smaller attractions. And, to avoid disappointments, don't wait to get to the parks to determine ride height restrictions.

Teens and tweens may want to head for some rides on their own. Determine theme-park meeting locations, and be sure everyone carries a cell phone in case they encounter longer ride lines and delays.

If some of your group are planning to hit the links and others want a spa day, don't wait until you're in town to reserve a tee time or a facial-mani-pedi package.

What follows are suggestions (and a few quick tips) on how you can do Orlando and the parks right—regardless of who's in your group. For more planning tips and insights, check out Experience Walt Disney World & Orlando.

Taumata Racer, Aquatica

Shamu's Happy Harbor play area, SeaWorld

FAMILIES WITH SMALL KIDS

Things will go more smoothly if you stick to routines. It's easier than you think. During naptime, for instance, you can relax on a bench while your toddler snoozes in her stroller and the rest of the family heads for a park attraction. Finding sights for wee ones is easy in the parks and outside.

Magic Kingdom. This is the top Disney destination for families with tots. Fantasyland has a treasure trove of age-appropriate attractions. Tom Sawyer Island lets squirmy kids burn up some energy.

SeaWorld. Dolphins, whales, and other marine mammals mesmerize young children. Most shows are captivating, and Shamu's Happy Harbor is a wet, wonderful play area.

Typhoon Lagoon. It sets an idyllic water-park scene for families with small children. Ketchakiddie Creek is a favorite splash zone.

Orlando Science Center. Exhibits—many of them interactive—at this center near downtown Orlando let kids experience science and the world around them.

Disney Springs. A kiddie carousel, splash fountains, a giant LEGO Store with a play area, Bibbidi Bobbidi Boutique (think princess makeovers) are among the attractions for kids.

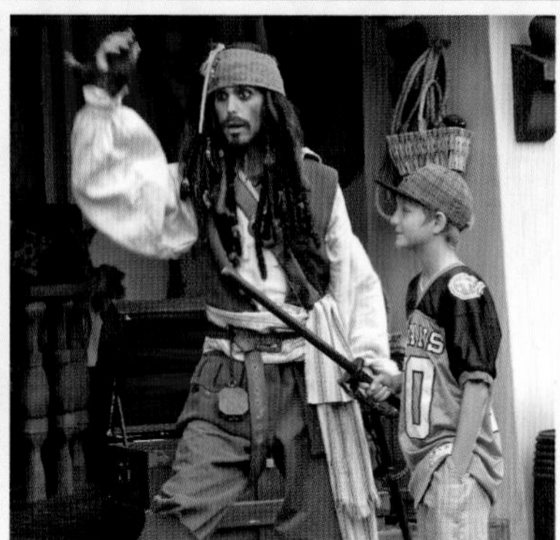

Pirates of the Caribbean, Magic Kingdom

FAMILIES WITH TWEENS

You and your tweens will have more fun together if you involve them in pre-trip planning. Let each child scope out best bets on Orlando- and theme-park Web sites, then gather to compare notes and create a rough itinerary. Here are a few suggestions to jumpstart the research.

Magic Kingdom. Who ever really outgrows this classic? Tweens love rides ending in "mountain"—Space, Splash, and Big Thunder. The Haunted Mansion and Pirates of the Caribbean are both cool.

Islands of Adventure. This theme-park will be a hit with tweens who love thrill rides and/or superheroes like Spider-Man. For muggle fans of J.K. Rowling's books, the Wizarding World of Harry Potter is a must-see.

Disney's Animal Kingdom. The exotic animals and safari are highlights, but so are scream-inducing Expedition Everest, DINOSAUR, Kali River Rapids, and Avatar Flight of Passage.

Hollywood Studios. The addition of Toy Story Land has brought a new family coaster (Slinky Dog Dash) and Alien Swirling Saucer. Star Wars: Galaxy's Edge offers a true immersive experience.

Fun Spot America. Tweens love the go-kart racetrack best, but the carnival-style rides and arcades are a big draw, too.

WonderWorks. Tweens can "build" their own coaster, and then ride it; lie on a bed of nails; and pilot a simulated fighter jet.

Incredible Hulk Coaster, Islands of Adventure

FAMILIES WITH TEENS

Let teens make their own "gotta do" list and head out on their own. (Chances are at least some of the sights below will make it to every list.) Stay in touch by texting updates and meeting for meals.

Disney's Hollywood Studios. Teens rave about The Twilight Zone Tower of Terror and Rock 'n' Roller Coaster Starring Aerosmith. They will love Star Wars: Rise of the Resistence.

Islands of Adventure. Older kids are drawn to the action here—from the Amazing Adventures of Spider-Man to the Incredible Hulk Coaster.

Universal Studios. Teens love Hollywood Rip Ride Rockit, Revenge of the Mummy, and The Wizarding World of Harry Potter.

Blizzard Beach and Volcano Bay. Blizzard stands out for its wintry theme, mix of thrills, and laid-back "beach" scene. Volcano Bay has loud music and big-thrill slides.

Universal CityWalk. It gets high marks for trendy shopping, movie theaters, and concerts. The theatrics of Blue Man Group is a big teen draw around the corner.

Spa with Mom. Mother-daughter facials and pedicures make for a fun morning or afternoon at Orlando spas like the Buena Vista Palace or Disney's Grand Floridian.

Sleuths Mystery Dinner Show, Orlando

LARGE, MIXED GROUPS

Look into Disney's vacation-planning program, Grand Gatherings. Just remember that group members will be happier campers with some "me" time factored in. Here are some suggestions for shared and individual experiences.

Behind-the-Scenes Park Tours. Tours at SeaWorld, Magic Kingdom, EPCOT, and Animal Kingdom are great shared experiences. Note that the more people you have on the expensive but oh-so-cool VIP tour at Universal, the better value it is.

Dinner shows. Some area favorites are Medieval Times in Kissimmee, Sleuths Mystery Dinner Show on I-Drive, and Disney's Hoop-Dee-Doo Revue.

Discovery Cove. Book a "beach" day here to share the experience of swimming with the dolphins. Meals and snacks are included.

EPCOT. Everyone can fan out here to take in the attractions and rides like Frozen Ever After and Remy's Rattatouille Experience and then gather for dinner at a reserved table to share experiences.

Spa Visits and Golf Expeditions. These are perfect "breakaway" activities. And there are options for both at Disney and in the greater Orlando area.

Spring Training. In March, it's easy to arrange a group outing to a ballgame in one of several central Florida locations.

Dudley Do-Right's Ripsaw Falls, Islands of Adventure

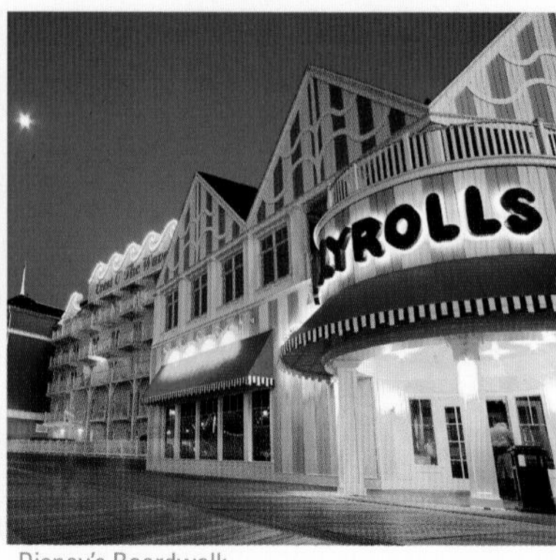

Disney's Boardwalk

COUPLES

Let us count the ways to be romantic in Orlando . . . there are too many to list here. Even if the kids are along for the trip, you can carve out time together by using a hotel's sitter service or by packing the children off to a resort kids' club.

Victoria & Albert's. Splurge on a dinner fit for royalty at the Grand Floridian's elegant eatery, central Florida's only AAA Five-Diamond restaurant. Reserve months ahead.

Spa Treatments for Two. Top spas for couples pampering include those in the Ritz-Carlton, Waldorf Astoria, Grand Floridian, Portofino Bay, Gaylord Palms, and Walt Disney World Dolphin, and the Four Seasons.

Wekiwa Springs State Park. Escape here for a picnic and/or to rent a canoe and share quiet time on the river.

Islands of Adventure and CityWalk. Plan a wild and crazy evening of roller-coaster thrills and then belly up to the bar for a cheeseburger in paradise at Jimmy Buffet's Margaritaville.

Lake Eola. Paddle a swan-shaped boat together at this lake in downtown Orlando. Then share flatbread and sip champagne at Eola Wine Company across the street.

SINGLES (OR GROUPS OF FRIENDS)

It's nice to have a traveling companion, but there's an advantage to visiting on your own—you can cover a lot more territory. Single but traveling with friends? You still may want to split up to sample from your own play list.

Animal Kingdom. Animal-loving singles can linger longer at this park to watch behaviors of many exotic creatures. Rough it on the excellent Wild Africa Trek for a fee.

Winter Park. On a day trip to this this town you can shop Park Avenue, take a scenic boat tour, and see the huge Tiffany collection at the Morse Museum of American Art.

Disney's Boardwalk. Let nostalgia take hold on a lakeside stroll. Or hop into a surrey or onto a bicycle built for two. Watch dueling pianos at Jellyrolls or a game at ESPN Club.

Run through the parks. Plan your visit in January and compete in the Walt Disney World Half- or Full Marathons—run both, and you'll go home with a Goofy medal as well as a Donald (half) and a Mickey (full)!

Tour new Worlds. Spend seven hours on Disney's Backstage Magic Tour of Magic Kingdom, EPCOT, and Hollywood Studios. Or take one of SeaWorld's Spotlight tours into the penguin or dolphin backstage habitats.

Chapter 3

THE MAGIC KINGDOM AND RESORT AREA

Updated by
Leigh Jenkins

Sights	Restaurants	Hotels	Shopping	Nightlife
★★★★★	★★★☆☆	★★★★★	★★★★☆	★★☆☆☆

PARK SNAPSHOT

TOP EXPERIENCES

■ **Buzz Lightyear's Space Ranger Spin.** A shoot-'em-up ride where space-ranger wannabes compete for the highest score (ages 7 and up).

■ **Dumbo the Flying Elephant.** The elephant ears get them every time, and the ride offers double the number of pachyderm vehicles as it did originally (ages 6 and under).

■ **Enchanted Tales with Belle.** Young girls and boys, and some parents, too, clamor to play characters from *Beauty and the Beast* in this well-done interactive story adventure (ages 6 and under).

■ **Seven Dwarfs Mine Train.** Train cars sway gently to and fro during the rollicking, musical ride through a mine full of glittery gems (ages 7 and up).

■ **Space Mountain.** The Magic Kingdom's scariest ride zips you along the tracks in near-total darkness except for the stars (ages 7 and up).

■ **Under the Sea: Journey of the Little Mermaid.** Wander past waterfalls and tide pools into the cave beneath Prince Eric's Castle for some interactive fun and a clamshell ride through Ariel's story (ages 6 and under).

GETTING HERE

If you're a Disney Resort guest, you can take a bus, monorail, or boat—depending on where you're staying—to the main gates of each park. However, getting to the entrance if you're not booked into a Disney Resort takes considerably more effort. Indeed, of the major Walt Disney World parks, the Magic Kingdom is the most difficult for off-site guests to reach. Guests not staying at a Disney hotel must park in a distant lot, take a tram or walk to the Ticket and Transportation Center (TTC), and then take the monorail or a boat to the entrance. The whole process could easily take a half-hour.

PLANNING YOUR TIME

■ Given its popularity with both non-resort and resort guests, the Magic Kingdom is the busiest of Disney's four major theme parks. It's usually the most crowded in the early afternoon, which is the best time for on-site guests who arrived at the park early to take a break. You can come back after 6, when the crowds have thinned. Just be sure to return in time for the nightly fireworks display.

QUICK BITES

■ **Aloha Isle.** Try the fresh pineapple spears, or sip the popular Frozen Dole Whip or just some fruit juice, while you relax on one of the benches scattered around Adventureland. ⌧ *Adventureland.*

■ **Gaston's Tavern.** Gaston's hunting lodge from *Beauty and the Beast* has giant cinnamon rolls big enough to share and LeFou's Brew, a frozen apple juice concoction that kids adore. ⌧ *Fantasyland.*

■ **Sleepy Hollow.** Quick pick-me-ups include funnel cakes, soft-serve ice cream, espresso drinks, and waffle sandwiches. ⌧ *Liberty Square.*

Cinderella Castle is likely the first image that comes to anyone's mind when thinking of Disney—it's even part of The Walt Disney Company logo. Roy Disney understood the importance of the castle as a symbol, so when construction began on Walt Disney World in 1967, he ordered that the first building completed should be this landmark.

When Walt Disney World first opened in 1971, the Magic Kingdom and the hotels around the Seven Seas Lagoon were the entirety of Walt Disney World. And through every expansion—through every new park or new hotel—the Magic Kingdom still inspires guests and their imaginations. No trip to Disney would be complete without visiting the resort's most iconic and popular park. The hotels that make up the resort area—the Grand Floridian, The Polynesian Village, The Contemporary, Wilderness Lodge, and Fort Wilderness—are the most popular (and expensive) hotels in Walt Disney World.

The Magic Kingdom sits at the northernmost point in all of Walt Disney World. In front of the park's entrance is the Seven Seas Lagoon, on whose shores can be found The Grand Floridian, The Polynesian Village, and the Contemporary resorts. Around the edge of the lagoon runs the monorail, a highway in the sky that visits the Magic Kingdom, each of the three hotels, and the TTC (aka, the parking lot). Adjacent to the Seven Seas Lagoon is Bay Lake, where Wilderness Lodge and Fort Wilderness are. Boats also travel from the five hotels to the Magic Kingdom.

Inside the Magic Kingdom, you will find a world of fantasy, just as Walt Disney imagined. Stepping onto Main Street, U.S.A. is like traveling back into the idyllic world of yesterday. Everything, from the steam trains to the pristine buildings waving American flags to the citizens roaming the streets, is designed to reflect middle-America at the turn of the 20th century. At the end of Main Street stands Cinderella Castle. From here, you can enter the rest of the lands that make up the Magic Kingdom—Adventureland, Frontierland, Liberty Square, Fantasyland, and Tomorrowland. They surround Cinderella Castle like spokes of a wheel.

Adventureland is a mix of Caribbean and Southeast Asia, home to the world-famous Jungle Cruise and Pirates of the Caribbean. In Frontierland you will encounter Splash Mountain and Big Thunder Mountain as you walk through the American West. Discover colonial America in Liberty Square, along with the spooky Haunted Mansion. Fantasyland, which now has three castles, is where you'll find princesses and storybook characters from famous Disney movies. Tomorrowland, with Space Mountain and

Buzz Lightyear's Space Ranger Spin, is every space ace's dream.

These six distinct lands make up the Magic Kingdom, but they have changed and grown over the last 40 years. The most notable expansion was a complete redesign of Fantasyland in 2013. And although it's smaller than the rest of the Walt Disney World parks, the Magic Kingdom remains the most popular (and has the most Fastpass attractions). Throughout the day, numerous parades and shows also take place, all designed to entertain kids of all ages.

Whether you arrive at the Magic Kingdom via monorail, boat, or bus, it's hard to escape that surge of excitement or suppress the sure smile you'll have upon sighting the towers of Cinderella Castle or the spires of Space Mountain. So what if it's a cliché by now? There's magic beyond the turnstiles, and you aren't going to miss one memorable moment.

Planning

Most visitors have some idea of what they'd like to see and do during their day in the Magic Kingdom. Popular attractions like Space Mountain and Splash Mountain are on the lists of any thrill seeker, and Fantasyland is Destination One for parents of small children and seekers of moderate thrills like the Seven Dwarfs Mine Train. Visitors who steer away from wilder rides are first in line at the Jungle Cruise or Pirates of the Caribbean in Adventureland.

It's great to have a strategy for seeing the park's attractions, grabbing a bite to eat, or scouring the shops for souvenir gold. But don't forget that Disney Imagineers—the creative pros behind every theme land and attraction—are famous for their attention to detail. Your experience will be richer if you take time to notice the extra touches—from the architecture to the music and the costumes. The same genius is evident even in the landscape, from the tropical setting of Adventureland to the red-stone slopes of Frontierland's Big Thunder Mountain Railroad. TIP→ **Be sure to download the Disney Play app before you leave home. Since Wi-Fi is free in Walt Disney World, while in the parks, you'll be able to play games and answer trivia questions to collect different badges. This is a great way to make those long lines seem a bit shorter, but be careful—the app can easily drain your battery. Bring a charger or a back-up battery just in case.**

Wherever you go, watch for hidden Mickeys—silhouettes and abstract images of Mickey Mouse—tucked by Imagineers into every corner of the Kingdom. For instance, at the Haunted Mansion, look for him in the place settings in the banquet scene.

Much of the Magic Kingdom's pixie dust is spread by the people who work here, the costumed cast members who do their part to create fond memories for each guest who crosses their path. Maybe the grim ghoul who greets you solemnly at the Haunted Mansion will cause you to break down and giggle. Or the sunny shop assistant will help your daughter find the perfect sparkly shoes to match her princess dress. You get the feeling that everyone's in on the fun; actually, you wonder if they ever go home!

Getting Oriented

The park is laid out like a wheel, with Cinderella Castle as the "hub" and the lands acting as the spokes of the wheel. As you pass underneath the railroad tracks, symbolically leaving behind the world of reality and entering a world of fantasy, you'll immediately notice the charming buildings lining Town Square and Main Street, U.S.A., which runs due north and ends at the Hub (also called Central Plaza), in front of Cinderella Castle. If you're lost or have questions, cast members are available at almost every turn to help you.

Park Amenities

Baby Care: The quiet baby-care center is next to the Crystal Palace between Main Street and Adventureland. Rocking chairs and low lighting make nursing comfortable, though it can get crowded. Toddler-size toilets are a hit with tots. There are also changing tables, formula, baby food, pacifiers, diapers, and children's pain relievers. Most park restrooms also have changing tables.

Cameras: The camera center at Town Square Theater (formerly Exposition Hall), opposite City Hall, sells batteries, digital memory cards, and film. If a Disney photographer took your picture in the park, you can buy digital copies here, or use the Memory Maker option ($169 in advance, $199 in park) to view and download all PhotoPass images. This area is a Mickey Mouse meet-and-greet spot and features a Fastpass+ ticket to meet Mickey.

First Aid: The first-aid center, staffed by registered nurses, is beside the Crystal Palace. More than a dozen automated external defibrillators are across the park.

Guest Relations: To the left in Town Square as you face Main Street, **City Hall** houses Guest Relations (aka Guest Services), the Magic Kingdom's principal information center (☎ *407/824–4521*). Here you can search for misplaced belongings or companions, ask questions of staffers, and pick up a guide map and a *Times Guide* with schedules of events and character-greeting information. **TIP→ If you're trying for a last-minute lunch or dinner reservation, you might be able to book it at City Hall.**

Lockers: Lockers ($10 to $15 per day, plus $5 deposit) are in an arcade under the Main Street railroad station. If you're park hopping, use your locker receipt to get a free locker at the next park; the fee is for the full day.

Lost People and Things: Instruct your kids to talk to anyone with a Disney name tag if they lose you. **City Hall** also has a Lost and Found and a computerized message center, where you can leave notes for your companions in the Magic Kingdom and other parks.

Main Lost and Found

After a day, found items across Walt Disney World are taken to the Lost and Found office at Disney Springs. If you realize you've lost an item, either visit Guest Relations or use the My Disney Experience app to fill out a lost-and-found claim form. Within 48 hours, you will receive an email stating if your item has been found or not. ✉ *City Hall, Main Street, U.S.A., Magic Kingdom* ☎ *407/824–4245* 🌐 *www.disneyworld.com.*

Package Pick-Up: Have large purchases sent to Package Pick-Up at the Chamber of Commerce next to City Hall, so you won't have to carry them around. Allow three hours for the delivery. You also can have packages delivered to your Disney hotel if you are a resort guest.

Services for People with Disabilities: The Magic Kingdom gets decent marks from visitors with disabilities. Level entrances and ramps provide wheelchair access. Frontierland is the only area of the park, aside from Main Street, that has sidewalk curbs; there are ramps in several locations.

Pick up a *Guide for Guests with Disabilities* at Guest Relations, or download it from the Disney website. It gives mobility details and notes where you can use handheld-captioning, assisted-listening, video-captioning, and other devices (which are available for free but require a deposit). The guide also indicates which attractions have sign-language interpretation and when, which attractions don't permit service animals, and locations of designated "break" areas for animals.

Braille maps of the park can be found near Guest Relations locations. You can rent wheelchairs only at the park's entrance before passing under the train station for $12 daily, $10 a day for multiday rental. Electronic convenience vehicles (ECV) are $50 per day plus a refundable $20 security deposit. **■ TIP→ Neither wheelchairs nor ECVs can be booked ahead, so arrive early to rent them—ECV availability is limited.**

Stroller Rentals: The Stroller Shop is near the entrance on the east side of Main Street. Single strollers are $15 daily, $13 for multiday rental; doubles are $31 daily, $27 for multiday rental. Keep your receipt; Disney will replace a lost stroller or will not charge you again if you move from park to park.

Wait-time Updates: Make sure you have downloaded the My Disney Experience app on your smartphone to receive up-to-the-minute wait times around the park.

Park Tours

Book any park tours ahead of your visit by calling ☎ *407/939–8687.*

Family Magic Tour

SPECIAL-INTEREST | It's a two-hour "surprise" scavenger hunt in which your guide encourages you to find things that have disappeared. Disney officials don't want to reveal the tour's components—after all, it's the Family "Magic" Tour—but they will say that a special character-greeting session awaits you at the end of the adventure. Tours leave the Chamber of Commerce adjacent to City Hall in Town Square daily ($39 for adults and children 3 and up). ✉ *Main Street, U.S.A., Magic Kingdom* ☎ *407/939–8687.*

Keys to the Kingdom Tour

SPECIAL-INTEREST | The five-hour tour gives you a feel for the Magic Kingdom's layout and what goes on behind the scenes. The walking tour, which costs $99, includes lunch. Park admission must be purchased separately. No one younger than 16 is allowed. Tours leave from the Chamber of Commerce adjacent to City Hall in Town Square several times daily. Included are visits to "backstage" zones: the parade staging area, the wardrobe area, and other locations in the web of tunnels beneath the Magic Kingdom. ✉ *Main Street, U.S.A., Magic Kingdom* ☎ *407/939–8687.*

Magic Behind Our Steam Trains

SPECIAL-INTEREST | This tour, which gives you an inside look at the daily operation of the WDW railroad, became so popular that it was lengthened from two to three hours and is offered on six days. Tours begin at the front-entrance turnstile at 7:30 am Monday through Saturday. Visitors 10 years old and up may participate. The cost is $54 per person, plus park admission. ✉ *Main Street, U.S.A., Magic Kingdom* ☎ *407/939–8687.*

Magic Kingdom Guided Tours

SPECIAL-INTEREST | Several Disney-run Magic Kingdom guided tours are available. Ask about discounts when booking, and arrive 15 minutes ahead of time to check in. Park admission is required in addition to the tour fee unless otherwise noted. ✉ *Magic Kingdom* ☎ *407/939–8687.*

Walt Disney: Marceline to Magic Kingdom Tour

SPECIAL-INTEREST | Walt Disney spent much of his early childhood in Marceline, Missouri, and this insider's walking tour offers insight into the boy who became the man behind the Disney kingdom. It also offers a peek at the design and operation of attractions. Open to ages 12 and up, tours ($49) leave from the Main Street Chamber of Commerce, next to City Hall, daily at 8 am. ✉ *Main Street, U.S.A., Magic Kingdom* ☎ *407/939–8687.*

Visiting Tips

Use insect repellent. Take advantage of the Disney-provided repellent at locations throughout the park, especially in the warm months.

Take advantage of parades. Ride a star attraction during a parade, when lines ease considerably. (But be careful not to get stuck on the wrong side of the parade route when it starts, or you may never get across.)

Pick up a map. You'll find maps at City Hall, near the park's Town Square entrance. Also get a *Times Guide,* which lists showtimes, character-greeting times, and hours for attractions and restaurants. If you are using your smartphone to access maps and wait times, bring a charger or back-up battery; the app can be draining.

Book character meals early. Main Street, U.S.A.'s The Crystal Palace, A Buffet with Character has breakfast, lunch, and dinner with Winnie the Pooh, Tigger, and friends. All three meals at the Fairy Tale Dining experience in Cinderella Castle are extremely popular—so much so that you should reserve your spot six months out. The same advice goes for booking the full-service dinner at Be Our Guest Restaurant in the Beast's Castle in Fantasyland. All meals can be booked 180 days in advance of your visit.

Main Street, U.S.A.

With its pastel Victorian-style buildings, antique automobiles ahoohga-oohga-ing, sparkling sidewalks, and an atmosphere of what one writer has called "almost hysterical joy," Main Street is more than a mere conduit to the other enchantments of the Magic Kingdom. It's where the spell is first cast.

You emerge from beneath the Walt Disney World Railroad Station into a realization of one of the most tenacious American dreams. The perfect street in the perfect small town in a perfect moment of time is burnished to jewel-like quality, thanks to a four-fifths-scale reduction, nightly cleanings with high-pressure hoses, and constant repainting. And it's a very sunny world, thanks to an outpouring of welcoming entertainment: live bands, barbershop quartets, and background music from Disney films and American musicals played over loudspeakers. Horse-drawn trolleys and omnibuses with their horns tooting chug along the street. Vendors in Victorian costumes sell balloons and popcorn. And Cinderella's famous castle floats enchantingly in the distance where Main Street disappears.

Although attractions with a capital "A" are minimal on Main Street, there are plenty of inducements—namely, shops and eateries—to while away your time and part you from your money. The largest of these, the Emporium, is often the last stop for souvenir hunters at day's end. At the Main Street Bakery, you can find your favorite Starbucks latte and a sandwich or baked treats like cupcakes and brownies. If you can't resist an interactive challenge while making your way through the park, head first to the Firehouse, next to City Hall, to join the legendary wizard Merlin in the Sorcerers of the Magic Kingdom role-playing game. For no extra charge, you can take ownership of special cards with "magic spells" that help you search for symbols and bring down Disney villains like Yzma and Kronk from the Disney film *The Emperor's New Groove.* Don't worry—you'll have time between fireball battles and cyclone spells to ride Space Mountain.

The Harmony Barber Shop lets you step back in time for a haircut ($18 for children 12 and under, $19 for anyone older). Babies or tots get free Mickey Ears, a souvenir lock of hair, and a certificate if it's their first haircut ever, but you pay $25 for the experience. At the Town

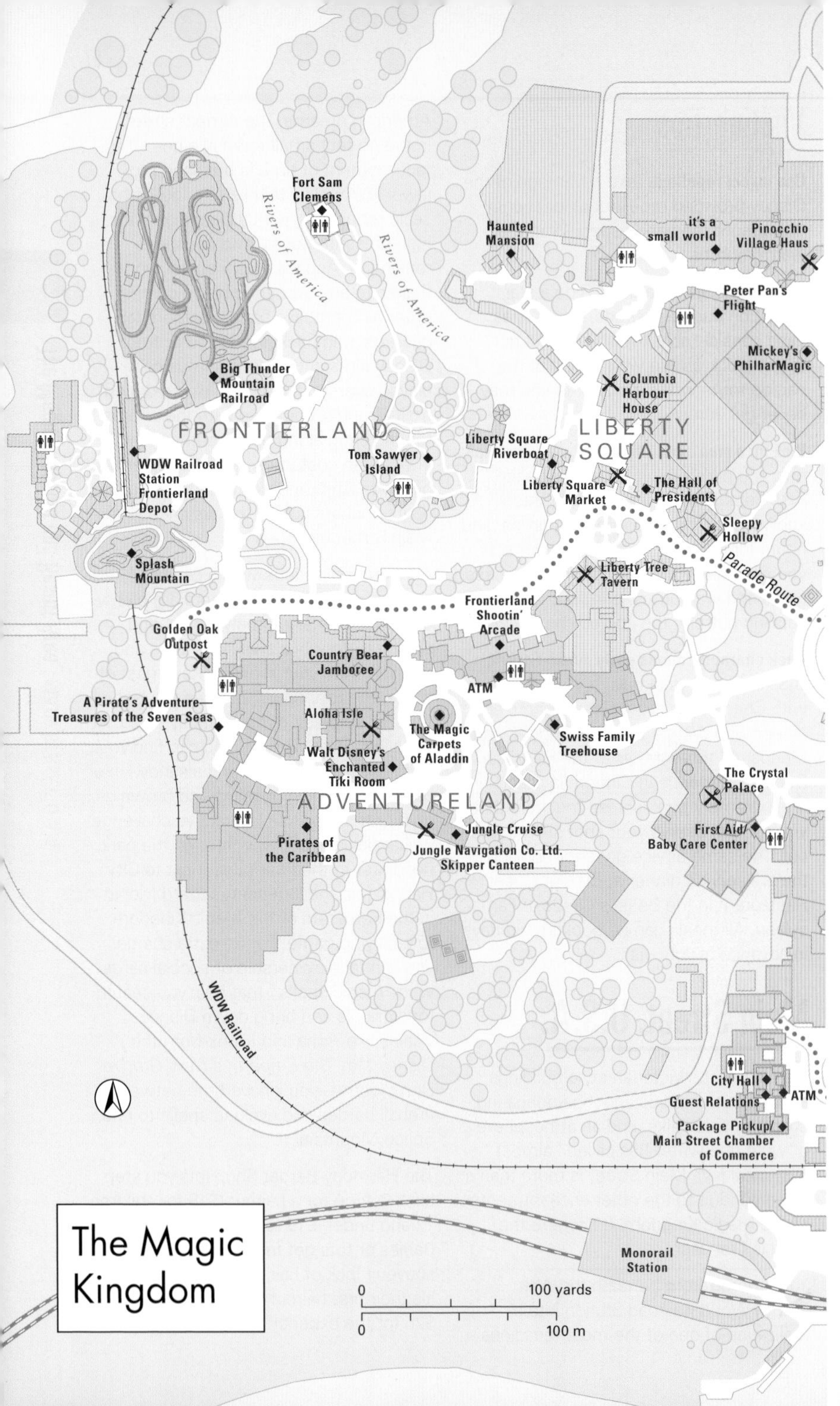

Fort Sam Clemens
Rivers of America
Rivers of America
Haunted Mansion
it's a small world
Pinocchio Village Haus
Peter Pan's Flight
Mickey's PhilharMagic
Big Thunder Mountain Railroad
Columbia Harbour House
FRONTIERLAND
LIBERTY SQUARE
Liberty Square Riverboat
Tom Sawyer Island
WDW Railroad Station Frontierland Depot
Liberty Square Market
The Hall of Presidents
Sleepy Hollow
Splash Mountain
Liberty Tree Tavern
Parade Route
Frontierland Shootin' Arcade
Golden Oak Outpost
Country Bear Jamboree
ATM
A Pirate's Adventure—Treasures of the Seven Seas
Aloha Isle
The Magic Carpets of Aladdin
Swiss Family Treehouse
Walt Disney's Enchanted Tiki Room
The Crystal Palace
ADVENTURELAND
Jungle Cruise
First Aid/ Baby Care Center
Pirates of the Caribbean
Jungle Navigation Co. Ltd. Skipper Canteen
WDW Railroad
City Hall
ATM
Guest Relations
Package Pickup/ Main Street Chamber of Commerce
The Magic Kingdom
Monorail Station
0
100 yards
0
100 m

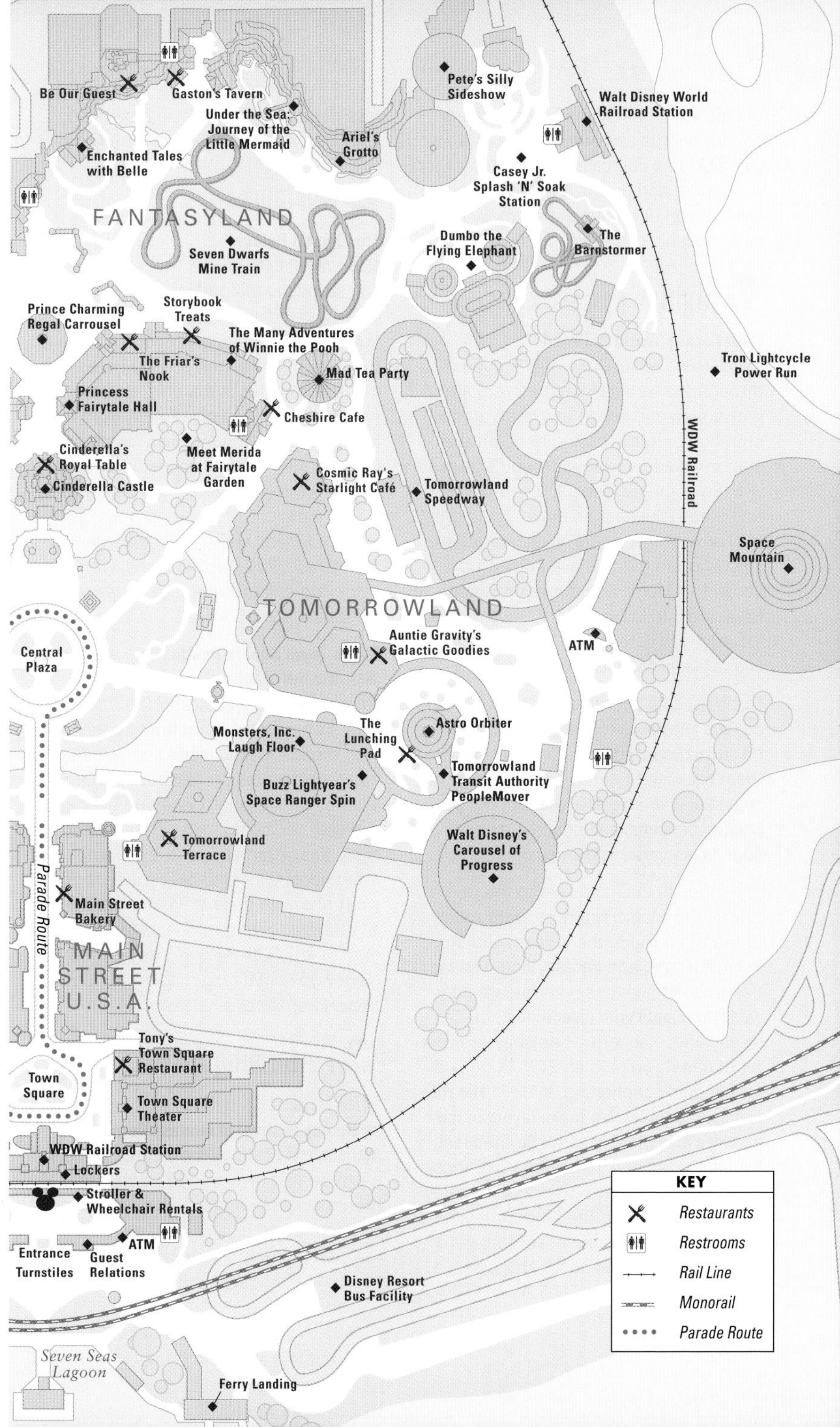

Be Our Guest
Gaston's Tavern
Under the Sea: Journey of the Little Mermaid
Ariel's Grotto
Pete's Silly Sideshow
Walt Disney World Railroad Station
Enchanted Tales with Belle
Casey Jr. Splash 'N' Soak Station
FANTASYLAND
Seven Dwarfs Mine Train
Dumbo the Flying Elephant
The Barnstormer
Prince Charming Regal Carrousel
Storybook Treats
The Many Adventures of Winnie the Pooh
The Friar's Nook
Mad Tea Party
Tron Lightcycle Power Run
Princess Fairytale Hall
Cheshire Cafe
WDW Railroad
Cinderella's Royal Table
Meet Merida at Fairytale Garden
Cosmic Ray's Starlight Café
Tomorrowland Speedway
Cinderella Castle
Space Mountain
TOMORROWLAND
Central Plaza
Auntie Gravity's Galactic Goodies
ATM
The Lunching Pad
Astro Orbiter
Monsters, Inc. Laugh Floor
Tomorrowland Transit Authority PeopleMover
Buzz Lightyear's Space Ranger Spin
Tomorrowland Terrace
Walt Disney's Carousel of Progress
Parade Route
Main Street Bakery
MAIN STREET U.S.A.
Tony's Town Square Restaurant
Town Square
Town Square Theater
WDW Railroad Station
Lockers
Stroller & Wheelchair Rentals
ATM
Entrance Turnstiles
Guest Relations
Disney Resort Bus Facility
Seven Seas Lagoon
Ferry Landing
KEY
Restaurants
Restrooms
Rail Line
Monorail
Parade Route

Square Theater, Mickey Mouse meets you for photos and autographs. And you can pick up a Fastpass+ appointment for such meet and greets. While you're here, stock up on batteries and memory cards or disposable cameras.

Sights

Walt Disney World Railroad

AMUSEMENT PARK/WATER PARK | If you click through the turnstile just before 9 am with young children in tow, wait at the entrance before crossing beneath the station. In a few moments, you'll hear a whistle in the distance and see the day's first steam-driven train arrive. For a great overview of the whole Magic Kingdom, step right up to the elevated platform above the Magic Kingdom's entrance for a ride into living history. Some of the locomotives date from 1928, the same year Mickey Mouse was created.

Disney scouts tracked down these vintage carriers in Mexico (where they transported sugarcane in the Yucatán), brought them back, and overhauled them. They're splendid, with striped awnings, brightly painted benches, authoritative "choo-choo" sounds, and hissing plumes of steam.

The 1½-mile track runs along the perimeter of the Magic Kingdom, with much of the trip through the woods, and stops in Frontierland and Fantasyland. The four trains run at five- to seven-minute intervals. **For people with disabilities:** You can remain in a standard wheelchair or transfer to one if you're in an ECV. Equipped for handheld-captioning. **TIP→ The ride is a good introduction to the layout of the park; it's also great as relief for tired feet.** You can't load bulky strollers—like those Disney rents. Go mid-afternoon to enjoy a leisurely circuit of the Kingdom while you rest. Since you are never forced to exit, it's a good chance for little ones to nap. ✉ *Main Street, U.S.A., Magic Kingdom* ☞ *Duration: 21 mins. or less depending where you disembark. Crowds: Moderate. Audience: All ages.*

Restaurants

The Crystal Palace

$$$$ | **AMERICAN** | **FAMILY** | A lovely Victorian setting is the perfect place for the old-fashioned and lovable Winnie the Pooh and friends to greet your kids via A Buffet with Character, offered here three meals a day. This is the only restaurant where you can find characters from the Hundred Acre Wood. **Known for:** character dining with Disney favorites; all-you-can-eat buffet; shrimp, meat-carving, and dessert stations. $ *Average main: $54* ✉ *Main Street, U.S.A., Magic Kingdom* ☎ *407/939–3463* 🌐 *disneyworld.disney.go.com/dining/magic-kingdom/crystal-palace.*

Tony's Town Square Restaurant

$$$ | **ITALIAN** | **FAMILY** | Inspired by the animated classic *Lady and the Tramp,* Tony's offers everything from spaghetti with meatballs to braised short ribs with mascarpone polenta to garlicky shrimp scampi with linguini. Wine and beer are available, including Italian Birra Moretti lager. **Known for:** Lady and the Tramp references; wine-and-beer menu; braised short ribs with polenta. $ *Average main: $27* ✉ *Main Street, U.S.A., Magic Kingdom* ☎ *407/939–3463* 🌐 *disneyworld.disney.go.com/dining/magic-kingdom/tonys-town-square-restaurant.*

Performing Arts

MAGIC KINGDOM SPECTACLES

★ **Disney Festival of Fantasy Parade**

AMUSEMENT PARKS | Who'd want to miss a parade that delivers in 12 entertainment-packed minutes a lineup of Disney characters and royalty, a Steampunk-inspired, fire-breathing dragon, elaborate towering floats, and handsome pairs of dancers twirling to some of Disney's best tunes? This daily 3 pm parade celebrates Walt's legacy with vignettes featuring the

Princesses Anna and Elsa are featured in Disney's Festival of Fantasy Parade.

glamour, drama, and fun of classic films like *Sleeping Beauty, Beauty and the Beast,* and *Peter Pan* while also catering to fans of contemporary box-office hits like *Brave* and *Frozen*. The colorful pageant of nine floats outperforms its predecessors with ubercreative costuming, inventive float technology, a cast of nearly 100 gung-ho performers, and a musical score that invites singing along with familiar medleys. From the 50-foot-long topiary garden float of Disney royal couples led by dancers in ball gowns with iridescent feathers to the 32-foot-tall Airship float finale with Mickey and Minnie, the parade energizes spectators as it rolls past. A Lost Boy from *Peter Pan* might grab your hand and kiss it. A stilt-walker might lean into your camera for a snapshot. You'll hear viewers gasp or shout when the towering 53-foot-long, green-eyed Maleficent Dragon, created with help from Tony Award–winning designer Michael Curry, rears its head and spews flames. **For people with disabilities:** There are viewing areas for guests in wheelchairs along the route; ask any cast member for guidance. A sign-language schedule is available at Guest Relations. **TIP→ The parade runs from Frontierland to Town Square. Check your guide map for the complete route. Disney distributes a limited number of Fastpass+ reservations, but book as far ahead as possible. Otherwise, find shade beneath a Frontierland porch at least an hour before showtime. If you've seen the parade, this is a good time to head for popular rides in Fantasyland or Tomorrowland while crowds gather along the route.** ✉ *Magic Kingdom* ☞ *Duration: 12 mins. Crowds: Heavy. Audience: All ages.*

Mickey's Royal Friendship Faire

AMUSEMENT PARKS | The Cinderella Castle forecourt provides the perfect location for several daily performances of this Disney character celebration of friendship starring Mickey Mouse, Minnie Mouse, Donald Duck, Daisy Duck, Goofy, and their friends. As the spectacle begins, the Duck and Mouse families along with pal Goofy bounce through the castle doors and announce they've invited new friends from afar to come to the fair: Tiana and friends from the Land of the Bewitching Bayous arrive with Goofy, to a Dixieland beat; Donald brings a troupe of rowdy Vikings, while Daisy's pals Rapunzel and Flynn encourage them to sing instead of carouse; the final newcomers are the popular *Frozen* characters Elsa, Anna, and Olaf the snowman. For the finale, everyone takes the stage for a waltz. If you want to sit (and don't mind an obstructed view), arrive 30 to 40 minutes before showtime to get a seat on a bench. ■ TIP→ **If you have children, plan to stand or sit on the pavement near the stage for an unobstructed view.** ✉ *Central Plaza, Magic Kingdom* ☞ *Duration: 20 mins. Crowds: Heavy. Audience: All ages.*

FIREWORKS AND NIGHTTIME SHOWS

Both in the theme parks and around the hotel-side waterways, Walt Disney World offers up a wealth of fabulous sound-and-light shows after the sun goes down. WDW is one of the Earth's largest single consumers of fireworks—perhaps even rivaling mainland China. Traditionally, sensational short shows have been held at the Magic Kingdom at 10. Starting times might vary throughout the year, so just ask a Disney host or Guest Relations for the evening's schedule.

Fireworks are only part of the evening entertainment. Disney's latest technology creates projections on Cinderella Castle, making it seem as if the icon is actually moving. Scenes of Disney movies play, characters scamper around the towers, at one point the turrets turn into a rocket ship ready to blast off. These effects are so jaw-dropping that Disney had to expand the Central Plaza in order to accommodate more guests. For the best viewing, stand in front Cinderella Castle or on Main Street. ■ TIP→ **If you've seen the nighttime shows before, either exit before they begin, or take the time to ride Big Thunder Mountain or Fantasyland attractions while most crowds are in another section of the park. You can continue to ride up until the park closes, so if you don't want to leave early, consider staying deep into the park until closing time and then exiting after most of the crowds are gone. Disney won't kick you out!**

★ Happily Ever After

SOUND/LIGHT SHOW | When the lights dim on Main Street and familiar film tunes fill the air, you know the fireworks extravaganza is about to begin. In Happily Ever After, popular Disney animated films are explored using song, fireworks, projections, and lasers. Cinderella Castle is transformed with spectacular projection technology for each musical segment of this 18-minute visual treat, from the title tune through familiar songs from nearly 20 Disney films. Snippets of the animated films appear on the castle's parapets and spires, and for some segments, the castle itself appears to become animated. Check the *Times Guide* for performance time, which varies seasonally. ■ TIP→ **You can book a Fastpass+ ahead of your visit for best viewing. The castle forecourt and surrounding bridges offer great views; or find a place near the front of the park for a quick postshow exit.** ✉ *Central Plaza, Magic Kingdom* ☞ *Duration: 18 mins. Crowds: Heavy. Audience: All ages.*

Once Upon a Time

SOUND/LIGHT SHOW | Before the popular fireworks show most evenings, and some nights twice, Cinderella Castle lights up to tell a story to park guests with the help of cutting-edge projector technology that wraps colorful images around the castle in sequences enhanced by music. For 14 minutes, the castle is a magical canvas that transforms into scenes from favorite Disney animated films like *Alice in Wonderland, Frozen, Peter Pan,* and more. **For people with disabilities:** Ask any cast member along Main Street for the best wheelchair viewing location; several areas are set aside. ■ TIP→ **Try for a better view and some breathing room away from the crowds**

by migrating to one of the walkways that lead from the castle hub to Tomorrowland or Adventureland. ✉ *Central Plaza, Magic Kingdom* ☞ *Duration: 14 mins. Crowds: Heavy. Audience: All ages.*

Shopping

Crystal Arts

CERAMICS/GLASSWARE | This shop dazzles with Arribas Brothers–engraved crystal pieces like a sparkling Cinderella coach or an iconic glass slipper in one of many sizes (though none will fit your foot!). ■ TIP→ **Be sure to visit the glass studio and its 2,100°F furnaces in the back, where a glassblower explains the process while creating wineglasses and bowls. Fascinating!** ✉ *Main Street, U.S.A., Magic Kingdom* 🌐 *www.disneyworld.disney.go.com/shops/magic-kingdom.*

The Emporium

GIFTS/SOUVENIRS | This 17,000-square-foot department store (strategically placed right before the exit) is one of the largest souvenir shops in any of the parks. You'll find thousands of Disney character products, from Disney pins to plush toys. Princess items rock for little girls, the costume jewelry is an inexpensive souvenir, and there seem to be enough Mickey sweatshirts and T's to clothe everyone in the entire park. Ask cast members about deals or marked-down merchandise. Also available here are MagicBands, colorful wristbands that can be linked with your My Disney Experience app to enter the parks, buy food and merchandise, set up Fastpass+ access, and even unlock your Disney resort room. ✉ *Main Street, U.S.A., Magic Kingdom* 🌐 *www.disneyworld.disney.go.com/shops/magic-kingdom/emporium.*

Uptown Jewelers

JEWELRY/ACCESSORIES | This upscale boutique is a treasure chest of jewelry, figurines, art, and designer handbags and accessories. It's here you can buy Pandora's Disney Park Collection gems and charms and order canvases from a computerized kiosk. ✉ *Main Street, U.S.A., Magic Kingdom* 🌐 *www.disneyworld.disney.go.com/shops/magic-kingdom/uptown-jewelers.*

Adventureland

From the scrubbed brick, manicured lawns, and meticulously pruned trees of the Central Plaza, an artfully dilapidated wooden bridge leads to the jungles of Adventureland. Here, South African cape honeysuckle droops, Brazilian bougainvillea drapes, Mexican flame vines cling, spider plants clone, and three varieties of palm trees sway. The bright, all-American, singalong tunes that fill the air along Main Street and Central Plaza are replaced by the recorded repetitions of trumpeting elephants, pounding drums, and squawking parrots. The architecture is a mishmash of the best of Thailand, the Middle East, the Caribbean, Africa, and Polynesia, arranged in an inspired disorder that recalls comic-book fantasies of far-off places.

Once contained within the Pirates of the Caribbean attraction, Captain Jack Sparrow and the crew of the Black Pearl are brazenly recruiting new hearties at the Pirates League, adjacent to the ride entrance. You can get pirate and mermaid makeovers (for lots of doubloons) here. At A Pirate's Adventure: Treasures of the Seven Seas, embark on an interactive quest with a pirate map and talisman to complete "raids" through Adventureland as you fight off pirate enemies along the way. Shiver me timbers—it's a pirate's life for ye!

Jungle Cruise

AMUSEMENT PARK/WATER PARK | Cruise through three continents and along four rivers: the Congo, the Nile, the Mekong, and the Amazon. The canopied launches are loaded, the safari-suited guides make a point of checking their pistols, and the

Adventureland Adventure Number 1: Being shipwrecked with the Swiss Family Robinson and exploring their tree house.

Irrawady Irma or *Mongala Millie* is off for another "perilous" journey. The guide's shtick is surprisingly funny in a wry and cornball way, provided he or she has mastered the art of enunciation. Along the way, you'll encounter Disney's famed Audio-Animatronics creatures of the African veld: bathing elephants, slinky pythons, an irritated rhinoceros, a tribe of hungry headhunters, and a bunch of hyperactive hippos (good thing the guide's got a pop pistol). Then there's Old Smiley, the crocodile, who's always waiting for a handout—or, as the guide quips, "a foot out."

The animals are early-generation and crude by Disney standards—anyone who's seen the real thing at the Animal Kingdom or even a good zoo won't be impressed. Unless you're an old-school Disney fan, the Jungle Cruise isn't really worth a Fastpass+. **For people with disabilities:** Several boats have lifts that allow wheelchair access; equipped for assisted-listening. Sign language is provided some days. **TIP→ Go during the afternoon parade, but not after dark—you miss too much.** ✉ *Adventureland, Magic Kingdom* ☞ *Duration: 10 mins. Crowds: Heavy. Audience: All ages.*

The Magic Carpets of Aladdin

AMUSEMENT PARK/WATER PARK | Brightening the lush Adventureland landscape is this jewel-tone ride around a giant genie's bottle. You can control your own four-passenger, state-of-the-art carpet with a front-seat lever that moves it up and down and a rear-seat button that pitches it forward or backward. Part of the fun is dodging the right-on aim of a water-spewing "camel." The ride is short but a big hit with kids, who are also dazzled by the colorful gems implanted in the surrounding pavement. Parents must ride with toddlers. **For people with disabilities:** There's ramp access for guests in wheelchairs. If you're in an ECV, you must transfer to a standard wheelchair. **TIP→ Fastpass+ is available here but you might not need one, as lines move fairly quickly.** ✉ *Adventureland, Magic Kingdom* ☞ *Duration: 3 mins. Crowds: Heavy. Audience: All ages.*

Pirates of the Caribbean

AMUSEMENT PARK/WATER PARK | FAMILY | This is one of the few rides in the world that inspired a film (*Haunted Mansion* with Eddie Murphy and *Jungle Cruise* with The Rock are the others) rather than the other way around. The gracious arched entrance soon gives way to a dusty dungeon, redolent of dampness and of a spooky, scary past. Lanterns flicker as your boat sails, and a ghostly voice intones, "Dead men tell no tales." Next, a deserted beach, strewn with shovels, a skeleton, and a disintegrating map indicating buried treasure prefaces this story of greed, lust, and destruction. You'll pass right through a water-mist screen featuring the maniacal mug of Davy Jones, complete with squirming tentacle beard and barnacle-encrusted hat. Emerging from a pitch-black tunnel after a mild, tummy-tickling drop, you're caught in the line of fire as a pirate ship cannon blasts away at a stone fortress. Look for Captain Barbossa, evil nemesis of Captain Jack Sparrow. Audio-Animatronics pirates hoist the Jolly Roger while brave soldiers scurry to defend the fort—to no avail.

The wild antics of the pirates—Captain Jack Sparrow pops up in several situations—result in a conflagration; the town goes up in flames, and all go to their just reward amid a catchy chorus of "A Pirate's Life for Me." **For people with disabilities:** Boarding requires transferring from a standard wheelchair to the ride vehicle; the very small flume drop may make the attraction inappropriate for those with limited upper-body strength or those wearing neck or back braces. Equipped for audio-description and handheld-captioning devices. **TIP→ A Fastpass+ is available but not always necessary. It's best to ride in the heat of the afternoon, and lines move steadily.** ✉ *Adventureland, Magic Kingdom* ☞ *Duration: 12 mins. Crowds: Moderate. Audience: All but very young kids.*

Swiss Family Treehouse

AMUSEMENT PARK/WATER PARK | Inspired by the classic novel by Johann Wyss about the adventures of the Robinson family, who were shipwrecked en route to America, the tree house shows what you can do with a big faux tree and a lot of imagination. Disney detail abounds: the kitchen sink is a giant clamshell; the boys' room, strewn with clothing, has two hammocks instead of beds; and an ingenious system of rain barrels and bamboo pipes provides running water in every room. As you clamber around the narrow wooden steps and rope bridges that connect the rooms in this split-level dwelling, take a look at the Spanish moss. It's real, but the tree itself—some 90 feet in diameter, with more than 1,000 branches—was constructed by the props department. The 300,000 leaves are vinyl. Toddlers unsteady on their feet might have trouble with the stairs. **For people with disabilities:** With its 100 steps and lack of narration, this attraction gets low ratings among those with mobility and visual impairments. **TIP→ If you're with children 4 to 12 who like to explore, plan to climb while you're already in Adventureland.** ✉ *Adventureland, Magic Kingdom* ☞ *Duration: Up to you. Crowds: Light to moderate. Audience: All ages.*

Walt Disney's Enchanted Tiki Room

AMUSEMENT PARK/WATER PARK | The latest version of Disney's first Audio-Animatronics attraction brings back the original show, Tropical Serenade. Winged hosts Jose, Fritz, Pierre, Michael, and the boys take you on a tour of the attraction while cracking lots of jokes. The original ditty "In the Tiki, Tiki, Tiki, Tiki, Tiki Room" is second only to "it's a small world" as the Disney song you most love to hate. Many people do hate this attraction, finding the talking birds obnoxious and the music too loud and peppy. But you can also hear old-timers singing along to "Let's All Sing Like the Birdies Sing," tweet, tweet tweet, tweet, tweet. Plus, it's a haven of cool in the summer heat. **For people**

Adventureland Adventure Number 2: Gliding through the muggy, steamy Caribbean world of pirates. Yo ho ho!

with disabilities: Accessible for those in standard wheelchairs; equipped for handheld-captioning, audio description, and assisted-listening devices. **TIP→ Go when you need to sit down with a/c.** ✉ *Adventureland, Magic Kingdom* ☞ *Duration: 12 mins. Crowds: Moderate. Audience: All ages.*

Shopping

Agrabah Bazaar

TOYS | A Hollywood-fantasized version of an open-air Arabian market, this wildly colorful shop is the retail equivalent of a maharaja's treasure. Shelves are replete with Aladdin wear and Jasmine costumes, maracas and other inexpensive percussion instruments, gold- and silver-plated bangles, collectible pins, sunglasses, housewares, plush toys, and snappy safari hats. ✉ *Adventureland, Magic Kingdom* 🌐 *www.disneyworld.disney.go.com/shops/magic-kingdom/agrabah-bazaar.*

Plaza del Sol Caribe Bazaar

TOYS | Just outside the Pirates of the Caribbean, you can stock up on pirate hats, swords, flintlocks, and hooks-for-hands. T-shirts, candy, and figurines are plentiful, but the ultimate scalawag topper is a Captain Jack Sparrow hat complete with braids. ✉ *Adventureland, Magic Kingdom* 🌐 *www.disneyworld.disney.go.com/shops/magic-kingdom/plaza-del-sol-caribe-bazaar.*

Frontierland

Frontierland recalls the American frontier and is planted with mesquite, twisted Peruvian pepper trees, slash pines, and cacti. The period evoked here is the latter half of the 19th century, and the West is being won by Disney cast members dressed in checked shirts, leather vests, cowboy hats, and brightly colored neckerchiefs. Banjo and fiddle music twangs from tree to tree, and every once in a while a line dance flash mob will erupt in front of the Country Bear Jamboree.

(Beware of hovering seagulls that migrate to the parks during cooler months—they've been known to snatch snacks.)

The screams that drown out the string music aren't the result of a horse throwing a cowboy. They come from two of the Magic Kingdom's more thrilling rides: Splash Mountain, an elaborate flume ride, and Big Thunder Mountain Railroad, a roller coaster. The Walt Disney World Railroad tunnels past a colorful scene in Splash Mountain and drops you off between it and Thunder Mountain.

Sights

★ Big Thunder Mountain Railroad
AMUSEMENT PARK/WATER PARK | Set in gold-rush days, this thrilling roller coaster simulates a runaway train. It's a bumpy ride with several good drops (pregnant women and guests wearing back, neck, or leg braces should avoid this one). There are moments when you feel like you're going to fly right off the tracks. Overall it's more fun than scary, and you'll see kids as young as 7 lining up to ride, though there is a 40-inch height requirement. The train rushes and rattles past 20 Audio-Animatronics figures—mostly critters—as well as $300,000 worth of genuine antique mining equipment, tumbleweeds, a derelict mining town, hot springs, and a flash flood.

The 197-foot mountain landscape is based on the windswept scenery of Arizona's Monument Valley, and thanks to 650 tons of steel, 4,675 tons of concrete, and 16,000 gallons of paint, it replicates the area's gorges, tunnels, caverns, and dry river beds. **For people with disabilities:** You must be able to step into the ride vehicle and walk short distances. Service animals aren't permitted. **TIP→ Use Fastpass+ unless you go first thing in the morning or during a parade. The ride is most exciting at night, when you can't anticipate the curves and the track's rattling really sounds as if something's about to give.** ✉ *Frontierland, Magic Kingdom* ☞ *Duration: 4 mins. Crowds: Absolutely. Audience: Not small kids.*

Country Bear Jamboree
AMUSEMENT PARK/WATER PARK | Wisecracking, cornpone, lovelorn Audio-Animatronics bears joke, sing, and play country music and 1950s rock and roll in this stage show. Even timid youngsters love them. The emcee, the massive but debonair Henry, leads the stellar cast of Grizzly Hall, which includes the robust Trixie, who laments love lost while perching on a swing suspended from the ceiling; Bubbles, Bunny, and Beulah, harmonizing on "All the Guys That Turn Me on Turn Me Down"; and Big Al, the off-key cult figure who has inspired his own shopping kiosk. **For people with disabilities:** Wheelchair accessible; reflective captioning provided; equipped for assisted-listening devices. If you lip-read, ask to sit up front. **TIP→ Visit during the afternoon parade or late in the day. Stand to the far left in the anteroom for the front rows and to the far right for the last row, where small kids can perch atop seats to see better.** ✉ *Frontierland, Magic Kingdom* ☞ *Duration: 17 mins. Crowds: Moderate. Audience: All ages.*

★ Splash Mountain
AMUSEMENT PARK/WATER PARK | One of the most popular thrill rides after Space Mountain, this log-flume water ride was based on animated sequences in Disney's 1946 film *Song of the South*. Disney announced in June 2020 that the ride would be re-themed with characters from The Princess and the Frog, including Princess Tiana and the alligator Louis. The ride did reopen in July 2020 but will close at a later date.

At this writing, the boat carries you up the mountain, Brer Rabbit's silhouette hops merrily ahead to the tune of the ride's theme song, "Time to Be Moving Along." Every time some critter makes a grab for the bunny, your log boat drops out of reach. But Brer Fox has been

Coasting down the popular Splash Mountain in Frontierland may get you wet.

studying his book *How to Catch a Rabbit*, and our lop-eared friend looks as if he's destined for the pot. Things don't look so good for the flumers, either. You get one heart-stopping pause at the top of the mountain—just long enough to grab the safety bar—and then the boat plummets about five stories at a 45-degree angle into a large, wet briar patch. It's enough to reach speeds of 40 mph—and makes you feel weightless. Clench your teeth and smile: as you begin to drop, a flashbulb pops. Another photographic memento for sale as you "Zip-a-Dee-Doo-Dah" your way to the next ride.

You might get wet, so plan accordingly. If you need to use Baby Swap you can take the young ones to a play area in a cave under the attraction; riders must be at least 40 inches tall. Do not ride if you're pregnant or have heart, back, or neck problems. **For people with disabilities:** You must be able to step into the ride vehicle and walk short distances. Service animals aren't permitted. **TIP→ Plan to use Fastpass+ or ride when the park opens or during meal or parade times.** ⊠ *Frontierland, Magic Kingdom* ☞ *Duration: 11 mins. Crowds: Yes! Audience: Not small kids.*

Tom Sawyer Island

AMUSEMENT PARK/WATER PARK | Tom Sawyer Island is a playground of hills, trees, rocks, and shrubs. Most attractions are on the main island, where your raft docks. The Mystery Mine is like a secret passageway to exploration. Children love Injun Joe's Cave, where there are lots of columns and crevices from which to jump out and startle siblings. As you explore the shoreline on the dirt paths, watch out for the barrel bridge—the whole contraption bounces at every step.

On the other island is Fort Langhorn, a log fortress from which you can fire air guns with great booms and cracks at the passing *Liberty Belle* riverboat. **For people with disabilities:** With its stairs, bridges, inclines, and narrow caves, this attraction isn't negotiable by those using a wheelchair. **TIP→ Get away from the crowds here. Watch toddlers closely, as it's easy to**

lose track of them. ✉ *Frontierland, Magic Kingdom* ☞ *Duration: Up to you. Crowds: Light. Audience: Kids and tweens.*

Shopping

Big Al's
TOYS | This merchandise cart across the walkway from the Country Bear Jamboree has Davy Crockett coonskin caps, cowboy hats like Woody wears in *Toy Story,* personalized sheriff's badges, and other gear that draws oohs and aahs from aspiring cowboys and cowgirls. ✉ *Frontierland, Magic Kingdom* 🌐 *www.disneyworld.disney.go.com/shops/magic-kingdom/big-als.*

Liberty Square

The rough-and-tumble West gently folds into Colonial America as Liberty Square picks up where Frontierland leaves off. The weathered siding gives way to solid brick and neat clapboard. The mesquite and cactus are replaced by stately oaks and masses of azaleas. The theme is Colonial history, which is portrayed here as solid Yankee. The buildings, topped with weather vanes and exuding prosperity, are pure New England.

A replica of the Liberty Bell, crack and all, seems an appropriate prop to separate Liberty Square from Frontierland. There's even a Liberty Tree, a more than 150-year-old live oak, transported here from elsewhere on Disney property. Just as the Sons of Liberty hung lanterns on trees as a signal of solidarity after the Boston Tea Party, the Liberty Tree's branches are decorated with 13 lanterns representing the 13 original colonies. Around the square are tree-shaded tables for an alfresco lunch and plenty of carts and fast-food eateries to supply the goods.

Did You Know?

It's hard to keep the Haunted Mansion's 200-odd trunks, chairs, harps, dress forms, statues, rugs, and knickknacks appropriately dusty. Disney buys its dust in five-pound bags and scatters it with a gadget resembling a fertilizer spreader. Word is, enough dust has been dumped since the park's 1971 opening to completely bury the mansion. Where does it all go? Perhaps the voice is right in saying that something will follow you home.

Sights

The Hall of Presidents
AMUSEMENT PARK/WATER PARK | With the latest in Disney Audio-Animatronics (this attraction introduced the technology in 1971, and underwent a total high-tech transformation in 2017) this show, housed in a redbrick building inspired by Philadelphia's Independence Hall, tells a moving story of the bond between the presidents and "We, the People." Producers reshot the accompanying film in high-definition video and added more than 130 images culled from the National Archives, Library of Congress, and other collections. A digital soundtrack, LED lighting, and a dramatic narration further enhance the experience. The film covers more than two centuries of U.S. history and emphasizes what it means to lead the nation. Both George Washington and Abraham Lincoln grab a bit of the spotlight, the latter by delivering his famous Gettysburg Address.

The best part of the show is a roll call of all 44 U.S. presidents. (Fun fact: Donald Trump is officially the 45th president because Grover Cleveland is counted twice due to his having served nonconsecutive terms.) The current president always recites the oath of office. Each chief executive responds with a nod, and those who are seated rise (except for wheelchair-bound Franklin Delano Roosevelt, of course). The robots nod and whisper to each other as the roll call proceeds. Anyone interested in presidential artifacts will enjoy the wait in the lobby area, where First Ladies' dresses, presidential portraits, and even George Washington's dental instruments are on display. **For people with disabilities:** Wheelchair accessible; enter through a door on the right. Reflective captioning available; equipped for assisted-listening devices. **TIP→ Visit in the afternoon when a chance to rest will be welcomed.** ✉ *Liberty Square, Magic Kingdom* ☞ *Duration: 22 mins. Crowds: Moderate to heavy. Audience: Not small kids.*

★ Haunted Mansion

AMUSEMENT PARK/WATER PARK | The special effects here are a howl. You're greeted at the creaking iron gates of this Gothic mansion by a lugubrious attendant, who has one of the few jobs at Disney for which smiling is frowned upon, and ushered into a spooky picture gallery. A disembodied voice echoes from the walls: "Welcome, foolish mortals, to the Haunted Mansion. I am your ghost host." An audio system with 30-plus surround-sound speakers ups the ghost-host fright factor. A scream shivers down, the room begins to "stretch," and you're off into one of Disney's classic attractions. Don't rush out of this room when other visitors depart; linger for some ghoulish bonus whispers.

Consisting mainly of a slow-moving ride in a cocoonlike "doom buggy," the Haunted Mansion is really scary only for younger children, and that's mostly because of the darkness. If the stretch room proves too scary, though, see a cast member to exit instead of riding. Everyone else will laugh while they gawk at the special effects. Watch the ghostly ballroom dancers, Madame Leota's talking head in the crystal ball, and ghostly footprints that move along a staircase. In the "bride in the attic" scene, keep an eye on the portraits. Just when you think the Imagineers have exhausted their bag of ectoplasmic tricks, you discover that your doom buggy has gained an extra passenger. This is a high-capacity, fast-loading ride, and lines usually move steadily. **For people with disabilities:** Those in wheelchairs must transfer to the doom buggies and take one or more steps; however, if you can walk up to 200 feet, you'll enjoy the preshow as well as the ride's sensations and eerie sounds. Equipped for handheld-captioning and audio-description devices. **TIP→ When you reach a fork in the queue before entering the mansion, go left through the cemetery for interactive graveyard fun. The Musical Crypt and Secret Library help you forget you're in line. Nighttime adds an extra fright factor.** ✉ *Liberty Square, Magic Kingdom* ☞ *Duration: 8 mins. Crowds: Heavy. Audience: Not small kids.*

Liberty Square Riverboat

AMUSEMENT PARK/WATER PARK | An old-fashioned steamboat, the *Liberty Belle* is authentic, from its calliope whistle and the gingerbread trim on its three decks to the boilers that produce the steam that drives the big rear paddle wheel. The boat misses authenticity on only one count: there's no mustachioed captain needed to guide it during the ride around the Rivers of America. That task is performed by an underwater rail. The 1½-mile cruise is slow and not exactly thrilling, but there are lovely views of Tom Sawyer Island and surrounding attractions. Children like exploring the boat. Lines move quickly. **For people with disabilities:** Wheelchair accessible; enter through exit on right or left. **TIP→ Come when you need a break from the crowds. Check the Times Guide—the riverboat is open seasonally.** ✉ *Liberty Square, Magic Kingdom* ☞ *Duration: 15 mins. Crowds: Light to moderate. Audience: All ages.*

Liberty Square's Haunted Mansion by day—pretty scary or just pretty? You decide.

Restaurants

★ Liberty Tree Tavern

$$$$ | AMERICAN | FAMILY | Now serving beer and wine, this formerly dry tavern holds a prime spot on the parade route, so you can have a good meal while you wait. Each of the six dining rooms commemorates a historical U.S. figure, like Betsy Ross or Benjamin Franklin. **Known for:** Patriot's Platter of roast turkey, sliced pot roast, and carved pork roast; multiroom, authentic-looking colonial decor; Samuel Adams Boston Lager and wine. *Average main: $36* ✉ *Liberty Square, Magic Kingdom* ☎ *407/939–3463* 🌐 *disneyworld.disney.go.com/dining/magic-kingdom/liberty-tree-tavern.*

Shopping

Memento Mori

GIFTS/SOUVENIRS | For those who can't get enough of the Haunted Mansion, visit the themed shop situated along the crosswalk between Liberty Square and Fantasyland. Here you'll find not only Haunted Mansion clothing and art prints, but also ghosts in a jar, mugs, and even Haunted Mansion themed salt and pepper shakers. ✉ *Liberty Square, Magic Kingdom* 🌐 *disneyworld.disney.go.com/shops/magic-kingdom/memento-mori.*

Ye Olde Christmas Shoppe

TOYS | You might think you've wandered into the North Pole at this quaint store, which sells character-themed stockings and ornaments, Mickey wedding top hats and Minnie bridal veils, plus art, housewares, and collectibles. ✉ *Liberty Square, Magic Kingdom* 🌐 *www.disneyworld.disney.go.com/shops/magic-kingdom/ye-olde-christmas-shoppe.*

Fantasyland

Walt Disney called this "a timeless land of enchantment," and Fantasyland does conjure pixie dust. Perhaps that's because the fanciful gingerbread houses, gleaming gold turrets, and, of course, the rides are based on Disney-animated movies.

Many of these rides, which could ostensibly be classified as rides for children, are packed with enough delightful detail to engage the adults who accompany them. Fantasyland has always been the most heavily trafficked area in the park, and its rides and shows are almost always crowded.

The good news for anyone who hasn't visited in a few years is that Fantasyland underwent the largest expansion in the park's history in 2012 to increase the number of attractions and experiences. Dumbo the Flying Elephant doubled in size, flying above circus-themed grounds that also include the Great Goofini coaster, starring Goofy as stuntman. There's also a Walt Disney World Railroad station in Fantasyland. And a circus-theme Casey Jr. Splash 'N' Soak Station provides water-play respite for kids. Ariel of *The Little Mermaid* invites you to her own state-of-the-art attraction, Under the Sea: Journey of the Little Mermaid. Disney princesses welcome you for a photo op in the glittering Princess Fairytale Hall. You can be part of the show when you join Belle, Lumiere, and Madame Wardrobe of *Beauty and the Beast* at the Enchanted Tales with Belle attraction for a story performance. Meanwhile, Beast might be brooding in his castle, where the Be Our Guest dining room beckons to lunch and dinner guests. The musical Seven Dwarfs Mine Train family coaster completes the expansion.

You can enter Fantasyland on foot from Liberty Square, Tomorrowland, or via the Walt Disney World Railroad, but the classic introduction is through Cinderella Castle. As you exit the castle's archway, look left to discover a charming and often overlooked touch: Cinderella Fountain, a lovely brass casting of the castle's namesake, who's dressed in her peasant togs and surrounded by her beloved mice and bird friends.

From the southern end of Liberty Square, head toward the park hub and stop at the Disney PhotoPass picture spot for one of the park's best, unobstructed ground-level views of Cinderella Castle. It's a great spot for that family photo.

Sights

Ariel's Grotto

AMUSEMENT PARK/WATER PARK | Every mermaid princess should have a giant seashell throne, and that's where Ariel fans can meet the fashionably finned, redheaded beauty. Built into the rock work of Prince Eric's castle, the grotto provides shade for those waiting in the queue and a more secluded experience for families who want to photograph or videotape the royal meet-up. **TIP→ Mermaid fans will be happy to know Fastpass+ is available. It's a natural to visit with young children before or after visiting Under the Sea: Journey of the Little Mermaid.** ✉ *Fantasyland, Magic Kingdom* ☞ *Duration: About 2 mins. Crowds: Yes. Audience: Young kids.*

The Barnstormer

AMUSEMENT PARK/WATER PARK | This coaster stars the Great Goofini, stunt master—a perfect fit for Fantasyland's Storybook Circus area. The twisting, turning roller coaster "flight" takes you high above the circus fun. It's perfect for young children's first thrill ride if they are 35 inches or taller. Circus props and theme posters tell Goofini's tale with references to some of the short films of Goofy's heyday. **For people with disabilities:** You must be able to walk a few steps from your wheelchair to board the ride. Service animals are not permitted. **TIP→ Book a Fastpass+ or, first thing in the morning, take the Walt Disney World Railroad to Fantasyland and hop in line before the crowds arrive.** ✉ *Fantasyland, Magic Kingdom* ☞ *Duration: 1 min. Crowds: Heavy. Audience: All but smallest kids. Height requirement: 35 inches.*

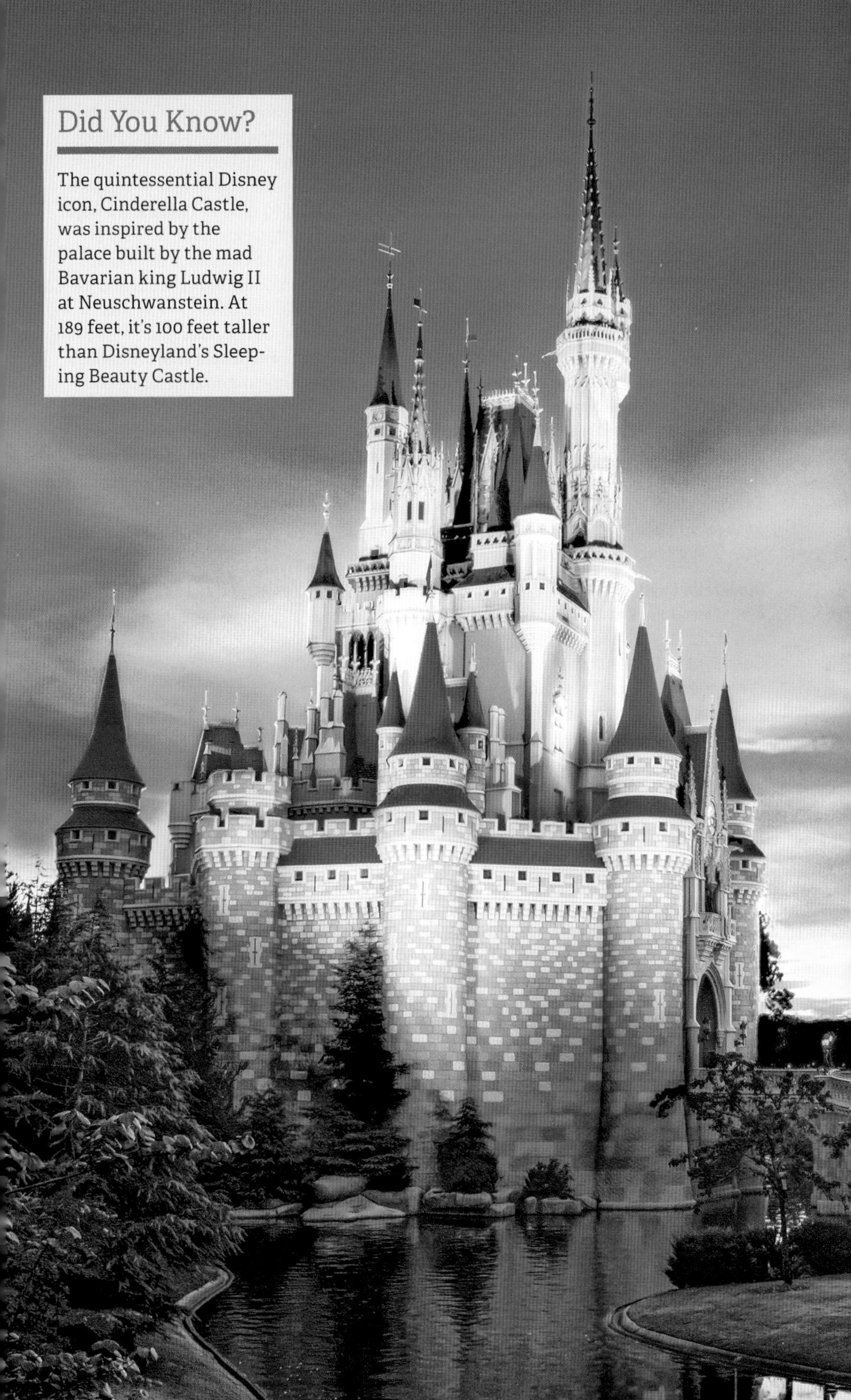

Did You Know?

The quintessential Disney icon, Cinderella Castle, was inspired by the palace built by the mad Bavarian king Ludwig II at Neuschwanstein. At 189 feet, it's 100 feet taller than Disneyland's Sleeping Beauty Castle.

Casey Jr. Splash 'N' Soak Station
AMUSEMENT PARK/WATER PARK | The Casey Jr. circus train has just pulled into town, and train cars full of faux circus animals are taking a break in this circus-theme play area across from Dumbo the Flying Elephant. The critters might not be real, but they sure do put out a lot of water as children run hooting and squealing past spitting camels, spraying elephants, and other water hazards. **For people with disabilities:** Wheelchair accessible. **TIP→ While the kids cool off and burn energy, parents can take a break and grab a hot dog or soft pretzel from nearby carts. Pack towels and fresh clothing for cooler days.** ✉ *Fantasyland, Magic Kingdom* ☞ *Duration: As long as you like. Crowds: Moderate to heavy. Audience: Young kids.*

Cinderella Castle
AMUSEMENT PARK/WATER PARK | Although similar to Disneyland's Sleeping Beauty Castle, at 189 feet this iconic castle is more than 100 feet taller; and with its elongated towers and lacy fretwork, it's more graceful. Don't miss the elaborate mosaics on the walls of the archway as you rush toward Fantasyland from the Hub. The five panels, measuring some 15 feet high and 10 feet wide were created from a million bits of multicolored Italian glass, silver, and 14-karat gold by mosaicist Hanns-Joachim Scharff. The mosaics tell the story of the little cinder girl as she goes from pumpkin to prince to happily ever after.

The fantasy castle has absolutely real foundations, made of solid steel beams, fiberglass, and 500 gallons of paint. Instead of dungeons, there are service tunnels for the Magic Kingdom's less-than-magical quotidian operations, such as Makeup and Costuming. These are the same tunnels that honeycomb the ground under much of the park.

Within the castle's archway is the **Bibbidi Bobbidi Boutique**, where the "royal treatment" transforms little girls age three and older into princesses or divas. Hair and makeup are by a Fairy Godmother-in-training. The valiant Knight Package offers a heroic makeover that includes hairstyle, sword, and shield. If you have reservations to dine at **Cinderella's Royal Table,** you enter the castle by way of an ascending spiral staircase. You are attended by costumed waiters and joined by Cinderella and other princesses in one of Disney's most popular character-dining experiences. **For people with disabilities:** For those with limited mobility, elevator access to the dining experience is provided. **TIP→ Call or book online 180 days ahead, if possible, to reserve the character breakfast, lunch, or dinner known as Fairytale Dining.** ✉ *Fantasyland, Magic Kingdom.*

Dumbo the Flying Elephant
AMUSEMENT PARK/WATER PARK | Based on the movie about the gigantic-eared baby elephant who learns he can fly, the ride consists of flying pachyderms, each packing a couple of kids and a parent. A joystick controls your Dumbo's up-and-down movement. A popular feature for parents and children: the Big Top "play while you wait" indoor area chock full of climbing equipment for kids of most ages. As you enter the colorful circus tent, a Disney "ringmaster" hands you a pager that buzzes when it's your turn to join the ride queue. Parents can supervise tots in a small circus ring of play equipment while older kids burn up energy on multilevel climbers like the Thrilling Tower of Flames. Adults enjoy the bench seating. **For people with disabilities:** If using a wheelchair, prepare to transfer to a ride vehicle. **TIP→ Get a Fastpass+ if you're in a hurry; otherwise, let the kids enjoy the play area before riding.** ✉ *Fantasyland, Magic Kingdom* ☞ *Duration: 2 mins. Crowds: Heavy. Audience: Young kids.*

★ Enchanted Tales with Belle
AMUSEMENT PARK/WATER PARK | Stroll the path through an artfully planted woodland and meadow to a rustic French cabin complete with waterwheel, where

See Lumiere chat with Belle at Enchanted Tales with Belle in Fantasyland.

Belle's father, Maurice, tinkers with his inventions. The small homestead oozes Belle's provincial life, with a giant pot hanging in the fireplace and books stacked on a simple wooden chair. Inside her father's workshop, amid blueprints and tools, a giant gold-framed mirror hangs. A costumed cast member welcomes your group to the workshop (*Bonjour!*) and implores everyone to chant, "Take me back to the day Belle and Beast fell in love!" *Voilà!* The mirror becomes an animated screen straight from the Disney film *Beauty and the Beast* before transforming into a portal that leads to an elegant room of Beast's Castle. Inside, an Animatronic Madame Armoire encourages you to grab props and play character roles from the "tale as old as time." Then it's on to the library, where a spot-on Audio-Animatronic Lumiere holds court from the mantle. Grab a cushy bench as a coiffed actress playing Belle joins you to perform a scene from the enchanted tale. You'll dance around the room to "Be Our Guest," and you might shed a tear as the interactive story unfolds. This live performance gets to the heart of Disney storytelling, and every participant poses for photos with Belle before a very happy ending. **For people with disabilities:** Wheelchair accessible; equipped for handheld captioning and assisted listening. **■ TIP→ This is a great use of a Fastpass+, since this is a slow-moving line that is mostly outside.** ✉ *Fantasyland, Magic Kingdom* ☞ *Duration: 15 mins. Crowds: Yes. Audience: All ages; perfect for families.*

it's a small world

AMUSEMENT PARK/WATER PARK | Visiting Walt Disney World and not stopping for this tribute to terminal cuteness—why, the idea is practically un-American. The attraction is essentially a boat ride through different bright-color lands, each representing a continent, complete with landmarks. First created for the 1964–65 New York World's Fair, the original ride opened in Disneyland with the same peppy theme song of international brotherhood and friendship written by the Sherman Brothers (of Mary Poppins fame). You'll float by 450 dolls created by Disney legend Mary Blair—Dutch babies in clogs, Spanish flamenco dancers, sari-wrapped Indians waving temple bells, Swiss yodelers, Japanese kite fliers, Middle East snake charmers, and young French cancan dancers, to name just a few—all singing the earworm song together. Take enchanted tots through again if the line is short.

For people with disabilities: You can board with your standard wheelchair through the designated entrance; if you use a scooter, transfer to one of the attraction's standard chairs available at the ride entrance. Equipped for handheld-captioning and audio-description devices. **TIP→ Fastpass+ is available, but lines usually move quickly for those in the standby queue.** ✉ *Fantasyland, Magic Kingdom* ☞ *Duration: 11 mins. Crowds: Heavy. Audience: All ages.*

Mad Tea Party

AMUSEMENT PARK/WATER PARK | This whirling carnival staple is for the vertigo addict looking for a fix. The Disney version is based on its own 1951 film *Alice in Wonderland*, in which the Mad Hatter hosts a tea party for his un-birthday. You hop into oversize, pastel-color teacups and whirl around a giant platter. Add your own spin to the teacup's orbit with the help of the steering wheel in the center. Check out the soused mouse that pops out of the teapot centerpiece. **For people with disabilities:** If using a wheelchair, enter through the exit on right, then transfer to a ride vehicle. **TIP→ Fastpass+ is available but not recommended unless you can't resist a good fast spin. Lines move slowly.** ✉ *Fantasyland, Magic Kingdom* ☞ *Duration: 2 mins. Crowds: Moderate. Audience: Small kids.*

★ The Many Adventures of Winnie the Pooh

AMUSEMENT PARK/WATER PARK | The famous honey lover and his exploits in the Hundred Acre Wood are the theme for this ride. You can read posted passages from A.A. Milne's stories as you wait in line. Once you board your "Hunny Pot," Pooh and his friends wish you a "happy windsday." Pooh flies through the air, held aloft by his balloon, in his perennial search for "hunny," and you bounce along with Tigger, ride with the Heffalumps and Woozles, and experience a cloudburst. This ride replaced Mr. Toad's Wild Ride; look for the painting of Mr. Toad handing the deed to Owl. **For people with disabilities:** If using a scooter, see a cast member about transferring to a standard wheelchair for the ride. Equipped for handheld-captioning and audio-description devices. **TIP→ Use a Fastpass+ if crowds are heavy.** ✉ *Fantasyland, Magic Kingdom* ☞ *Duration: 3 mins. Crowds: Heavy. Audience: Small kids.*

Mickey's PhilharMagic

AMUSEMENT PARK/WATER PARK | Mickey Mouse might be the headliner here, but it's Donald Duck's misadventures—reminiscent of Mickey's as the sorcerer's apprentice in *Fantasia*—that set the comic pace in this 3-D animated film. As you settle into your seat, the on-screen action takes you behind the curtains at a grand concert hall where Donald and Mickey are preparing for a musical performance. But when Donald misuses Mickey's sorcerer's hat, he finds himself on a whirlwind journey that includes a magic carpet ride and an electrifying dip under the sea. And you go along for the ride. On the way, you meet Ariel, Simba, Aladdin, Jasmine, Peter Pan, Tinker Bell, and others.

The film startles with its special-effects technology—you'll smell a fresh-baked apple pie, feel the rush of air as champagne corks pop, and get lost in the action on the 150-foot-wide screen. The 3-D film marks the first time that classic Disney characters appear in a computer-generated animation attraction. Some of the effects can startle small children, and some of the darker scenes are a bit muddy through the recycled 3-D glasses. **For people with disabilities:** There's a special viewing area for guests in wheelchairs. Reflective captioning is provided; equipped for assisted-listening and audio-description devices. **TIP→ Fastpass+ is offered, but it's a big theater, so waits aren't long.** ✉ *Fantasyland, Magic Kingdom* ☞ *Duration: 12 mins. Crowds: Heavy. Audience: All ages.*

Peter Pan's Flight

AMUSEMENT PARK/WATER PARK | This sweet indoor ride was inspired by Sir James M. Barrie's 1904 novel about the boy who wouldn't grow up, which Disney animated in 1953. Aboard two-person magic sailing ships with brightly striped sails, you soar into the skies above London en route to Neverland. Along the way you can see Wendy, Michael, and John get sprinkled with pixie dust while Nana barks below, wave to the Lost Boys, spot the evil Captain Hook, and cheer for the ticktocking, clock-swallowing crocodile who breakfasted on Hook's hand.

Children—especially preschoolers—love this ride. Adults enjoy the dreamy views of London by moonlight. The downsides are the ride's brevity and its low-tech look. **For people with disabilities:** You must transfer from your wheelchair to the ride vehicle. Service animals aren't permitted. Equipped for handheld-captioning and audio-description devices. **TIP→ Use Fastpass+ here or ride early, late, or during the parade.** ✉ *Fantasyland, Magic Kingdom* ☞ *Duration: 2½ mins. Crowds: Heavy. Audience: Small kids.*

Pete's Silly Sideshow

AMUSEMENT PARK/WATER PARK | No other Disney character meet-and-greet location is quite as much fun as Pete's Silly Sideshow, named after the Mickey Mouse archenemy created in 1925. But you won't meet Strongman Pete under this big top, although he does make a poster appearance; instead, you'll grip and grin with Goofy, Minnie Mouse, Donald Duck, and his sweetheart, Daisy. Each character poses for photos and signs autographs against a sideshow backdrop: the Great Goofini, "Broken Bone Record Holder," in his stunt garb; the Astounding Donaldo dressed as a snake charmer; Minnie Magnifique, pretty in pink feathers, and her "pirouetting Parisian poodles," and Madame Daisy Fortuna with crystal ball as "seer of all fate and destinies." Two queues move guests along fairly quickly, and elaborate themed backdrops offer extra-fun photo ops. **TIP→ Line up your Fastpass+ for Enchanted Tales with Belle or Under the Sea: Journey of the Little Mermaid, then head back to the Storybook Circus area to meet these characters and ride Dumbo the Flying Elephant.** ✉ *Fantasyland, Magic Kingdom* ☞ *Duration: About 1–2 mins. per character meet and greet. Crowds: Yes, but double queue makes wait shorter. Audience: Young kids.*

Prince Charming Regal Carrousel

AMUSEMENT PARK/WATER PARK | This ride is great for families and for romantics, young and old. Seventy-two of the 90 dashing wooden steeds date from the original carousel built in 1917 by the Philadelphia Toboggan Company; additional mounts were made of fiberglass. All are meticulously painted, and each one is completely different. One wears a collar of bright yellow roses; another, a quiver of Native American arrows. For a bit of extra magic, look for the horse with a golden ribbon in its tail: this is Cinderella's horse. Eighteen panels beneath the wooden canopy depict scenes from Disney's 1950 film *Cinderella*. As the ride spins, the mirrors sparkle, the fairy lights glitter, and the band organ plays favorite Disney movie tunes. **For people with disabilities:** If using a wheelchair, or if you have a service animal, check with a host for boarding information. **TIP→ Lines move quickly. Come while waiting for your Peter Pan's Flight Fastpass+ reservation.** ✉ *Fantasyland, Magic Kingdom* ☞ *Duration: 2 mins. Crowds: Moderate to heavy. Audience: Families.*

★ Seven Dwarfs Mine Train

AMUSEMENT PARK/WATER PARK | Quick! Can you name all Seven Dwarfs in seven seconds? Sleepy, Doc, Grumpy, Bashful, Sneezy, Happy, and Dopey. Snow White's hardworking pals display impressive Audio-Animatronics flair as they mine a mountain full of glittering gems and "Heigh-ho" their way into theme-park fans' hearts at the Seven Dwarfs Mine Train. Set amid a steep Enchanted Forest landscaped with red poppies, cedars, and birch trees, the attraction is a visual feast of LED-illuminated gems, playful woodland creatures, and beloved characters from Walt Disney's 1937 animated film classic, *Snow White and the Seven Dwarfs.* A rough-hewn entrance to the mine leads to a covered queue designed to keep you occupied as you wend your way toward the train load area. Fun interactive diversions include animated "floating" gems that you can catch and match in a touch-screen jewel-washing trough. The musical family coaster serves up thrills, but no stomach-churning plunges, with cars that twist, climb, drop rapidly, and rock gently when slowing down for you to enjoy the artfully crafted scene of the dwarfs at work in the mine. As the train rounds its final curve, you'll see Snow White dancing with her diminutive pals in the storybook cottage as the Wicked Queen, disguised as an old hag, lurks outside. The ride is not appropriate if you're pregnant or have heart, back, or neck problems, and although it's billed as a family coaster, there's a 38-inch height requirement. **For people with disabilities:** You must transfer from wheelchair to ride vehicle. ■ TIP→ **Book your Fastpass+ at the closest park kiosk if you didn't reserve it via the My Disney Experience website or mobile app. If circumstances deposit you in the stand-by queue, enjoy the clever hands-on activities along the way.** ✉ *Fantasyland, Magic Kingdom* ☞ *Duration: 2½ mins. Crowds: Heavy. Audience: All ages.*

Under the Sea: Journey of the Little Mermaid

AMUSEMENT PARK/WATER PARK | The shipwreck theming, craggy grotto rock work, waterfalls, lagoons, and magical landscape of this attraction draw you into Ariel's world long before you board a giant clamshell for a journey under the sea. As you wend your way through the long queue, you'll see starfish embedded in rocks, a sandy beach, palm trees, sea-grape plants, and other authentic seaside touches. Once inside the cavern beneath Prince Eric's Castle, you can join in an interactive game that plays out around every corner and stars Scuttle the seagull and his animated crab pals. Through a cave portal, you enter the castle's stone hallways, where you hop aboard a clamshell ride vehicle and, thanks to cold air and light effects, feel the sensation of descending under the sea. You then float past animated and Audio-Animatronic scenes from *The Little Mermaid* film, including a Broadway-style "Under the Sea" number with Sebastian conducting the undersea orchestra. There are fish conga lines and ominous scenes starring villainess Ursula but, of course, a fairy-tale ending is in store featuring Menken-Ashman show-stopper "Kiss the Girl." Most children love this ride, but some tots are afraid in the dark Ursula scene. **For people with disabilities**: Guests in scooters must transfer to a standard wheelchair to ride; equipped for handheld captioning and audio description. ■ TIP→ **You can get a Fastpass+, but you'll miss the fun of the interactive stand-by queue, and the line moves swiftly.** ✉ *Fantasyland, Magic Kingdom* ☞ *Duration: 7 mins. Crowds: Absolutely! Audience: All ages.*

Restaurants

★ Be Our Guest

$$$$ | FRENCH | This massive restaurant offers a *Beauty and the Beast* theme, French flair, and the Magic Kingdom's first wine and beer served at lunch and dinner; breakfast and lunch remain a fast-casual affair. Prix-fixe menus are served at dinner, while breakfast and lunch are à la carte. **Known for:** the best French dip sandwich in town; dessert platter; character appearances. $ *Average main: $55* ✉ *Fantasyland, Magic Kingdom* ✣ *North end of Fantasyland* ☎ *407/939–3463* ⊕ *disneyworld.disney.go.com/dining/magic-kingdom/be-our-guest-restaurant.*

Cinderella's Royal Table

$$$$ | AMERICAN | FAMILY | Cinderella and other Disney princesses appear at this eatery in the castle's old mead hall, offering prix-fixe Fairyland dining as only Disney can supply. The Fairytale Breakfast offers all-you-can-eat options such as beef tenderloin and eggs and caramel apple–stuffed French toast. **Known for:** breakfasts from oatmeal to shrimp and grits; character appearances and autograph signings; distinctive medieval castle decor. $ *Average main: $59* ✉ *Cinderella Castle, Magic Kingdom* ☎ *407/939–3463* ⊕ *disneyworld.disney.go.com/dining/magic-kingdom/cinderella-royal-table.*

Shopping

Castle Couture

TOYS | This shop on the corner near Cinderella Castle markets to little princesses with sparkly, shimmery dresses, bows, hats, and T-shirts as well as dolls, slippers, and jewelry. Taking the Fantasyland fantasy a step further is the Bibbidi Bobbidi Boutique next door, where little ones ages 3 to 12 can walk into a full-scale salon and, after being attended to by hair stylists and makeup artists, walk out as their favorite princess or knight. ✉ *Fantasyland, Magic Kingdom* ⊕ *www.disneyworld.disney.go.com/shops/magic-kingdom/castle-couture.*

Tomorrowland

The "future that never was" spins boldly into view as you enter Tomorrowland, where Disney Imagineers paint the landscape with whirling spaceships, flashy neon lights, and gleaming robots. This is the future as envisioned by sci-fi writers and moviemakers in the 1920s and '30s, when space flight, laser beams, and home computers were fiction, not fact. Retro Jetsonesque styling lends the area lasting chic. **TIP→ Though Tomorrowland Transit Authority (TTA) PeopleMover isn't a big-ticket ride, it's a great way to check out the landscape from above as it zooms in and out of Space Mountain and curves around the entire land, and there's usually no big line.**

Coming in 2021 will be a new thrill ride for the Magic Kingdom, the TRON Lightcycle/Run. Based on the popular attraction of the same name in Shanghai Disneyland, it will let you race lightcycles along an intense track being built behind Space Mountain. If you're visiting after the ride has opened, make sure you book a Fastpass+ early.

Sights

Astro Orbiter

AMUSEMENT PARK/WATER PARK | This gleaming superstructure of revolving planets has come to symbolize Tomorrowland as much as Dumbo represents Fantasyland. Passenger vehicles, on arms projecting from a central column, sail past whirling planets; you control your car's altitude but not the velocity. The line is directly across from the entrance to the TTA PeopleMover. **For people with disabilities:** You must be able to walk several steps and transfer to the vehicle. **TIP→ The line moves slowly; come while waiting for a Space Mountain Fastpass+ appointment or if there's a short**

In Tomorrowland, interplanetary travel is within your reach on the Astro Orbiter.

line. Skip on your first visit if time is limited. ✉ *Tomorrowland, Magic Kingdom* ☞ *Duration: 2 mins. Crowds: Moderate to heavy. Audience: All ages.*

★ **Buzz Lightyear's Space Ranger Spin**
AMUSEMENT PARK/WATER PARK | Based on the wildly popular *Toy Story*, this ride gives you a toy's perspective as it pits you and Buzz Lightyear against the evil Emperor Zurg. You're seated in a fast-moving two-passenger Star Cruiser vehicle with an infrared laser gun and a centrally located lever for spinning your ship to get a good vantage point. Throughout the ride, you shoot at targets to help macho space toy, Buzz, defeat the emperor and save the universe. You have to hit the targets marked with a "Z" to score, and the rider with the most points wins. To infinity and beyond! **For people with disabilities:** To board you must transfer to a standard wheelchair. Equipped for audio-description and handheld-captioning devices. **■ TIP→ Use Fastpass+ or go during a parade. If you're with kids, time the wait and—if it's only 15 or 20 minutes—ride twice so they can have a practice run.** ✉ *Tomorrowland, Magic Kingdom* ☞ *Duration: 5 mins. Crowds: Heavy. Audience: All ages—truly.*

Monsters, Inc. Laugh Floor
AMUSEMENT PARK/WATER PARK | The joke's on everyone at this interactive attraction starring Mike Wazowski, the one-eyed hero from Disney-Pixar's hit film *Monsters, Inc.* In the 400-seat theater, you can interact with an animated Mike and his sidekicks in the real-time, unscripted way that the character Crush from *Finding Nemo* performs at Epcot in Turtle Talk with Crush at The Seas with Nemo & Friends. Here the premise is that Mike realizes laughter can be harnessed as a power source, and Mike's new comedy club is expected to generate power for the future. The more the audience yuks it up, the greater the power produced. You can text-message jokes from cell phones to the show's producer; they might even be used in the show. **For people with disabilities:** Wheelchair accessible. Sign language is available some days. Equipped

for assisted-listening and video-captioning devices. ■ **TIP→ Skip the Fastpass+ for this show; come when you're waiting for your Buzz Lightyear or Space Mountain Fastpass+ appointment.** ✉ *Tomorrowland, Magic Kingdom* ☞ *Duration: 15 mins. Crowds: Heavy. Audience: All ages.*

★ Space Mountain

AMUSEMENT PARK/WATER PARK | The needlelike spires and gleaming, white, concrete cone of this 180-foot-high attraction are almost as much a Magic Kingdom landmark as Cinderella Castle. Inside is what is one of the world's most imaginative roller coasters, one that had a real astronaut, Gordon Cooper, for a creative consultant. Although there are no loop-the-loops or high-speed curves, the thrills are many as you take a trip into the depths of outer space—in the dark.

You can pass the wait time playing one of the many games on the Disney Play app. As you walk to the loading area, you'll pass whirling planets and hear the screams and shrieks of the riders, pumping you up for your own launch. Once you blast off, the ride lasts only two minutes and 38 seconds, with a top speed of 28 mph, but the devious twists and invisible drops in the dark make it seem twice as long. You can hear the screams from other cars, but you don't know where they are, adding an additional fright factor. Stow personal belongings securely. Not appropriate for pregnant women or guests wearing back, neck, or leg braces. **For people with disabilities:** You must be able to step into the ride vehicle and walk short distances. Guests in wheelchairs should see a cast member for boarding options. Service animals aren't permitted. ■ **TIP→ The wait can be long. Get a Fastpass+, or come early, late, or during a parade.** ✉ *Tomorrowland, Magic Kingdom* ☞ *Duration: 2½ mins. Crowds: You bet! Audience: Not young kids. Height requirement: 44 inches.*

Tomorrowland Speedway

AMUSEMENT PARK/WATER PARK | This is one of those rides that incites instant addiction in children and immediate regret in their parents. The reasons for the former are evident: the children drive brightly colored Mark VII model cars that swerve around the four 2,260-foot tracks with much *vroom-vroom-vrooming*. Like real sports cars, the vehicles are equipped with rack-and-pinion steering and disc brakes; unlike the real thing, these run on a track. But the track is so twisty that it's hard to keep the car on a straight course. Expect to spend a lot of time waiting your turn on the track and returning your vehicle after your lap. All this for a ride that achieves a top speed of 7 mph.

For people with disabilities: To drive the cars, you must be able to steer, press the gas pedal, and transfer into the low car seat. ■ **TIP→ Don't waste a Fastpass+ on this one; skip on a first-time visit unless you'll break your child's heart.** ✉ *Tomorrowland, Magic Kingdom* ☞ *Duration: 5 mins. Crowds: Moderate. Audience: Young kids and tweens. Height requirements: With an adult must be at least 32 inches; those who wish to drive must reach 54 inches.*

Tomorrowland Transit Authority PeopleMover

AMUSEMENT PARK/WATER PARK | A reincarnation of what Disney old-timers might remember as the WEDway PeopleMover, the TTA PeopleMover gives you a nice, leisurely ride with great views of Tomorrowland, circling the Astro-Orbiter and gliding through the middle of Space Mountain. Disney's version of future mass transit is smooth and noiseless, thanks to an electromagnetic linear induction motor that has no moving parts, uses little power, and emits no pollutants. **For people with disabilities:** You must be able to walk several steps and step on and off a moving ramp to transfer to a ride vehicle. Equipped for handheld-captioning and audio-description

Magic Kingdom Kids Tour

The Magic Kingdom is alive with thrilling distractions for young children, so let them take the lead now and then. Toddlers might want to jump from their strollers and dance along to the barbershop quartet on Main Street. Children who love to explore will have a ball scrambling around Frontierland and hopping a raft to Tom Sawyer's playground.

Stop and Smell the Roses

Head down Main Street, U.S.A., and, if you're lucky, the park's **Dapper Dan's Barbershop Quartet** will be harmonizing sweet tunes and tossing out one-liners from a small alcove along the street (check the park's *Times Guide* for performances). Young children are thrilled with the music and colorful costumes of these talented singers.

As you continue on, veer right toward the rose garden for a scenic picture spot where you can snap one of the prettiest shots in the park: the kids by the garden amid Mickey and Minnie topiaries, with Cinderella Castle in the background.

Fantasyland is dead ahead, and after you've soared on **Dumbo the Flying Elephant**, head straight to **Enchanted Tales with Belle**, where the kids get to participate. Use one of your coveted Fastpass+ reservations on **The Seven Dwarfs Mine Train** family coaster. Then try to catch a character performance in front of **Cinderella Castle** or during one of the daily parades or street parties.

Put the Zip in Your Doo-Dah

With little ones in tow, when it's time for food, fast is best. **Cosmic Ray's Starlight Café** is a high-energy quick stop with multiple choices for the entire family. Kids can head straight to the dance floor where Audio-Animatronics entertainer Sonny Eclipse keeps the tunes coming. After refueling, board the **Walt Disney World Railroad** at Main Street, U.S.A., Fantasyland, or Frontierland. While in Frontierland, too-short-to-ride kids can burn energy in the cavelike play area beneath **Splash Mountain** while parents take turns riding. The short raft trip to **Tom Sawyer Island** is worth it for kids who like exploring. Not far from the Country Bear Jamboree, sure shots can take aim at Western-style targets in the often-missed **Frontierland Shootin' Arcade**—at about $1 per 35 shots, it's a blast for any aspiring sheriff.

Become the Character

Get the makeover of a lifetime ($74.95–$229.95) at **Bibbidi Bobbidi Boutique**, in Cinderella Castle. Hair, nails, makeup—even a sprinkling of pixie dust—it's all here.

Afterward, be sure to catch a character meet and greet (see *Times Guide* for schedule) so the little rascals get all the hugs, autographs, photos, and magical memories they deserve.

Magic Kingdom Grown-Up Tour 

The kids are older, and they're interested in thrills not magic. Or there aren't any kids in tow, and this is your golden opportunity to enjoy me time. Seize the day! The Magic Kingdom is a whole new experience without young children. Maximize the big adventures, take time to dine and shop, and discover your own brand of magic along the way.

Classic Thrills

As you pass beneath the train station and into Town Square, you're entering the Happiest Place on Earth, and it's time to grab the golden ring. If thrill riding tops your list, work that cardio for a power walk northwest from the park hub through Liberty Square to Frontierland, where you can ride **Splash Mountain**, then go next door to dry off on the bumpy, scenic, runaway train at **Big Thunder Mountain Railroad.** The next hot ticket on your must-ride list is the **Seven Dwarfs Mine Train** family coaster in Fantasyland.

For many, just seeing the Johnny Depp look-alike, Audio-Animatronics Captain Jack Sparrow is reason enough to ride **Pirates of the Caribbean** in Adventureland, a short stroll from Splash Mountain. Cut back through the park hub and straight to **Space Mountain** in Tomorrowland for your other big-deal Fastpass+. While you wait, sip an iced cappuccino or smoothie from **Auntie Gravity's Galactic Goodies** and/or experience the interactive **Buzz Lightyear's Space Ranger Spin**, which is addictive for competitive types, who will probably want to ride more than once for a chance to raise their space ranger profile.

Play, Dine, Shop

Chill out afterward at **Tony's Town Square Restaurant**, a great, full-service, late-lunch spot where you can feast on pasta. Burn off the calories shopping on Main Street for a make-your-own Mouse Ears souvenir from **The Chapeau** or some character bling from **Uptown Jewelers.**

At **Crystal Arts**, you can buy a fluted glass bowl and then mosey to the rear of the glass shop to see an Arribas Brothers glassblower craft a piece using 2,100°F furnaces, a heated glass rod, and lots of talent. It takes about 20 minutes for the glassblower to shape a piece of glass and explain each step along the way.

Catch the Spirit(s)

You can skip the 3 pm parade crowds and join 999 grim-grinning ghouls at the **Haunted Mansion** in Liberty Square. Afterward, stroll several paces to the Hall of Presidents and catch the patriotic spirit. Just around the corner in Fantasyland, don your goofy 3-D glasses for **Mickey's PhilharMagic**, starring the largest cast of Disney animated stars performing in a single show. Cap the evening with the **Happily Ever After** fireworks, lasers, and projections display, featuring themes from more than a dozen Disney animated films. You'll be glad you stayed for the fairy-tale ending.

devices. **TIP→ Come to view Tomorrowland, to preview Space Mountain, if you have young children, or if you need a relaxing ride.** If there is no line, this is a great nap spot for toddlers. ✉ *Tomorrowland, Magic Kingdom* ☞ *Duration: 10 mins. Crowds: Light. Audience: All ages.*

Walt Disney's Carousel of Progress
AMUSEMENT PARK/WATER PARK | Originally seen at New York's 1964–65 World's Fair, this revolving theater traces the impact of technological progress on the daily lives of Americans from the turn of the 20th century into the near future. Representing each decade, an Audio-Animatronics family sings the praises of modern-day gadgets that technology has wrought. **For people with disabilities:** Wheelchair accessible; equipped for assisted-listening, hand-held-captioning, audio-description, and video-captioning devices. **TIP→ Skip on a first-time visit unless you adore nostalgia. It might close early or entirely in low season.** ✉ *Tomorrowland, Magic Kingdom* ☞ *Duration: 20 mins. Crowds: Moderate. Audience: All ages.*

Shopping

Mickey's Star Traders
TOYS | One of the largest shops in the Magic Kingdom, Star Traders trades on the purchase of all things Disney. Toys, pins, T-shirts featuring favorite characters like Mickey, Stitch, and Mike from Monsters Inc. can be found here, as well as Goofy caps and oversize Mickey gloves. So much to see—so much to buy! ✉ *Tomorrowland, Magic Kingdom* 🌐 *www.disneyworld.disney.go.com/shops/magic-kingdom/mickeys-star-traders.*

Magic Kingdom Resort Area

Despite being the oldest hotels on Disney property, the five properties in the Magic Kingdom Resort Area are some of the nicest. Those looking for a more upscale experience should consider the three hotels that are all connected to the Magic Kingdom by monorail—The Grand Floridan, The Polynesian Village Resort, and The Contemporary. Connected by boat are the Wilderness Lodge and the only camping location on Disney property, Fort Wilderness. While these are not as pricey or upscale, you are still paying for easy transportation to the Magic Kingdom. Adults looking for a nice night out will be thrilled with the many dining options at the Grand Floridan and the California Grill at the Contemporary. If you're traveling with a big group, look into the newly built bungalows at the Polynesian Village Resort or the Boulder Ridge Villas at Fort Wilderness Lodge. From those looking for a bar complete with a big band to families hoping to watch the fireworks while eating sushi, staying at the Magic Kingdom Resort Area makes everyone feel as if they're in the middle of all the action.

Restaurants

★ California Grill
$$$$ | **AMERICAN** | The view of the surrounding Disney parks from this 15th-floor restaurant—the World's signature dining establishment since 1995—is as stunning as the food, especially after dark, when you can watch the nightly Magic Kingdom fireworks from an outdoor viewing area. The space has stylish mid-century modern furnishings and chandeliers, and the exhibition kitchen is so well equipped that it has a cast-iron flat grill designed specifically for cooking fish. **Known for:** stunning views of the parks and fireworks; wild game

charcuterie and fresh sushi; Sunday brunch. *Average main: $47* ✉ *Disney's Contemporary Resort, 4600 N. World Dr., Magic Kingdom Resort Area* ☎ *407/939–3463* 🌐 *disneyworld.disney.go.com/dining/contemporary-resort/california-grill* ⊗ *No lunch.*

★ Capa

$$$$ | **STEAKHOUSE** | Billed as a Spanish steak house, Capa is a concept cleverly executed in a chic, modern dining area. The menu spans the culinary culture gap by starting with tapas, most of them authentically Spanish, and continuing with exceptional steaks worthy of the luxury setting. **Known for:** superb steaks and seafood; grilled duck, lamb, and pork chops; enviable view of fireworks from the outdoor patio. *Average main: $52* ✉ *Four Seasons Resort, 10100 Dream Tree Blvd., Magic Kingdom Resort Area* ☎ *407/313–7777* 🌐 *www.fourseasons.com/orlando/dining* ⊗ *No lunch.*

Chef Mickey's

$$$$ | **AMERICAN** | **FAMILY** | The fact that the Disney monorail zooms overhead right through the Contemporary Resort, and that Mickey, Minnie, or Goofy hang around for breakfast and dinner, would be enough to make it popular, but the food here is surprisingly good. Chef Mickey's is shiny and bright, still offering a breakfast buffet and brunch that includes French toast, scrambled hash, and even a create-your-own waffle station. **Known for:** character meals and Storybook Moments; family-fare buffet and lots of it; specialty cocktails for the grown-ups. *Average main: $59* ✉ *Disney's Contemporary Resort, 4600 N. World Dr., Magic Kingdom Resort Area* ☎ *407/939–3463* 🌐 *disneyworld.disney.go.com/dining/contemporary-resort/chef-mickeys* ⊗ *No lunch.*

Citricos

$$$$ | **ECLECTIC** | With an ambitious menu that's fundamentally American with influences of Tuscan, Provençal, and Spanish-Mediterranean cuisine, this Grand Floridian restaurant is one of the resort's best dollar-to-dining options. Standout entrées include Florida red snapper with shrimp, mussels, and clams, and the red wine–braised beef short ribs with hand-harvested mushrooms. **Known for:** superb cheese-course selections; oak-grilled meats; casually elegant atmosphere. *Average main: $47* ✉ *Disney's Grand Floridian Resort & Spa, 4401 Floridian Way, Magic Kingdom Resort Area* ☎ *407/939–3463* 🌐 *disneyworld.disney.go.com/dining/grand-floridian-resort-and-spa/citricos* ⊗ *No lunch.*

Garden View Tea Room

$$$$ | **BRITISH** | Disney's Perfectly Princess Tea Party is afternoon tea at its grandest as children ages 3 to 9 enjoy the royal treatment with Mom (or Dad). Dressing up is encouraged, and an early 9 am meal, featuring tea and sandwiches, is served on china plates (apple juice, peanut butter, and ham-and-cheese sandwiches for the kids; cheeses and finger sandwiches for adults). **Known for:** highly elegant tea for young princesses and princes and refined adults; character appearances; house-made scones, sandwiches, and sweets. *Average main: $150* ✉ *Disney's Grand Floridian Resort & Spa, 4401 Floridian Way, Magic Kingdom Resort Area* ☎ *407/939–3463* 🌐 *disneyworld.disney.go.com/dining/grand-floridian-resort-and-spa/perfectly-princess-tea-party.*

Narcoossee's

$$$$ | **SEAFOOD** | The dining room, with Victorian-style columns, high ceilings, and hardwood floors, makes a great place not only to enjoy "coastal cuisine"—especially steaks and seafood—but to gaze out at the nightly fireworks over the Seven Seas Lagoon; an announcement is made when fireworks commence and music is piped in. The menu changes regularly. **Known for:** intimate and well-stocked bar; seafood flown in daily; black Angus steaks. *Average main: $54* ✉ *Disney's Grand Floridian Resort & Spa, 4401*

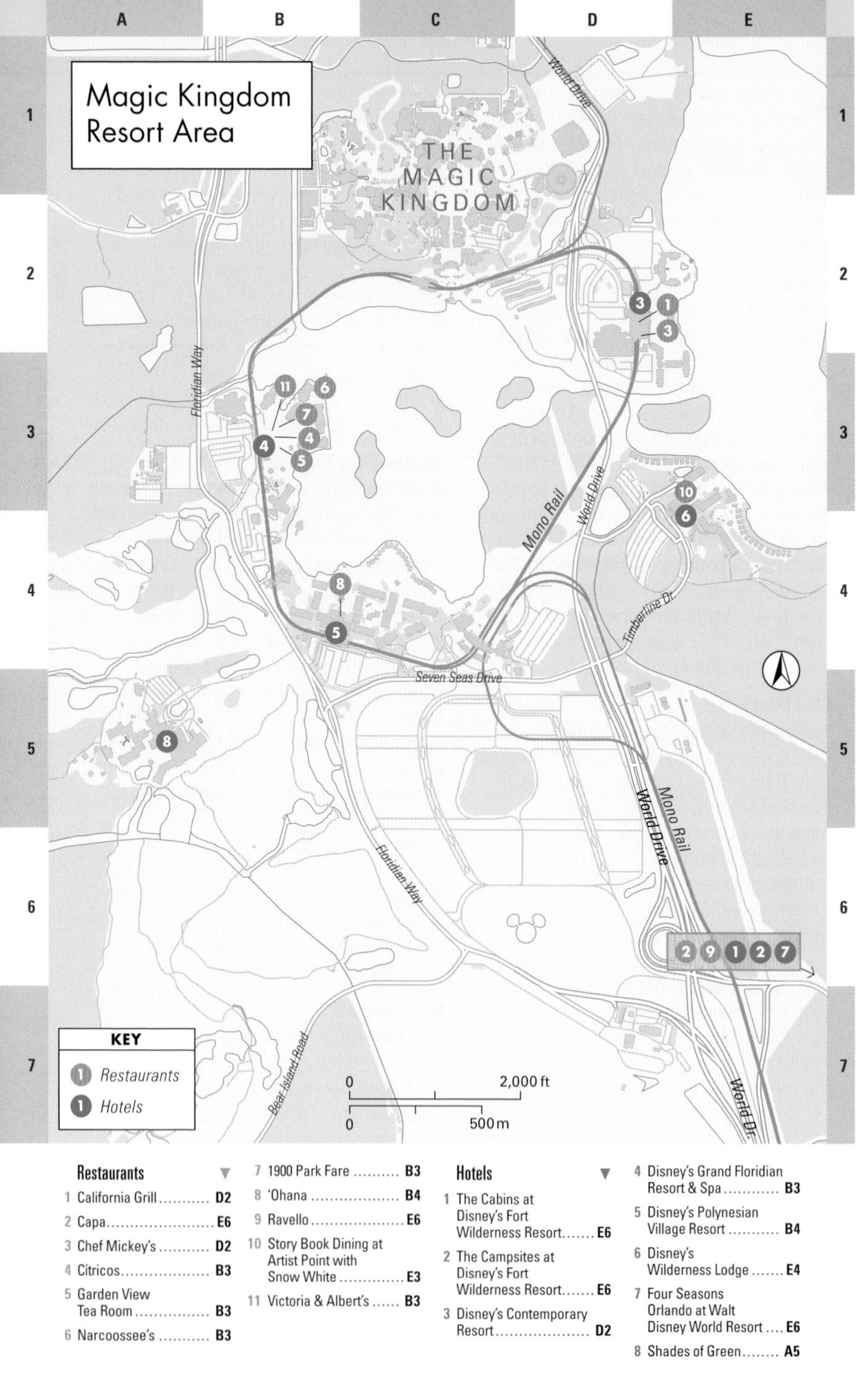

Restaurants

1 California Grill **D2**
2 Capa **E6**
3 Chef Mickey's **D2**
4 Cítricos **B3**
5 Garden View Tea Room **B3**
6 Narcoossee's **B3**
7 1900 Park Fare **B3**
8 'Ohana **B4**
9 Ravello **E6**
10 Story Book Dining at Artist Point with Snow White **E3**
11 Victoria & Albert's **B3**

Hotels

1 The Cabins at Disney's Fort Wilderness Resort....... **E6**
2 The Campsites at Disney's Fort Wilderness Resort....... **E6**
3 Disney's Contemporary Resort..................... **D2**
4 Disney's Grand Floridian Resort & Spa **B3**
5 Disney's Polynesian Village Resort **B4**
6 Disney's Wilderness Lodge **E4**
7 Four Seasons Orlando at Walt Disney World Resort **E6**
8 Shades of Green........ **A5**

Floridian Way, Magic Kingdom Resort Area ☎ 407/939–3463 🌐 disneyworld.disney.go.com/dining/grand-floridian-resort-and-spa/narcoossees ⏲ No lunch.

1900 Park Fare

$$$$ | **AMERICAN** | Disney characters delight guests throughout the day at this sprawling, though dainty, lobby restaurant. Mary Poppins and friends join guests during the Supercalifragilistic Breakfast, posing for pics while cheerful tunes are played on an antique organ called Big Bertha. **Known for:** Florida strawberry soup; character dining buffets throughout the day; Wonderland Tea Party. [$] *Average main: $45* ✉ *Disney's Grand Floridian Resort & Spa, 4401 Floridian Way, Magic Kingdom Resort Area* ☎ *407/939–3463* 🌐 *disneyworld.disney.go.com/dining/grand-floridian-resort-and-spa/1900-park-fare* ⏲ *No lunch.*

'Ohana

$$$$ | **SOUTH PACIFIC** | **FAMILY** | This Polynesian-themed restaurant offers two thoroughly entertaining, though incredibly different, experiences. Early in the day, the Best Friends Breakfast with Lilo & Stitch is destination-worthy; by night you'll find a Hawaiian-theme dinner. **Known for:** storytelling, shows, and games between courses; chicken, seafood, and steak skewers; full bar for adults. [$] *Average main: $54* ✉ *Disney's Polynesian Village Resort, 1600 Seven Seas Dr., Magic Kingdom Resort Area* ☎ *407/939–3463* 🌐 *disneyworld.disney.go.com/dining/polynesian-resort/ohana* ⏲ *No lunch.*

Ravello

$$$$ | **MODERN ITALIAN** | **FAMILY** | Under the leadership of Neapolitan chef Fabrizio Schenardi, Ravello is a chic modern Italian restaurant after dark. Hand-tossed pizzas emerge from the oven—perhaps finished with house-made ricotta, arugula, and truffle oil. **Known for:** superbly executed cuisine of Naples; grilled lamb chops; Disney character breakfast. [$] *Average main: $32* ✉ *Four Seasons Orlando, 10100 Dream Tree Blvd., Magic Kingdom Resort Area* ☎ *407/313–6161* 🌐 *www.fourseasons.com/orlando* ⏲ *No lunch.*

Story Book Dining at Artist Point with Snow White

$$$$ | **AMERICAN** | **FAMILY** | This family-style restaurant deep inside the Wilderness Lodge now has a new theme and offers character dining with Snow White and Dopey. The prix-fixe menu includes a shared appetizer, a single entrée per person, and then a shared dessert. **Known for:** slow-braised pork shank; butter-poached sustainable fish; shrimp cocktail. [$] *Average main: $60* ✉ *Disney's Wilderness Lodge, 901 Timberline Dr., Magic Kingdom Resort Area* ☎ *407/939–3463* 🌐 *disneyworld.disney.go.com/dining/wilderness-lodge-resort/artist-point* ⏲ *No lunch.*

★ Victoria & Albert's

$$$$ | **MODERN AMERICAN** | At this ultraposh restaurant, a well-polished service team will anticipate your every need, providing one of the plushest fine-dining experiences in Florida; the setting is so sophisticated that children under 10 aren't on the guest list. There's nothing quick about sitting down for dinner in the 7- and 10-course main dining room, the 10-course intimate Queen Victoria's Room, or the over-the-top Chef's Table, which is actually in the restaurant's kitchen. **Known for:** highest-priced restaurant at WDW; enormous and expensive wine list; exclusive additions like Osetra caviar and Miyazaki beef. [$] *Average main: $200* ✉ *Disney's Grand Floridian Resort & Spa, 4401 Floridian Way, Magic Kingdom Resort Area* ☎ *407/939–3862* 🌐 *disneyworld.disney.go.com/dining/grand-floridian-resort-and-spa/victoria-and-alberts* ⏲ *No lunch* *Jacket required.*

Hotels

The Cabins at Disney's Fort Wilderness Resort

$$$$ | **RESORT** | **FAMILY** | The cabins in this 750-acre resort campground just a boat ride away from the Magic Kingdom don't exactly constitute roughing it, as they are compact, air-conditioned log homes that accommodate four grown-ups and two youngsters. **Pros:** lots of traditional camping activities and a real campground community feel; you can save money by cooking, but you don't have to, as there is a three-meals-a-day restaurant; nightly family-oriented entertainment options. **Cons:** shuttle to parks is free but slow; pricey for what is really just a mobile home encased in logs; it's a long hike to many of the campground entertainment and dining sites. *Rooms from: $435 4510 N. Fort Wilderness Trail, Magic Kingdom Resort Area 407/824–2900 disneyworld.disney.go.com/resorts/cabins-at-fort-wilderness-resort 421 cabins No meals.*

★ The Campsites at Disney's Fort Wilderness Resort

$ | **RESORT** | One of the cheapest ways to stay on WDW property is in your own tent or RV, which can be set up in one of four different areas, from bargain-priced tent sites with water and electricity to deluxe RV sites equipped with electric, cable TV, Internet access, water and sewage hookups, outdoor charcoal grills, and picnic tables. **Pros:** Disney's most economical lodging; pets allowed; wide choice of recreation and entertainment options. **Cons:** amount of walking to reach the store, restaurants, and so on, can be a bit much; shuttle rides to Disney parks take a long time; the mosquitoes can be irritating, except in winter. *Rooms from: $128 4510 N. Fort Wilderness Trail, Magic Kingdom Resort Area 407/939–6244, 407/824–2742 disneyworld.disney.go.com/resorts/campsites-at-fort-wilderness-resort 799 campsites No meals.*

Disney's Contemporary Resort

$$$$ | **RESORT** | You're paying for location at this sleek, modern, luxury resort next to the Magic Kingdom that despite having opened in 1971, still lives up to its name; park hopping is a breeze, as the monorail runs through the lobby. **Pros:** monorail access; Chef Mickey's, the epicenter of character-meal world; health and wellness suites. **Cons:** the mix of conventioneers and vacationers can make for chaos in the lobby; fee for self-parking; lobby eateries can be crowded and noisy. *Rooms from: $534 4600 N. World Dr., Magic Kingdom Resort Area 407/824–1000 disneyworld.disney.go.com/resorts/contemporary-resort 1,028 rooms No meals.*

★ Disney's Grand Floridian Resort & Spa

$$$$ | **RESORT** | So close to the Magic Kingdom you can see the colors change on the Cinderella Castle, this red-roofed Victorian-style resort emulates the look of the great railroad resorts of the past with beautifully appointed rooms, rambling verandas, delicate, white-painted woodwork, and brick chimneys. **Pros:** one monorail stop from the Magic Kingdom; Victoria & Albert's offers an evening-long experience in fine dining; if you're a couple with no kids, this is definitely the most romantic on-property hotel. **Cons:** pricey; draws a large convention clientele; vacationing couples might be more comfortable than families with young children. *Rooms from: $708 4401 Floridian Way, Magic Kingdom Resort Area 407/824–3000 disneyworld.disney.go.com/resorts/grand-floridian-resort-and-spa 867 rooms No meals.*

Disney's Polynesian Village Resort

$$$$ | **RESORT** | **FAMILY** | This South Pacific–themed resort, with its tropical backdrop of orchids, ferns, and palms, lies directly across the lagoon from the Magic Kingdom; it's on the monorail and water taxi routes and has lots of kids activities, making it a good family choice. **Pros:** on the monorail line; great atmosphere; kids'

The Grand Floridian is one of Walt Disney World's original hotels and also one of its most luxurious and expensive.

activities. **Cons:** pricey; lots of loud children; Magic Kingdom ferry noise affects some bungalows. $ *Rooms from: $703* ✉ *1600 Seven Seas Dr., Magic Kingdom Resort Area* ☎ *407/824–2000* 🌐 *disneyworld.disney.go.com/resorts/polynesian-resort* *844 rooms* *No meals.*

Disney's Wilderness Lodge

$$$$ | RESORT | FAMILY | The architects designed this seven-story luxury resort to mimic the majestic turn-of-the-20th-century lodges of the American West. **Pros:** boarding point for romantic cruises or free water taxi to Magic Kingdom; good dining options; children's activity center. **Cons:** no direct bus to Magic Kingdom; no monorail access; noise from the antics at Whispering Canyon Cafe can be annoying. $ *Rooms from: $508* ✉ *901 Timberline Dr., Magic Kingdom Resort Area* ☎ *407/824–3200* 🌐 *disneyworld.disney.go.com/resorts/wilderness-lodge-resort* *716 rooms* *No meals.*

Four Seasons Orlando at Walt Disney World Resort

$$$$ | RESORT | The award-winning Four Seasons presides majestically over Disney's exclusive Golden Oak community, and its luxurious amenities and dedication to service are clear from the moment you step into the marble, flower-bedecked lobby and head for your room. **Pros:** free transportation to Disney parks; lots of on-site kids' entertainment and an exclusive golf course; no resort fee. **Cons:** pricey, but then, it is the Four Seasons; a long way from Universal or SeaWorld; remote from Disney parks. $ *Rooms from: $769* ✉ *10100 Dream Tree Blvd., Magic Kingdom Resort Area* ☎ *407/313–7777* 🌐 *www.fourseasons.com/orlando* *444 rooms* *No meals.*

Shades of Green

$ | HOTEL | FAMILY | Operated by the U.S. Armed Forces Recreation Center, this resort is open only to active-duty and retired personnel from the armed forces, reserves, and National Guard, their families, and others connected with the military. **Pros:** large standard rooms; monorail a short walk away; Army–Air Force Exchange store discounts deeply for people with military IDs. **Cons:** prices vary based on rank; no MagicBands or Cards; can be very crowded during holidays. *Rooms from: $115* *1905 W. Magnolia Palm Dr., Magic Kingdom Resort Area* *407/824–3600, 888/593–2242* *www.shadesofgreen.org* *597 rooms* *No meals.*

Activities

SPAS

Senses—A Disney Spa at Disney's Grand Floridian Resort

FITNESS/HEALTH CLUBS | All the senses—sound, sight, smell, touch, and taste—are engaged when you enter this Disney-designed-and-owned spa near the Wedding Pavilion at the Grand Floridian Resort. Soothing fruit-based elixirs start the journey toward serenity, while soft lighting, gentle music, and the aroma of lavender encourage you to shed your stress (along with most of your clothes). Lounge chairs in separate and secluded men's and women's relaxation areas offer you a spot to further unwind as you wait. Massage tables are heated, as are the lounge chairs in the restful wet room (spend some time looking for the hidden Mickey on the wall). Swimsuits are required in all wet relaxation areas. Treatments include facials, scrubs, and many massages. A whimsical Mad Hatter chair offers little princesses a special place for a pedicure. Prices do not include the 20% gratuity. *Grand Floridian Resort, 4401 Floridian Way, Magic Kingdom Resort Area* *407/824–3000* *www.disneyworld.disney.go.com/spas/grand-floridian-resort-and-spa/senses-spa* *Parking: complimentary self-parking.*

Chapter 4

EPCOT AND RESORT AREA

Updated by
Leigh Jenkins

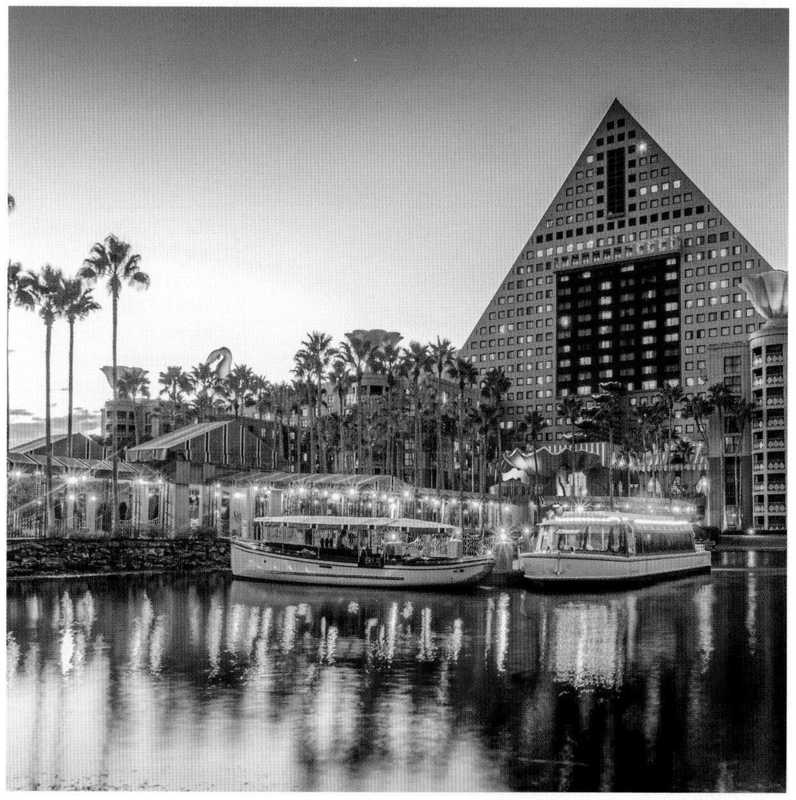

Sights ★★★★★ | Restaurants ★★★★★ | Hotels ★★★★☆ | Shopping ★★★★★ | Nightlife ★★★☆☆

EPCOT INTERNATIONAL FOOD AND WINE FESTIVAL

A wine-and-cheese tasting at the EPCOT International Food and Wine Festival.

For an ever-increasing number of autumn weeks, EPCOT hosts the EPCOT International Food and Wine Festival, attracting folks more interested in a fine phyllo than a photo op with Cinderella.

The festival is essentially a compendium of food- and beverage-related offerings, some free with the price of EPCOT admission, others costing anywhere from $3.75 for a piece of cake to several hundred dollars for extravagant wine dinners. Mixology or cheese seminars compete with cookbook signings by famous chefs, and tapas-size portions of foods served from about 30 international theme stalls encircle the World Lagoon. Throughout the event, guest chefs host brunches, lunches, and wine-pairing dinners—casual, posh, or festive—at EPCOT and in hotels. The headliners change annually but might include names like chef Masaharu Morimoto or Rick Bayless. The festival's food and beverage lineup changes every year, too, so for more information and to make reservations (during festival season only, generally midsummer through early November), call *407/939–3378* or visit *www.disneyworld.com/foodandwine*.

GARDEN OF EATING

EPCOT has expanded the offerings at its annual Flower & Garden Festival, which ran for a staggering 90 days in 2018. The springtime celebration of all things green and floral features more than a dozen outdoor kitchens whose dishes are inspired by produce and fresh foods from around the world, and are served throughout the World Showcase—with paired beverages, of course.

SHOPPING FOR A SNACK

The heart of the Food and Wine Festival—and the most approachable event for hungry tourists on a budget—takes place around EPCOT's World Showcase. Ordinarily a miniature world of 11 pavilions themed around one country apiece, the area takes on new life when as many as 36 "international marketplaces" take up residence.

Most of the marketplaces, from Brazil to South Korea, offer a taste of one country, selling several appetizer-size food items and beverages—nearly all for $3.25 to $10 apiece. Indisputably popular creations like the cheddar soup ladled out endlessly at Canada are perennials. Still, a majority of the menu will change from year to year. Attendees might taste Brazilian crispy pork belly with black beans (paired with Xingu Black beer), Beijing roasted duck bao with hoisin sauce (with vodka "Kung Fu Punch"), or chicken with red-eye gravy and griddled corn cakes (with a Florida Orange Groves mango wine).

A few marketplaces feature items instead of locales. The Desserts and Champagne booth, for instance, pours a bounty of bubbly and serves special sweets.The craft beer marketplace puts out several regional brews along with complementary snacks like spicy pimento cheese with crackers. And the all-American Craft Beers market often specializes in fare U.S. citizens can be proud of, such as the Zesty Cheeseburger Handwich and Cigar City Brewing's Invasion Pale Ale from Tampa.

Lines get long, especially on weekends, when locals pour in for their regular fix of foreign fare, so consider timing your tour during the day or on a weekday evening, when most spots have shorter waits. And keep an eye on the budget: those little dishes can add up quickly.

Diners at EPCOT's Teppan Edo.

Marinated strawberries with basil served at the Argentina kiosk.

FESTIVAL OF THE SENSES

Several evenings throughout the festival, food and wine enthusiasts clad in cocktail attire saunter into the gala called Party for the Senses. Billed as a "grand tasting," the upscale bash starts booking in July and sells out within days. In a dramatically decorated, high-ceiling room, 10 to 15 chefs from around the country host as many as 50 food stations, serving a hearty appetizer-size portion of one passionately prepared dish. Some are Disney chefs eager to show their talents, and others are known nationally. Big names such as François Payard, Allen Susser, and Walter Staib have participated. Reserved seating for all guests is now offered, a welcome reprise from the "stand and carry" model. Live entertainment such as acrobats and vocalists gives attendees something to watch while taking a break between bites. Seats in the Wine View Lounge include early entrance and private transport.

PARK SNAPSHOT

TOP EXPERIENCES

■ **Frozen Ever After.** *Frozen* fans line up in droves to hop in a longboat and join Elsa and Anna in this chilly adventure based on the film.

■ **Mission: SPACE.** Blast off on a simulated ride to Mars, if you can handle the turbulence.

■ **Remy's Ratatouille Adventure.** EPCOT's newest attraction uses 4-D technology to make you feel like you're really scurrying around the kitchens of Paris.

■ **Soarin' Around the World.** Everyone's hands-down favorite: feel the breeze as you hang glide over spectacular global scenery.

■ **Test Track.** Design your concept car, then rev up to 60 mph on a hairpin turn in this wild ride on a Chevrolet proving ground.

GETTING HERE

Disney's monorail and buses drop you off at the main entrance in front of World Celebration. But if you're staying at one of the EPCOT resorts (the BoardWalk, Yacht Club, Beach Club, Dolphin, or Swan), you can take a boat to the International Gateway entrance. The Disney Skyline, a large gondola system, also brings guests of the Caribbean Beach, Pop Century, Riviera Resort, and Art of Animation resorts to this back entrance.

PLANNING YOUR TIME

EPCOT is vast and generally requires two days to do it justice, one for World Celebration, World Discovery, and World Nature, and another full day for World Showcase. Because World Showcase doesn't usually open until 11, make sure you ride any other top rides early in the day so you'll be prepared for the second rope drop, when you should head straight to Norway for Frozen Ever After or France for Remy's Ratatouille Adventure. (These rides sometimes open early.) It's easier to get a reservation for lunch at one of the better restaurants. If you want to have dinner in the park, eat during the fireworks.

QUICK BITES

■ **Kingla Bakeri Og Kafe.** Looking for a sweet bite or maybe a bit of smoked salmon? This café offers both. The Norwegian school bread and *lefse*, a soft bread rolled in cinnamon and sugar, are both guest favorites, and adults will enjoy their Viking Coffee, spiked with Baileys Irish Creme and Kamora coffee liqueur. ⊠ *World Showcase, Norway.*

■ **Les Halles Boulangerie-Patisserie.** At this French patisserie, expect to choose from eclairs, macarons, and napoleons. And what could be more French than finishing off your treat with a glass of champagne? ⊠ *World Showcase, France.*

■ **Sunshine Seasons.** Talk about a self-contained ecosystem: The Land pavilion grows its own produce, including tomatoes and cucumbers, some of which show up on the menu at the healthful food court. Much of the fare is cooked on a 48-inch Mongolian grill. ⊠ *World Nature, The Land.*

Walt Disney said that EPCOT would "take its cue from the new ideas and new technologies that are now emerging from the creative centers of American industry."

He wrote that EPCOT—never completed, always improving—"will never cease to be a living blueprint of the future, a showcase to the world for the ingenuity of American free enterprise." That statement has never been more true than now, as so much in EPCOT is undergoing big changes. Several attractions have closed, and Disney officials have announced new, and often more kid-friendly, attractions to be open by 2021.

The permanent settlement that Disney envisioned wasn't to be. EPCOT opened in 1982—16 years after his death—as a showcase, ostensibly, for the concepts that would be incorporated into the real-life EPCOTs of the future. (Disney's vision *has* taken an altered shape in the self-contained city of Celebration, an urban-planner's dream opened in 1996 on Disney property near Kissimmee.)

EPCOT theme park, opened with two key areas: Future World, with pavilions—collaborations between Walt Disney Imagineering and U.S. corporations—demonstrating technological advances through innovative shows and attractions, and World Showcase, where microcosms of 11 countries from four continents feature shops, restaurants, attractions, and live entertainment. During the next couple of years, Future World, will be remade into three new areas—World Celebration, World Discovery, and World Nature—and the World Showcase will be expanded with new rides and attractions.

For years, EPCOT was considered the more staid park, a place geared toward adults. But after its 10th anniversary, EPCOT began to evolve into a livelier, more child-friendly park, with such wow attractions as Test Track, Mission: SPACE, and Soarin'.

There's something for everyone here. The World Showcase appeals to younger children with the Kidcot Fun Stop craft stations and the Norway pavilion's Frozen Ever After ride. Soarin', in The Land pavilion, is a family favorite. And the Seas with Nemo & Friends—with one of the world's largest saltwater aquariums and a Nemo-theme ride—is a must-see for all. Adrenaline junkie? Don't miss Test Track presented by Chevrolet, where you can design your own custom concept car, then put it through its high-speed paces.

Wear comfortable shoes—there's *a lot* of territory to cover here. Arrive early, and try to stay all day, squeezing in extras like Bruce's Shark World and a relaxing meal. If you enter through International Gateway before 11 am, cast members will direct you to World Nature, as World Showcase opens just before lunch, or you can indulge in a latte and éclair at the France bakery, the sole quick-service eatery open early in World Showcase.

Planning

Getting Oriented

EPCOT is undergoing a massive transformation in time for Walt Disney World's 50th anniversary in 2021. Over the next couple years, the park will be divided into four sections, including the beloved World Showcase, as well as the new World Celebration, World Nature, and World Discovery areas in what was (and some might still refer to as) Future World. Of course, amid the park's classic offerings, you can expect to find plenty of new, innovative, and thrilling attractions.

At the entrance of the park is the recently created World Celebration area, home to Spaceship Earth, a new festival space, and Dreamers Point, which will honor Walt Disney's vision for EPCOT. This area will also have everything you need for your day at EPCOT, including stroller and wheelchair rentals, maps, and Guest Relations (aka Guest Services).

To the east, World Nature will keep favorites such as Soarin' and The Seas with Nemo & Friends. In The Land pavilion the new *Awesome Planet* film has opened to complement Soarin' and Living with the Land. Soon to be added is the Journey of Water, a "Moana"-themed exploration trail; updates to the Imagination pavilion are also in the works.

In the west is World Discovery, which, with the help of Test Track and Mission: SPACE, will focus on science and technology. This is where the highly anticipated Guardians of the Galaxy: Cosmic Rewind will be. A new restaurant called Space 2020, beside Mission: SPACE, gives guests views of the celestial. The PLAY! pavilion is full of interactive games based off the latest Disney Channel hits.

World Showcase pavilions are on the promenade that circles the World Showcase Lagoon. Each houses architectural examples of a country, with shops, restaurants, and friendly international staffers; some have films or displays. Live entertainment is scheduled at several pavilions. New attractions, such as Remy's Ratatouille Adventure in France and a Mary Poppins–inspired attraction in Great Britain, are expanding the ride options in this section of the park.

Park Amenities

Baby Care: The baby-care center at Odyssey Center in World Discovery has rocking chairs and low lighting. The center sells formula, baby food, pacifiers, and disposable diapers. Changing tables are available here, as well as in all women's and some men's restrooms.

Cameras: Disposable cameras and memory cards are widely available, and you can use the Disney PhotoPass Service to gather memories throughout the park. Other photo services are available at the Imagination! pavilion.

First Aid: Staffed by registered nurses, first aid is in the Odyssey Center. More than a dozen automated external defibrillators are located across the park.

Guest Relations: The two locations where you can pick up schedules and maps are to the right of the ticket windows at the park entrance and to the left of Spaceship Earth inside the park. You can also get maps at the park's International Gateway entrance and most shops. Guest Relations will also assist with dining reservations, ticket upgrades, and services for guests with disabilities.

Lockers: Lockers ($10 to $15 depending on size, with $5 refundable deposit) are at the International Gateway and to the west of Spaceship Earth. Coin-operated lockers also are at the bus information center by the bus parking lot.

Lost People and Things: Instruct children to speak to someone with a Disney name tag if you become separated. If you have lost an item, check the park's Guest Relations office.

EPCOT Lost and Found
Located in the Guest Relations lobby east of Spaceship Earth. ✉ *World Celebration, EPCOT* ☎ *407/560–7500.*

Main Lost and Found Office
After one day, all articles are sent here and can be retrieved between 9 am and 7 pm daily. ✉ *Disney Springs, Disney Springs* ☎ *407/824–4245.*

Package Pick-Up: Ask shop clerks to forward large purchases to Package Pick-Up at the Gift Stop in the Entrance Plaza and at the World Traveler at International Gateway. Allow three hours for delivery. You also can have packages sent to your Disney hotel.

Services for People with Disabilities:
Accessibility standards are high. Many attractions and most restaurants and shops are fully wheelchair accessible. There are large Braille park maps at Guest Relations in World Celebration and International Gateway as well as to the left of the walkway from World Celebration to the World Showcase Plaza.

At Guest Relations, there's a schedule for sign-language presentations at some of the park attractions; you can also pick up special devices for hearing- and sight-impaired visitors.

At World Showcase most people stroll around the promenade, but there are also Friendship boats, which require visitors using oversize wheelchairs or scooters to transfer to Disney chairs.

You can rent wheelchairs at the gift stop outside the main entrance, at the Stroller & Wheelchair Rental Shop to the left of Spaceship Earth, or at the International Gateway. A limited number of electronic convenience vehicles (ECVs) are available only at the Stroller & Wheelchair Rental. Wheelchairs are $12 daily, $10 for multiday rental. ECVs are $50 per day plus a refundable $20 security deposit. Arrive early, because neither conveyance can be reserved. Several Orlando-area companies also rent and deliver ECVs.

Stroller Rentals: You can rent strollers on the east side of the World Celebration and at the International Gateway. Singles are $15 daily, $13 for multiday rental; doubles cost $31 daily, $27 for multiple days. Even preschoolers will be glad for a stroller in this large park.

Park Tours

Backstage Magic
GUIDED TOURS | This tour begins at EPCOT and continues to the Magic Kingdom, Disney's Hollywood Studios, Disney's Animal Kingdom, and several behind-the-scenes areas, including costuming and central shops, where most of the Disney magic is made. Tours depart at 9 am Monday through Friday. The cost for the seven-hour tour (12 and older only) includes lunch at Tiffin's in Disney's Animal Kingdom and bus transportation but does not include park admission, which isn't required for the tour itself. Those using wheelchairs or ECVs need to inform Disney at the time of booking. ✉ *EPCOT* ☎ *407/939–8687* 🌐 *disneyworld.disney.go.com/events-tours/backstage-magic* 🎫 *$275.*

Dolphins in Depth
GUIDED TOURS | During this three-hour experience ($199), guides escort you from EPCOT Guest Relations outside the main park entrance backstage to the Caribbean Coral Reef. This 5.7-million-gallon, man-made saltwater aquarium is home to The Seas with Nemo & Friends at EPCOT, as well as several bottle-nosed dolphins. You must bring your own bathing suits to wade into the water to meet, but not swim with, the dolphins. Children must be 13 years or older, and neither park admission nor a diving certificate

is required. ✉ *EPCOT* ☎ *407/939–8687* 🌐 *disneyworld.disney.go.com/events-tours/epcot/dolphins-in-depth* 🎫 *$199.*

EPCOT Seas Adventures—DiveQuest
ECOTOURISM | The three-hour EPCOT DiveQuest (park admission not required or included) begins with a guide collecting you at Guest Relations outside the entrance. You spend 40 minutes in the 5.7-million-gallon saltwater aquarium under the supervision of a master diver. Family and friends with EPCOT admission can view your dive through the huge windows that line the aquarium. The tour takes place Tuesday through Saturday in the afternoon. Guests ages 10 and up must have open-water adult scuba certification; children 10 to 12 must dive with a parent or legal guardian. Diving equipment is supplied. ✉ *EPCOT* ☎ *407/939–8687* 🌐 *disneyworld.disney.go.com/events-tours/epcot/epcot-divequest* 🎫 *$179.*

EPCOT Seas Adventures—Aqua Tour
ECOTOURISM | For this tour (no park admission required or included) you wear a flotation device and snorkel gear, and you remain on the water's surface. Anyone age 8 and older can join the tour (those under 12 must be with a parent or legal guardian). Tours are limited to 12 guests, meet Tuesday through Saturday, and run about 2½ hours, with 30 minutes in the water. ✉ *EPCOT* 🌐 *disneyworld.disney.go.com/events-tours/epcot/epcot-seas-aqua-tour* 🎫 *$145.*

Gardens of the World Tour
GUIDED TOURS | Plant lovers of all levels will enjoy this three-hour tour (not including park admission) with a Disney Horticulturist to see the World Showcase's wide range of exotic plantings and to learn about the role landscaping plays in Disney parks and resorts. Tours run on select days during the EPCOT International Flower and Garden Festival from January through late May or during the EPCOT International Food and Wine Festival in the fall. For ages 12 and up. ✉ *EPCOT* ☎ *407/939–8687* 🌐 *disneyworld.disney.go.com/events-tours/gardens-of-the-world* 🎫 *$85.*

UnDISCOVERed Future World
GUIDED TOURS | This tour (plus park admission) leaves at 8:30 am weekdays from a meeting spot between Fountain View and Club Cool. The four-hour behind-the-scenes walk for guests 16 and older covers Future World pavilions and some backstage areas, including the EPCOT wardrobe department. Be aware that as Future World changes its name, this tour's name will also likely change, so call well in advance to see if it's being offered and what it is called. ✉ *EPCOT* ☎ *407/939–8687* 🌐 *disneyworld.disney.go.com/events-tours/epcot/undiscovered-future-world* 🎫 *$69.*

EPCOT by Boat 

EPCOT is a big place at 305 acres, and while the most efficient way to get around is to walk, you can save some time by boating across the lagoon. Also called Friendship Boats, the 65-foot water taxis depart every 12 minutes from four World Showcase Plaza docks spaced around the lagoon. The boat closer to Mexico zips to a dock by the Germany pavilion; the one closer to Canada heads to Morocco.

Visiting Tips

Take your time. EPCOT is so vast and varied that you really need two days to explore. With just one day, you'll have to be highly selective.

Shop in the World Showcase. While shopping is thin on the ground in the rest of the park, the country-specific shops in the World Showcase have unique items from around the globe.

Go early in the week. Magic Kingdom tends to be busiest in early in the week, making it the perfect time to visit EPCOT

Plan for the special events. If you like a good festival, visit during the International Flower and Garden Festival (early March through mid-May) or the International Food and Wine Festival (September through mid-November).

Ride the popular rides early. Once through the turnstiles at either the main World Celebration entrance or the back World Showcase entrance, make a beeline for the popular Mission: SPACE and Test Track (for fast-paced thrills) or Frozen Ever After and Soarin' (for family fun). Or book a Fastpass+ for the afternoon.

World Celebration

World Celebration's centerpiece is the iconic Spaceship Earth geosphere and, beyond it, a plaza anchored by a new pavilion for live events. Three stories high, this architectural masterpiece adds some much needed space for EPCOT's many festivals. And fans of Walt Disney will be thrilled with Dreamers Point, containing a statue and story fountain celebrating Walt Disney and his vision for the future.

Also in World Celebration are Guest Relations, wheelchair and stroller rental, and lockers. If you haven't already done so, you can purchase Memory Maker at the Camera Center ($199 in the park, $169 in advance). It gives you access to all Disney PhotoPass photos of your group shot by Disney photographers, which you can view here in person or through the My Disney Experience app.

Sights

Balanced like a giant golf ball waiting for some celestial being to tee off, the multifaceted silver geosphere of Spaceship Earth is to EPCOT what Cinderella Castle is to the Magic Kingdom. As much a landmark as an icon, it can be seen on a clear day from an airplane flying down either coast of Florida.

Spaceship Earth

AMUSEMENT PARK/WATER PARK | Inside the giant geosphere you are transported past a series of tableaux that explores human progress and the continuing search for better forms of communication. The journey begins in the darkest tunnels of time, proceeds through history, and ends poised on the edge of the future. Revered author Ray Bradbury helped design the iconic ball and wrote the original story. Ten-time Emmy winner Bruce Broughton composed the musical score.

Audio-Animatronics figures present Cro-Magnon man daubing mystic paintings on cave walls, Egyptian scribes scratching hieroglyphics on papyrus, Roman centurions building roads, Islamic scholars mapping the heavens, and 11th- and 12th-century Benedictine monks hand-copying manuscripts. As you move into the Renaissance, there's Michelangelo and Gutenberg, and, in rapid succession, the telegraph, radio, television, and computer come into being. A family views the moon landing on TV, and soon the personal computer is born.

This ride has been updated multiple times over the years, always trying to incorporate the newest ideas for the future. The current Spaceship Earth emphasizes storytelling as what connects humanity, culminating in guests exiting at Dreamers Point, which honors Walt Disney who had his own gift for storytelling. **For people with disabilities:** You must be able to transfer to a standard wheelchair, then walk four steps to the ride vehicle. Guests with service animals should check with an attraction host for boarding information. The ride is equipped for handheld-captioning and audio-description devices available at Guest Relations. **TIP→ Ride while waiting for a Mission: SPACE or Soarin'**

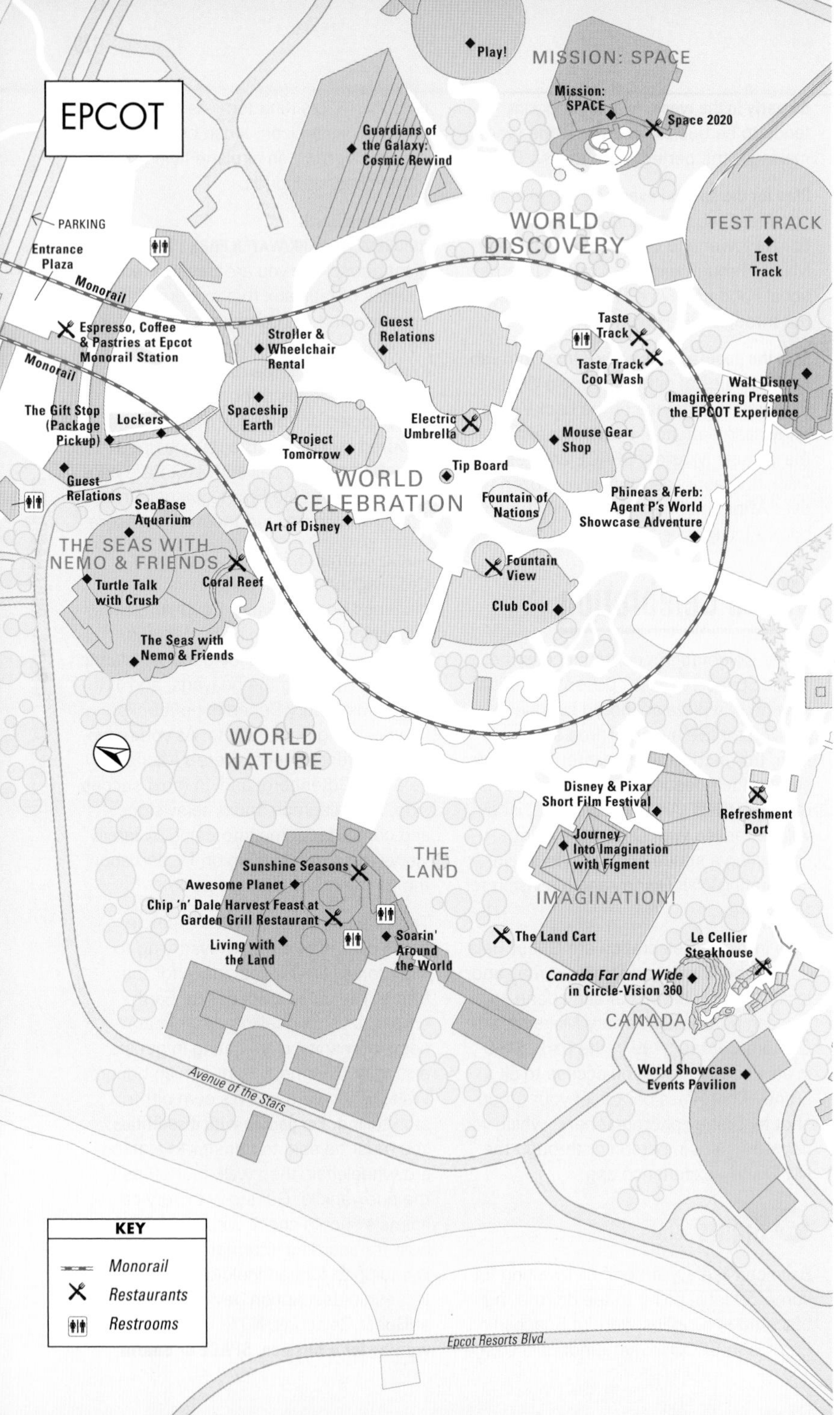
EPCOT
Play!
MISSION: SPACE
Mission: SPACE
Space 2020
Guardians of the Galaxy: Cosmic Rewind
PARKING
Entrance Plaza
Monorail
WORLD DISCOVERY
TEST TRACK
Test Track
Espresso, Coffee & Pastries at Epcot Monorail Station
Monorail
Stroller & Wheelchair Rental
Guest Relations
Taste Track
Taste Track Cool Wash
Walt Disney Imagineering Presents the EPCOT Experience
The Gift Stop (Package Pickup)
Lockers
Spaceship Earth
Project Tomorrow
Electric Umbrella
Mouse Gear Shop
Guest Relations
Tip Board
WORLD CELEBRATION
Fountain of Nations
Phineas & Ferb: Agent P's World Showcase Adventure
SeaBase Aquarium
THE SEAS WITH NEMO & FRIENDS
Art of Disney
Fountain View
Coral Reef
Turtle Talk with Crush
Club Cool
The Seas with Nemo & Friends
WORLD NATURE
Disney & Pixar Short Film Festival
Refreshment Port
Journey Into Imagination with Figment
THE LAND
Sunshine Seasons
Awesome Planet
Chip 'n' Dale Harvest Feast at Garden Grill Restaurant
IMAGINATION!
Living with the Land
Soarin' Around the World
The Land Cart
Le Cellier Steakhouse
Canada Far and Wide in Circle-Vision 360
CANADA
World Showcase Events Pavilion
Avenue of the Stars
KEY
Monorail
Restaurants
Restrooms
Epcot Resorts Blvd.

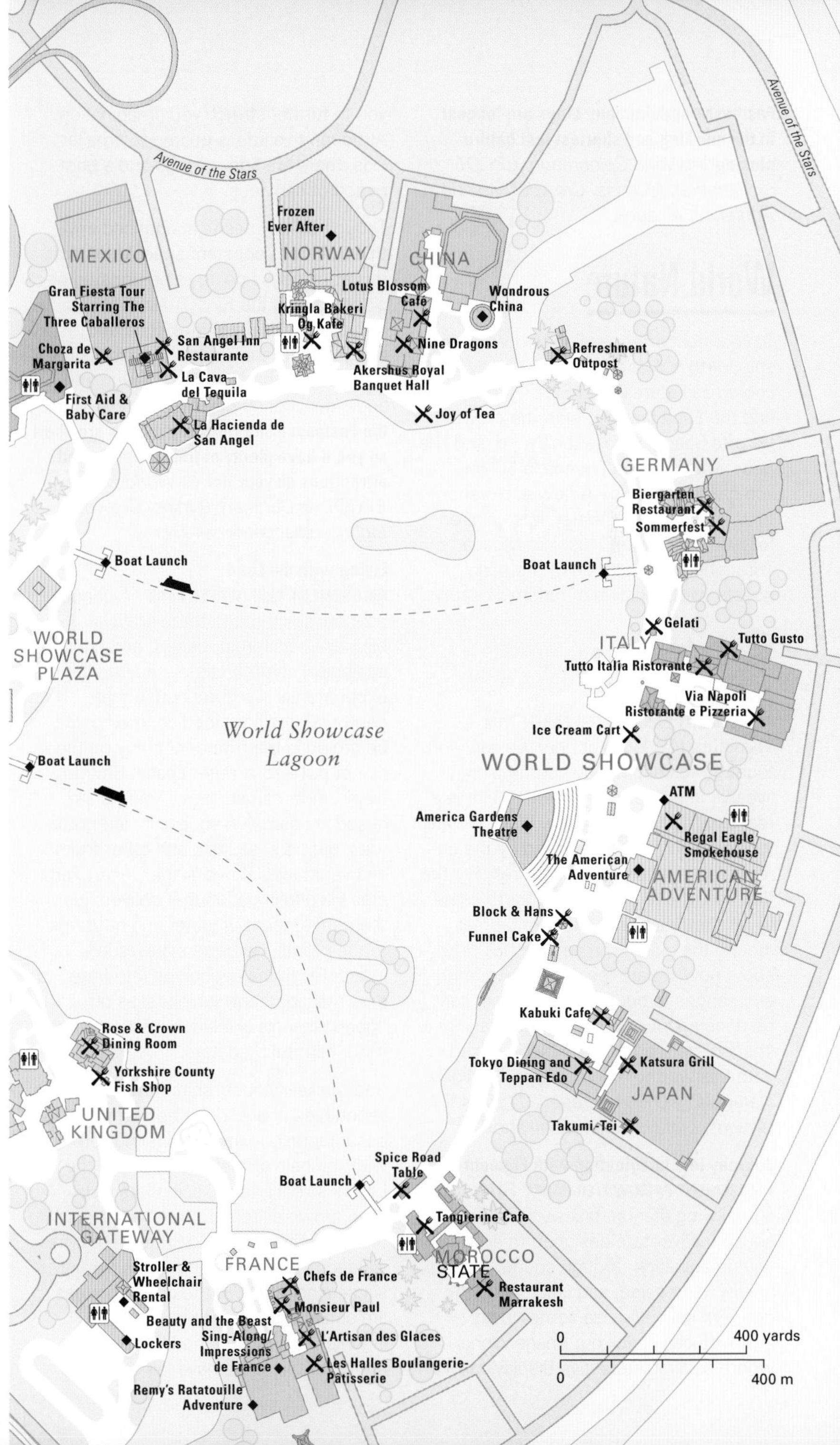
Avenue of the Stars
Avenue of the Stars
MEXICO
NORWAY
CHINA
Frozen Ever After
Gran Fiesta Tour Starring The Three Caballeros
Kringla Bakeri Og Kafe
Lotus Blossom Café
Wondrous China
Choza de Margarita
San Angel Inn Restaurante
La Cava del Tequila
Nine Dragons
Akershus Royal Banquet Hall
Refreshment Outpost
First Aid & Baby Care
La Hacienda de San Angel
Joy of Tea
GERMANY
Biergarten Restaurant
Sommerfest
Boat Launch
Boat Launch
WORLD SHOWCASE PLAZA
Gelati
ITALY
Tutto Gusto
Tutto Italia Ristorante
Via Napoli Ristorante e Pizzeria
World Showcase Lagoon
Ice Cream Cart
WORLD SHOWCASE
Boat Launch
ATM
America Gardens Theatre
Regal Eagle Smokehouse
The American Adventure
AMERICAN ADVENTURE
Block & Hans
Funnel Cake
Kabuki Cafe
Rose & Crown Dining Room
Tokyo Dining and Teppan Edo
Katsura Grill
Yorkshire County Fish Shop
JAPAN
UNITED KINGDOM
Takumi-Tei
Spice Road Table
Boat Launch
Tangierine Cafe
INTERNATIONAL GATEWAY
MOROCCO STATE
FRANCE
Stroller & Wheelchair Rental
Chefs de France
Restaurant Marrakesh
Monsieur Paul
Beauty and the Beast Sing-Along/ Impressions de France
L'Artisan des Glaces
Lockers
Les Halles Boulangerie-Pâtisserie
0
400 yards
0
400 m
Remy's Ratatouille Adventure

Fastpass+ appointment. Lines are longest in the morning and shortest just before closing. ✉ *World Celebration, EPCOT* ☞ *Duration: 15 mins. Crowds: Moderate. Audience: All ages.*

World Nature

To your right after passing under Spaceship Earth is World Nature, formerly known as Future World East. Here you'll find the Land pavilion, with the crowd favorite Soarin' Across the World, and The Seas with Nemo & Friends, a 5.7-million-gallon aquarium. A new exploration trail, the Journey of Water, lets children follow "living water," just like Moana. Throughout this section of the park, guests will be in awe of nature's beauty.

Sights

Awesome Planet

AMUSEMENT PARK/WATER PARK | This 11-minute film looks at how we can work together to keep our awesome planet liveable in the future. The entire film is a real-estate pitch about how lucky we are to live on our planet, narrated by the ultimate real estate agent, Ty Burrell. For the first half, you're shown how Earth came to take form and the different biomes around the globe. The second half talks about how we are facing unprecedented changes to our planet and what can be done about it. There is breathtaking imagery from around the globe mixed in with this worthwhile message. ✉ *World Nature, EPCOT* ☞ *Duration: 11 mins. Crowds: Light. Audience: All ages.*

Journey into Imagination with Figment

AMUSEMENT PARK/WATER PARK | Figment, a fun-loving dragon, takes you on a sensory adventure designed to engage your imagination through sound, illusion, gravity, dimension, and color. After the ride—which could use some updating—you can check out Image Works, where several interactive displays allow you to further stretch your imagination. Although this ride is geared to smaller kids, there are a few bangs and a brief period of darkness.

Though Disney hasn't announced anything, there is constant speculation that this attraction is going to be updated or closed during the EPCOT renovations. **For people with disabilities:** Ride and Image Works are wheelchair accessible. Equipped for handheld-captioning and audio-description devices. **TIP→ Skip the Fastpass+ and ride only if lines are short so you'll have plenty of time for preferred attractions on your list.** ✉ *World Nature, EPCOT* ☞ *Duration: 8 mins. Crowds: Light. Audience: Small kids.*

Living with the Land

AMUSEMENT PARK/WATER PARK | A canopied boat cruises through three artificial biomes—rain forest, desert, and prairie ecological communities—and into an experimental live greenhouse that demonstrates how food sources might be grown in the future, not only on the planet but also in outer space. Shrimp, tilapia, eels, catfish, and alligators are raised in controlled aquacells, and tomatoes, peppers, squash, and other fruits and vegetables thrive in the Desert Farm area via drip irrigation that delivers just the right amount of water and nutrients to their roots. Gardeners are usually interested in the section on integrated pest management, which relies on "good" insects like ladybugs to control more harmful predators.

See Mickey Mouse–shape fruits and vegetables (there might be pumpkins, cucumbers, or watermelons) nurtured with the help of molds created by the Land's science team; scientists also have grown a "tomato tree"—the first of its kind in the United States—that has yielded thousands of tomatoes from a single vine. Many of the growing areas are actual experiments-in-progress, in which Disney and the U.S. Department of Agriculture have joined forces to produce, say, a sweeter pineapple or a faster-growing pepper. The plants (including the tomato tree's golf-ball-size tomatoes) and fish that grow in the greenhouse are regularly harvested for use in The Land's restaurants. **For people with disabilities:** Those using an oversize wheelchair or ECV must transfer to a standard wheelchair. Equipped for hand-held-captioning and audio-description devices. **TIP→ If your party finds Living with the Land interesting, check out Behind the Seeds, an hour-long tour providing a more detailed look at the greenhouse. Offered every 45-minutes, this tour is $25 for adults and $20 for children. A sign-up desk is beside the ride's exit.** ✉ *World Nature, EPCOT* ☞ *Duration: 14 mins. Crowds: Moderate. Audience: All ages.*

The Seas with Nemo & Friends

AMUSEMENT PARK/WATER PARK | Hop into a "clamobile" and take a ride under the sea to look for Nemo, who has wandered off from Mr. Ray's class field trip. This ride adds clever fun to the aquarium attraction—an astonishing animation-projection effect makes it appear as if Nemo and his pals are swimming among the marine life of the actual Seas aquarium. As your ride progresses, Dory, Nemo's spacey sidekick, helps Bruce, Squirt, and other pals find him. After the ride, walk around the tank to Bruce's Shark World for some fun photo ops and shark facts, discover how dolphins communicate, and visit an endangered Florida manatee rehabilitation center. **For people with disabilities:** Guests in standard wheelchairs can wheel onto an accessible "clamshell" vehicle; those in ECVs must transfer to a standard wheelchair or the ride vehicle. Equipped for audio-description and hand-held-captioning devices. **TIP→ Though lines can be long, the queue moves quickly. Only use a Fastpass+ during the busiest times.** ✉ *World Nature, EPCOT* ☞ *Duration: Up to you. Crowds: Moderate to heavy. Audience: All ages.*

★ **Soarin' Around the World**

AMUSEMENT PARK/WATER PARK | If you've ever wondered what it's like to fly, or at least hang glide, this attraction is your chance to enjoy the sensation without actually taking the plunge. It uses motion-based technology to literally lift you in your seat 40 feet into the air within a giant projection-screen dome.

As you soar above the wonders of the world, from the sharp peaks of the Alps, to the Great Wall of China, to Sydney Harbor in Australia, and the spires of Neuschwanstein Castle in Bavaria, you feel the wind and dodge the spray of leaping whales.

The flight is so mild (and the view so thrilling) that even very timid children love it. **For people with disabilities:** Those with mobility impairments must transfer from their wheelchairs to the ride system. Equipped for video-captioning devices. Service animals aren't permitted on the ride. **TIP→ Book your Fastpass+ early or plan to wait an hour or longer in the standby queue.** ✉ *World Nature, EPCOT* ☞ *Duration: 5 mins. Crowds: Heavy. Audience: All ages. Height requirement: 40 inches.*

Turtle Talk with Crush

AMUSEMENT PARK/WATER PARK | Head for the Sea Base area to line up for this real-time animated show starring Crush, the ancient sea turtle from *Finding Nemo*. Crush chats and jokes with kids so convincingly that young children, eyes wide as sand dollars, have walked up and touched the screen where Crush "swims." It's in a small theater, and there's often a wait, but it's a hit with young children as well as their parents. **For people with disabilities:** The theater is wheelchair accessible, and assisted-listening devices can be used. **TIP→ Check the Times Guide for show schedule; use a Fastpass+ or come early and prepare to be amazed.** ✉ *World Nature, EPCOT* ☞ *Duration: 15 mins. Crowds: Moderate to heavy. Audience: Small kids, but great for all ages.*

Restaurants

Chip 'n' Dale Harvest Feast at Garden Grill Restaurant

$$$$ | **AMERICAN** | Family-style dinner fare is served here as the restaurant revolves, giving you an ever-changing backstage view of the Living with the Land boat ride. Offering quantity over quality, the restaurant serves all-you-can-eat meals with visits from Chip 'n' Dale, Pluto, and occasionally Mickey. **Known for:** character dining; unusual revolving restaurant within the Land pavilion; family-style servings with beer and wine available. *Average main: $54 World Nature, EPCOT 407/939–3463 disneyworld.disney.go.com/dining/epcot/garden-grill-restaurant.*

Coral Reef

$$$ | **AMERICAN** | With stunning views of the 5.7-million-gallon aquarium, dining at Coral Reef is as entertaining as it is delicious. As you watch marine life—and sometimes scuba divers—swim by, enjoy offerings from the seasonal menu heavy on seafood offerings. **Known for:** lobster bisque; scenic aquarium views; Bailey's almond and Jack Daniel's mousse. *Average main: $30 World Nature, EPCOT 407/939–3463 disneyworld.disney.go.com/dining/epcot/coral-reef-restaurant.*

World Discovery

World Discovery is to the left of World Celebration, and was formerly called Future World West. The sleek lines and out of this world atmosphere helps tell the stories of science, technology, and space. The main rides here are Test Track and Mission: SPACE, but EPCOT's newest thrill ride, Guardians of the Galaxy: Cosmic Rewind will premier here in 2021, replacing Ellen's Energy Adventure. An entire showcase pavilion dedicated to learning about the planet Xander, from the first *Guardians of the Galaxy* movie, will immerse guests in a different world. This coaster will rotate 360 degrees and include a reverse launch. Also in time for the 50th Anniversary will be the PLAY! avilion, an interactive digital metropolis for gamers. Here kids will enjoy virtual interactions with characters from *The Incredibles* and DuckTales.

Sights

★ Mission: SPACE

AMUSEMENT PARK/WATER PARK | It took five years for Disney Imagineers, with the help of 25 experts from NASA, to design Mission: SPACE, the first ride ever to take people "straight up" in a simulated rocket launch. The story transports you and co-riders to the year 2036 and the International Space Training Center, where you are about to embark on your first launch. Before you board the four-person rocket capsule, you're assigned to a position: commander, navigator, pilot, or engineer. And at this point, you're warned several times about the intensity of the ride and the risks for people with health concerns. After many guests became sick after riding, Disney created an "orange" and a "green" mission. The Orange mission heads to Mars and has a height-requirement of 44 inches. A spinning motion creates the feeling of a rocket launch and weightlessness (the effect is also cumulative, so stick with one go-round unless you have particularly hardy constitution). The green mission on Earth, with a height-requirement of 40 inches, is still plenty bumpy, but doesn't use spinning to create special effects. Pregnant women and anyone with heart, back, neck, balance, blood-pressure, or motion-sickness problems shouldn't ride either version.

For those who can handle the intense spinning, the sensation of liftoff is a turbulent, heart-pounding experience that flattens you against your seat. Once you break into outer space, you'll even feel weightless. After landing, you exit your capsule into the Advanced Training Lab, where you can play some very entertaining space-related games. **For people with disabilities:** This ride requires a transfer from wheelchair to seat. Service animals aren't permitted to board. Video-captioning devices can be used on the ride; assisted-listening devices can be used in the postshow Training Lab. ■ TIP→ **Arrive before 10 am or use Fastpass+ during peak season. Don't ride on a full stomach.** ✉ *World Discovery, EPCOT* ☞ *Duration: 4 mins. Crowds: You bet! Audience: Not small kids. Height requirement: 40 inches.*

★ **Test Track**

AMUSEMENT PARK/WATER PARK | The white-knuckle finale of this fan favorite is as thrilling as ever. Create a custom concept vehicle at an interactive design station, and then buckle up in a six-person SimCar to put the design through its paces in a neon-splashed, futuristic setting that surrounds the attraction's original hills and mountain switchbacks. Everyone can create their own design and see how it compares to everyone else's—first in their car and then at the end of the ride.

The High-Speed Test is last: your vehicle bursts through an opening in the Test Track building to negotiate a steeply banked loop at a speed of nearly 60 mph. At the special effects–laden postshow, you can check out how your custom car performed and create your own car commercial. The speeds and some jarring effects might prove unsettling. The ride isn't suitable for pregnant women or guests wearing back, neck, or leg braces. **For people with disabilities:** Visitors in wheelchairs are provided a special area in which to practice transferring into the ride vehicle before actually boarding. One TV monitor in the preshow area is closed-captioned. Service animals aren't permitted onboard. ■ TIP→ **The Single Rider queue has been eliminated. The ride won't function on wet tracks, so don't head here after a downpour.** ✉ *World Discovery, EPCOT* ☞ *Duration: 5 mins. Crowds: Heavy. Audience: Not small kids. Height requirement: 40 inches.*

Restaurants

Space 2020

$$$$ | **MODERN AMERICAN** | EPCOT's newest restaurant is literally out of this world. Upon arriving you'll board a special elevator to travel 220 miles above the planet, where you'll enjoy panorama views of Earth as you dine. **Known for:** real-time views from space; unique craft beer; newest restaurant at Disney. $ *Average main: $45* ✉ *World Discovery, EPCOT* ☎ *407/939–3463* 🌐 *disneyworld.disney.go.com/dining/epcot/space-220.*

World Showcase

Nowhere but at EPCOT can you explore nearly a dozen countries in one day. As you stroll the 1.3 miles around the 40-acre World Showcase Lagoon, you circumnavigate the globe-according-to-Disney by experiencing native food, entertainment, culture, and arts and crafts at pavilions representing countries in Europe, Asia, North Africa, and the Americas. Pavilion employees are from the countries they represent—Disney hires them as part of its international college program.

By far the most popular attraction among youngsters is the Frozen Ever After ride in the Norway pavilion. The new Remy's Ratatouille Adventure will have you scurrying around the kitchens of France. You'll see solid film attractions, as well as several art exhibitions, at the Canada, China, and France pavilions, and you can try your foreign language skills with the staff. Each pavilion also has a designated Kidcot Fun Stop, open daily from 11 or noon until about 8 or 9, where youngsters can try a cultural crafts project. Live entertainment is an integral part of the

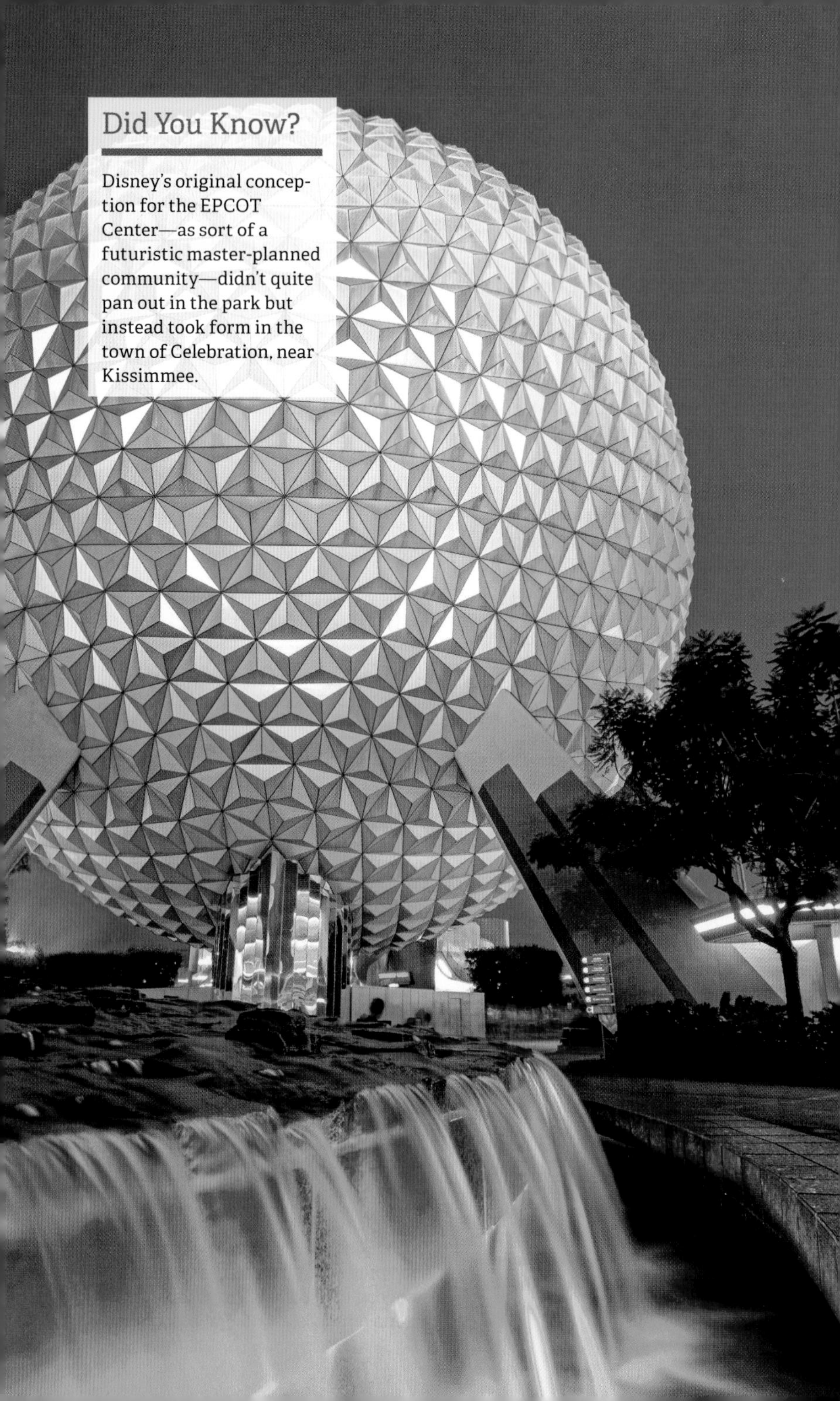

Did You Know?

Disney's original conception for the EPCOT Center—as sort of a futuristic master-planned community—didn't quite pan out in the park but instead took form in the town of Celebration, near Kissimmee.

experience, and you'll enjoy watching the incredibly talented Jeweled Dragon Acrobats in China and the Matsuriza Taiko drummers in Japan or laughing along with Sergio, the mime and juggler in the Italy courtyard.

Dining is another favorite pastime at EPCOT, and the World Showcase offers tempting tastes of the authentic cuisines of the countries here. Drinking is another draw, and there are plenty of theme bars and international drinks on hand to try.

For People with Disabilities: Attractions at Mexico, American Adventure, France, China, and Canada are all wheelchair accessible, as are the plaza areas where shows are presented. Mexico's Gran Fiesta Tour boat ride also is wheelchair accessible; personal-translator units amplify soundtracks. Most of the live entertainment around the World Showcase features strong aural as well as visual elements.

Canada

"Oh, it's just our Canadian outdoors," said a typically modest native guide upon being asked about the model for the striking rocky chasm and tumbling waterfall that represent just one of the pavilion's high points. The beautiful formal gardens do have an antecedent: Butchart Gardens, in Victoria, British Columbia. And so does the Hôtel du Canada, a French Gothic mansion with spires, turrets, and a mansard roof; anyone who's ever stayed at Québec's Château Frontenac or Ottawa's Château Laurier will recognize the imposing style favored by architects of Canadian railroad hotels.

Like the size of the Rocky Mountains, the scale of the structures seems immense; unlike the real thing, it's managed with a trick called forced perspective, which exaggerates the smallness of the distant parts to make the entire thing look gigantic.

Water Play 

Preschoolers love to play in the interactive fountains in front of Mission: SPACE and in the walkways between World Celebration and the World Showcase. Bring swimsuits and a towel!

You can browse shops that sell maple syrup; Canadian sports jerseys; and plush huggable bears, beavers, and huskies. Le Cellier Steakhouse is a great place for a relaxing lunch or dinner; due to its increasing popularity, you should book reservations far ahead.

Sights

Canada Far and Wide in Circle-Vision 360
AMUSEMENT PARK/WATER PARK | Disney has updated and expanded this attraction, which uses 12 surrounding screens to give guests a full 360-degree view of Canada's majestic landscape. The narrators break Canada down province by province, sharing knowledge, along with breath-taking views, about this majestic country. The only downside: this is a standing-only theater, strollers aren't permitted, and toddlers and small children can't see unless they're held aloft. **For people with disabilities:** Wheelchair and ECV accessible; reflective captioning and equipped for assisted-listening and audio-description devices. ✉ *World Showcase, Canada Pavilion, EPCOT* ☞ *Duration: 14 mins. Crowds: Moderate to heavy. Audience: All ages.*

Restaurants

Le Cellier Steakhouse
$$$$ | **CANADIAN** | This popular, charming eatery with stone arches and dark woods transports diners to a well-heeled setting similar to a cozy Canadian château,

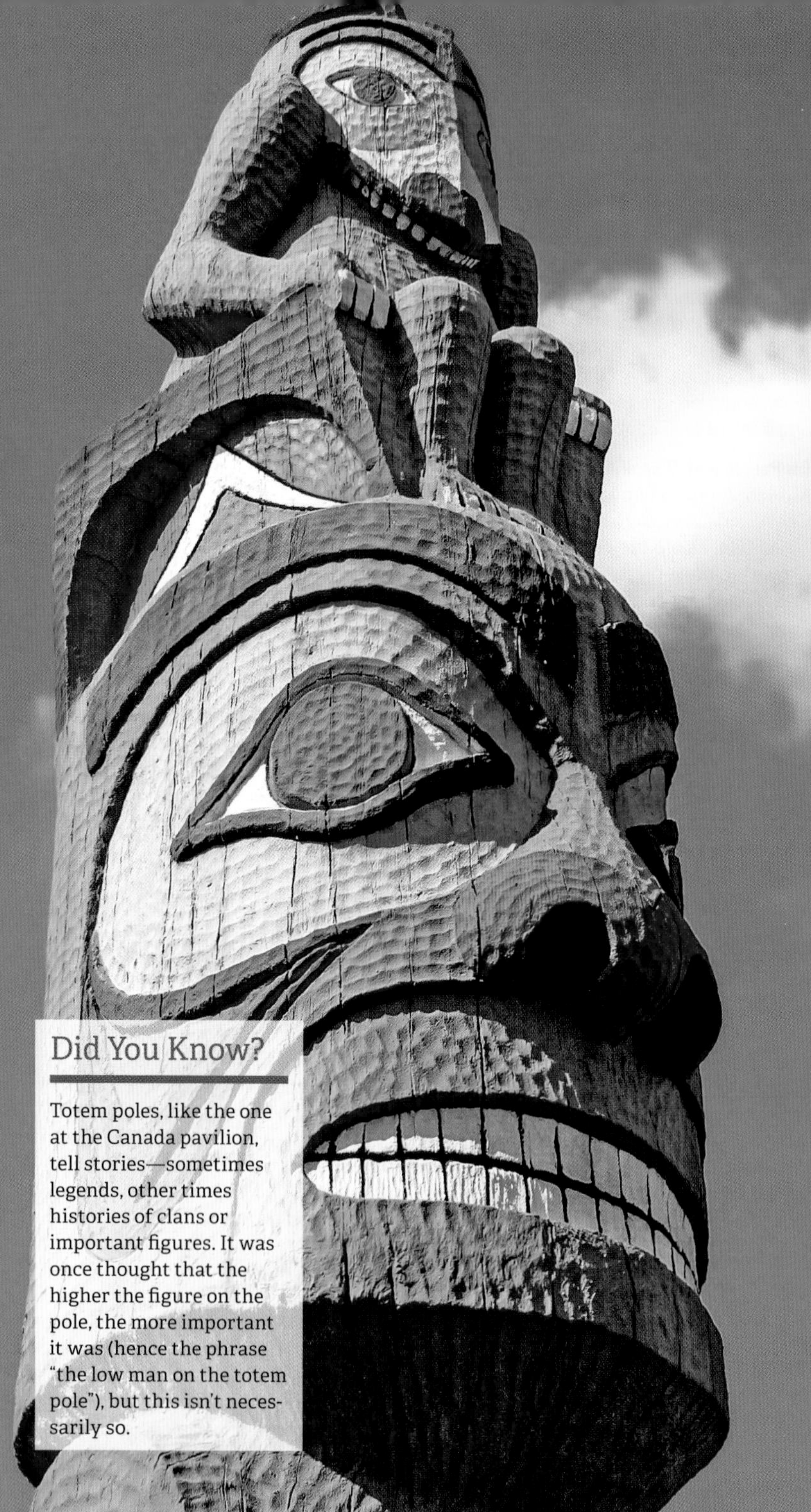

Did You Know?

Totem poles, like the one at the Canada pavilion, tell stories—sometimes legends, other times histories of clans or important figures. It was once thought that the higher the figure on the pole, the more important it was (hence the phrase "the low man on the totem pole"), but this isn't necessarily so.

EPCOT Family Tour

A trip to Italy is on hold, but Mom knows she can find a taste of Venice in the World Showcase. Dad, the *Popular Mechanics* devotee, can't wait to check out Test Track. Each can have a great day—in his or her own way.

Strategize

Devise a plan before pushing through the EPCOT turnstiles. Everyone will probably want to take off at Soarin' in The Land for the one-ride-fits-all thrill of simulated hang gliding (there are even special safety restraints for little ones). If your kids are too small for the height restrictions at Test Track, let Dad use the single rider line while Mom takes the kids to the PLAY! pavilion. Meet up with the riding parent at the Imagination! pavilion to ride along with Figment, the purple dragon, or head back to The Land for a Sunshine Seasons treat. Don't miss an under-the-sea ride at the Seas with Nemo & Friends before meeting the coolest dude of all at Turtle Talk with Crush.

Get Your World Showcase Passports

On the way into the World Showcase, let the kids get their own passports, complete with stickers, at any merchandise location. As you visit each country, they can get their passports stamped—not only a fun lesson in geography but a great keepsake. Before you cross the border, stop and let young kids play in the dancing fountains if they're operating—it'll be one of their happiest memories. Bring a towel and a change of clothing, and you'll be happy, too.

For the Little Ones (and Mom)

Younger children can be creative at Kidcot Fun Stops, where a Disney cast member gets them started on a craft activity, such as coloring a Carnivale-style mask on a stick. At each of 11 Fun Stops, the kids can add something to the mask, such as a Viking ship at Norway after the Frozen Ever After ride. Children love Mexico because they can ride the boats at Gran Fiesta Tour starring the Three Caballeros. Now it's your turn, Mom. Italy is right around the corner, and the kids can watch a juggler or comedy troupe in the courtyard while you sip some wine at Enoteca Castello or go shopping.

Live Performances

The Beatles, the Rolling Stones, Elton John, and more: hear top hits by iconic British musicians when the tribute band British Revolution amps up the fun outside the United Kingdom showcase five days each week. Grab a bench or dance to favorite tunes. Young children are thrilled to explore hedge mazes that surround the gazebo stage.

Live entertainment is one of EPCOT's strong suits—best shows for younger kids are the Jeweled Dragon Acrobats at China, Mariachi Cobre musicians at Mexico, Sergio the clown and juggler at Italy, and the JAMMitors percussion group at World Celebration (check the daily *Times Guide*).

EPCOT Adult Tour

Hang glide over a mountain, blast off into space, then journey to Mexico for a tequila flight and a "moonlit" dinner. Even if the adventures are faux fun, there's so much to soak up here that you'll want to return later to catch up on whatever you missed.

A Ticket to Ride

If you're aiming for high adventure, Fastpass+ is your ticket to Mission: SPACE or Soarin', especially during peak season. With a Fastpass+ appointment safely pocketed, you can make tracks for Test Track.

Look for more interactive challenges in the Advanced Training Lab at the end of your Mission: SPACE ride and in the Spaceship Earth postride show by Siemens.

World Travel

You can be in Canada one minute and England the next, once you cross into the World Showcase. Authentic replicas of famous landmarks like Venice's Piazza San Marco or Norway's 13th-century stave church will grab you. Once inside, you can practice your Italian, French, Spanish—Norwegian, even—with representatives of those countries.

You can also eat your way around the globe from a biergarten in Germany to a French bistro, and beyond. The margherita pizza delivers the flavor of Italy at Via Napoli. Enjoy a glass of prosecco as you watch passersby in the courtyard, or buy a wine-tasting pass for two tastes at each wine shop in Italy, Germany, and France. You'll find silk (or washable poly) kimonos in Japan's Mitsukoshi store, hefty beer steins at Die Weihnachts Ecke in Germany, and belly-dancing garb and finger cymbals at Morocco. For those really looking to eat around the world, visit during the Food and Wine Festival in the fall, where more than 30 booths offer tasty treats from around the globe.

Applause and a Toast

Too many people miss the great daily live acts around the park, so take time to check your *Times Guide* and choose a performance or two. Top acts include the Voices of Liberty at the American Adventure, a traditional Berber music and dance troupe at Morocco, and the British Revolution rock-and-roll cover band as well as a Celtic folk music ensemble at United Kingdom. The park's comedy troupes are a hoot, and the Matsuriza drummers at Japan are mesmerizing.

Before you venture to the edge of the lagoon for the fireworks-filled closing show, check out one of EPCOT's great watering holes. Cava del Tequila in Mexico serves 90 tequila choices, tequila flights, and specialty margaritas, including unexpected flavors like jalapeño and cucumber. The Rose & Crown pub in the United Kingdom is EPCOT's most boisterous spot, where the pianist takes requests for piano numbers—and it's standing-room-only at the bar. Finally, grab a spot at the Spice Road Table in Morocco, and order a beer or wine flight and some tapas for lagoon-side fireworks viewing. Cheers! *Salud! Prosit!* And take a bus or taxi back to your resort.

offering a menu heavy on meat and a good selection of wines and Canadian beer. The à la carte menu includes signature Canadian specialties such as Prince Edward Island mussels, the mandatory cheddar cheese soup, and an indulgent bison strip loin for two. **Known for:** Le Cellier signature coffee-rubbed venison osso buco; macaroni and cheese with Canadian lobster; exceptional personalized service. *$ Average main: $55 ✉ Canada Pavilion, World Showcase, EPCOT ☎ 407/939–3463 🌐 disneyworld.disney.go.com/dining/epcot/le-cellier-steakhouse.*

Shopping

Northwest Mercantile

GIFTS/SOUVENIRS | Along with an abundance of hockey-related merchandise and maple syrup, the shop offers a number of Canadian-centric items not otherwise available in the United States. You'll find plenty of teddy bears (and far more moose) on the shelves, as well as mugs and clothing celebrating Canadian brews. *✉ World Showcase, Canada Pavilion, EPCOT 🌐 www.disneyworld.disney.go.com/shops/epcot.*

United Kingdom

The United Kingdom rambles between the elegant mansions lining a London square to the bustling, half-timber shops of a village High Street to thatched-roof cottages from the countryside. (The thatch is made of plastic broom bristles due to local fire regulations.) And, of course, there's a pair of iconic red phone booths.

Part of EPCOT's expansion is a Mary Poppins–inspired experience, due to open in 2021. Around 17 Cherry Tree Lane, you wander through shops selling tea, Welsh handicrafts, Scottish tweed, and English lavender fragrance by Taylor of London. There's a store with Beatles T-shirts, CDs, and memorabilia. Next door is the Historic Research Center, where you can research your family name and purchase printed, hand-painted, or embroidered versions of your family coat of arms.

Get a Passport

A World Showcase Passport ($13) is a wonderful way to keep a kid interested in this more adult area of EPCOT. The passports, available at vendor carts, come with stickers and a badge, and children can have them stamped at each pavilion. The World Showcase is also a great place to look for unusual gifts—you might pick up a Oaxacan wood carving in Mexico, a tea set in China, or a kimonoed doll in Japan.

Tucked in the back are a lovely, though easy-to-miss, garden and park with benches—relax and kick back to the tunes of the British Revolution, a band known for its on-target Beatles and other Brit-band performances. Kids love to run through the hedge maze as their parents travel back in time to "Yesterday." Check the *Times Guide,* and arrive 30 minutes early for a bench or 15 minutes early for a curb. Restrooms are near the red phone booths.

Restaurants

Rose & Crown Dining Room

$$$ | **BRITISH** | **FAMILY** | If you're an Anglophile and you love a beer so thick you could stand a spoon up in your mug, this is the place to soak up both the suds and British street culture and get the best fish-and-chips in town. Try the traditional English fare—cottage or shepherd's pie, and, at times, the ever-popular bangers-and-mash (sausage over mashed potatoes). **Known for:** beer-battered fish-and-chips; Angus beef burger with Welsh rarebit sauce; wide selection of beers

and ciders from the pub. *Average main: $24 ✉ World Showcase, United Kingdom Pavilion, EPCOT ☎ 407/939–3463 🌐 disneyworld.disney.go.com/dining/epcot/rose-and-crown-dining-room.*

Coffee and Quick Bites

Revive yourself with a pint of the best at the **Rose & Crown,** a pub where you'll jostle for space any evening the pianist is in the house. The dining room serves hearty fare for lunch and dinner (reservations often required). The outdoor terrace is one of the best spots for watching **HarmonioUS.** Arrive at least an hour or so in advance for a seat. For more room, order your beer to go and wander over to watch the British Revolution. If you're in a hurry, grab fish-and-chips to go from **Yorkshire County Fish Shop,** then nab a lagoon-side table.

Nightlife

BARS

Rose & Crown Pub

BARS/PUBS | In this rollicking pub in the United Kingdom, patrons come to sing along with the piano or just hear a jazzy version of last year's hits. On busy nights, people stand four- to six deep at the bar. The fish-and-chips are first-rate; think about pairing them with one of the many unique "pub blends". Grab a pint and let the fun begin! *✉ World Showcase, United Kingdom Pavilion, EPCOT 🌐 disneyworld.disney.go.com/dining/epcot/rose-and-crown-pub.*

Performing Arts

HarmonioUS

SOUND/LIGHT SHOW | The largest fireworks show ever created for a Disney park (a replacement for the long-lived and well-loved IllumiNations), this all new night-time closing show is a spectacular ending to the day. Large barges combine LED panels, fountains, lights, lasers, and fireworks to create a show using the most inspiring music Disney has to offer. While this show can be viewed anywhere around the World Showcase Lagoon, arrive an hour before showtime at either World Showcase Plaza or by the International Gateway if you want to exit swiftly. Or take the other extreme, and find a seat deep into the park and plan to meander out slowly after the show. Want a guaranteed seat? Book a reservation at the Rose & Crown, La Cantina de San Angel, or Spice Road Table to eat while you view the fireworks. *✉ World Showcase, World Showcase Lagoon, EPCOT.*

Shopping

Anglophiles will feel as if they've crossed the Atlantic upon entering the cobblestoned village at the United Kingdom, where an English pub sits on one side, and a collection of British, Irish, and Scottish shops beckons you on the other. The Toy Soldier carries popular British toys and memorabilia known by all Brits; the Sportsman Shoppe has books and team apparel from various U.K. football (aka: soccer) teams; and the Tea Caddy sells Twinings tea, teacups, teapots, and British sweets.

The Crown & Crest

SPECIALTY STORES | This shop carries the widest range of items in the U.K. pavilion, from woolen sweaters from Scotland to Beatles-theme gifts and memorabilia. *✉ World Showcase, United Kingdom Pavilion, EPCOT 🌐 www.disneyworld.disney.go.com/shops/epcot/the-crown-and-crest.*

Historic Research Center

SPECIALTY STORES | The focus at this U.K. outpost in the Crown & Crest is tracking down your family name and coat of arms. Take home a printout of both for about $70. Drop the bigger bucks for a framed, embroidered, or hand-painted version. *✉ World Showcase, United Kingdom Pavilion, EPCOT.*

France

You don't need the scaled-down model of the Eiffel Tower to tell you that you've arrived in France, specifically Paris. There's the poignant accordion music wafting out of concealed speakers, the trim sycamores pruned in the French style to develop signature knots at the end of each branch, and the delicious aromas surrounding Les Halles Boulangerie & Pâtisserie bakeshop. This is the Paris of dreams, a Paris of the years just before World War I, when solid mansard-roof mansions were crowned with iron filigree, when the least brick was drenched in romanticism. Another dream has arrived in the France pavilion, Remy's Ratatouille Adventure has just opened, as has a Beauty and the Beast singalong show.

Here's a replica of the original Les Halles—the iron-and-glass barrel-roof market that no longer exists in the City of Light; there's an arching footbridge; and all around, of course, there are shops. You can inspect Parisian Impressionist artwork at Galerie des Halles; sample perfume at the Guerlain shop; and acquire a Julia Child cookbook or bottle of Pouilly-Fuisse at Les Vins de France. If you plan to dine at Les Chefs de France, make a reservation for a late lunch or dinner; the second-floor Monsieur Paul (dinner only) is a gourmet treat.

Sights

Beauty and the Beast Sing-Along

AMUSEMENT PARK/WATER PARK | **FAMILY** | Make sure to take your children to this all-new show, which plays in the same theater as Impressions de France. As the name implies, little ones will love singing along with the beloved classic songs from Beauty and the Beast, but the traditional story comes with a little twist. As Mrs. Potts narrates, you realize that LeFou, best known as Gaston's side-kick, was actually working behind the scenes to help Belle and the Beast fall in love. This 15-minute film is great for younger kids, and everyone will appreciate getting a chance to sit down and enjoy the cute story line. ✉ *World Showcase, France Pavilion, EPCOT* ☞ *Duration: 15 mins. Crowds: Moderate. Audience: All ages.*

Impressions de France

AMUSEMENT PARK/WATER PARK | The intimate Palais du Cinema, inspired by the royal theater at Fontainebleau, screens this homage to the glories of the country. Shown on five screens spanning 200 degrees, in an air-conditioned, sit-down theater, the film takes you to vineyards at harvest time, Paris on Bastille Day, the Alps, Versailles, Normandy's Mont-Saint-Michel, and the stunning châteaux of the Loire Valley. The music sweeps you away with familiar segments from Offenbach, Debussy, and Saint-Saëns, all woven together by longtime Disney musician Buddy Baker. **For people with disabilities:** Wheelchair- and ECV-accessible; reflective captioning and equipped for assisted-listening and audio-description devices. **TIP→ Visit anytime during your stroll around the World Showcase; theater seats are comfy and a great way to rest weary legs.** ✉ *World Showcase, France Pavilion, EPCOT* ☞ *Duration: 20 mins. Crowds: Moderate. Audience: All ages.*

Remy's Ratatouille Adventure

AMUSEMENT PARK/WATER PARK | **FAMILY** | In the newest ride in EPCOT, it's Remy's big night, and he's cooking to impress the food critic Anton Ego. To succeed, he needs the help of all his rat friends, including you! The four-person cars shaped like rats begin by meandering through the oversized rooftops of Paris. Gusteau quickly takes you to his restaurant so you can assist Remy and Linguini with the cooking, all the while trying to avoid the gaze of Skinner, the head chef with a terror of rats. Combined 3-D screens along with a giant kitchen create a 4-D effect so real it feels like you're really scurrying around. The trackless ride system furthers the notion of independence; often you and your fellow rats will hide in different places and then meet back up to help Remy. ✉ *World Showcase, France Pavilion, EPCOT* ☞ *Duration: 5 mins. Crowds: Heavy. Audience: All ages.*

Restaurants

Chefs de France

$$$ | **FRENCH** | A busy, bustling brasserie with a plush look, this French café maintains its original spirit, which was created by three of France's most famous chefs at the time: Paul Bocuse, Gaston Lenôtre, and Roger Vergé—Bocuse's son, Jerome, continues to run the restaurant. Classic escargots, a good starter, are prepared in a casserole with garlic butter; you might follow up with roasted breast and leg of duck confit l'orange or grilled beef tenderloin with green peppercorn sauce. **Known for:** sophisticated, classic French cuisine; beef bourguignon; duck confit. [$] *Average main: $30* ✉ *World Showcase, France Pavilion, EPCOT* ☎ *407/939–3463* 🌐 *disneyworld.disney.go.com/dining/epcot/chefs-de-france.*

★ **Monsieur Paul**

$$$$ | **FRENCH** | A mere staircase away from EPCOT's busy World Showcase, Monsieur Paul is a subdued, sophisticated (and not very kid-friendly) French restaurant. Make a reservation here if you are looking for an expensive, polished, and delightful diversion from the theme park's bustle. **Known for:** the service is so good you'll think you're at a Michelin-starred restaurant; magret de canard (roasted duck breast); an extensive wine list. [$] *Average main: $42* ✉ *World Showcase, France Pavilion, EPCOT* ☎ *407/939–3463* 🌐 *disneyworld.disney.go.com/dining/epcot/monsieur-paul.*

Coffee and Quick Bites

It's worth it to brave the lines at **Les Halles Boulangerie & Pâtisserie,** a large Parisian-style counter-service café. Have wine with a cheese plate, quiche, or sandwich on crusty French bread. Or go for a creamy café au lait and a napoleon. The new **L'Artisan des Glaces** ice cream–and-sorbet shop is praiseworthy for its ultracreamy treats that include an ice cream "martini" with Grand Marnier and flavor-customized ice-cream sandwiches made with brioche or French *macaron.*

Looking to taste the best wines around the world? EPCOT's "Wine Walk" includes tastings in the France, Italy, and Germany pavilions. For $32, you receive two plastic wine glasses and tastings in all three countries.

Shopping

La Signature

PERFUME/COSMETICS | In the France pavilion, follow your nose for a sniff and a spritz of high-end French perfumes. Guerlain fragrances, cosmetics, and skin-care products like the Orchidée Impériale eye cream (most recently selling for a whopping $200 apiece) draw fans from around the globe. ✉ *World Showcase, France Pavilion, EPCOT* 🌐 *disneyworld.disney.go.com/shops/epcot/la-signature.*

Morocco

Walk through the pointed arches of the Bab Boujouloud Gate, and you're transported to this strikingly beautiful North African country. The arches are ornamented with wood carvings and encrusted with mosaics made of 9 tons of handmade, hand-cut tiles; 19 native artisans were sent to EPCOT to install them and to create the dusty stucco walls that seem to have withstood centuries of sandstorms. Look closely and you'll see that every tile has a small

Morocco's open-air market is like something out of an Indiana Jones movie. It's a maze of shops selling straw bags, colorful carpets, leather goods, and, of course, ceramics.

crack or other imperfection, and no tile depicts a living creature—in deference to the Islamic belief that only Allah creates perfection and life.

Koutoubia Minaret, a replica of the prayer tower in Marrakesh, acts as Morocco's landmark. Winding alleyways—each corner bursting with carpets, brasses, leatherwork, and other wares—lead to a tiled fountain and lush gardens. A highlight is Restaurant Marrakesh. Enjoy couscous and roast lamb while a belly dancer performs traditional dances. One of the hottest fast-food spots in EPCOT is Tangierine Café, with tasty Mediterranean specialties like pita-pocket lamb and chicken sliders, killer baklava, and share-worthy vegetable platters with hummus, tabbouleh, falafel, lentils, and couscous. Spice Road Table is the ideal lagoon-side spot for tapas and the best sangria in Orlando. All eateries are open for lunch and dinner. Restrooms on the France side of the pavilion offer quick access.

Restaurants

Restaurant Marrakesh

$$$ | **MOROCCAN** | **FAMILY** | Deep inside the Moroccan pavilion is Restaurant Marrakesh, an authentic Moroccan experience that combines delicious food and entertainment. Children and adults will enjoy watching the belly dancers and listening to the Moroccan band. **Known for:** authentic entertainment; bastilla, a crispy pastry; beef couscous m'rouzia. *Average main: $28 World Showcase, Morocco Pavilion, EPCOT 407/939-3463 disneyworld.disney.go.com/dining/epcot/restaurant-marrakesh.*

Spice Road Table

$$$ | **MOROCCAN** | To accommodate guest's clamour for more fireworks dining, this new restaurant was built along World Showcase Lagoon, and it's a great place to catch a meal and watch HarmonioUS at 9 pm. Here you'll find the food to be more Moroccan-American cuisine, so listed among the rice-stuffed grape leaves and three lamb sliders, you'll

find a New York strip steak and spicy fried calamari. **Known for:** pistachio and saffron custard; hummus fries; fireworks viewing. $ *Average main: $27* ✉ *World Showcase, Morocco Pavilion, EPCOT* ☎ *407/939–3463* 🌐 *disneyworld.disney.go.com/dining/epcot/spice-road-table.*

Shopping

Tangier Traders

OUTDOOR/FLEA/GREEN MARKETS | Morocco's open-air market is like something out of an Indiana Jones movie. It's a maze of shops selling straw bags and colorful carpets. It's also a great place to pick up something really different, like a Moroccan fez or belly-dancing gear, including a bright scarf, finger cymbals, and a CD with all the music you need to wow your audience. ✉ *World Showcase, Morocco Pavilion, EPCOT* 🌐 *disneyworld.disney.go.com/shops/epcot.*

Japan

A brilliant vermilion torii gate, based on Hiroshima Bay's much-photographed Itsukushima Shrine, frames the World Showcase Lagoon and stands as an emblem of Disney's serene version of Japan.

Disney horticulturists deserve a hand for authenticity: 90% of the plants they used are native to Japan. Rocks, pebbled streams, pools, and pruned trees and shrubs complete the meticulous picture. At sunset, or during a rainy dusk, the twisted branches of the corkscrew willows frame a perfect Japanese view of the five-story winged pagoda that is the heart of the pavilion. Based on the 8th-century Horyuji Temple in Nara, the brilliant blue pagoda has five levels, symbolizing the five elements of Buddhist belief—earth, water, fire, wind, and sky. The peace is occasionally interrupted by performances on drums and gongs. Mitsukoshi, an immense retail firm known as Japan's Sears Roebuck, carries everything from T-shirts to kimonos and rows of Japanese dolls. For lunch and dinner, you'll be entertained by the culinary feats of chefs at Teppan Edo (which carries on the chop-toss-applaud antics of the original Teppanyaki Dining Room). Tokyo Dining focuses on presentation of traditional ingredients and cuisine from Japan, including sushi. At the pavilion's rear is a sake tasting bar that you'll miss if you don't look for it. The newest addition is Takumi-Tei, offering a high-end (and high-priced) omakase menu or equally expensive à la carte dining of superb quality and with excellent service.

Restaurants

Tokyo Dining and Teppan Edo

$$$ | **JAPANESE** | **FAMILY** | Above the Mitsukoshi department store in EPCOT's Japan pavilion are sister restaurants Teppan Edo, a teppanyaki steak house where chefs do performance cooking at 20 grills, and Tokyo Dining, for sushi and preplated meals. Menu standouts at Teppan Edo include the filet mignon and the Tori chicken breast. **Known for:** amazingly fresh sushi; attentive and knowledgeable service; family-fun teppanyaki meals. $ *Average main: $30* ✉ *World Showcase, Japan Pavilion, EPCOT* ☎ *407/939–3463* 🌐 *disneyworld.disney.go.com/dining/epcot/teppan-edo.*

Coffee and Quick Bites

Tucked behind the pagoda is **Katsura Grill,** home to hand-rolled sushi or teriyaki plates if you're looking for a full meal. If you just want a quick drink, stop by **Kabuki Cafe** to try kakigori, Japanese shaved ice or a Japanese beer.

Shopping

Mitsukoshi Department Store

TOYS | Hello Kitty, one of Japan's most popular toys, is on hand here, as are the Transformers and Godzilla. Dress up with a washable poly kimono or a more luxurious silk version, or check out the shimmering pearl jewelry. Other popular items include animé art, chopsticks, and Kit Kat bars in assorted flavors. You'll be tempted to take home some sweets after watching a Japanese Candy Art demonstration just outside the store (see *Times Guide* for demo schedule). ✉ *World Showcase, Japan Pavilion, EPCOT* 🌐 *www.disneyworld.disney.go.com/shops/epcot/mitsukoshi-kiosk.*

American Adventure

In a Disney version of Philadelphia's Independence Hall, the Imagineers prove that their kind of fantasy can beat reality hands down. The 110,000 bricks, made by hand from soft, pink Georgia clay, sheathe the familiar structure, which acts as a beacon for those across EPCOT's lagoon. The pavilion includes an all-American fast-food restaurant, a shop, lovely rose gardens, and an outdoor theater. Restrooms are tucked away along the far left side of the restaurant; there's also a roomier restroom accommodation by the gift shop.

Sights

★ The American Adventure

AMUSEMENT PARK/WATER PARK | The pavilion's key attraction is this 100-yard dash through history, and you'll be primed for the lesson after reaching the main entry hall and hearing the stirring a cappella Voices of Liberty. Inside the theater, the main event begins to the accompaniment of "The Golden Dream," performed by the Philadelphia Orchestra. This show combines evocative sets, a rear-projection screen (72 feet wide), enormous movable stages, and 35 Audio-Animatronics players.

Photo Tip

You'll get a great shot of Spaceship Earth across the lagoon by framing it in the torii gate at the entrance to the Japan pavilion.

Beginning with the arrival of the Pilgrims at Plymouth Rock and their grueling first winter, Benjamin Franklin and a wry, pipe-smoking Mark Twain narrate the episodes, both praiseworthy and shameful, that have shaped the American spirit. Each speech and scene seems polished like a little jewel. You feel the cold at Valley Forge. You're moved by Nez Percé Chief Joseph's forced abdication of Native American ancestral lands, by Frederick Douglass's reminder of the miseries of slavery, and by women's rights campaigner Susan B. Anthony's speech. You laugh with Will Rogers's aphorisms and learn about the pain of the Great Depression through an affecting radio broadcast by Franklin Delano Roosevelt. **For people with disabilities:** Wheelchair- and ECV-accessible; reflective captioning and equipped for assisted-listening and audio-description devices. **TIP→ Check your "Times Guide" and arrive 10 minutes before the Voices of Liberty are slated to perform, then head inside to enjoy the a cappella tunes.** ✉ *World Showcase, America Pavilion, EPCOT* ☞ *Duration: 30 mins. Crowds: Heavy. Audience: All ages.*

America Gardens Theatre

AMUSEMENT PARK/WATER PARK | On the edge of the lagoon, directly opposite Disney's magnificent bit of colonial imagery, is this open-air, partially tree-shaded venue for concerts and shows. Most performances are hot tickets with themes tied to EPCOT events, such as "Garden Rocks" concerts with pop legends during the March through May EPCOT International Flower and Garden Festival and Eat to the Beat concerts during the late-September through mid-November EPCOT International Food and Wine Festival. Check the festival schedules before your trip, and plan to visit EPCOT on an evening with a musical guest you'll enjoy. This is also the setting for the annual yuletide Candlelight Processional—a not-to-be-missed event if you're at WDW during the holidays. The Candlelight Dinner Package (available through Disney's dining reservations hotline) includes lunch or dinner in a select World Showcase restaurant and preferred seating for the moving performance. Roomy restrooms are behind the Kidcot Fun Stop. **TIP→ Arrive more than an hour ahead of time for holiday and celebrity performances, though the first show is always the least crowded.** ✉ *World Showcase, America Pavilion, EPCOT* ☞ *Duration: Performances vary. Crowds: Vary. Audience: Varies.*

Restaurants

Regal Eagle Smokehouse

$ | **BARBECUE** | Brand new for 2020 is the Regal Eagle Smokehouse, an American smokehouse that combines barbecue from Texas, Kansas, Memphis, and the Carolinas. This might sound sacrilegious, but get the American platter and try all three to see which area should reign supreme with its barbecue. **Known for:** gluten-free, egg-free, and shellfish-free friendly; American beers; s'mores brownie. $ *Average main: $14* ✉ *World Showcase, America Pavilion, EPCOT* ☎ *407/939–3463* 🌐 *disneyworld.disney.go.com/dining/epcot/regal-eagle-smokehouse.*

Italy

Architectural reproductions of Venice's Piazza San Marco and the Doge's Palace are accurate right down to the gold leaf on the ringlets of the angel perched 100 feet atop the Campanile; the seawall stained with age, with barbershop-stripe poles to which two gondolas are tethered; and the Romanesque columns, Byzantine mosaics, Gothic arches, and stone walls that have all been carefully antiqued. Mediterranean plants such as grapevines, kumquat, and olive trees add verisimilitude. Shops sell Venetian beads and glasswork, leather purses, perfumes, olive oils, pastas, and Perugina cookies and chocolate kisses.

At Tutto Italia Ristorante, the cuisine—wines, handmade mozzarella, and fresh bread—is from several regions of Italy. Limited outdoor dining beneath umbrellas is lovely. The hot ticket is on the edge of the piazza: Via Napoli is a casual 300-seat pizzeria with wood-burning ovens and an airy, noisy dining room. Chefs use Caputo flour, San Marzano tomatoes, and fresh, handmade mozzarella to craft some of the best margherita pizza outside Naples! The Tutto Gusto Wine Cellar is a cool escape for a glass of prosecco and a small plate.

Sergio, a clown–juggler brings crowds to the piazza several times each day. This is a great spot for viewing HarmonioUS if you're in the vicinity.

Restaurants

Tutto Italia Ristorante

$$$ | **ITALIAN** | It's sometimes difficult to shake off the illusion that this is a restaurant in Venice or Rome; the service and food are that good. Offerings include lobster ravioli, grilled salmon in citrus butter sauce, and seafood stew. **Known for:** generous antipasto platter; handmade

pasta; casual but attentive service. $ *Average main: $28* ✉ *World Showcase, Italy Pavilion, EPCOT* ☎ *407/939–3463* 🌐 *disneyworld.disney.go.com/dining/epcot/tutto-italia-ristorante.*

Via Napoli Ristorante e Pizzeria
$$$ | **PIZZA** | **FAMILY** | Loud, mad, bustling, and chaotic, this casual, family-friendly restaurant features a menu of authentic, thin-crust Neapolitan-style pizzas from massive ovens named after Italian volcanoes that's supplemented by a large selection of southern Italian favorites. Pizzas come topped with pepperoni, mushrooms, or eggplant, artichokes, cotto ham, cheese, and even prosciutto and melon. **Known for:** pizzas from wood-fired ovens; spaghetti with veal meatballs; generous kid portions. $ *Average main: $30* ✉ *World Showcase, Italy Pavilion, EPCOT* ☎ *407/939–3463* 🌐 *disneyworld.disney.go.com/dining/epcot/via-napoli.*

Nightlife

BARS

Tutto Gusto
BARS/PUBS | This cool and cozy wine cellar adjoining Tutto Italia is an ideal place to escape the crowds. You can order from among 200 varieties of wine; switch things up with a cold beer; and complement either with a small-plate selection of meats, cheeses, panini, pastas, and desserts. The gnocchi is delicious, and a small flight of desserts is the perfect way to end the meal. Wine flights from around Italy are offered, ask your server for their favorite. This is the only sit-down restaurant in Walt Disney World that does not take reservations, so if you show up and are willing to wait around 20 or 30 minutes, you can usually get a table. Be aware that there are no kid menus, and smaller kids might not be thrilled with the adult ambience or food. ✉ *World Showcase, Italy Pavilion, EPCOT* 🌐 *disneyworld.disney.go.com/dining/epcot/tutto-gusto-wine-cellar.*

Shopping

Il Bel Cristallo
JEWELRY/ACCESSORIES | Just like an elegant boutique in Milan, this shop sells chic Italian totes, designer handbags, clothing, collectibles, and fragrances by Fendi, Prada, and Bulgari. You'll also find porcelain, crystal, and Murano glass. ✉ *World Showcase, Italy Pavilion, EPCOT* 🌐 *disneyworld.disney.go.com/shops/epcot/il-bel-cristallo.*

Tutto Gusto Wine Cellar
FOOD/CANDY | This café and wine bar iis an exclusive seller of some of Italy's unique wines. ✉ *World Showcase, Italy Pavilion, EPCOT* 🌐 *disneyworld.disney.go.com/dining/epcot/tutto-gusto-wine-cellar.*

Germany

Germany, a make-believe village that distills the best folk architecture from all over that country, is so jovial that you practically expect the Seven Dwarfs to come "heigh-ho"-ing out to meet you. If you time it right, you will spot Snow White as she poses for photos and signs autographs. The fairy tale continues as a specially designed glockenspiel on the clock tower chimes on the hour. You'll also hear musical toots and tweets from cuckoo clocks, folk tunes from the spinning dolls sold at Der Teddybär, and the satisfied sighs of hungry visitors chowing down on hearty German cooking.

The Biergarten's wonderful buffet serves several sausage varieties, as well as sauerkraut, spaetzle, roasted potatoes, rotisserie chicken, and German breads—all accompanied by yodelers, dancers, and other lederhosen-clad musicians who perform a year-round Oktoberfest show. There are shops aplenty, including Die Weihnachts Ecke (the Christmas Corner), which sells nutcrackers and other Christmas ornaments. It's hard to resist watching the miniature trains that choo-choo along a garden track dotted with tiny villages. Restrooms are just steps away.

Restaurants

Biergarten Restaurant
$$$$ | **GERMAN** | Oktoberfest runs 365 days a year here, where cheerful crowds and an oompah band set the stage for a buffet of German specialties. The menu and level of frivolity are the same at lunch and dinner. **Known for:** bratwurst, sausages, and other German specialties; lively oompah band music; buffet-style servings, including dessert bar. *Average main: $47 World Showcase, Germany Pavilion, EPCOT 407/939–3463 disneyworld.disney.go.com/dining/epcot/biergarten-restaurant.*

Coffee and Quick Bites

Refreshment Outpost
$ | **AMERICAN** | The Refreshment Outpost, between Germany and China, isn't one of the 11 World Showcase pavilions, but kids love to test their drumming skills on the large authentic drums that invite players to improvise their own African folklore performances. Village Traders sells African handicrafts and—you guessed it—souvenirs relating to *The Lion King*. Buy an ice cream or frozen yogurt, and enjoy the break at a table by the lagoon. **Known for:** panna cotta; short lines; ice cream. *Average main: $8 World Showcase, EPCOT.*

Sommerfest
$ | **GERMAN** | Bratwurst and cold beer from the Sommerfest counter at the entrance of the Biergarten restaurant make a perfect quick and hearty lunch, while the apple strudel and Black Forest cake are ever-popular sweets. There's not much seating, so you might have to eat on the run. **Known for:** beer flight; bratwurst; sauerkraut. *Average main: $14 World Showcase, Germany Pavilion, EPCOT disneyworld.disney.go.com/dining/epcot/sommerfest.*

Shopping

Der Teddybår
WINE/SPIRITS | Although you can buy wines and beer steins in the Germany pavilion, none give the warm, fuzzy feelings the teddy bears on display here do. Bears (or "bårs") share the boutique with Rapunzel and Snow White snow globes and plush toys, Minnie dolls and figurines, and German confections. *World Showcase, Germany Pavilion, EPCOT disneyworld.disney.go.com/shops/epcot/der-teddybar-toyshop.*

China

A shimmering red-and-gold, three-tier replica of Beijing's Temple of Heaven towers over a serene Chinese garden, an art gallery displaying treasures from the People's Republic, a spacious emporium devoted to Chinese goods, and two restaurants. The gardens—planted with a native Chinese tallow tree, water lilies, bamboo, and a 100-year-old weeping mulberry tree—are tranquil. Inside, learn more about the newest Disneyland resort in Shanghai.

Piped-in traditional Chinese music flows gently over the peaceful hush of the gardens, which come alive with applause and cheers when the remarkable Jeweled Dragon Acrobats tumble into a roped-off area for their breathtaking act. At China's popular Nine Dragons Restaurant, try the shrimp and chicken egg rolls or the peppery shrimp with spinach noodles; there are also several chicken and stir-fry favorites.

Sights

Wondrous China
AMUSEMENT PARK/WATER PARK | The Temple of Heaven houses another of EPCOT's improvements, the new *Wondrous China* film. Now presented on a seamless 360-degree screen in digital format, this

film highlights China's iconic images, both old and new. However, be prepared to stand and possibly hold children: strollers aren't permitted, and there are no seats. **For people with disabilities :** Wheelchair- and ECV-accessible; reflective captioning and equipped for assisted-listening and audio-description devices.

■ TIP→ Come anytime, and, before the show, visit the Tomb Warriors gallery, where you can see replicas of the terracotta soldiers unearthed by farmers in Xi'an, China, in 1974. ✉ *World Showcase, China Pavilion, EPCOT* ☞ *Duration: 14 mins. Crowds: Moderate. Audience: All Ages.*

Coffee and Quick Bites

Lotus Blossom Café
$$ | CHINESE | The open-air Lotus Blossom Café offers some authentic Chinese fare: pot stickers, soups, and egg rolls. Entrées include orange chicken with steamed rice, vegetable stir-fry, and a beef noodle soup bowl. **Known for:** pot-stickers; Chinese beer; caramel-ginger ice cream. Ⓢ *Average main: $15* ✉ *World Showcase, China Pavilion, EPCOT* 🌐 *disneyworld.disney.go.com/dining/epcot/lotus-blossom-cafe.*

Shopping

House of Good Fortune
HOUSEHOLD ITEMS/FURNITURE | China's sprawling bazaar has a huge selection of tea sets ranging in style from traditional to contemporary, intricately embroidered robes, and fragrance candles that are sure to align your chi. Butterfly hair combs are beautiful, but the hottest items are little Buddha statues, available for less than $10. ✉ *World Showcase, China Pavilion, EPCOT* 🌐 *disneyworld.disney.go.com/shops/epcot.*

Norway

Although most visitors to the Norway pavilion are on their way to the Frozen Ever After ride, there's plenty to look at while waiting in line. Among the rough-hewn timbers and sharply pitched roofs here—softened and brightened by bloom-stuffed window boxes and figured shutters—are lots of smiling young Norwegians, all eager to speak English and show off their country. The pavilion complex contains a 14th-century, fortresslike castle that mimics Oslo's Akershus; cobbled streets; rocky waterfalls; and a stave church modeled after one built in 1250, with wood dragons glaring from the eaves. The church houses an exhibit called Gods and Vikings, which uses vintage artifacts to tell the legends of Odin, Thor, Loki, and Freya. It all puts you in the mood for the pavilion's shops, which sell *Frozen* souvenirs, spears, shields, and other Viking necessities perfect for next Halloween.

At Akershus Royal Banquet Hall, Princess Storybook Dining is a big deal. Visit the Norwegian *koldtbord* (buffet) for smoked salmon, fruit, and pastries, followed by a family-style hot breakfast of eggs, meats, and other treats served at the table. For lunch and dinner, you'll find traditional treats like chilled shrimp, salads, meats, and cheeses. Hot entrées served à la carte might include oven-roasted chicken breast, venison stew, or the traditional Scandinavian meatball dish called *kjottkake*. Family-style dessert is a treat with three of the chef's sweet specialties.

■ TIP→ The restaurant is the only one in the park where you can dine with Disney princesses, who might include Aurora, Belle, or Snow White. You can reserve up to 180 days in advance (booking as early as possible). If you haven't made a reservation, it's worth checking at Guest Relations for seats left by cancellations.

Frozen Ever After has become a favorite ride at EPCOT.

Sights

★ **Frozen Ever After**

AMUSEMENT PARK/WATER PARK | In Norway's dandy boat-ride homage to the popular *Frozen* film, which replaced the Maelstrom ride in 2016, you pile into a 16-passenger, dragon-headed longboat for a dark-ride voyage around Arendelle. The familiar form of Olaf welcomes you as you enter the frozen willow forest and head to Queen Elsa's ice palace, meeting up with Anna and many familiar *Frozen* characters along the way, and hearing the popular songs from the film. The animated figures are amazing, featuring Disney's first all-electric Audio-Animatronics, allowing much more fluid and graceful movement and utilizing projection-mapped faces, which make the figures look exactly like their animated counterparts. For fans who miss the Maelstrom ride, keep a sharp eye open for Easter eggs that remain, particularly in the castle finale. **For people with disabilities:** You must step down into and up out of a boat to ride. Equipped with reflective captioning and for assisted-listening, audio-description, or handheld-captioning devices. **TIP→ Make a Fastpass+ appointment, or come here first thing in the morning.** ✉ *World Showcase, Norway Pavilion, EPCOT* ☞ *Duration: 10 mins. Crowds: Moderate to heavy. Audience: All ages.*

Restaurants

Akershus Royal Banquet Hall

$$$$ | **SCANDINAVIAN** | **FAMILY** | This restaurant has character buffets at all three meals, with an array of Disney princesses, including Ariel, Belle, Jasmine, Snow White, Aurora, Mary Poppins, and even an occasional cameo appearance by Cinderella. The breakfast menu is American, but lunch and dinner find an ever-changing assortment of Norwegian specialties, which might be foreign to children. **Known for:** an expansive buffet of Nordic specialties; Scandinavian appeal; character dining with the princesses. [$] *Average main: $62* ✉ *World Showcase, Norway Pavilion, EPCOT* ☎ *407/939–3463*

 *disneyworld.disney.go.com/dining/epcot/akershus-royal-banquet-hall.*

Coffee and Quick Bites

Kringla Bakeri Og Kafe

$ | NORWEGIAN | You can order smoked salmon, sandwiches, and a salmon and egg bagel, as well as wine, beer, and the potent Viking coffee at Kringla Bakeri Og Kafe. Sweet pretzels, pastries, and cookies satisfy sugar cravings. **Known for:** smoked salmon; Norwegian sweet treats; coffee. *Average main: $14* *World Showcase, Norway Pavilion, EPCOT disneyworld.disney.go.com/dining/epcot/kringla-bakeri-og-kafe.*

Puffin's Roost

TOYS | Viking wannabes go crazy for the soft toy spears and shields. The plush seals are sweet for tots, and you can find Norwegian pewter, leather goods, and colorful woolen sweaters and knit caps, along with a wide variety of character goods from the hit movie *Frozen*.The shop's larger-than-life troll is always ready for a selfie. *World Showcase, Norway Pavilion, EPCOT disneyworld.disney.go.com/shops/epcot/puffins-roost.*

Mexico

Housed in a spectacular Mayan pyramid surrounded by dense tropical plantings and brilliant blossoms, Mexico welcomes you onto a "moonlit" plaza that contains the Gran Fiesta Tour boat ride; an exhibit of pre-Columbian art; a very popular restaurant; and, of course, shopping kiosks where you can unload many, many pesos.

Modeled on the market in the town of Taxco, Plaza de los Amigos is well named: there are lots of friendly people—the women dressed in peasant blouses and bright skirts, the men in white shirts and dashing sashes—all eager to sell you trinkets from a cluster of canopied carts. The perimeter is rimmed with stores with tile roofs, wrought-iron balconies, and flower-filled window boxes. What to buy? Sombreros, baskets, pottery, jewelry, and maracas.

One of the pavilion's key attractions is the San Angel Inn, featuring traditional Mexican cuisine and wine and beer, and overlooking the faux-moonlit waterway traversed by Gran Fiesta Tour boats. The pavilion's La Cava del Tequila bar serves up tequila flights, exotic blended margaritas, and light snacks like guacamole with corn chips. The casual, outdoor La Cantina de San Angel is a 150-seat quick-service eatery adjacent to La Hacienda de San Angel, a 250-seat table-service restaurant with a waterside view. You won't want to miss trying Mexican treats like the Queso Fundido, melted cheese with poblano peppers, chorizo, and tortillas, or La Hacienda mixed grill served with beans and fresh salsa.

Gran Fiesta Tour Starring the Three Caballeros

AMUSEMENT PARK/WATER PARK | In this attraction—which shines with the polish of enhanced facades, sound system, and boat-ride props—Donald teams with old pals José Carioca (the parrot) and Panchito (the Mexican charro rooster) from the 1944 Disney film *The Three Caballeros*. The Gran Fiesta Tour film sweeps you along for an animated jaunt as the caballeros are reunited for a grand performance in Mexico City. Donald manages to disappear for his own tour of the country, leaving José and Panchito to search for their missing comrade. **For people with disabilities:** The boat is accessible to guests using wheelchairs, but those using ECVs or oversize chairs must transfer to a Disney model. Equipped for handheld-captioning and audio-description devices. **TIP→ It's worth a**

The Temple of Quetzalcoatl (ket-zal-co-WAH-tal) at Teotihuacán (tay-o-tee-wah-CON), just outside Mexico City, is the model for the pyramid at the Mexico pavilion.

visit if lines aren't long, especially if you have small children, who usually enjoy the novelty of a boat ride. ✉ *World Showcase, Mexico Pavilion, EPCOT* ☞ *Duration: 9 mins. Crowds: Moderate. Audience: All ages.*

Restaurants

La Hacienda de San Angel

$$$ | **MEXICAN** | Open only for dinner, this restaurant combines authentic Mexican entrees with a perfect location to view the fireworks. The *alambre de res* (flank steak with bacon in poblano and bell peppers) is delicious, while the *chili relleno con camaron* (chili relleno with shrimp) is a nice twist on an old favorite. **Known for:** Mexican sorbets; premium margaritas; fireworks viewing. $ *Average main: $29* ✉ *World Showcase, Mexico Pavilion, EPCOT* ☎ *407/939–3463* 🌐 *disneyworld.disney.go.com/dining/epcot/hacienda-de-san-angel.*

San Angel Inn Restaurante

$$$ | **MEXICAN** | **FAMILY** | Set at a Mexican market in perpetual twilight, this restaurant gets high marks from guests for its food and atmosphere. Especially in the summer, you'll appreciate the dimmed lights, and everyone enjoys sharing the guacamole or ordering the *tacos el pastor* (with pork with pineapple). **Known for:** darkened atmosphere; many healthy eating options; chiles rellenos. $ *Average main: $28* ✉ *World Showcase, Mexico Pavilion, EPCOT* ☎ *407/939–3463* 🌐 *disneyworld.disney.go.com/dining/epcot/san-angel-inn-restaurante.*

Coffee and Quick Bites

The line for **Choza de Margarita** can seem longer than any other in EPCOT, and for good reason. With eight different margaritas, this is the first stop for a drink in your lap around the World Showcase, and with options like spicy blackberry or "mango loco," you'll want to line up, too. If you just want a side of guacamole, stop by **La**

Cantina de San Angel for a snack or to split an order of empanadas con queso.

Nightlife

BARS

La Cava del Tequila

BARS/PUBS | This intimate bar serves more than 200 tequilas along with Mexican beers, wines, top-shelf cocktails, and a colorful array of margaritas. Try a tequila flight while snacking on tapas, chips, guacamole, and queso. ✉ *World Showcase, Mexico Pavilion, EPCOT* 🌐 *disneyworld.disney.go.com/dining/epcot/cava-del-tequila.*

Shopping

Plaza de Los Amigos

ART GALLERIES | As you enter the Mexico pavilion and descend the staircase, stop in the village square here to browse the hand-painted wood carvings crafted by Zapotec Indians of Oaxaca in southern Mexico. Vendors' carts offer silver jewelry, leather goods, sombreros, piñatas, pottery, home decor, and more. Don't miss indoor shops including La Princesa de Cristal, which sells sparkling jewelry, etched glass, and Disney figurines cast in crystal, and La Tienda Encantada with fine jewelry, leather goods, and colorful accessories. Outside on the promenade is El Ranchito del Norte, a bazaar well stocked with similar items. ✉ *World Showcase, Mexico Pavilion, EPCOT* 🌐 *disneyworld.disney.go.com/shops/epcot/plaza-de-los-amigos.*

EPCOT Resort Area

For those looking for the best location on Disney property, the EPCOT resort area is the place to be. Three different properties, Disney's BoardWalk Inn & Villas, Disney's Yacht and Beach Club resorts, and the Swan and Dolphin resorts, surround Crescent Lake, which also provides access to Hollywood Studios and the International Gateway at EPCOT. Although the area is walkable, boats also stop at all three locations plus the two theme parks. Also in this area are Pop Century, the brand-new Riviera Resort, Caribbean Beach, and Art of Animation, lower priced hotels that are great for families on a budget.

Disney's BoardWalk Inn & Villas is fronted by a charming, ¼-mile-long promenade along the lake—minutes from the International Gateway at EPCOT—that is rich with architecture and signage recalling the turn-of-the-20th-century esplanades all along the Atlantic seaboard. Boats chug across Crescent Lake toward Hollywood Studios or EPCOT, lights outline the buildings, bicycle surreys with a fringe on top pedal along the waterfront, making this a delightful place for dining, meandering, or watching EPCOT fireworks. Here guests can find midway games, magicians, the ESPN sports bar, a piano bar, and the only dance club on Disney property. Flying Fish, a guest favorite, is the crowning restaurant of the BoardWalk. The action here, for better or worse, never stops.

Across Crescent Lake, the twin Yacht and Beach Club hotels feature a more relaxed atmosphere in an excellent location. Easily the highlight is Stormalong Bay, a 3-acre water area that features a sand-bottom pool, lazy river, towering waterslide, and three separate hot tubs. A large beach, which hosts movies and campfires and offers volleyball, sits along the Beach Club, while an array of watercraft is offered outside the Yacht Club. Don't be fooled by the simplicity of Beaches and Cream, the old-time soda shop, or the character breakfast at Cape May Cafe. Plus, Yachtman Steakhouse is one of the best restaurants on Disney property. A bonus of the Yacht and Beach—as well as the Swan and Dolphin—is that guests can easily get to the entertainment at the BoardWalk and then retreat to quieter rooms at night.

Though not owned by Disney, the Swan and Dolphin hotels are large convention hotels that are excellent choices for adults looking for time away from Disney between park visits. Restaurants here, such as Tony English's bluezoo, offer upscale dining in a calm setting. Between a sushi bar, a sports bar, and pool side cabanas, it is easy to forget that both Hollywood Studios and EPCOT are only a stone's throw away from these more traditional hotels. Those looking for a supreme spa experience will want to check into the Mandara Spa.

Caribbean Beach and the Riviera Resort are both moderately priced hotels that offer plenty of activities at a lower price point. Elaborate pools are highlights of both hotels, and those looking for upscale suites will love those at the Riviera. Also unique to the Riviera are the Tower Studio rooms, designed for only two guests, each with a small kitchenette in the room. Though tight, they are the perfect option for those looking for elegance on a budget. One downside of the Caribbean Beach Resort has always been transportation, but the new Disney Skyliner, a gondola that connects them to both EPCOT and Hollywood Studios, is now a highlight of both resorts.

In the far corner of Disney's property are Art of Animation and Pop Century. Connected by Hourglass Lake, these two resorts emphasize value. The Art of Animation, brilliantly bright, carries Disney all the way into guests' rooms, with themed shower curtains, Disney pictures on the table, and other little touches. Here are family suites at a reasonable price, rooms able to sleep six, with two separate bathrooms and a small kitchenette. Pop Century, a traditional hotel, is used most often for cheerleading and sports teams that come to compete at Walt Disney World. Though farther out, these resorts are also connected to the Disney Skyliner, meaning travel to EPCOT and Hollywood Studios is a breeze.

Restaurants

Big River Grille & Brewing Works

$$ | **AMERICAN** | **FAMILY** | Strange but good brews, like Rocket Red Ale, Southern Flyer Light Lager, Steamboat Pale Ale, and Gadzooks Pilsner, abound here at Walt Disney World's only microbrewery. You can dine inside among the giant stainless-steel brewing tanks or sip your suds outside on the lake-view patio. **Known for:** massive burgers; Disney's only microbrewery; ribs, steaks, and flame-grilled meat loaf. *Average main: $19* *Disney's BoardWalk, 2101 EPCOT Resorts Blvd., EPCOT Resort Area* *407/560–0253* *www.bigrivergrille.com.*

Cape May Cafe

$$$$ | **SEAFOOD** | **FAMILY** | With the feel of a New England seafood house—the type your grandma might enjoy—this bustling spot in the Beach Club Resort features popular buffet meals. For breakfast, Minnie and other cast classics visit tables while families help themselves to American classics from waffles to sausage links from the buffet. **Known for:** character breakfast; seafood buffet; casual atmosphere in an out-of-the-way setting. *Average main: $54* *Beach Club Resort, 1800 EPCOT Resorts Blvd., EPCOT Resort Area* *407/939–3463* *disneyworld.disney.go.com/dining/beach-club-resort/cape-may-cafe* *No lunch.*

ESPN Club

$$ | **AMERICAN** | Not only can you watch every possible televised sporting event on a big-screen TV here (the restaurant has about 100 monitors), but you can also periodically see ESPN programs being taped in the club itself. Food ranges from a variety of half-pound burgers, made with Angus chuck, to Guinness beer-battered fish-and-chips and buttermilk fried chicken. **Known for:** gigantic space that still fills up on game days; pub food: nachos, onion rings, big burgers; wine and regional beers. *Average main: $19* *Disney's BoardWalk, 2101 EPCOT*

Flying Fish is one of the original restaurants along Disney's Boardwalk. Opened in 1996, it was refurbished and reopened in 2016 with a new upscale seafood menu.

Resorts Blvd., EPCOT Resort Area ☎ *407/939–3463* 🌐 *disneyworld.disney.go.com/dining/boardwalk/espn-club.*

★ Flying Fish

$$$$ | SEAFOOD | Flying Fish has maintained its place as one of Disney World's finest restaurants, with a menu heavy on the freshest seasonal seafood as well as steaks. Options include as oak-grilled salmon, swordfish, and even exotic fare like Kurabuta pork belly and Hokkaido scallops. **Known for:** sophisticated dining on the Disney BoardWalk; fresh daily local and international seafood; AbracadaBAR cocktail lounge next door. 💲 *Average main: $48* ✉ *Disney's BoardWalk, 2101 EPCOT Resorts Blvd., EPCOT Resort Area* ☎ *407/939–2359* 🌐 *disneyworld.disney.go.com/dining/boardwalk/flying-fish* ⏲ *No lunch.*

Garden Grove

$$$$ | AMERICAN | FAMILY | With twinkling lights hung amid the branches of its oversize, 25-foot, signature tree, this restaurant, designed to resemble New York's Central Park, specializes in character meals. Monday, Tuesday, and Wednesday night, guests dine on classic American fare like prime rib while Goofy and his buddies make their rounds. **Known for:** character meals; cedar plank–blackened salmon; seafood buffet. 💲 *Average main: $34* ✉ *Walt Disney World Swan, 1200 EPCOT Resorts Blvd., EPCOT Resort Area* ☎ *407/934–1618* 🌐 *www.swandolphinrestaurants.com.*

Kimonos

$$$ | JAPANESE | Knife-wielding chefs prepare world-class sushi and sashimi but also other Japanese treats like soups and salads at this sleek hotel sushi bar, where bamboo-style floor tiles and dark teakwood furnishings create an inviting environment. Popular rolls include the Dragon Roll (giant shrimp and tuna), Banzai Roll (spicy tuna, avocado, and eel), and the Bagel Roll (smoked salmon, cream cheese, and cucumber). **Known for:** open until midnight; nightly karaoke; extensive sushi menu. 💲 *Average main: $24* ✉ *Walt Disney World Swan, 1200 EPCOT Resorts Blvd., EPCOT Resort*

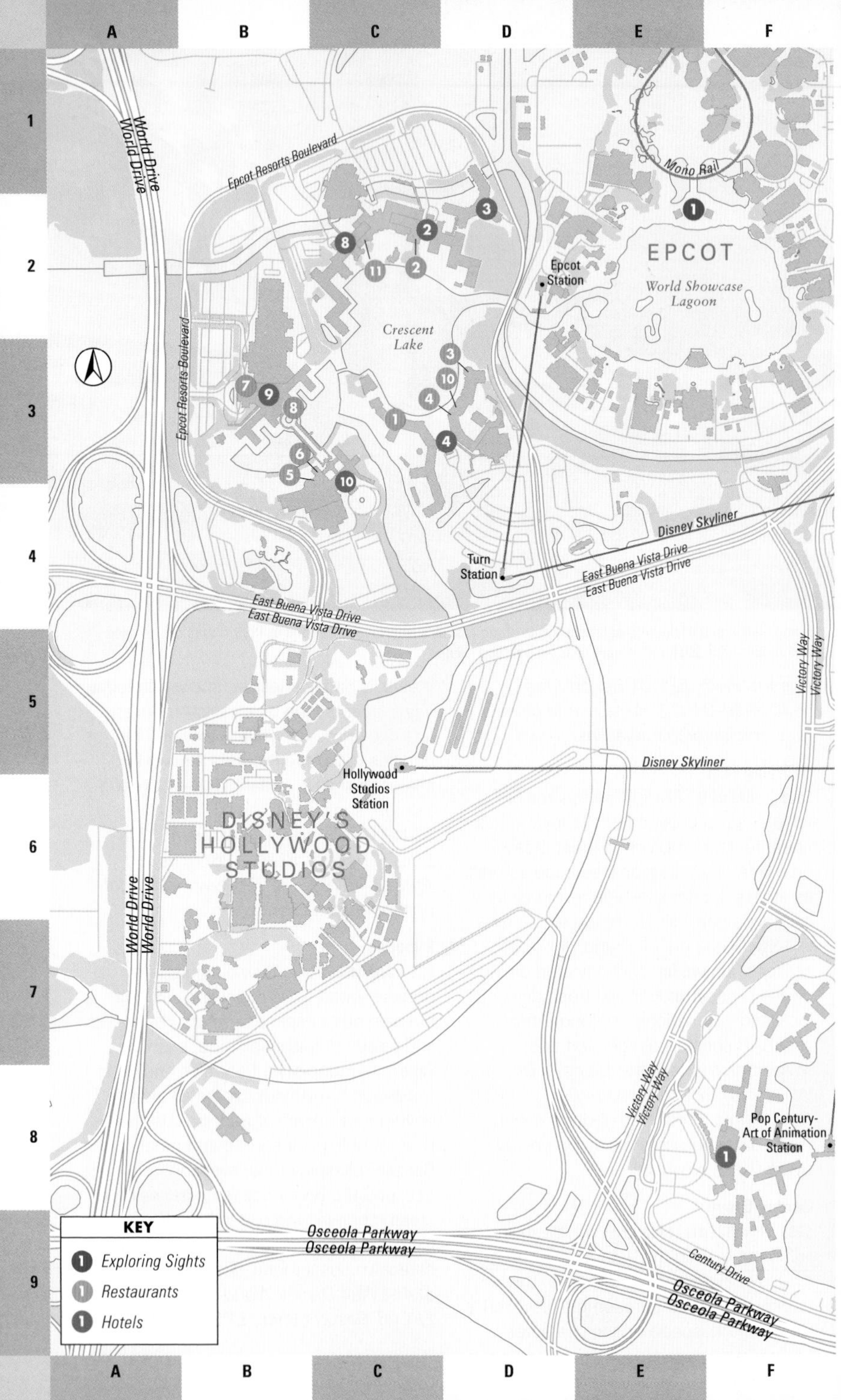

A
B
C
D
E
F
1
2
3
4
5
6
7
8
9
World Drive
Epcot Resorts Boulevard
Mono Rail
EPCOT
World Showcase Lagoon
Epcot Station
Crescent Lake
Disney Skyliner
Turn Station
East Buena Vista Drive
Victory Way
Hollywood Studios Station
DISNEY'S HOLLYWOOD STUDIOS
Pop Century-Art of Animation Station
Osceola Parkway
Century Drive
KEY
Exploring Sights
Restaurants
Hotels

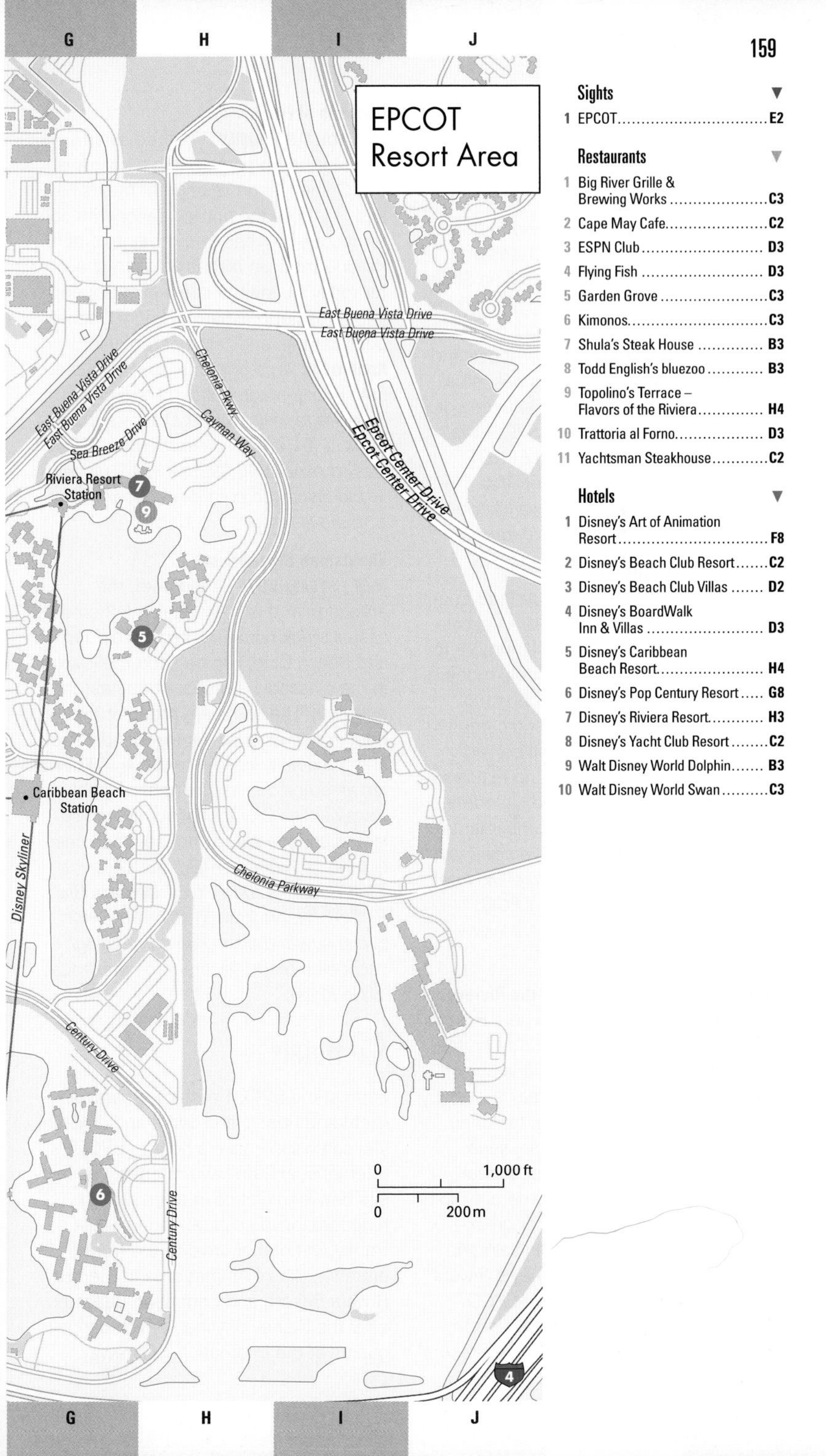

Sights

1 EPCOT................................E2

Restaurants

1 Big River Grille & Brewing Works......................C3

2 Cape May Cafe.......................C2

3 ESPN Club.......................... D3

4 Flying Fish D3

5 Garden Grove C3

6 Kimonos..............................C3

7 Shula's Steak House B3

8 Todd English's bluezoo B3

9 Topolino's Terrace – Flavors of the Riviera.............. H4

10 Trattoria al Forno................... D3

11 Yachtsman Steakhouse............C2

Hotels

1 Disney's Art of Animation Resort................................F8

2 Disney's Beach Club Resort.......C2

3 Disney's Beach Club Villas D2

4 Disney's BoardWalk Inn & Villas D3

5 Disney's Caribbean Beach Resort....................... H4

6 Disney's Pop Century Resort G8

7 Disney's Riviera Resort............ H3

8 Disney's Yacht Club Resort C2

9 Walt Disney World Dolphin....... B3

10 Walt Disney World Swan..........C3

Area ☎ *407/934–1609* 🌐 *www.swandolphinrestaurants.com/kimonos* ⏲ *No lunch.*

Shula's Steak House

$$$$ | STEAKHOUSE | The hardwood floors, dark-wood paneling, and pictures of former Miami Dolphins coach Don Shula make this restaurant resemble an annex of the NFL Hall of Fame. Among the best selections are the porterhouse and prime rib. **Known for:** steak, steak, steak; extensive whiskey menu; 48-ounce porterhouse. [$] *Average main: $79* ✉ *Walt Disney World Dolphin, 1500 EPCOT Resorts Blvd., EPCOT Resort Area* ☎ *407/934–1362* 🌐 *www.swandolphinrestaurants.com/shulas* ⏲ *No lunch.*

Todd English's bluezoo

$$$$ | SEAFOOD | Celebrity chef Todd English designed the menu for this upscale seafood eatery, known perhaps more for style than substance. The sleek, modern restaurant resembles an underwater dining hall, with blue walls and carpeting, aluminum fish along the wall behind the bar, and bubblelike lighting fixtures. **Known for:** variety of seafood; celebrity chef dining; two hours of complimentary child care while dining. [$] *Average main: $44* ✉ *Walt Disney World Dolphin Hotel, 1500 EPCOT Resorts Blvd., EPCOT Resort Area* ☎ *407/934–1111* 🌐 *www.thebluezoo.com* ⏲ *No lunch.*

Topolino's Terrace–Flavors of the Riviera

$$$$ | ITALIAN | At the new Riviera Resort is Topolino's Terrace, a restaurant on the 10th floor that offers fantastic views of the resort and EPCOT. At breakfast, enjoy a family-style character meal featuring sour cream waffles, spiced sausage hash, and wood-fired butcher's steak, while Mickey and friends come right to the table. **Known for:** character breakfast; hand-crafted pasta; King salmon. [$] *Average main: $50* ✉ *Disney's Riviera Resort, 1080 Esplanade Ave., EPCOT Resort Area* ☎ *407/828–7030* 🌐 *disneyworld.disney.go.com/dining/riviera-resort/topolinos-terrace.*

Trattoria al Forno

$$$ | ITALIAN | FAMILY | Themed as an old-time Italian home along a boardwalk, this Disney resort restaurant melds new and old, from the homey decor with contemporary touches to the menu, where Italian-American dishes are refreshed for today's tastes. Share a pizza topped with prosciutto di parma, Laura Chenel goat cheese, and caramelized onion. **Known for:** large portions; whole roasted fish; house-made desserts and gelato. [$] *Average main: $27* ✉ *Disney's BoardWalk, 2101 EPCOT Resorts Blvd., EPCOT Resort Area* ☎ *407/939–3463* 🌐 *disneyworld.disney.go.com/dining/boardwalk/trattoria-al-forno* ⏲ *No lunch.*

Yachtsman Steakhouse

$$$$ | STEAKHOUSE | Aged beef, the attraction at this New England–themed casual steak house in the upscale Yacht and Beach Club, can be seen mellowing in the glassed-in butcher shop near the entryway. The chefs are proud of their beef in this woodsy, family-friendly spot, and the quality seems to prove it. **Known for:** an ambitious assortment of steaks from Kansas City to Wagyu; artisan-selected cheese plates; house-made charcuterie. [$] *Average main: $50* ✉ *Yacht Club Resort, 1700 EPCOT Resorts Blvd., EPCOT Resort Area* ☎ *407/939–3463* 🌐 *disneyworld.disney.go.com/dining/yacht-club-resort/yachtsman-steakhouse* ⏲ *No lunch.*

Hotels

From some EPCOT resorts (Boardwalk, Yacht and Beach, and Swan and Dolphin), you can walk or take a boat to EPCOT's International Gateway entrance, which sits between France and the United Kingdom, or you can take the shuttle from your hotel or drive to the front entrance. Art of Animation, Pop Century, Riviera Resort, and Caribbean Beach now offer the Disney Skyliner, which deposits guests at the International Gateway.

The Disney Skyliner opened in September 2019, connecting EPCOT, Hollywood Studios, and several EPCOT Resort Area hotels.

Disney's Art of Animation Resort

$$ | **RESORT** | **FAMILY** | This brightly colored, three-story resort is a kid's version of paradise: each of its four wings features images from *Finding Nemo, Cars, The Lion King,* or *The Little Mermaid,* and in-room linens and carpeting match the wing's new theme. **Pros:** splash pad at the pool; reasonably priced family suites; images that kids adore. **Cons:** can be crowded; standard rooms fill up fast; the only on-site dining options are quick-service. *Rooms from: $195* *1850 Animation Way, EPCOT Resort Area* *407/938–7000* *www.disneyworld.disney.go.com/resorts* *1,984 rooms* *No meals.*

Disney's Beach Club Villas

$$$$ | **RESORT** | **FAMILY** | Each villa in this pale-turquoise-and-white waterfront area next to the Yacht and Beach Club Resort has a separate living room, kitchen, and one or two bedrooms, offering families some space, along with easy access to Disney's BoardWalk, Hollywood Studios, and EPCOT. **Pros:** short walk or boat ride to the BoardWalk, EPCOT, and Hollywood Studios; access to Stormalong Bay water park; in-suite kitchens let you save money on meals. **Cons:** boat traffic can be noisy; not close to Magic Kingdom or Animal Kingdom; pricey. *Rooms from: $950* *1800 EPCOT Resorts Blvd., EPCOT Resort Area* *407/934–8000* *www.disneyworld.disney.go.com/resorts* *576 units* *No meals.*

Disney's BoardWalk Inn & Villas

$$$$ | **RESORT** | Harking back to Atlantic City in its heyday, the striking red-and-white hotel has a wood-floor lobby filled with potted palms that looks over a classic waterfront promenade. **Pros:** casual, upscale atmosphere; lots of activities just outside the door; adjacent to EPCOT and Hollywood Studios. **Cons:** pricey; long bus ride to Magic Kingdom; boat whistles can intrude if you have a waterfront room. *Rooms from: $619* *2101 EPCOT Resorts Blvd., EPCOT Resort Area* *407/939–5100* *www.disneyworld.disney.go.com/resorts* *372 rooms* *No meals.*

Disney's Pop Century Resort, in the EPCOT Resort Area, is one of the hotels on a Disney Skyliner route.

Disney's Caribbean Beach Resort

$$$ | RESORT | FAMILY | A series of five palm-studded island "villages," this charming and moderately priced Disney resort with a 42-acre lake and white sand beaches is labeled with names straight from Pirates of the Caribbean. **Pros:** plenty of on-site outdoor activities give the place a lush summer-camp feel; convenient to EPCOT, Hollywood Studios, and Disney Springs; moderate price. **Cons:** you don't truly feel swept away to a tropical island; the beach is for sitting on, as the only swimmable waters are in the pools, not the lake; walks from your room to the beach or a restaurant can take up to 15 minutes. *Rooms from: $259 900 Cayman Way, EPCOT Resort Area 407/934–3400 www.disneyworld.disney.go.com/resorts 1,536 rooms No meals.*

Disney's Pop Century Resort

$ | RESORT | FAMILY | Giant jukeboxes, 65-foot-tall bowling pins, an oversize Big Wheel and Rubik's Cube, and other pop-culture memorabilia are scattered throughout the grounds of this value resort. **Pros:** great room rates; coffeemakers in most rooms; proximity to EPCOT, ESPN Wide World of Sports, and Disney's Hollywood Studios. **Cons:** having close to 3,000 rooms means big crowds at the front desk and in the food court; small rooms; lots of small kids around. *Rooms from: $153 1050 Century Dr., EPCOT Resort Area 407/938–4000, 407/934–4639 www.disneyworld.disney.go.com/resorts 2,880 rooms No meals.*

Disney's Riviera Resort

$$$$ | RESORT | FAMILY | Designed to evoke a resort along the European Riviera, this property offers its guests a multitude of room choices, ranging from tower studios (small rooms designed for only two guests but with a kitchenette) to grand, three-bedroom villas. **Pros:** newly built; large range of room options; lush gardens with bocci and chess boards. **Cons:** expensive for smaller rooms; far from Magic Kingdom; small pool. *Rooms from: $356 1080 Esplanade Ave., Lake*

Buena Vista ☎ 407/828–7030 🌐 www.disneyworld.disney.go.com/resorts ⇒ 300 rooms 🍴 No meals.

Disney's Yacht Club and Beach Club Resorts
$$$$ | RESORT | FAMILY | These big Crescent Lake inns adjacent to EPCOT and Hollywood Studios seem straight out of a Cape Cod summer, with their nautical decor, waterfront locale, light-filled rooms, rocking-chair porches, and family-friendly water-based activities. **Pros:** it's easy to walk or hop a ferry to EPCOT or Hollywood Studios; gracious atmosphere; adjacent to BoardWalk entertainment and dining. **Cons:** distances within the resort can seem vast; remote from other parks; bus transportation is slow. *$ Rooms from: $593 ✉ 1700 EPCOT Resorts Blvd., EPCOT Resort Area ☎ 407/934–8000 Beach Club, 407/934–7000 Yacht Club 🌐 www.disneyworld.disney.go.com/resorts ⇒ 1,200 rooms 🍴 No meals.*

Walt Disney World Dolphin
$$$$ | RESORT | A pair of 56-foot-tall sea creatures bookends this 25-story glass pyramid, a luxe resort designed, like the adjoining Swan (which is also on Disney property but not a Disney-owned resort), by world-renowned architect Michael Graves, and set close enough to the parks that you can escape the midday heat for a dip in the pool. **Pros:** character meals available; access to all facilities at the Swan; free boat to BoardWalk, EPCOT, and Hollywood Studios, buses to other parks. **Cons:** daily self-parking fee; a daily resort fee; no charging to room key at parks. *$ Rooms from: $635 ✉ 1500 EPCOT Resorts Blvd., EPCOT Resort Area ☎ 407/934–4000, 800/227–1500 🌐 www.swandolphin.com ⇒ 1,509 rooms 🍴 No meals.*

Walt Disney World Swan
$$$ | RESORT | This luxurious hotel, like its sister hotel the Dolphin, is not owned by Disney but still receives many of the same Disney perks, including Extra Magic Hours and an extended window to book Fastpass+. **Pros:** boat service to EPCOT and Hollywood Studios; adult-oriented; refurbished in 2019. **Cons:** no charging to room key at the parks; daily resort fee; self-parking fee. *$ Rooms from: $320 ✉ 1200 EPCOT Resorts Blvd., Lake Buena Vista ☎ 407/934–4000, 888/828–8850 🌐 www.swandolphin.com ⇒ 758 rooms 🍴 No meals.*

Nightlife

In the good ol' days, folks in New York and New Jersey escaped their city routines for breezy seaside boardwalks. That era is re-created on the shores of Crescent Lake at Disney's BoardWalk, just a short walk from EPCOT. The ¼-mile promenade becomes a festive setting after sunset, where you can stroll past shops, bars, boutiques, nightlife, and street performances. And if you'd like to see the EPCOT fireworks, you'll find a nice view from the bridge that connects the BoardWalk with the Yacht and Beach Club resorts just across the lake.

Atlantic Dance Hall
DANCE CLUBS | This popular, high-energy dance club plays music from the '80s onward, with a huge screen showing videos requested by the crowd. The parquet dance floor is set off by furnishings of deep blue, maroon, and gold, and the ceiling glows with stars and twinkling lights. Signature cocktails are in demand, and you can sip a cognac or choose from a selection of popular beers to inspire your dance floor moves. *✉ Disney's BoardWalk, 2101 EPCOT Resorts Blvd., EPCOT Resort Area ☎ 407/939–2444 🌐 www.disneyworld.disney.go.com/entertainment/boardwalk/atlantic-dance-hall.*

Big River Grille & Brewing Works
BARS/PUBS | The BoardWalk's only brewpub welcomes families with intimate tables and a waterfront patio; either is a splendid place to sample craft brews and upscale American pub grub like barbecued ribs or blackened

Creole salmon. House brews on tap might include Southern Flyer Light Lager, Rocket Red Ale, and the seasonal Sweet Magnolia American Brown Ale. ✉ *Disney's BoardWalk, 2101 EPCOT Resorts Blvd., EPCOT Resort Area* ☎ *407/560–0253* 🌐 *www.disneyworld.disney.go.com/dining/boardwalk/big-river-grille-and-brewing-works.*

ESPN Club

BARS/PUBS | The sports motif here is carried into every nook and cranny—the main dining area looks like an arena, with a basketball-court hardwood floor and a giant scoreboard that projects the day's big game. While you watch, you can munch on wings, nachos, and linebacker-size burgers. More than 100 TVs throughout the 13,000-square-foot hall (even in the restrooms) carry satellite feeds of games from around the world, so you won't miss one action-packed minute. **TIP→ The place is packed for big games, so plan to arrive early: seats are first come, first served.** ✉ *Disney's BoardWalk, 2101 EPCOT Resorts Blvd., EPCOT Resort Area* ☎ *407/939–1177* 🌐 *www.disneyworld.disney.go.com/dining/boardwalk/espn-club.*

Jellyrolls

BARS/PUBS | In this rockin', boisterous piano bar, comedians double as emcees as they play dueling grand pianos nonstop. Their speed and intricacy is impressive, as is the depth of their playlists. The steady stream of conventions at Disney makes this the place to catch CEOs doing the conga to Barry Manilow's "Copacabana" (if that's your idea of a good time) and young Disney cast members checking in after they clock out. There's a nightly cover charge. ✉ *Disney's BoardWalk, 2101 EPCOT Resorts Blvd., EPCOT Resort Area* ☎ *407/560–8770* 🌐 *www.disneyworld.disney.go.com/entertainment/boardwalk/jellyrolls* ☞ *Guests must be 21 and over.*

Chapter 5

DISNEY'S HOLLYWOOD STUDIOS

WITH BLIZZARD BEACH

Updated by
Leigh Jenkins

Sights	Restaurants	Hotels	Shopping	Nightlife
★★★★★	★★★★☆	★★★☆☆	★★★★☆	★★☆☆☆

CHARACTER MEALS

Character meals are larger-than-life experiences that might be the high point of your child's visit to Walt Disney World or Universal. Mickey, Minnie, and more come alive and welcome your kids as if they were old friends.

TOP PICKS FOR BREAKFAST

WALT DISNEY WORLD

Chef Mickey's Fun Time Buffet, Disney's Contemporary Resort. This breakfast combines space-age Disney styling with Mickey Mouse, Donald, and the gang, plus the ever-popular Mickey-shaped waffles.

'Ohana's Best Friends Breakfast with Lilo & Stitch, Disney's Polynesian Resort. The intergalactic Stitch and his human friend, Lilo, join your family in a tropical setting for this very popular breakfast. Every 30 minutes, Mickey and Pluto join in while kids parade around the restaurant with maracas and wide grins.

Topolino's Terrace–Flavors of the Riviera, Disney's Riviera Resort. Mickey, Minnie, Donald, and Daisy are dressed with European elegance as you dine on the top floor of Disney's newest restaurant. Entrées such as sour cream waffles, quiche Gruyère, and wild mushroom scrambles elevate this meal above other character dining.

UNIVERSAL

Despicable Me Character Breakfast, Loews Royal Pacific Resort. Every Saturday morning Gru, his three girls, and the lovable minions rotate around Royal Pacific's Tahitian Room while you dine on pancakes, bacon, and scrambled eggs.

TOP PICKS FOR LUNCH WALT DISNEY WORLD

The Crystal Palace Character Meal, Magic Kingdom. A lovely Victorian setting is the perfect place for the old-fashioned and lovable Winnie the Pooh and friends to greet your kids. This is the only meal at which you'll find characters from the Hundred Acre Wood.

My Disney Girl's Perfectly Princess Tea Party, Disney's Grand Floridian Resort. Girls ages 3 to 11 enjoy the princess experience here. Dressing up is encouraged, and lunch, featuring tea and sandwiches, is served on china plates. Princess Aurora (Sleeping Beauty herself) will make an appearance. Little ones receive a special Disney Girl Princess doll, jewelry, a ribbon tiara, and a photo scrapbook page.

TOP PICKS FOR DINNER WALT DISNEY WORLD

Cinderella's Happily Ever After Dinner, Disney's Grand Floridian Resort. A dinner buffet of worldly cuisine is complete with Cinderella, Prince Charming, and their family (including the wicked steps) making the rounds.

Princess Storybook Dining at Akershus Royal Banquet Hall, EPCOT. Belle, Jasmine, Snow White, the *Little Mermaid*'s Ariel and many more princesses could appear at this medieval castle–style Norwegian building.

Tusker House Restaurant, Disney's Animal Kingdom. With selections such as peri peri salmon, spit-roasted chicken, and African side dishes, the option offers some of the best food at any character meal while Minnie, Daisy, and Donald mingle in their safari gear.

UNIVERSAL

Halloween Horror Nights Scareactor Dining Experience, Universal Studios. During Halloween Horror Nights in the fall, a character experience unlike any other is available at Classic Monster Cafe. Character actors from the haunted park will visit your table in an experience so intense it's not recommended for anyone under age 13.

Marvel Character Dinner, Islands of Adventure. On Thursday–Sunday night Captain America, Spider-Man, Wolverine, Storm, and Rogue can be found at Cafe 4, while you enjoy specialty pizzas and pastas.

PARK SNAPSHOT

TOP EXPERIENCES

■ **Disney Junior Dance Party!** The preschool crowd can't get enough of the characters here from Disney Junior shows like *Vampirina, Mickey and the Roadster Racers, Doc McStuffins,* and *The Lion Guard* (ages 7 and under).

■ **For the First Time in Forever: A "Frozen" Sing-Along Celebration.** Every audience member can "Let It Go" and sing along to the popular tunes from Disney's blockbuster film *Frozen* (ages 7 and under).

■ **Slinky Dog Dash.** In the spirit of the Seven Dwarfs Mine Train, this new family coaster offers some speed and thrills but no real scares (ages 8 and up).

■ **Star Wars: Rise of the Resistance.** Try to avoid the First Order while helping Rey, Finn, and Poe on a resistance mission (ages 8 and up).

■ **Toy Story Mania!** 3-D glasses? Check. Spring-action shooter? Check. Ride and shoot your way through the midway with Buzz, Woody, and others (ages 8 and up).

PLANNING YOUR TIME

Since the opening of Star Wars: Galaxy's Edge, Hollywood Studios has become incredibly crowded. If you want to ride **Rise of the Resistance,** plan to be at the park at opening or 30 minutes before during busy times. Secure a boarding group to get a two-hour window in which to experience the attraction. Younger kids and parents should go to **Toy Story Land.** The other hot ticket is **Mickey and Minnie's Runaway Railway.**

For dinner, make reservations well in advance for **50's Prime Time Café,** where you'll dine in the setting of a classic '50's sit-com. Those wanting an upscale experience should look at the **Brown Derby Restaurant.** Finally, make sure to catch ***Fantasmic!*** by either reserving a *Fantasmic!*dining package or showing up 30 minutes before show time.

GETTING HERE

■ Most guests staying at a Disney resort hotel will take a Disney bus to the entrance of Hollywood Studios. If you're at BoardWalk, Yacht and Beach Club, or Swan and Dolphin, a ferry leaves about every 15 minutes for the park. Guests at Pop Century, Art of Animation, Caribbean Beach, and Riviera Resort can take advantage of the new Disney Skyliner. Parking for those not staying in a Disney resort is $25 per day. If you're at a hotel near the Magic Kingdom, consider driving; the parking lot is compact and will save you a long bus ride.

QUICK BITES

■ **BaseLine Tap House.** With more than a dozen American beers and ciders on tap, this is a great place to pop in for a quick drink, a California cheese plate, or coffee-rubbed steak puff. ✉ *Grand Avenue*

■ **Epic Eats.** Sweet tooth acting up? Funnel cakes and soft-serve ice cream might be the ticket. ✉ *Echo Lake.*

■ **Milk Stand.** For *Star Wars* fans, this is your one chance to try the legendary "blue milk" from the movies. ✉ *Star Wars: Galaxy's Edge.*

The first thing you notice when you pass through the Hollywood Studios turnstiles is the laid-back California attitude. Palm-lined Hollywood Boulevard oozes old-time glamour.

The second thing you notice is that nostalgia for the past glories of Hollywood film is giving way to nostalgia for its depiction of the future and toward a more Disney-centric vision of the movies. As interest in *Star Wars* has grown, the newest land—called Star Wars: Galaxy's Edge—has transformed the park in many ways.

Rather than offering a visit to a working movie studio, as the park's original concept called for, Disney is looking to immerse you in the world of beloved movies. In addition, the popularity of the *Toy Story* film series brought another big change. Toy Story Land, which opened in 2018, takes visitors into Andy's backyard, and brings Woody, Buzz, and a host of familiar characters to life. A new indoor attraction, **Mickey and Minnie's Runaway Railway,** sits inside Grauman's Chinese Theatre, taking the spot once occupied by the Great Movie Ride.

When the park opened in May 1989, its name was Disney–MGM Studios. Disney changed the name in 2008 to broaden its appeal. Another name change in the near future is not outside the realm of possibility. But no matter the name, the inspiration springs from the same place: America's love affair with the movies.

Although the park was built with real film and television production in mind, that has mostly halted. There are still attractions that showcase how filmmakers practice their craft, so if you're wowed by action-film stunts, you can learn the tricks of the trade at the Indiana Jones Epic Stunt Spectacular!, then you can take a close look at the legend himself, at Walt Disney Presents, where sketches, artwork, and early animation join previews of what's coming next. But the focus has shifted toward transporting you directly into the action through such big-hit attractions as Toy Story Mania!; the 3-D, *Star Wars*–themed simulator ride, Star Tours—The Adventures Continue; The Twilight Zone Tower of Terror; and Rock 'n' Roller Coaster starring Aerosmith.

Planning

Getting Oriented

The park is divided into sightseeing clusters. **Hollywood Boulevard** is the main artery to the heart of the park and is where you find the glistening replica of Grauman's Chinese Theatre.

Encircling it are **Sunset Boulevard,** the **Animation Courtyard, Toy Story Land, Pixar Place, Commissary Lane, Grand Avenue, Star Wars: Galaxy's Edge,** and **Echo Lake.**

The entire park is 135 acres, but it has fewer than 20 attractions (compared with Magic Kingdom's 40-plus). It's small enough to cover in a day and even repeat a favorite ride or two.

If you're staying at one of the EPCOT resorts (BoardWalk, Yacht or Beach Club, Swan, or Dolphin), getting to the

Entrance Plaza on a motor launch is part of the fun. Disney resort buses also drop you at the entrance. Those staying at Pop Century, Art of Animation, Caribbean Beach, and the Riviera Resort can take the new Disney Skyliner to the parks.

If you're staying off-property and driving, your $25 parking ticket will remain valid for parking at another Disney park later in the day—provided, of course, you have the stamina.

Park Amenities

Baby Care: The small baby-care center next to Guest Relations (aka Guest Services) has nursing and changing facilities. Formula, baby food, pacifiers, and disposable diapers are for sale next door at Movieland and at Oscar's Super Service. There are also diaper-changing areas in all women's and some men's restrooms.

Cameras: At the Darkroom (or next door at Cover Story) on Hollywood Boulevard, you can buy memory cards and disposable cameras. And if a Disney photographer takes your picture in the park, you can pick up a Disney PhotoPass from him or her that lets you see the pictures online. Memory Maker, digital copies of your photos, are $169 in advance and $199 in the parks, and you can purchase prints ($20.95 for an 8–by-10-inch photo; other sizes available).

First Aid: The station is in the Entrance Plaza adjoining Guest Relations.

Tip Board: Small tip boards are located at the end of **Hollywood Boulevard,** by Back-Lot Express, near Tower of Terror, and at the entrance to Toy Story Land. These are especially helpful while waiting for your Rise of the Resistance boarding number.

Guest Relations: You'll find it just inside the turnstiles on the left side of the Entrance Plaza.

Lockers: You can rent lockers at the Crossroads of the World kiosk in the center of the Entrance Plaza. The cost is $10 to $15 with a $5 refundable key deposit. The lockers themselves are at Oscar's Super Service.

Lost People and Things: Instruct your kids to go to a Disney staffer with a name tag if they can't find you. If you lose them, ask any cast member for assistance; logbooks of lost children's names are kept at Guest Relations, which also has a computerized message center where you can leave notes for companions.

Disney's Hollywood Studios Lost and Found
Report lost or found articles at Guest Relations. ✉ *Hollywood Boulevard, Disney's Hollywood Studios* ☎ *407/560–4666.*

Main Lost and Found
Seek out articles lost for more than one day here. ✉ *Disney Springs, Disney Springs* ☎ *407/824–4245.*

Package Pick-Up: You can ask shop clerks to forward purchases to your hotel if you're staying on Disney property or to Package Pick-Up next to Oscar's Super Service in the Entrance Plaza, so you won't have to carry them around. Allow three hours for delivery.

Services for People with Disabilities: The Studios' restaurants, shops, theaters, and attractions are wheelchair accessible, although there are boarding restrictions on some rides. Some theater-type attractions, including Muppet*Vision 3-D, have reflective captioning, and most other attractions are equipped for assisted-listening and video- or handheld-captioning devices. There are large Braille park maps near the Guest Relations lobby and near the Tip Board at Hollywood and Sunset. Note that restaurants don't have Braille menus.

You can pick up Braille guides ($25 same-day refundable deposit) and assisted-listening devices (also $25 deposit) and

Dinner and a Show

Call or check ahead to visit on a day when you can see the after-dark Fantasmic! show, with its 30 powerful minutes of Disney characters, special effects, fireworks, flames, fountains, and even animation sequences projected onto water screens. If you're not crazy about the idea of arriving at the huge Hollywood Hills Amphitheater more than an hour ahead of showtime for a good seat, it's worth booking a Fantasmic! lunch or dinner package.

You get a prix-fixe meal at buffet-style Hollywood & Vine or a full table-service lunch or dinner at Hollywood Brown Derby or Mama Melrose's, along with a preferred-entry pass to the VIP seating area at the Fantasmic! show. Each dinner includes appetizer, entrée, dessert (the Brown Derby's grapefruit cake is a sweet-tart wonder), and a nonalcoholic beverage.

There's a small catch (well, actually, there are three):

If you choose to book dinner, allow plenty of time between your dining time and your arrival for showtime. (Disney recommends that you show up at the theater 30 or more minutes ahead of time to choose your seat.)

The dinner package is offered only for the first show on peak nights when Fantasmic! is performed twice.

If it rains, Fantasmic! might be canceled. You still get dinner, but you lose out on seeing the show with preferred seating.

The cost is $44 to $63 for adults, $18 to $36 for children. It's best to reserve the package 180 days or at least several months in advance. You'll have to provide a credit-card number and, if you cancel 48 hours or less before the show, your card will be charged $10 per person.

Sound like too much? Consider the Fantasmic! Dessert and VIP Viewing Experience. You'll receive a plate of unique tasty treats inspired by the show, adults will receive a specialty cocktail, and children will love their make-your-own worms and dirt pudding. Then your party will be led to a private viewing section of the show. The price is $39 for adults and $19 for children.

check on sign-language interpretation schedules at Guest Relations. Although interpreters appear only two days each week, you can request them (at least 14 days in advance) on other days by calling ☎ *407/560–2547* or TTY ☎ *407/827–5141*.

Oscar's Super Service, to the right in the Entrance Plaza, rents wheelchairs ($12 daily, $10 multiday) and electronic convenience vehicles (ECVs; $50 per day plus a refundable $20 security deposit). Reservations aren't an option, so arrive early, especially to snag an ECV.

Stroller Rentals: Oscar's Super Service rents strollers. Single strollers are $15 daily, $13 for more than one day; doubles are $31 daily, $27 multiday.

Visiting Tips

Visit early in the week. That's when most other people are at Magic Kingdom and Animal Kingdom.

Arrive 30 minutes before opening. Those wanting to snag a boarding time for Rise of the Resistance should arrive before park opening.

Keep your eyes open. Look for attractions displaying short wait times to visit between Fastpass+ appointments.

Arrive early for Fantasmic! Be at the Fantasmic! amphitheater at least an hour before showtime if you didn't book the lunch or dinner package.

Grab a bite. Need a burst of energy? On-the-run hunger pangs? Try Fairfax Fare on Sunset. Alternatively, Hollywood Scoops ice cream next door is the place to be on a hot day.

Disney's Hollywood Studios

Hollywood Boulevard

With its palm trees, pastel buildings, and flashy neon, Hollywood Boulevard paints a rosy picture of midcentury Tinseltown. There's a sense of having walked right onto a movie set of old, with art deco storefronts and roving starlets and nefarious agents—actually costumed actors known as the Citizens of Hollywood. Throughout the park, characters from Disney movies new and old—from *Mickey Mouse* to *Toy Story* friends—pose for photos and sign autographs.

A new ride called Mickey and Minnie's Runaway Railway just opened within the centerpiece of Grauman's Chinese Theatre.

TIP→ Dinner packages that include the Fantasmic! after-dark show can be booked by phone or online, in person at a Disney hotel, or at the park's Guest Relations.

★ **Mickey and Minnie's Runaway Railway**
AMUSEMENT PARK/WATER PARK | FAMILY | Inspired by the newest Mickey and Minnie shorts, this ride starts with you watching a new cartoon about Mickey and Minnie's desire for a perfect picnic. But all does not go according to plan, and when Pluto steals their picnic basket, that's when you're off. Aboard Engineer Goofy's railway, you'll chase after the picnic basket, twisting and turning inside the cartoon. Don't fret, though: despite the "runaway" part of the name, this is a tame ride that any age can enjoy. ✉ *Hollywood Boulevard, Disney's Hollywood Studios* ☞ *Duration: 5 mins. Crowds: Heavy. Audience: All ages.*

Hollywood Brown Derby
$$$$ | AMERICAN | At this reproduction of the famous 1940s Hollywood favorite, the walls are lined with caricatures ofold-time movie stars. The specialty is a Cobb salad, which was invented by Brown Derby founder Robert Cobb and still tossed table-side. While waiting for a table (it might take a while), or as an alternative, try the outdoor lounge, where appetizers and drinks may be ordered. Other menu choices include grilled salmon with braised lentils and Brussel sprouts, and duck breast with butter-braised bok choy. Dining with an Imagineer is a special option; you will have lunch or dinner with one of Disney's creative engineers while enjoying a set-price four-course meal including soup, salad, entrée, and dessert. If you request the Fantasmic! dinner package, make a reservation for no later than two hours before the start of the show. **Known for:** old-Hollywood atmosphere; the Cobb salad; grapefruit cake. [$] *Average main: $40* ✉ *Hollywood Boulevard, Disney's Hollywood Studios* ☎ *407/939–3463* 🌐 *disneyworld.disney.go.com/dining/hollywood-studios/hollywood-brown-derby.*

Performing Arts

Star Wars: A Galactic Spectacular

SOUND/LIGHT SHOW | Combining imagery, lasers, and fireworks, this 14-minute show covers everyone's favorite *Star Wars* characters, from Darth Maul to Rey. Similar to the technology used on Cinderella Castle, images are projected onto Grauman's Chinese Theatre and the surrounding buildings, showing beloved characters and famous fight scenes. Sometimes this show will run at the same time as Fantasmic!, other times they are staggered. Those with younger kids will prefer Fantasmic! while older kids and *Star Wars* fans will prefer this spectacular. ✉ *Hollywood Boulevard, Disney's Hollywood Studios* ☞ *Duration: 14 mins. Crowds: Moderate. Audience: Not small kids.*

Wonderful World of Animation

SOUND/LIGHT SHOW | This 12-minute nighttime projection show lights up the facade of the iconic Grauman's Chinese Theatre and begins with Mickey Mouse and his cartoon debut. Classic scenes from *Aladdin, The Little Mermaid,* and *The Incredibles* are projected across the entire theater, ending with, of course, Steamboat Willie and Mickey Mouse reminding you who started it all. ✉ *Hollywood Boulevard, Disney's Hollywood Studios.*

Shopping

You can upgrade your look at Keystone Clothiers. Mickey's of Hollywood has something for everyone in the family.

Keystone Clothiers

CLOTHING | This shop pops with stylish clothing and accessories for adults. Disney characters are emblazoned on T-shirts and button-up-shirts, ties, and accessories, while handbags and totes sport classic Mickey Mouse artwork. Colorful scarves with hidden Mickeys and other designs are popular buys. ✉ *Hollywood Boulevard, Disney's Hollywood Studios* 🌐 *disneyworld.disney.go.com/shops/hollywood-studios/keystone-clothiers.*

Mickey's of Hollywood

CLOTHING | The largest store in Hollywood Studios is a miniversion of the Magic Kingdom's Emporium with toys, T-shirts, and doodads. Blue velvety *Sorcerer's Apprentice* hats have Mouse ears, plus a moon and stars that light up. You'll also find Minnie Mouse and Donald Duck character key chains and lots of Disney-character-embossed tech accessories, including the MagicBand, a wristband that links to your charge account so you can purchase meals, merchandise, and even Fastpasses. ✉ *Hollywood Boulevard, Disney's Hollywood Studios* 🌐 *disneyworld.disney.go.com/shops/hollywood-studios/mickeys-of-hollywood.*

Sunset Boulevard

This avenue honors Hollywood with facades derived from the Carthay Circle Theatre, Fox Wilshire Theatre, and other City of Angels landmarks.

Sights

Beauty and the Beast—Live on Stage!

AMUSEMENT PARK/WATER PARK | This popular stage show takes place at the Theater of the Stars, a re-creation of the famed Hollywood Bowl. The actors playing a luminous Belle and delightfully vain Gaston sing with passion with a lively cast of characters and dancers. The enchanted prince (Beast) and household characters (Mrs. Potts, Chip, Lumiere, and Cogsworth) deftly navigate the stage despite their bulky costumes. Even some set pieces sway along during the charming "Be Our Guest" number. There's high drama during the mob scene and a sweet ending when ballroom dancers in frothy pink and purple waltz along with the fairy-tale couple.

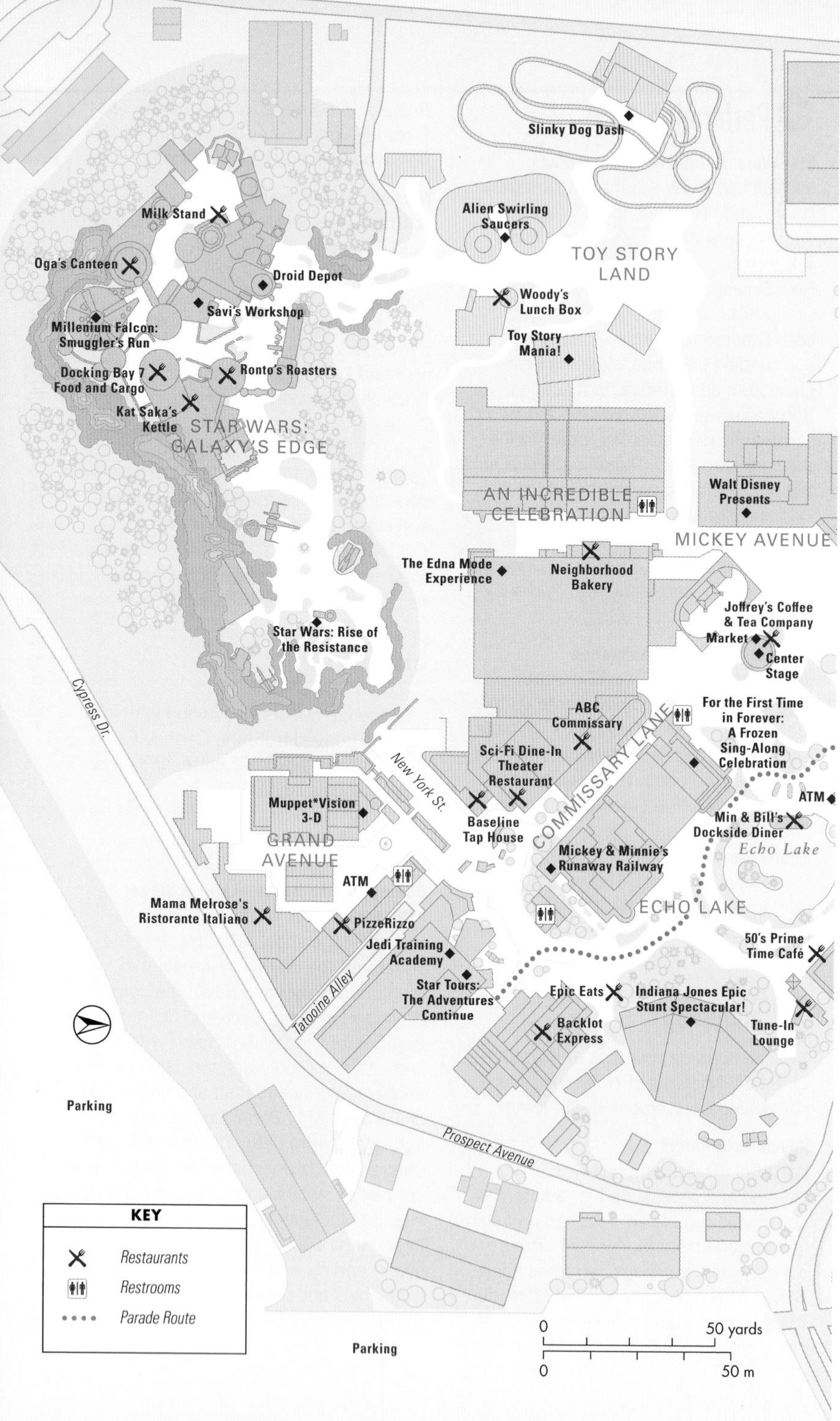
Slinky Dog Dash
Alien Swirling Saucers
TOY STORY LAND
Milk Stand
Oga's Canteen
Droid Depot
Savi's Workshop
Millenium Falcon: Smuggler's Run
Woody's Lunch Box
Toy Story Mania!
Docking Bay 7 Food and Cargo
Ronto's Roasters
Kat Saka's Kettle
STAR WARS: GALAXY'S EDGE
AN INCREDIBLE CELEBRATION
Walt Disney Presents
MICKEY AVENUE
The Edna Mode Experience
Neighborhood Bakery
Joffrey's Coffee & Tea Company
Market
Center Stage
Star Wars: Rise of the Resistance
Cypress Dr.
ABC Commissary
For the First Time in Forever: A Frozen Sing-Along Celebration
COMMISSARY LANE
Sci-Fi Dine-In Theater Restaurant
New York St.
Muppet*Vision 3-D
ATM
Min & Bill's Dockside Diner
Baseline Tap House
GRAND AVENUE
Echo Lake
Mickey & Minnie's Runaway Railway
ATM
Mama Melrose's Ristorante Italiano
ECHO LAKE
PizzeRizzo
Jedi Training Academy
50's Prime Time Café
Star Tours: The Adventures Continue
Epic Eats
Indiana Jones Epic Stunt Spectacular!
Tatooine Alley
Backlot Express
Tune-In Lounge
Parking
Prospect Avenue
KEY
Restaurants
Restrooms
Parade Route
Parking
0
50 yards
0
50 m

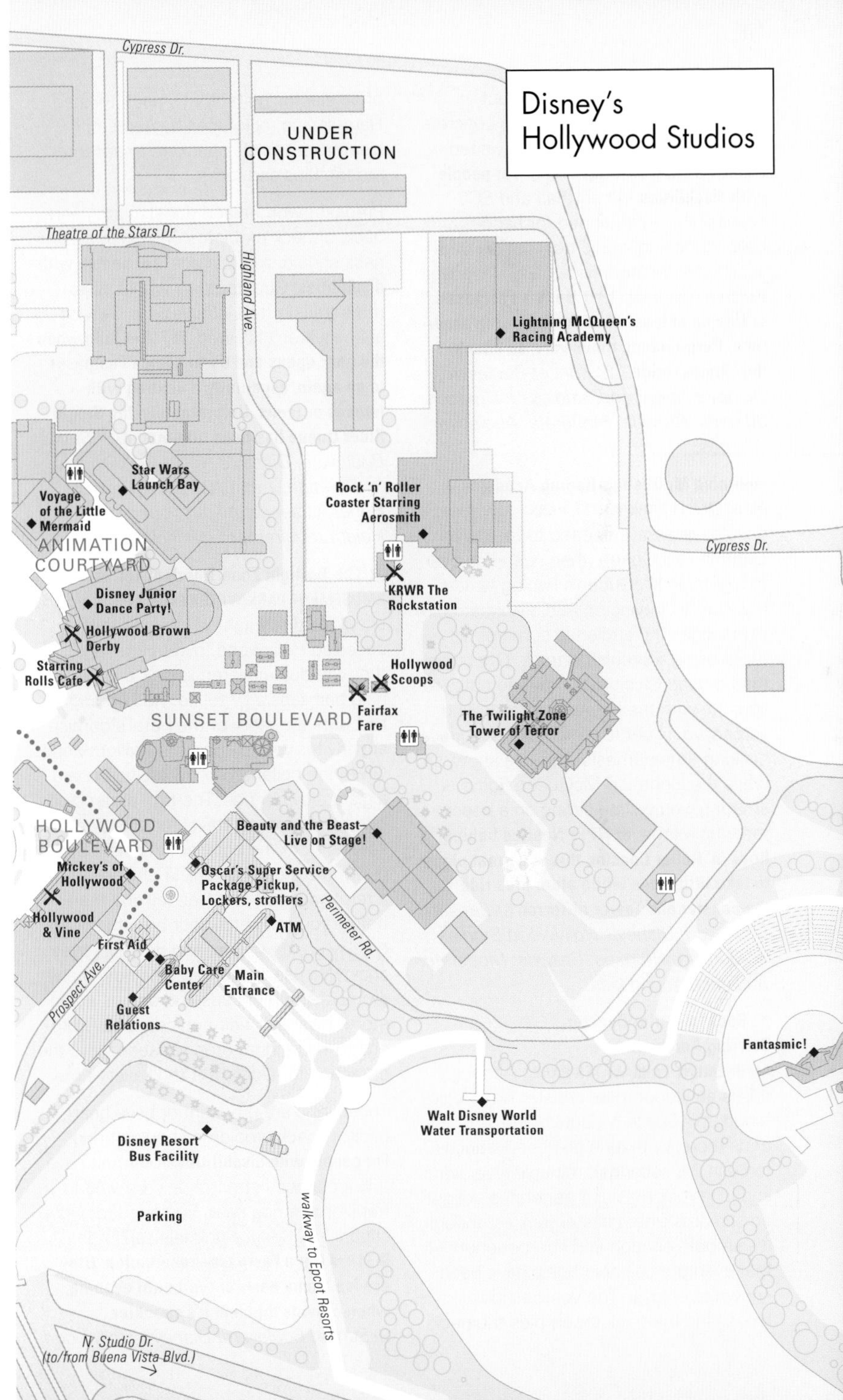
Disney's Hollywood Studios
Cypress Dr.
UNDER CONSTRUCTION
Theatre of the Stars Dr.
Highland Ave.
Lightning McQueen's Racing Academy
Star Wars Launch Bay
Voyage of the Little Mermaid
ANIMATION COURTYARD
Rock 'n' Roller Coaster Starring Aerosmith
Cypress Dr.
KRWR The Rockstation
Disney Junior Dance Party!
Hollywood Brown Derby
Starring Rolls Cafe
Hollywood Scoops
Fairfax Fare
SUNSET BOULEVARD
The Twilight Zone Tower of Terror
HOLLYWOOD BOULEVARD
Beauty and the Beast–Live on Stage!
Mickey's of Hollywood
Oscar's Super Service Package Pickup, Lockers, strollers
Perimeter Rd.
Hollywood & Vine
ATM
First Aid
Baby Care Center
Main Entrance
Prospect Ave.
Guest Relations
Fantasmic!
Walt Disney World Water Transportation
Disney Resort Bus Facility
Parking
walkway to Epcot Resorts
N. Studio Dr. (to/from Buena Vista Blvd.)

As you arrive or depart, check out handprints and footprints set in concrete of the TV personalities who've visited Disney's Hollywood Studios. **For people with disabilities:** Wheelchair and ECV accessible and equipped for hand-held-captioning, audio-description, and assisted-listening devices. Sign language twice a week. **TIP→ Book a Fastpass+ or line up at least 30 minutes prior to show-time. Performance times vary, so check the "Times Guide."** ✉ *Sunset Boulevard, Disney's Hollywood Studios* ☞ *Duration: 30 mins. Crowds: Moderate. Audience: All ages.*

Lightning McQueen's Racing Academy
AMUSEMENT PARK/WATER PARK | If your little ones have always wanted to race with Lightning McQueen, then speed on over to Lightning McQueen's Racing Academy. A very convincing Audio-Animatronic car teaches the audience some of his tricks using a simulated track. Of course, the no-good Chick Hicks tries to out-race you, so, with the help of a wraparound screen, you'll get to watch Lightning race his long-time nemesis. This is a show, so while the Lightning McQueen figure is amazing, you will be sitting on a bench the whole time. **TIP→ Nestled behind Rock 'n' Roller Coaster, this is a great place to take little ones while older kids ride the coaster and Tower of Terror.** ✉ *Sunset Boulevard, Disney's Hollywood Studios* ☞ *Duration: 10 mins. Crowds: Moderate. Audience: Young kids.*

★ Rock 'n' Roller Coaster Starring Aerosmith
AMUSEMENT PARK/WATER PARK | Although this is an indoor roller coaster like Magic Kingdom's Space Mountain, the similarity ends there. With its high-speed launch (0 to 60 in 2.8 seconds), multiple inversions, and loud rock music, it generates delighted screams from coaster junkies, though it's smooth enough and short enough that even the coaster-phobic have been known to enjoy it. The vehicles look like limos, and the track resembles the neck of an electric guitar that's been twisted. Hard-driving rock tunes by Aerosmith blast from vehicle speakers to accentuate the flips and turns.

Pregnant women and guests with heart, back, or neck problems or motion sickness should skip this one. **For people with disabilities:** Guests using wheelchairs must transfer to a ride vehicle. Service animals aren't allowed. **TIP→ Ride when the park opens and try to book a Fastpass+ to go again, especially if visiting with tweens or teens. Unfortunately, the Single Rider Queue has been eliminated.** ✉ *Sunset Boulevard, Disney's Hollywood Studios* ☞ *Duration: 1 min., 22 secs. Crowds: Huge. Audience: All but young kids. Height requirement: 48 inches.*

★ The Twilight Zone Tower of Terror
AMUSEMENT PARK/WATER PARK | After you enter the dimly lighted lobby of the deserted Hollywood Tower Hotel and then the dust-covered library, a lightning bolt zaps a TV to life. Rod Serling recounts the story of the hotel's demise and invites you to enter the Twilight Zone. On to the boiler room, where you board a giant elevator ride. The fifth dimension awaits, where you travel forward past scenes from the popular TV series. Suddenly, the creaking vehicle plunges into a terrifying, 130-foot free fall and then, before you can catch your breath, shoots quickly up, down, up, and down all over again. No use trying to guess how many stomach-churning ups and downs are in store—Disney's ride engineers have programmed random drop variations into the attraction for a different thrill every time.

Those who are pregnant or have heart, back, or neck problems shouldn't ride. **For people with disabilities:** You must have full upper-body strength and be able to transfer to a ride seat. Equipped for video captioning. Service animals can't ride. **TIP→ Get a Fastpass+ reservation. Otherwise, come early or wait until evening, when crowds thin and it's spookier.** ✉ *Sunset Boulevard, Disney's Hollywood*

Studios ☞ Duration: 10 mins. Crowds: You bet! Audience: All but young kids. Height requirement: 40 inches.

Shopping

Once Upon A Time
GIFTS/SOUVENIRS | It's the one shop you don't want to miss on Sunset Boulevard. Vintage-style T-shirts of Mickey, Pluto, Donald, and Grumpy are classy alternatives to standard-issue T's, and a white-sequined Mickey hat adds flair to any outfit. Women's fashion T's and costume bling draw lots of shoppers. Customized watches, like those sold at the Magic Kingdom's Uptown Jewelers, as well as purses and totes are sold here, too. ✉ *Sunset Boulevard, Disney's Hollywood Studios* 🌐 *disneyworld.disney.go.com/shops/hollywood-studios/once-upon-a-time.*

Tower Hotel Gifts
CLOTHING | After the screams and thrills of the Tower of Terror, what could be better than a mug from the hotel bar, the actual bell from the front desk, or a leather key fob from "your" room. In addition to leather handbags and bellboy hats, you can find some rather macabre takes on Disney characters that are exclusive to this shop. ✉ *Sunset Boulevard, Disney's Hollywood Studios* 🌐 *disneyworld.disney.go.com/shops/hollywood-studios/tower-shop.*

Performing Arts

Fantasmic!
AMUSEMENT PARK/WATER PARK | The Studios' after-dark show wows huge audiences with its special effects and Disney characters. The omnipresent Mickey, in his sorcerer's apprentice costume, plays the embodiment of Good in the struggle against forces of Evil, personified by Disney villains such as Cruella DeVil, Scar, and Maleficent. Animated clips of these famous baddies, alternating with clips of Disney sweethearts, are projected onto screens made of water—high-tech fountains surging high in the air. The epic battle plays out amid water effects and flames, explosions, and fireworks worthy of a Hollywood shoot-'em-up. All this, plus the villainous action, is why small kids may find this show frightening.

Arrive early at the Hollywood Hills Amphitheater opposite the Twilight Zone Tower of Terror. Check ahead for information on show days and times. This show often runs twice nightly during peak season; fewer times during nonpeak periods. **For people with disabilities:** Wheelchair and ECV accessible. Equipped with reflective captioning and for assisted-listening, handheld-captioning, and audio-description devices. **TIP→ Fastpass+ seating is available. If you didn't book it, arrive at least an hour early and sit toward the rear, near the entrance/exit. Or consider the lunch or dinner package, which includes a special block of seating for the show. If you sit in front rows, you will get wet.** ✉ *Sunset Boulevard, Disney's Hollywood Studios ☞ Duration: 30 mins. Crowds: Heavy. Audience: Not small kids.*

Animation Courtyard

As you exit Sunset Boulevard, veer right through the high-arched gateway to the Animation Courtyard. Straight ahead are Disney Junior Dance Party!, Star Wars Launch Bay, and Voyage of the Little Mermaid.

Sights

Disney Junior Dance Party!
AMUSEMENT PARK/WATER PARK | **FAMILY** | This is one of Walt Disney World's best shows for tots and preschoolers. DJ Deejay spins familiar Disney Junior tunes while Finn Fiesta acts as host for Doc McStuffins, Timon, and Vampirina. Kids are encouraged to get up and dance along with the characters as they lead the group in popular songs from the

shows. The entire event is capped off with Mickey appearing in his racing gear from *Mickey and the Roadster Racers.*

Throughout the 25-minute show, preschoolers sing and dance along as the characters cha-cha-cha their way through the fun. Special effects help the kids want to get up and dance. **For people with disabilities:** Wheelchair and ECV accessible, equipped with preshow-area TV monitors with closed captioning, and equipped for assisted-listening, audio-description, and video- and handheld-captioning devices. **TIP→ Fastpass+ is offered; or come early, when your child is most alert and lines are shorter. Be prepared to sit on the carpet. Don't miss character meet and greets before or after the show.** ✉ *Animation Courtyard, Disney's Hollywood Studios* ☞ *Duration: 25 mins. Crowds: Moderate. Audience: Young kids.*

Star Wars Launch Bay

AMUSEMENT PARK/WATER PARK | This is the spot to check out costumes, concept art work, replica props, models, and artifacts from the *Star Wars* films on display in several galleries. A 10-minute film runs continuously in the Launch Bay Theater, documenting the creation of *Star Wars* through interviews with the directors, writers, and producers of this wildly popular film series. There's also an area where you can meet and have your photo taken with *Star Wars* characters. ✉ *Animation Courtyard, Disney's Hollywood Studios* ☞ *Duration: Up to you. Crowds: Moderate. Audience: All ages.*

Voyage of the Little Mermaid

AMUSEMENT PARK/WATER PARK | You join Ariel, Sebastian, and the underwater gang in this stage show, which condenses the movie into a marathon presentation of the greatest hits. In an admirable effort at verisimilitude, a fine mist sprays the stage; if you're sitting in the front rows, expect to get spritzed. Although this show is suitable for all ages, smaller children might be frightened by the dark theater and the evil, larger-than-life Ursula. **For people with disabilities:** Wheelchair accessible, has reflective captioning and preshow-area TVs with closed captioning, and equipped for audio-description and assisted-listening devices. **TIP→ If you're not riding Rock 'n' Roller Coaster or Tower of Terror, come while braver members of your party ride. Or wait until the stroller brigade's exodus later in the day.** ✉ *Animation Courtyard, Disney's Hollywood Studios* ☞ *Duration: 17 mins. Crowds: Moderate. Audience: All ages.*

Walt Disney Presents

AMUSEMENT PARK/WATER PARK | A self-guided tour through a treasure trove of Walt Disney memorabilia follows his life from early boyhood, through the founding of his first studio, to Disneyland, and then to Disney World. **For people with disabilities:** Wheelchair and ECV accessible. **TIP→ Come in the afternoon, this attraction is rarely busy.** ✉ *Animation Courtyard, Disney's Hollywood Studios* ☞ *Duration: 15+ mins. Crowds: Light to moderate. Audience: Not young kids.*

Shopping

In Character

TOYS | Little girls love this open-air shop next to the Voyage of the Little Mermaid for the dolls, plush princess toys, and dress-up costumes. You can drop a small bundle on glass (plastic) slippers and a magical light-up wand, or spring for the coveted Ariel mermaid costume gown. ✉ *Animation Courtyard, Disney's Hollywood Studios* 🌐 *disneyworld.disney.go.com/shops/hollywood-studios/in-character-disneys-costume-shop.*

Toy Story Land

Pixar Place leads you to one of the park's most popular attractions, Toy Story Mania! As of June 2018, it also leads to Toy Story Land, where you enter Andy's backyard for adventures with Woody,

Did You Know?

Toy Story Land's Toy Story Mania! combines the fun of a video game with 3-D technology *and* interaction with favorite *Toy Story* characters, like Mr. Potato Head. Man your spring-action shooter and take aim at playful targets along the colorful ride route. Scores are tallied at the end—will yours make you master of the midway?

Buzz, Slinky Dog, Rex, the Aliens, and many other beloved *Toy Story* characters. The land has two other major attractions: a coaster called Slinky Dog Dash and a dizzying ride called Alien Swirling Saucers, which is reminiscent of the Mad Hatter's Teacups at the Magic Kingdom.

Sights

Alien Swirling Saucers
AMUSEMENT PARK/WATER PARK | FAMILY | Based on the toys Andy got from the Pizza Planet claw machine in the first *Toy Story* movie, this ride puts you on a rocket being driven by aliens in flying saucers, who are trying to have their rocket chosen by The Claw. Rather than just spinning, the cars swirl about in figure eight formations, sending passengers back and forth within the car. Kids love the unexpected twist, so consider booking a Fastpass+ and plan on waiting in line! **For people with disabilities:** You must transfer from a wheelchair to ride. ✉ *Toy Story Land, Disney's Hollywood Studios* ☞ *Duration: 2 mins. Crowds: Moderate. Audience: All ages.*

★ **Slinky Dog Dash**
AMUSEMENT PARK/WATER PARK | FAMILY | This family-friendly ride is the centerpiece of Toy Story Land, and is meant to be a roller coaster built by Andy using his Mega Coaster Play Kit. The bright-red track surrounds a primary-color building-block city with towers featuring *Toy Story* icons such as Cowgirl Jessie and Rex the dinosaur. The coaster vehicles are Slinky Dogs, whose slinky springs surround the cars. Watch this ride a couple of times before boarding, it is faster than it looks! Kids who did well on Goofy's Barnstormer at the Magic Kingdom will love this longer coaster. **For people with disabilities:** You must transfer from a wheelchair to ride. ✉ *Toy Story Land, Disney's Hollywood Studios* ☞ *Duration: 2 mins. Crowds: Heavy. Audience: All ages.*

★ **Toy Story Mania!**
AMUSEMENT PARK/WATER PARK | Great toys like Mr. Potato Head, Woody, and Buzz Lightyear from Disney's hit film *Toy Story* never lose their relevance. The action here involves these beloved characters and takes place inside the toy box of Andy, the boy whose toys come to life when he's gone. Step right up and grab a pair of 3-D glasses before boarding your jazzed-up carnival tram. Soon you're whirling onto the midway where you can use your spring-action shooter to launch darts at balloons, toss rings at aliens, and splatter eggs at barnyard targets.

You'll rack up points for targets hit and see your tally at ride's end. Try to hone a rat-a-tat shooting system to increase your score. Don't let Rex's fear of failure slow you down—shoot for the stars, and you'll deserve a salute from the Green Army Men. **For people with disabilities:** Guests using ECVs must transfer to a standard wheelchair. Equipped for video-captioning and audio-description devices. Check with a host about boarding with a service animal. **TIP→ It's so addictive, you might want to come first thing, ride, and get a Fastpass+ for another go.** ✉ *Toy Story Land, Disney's Hollywood Studios* ☞ *Duration: 7 mins. Crowds: Heavy. Audience: All ages.*

Coffee and Quick Bites

Woody's Lunch Box is your spot to grab a quick-service meal. The outdoor stand sells sandwiches (including a delicious brisket melt and an excellent grilled cheese on sourdough). For dessert, you can get a pop-tart inspired chocolate-hazelnut tart.

Grand Avenue

Formerly Streets of America, this area of the park has changed most in the past year, with many of the familiar facades fallen to Toy Story Land and Star Wars. But Miss Piggy, Kermit, and their Muppet pals are still entertaining their fans at the theater on Grand Avenue.

Sights

Muppet*Vision 3-D

AMUSEMENT PARK/WATER PARK | FAMILY | You don't have to be a Miss Piggyphile to get a kick out of this combination 3-D movie and musical revue. All the Muppet characters make appearances, including Miss Piggy in roles that include the Statue of Liberty. In the waiting area, movie posters advertise the world's most glamorous porker in *Star Chores* and *To Have and Have More,* and Kermit the Frog in an Arnold Schwarzenegger parody, *Kürmit the Amphibian,* who's "so mean, he's green." Special effects are built into the walls and ceilings of the theater; the 3-D effects are coordinated with other sensory stimulation. **For people with disabilities:** Wheelchair accessible; has reflective captioning and preshow-area TVs with closed captioning; and equipped for assisted-listening, video-captioning, and audio-description devices. **TIP→ No need for a Fastpass+ for this attraction: continuous shows means a short wait here. And don't worry—there are no bad seats.** ✉ *Grand Avenue, Disney's Hollywood Studios* ☞ *Duration: 25 mins. Crowds: Moderate to heavy. Audience: All ages.*

Restaurants

Baseline Tap House

$$$ | AMERICAN | Part of the new Grand Avenue area of Hollywood Studios, Base Line Tap House (re)creates a downtown Los Angeles corner pub, serving California wines and craft beers. Charcuterie boards featuring California cheeses and Bavarian pretzels with fondue are snackable highlights. **Known for:** urban Los Angeles feel; casual snacks; California beers, ciders, and wines. $ *Average main: $25* ✉ *Grand Avenue, Disney's Hollywood Studios* ☎ *407/939–3463* 🌐 *disneyworld.disney.go.com/dining/hollywood-studios/baseline-tap-house.*

Mama Melrose's Ristorante Italiano

$$$ | ITALIAN | FAMILY | To replace the energy you've no doubt depleted by miles of theme-park walking, you can load up on carbs at this casual Italian restaurant that looks like a classic San Francisco Italian eatery. Good main courses include spaghetti with meatballs, and wood-grilled chicken in a four-cheese sauce with pasta and vegetables. Wood-fired flatbreads are available as an entrée choice here and are a great bargain, with toppings ranging from pepperoni to house-made sausage to wild mushrooms. The sangria is popular. Ask for the Fantasmic! dinner package if you want priority seating for the show. **Known for:** old-fashioned-Italian-restaurant atmosphere; Fantasmic! dining package; authentic San Francisco seafood cioppino. $ *Average main: $25* ✉ *Grand Avenue, Disney's Hollywood Studios* ☎ *407/939–3463* 🌐 *disneyworld.disney.go.com/dining/hollywood-studios/mama-melrose-ristorante-italiano.*

Sci-Fi Dine-In Theater Restaurant

$$$ | AMERICAN | FAMILY | If you don't mind zombies leering at you while you eat, then head to this enclosed faux drive-in, where you can eat in a booth that looks like a candy-color 1950s convertible while watching clips from classics like *Attack of the Fifty-Foot Woman* and *Teenagers from Outer Space.* The menu includes choices like steak and roasted potatoes, an Angus or veggie burger, shrimp with whole-grain pasta, and a huge cheese steak sandwich; end with a hot-fudge sundae. **Known for:** menu of American classics like cheese steak sandwich; specialty chef burgers; wine, sangria, and fun cocktails. $ *Average main: $25* ✉ *Commissary Lane, Disney's Hollywood Studios* ☎ *407/939–3463* 🌐 *disneyworld.disney.go.com/dining/hollywood-studios/sci-fi-dine-in-theater.*

Echo Lake

In the center of an idealized slice of Southern California is a cool, blue lake—an oasis fringed with trees, benches, and things like pink-and-aqua, chrome-trimmed restaurants with sassy waitresses and tableside black-and-white TVs. In addition to the shipshape Min & Bill's Dockside Diner, there's Tatooine Traders, where kids can build their own lightsabers and browse a trove of *Star Wars*–inspired goods. You'll also find two of the park's longest-running attractions, the Indiana Jones Epic Stunt Spectacular! and Star Tours—The Adventures Continue, where a 3-D attraction transformation jazzes up the galaxy.

Sights

For the First Time in Forever: A "Frozen" Sing-Along Celebration
AMUSEMENT PARK/WATER PARK | Ever since the Disney film *Frozen* hit the jackpot, Disney's theme parks have been mining the blockbuster with character meet and greets, entertainment vignettes, a ride, and a half-hour show that's packing the house up to 10 times a day. The comical emcees are two costumed "Royal Historians" of Arendelle, who pepper the 30-minute show with witticisms as they narrate the *Frozen* story. Animated segments of the film accompany the narration on a giant screen as the story unfolds and the audience sings along to the film's playlist. Live actors portray Anna, Elsa, and Kristoff convincingly as they interact with the "historians" and audience, which rocks the Academy Award–winning "Let It Go" most enthusiastically and can't resist the sweetly melodic "Do You Want to Build a Snowman?" Song lyrics, including those for Olaf's whimsical anthem, "In Summer," as well as "For the First Time in Forever" and "Love Is an Open Door," are displayed for the audience on two additional video screens. **For people with disabilities**: Wheelchair accessible. **■ TIP→ Fastpass+ is available but rarely needed as the Itheater is so large.** ✉ *Echo Lake, Disney's Hollywood Studios* ☞ *Duration: 30 mins. Crowds: Moderate. Audience: All ages.*

★ **Indiana Jones Epic Stunt Spectacular!**
AMUSEMENT PARK/WATER PARK | The rousing theme music from the *Indiana Jones* movies heralds action delivered by veteran stunt coordinator Glenn Randall, whose credits include *Raiders of the Lost Ark*, *E.T.*, and *Jewel of the Nile*. Presented in a 2,200-seat amphitheater, the show starts with a series of near-death encounters in an ancient Mayan temple. Indy slides down a rope from the ceiling, dodges spears, avoids getting chopped by booby-trapped idols, and snags a forbidden gemstone, setting off a gigantic boulder that threatens to flatten him.

Next comes the Cairo street scene, circa 1940, where lucky audience members are chosen to perform as extras. When the nasty Ninja-Nazi stuntmen come out, you start to think that it's probably better to be in the audience.

Eventually Indy returns with his redoubtable girlfriend, Marian Ravenwood, portrayed by a Karen Allen look-alike. She's kidnapped and tossed into a truck while Indy fights his way free with bullwhip and gun, and bad guys tumble from every corner and cornice.

The actors do a commendable job of explaining their stunts, and you'll learn how cameras are camouflaged for trick shots. Only one stunt remains a secret: how do Indy and Marian escape the grand finale explosion? That's what keeps 'em coming back. **For people with disabilities:** Wheelchair accessible. Equipped for assisted-listening, audio-description, and handheld-captioning devices. There's sign language interpretation twice weekly.
Be aware that there are constant rumors that this show will be updated, or possibly removed, to keep with Disney's new "immersive" theme. **■ TIP→ Don't waste**

your Fastpass+ here; there's plenty of room. Come at night to see the idols' eyes glow. ✉ *Echo Lake, Disney's Hollywood Studios* ☞ *Duration: 30 mins. Crowds: Moderate. Audience: All but very young kids.*

★ **Star Tours: The Adventures Continue**
AMUSEMENT PARK/WATER PARK | *Star Wars* fans, wield those lightsabers! This fan favorite multiplies the thrills with more than 50 ride scenarios powered up by Dolby 3-D video combined with motion-simulator technology. Here's the basic storyline: C-3PO and R2-D2, at the helm of a misappropriated spaceship, must navigate the galaxy with a rebel spy on board (it could be you!) while Imperial forces try to thwart the journey.

Each ride is different: you'll encounter multiple thrills from the *Star Wars* universe including the lush Wookiee planet Kashyyyk and the underwater world of Naboo. Recently, Kef Bir, the water moon with a destroyed Death Star, has been added to the line-up. One flight takes you to the climatic battle from *The Rise of Skywalker*. You might come face-to-menacing-mask with Kylo Ren or be recruited by Lando Calrissian. Other characters sprinkled throughout the different films include Admiral Ackbar, Chewbacca, and Boba Fett. Your 40-passenger Starspeeder 1000 rockets through space with enough high-speed twists, turns, and nosedives to guarantee that the Force is, indeed, with you.

Those who are pregnant or have heart, back, neck, or motion-sickness issues shouldn't ride. Children less than 40 inches tall may not ride. **For people with disabilities:** Guests using wheelchairs must transfer to a ride seat. Equipped for handheld-captioning and video-captioning devices. Service animals aren't allowed. **TIP→ Lines swell when the Indiana Jones show lets out. Use a Fastpass+, or visit early or late. For the wildest ride, sit in the back.** ✉ *Echo Lake, Disney's Hollywood Studios* ☞ *Duration: 6 mins. Crowds: Heavy. Audience: All but young kids.*

Restaurants

50's Prime Time Café
$$ | **AMERICAN** | **FAMILY** | If you grew up in middle America in the 1950s—or if you're just a fan of classic TV shows like *I Love Lucy* and *The Donna Reed Show*—you'll appreciate the vintage atmosphere and all-American classic menu at this diner-style restaurant. Clips of old TV shows will welcome you as you feast on meat loaf, pot roast, or fried chicken, all served on a Formica tabletop. The meat loaf is one of the best inexpensive, filling dinners in any local theme park. Enjoy it with a malted-milk shake or root-beer float (or a bottle of wine or cocktail from the Tune-In Lounge next door). The place offers some fancier dishes, like grilled salmon with maple bourbon butter sauce, which is a good choice for lighter eaters. If you're not feeling totally wholesome, go for Dad's Electric Lemonade (rum, vodka, blue curaçao, sweet-and-sour mix, and Sprite). Just like Mother, the menu admonishes, "Keep your elbows off the table." **Known for:** showing clips of classic TV shows during dinner; "Mom" wandering around tables telling kids to eat their veggies; golden-fried chicken, pot roast, and meat loaf sampler. $ *Average main: $18* ✉ *Echo Lake, Disney's Hollywood Studios* ☎ *407/939–3463* 🌐 *disneyworld.disney.go.com/dining/hollywood-studios/50s-prime-time-cafe.*

Hollywood & Vine
$$$$ | **AMERICAN** | **FAMILY** | Disney Channel stars come to life at this restaurant through its Disney Junior Play 'n Dine meals for breakfast and lunch. Vampirina, along with friends of *Sofia the First* and *Doc McStuffins*, are among the cheerful characters marching around the room, singing and dancing to the delight of energetic fans. This is a great choice for toddlers. At night, the buffet format transforms into a more upscale all-you-can-eat affair with cooking stations and buffet. **Known for:** character breakfasts; meat, shrimp, and salad

Hollywood Studios Kids Tour

Young children always get a kick out of Hollywood Boulevard's wacky street performers and the park's energetic stage shows.

The minute you enter, head straight to Toy Story Mania! and get in line (unless you made a Fastpass+ reservation). Everyone loves this busy ride—even young children who have to learn how to operate their spring-action shooters to rack up midway points. If you can ride *and* come back for your Fastpass+ reservation, you'll be your kids' hero. Then head deeper into Toy Story Land for Alien Swirling Saucers or Slinky Dog Dash for the brave at heart.

Combine lunch with more playtime at the Disney Junior Play 'n Dine at Hollywood & Vine family buffet, where characters from Disney Junior Dance Party! mix and mingle with the children. Don't forget your camera and the kids' autograph books!

See the Characters Come to Life

Shows and attractions based on Disney films and TV series really grab young children. Check your *Times Guide* for performances of Beauty and the Beast: Live on Stage and Disney Junior Dance Party! After tots and preschoolers have danced along at the Disney Junior show, they can meet the characters in the Animation Courtyard, then catch a Beauty and the Beast performance or watch Ariel "under the sea" in Voyage of the Little Mermaid.

Check other character greeting locations and times—the Green Army Men from *Toy Story* put the kids through their marching paces on Pixar Place, Mickey and Minnie Mouse can be found along Commissary Lane, and The Incredibles pose for photos at the end of Pixar Place. Make time to catch Lightning McQueen at Lightning McQueen's Racing Academy. Then watch Kermit display his wry wit and Miss Piggy steal the show at Muppet*Vision 3-D. It's not easy being green. ...

Grab the Spotlight

Jedi wannabes can suit up to clash with the dark side at Jedi Training: Trials of the Temple, which is scheduled throughout the day. As soon as you enter, head toward 50's Prime Time so children ages 4–12 can sign up early in the day for a chance to grab a lightsaber and let the Force be with them. During each 20-minute show, crowds gather and cheer the kids as they learn to "cut to the left shoulder, step back, and duck!" when clashing with a costumed Darth Vader. Needless to say, the dark side can't compete.

buffets; VIP dining package for Fantasmic! nighttime show. $ *Average main: $54* ✉ *Echo Lake, Disney's Hollywood Studios* ☎ *407/939–3463* 🌐 *disneyworld.disney.go.com/dining/hollywood-studios/hollywood-and-vine.*

Two hyperpopular movie franchises—*Star Wars* and *Indiana Jones*—command attention in this section of the studios.

Hollywood Studios Grown-Up Tour

At the Studios, the best of Disney animation—from *Toy Story* to *Beauty and the Beast*—is reborn as park attractions. The old small-screen favorite *The Twilight Zone* is taken to new heights, and Indiana Jones performs action-packed stunts to bring famous film moments to life.

Find Your Adrenaline Rush

Two words—thrills and chills—define the top two attractions for older kids and adults. Head straight to Sunset Boulevard and grab the thrills at Rock 'n' Roller Coaster Starring Aerosmith, where multiple inversions, twists, and turns rock to the tune of "Dude (Looks Like a Lady)." Feel the chills at the Twilight Zone Tower of Terror, when something goes terribly wrong with your elevator car, and it veers off its ghostly course.

A quick walk to Echo Lake lands you in Wookiee territory, where you can climb aboard the Star Tours flight simulator for a wild flight themed to the latest *Star Wars* movies; 3-D upgrades and more than 50 different ride scenarios increase the thrill factor.

Discover A New World

In the morning, make sure to set up a boarding pass for Star Wars: Rise of the Resistance and a Fastpass+ for Millennium Falcon: Smugglers Run. Leave plenty of time to take in the sights and sounds of Batuu!

Tastes of the Past

Refuel at one of the park's many quick-service stands, let "Mom" serve you meat loaf and a peanut butter–and-jelly shake at the 50s Prime Time Café, or boost your image with a plush booth and a Cobb salad at the Hollywood Brown Derby.

Back at Echo Lake, the Tune-In Lounge is a great place to grab a mojito or margarita before heading to the nighttime extravaganza Fantasmic! That's a wrap.

Indiana Jones Adventure Outpost

TOYS | Almost as popular as the pirate hats in the Magic Kingdom are the Indiana Jones felt fedoras sold at this outpost near the stunt amphitheater. Small kids can get a complete Indy play set with fedora, machete, pistol, and gems for about $20. You can also find crystal skulls, plush exotic animals, polished rocks, and Raiders of the Lost Ark action figures. ✉ *Echo Lake, Disney's Hollywood Studios* 🌐 *disneyworld.disney.go.com/shops/hollywood-studios.*

Tatooine Traders

TOYS | The *Star Wars* theme is strong in this desert dome shop outside the Star Tours ride. Guests of all ages can build their own single or double lightsabers complete with crystals, hilts, and blades. And what's a lightsaber without a droid to share it with? So build a droid as well. Collectible pins, books, action figures, art, clothing, and Vinylmation characters are also popular here. **TIP→ Don't feel up to the long line and price of building a lightsaber in Galaxy's Edge? The lightsabers here might not be as intricate, but will still please younglings and their parent's wallet.** ✉ *Echo Lake, Disney's Hollywood Studios* 🌐 *disneyworld.disney.go.com/shops/hollywood-studios/tatooine-traders.*

Star Wars: Galaxy's Edge

A gray, unmarked subway entrance gives way to otherworldly slabs of concrete and rock formations. Emerging from the tunnel, you find you've entered Batuu, a special planet from the *Star Wars* universe, created just for the Disney theme parks. Everywhere you look, you'll see tiny details, from the droid prints in the concrete to signs written in Aurebesh, the language of Batuu (if you want to know what the signs say, there is a translator within the Disney Play app). Parked X-wings and droids provide atmosphere as you walk deeper and deeper into this fully immersive world. The area's two rides, Millennium Falcon: Smuggler's Run and Star Wars: Rise of the Resistance are both popular and spectacular attractions, but make sure to take time to walk through the marketplace, visit Og's Cantina, and build your own droid at the Droid Depot. This land is so popular that even shops and restaurants can draw lines, so head here first thing in the morning once you've entered Hollywood Studios.

Sights

★ **Millennium Falcon: Smuggler's Run**
AMUSEMENT PARK/WATER PARK | *Star Wars* fans will love being able to actually pilot the Millennium Falcon on a supply run. Hondo Ohnaka, who fans will recognize from *Star Wars: The Clone Wars,* has hired you to fetch "precious cargo" that will bring him big profits and help the Resistance by providing much-needed supplies. Chewie has offered use of the Millennium Falcon, but it will take a team of six to complete the mission. Groups are split into two pilots, who drive the Falcon; two gunners, who defend the Falcon; and two engineers, who rope in the cargo. The effects, first with the Audio-Animatronic Hondo Ohnaka, and then walking through the ship itself, are incredible. Make sure to take a moment to capture a picture at the legendary Dejarik (chess) table.

Once onboard, your crew must work together to retrieve the cargo and bring the Millennium Falcon back with minimal damage. At the end of your mission, Hondo tallies up how you did, minus repairs to the Falcon and his profit, of course. This means most guests will want to ride again to improve their score! **TIP→ Make sure to book a Fastpass+ as early as possible for this ride, and then plan to wait to ride again.** ✉ *Star Wars: Galaxy's Edge, Disney's Hollywood Studios* ☞ *Duration: 4½ mins. Crowds: Heavy. Audience: All ages.*

★ **Star Wars: Rise of the Resistance**
AMUSEMENT PARKS | The crowning jewel of Galaxy's Edge, Rise of the Resistance is more experience than ride. You, along with other residents of Batuu, are led to a briefing room to join Rey and the rest of the Resistance off-planet. A holographic transmission, just like in the movies, appears before your group to explain that you'll be lead by Lieutenant Bek to a rendezvous point with General Leia Organa. You'll then board a transport, walking outside past Poe Dameron's X-wing, all the while being rushed along by Resistance fighters. Aboard the transport, similar to a subway car, Lieutenant Bek flies you to outer space while Poe provides cover. But—surprise—the First Order is waiting for you! General Hux catches you in the tractor beam and pulls you into the hanger bay of his Star Destroyer.

Upon exiting, you'll be inside the hanger bay, with First Order officers barking commands at you while you file past impressive rows of stormtroopers. You're broken into groups to be placed in containment cells, where first General Hux and then Kylo Ren show up to convince you to turn over the location of the rebel base you were heading to. When he's called away, you're rescued by the Resistance, led by Finn, and placed onto First Order Fleet Transports, each piloted by a reprogrammed droid. Kylo Ren isn't going to give up easily, though, and you're chased throughout the Star Destroyer, passing under AT-AT walkers, past turbo-laser cannons and coming face to face with Kylo. Don't worry, you'll end up safely back on Batuu, but be prepared for a truly thrilling adventure.

This multipart experience is so popular that currently Disney has guests sign up for "boarding groups" through the My Disney Experience app upon entering the park. Guests arrive at Rise of the Resistance within a two-hour window to board the ride. Check while planning your trip to see if Fastpass+ is offered, or if you will need to arrive at park opening to grab a spot. Also note that though the ride itself is 18 minutes, the entire experience can be longer. Many of the effects can be jarring, and cast members acting as the First Order can be intense. Make sure to reassure younger riders that you're on a make-believe mission.

For people with disabilities: Guests in an ECV or wheelchair must be able to transfer. ✉ *Star Wars: Galaxy's Edge, Disney's Hollywood Studios* ☞ *Duration: 18 mins. Crowds: Heavy. Audience: All ages. Height requirement: 40 inches.*

Restaurants

Docking Bay 7 Food and Cargo

$$ | **AMERICAN** | Plan to eat in this hanger-bay turned quick-service restaurant by Chef Strono "Cookie" Tuggs, for an out-of-this world meal. Try the braised beef pot roast with cavatelli pasta or the fried chicken tip yip with roasted vegetables. Those with egg or gluten allergies will find multiple options here that they'll enjoy. If the line looks over-whelming, order online with the My Disney Experience app. **Known for:** vegetarian hummus spread on pita; gluten-free options; authentic Star Wars atmosphere. $ *Average main: $16* ✉ *Star Wars: Galaxy's Edge, Disney's Hollywood Studios* 🌐 *disneyworld.disney.go.com/dining/hollywood-studios/docking-bay-7-food-and-cargo.*

Ronto's Roasters

$$ | **AMERICAN** | If you're looking for a quick meal in Galaxy's Edge, this the place to go. Among the meats that have been "roasted over a pod racer engine," you'll find turkey jerky, roasted pork, and marinated chicken. Groups who just want a small bite should consider the snack sampler in a droid bucket. **Known for:** turkey jerky; specialty beverages; quick meal. $ *Average main: $15* ✉ *Star Wars: Galaxy's Edge, Disney's Hollywood Studios* 🌐 *disneyworld.disney.go.com/dining/hollywood-studios/ronto-roasters.*

Coffee and Quick Bites

Everyone will want to stop by the **Milk Stand** near **Millennium Falcon: Smuggler's Run** to grab their own glass of blue milk, Luke Skywalker's favorite drink. And who knew: green milk is available, too! Both drinks are made with coconut and rice milk, mixed with different fruits. You'll also find *Star Wars*–themed, globe-shape Coke bottles at stands throughout this section of the park, but beware: unless you want this for its noteworthy souvenir value, you'll be paying $6 for a tiny drink.

Shopping

Whether you choose to build a droid (starting at $99.99) or a lightsaber (starting at $199), Star Wars: Galaxy's Edge gives you plenty of opportunities to part with your money. MultipleBlack Spire Outpost shops offer Batuu-theme gifts, and keep an eye out for a stall of stuffed *Star Wars* creatures to call your own. And while Resistance paraphernalia is "hidden" at stalls along the streets, those looking to join the dark side can visit the First Order Cargo for their gear.

Black Spire Outfitters

CLOTHING | If you're visiting Galaxy's Edge to get in character, stop by Black Spire Outfitters for the perfect costume. Here you'll find everything from blaster belts to full Jedi robes. How "in character" you go is up to you. Many of the shirts are stylish on their own, and who doesn't need a good cloak when visiting the cliffs of Ahch-To? ✉ *Star Wars: Galaxy's Edge, Disney's Hollywood Studios* 🌐 *disneyworld.disney.go.com/shops/hollywood-studios/black-spire-outfitters.*

Droid Depot

TOYS | Here you can build your very own droid, on a miniature scale at least. Upon arriving, choose between a BB-series (like BB-8) or R-series (like R2-D2), then select your own color scheme and accessories. Once built, droids can communicate with one another using Bluetooth technology, or be driven by their owners with a remote control. Droids are not cheap, and reservations can be made up to 180 days before you visit on the My Disney Experience app. Without a reservation, expect to wait just to enter the store. ✉ *Star Wars: Galaxy's Edge, Disney's Hollywood Studios* 🌐 *disneyworld.disney.go.com/shops/hollywood-studios/droid-depot.*

Savi's Workshop–Handbuilt Lightsabers

TOYS | If you're an aspiring Jedi, plan a trip to Savi's Workshop to build a lightsaber. More intense than just a toy from the store, this lightsaber allows its wielder to choose different themes and kyber crystals, creating a truly unique design. Reservations are highly recommended and can be made 180 days out on the My Disney Experience app. ✉ *Star Wars: Galaxy's Edge, Disney's Hollywood Studios* 🌐 *disneyworld.disney.go.com/shops/hollywood-studios/savis-workshop-handbuilt-lightsabers.*

Blizzard Beach

With its oxymoronic name, Blizzard Beach promises the seemingly impossible—a seaside playground with an alpine theme. As with its older cousin, Typhoon Lagoon, Disney Imagineers have created a legend to explain the park's origin.

The story goes that after a freak winter storm dropped snow over the western side of Walt Disney World, entrepreneurs created Florida's first downhill ski resort. Saunalike temperatures soon returned. But as the 66-acre resort's operators were ready to close up shop, they spotted a playful alligator sliding down the 120-foot-tall "liquid ice" slopes. The realization that the melting snow had created the world's tallest, fastest, and most exhilarating water-filled ski and toboggan runs gave birth to the ski resort–water park.

From its imposing ski-jump tower to its 1,200-foot series of rushing waterfalls, Blizzard Beach delivers cool fun even in the hot summertime. Where else can you wear your swimsuit on the slopes?

GETTING ORIENTED

The park layout makes it fairly simple to navigate. Once you enter and rent a locker, you'll cross a small bridge over Cross Country Creek before choosing a spot to park your towels and cooler. To the left is the Melt-Away Bay wave pool. Dead ahead you can see Mt. Gushmore, a chairlift to the top, and the park's many slopes and slides.

If thrills are your game, come early and line up for Summit Plummet, Slush Gusher, and Downhill Double Dipper before wait times go from light to moderate (or heavy). Anytime is a good time for a dip in Melt-Away Bay or a tube trip around Cross Country Creek. Parents with young children should claim their spot early at Tike's Peak, to the park's right even before you cross the bridge.

Blizzard Beach's Toboggan Racers accommodates eight sliders at a time, who get to race 250 feet to the bottom of Mt. Gushmore.

You can take Disney bus transportation or drive to Blizzard Beach. There's no charge for parking. Once inside, your options are to walk, swim, or slide.

WHAT TO EXPECT

Disney Imagineers have gone all out here to create the paradox of a ski resort in the midst of a tropical lagoon. Lots of verbal puns and sight gags play with the snow-in-Florida motif. The centerpiece is Mt. Gushmore, with its 120-foot-high Summit Plummet. Attractions have names like Teamboat Springs, a white-water raft ride. Themed speed slides include Toboggan Racers, Slush Gusher, and Snow Stormers. Between Mt. Gushmore's base and its summit, swim-skiers can also ride a chairlift converted from ski-resort to beach-resort use—with multihue umbrellas and snow skis on their undersides. Older kids and devoted waterslide enthusiasts generally prefer Blizzard Beach to other water parks.

PARKS AMENITIES

Dining: You can't bring oversize coolers, glass containers, or your own alcoholic beverages into the park. Picnicking is welcome, however, and there are several pleasant pavilions and other spots, most notably the terrace outside Lottawatta Lodge. This is also where you can reserve your own lodge umbrella ($40–$60 for a day), which includes chairs (two of them loungers), an umbrella and small table, and four beach towels. Arrive early enough, and you'll snag your ideal spot in the park for free. You can get burgers, hot dogs, and salads at Lottawatta Lodge or other eateries and food stands. You could go for the usual snacks—snowballs or ice cream. But a truly sublime nibble is the melt-in-your-mouth mini-doughnut from the Mini Donuts stand across from Lottawatta Lodge.

Dressing Rooms and Lockers: Dressing rooms, showers, and restrooms are in the village area, just inside the main entrance. There are other restrooms in Lottawatta Lodge, at the Ski Patrol

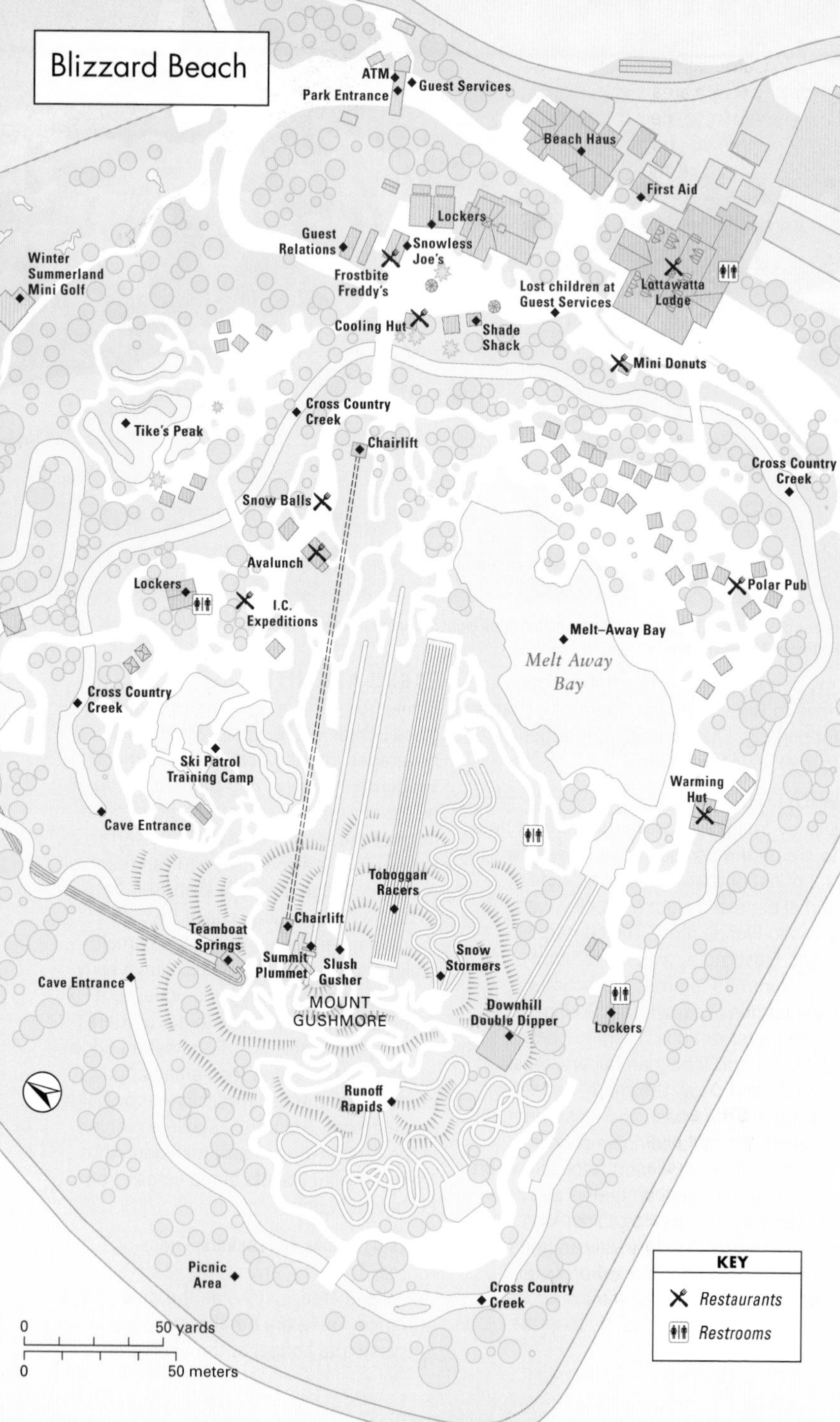
Blizzard Beach
ATM
Guest Services
Park Entrance
Beach Haus
First Aid
Lockers
Guest Relations
Snowless Joe's
Frostbite Freddy's
Winter Summerland Mini Golf
Lost children at Guest Services
Lottawatta Lodge
Cooling Hut
Shade Shack
Mini Donuts
Cross Country Creek
Tike's Peak
Chairlift
Cross Country Creek
Snow Balls
Avalunch
Polar Pub
Lockers
I.C. Expeditions
Melt–Away Bay
Melt Away Bay
Cross Country Creek
Ski Patrol Training Camp
Warming Hut
Cave Entrance
Toboggan Racers
Chairlift
Teamboat Springs
Summit Plummet
Slush Gusher
Snow Stormers
Cave Entrance
MOUNT GUSHMORE
Downhill Double Dipper
Lockers
Runoff Rapids
Picnic Area
Cross Country Creek
KEY
Restaurants
Restrooms
0
50 yards
0
50 meters

Training Camp, and just past the Melt-Away Bay beach area. Lockers are near the entrance, next to Snowless Joe's Rentals, and near Tike's Peak (the children's area and the most convenient if you have little swim-skiers in tow). It costs $8 to rent a small locker and $10 for a large one, and there's a $5 deposit. Note that there are only small lockers at Tike's Peak. The towels for rent ($2) at Snowless Joe's are tiny. If you forgot yours, you're better off buying a proper one at the Beach Haus.

First Aid: The first-aid stand, overseen by a registered nurse, is in the village, between Lottawatta Lodge and the Beach Haus.

Guest Services: Disney staffers at Blizzard Beach's Guest Services window, to the left of the ticket booth as you enter the park, can answer most of your questions. Get free life vests or rent towels and lockers at **Snowless Joe's.** Inner tubes, rafts, and slide mats are provided at the rides. Buy beach gear or rent towels or lockers at **Beach Haus. Shade Shack** is the place for a new pair of sunglasses.

Lost People and Things: Instruct youngsters to let a lifeguard know if they get lost. The lost-children station is beneath a large beach umbrella near the front of the park. And don't worry about the kids—a Disney cast member will keep them busy with activities.

Private Patios: The park has 14 Polar Patios to rent to groups of as many as six people. For $325 a day in peak season (usually March through late August) and between $160 and $240 at other times of the year, you get plush loungers, chairs, a table with umbrella, refillable beverage mugs, an ice chest with two water bottles per person, a group locker, and an attendant who will take your orders for and deliver lunch and snacks (food costs extra). It's best to book a patio far ahead of time (*407/939–8687*). If you arrive early enough, though, there might be an open patio; check at the Shade Shack.

SERVICES FOR PEOPLE WITH DISABILITIES

Most of Blizzard Beach's paths are flat and level. If you can transfer from your chair a short distance, you can also access all the waterslides except Summit Plummet. Or settle into a large inner tube and float in Cross Country Creek.

A limited number of wheelchairs—some suitable for the water—are available near the park entrance and are free if you leave an ID.

Sights

Chairlift

AMUSEMENT PARK/WATER PARK | No subtropical skiing paradise would be complete without a chairlift, and this one is an attractive alternative to trekking to the top of Mt. Gushmore over and over again. The two-minute chairlift ascent is a great opportunity to scout out other slides and to enjoy the "ski beach" scenery. **For people with disabilities:** Guests using wheelchairs must transfer to a ride seat and subsequent attractions. A companion will have to meet you with the wheelchair at the base of Mt. Gushmore. **TIP→ If the wait is too long or you have children under 32 inches tall, hiking up is good exercise.** ✉ *Blizzard Beach* ☞ *Duration: 2 mins. Crowds: Light to moderate. Audience: Not young kids. Height requirement: 32 inches.*

Cross Country Creek

AMUSEMENT PARK/WATER PARK | Just grab an inner tube, hop on, and circle the entire park during a leisurely 25-minute float on this 3,000-foot-long creek. Along the way, you'll get doused with frigid water in an ice cave—wonderful on a steamy Florida day. Tubes are provided at seven launch sites, but they're not required. Kids soon discover that the fastest and most enjoyable way to get around the park is to glide with the current and hop off at whichever landing they wish. **For people with disabilities:** Guests using wheelchairs must transfer to inner tubes. ■ TIP→ **There are landings near most thrill rides, and moving through the park this way is oodles more fun than walking.** ✉ *Blizzard Beach* ☞ *Duration: 25 mins. Crowds: Vary by season. Audience: All ages.*

★ Downhill Double Dipper

AMUSEMENT PARK/WATER PARK | If you're on your way to Snow Stormers or Toboggan Racers on the purple slopes, you might notice a cool-looking slide on the left. This is the Downhill Double Dipper, and it's well worth the stop. The best thing about this slide is that you are timed from blastoff to finish line! Competition can get heated as kids (48 inches or taller) vie for the glory of fastest speed slider, but even the least competitive will enjoy tearing down Mt. Gushmore in their racing tubes. Expectant mothers shouldn't ride, nor should guests with heart conditions or neck or back problems. **For people with disabilities:** Guests using wheelchairs must transfer to the tube-launch site. ■ TIP→ **Ride early; this popular purple-slope attraction gets crowded after lunch.** ✉ *Blizzard Beach* ☞ *Duration: Under 10 secs. Crowds: Heavy. Audience: Not young kids. Height requirement: 48 inches.*

Melt-Away Bay

AMUSEMENT PARK/WATER PARK | The park's main pool is a 1-acre oasis that's constantly fed by "melting snow" waterfalls. The man-made waves are positively oceanlike. If you're not a strong swimmer, stay away from the far end of the pool, where the waves originate. You can get temporarily stuck in a pocket even if your head is still above water. If you prefer to stay beached, there are plenty of recliner chairs spread out around the bay. This is where moms and dads often relax and watch their kids swim in the lifeguard-protected waters. **For people with disabilities:** Guests using water-appropriate wheelchairs can enjoy shallow waters here. ■ TIP→ **Get an inner tube if you plan to venture to deeper waters, and arrive early if you want to find a shady spot (there are limited giant umbrellas).** ✉ *Blizzard Beach* ☞ *Duration: Up to you. Crowds: Vary by season. Audience: All ages.*

Runoff Rapids

AMUSEMENT PARK/WATER PARK | It's easy to overlook this three-track flume ride hidden on the far red slope of Mt. Gushmore. Yet if you have the courage to carry your tube all the way up to the top, you'll eventually come upon three twisting, turning, 600-foot-long flumes—even one that's in the dark (keep in mind the tunnel slide is for single riders only, while the open slides are for one- or two-passenger tubes). Once you're in, it's way more fun than scary. Still, guests who are pregnant or who have heart, neck, or back problems should skip it. **For people with disabilities:** Guests using wheelchairs must transfer to inner tubes. ■ TIP→ **It's worth riding both an open slide and the tunnel slide, but remember that the tunnel slide is only for single riders.** ✉ *Blizzard Beach* ☞ *Duration: 35 secs. Crowds: Light to moderate. Audience: Not young kids.*

Ski Patrol Training Camp

AMUSEMENT PARK/WATER PARK | Preteens might want to spend most of their time on the T-bar drop, Cool Runners slides, and Snow Falls downhill body slide. In addition, there's a chance to take on the Thin Ice Training Course, a wide-open area where kids can jump from one slippery mogul to the next. The moguls really look more like bobbing baby icebergs, and kids don't mind when they miss a berg and plop into the pool. **For people with disabilities:** Guests using water-appropriate wheelchairs can enjoy wading areas here. ■ TIP→ **The optimum time to come is early in the day or after a thunderstorm, when crowds thin out. That said, lines are often short at the zipline drop and the iceberg obstacle course.** ✉ *Blizzard Beach* ☞ *Duration: Up to you. Crowds: Light to moderate. Audience: Tweens.*

★ Slush Gusher

AMUSEMENT PARK/WATER PARK | This speed slide, which drops through a snow-banked mountain gully next door to Summit Plummet on the green slopes, isn't quite as intimidating, but it's a real thriller nonetheless. Instead of one scream-inducing steep drop, the Slush Gusher features a fast, hilly descent to the base of Mt. Gushmore. Although the Slush Gusher will not disappoint thrill seekers, it is perfect for those who want some adventure but tremble at the sight of Summit Plummet. For guests who are pregnant or who have heart, back, or neck problems, this ride is not recommended. **For people with disabilities:** Guests using wheelchairs must transfer to the slide. ■ TIP→ **The earlier you ride, the better. On crowded days waits can last up to 90 minutes.** ✉ *Blizzard Beach* ☞ *Duration: 15 secs. Crowds: You bet! Audience: Not young kids. Height requirement: 48 inches.*

Snow Stormers

AMUSEMENT PARK/WATER PARK | No water park would be complete without a meandering waterslide, and Blizzard Beach has one. Here three flumes, each 350 feet long, descend from the top of Mt. Gushmore along a switchback course of ski-type slalom gates on the purple slopes. Snow Stormers offers an exciting change of pace from the straight-down slides of the green slopes, and riders are in for a grand total of eight hairpin turns before finally splashing into the pool at the bottom. This ride isn't appropriate for guests who are pregnant or who have heart, neck, or back problems. **For people with disabilities:** Guests using wheelchairs must transfer to a toboggan-style slide mat with handles. ■ TIP→ **This is a belly-down ride. Hold on tight!** ✉ *Blizzard Beach* ☞ *Duration: 20 secs. Crowds: Moderate to heavy. Audience: All Ages.*

★ Summit Plummet

AMUSEMENT PARK/WATER PARK | This is Mt. Gushmore's big gun, one of the world's tallest, fastest free-fall speed slides. From Summit Plummet's "ski jump" tower at the very top of the green slopes, it's a wild, 55-mph, 12-story plunge straight down, then into a tunnel before a white-water splash landing at the end of the 360-foot-long run. It looks almost like a straight vertical drop, and you can't help but feel like a movie stunt double as you take the plunge. If you're watching from the beach below, you can't hear the yells of the participants, but you can bet many of them are screaming their heads off. The ride is not for guests who are pregnant or who have heart, back, or neck problems. ■ TIP→ **Make this one of your first stops. The line will only get longer as the day goes on. (Summer afternoon waits can be up to two hours.)** ✉ *Blizzard Beach* ☞ *Duration: 10 crazy secs. Crowds: Absolutely. Audience: Not young kids. Height requirement: 48 inches.*

Teamboat Springs

AMUSEMENT PARK/WATER PARK | Six-passenger rafts zip along green slopes in one of the world's longest family whitewater raft rides. Since its original construction, it has doubled its speed of departure onto its twisting, 1,200-foot channel of rushing water, which ends with a refreshing waterfall dousing. This ride is a good place for kids too big for Tike's Peak to test more grown-up waters. Those who are pregnant or have heart, neck, or back problems should avoid this one. **For people with disabilities:** Guests using wheelchairs must transfer to the ride. ■ TIP→ **This is an excellent ride for the whole family: there are no age or height requirements (other than "No Infants"), tubes seat four to six people, and lines generally move quickly.** ✉ *Blizzard Beach* ☞ *Duration: 1½ mins. Crowds: Moderate. Audience: Families.*

★ Tike's Peak
AMUSEMENT PARK/WATER PARK | Disney never leaves the little ones out of the fun, and this junior-size version of Blizzard Beach, set slightly apart from the rest of the park, has scaled-down elements of Mt. Gushmore, with sand, slides (including one with tubes), faux snow drifts, and igloolike tunnels. Parents can find sun or shade beneath lean-tos while watching over the little ones. Several lifeguards are on hand, but parents should still watch their youngsters at all times. **For people with disabilities:** Guests using water-appropriate wheelchairs can enjoy the wading areas. **TIP→ Stake out lounge chairs early, especially for a shady spot. If your tykes don't swim well, get them fitted with a free life vest, and pull your chair up to the water's edge.** ✉ *Blizzard Beach* ☞ *Duration: Up to you. Crowds: Vary by season. Audience: Small kids. Height requirement: Children must be shorter than 48 inches and accompanied by adults.*

Toboggan Racers
AMUSEMENT PARK/WATER PARK | Grab your mat, wait for the signal, and go. You and eight other racers whiz simultaneously down the watery trail on the purple slopes toward the finish line at the base of the mountain. The racing aspect and dips along the 250-foot-long slope make the ride fun, but it lacks the speed of single-rider green-slope rides like Slush Gusher. For a ride combining speed and friendly competition, check out the Downhill Double Dipper. Expectant mothers shouldn't ride, nor should guests with heart, neck, or back problems. **For people with disabilities:** Guests using wheelchairs must transfer to slide mats. **TIP→ It's more fun when you race family members or friends—up to eight people can ride at the same time.** ✉ *Blizzard Beach* ☞ *Duration: 10 secs. Crowds: Moderate to heavy. Audience: Not young kids.*

Restaurants

Lottawatta Lodge—a North American ski lodge with a Caribbean accent—is the park's main emporium of fast food. Lines are long at peak feeding times. The **Warming Hut,** which is open seasonally, offers salads, sandwiches, and ice cream. Specialty hot dogs and salads are on the menu at **Avalunch. Frostbite Freddy's** and **Polar Pub,** on the main beach, both sell frozen drinks and spirits.

Chapter 6

DISNEY'S ANIMAL KINGDOM AND RESORT AREA

Updated by
Leigh Jenkins

Sights	Restaurants	Hotels	Shopping	Nightlife
★★★★★	★★★☆☆	★★★★★	★★★★☆	★★☆☆☆

PARK SNAPSHOT

TOP EXPERIENCES

■ **Avatar: Flight of Passage.** It's simply one of the most exciting theme-park rides you'll experience.

■ **Expedition Everest.** This roller coaster is a spine-tingling trip into the snowy Himalayas to find the abominable snowman. It's best reserved for brave riders 7 and up.

■ **Festival of the Lion King.** Singers and dancers dressed in fantastic costumes representing many wild animals perform uplifting dance and acrobatics numbers and interact with children in the audience.

■ **Finding Nemo: The Musical.** Don't miss a performance of this outstanding musical starring the most charming, colorful characters ever to swim their way into your heart.

■ **Kilimanjaro Safaris.** You're guaranteed to see dozens of wild animals, including giraffes, gazelles, hippos, rhinos, zebras, and elephants, living in authentic, re-created African habitats. If you're lucky, the lions and cheetahs will be stirring, too.

■ **Tree of Life: It's Tough to Be a Bug!** This clever and very funny 3-D movie starring Flik from the Disney film *A Bug's Life* is full of surprises, including "shocking" special effects. Some young children are scared of the loud noises.

■ **Wild Africa Trek.** The price tag is hefty, but this behind-the-scenes wild-animal adventure is a memory maker.

PLANNING YOUR TIME

With the addition of the new Pandora–The World of Avatar, Animal Kingdom has definitely earned its full-day badge of honor, and now that the park closes late most nights, there are reasons to stay (or come back) after the sun goes down to watch the Tree of Life come alive before heading over to watch Rivers of Light. With its bioluminescent flora, Pandora itself really does come alive in a different way at night, and the Kilamanjaro Safari is a completely different experience.

GETTING HERE

■ Animal Kingdom is the most isolated of the parks, reachable by buses but no other transportation. It's near only the Animal Kingdom Lodge and Villas but not really any other hotels. If you are staying at another Walt Disney World resort and have a car, it's worth driving, especially if you are staying after dark.

QUICK BITES

■ **Kusafiri Coffee Shop & Bakery.** The tantalizing aroma of fresh-baked cinnamon buns leads here, where, after just one look, you might give in to the urge. These buns are worth the banknotes, and they pair well with a cappuccino or espresso. Kids might opt for a giant cookie and milk. ✉ *Africa.*

■ **Pongu Pongu.** If you need a pick-me-up after Avatar Flight of Passage, stop by Pangu Pongu for a pineapple cream cheese spring roll. Kids adore the Night Blossom, a bubble tea drink, while adults are thrilled with the craft beers. ✉ *Pandora–The World of Avatar.*

■ **Restaurantosaurus.** Famished but not much time for lunch? Make tracks for a counter-service burger and fries or a hearty salad at Restaurantosaurus and you'll be ready to take on T. rex. ✉ *DinoLand U.S.A.*

If you're thinking, "Oh, it's just another zoo, let's skip it," think again. Walt Disney World's fourth theme park, opened in 1998, takes its inspiration from humankind's enduring love for animals and the environment and pulls out all the stops. Your day will be packed with unusual animal encounters, enchanting entertainment, and theme rides, one of them out of this world, that'll leave you breathless.

A large chunk of the park is devoted to animal habitats, especially the forest and savanna of Africa's Kilimanjaro Safaris. Towering acacia trees and tall grasses sweep across the land where antelopes, giraffes, and wildebeests roam. A lion kopje, warthog burrows, a zebra habitat, and an elephant watering hole provide ample space for inhabitants.

About 94 acres contain foliage like hibiscus and mulberry, perfect for antelope and many other species. The largest groups of Nile hippos and African elephants in North America live along the winding waterway that leads to the savanna. The generously landscaped Pangani Forest Exploration Trail provides roaming grounds for troops of gorillas and authentic habitats for meerkats, birds, fish, and other creatures.

Beyond the park's Africa territory, similar large spaces are set aside for the homes of Asian animals like tigers and giant fruit bats, as well as for creatures such as Galápagos tortoises and a giant anteater.

Disney Imagineers didn't forget to incorporate their trademark thrills, including the astonishing Avatar Flight of Passage in Pandora; the Kali River Rapids ride in Asia; the fast-paced DINOSAUR journey in DinoLand U.S.A.; and Expedition Everest, a "runaway" train ride on a faux rugged mountain complete with icy ledges, dark caves, and a yeti legend.

The latest land to open takes you totally off-planet to a world inspired by the film *Avatar.* Opened in 2017, Pandora–The World of Avatar is filled with breathtaking technology, astonishing alien beauty, and the park's biggest thrill attraction, Avatar Flight of Passage. The whole park is open at night allowing for the best views of the lighted alien landscape.

The only downside to the Animal Kingdom layout is that walking paths and spaces can get very crowded and hot in the warmest months. Your best bet is to arrive very early and see the animals first before the heat makes them (and you) woozy.

Keep an eye peeled throughout the day for the spectacular appearance of a flock of macaws soaring overhead. The brightly colored birds—scarlet, hyacinth, blue, and gold and more—make periodic flights throughout the park.

Planning

Getting Oriented

Animal Kingdom's hub is the Tree of Life, in the middle of Discovery Island. The park's lands, each with a distinct personality, radiate from Discovery Island. To the southwest, lies Pandora–The World of Avatar, inspired by *Avatar* and its upcoming sequels. The area is best viewed after dark, when the alien landscape lights up, but the floating islands are spectacular at any time of day. North of the hub is Africa, where Kilimanjaro Safaris travel across extensive savanna. In the northeast corner is Rafiki's Planet Watch with conservation activities.

Asia, with thrills like Expedition Everest and Kali River Rapids, is east of the hub, and DinoLand U.S.A. brings T. rex and other prehistoric creatures to life in the park's southeast corner.

If you're staying on Disney property, you can take a Disney bus to the Entrance Plaza. If you drive, the $25 parking fee allows you to park at other Disney lots throughout the day.

Although this is technically Disney's largest theme park, most of the land is reserved for the animals. Pedestrian areas are actually quite compact, with relatively narrow passageways. The only way to get around is on foot or in a wheelchair or electronic convenience vehicle (ECV).

Park Amenities

Baby Care: At Discovery Island, you can stop in to nurse babies in the quiet baby-care center, which is equipped with rocking chairs and low lighting. There are changing tables, which are also available in restrooms (including some men's restrooms), and you can buy disposable diapers, formula, baby food, and pacifiers.

Cameras: You can buy film and digital memory cards at several shops throughout the park. If a Disney photographer takes your picture, sign up for a Disney PhotoPass—later, you can view and purchase the pictures online ($199 for full digital Memory Maker access) or at the park's photo center in the Oasis.

First Aid: The first-aid center, staffed by registered nurses, is in Discovery Island, and at least a dozen automated external defibrillators are in key park areas.

Mosquito Control: Disney offers complimentary insect repellent for guests throughout all its parks.

Guest Relations (aka Guest Services): This office will help with tickets at a window to the left just before you pass through the turnstile. Once you've entered, Guest Relations staffers in the Oasis can provide park maps, schedules, and answers to questions. They can also assist with dining reservations, ticket upgrades, and services for guests with disabilities.

Lockers: Lockers are in Guest Relations in the Oasis. Rental fees are $10 to $15 (depending on size) for a day plus a $5 key deposit. Lockers located immediately outside Kali River Rapids will help you keep bags and belongings from getting wet. Standard lockers are free for the first two hours; large lockers are $4.

Lost People and Things: Instruct your kids to speak to someone with a Disney name tag if you become separated. Lost children are taken to the baby-care center, where they can watch Disney movies, or to Guest Relations, whichever is closer. If you do lose your child, contact any cast member immediately and Disney security personnel will be notified.

Animal Kingdom Lost and Found
To retrieve lost articles on the same day, visit or call Lost and Found, which is in the lobby of Guest Relations, just inside the park. ✉ *Oasis, Animal Kingdom* ☎ *407/938–2785.*

Main Lost and Found
If more than a day has passed since you've lost something, contact the Main Lost and Found office at Disney Springs. ☎ *407/824–4245.*

Package Pick-Up: You can have shop clerks forward purchases to Package Pick-Up near the Main Entrance in the Oasis, so that you won't have to carry them around all day. Allow three hours for the journey. If you're staying at a Disney hotel, you can also have packages delivered there.

Services for People with Disabilities:
Guests using wheelchairs will have ready access to restaurants, shops, and most attractions—including the Finding Nemo: The Musical theater in DinoLand U.S.A. and the Tree of Life theater showing It's Tough to Be a Bug! (Theaters also are accessible to ECVs.) Some monitor-equipped attractions have reflective-captioning boxes.

Scripts and story lines for all attractions are available, and you can book sign-language interpreters with notice of two or more weeks. Large Braille park maps are by Guest Relations and near the Tip Board at the entrance to Discovery Island. Guest Relations is also where you can borrow assisted-listening, handheld-captioning, and video-captioning devices with a refundable deposit. Service animals are allowed in most, but not all, areas of the park.

You can rent wheelchairs ($12 daily, $10 for multiple days) and ECVs ($50 per day plus a refundable $20 security deposit) at Garden Gate Gifts in the Oasis. You can't, however, reserve these items, so arrive early to get one—particularly if you want an ECV.

Stroller Rentals: Garden Gate Gifts in the Oasis rents strollers. Singles are $15 daily, $13 multiday; doubles run $31 daily, $27 multiday.

Tours

Caring for Giants
ECOTOURISM | **FAMILY** | During this 60-minute tour ($30), you'll learn about the African elephant herd that calls Animal Kingdom home. Animal specialists explain the daily care that the elephants receive, while an African cultural representative talks about conservation efforts Disney has started in Africa. For safety reasons, you view the elephants from 80 to 100 feet away and do not actually interact with them. Children must be 4 and over to participate; those under 18 must have adult supervision. Standard wheelchairs are allowed if Disney is notified in advance, but ECVs cannot be used on the tour. ✉ *Animal Kingdom* ☎ *407/939–8687* 🌐 *www.disneyworld.disney.go.com/events-tours/animal-kingdom/caring-for-giants.*

Up Close with Rhinos
ECOTOURISM | This 60-minute tour ($40) takes you behind the scenes to meet the white-rhinoceros that live at the Animal Kingdom. Disney's rhino handlers share their knowledge about rhinos and the extinction threat they face, while also demonstrating how the animals have been trained to cooperate with the handlers. If the rhinos are having a good day, you'll be allowed to pet them, but that's not guaranteed because these animals can be cantankerous at times. Children must be 4 and over to experience this tour, and it's only offered at

certain times during the year. ✉ *Animal Kingdom* ☎ *407/939–8687* 🌐 *www.disneyworld.disney.go.com/events-tours/animal-kingdom/up-close-with-rhinos.*

★ Wild Africa Trek

ECOTOURISM | You will cover exciting ground on this three-hour, walking-riding adventure ($189 to $249 per person depending on season) into unexplored areas of the park. For a close-up view of the hippos, you'll wear a special vest with a harness that's tethered to a rail at the edge of a bluff. You'll cross a rope bridge above a pool of Nile crocodiles. Your exclusive open-air safari vehicle makes multiple stops for leisurely viewing of giraffes, wildebeests, cheetahs, and other creatures of the savanna. Burning all those calories pays off when breakfast or lunch treats are served (think prosciutto, salmon, brie, and fresh fruit) at the open-air Boma Landing on the edge of the savanna. The tour is good for anyone age 8 and older who's fit. Included in the admission price is a CD-photo souvenir of your trek. A portion of the tour price is donated to the Disney Worldwide Conservation Fund. ✉ *Animal Kingdom* ☎ *407/939–8687.*

Visiting Tips

Try to visit during the week. Pedestrian areas are compact, and the park can feel uncomfortably packed on weekends.

Plan on a full day here. That way, while exploring Africa's Pangani Forest Exploration Trail, say, you can spend 10 minutes (rather than just two) watching vigilant meerkats stand sentry or tracking a mama gorilla as she cares for her youngster.

Arrive a half-hour before the park opens. That way you'll see the animals at their friskiest (first thing in the morning or at night are the best times to do the safari ride) as you get a jump on the crowds.

Eat here. Animal Kingdom has some of Disney World's best food, including Tiffins, which might be the best upscale restaurant anywhere in Walt Disney World.

Plan your meet-up. Good places to rendezvous include the outdoor Dawa Bar or Tamu Tamu Refreshments areas in Africa, in front of DinoLand U.S.A.'s Boneyard, or on one of the benches outside Expedition Everest in Asia.

The Oasis

This entrance makes you feel as if you've been plunked down in the middle of a rain forest. Cool mist, the aroma of flowers, playful animals, and colorful birds enliven a miniature landscape of streams and grottoes, waterfalls, and glades fringed with banana leaves and jacaranda. It's also where you can take care of essentials before entering. Here you'll find guide maps, stroller and wheelchair rentals, Guest Relations, and an ATM.

Discovery Island

The park hub and site of the Tree of Life, this island is encircled by Discovery River, which isn't an actual attraction but makes for attractive views from the bridge to Harambe and another between Asia and DinoLand U.S.A. The amphitheater on the east side of the river is home to the nighttime attraction Rivers of Light. The island's whimsical architecture, with wood carvings from Bali, lends charm and a touch of fantasy. The Discovery Island Trails that lead to the Tree of Life provide habitats for African crested porcupines, lemurs, Galápagos tortoises, and other creatures you won't want to miss.

As you are walking through this area, watch for the awe-inspiring sight of a flock of multicolor macaws flying free

At Disney's Animal Kingdom, entertainment, including street performers, is nonstop throughout the day (and also now at night).

over your head. Check with a cast member to see what time and where these majestic birds will be flying.

You'll discover some great shops and good counter-service eateries here. Visitor services that aren't in the Oasis are here, on the border with Harambe, including the baby-care center and the first-aid center.

Sights

It's Tough to be a Bug!

AMUSEMENT PARK/WATER PARK | FAMILY | A monument to all of Earth's creatures, the park's centerpiece is an imposing 14 stories high and 50 feet wide at its base. Its 100,000-plus leaves are several shades of green fabric, each carefully placed for a realistic effect. Carved into its thick trunk, gnarled roots, and soaring branches—some of which are supported by joints that allow them to sway in a strong wind—are nearly 350 intricate animal forms that include a baboon, a whale, a horse, the mighty lion, and even an ankylosaurus. At night, the tree is lit up by projections onto the vast trunk and leaves. Outside, paths tunnel underneath the roots as the fauna-encrusted trunk towers overhead.

The path leads you inside the tree trunk, where you get a bug's-eye view of life. The witty 3-D film adventure *It's Tough to Be a Bug!* is modeled on the animated film *A Bug's Life* from Disney-Pixar . Special effects spray you with "poison," zap you with a swatter, and even poke you with a stinger—all in good fun.

Although the show has something for all ages, it's very loud, and some effects frighten young children (during the hornet attack, have children lean forward to avoid a "sting"). **For people with disabilities:** Wheelchair accessible, but, to fully experience all the special effects, guests using wheelchairs should transfer to a seat. Equipped with reflective captioning and for audio-description and assisted-listening devices. If you have a service animal, check with a host before entering the theater. **TIP→ Fastpass+ is offered,**

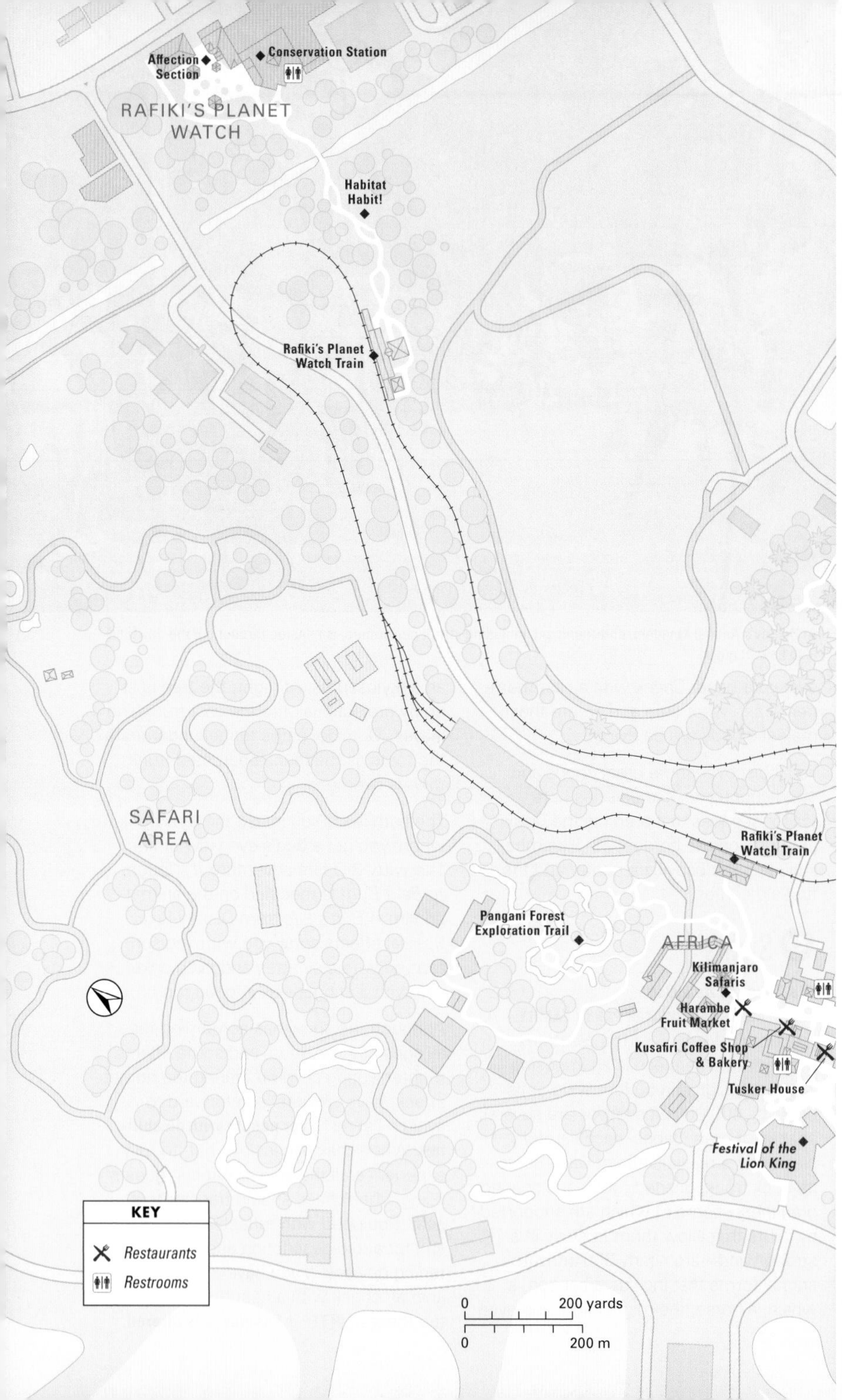

Affection Section
Conservation Station
RAFIKI'S PLANET WATCH
Habitat Habit!
Rafiki's Planet Watch Train
SAFARI AREA
Rafiki's Planet Watch Train
Pangani Forest Exploration Trail
AFRICA
Kilimanjaro Safaris
Harambe Fruit Market
Kusafiri Coffee Shop & Bakery
Tusker House
Festival of the Lion King
KEY
Restaurants
Restrooms
0
200 yards
0
200 m

Disney's Animal Kingdom

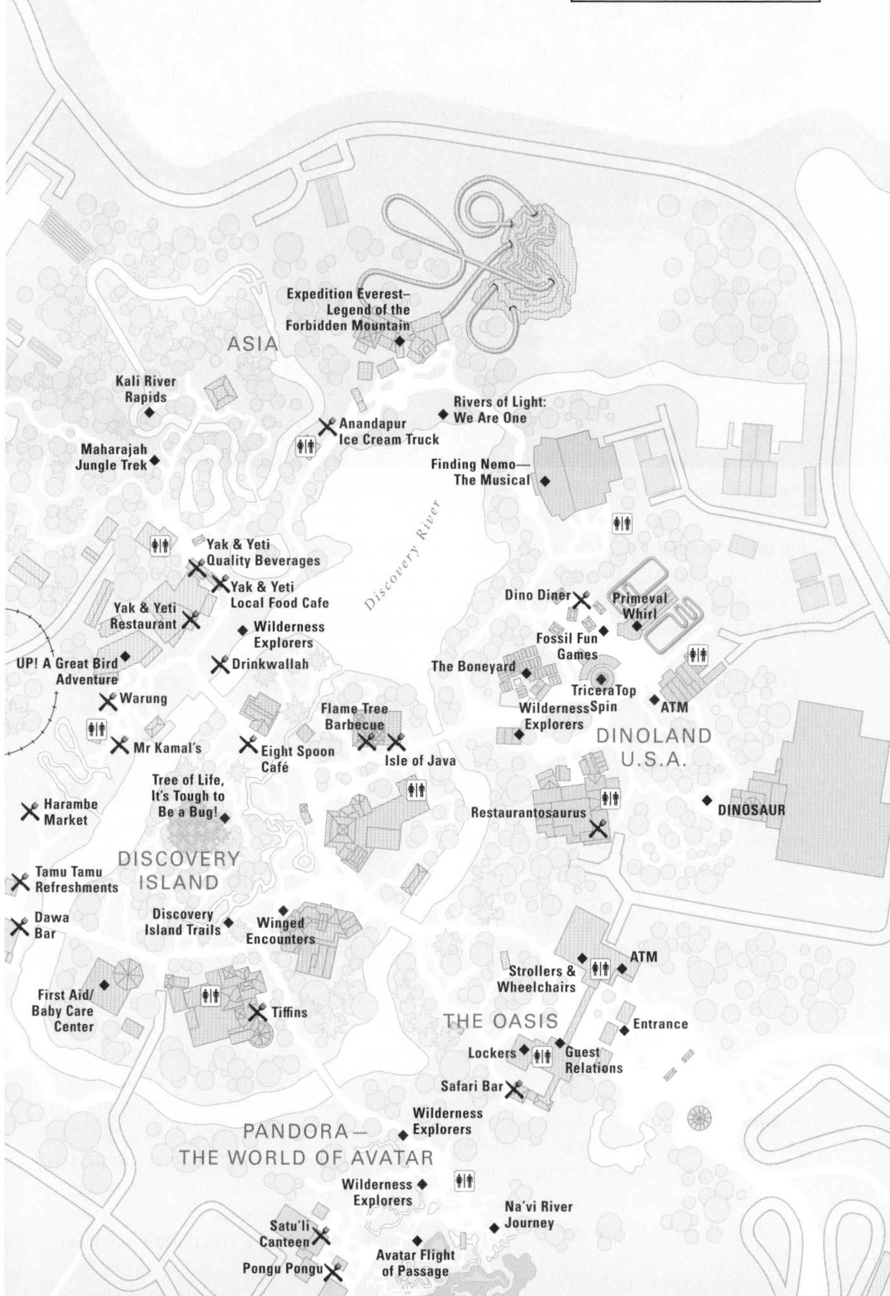

The Tree of Life is the iconic centerpiece of Disney's Animal Kingdom.

but rarely needed. ✉ *Discovery Island, Animal Kingdom* ☞ *Duration: 20 mins. Crowds: Moderate to heavy. Audience: All but young kids.*

Restaurants

Flame Tree Barbecue

$ | **FAST FOOD** | **FAMILY** | This quick-service eatery is one of the relatively undiscovered gems of Disney's culinary offerings; there's nothing fancy here, but you can dig into ribs, chicken, and pulled-pork sandwiches. And yes, you can still get those giant turkey legs. **Known for:** reasonably priced barbecue in an Animal Kingdom setting; ribs, chicken, and pulled-pork sampler; variety of beer and wine. [$] *Average main: $12* ✉ *Discovery Island, Animal Kingdom* 🌐 *disneyworld.disney.go.com/dining.*

★ Tiffins

$$$$ | **INTERNATIONAL** | **FAMILY** | Inspired by the worldwide journeys of Disney Imagineers, Tiffins is the theme-parks' newest upscale sit-down restaurant and possibly the best theme-park eatery, period. With a wide-ranging international menu that changes constantly, this gateway to Pandora has become intensely popular. **Known for:** superbly cooked, changing menu with Asian, Latin, and African flavors; elaborate decor; kids meals that aren't dumbed down. [$] *Average main: $41* ✉ *Discovery Island, Animal Kingdom* ☎ *407/939–1947* 🌐 *disneyworld.disney.go.com/dining.*

Performing Arts

Rivers of Light

SOUND/LIGHT SHOW | As dusk falls, radiance lights up the waterfront Discovery River amphitheater in a tranquil 15-minute performance that combines video, fountain projections, floats, and an original musical score. Lanterns transform into animal spirit forms—the Elephant, the Tiger, the Turtle, and the Owl—while flowers open to create an intricate water show. The projections move across jungles, oceans, savannas, and mountains, using curtains of mist as screens. ✉ *Discovery River, Animal Kingdom* ☞ *Duration: 15 mins. Crowds: Heavy. Audience: All ages.*

Tree of Life Awakenings

SOUND/LIGHT SHOW | The iconic tree has developed a nighttime persona now that the park stays open after dark. As night falls, fireflies begin to flicker among the leaves of the tree. The tiny lights expand, and through the magic of high-tech projections, the animals carved into the trunk—from dinosaurs to gorillas to tropical birds to a deer—begin to awaken in a swirl of color, until the whole tree is alive with light. The experience repeats every 10 minutes from dark until park closing time. ✉ *Discovery Island, Animal Kingdom.*

DinoLand U.S.A.

Just as it sounds, this is the place to come in contact with re-created prehistoric creatures, including the fear-inspiring carnotaurus and the gentle iguanodon. The landscaping includes live plants that have evolved over the last 65 million years. In collaboration with Chicago's Field Museum, Disney displays a complete, full-scale skeleton cast of Dino-Sue—also known as "Sue"—the 65-million-year-old *Tyrannosaurus rex* discovered near the Black Hills of South Dakota.

After admiring Sue, you can go on the thrilling DINOSAUR ride, play in the Boneyard, or take in the Finding Nemo: The Musical show at the Theater in the Wild. Kids will want to try the TriceraTop Spin and the Primeval Whirl family coaster, which has spinning "time machines." There's no need to dig for souvenirs at Chester and Hester's Dinosaur Treasures gift shop—all you need is your wallet.

Timing Tip: Because of the proximity of the two attractions, Finding Nemo: The Musical is a good place to take younger kids while older siblings do Expedition Everest.

Sights

The Boneyard

AMUSEMENT PARK/WATER PARK | Youngsters can slide, dig, bounce, slither, and stomp around this archaeological dig site–cum–playground, the finest play area in any of the four Disney parks. In addition to a huge sand pit where children can dig for mammoth bones, there are twisting short and long slides, climbing nets, caves, a maze, and a jeep to climb on. Stomp on the dino footprints to make 'em roar. **For people with disabilities:** This fossil play maze is wheelchair accessible. **TIP→ Let the kids burn off energy here while waiting for a Fastpass+ appointment. Or head over late in the day when kids need to run free. As one of the few shaded play areas, this is a perfect spot in the afternoon.** ✉ *DinoLand U.S.A., Animal Kingdom* ☞ *Duration: Up to you. Crowds: Moderate to heavy. Audience: Young kids.*

DINOSAUR

AMUSEMENT PARK/WATER PARK | This wild adventure through time puts you face-to-face with huge dinosaurs that move and breathe with uncanny realism. When a carload of guests rouses a cantankerous carnotaurus from his Cretaceous slumber, it's showtime. You travel back 65 million years on a fast-paced, twisting adventure and try to save the last living iguanodon as a massive asteroid hurtles toward Earth. Exciting Audio-Animatronics and special effects bring to life dinosaurs like the raptor, pterodactyl, styracosaurus, alioramus, and compsognather. Be prepared for a short but jolting drop toward the end of the ride.

Guests who are pregnant or have back, neck, or heart problems should avoid this very bumpy ride. The jostling and realistic carnivores might frighten young children. **For people with disabilities:** You must transfer from your wheelchair to board this ride. Equipped for video-captioning and assisted-listening devices. No service animals. **TIP→ Come first thing**

in the morning or at the end of the day, or use Fastpass+. ✉ *DinoLand U.S.A., Animal Kingdom* ☞ *Duration: Under 4 mins. Crowds: Heavy. Audience: All but young kids. Height requirement: 40 inches.*

★ Finding Nemo–The Musical

AMUSEMENT PARK/WATER PARK | The performance of this fish tale is so creative and fun that many have likened it to a first-rate Broadway show. Indeed, Disney Imagineers collaborated with several Broadway talents to produce it. Original songs by Tony Award–winning *Avenue Q* co-composer-creator Robert Lopez and a cappella musical *Along the Way* co-creator Kristen Anderson-Lopez add depth and energy. Michael Curry, who co-designed the character puppets of Broadway's *The Lion King,* also created this show's eye-popping puppetry.

Multigenerational humor, special effects, and larger-than-life puppets wielded by gifted performers, dancers, and acrobats all bring you into Nemo's world. The sweet story remains the same as in the movie—Nemo and his father, Marlin, go on separate journeys that teach them how to understand each other. Zany Dory, with her memory lapses, Crush the sea turtle dude, tap-dancing sharks, and others make memorable supporting-role appearances. **For people with disabilities:** Wheelchair accessible. Equipped with reflective captioning and for audio-description and assisted-listening devices. Check with Guest Relations for sign-language schedule. **TIP→ Arrange a Fastpass+ or arrive 30 to 40 minutes before showtime. Bring little kids here while older tweens and teens ride Expedition Everest.** ✉ *DinoLand U.S.A., Animal Kingdom* ☞ *Duration: 40 mins. Crowds: Heavy. Audience: All ages.*

Fossil Fun Games

AMUSEMENT PARK/WATER PARK | A carnival-style midway in the middle of DinoLand U.S.A., this fun fair draws crowds with games like Whack a Packycephalosaur and the basketball-inspired Bronto-Score. The prehistoric fun comes at a price, however, and stone currency is not accepted. Prizes are mostly of the plush-character variety—you might win your sweetheart a stuffed Nala. **For people with disabilities:** Wheelchair accessible. **TIP→ It costs $5 a game, $10 for 3 games, or $30 for 10 games. Vouchers can be purchased at a stand amid the games.** ✉ *DinoLand U.S.A., Animal Kingdom* ☞ *Duration: Up to you. Crowds: Light. Audience: All ages.*

Primeval Whirl

AMUSEMENT PARK/WATER PARK | In a free-spinning, four-passenger vehicle, you head on a brief journey back in time on this outdoor open-air coaster, twisting, turning, and even venturing into the jaws of a dinosaur "skeleton." Crazy cartoon dinosaurs in shades of turquoise, orange, yellow, and purple pop up along the track bearing signs that warn "The End Is Near." More signs alert you to incoming "Meteors!" and suggest that you "Head for the Hills!"—coaster hills, that is. Halfway through the ride, your car seems to spin out of control, and you take the next drop backward. The more weight in the vehicle, the more you spin.

Pregnant women or guests with back, neck, or heart problems should skip this one. **For people with disabilities:** Guests using wheelchairs must transfer to the ride vehicle. No service animals. **TIP→ Fastpass+ is recommended. Kids might want to ride twice if the wait isn't long.** ✉ *DinoLand U.S.A., Animal Kingdom* ☞ *Duration: 2½ mins. Crowds: Heavy. Audience: All but young kids. Height requirement: 48 inches.*

TriceraTop Spin

AMUSEMENT PARK/WATER PARK | TriceraTop Spin is designed for playful little dinophiles who ought to get a kick out of whirling around this ride's giant spinning toy top and dodging incoming comets in their dino mobiles. "Pop!" goes the top, and out comes a grinning dinosaur as four passengers in each vehicle fly

On Asia's Expedition Everest, you'll chug, twist, turn, and plunge up, through, and down Mt. Everest on nearly a mile of track. Oh, yeah, and beware of the yeti!

in a circle and maneuver up and down. **For people with disabilities:** Wheelchair accessible, but guests using ECVs must transfer to standard wheelchairs. **■ TIP→ Ride early, or take little ones while older kids are riding DINOSAUR or Primeval Whirl.** ✉ *DinoLand U.S.A., Animal Kingdom* ☞ *Duration: 2 mins. Crowds: Heavy. Audience: Young kids.*

Asia

Meant to resemble an Asian village, this land is full of remarkable rain-forest scenery and ruins. Groupings of trees grow from a crumbling shrine populated by roaming tigers, and massive towers—representing Thailand and Nepal—are the habitat for gibbons, whose hooting fills the air.

Sights

★ Expedition Everest—Legend of the Forbidden Mountain

AMUSEMENT PARK/WATER PARK | A fierce yeti guards the route to Mt. Everest. Of course, you're willing to risk running across the big guy in your roller-coaster quest to reach the summit. So, you board an "aging," seemingly innocuous, 34-passenger, steam-engine train into the mountains. You roll past bamboo forests, waterfalls, and glacier fields as you climb higher through snowcapped peaks. Suddenly, the train becomes a runaway, barreling forward then backward around icy ledges and through dark snowy caverns.

Nearly a mile of twists and turns cut through the dark mountain, and, at one point, your train plunges a harrowing 80 feet. Will you find the yeti? Buildings along the queue look like Himalayan mountain dwellings and teem with things like prayer flags, totems, and other artifacts from Tibet, Nepal, and the entire region.

Pandora–The World of Avatar is the newest addition to Animal Kingdom.

Because of the backwards portion of the ride, those wanting a wilder experience should ride up front instead of in the back. There is a 44-inch height requirement to ride. Pregnant women or guests with back, neck, or heart problems shouldn't ride. **For people with disabilities:** You must transfer from your wheelchair to a ride vehicle; ask a cast member about the Transfer Practice Vehicle. No service animals. ▮▮▮ TIP→ **Unless you prefer to see the animals first, rush here as soon as the park opens , when the wait won't be too long. Otherwise, arrange a Fastpass+.** ✉ *Asia, Animal Kingdom* ☞ *Duration: 2½ mins. Crowds: Huge. Audience: All but young kids. Height requirement: 44 inches.*

Kali River Rapids

AMUSEMENT PARK/WATER PARK | Asia's thrilling water adventure ride mixes the fun of a rafting experience with a solemn message to save pristine lands and animal habitats that are threatened by development. Aboard a round raft that seats 12, you run the Chakranadi River. After passing through a huge bamboo tunnel filled with jasmine-scented mist, your raft climbs 40 feet upriver, lurches and spins through sharp twists and turns, and then approaches an immense waterfall, which curtains a giant carved tiger face. Past rain forests and temple ruins, you find yourself face-to-face with the denuded slope of a logged-out woodland burning out of control. There are many more thrills, but why spill the beans?

You will get wet—possibly even soaked. Unless you want to wring out your clothing in the nearest restroom afterward, bring a poncho. Better yet, bring a change of clothing in a plastic bag. Nearby lockers can keep bags dry while you ride. The ride-height minimum is 38 inches. If you are pregnant or have heart, back, neck, or motion-sickness problems, sit this one out. **For people with disabilities:** Guests using wheelchairs must transfer to a ride raft. No service animals. ▮▮▮ TIP→ **Use Fastpass+ to avoid a long wait.** ✉ *Asia, Animal Kingdom* ☞ *Duration: 7 mins. Crowds: Heavy. Audience: All but young kids.*

Maharajah Jungle Trek

AMUSEMENT PARK/WATER PARK | Along this trail, you get an up-close view of some unusual animals, including giant fruit bats that hang to munch fruit from wires and fly very close to the open and glass-protected viewing areas and Bengal tigers in front of a maharajah's palace ruins. The tigers have their own view (with no accessibility, of course) of Asian deer and black buck, an antelope species. At the end of the trek, you walk through an aviary with a lotus pool. Disney animal experts are on hand to answer questions. **For people with disabilities:** Wheelchair accessible; equipped for audio-description devices. Guests with service animals should check with a host before entering the aviary. **TIP→ Come anytime. Crowds stay fairly light, as people are constantly on the move.** ✉ *Asia, Animal Kingdom* ☞ *Duration: Up to you. Crowds: Light. Audience: All ages.*

UP! A Great Bird Adventure

AMUSEMENT PARK/WATER PARK | **FAMILY** | During this 25-minutes show, Russell and Doug from Disney's *Up* are trying to earn their Bird Badge from their wacky Wilderness Explorer troop leader. Fortunately, a bird expert is on hand to teach them about vultures, macaws, cranes, and even a singing parrot. Adults might groan at some of the corny jokes, but everyone will be amazed as the birds soar right overhead. Those with questions, or who want a closer look at the birds, can walk down to the stage after the show. **For guests with disabilities:** Wheelchair- and ECV-accessible. **TIP→ Guests who don't want birds directly overhead should sit in the elevated bleachers in the back.** ✉ *Asia, Animal Kingdom* ☞ *Duration: 25 mins. Crowds: Moderate. Audience: Kids.*

Restaurants

Yak & Yeti

$$$ | **ASIAN** | This large, sit-down, pan-Asian restaurant in a two-story, 250-seat venue offers everything from noodles to curries to Korean barbecued ribs. The decor is pleasantly faux-Asian, with cracked plaster walls, wood carvings, and tile mosaic tabletops. **Known for:** large menu with Indian, Japanese, Chinese, and Korean influences; welcoming lounge for escaping the weather; shareable dim sum and appetizer baskets. $ *Average main: $22* ✉ *Asia, Animal Kingdom* ☎ *407/939–3463* 🌐 *disneyworld.disney.go.com/dining.*

Pandora—The World of Avatar

As you cross the bridge from the hub into Pandora, you sense an immediate change, in landscape, in lighting fixtures, in tone. The details are important, and they leave no doubt you are entering another world. Disney Imagineers—along with *Avatar* film creator James Cameron and his Lightstorm Entertainment—worked for yearsto create the inventive, sometimes surreal, landscape of Pandora. The experience is set far in the future, far beyond the war between the Na'vi and humans depicted in the film. Instead, Alpha Centauri Expeditions (ACE) are bringing humans back to the planet. The emphasis now is on cooperation between human and Na'vi to ensure the environment is protected. In the daytime, you'll be awe-struck by the gravity defying floating islands and the lush plants, both earthlike and unearthly, that envelop the land. At night, when the bioluminescence cranks up, you feel slightly off balance, as if you were truly on an alien world, seeing alien things for the first time. That feeling only grows with a trip along the Na'vi River or deeper into the jungle, where the Avatar Flight of Passage puts you atop a banshee for a stomach-lurching journey. But don't make the mistake of rushing to the thrill ride and missing all the beauty along the way. Be sure to stop by Satu'li Canteen, where you can refuel with a delicious and healthy bowl of grains or noodles topped with grilled meats and a variety of vegetables, or Pongu Pongu, where drinks have been known to glow in the dark.

Sights

★ Avatar Flight of Passage

AMUSEMENT PARK/WATER PARK | This stunning thrill ride puts you atop a dragonlike mountain banshee for the ride of your life. After a trek deep into the jungles of Pandora, you enter a room where scientists are pairing up banshees and visitors. On instruction, you board a vehicle resembling a motorcycle that faces a blank wall. After hopping on, you don special 3-D goggles, the action begins, and you are one with your banshee. You feel it come to life beneath you, as Pandora comes to life before your eyes. The banshee's wing muscles pump as you hurtle down cliff faces and soar above the floating islands familiar from the film. The visuals are breathtaking, with dense jungles, seascapes, vast waterfalls, and alien plant life passing rapidly before your eyes. Even more astonishing, however, are the subtle smells and temperature changes that accompany different landscapes, immersing you totally in the experience. **For guests with disabilities:** Guests must transfer to a standard wheelchair and then on to ride vehicle. ✉ *Pandora–The World of Avatar, Animal Kingdom* ☞ *Duration: 4½ mins. Crowds: Heavy. Audience: All but young kids.*

★ Na'vi River Journey

AMUSEMENT PARK/WATER PARK | To enter this gentle river ride, you must first wander through the inventive landscape of Pandora, designed by Disney Imagineers to include many tropical and subtropical plants found in Florida,as well as creatively imagined alien plants, many of which light up at night. After entering the cavern and boarding a reed raft, you drift slowly past a bioluminescent rain forest, with an even more diverse range of flora and fauna. The object of your quest is to find the Na'vi Shaman of Songs, the life force of Pandora, but you'll be so caught up in the stunning details of the landscape that you'll be surprised when the Audio-Animatronic Shaman shows up. **For guests with disabilities:** Guests must transfer from a wheelchair or ECV. ✉ *Pandora–The World of Avatar, Animal Kingdom* ☞ *Duration: 4½ mins. Crowds: Heavy. Audience: Young kids, adults, fans of Avatar.*

Restaurants

★ Satu'li Canteen

$ | INTERNATIONAL | FAMILY | Situated in the heart of Pandora, Satu'li walks a line between fast-casual and fine dining with counter service and surprisingly sophisticated (and healthy), internationally inspired dishes. The menu features grain bowls with fresh-cooked ingredients and kids meals that are actually nutritious. **Known for:** grain bowls; fresh cooked, high-quality chicken, beef, and tofu; phone-app ordering eliminates waiting. [$] *Average main: $14* ✉ *Pandora–The World of Avatar, Animal Kingdom* ☎ *407/939–1947* 🌐 *disneyworld.disney.go.com/dining.*

Africa

The largest of the lands is an area of forests and grasslands, predominantly an enclave for wildlife from the continent. Harambe, on the northern bank of Discovery River, is Africa's starting point. Inspired by several East African villages, this Disney town has so much detail that it's mind-boggling to try to soak it all up. Signs on the apparently peeling stucco walls are faded, as if bleached by the sun, and everything has a hot, dusty look. For souvenirs with Disney and African themes, browse through the Mombasa Marketplace and Ziwani Traders.

A silverback gorilla at Gorilla Falls Exploration Trail

Sights

★ ***Festival of the Lion King***
AMUSEMENT PARK/WATER PARK | If you think you've seen enough *Lion King* to last a lifetime, you're wrong—unless you've seen this show. Disney presents a delightful tribal celebration of song, dance, and acrobatics that uses huge moving stages and floats. The show's singers are first-rate; lithe dancers wearing exotic animal-theme costumes portray creatures in the wild. Timon, Pumba, and other *Lion King* stars have key roles. The show is presented in the Harambe Theater in the park's Africa area. **For people with disabilities:** Wheelchair and ECV accessible; equipped for assisted-listening and handheld-captioning devices; sign-language interpretation is sometimes offered. **■ TIP→ Fastpass+ is offered. Without one, arrive 30–40 minutes before showtime. If you have a child who might want to go on stage, try to sit up front to increase his or her chance of getting chosen.** ✉ *Africa, Animal Kingdom* ☞ *Duration: 30 mins. Crowds: Moderate to heavy. Audience: All ages.*

★ **Kilimanjaro Safaris**
AMUSEMENT PARK/WATER PARK | A giant Imagineered baobab tree is the starting point for exploring this animal sanctuary. Although re-creating an African safari in the United States isn't a new idea, with this one, great pains were taken to create an authentic environment, allowing you to observe rhinos, hippos, antelopes, wildebeests, giraffes, zebras, cheetahs, elephants, lions, and the like as if you were seeing them in the wild. Illustrated game-spotting guides are available above the seats in the open-air safari vehicles, and as you lurch and bump over some 110 acres of savanna, forest, rivers, and rocky hills, you'll see most of the Harambe Reserve's 34 species of animals—sometimes so close you feel that you could reach out and touch them. It's easy to suspend disbelief here because the landscape and habitats are so effectively modeled and replenished by Disney horticulturists. Keep an eye

Animal Kingdom Kids' Tour

Animals fascinate young children, but when their attention wanes, you'll find plenty of other diversions: stage shows, fun-filled rides, and one very imaginative playground.

It's a Creatures Great and Small World

Upon entering, stop at the Wilderness Explorer kiosk to the right and sign kids up to earn their Wilderness Explorer badges. Badge stations around the park will help teach kids about wildlife, conservation, and culture. When you're traveling with young children, there's no better way to kick off a visit to this park than with a ride aboard **Kilimanjaro Safaris.** Your kids will enjoy seeing live hippos, rhinos, crocodiles, giraffes, gazelles, wildebeests, zebras, and elephants roaming their natural habitats. Hang on to toddlers, though—it's a bumpy ride!

When you disembark, go straight to **Pangani Forest Exploration Trail,** where kids can see gorillas and the real meerkats behind the animated character Timon from *The Lion King.* Children flock to the glass-walled habitat where tiny hairless mole rats scurry through tunnels.

Turn the kids loose on the **Maharajah Jungle Trek** in the park's Asia area to see giant fruit bats, Eld's deer, and Bengal tigers. Aviaries on both Pangani and Maharajah walks offer bird-spotting guides, so your family can find and compare different species.

Ride, Play, See a Show, Meet a Mouse

If the kids meet height requirements (38 inches) and are ready for some adventure, head for **Kali River Rapids**—an exciting family raft ride. Steer smaller children toward **DinoLand U.S.A.,** where they'll be happy whirling around TriceraTop Spin and exploring the Boneyard play maze with its cool slides and its climbing and sandy fossil-dig areas.

Break for lunch at **Flame Tree Barbecue,** and then head around the corner to **Finding Nemo: The Musical,** where kids love the character puppets and lively, Broadway-style music. Toddlers may use this stop to nap in your arms.

Afterward, visit one of the park's character meet-and-greet areas, where you might find Mickey or Chip 'n' Dale. Back in Africa, you can take in **Festival of the Lion King,** where several children get to join "animal" dancers for one show number. Or take a break at **UP! A Great Bird Adventure** to marvel at the high-flying birds.

Board a Train, Save the Planet

Try to find time to board the Wildlife Express Train to **Rafiki's Planet Watch,** where the kids can see cotton-top tamarins and learn about taking care of the world's animals. You might be able to take part in a critter encounter with a Disney animal-care specialist at Conservation Station. The Affection Section petting yard is a comfortable place to meet domesticated animals from around the world.

Wrap up your day in **Pandora,** where the kids will marvel at the alien plant-life on the gentle Na'vi River Journey. Dinner at Satu'li Canteen offers a healthy but kid-pleasing bowl of roasted meats or grains, and a drink that might glow in the dark.

Animal Kingdom Grown-Up Tour

Thrill rides, a hilarious 3-D film, and two Broadway-style shows can fill a memorable day.

Adventure Seekers Wanted

The park's most popular thrill ride is **Avatar Flight of Passage** in Pandora, which puts you aboard a mountain banshee for a heart-stopping 3-D experience that takes you soaring above floating islands and plummeting down cliffs.

Next, make a beeline for Asia and **Expedition Everest.** If there's a wait for the attraction's high-speed train ride, the queue snakes through authentic rammed-earth and stacked-stone buildings of a Himalayan village. While in Asia, pile into a **Kali River Rapids** raft for a whitewater ride on the park's Chakranadi River (take off your shoes so they don't get wet).

Time-travel back to **DinoLand U.S.A.** for a DINOSAUR journey through a primeval forest and white-knuckle encounters with carnivorous creatures like the razor-toothed carnotaurus and other menacing creatures of prehistoric doom.

If it's a cool day, the park's animals should be active, so head to Africa. Your **Kilimanjaro Safaris** open-air journey is a bumpy 20-minute quest to sight exotic animals, and you won't be disappointed. Adventurous guests with dollars to spare should sign up for the park's Wild Africa Trek, one of Disney's most thrilling guided tours.

Eat, Shop, Laugh

Animal Kingdom has some of the best food at Walt Disney World. **Tusker House Restaurant,** in Africa, offers a colorful buffet of vegetables and carved meats enhanced with African-inspired chutneys, hummus, spiced tandoori tofu, and couscous salad.

At **Tiffins,** on Discovery Island at the bridge to Pandora, the cuisine (it deserves the term) is inspired by adventure travel, and the globetrotting menu is served with style. It might very well be the best restaurant in all of Walt Disney World.

Burn the calories during a shopping excursion to **Mombasa Marketplace,** where you can buy a bottle of South African wine or pick up hand-painted dishes from Zimbabwe. Onward to Discovery Island for a stroll along Discovery Island Trails into the Tree of Life show It's Tough to Be a Bug! Expect to laugh a lot.

Discover Animal Attraction

Along the **Pangani Forest Exploration Trail,** you can view families of mountain gorillas through a glassed-in area or from a bridge. It's inspiring to see these magnificent primates move among the rocks and lush greenery.

Although you feel safe from Bengal tigers on the **Maharajah Jungle Trek,** several raised viewing spots offer clear views with no glass or fence to mar your photos. Backdrops like the Maharajah palace ruins create scenic props.

If you can squeeze in only one live show, make it **Festival of the Lion King.**

Experts are always on hand to tell you more about all the animal species.

out for animal babies here and on the postsafari Pangani Forest Exploration Trail; the park's breeding programs have been extremely successful, with new additions including elephants, rhinos, okapi, giraffes, and several gorillas. It's a completely different experience at night, and the animals are often much more lively and interesting, so this experience definitely deserves a revisit. If you have to choose, the nighttime experience is probably superior.

Parents should hang on tightly to their small tykes. The ride is very bumpy and should be avoided by expectant guests or those with heart, back, or neck problems. **For people with disabilities:** Wheelchair accessible, but ECV users must transfer to standard wheelchairs. Equipped for assisted-listening and video-captioning devices. Guests with service animals should check with a host for boarding information. **TIP→ During the hottest months, come first thing in the morning when animals are most active, using Fastpass+ if necessary. Otherwise come at day's end when it cools down a bit or at night. For best photo ops, ask to be seated in the very last row of seats (you might have to wait for the next vehicle) where you can pivot for an unobstructed view of the animals you just passed.** ✉ *Africa, Animal Kingdom* ☞ *Duration: 18 mins. Crowds: Moderate to heavy. Audience: All ages.*

Pangani Forest Exploration Trail

AMUSEMENT PARK/WATER PARK | Calling this a nature walk doesn't really do it justice. A path winds through dense foliage, alongside streams, and past waterfalls. En route there are viewing points where you can watch a beautiful rare okapi (a member of the giraffe family) munching the vegetation, a family and a separate bachelor group of lowland gorillas, hippos (which you usually can see underwater), comical meerkats (a kind of mongoose), exotic birds, and a bizarre colony of hairless mole rats. Disney animal experts are at many viewing points to answer questions. **For people with disabilities:**

Wheelchair accessible and equipped for audio-description devices. Guests with service animals should check with a host before entering. **TIP→ Come while awaiting a Kilimanjaro Safaris Fastpass+ appointment or just after you exit your safari vehicle; avoid coming at the hottest time of day, when the gorillas like to nap.** ✉ *Africa, Animal Kingdom* ☞ *Duration: Up to You. Crowds: Moderate to heavy. Audience: All ages.*

Restaurants

★ Harambe Market
$ | AFRICAN | FAMILY | Carved into the walkway leading to the Wildlife Express train, this four-station food mart offers a selection of gyros, pork sausage on naan bread, and a ribs or chicken bowls. Everyone will want their own watermelon or pineapple-coconut shave ice. **Known for:** shaded, family-size, outdoor-market seating; African-inspired chicken, sausage, and ribs; appealing kids meals. $ *Average main: $12* ✉ *Africa, Animal Kingdom* ☎ *407/939–5277* 🌐 *disneyworld.disney.go.com/dining.*

★ Tusker House
$$$$ | AFRICAN | FAMILY | This good-value restaurant offers all-buffet dining three meals a day, and a Donald's safari-theme character crew complements the African-esque decor and menu. In addition to standard kids fare, the menu has healthy dishes like curry chicken, *peri-peri* (African hot pepper) marinated salmon, strip loin rubbed with *berbere* (an African spice mix), and saffron-infused root vegetables. **Known for:** great food with reasonable prices; character appearances; wide-ranging buffet choices. $ *Average main: $54* ✉ *Africa, Animal Kingdom* ☎ *407/939–3463* 🌐 *www.disneyworld.disney.go.com/dining.*

Rafiki's Planet Watch

While in Africa's Harambe section, board the 250-passenger rustic Wildlife Express steam train for a ride to a unique center of eco-awareness named for the wise baboon from *The Lion King*. Young children especially enjoy the chance to explore these three animal-friendly areas.

Sights

Affection Section
AMUSEMENT PARK/WATER PARK | In this petting zoo, children and adults can pet and even borrow brushes to groom goats, sheep, donkeys, and other domesticated creatures. **For people with disabilities:** Guests must transfer from ECVs to standard wheelchairs. No service animals are allowed in this area. **TIP→ If you visit at the right time, you might see pigs demonstrate how they've learned to paint with their snouts.** ✉ *Rafiki's Planet Watch, Animal Kingdom* ☞ *Duration: Up to you. Crowds: Light to moderate. Audience: All ages, mostly children.*

Conservation Station
AMUSEMENT PARK/WATER PARK | This is a great place to meet some of the park's animal handlers and to gather round for a critter encounter. You'll learn about the park's veterinary care, ongoing research, and food preparation for hundreds of animal inhabitants. Interactive exhibits are simple fun for younger children and have messages about worldwide efforts to protect endangered species and their habitats. Here, you also can find out how to connect with conservation efforts in your own community. You can now use your Fastpass+ at The Animation Experience at Conservation Station, where a Disney artist leads a class in drawing a famous (animal) Disney character. **For people with disabilities:** Guest may remain in wheelchairs or ECVs. **TIP→ This is a great place to begin a family conservation**

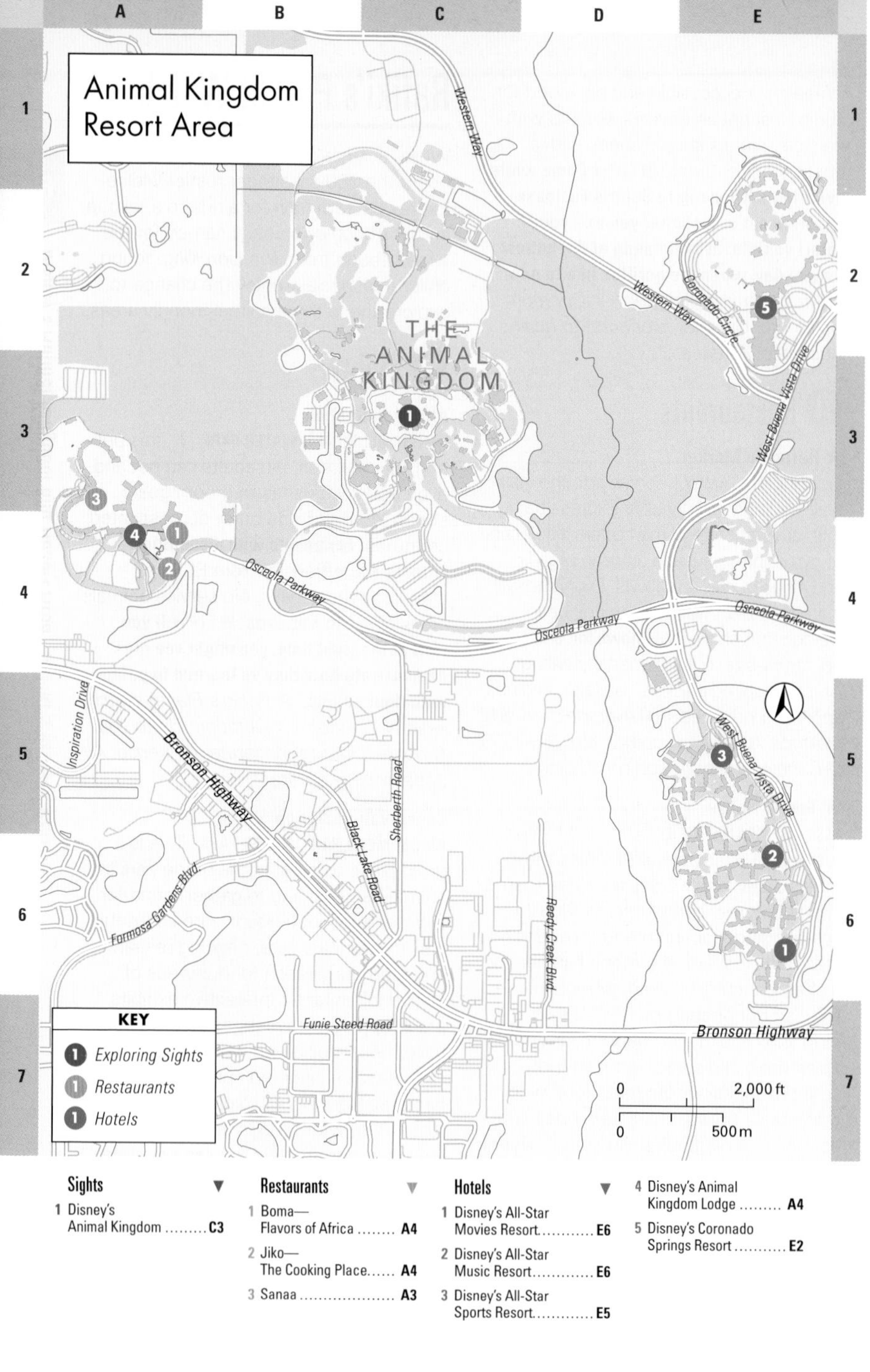

Sights

1 Disney's Animal Kingdom C3

Restaurants

1 Boma—Flavors of Africa A4

2 Jiko—The Cooking Place...... A4

3 Sanaa A3

Hotels

1 Disney's All-Star Movies Resort........... E6

2 Disney's All-Star Music Resort............ E6

3 Disney's All-Star Sports Resort............ E5

4 Disney's Animal Kingdom Lodge A4

5 Disney's Coronado Springs Resort E2

Disney's Animal Kingdom Lodge

project. ✉ *Rafiki's Planet Watch, Animal Kingdom* ☞ *Duration: Up to you. Crowds: Light to moderate. Audience: All ages.*

Habitat Habit!

AMUSEMENT PARK/WATER PARK | On this educational wildlife trail that focuses heavily on animal conservation efforts, you get a close-up look at the entertaining antics of cotton-top tamarins—small South American primates named for their flowing white manes—while you learn how to live with all of the Earth's animals. **For people with disabilities:** Wheelchair accessible. **TIP→ Ask questions; the animal-care cast members enjoy telling you about these cute critters.** ✉ *Rafiki's Planet Watch, Animal Kingdom* ☞ *Duration: Up to you. Crowds: Light to moderate. Audience: All ages.*

Animal Kingdom Resort Area

The Animal Kingdom Resort Area is a mix of an immersive luxury resort, well-priced value resorts, and an elaborate moderately priced resort. Nearest to the park, the Animal Kingdom Lodge is an experience in and of itself, with some of the best restaurants on Disney property, great informational programs, and proximity to the savanna, where live animals roam their own enclosure, so it's easy to hop from the pool to a viewing platform. Animal experts are on hand throughout the day to provide information about what you're seeing, and after dark, night-vision googles are available for further animal viewing. Coronado Springs offers beautiful, recently renovated rooms for an excellent price in a lively Mexican setting, complete with a Mayan-themed waterslide. On the other end of the spectrum are the no-frills, best value for your dollar, All-Star Resorts, three hotels that are usually the cheapest on Disney property. Here you'll find few amenities beyond a pool and a food court, but you can still take advantage of the extra-Magic hours, free Disney bus service, and early Fastpass+ reservations.

Restaurants

★ Boma–Flavors of Africa

$$$$ | AFRICAN | FAMILY | Boma takes Western-style ingredients and prepares them with an African twist. You walk through an African marketplace–style dining room to help yourself at counters piled high with flavor from an upscale buffet like no other. **Known for:** superb food both the timid and adventurous will like; African flavors and dishes; endless buffet with wonderful service that appeals to kids. *$ Average main: $49 ✉ Animal Kingdom Lodge, 2901 Osceola Pkwy., Animal Kingdom Resort Area ☎ 407/939–3463 🌐 disneyworld.disney.go.com/dining ⏲ No lunch.*

★ Jiko—The Cooking Place

$$$$ | AFRICAN | "Jiko" means "the cooking place" in Swahili, and this restaurant is certainly that, offering a menu that is more African-inspired than purely African, as well as a strong selection of South African wines. The dining area surrounds two big, wood-burning ovens and a grill area where you can watch cooks in North African–style caps working on your meal. **Known for:** African cuisine with an American flair and Indonesian accents; sophisticated surroundings and decor; Moroccan lamb. *$ Average main: $45 ✉ Animal Kingdom Lodge, 2901 Osceola Pkwy., Animal Kingdom Resort Area ☎ 407/939–3463 🌐 disneyworld.disney.go.com/dining ⏲ No lunch.*

★ Sanaa

$$$ | AFRICAN | FAMILY | Most of the flavors are from India, yet Sanaa is really a celebration of the Spice Islands—locales off the coast of Africa that for centuries hosted traders from the world's corners. Exotic yet approachable lunches and dinners make it a true find on the outer edges of the Disney empire; views of zebras and giraffes on the savanna right out the picture windows are another draw. **Known for:** surprising combinations of African and Indian flavors; Indian style bread service; African inspired biryani. *$ Average main: $26 ✉ Animal Kingdom Villas—Kidani Village, 3701 W. Osceola Pkwy., Animal Kingdom Resort Area ☎ 407/989–3463 🌐 www.disneyworld.disney.go.com/dining.*

Hotels

Disney's All-Star Movies Resort

$ | RESORT | FAMILY | Scenes and characters from favorite Disney movies dot the landscape of this large, value-priced, family resort: *101 Dalmatians* of all sizes scamper along railings; Mickey, in his *Sorcerer's Apprentice* robes, commands the waters at the *Fantasia* pool, and a larger-than-life Woody cavorts with his *Toy Story* pals. **Pros:** familiar characters and lots of activities to amuse kids; room rates among lowest at Disney; easy access to Animal Kingdom. **Cons:** at the opposite end of WDW from Magic Kingdom; rooms and decor need refreshing; few plugs for charging phones or tablets. *$ Rooms from: $138 ✉ 1901 W. Buena Vista Dr., Animal Kingdom Resort Area ☎ 407/939–7000 🌐 www.disneyworld.disney.go.com/resorts 1,920 rooms No meals.*

Disney's All-Star Music Resort

$ | RESORT | FAMILY | Music rules in this colorful, value-priced, family-centric resort that resembles a Florida beach hotel of the 1950s. **Pros:** good value for family holidays; music theme is carried throughout; two heated pools. **Cons:** suites have sleeper chair and sleeper ottoman; long way to Magic Kingdom; rooms and bathrooms are basic and small. *$ Rooms from: $139 ✉ 1801 W. Buena Vista Dr., Animal Kingdom Resort Area ☎ 407/939–6000 🌐 www.*

Did You Know?

The All-Star Sports, Music, and Movies Resorts and the Art of Animation Resort are all thematically designed. Goofy is the pitcher in the baseball diamond–shaped pool at the Sports resort, a piano-shaped pool can be found at the Music resort, a huge Buzz Lightyear figure stands tall at the Movies resort, and Disney and Pixar animation classics star at Art of Animation.

disneyworld.disney.go.com/resorts *1,704 rooms* *No meals.*

Disney's All-Star Sports Resort
$ | RESORT | FAMILY | Stay here if you want the All-American, sports-mad, quintessential Disney-with-your-kids experience, or if you're a couple to whom all that pitter-pattering of little feet is a reasonable trade-off for a good deal on a room, albeit a small one. **Pros:** unbeatable price for a Disney property; kids love sports themes; close to Disney's ESPN Wide World of Sports Complex. **Cons:** no kids clubs or programs; distances between rooms and on-site amenities can seem vast; farthest resort from Magic Kingdom means you'll spend time on the bus. *Rooms from: $139* *1701 W. Buena Vista Dr., Animal Kingdom Resort Area* *407/939–5000* *www.disneyworld.disney.go.com/resorts* *1,704 rooms* *No meals.*

★ Disney's Animal Kingdom Lodge
$$$$ | RESORT | FAMILY | Entering the vast atrium lobby of this African-inspired lodge is like entering a cathedral with a roof formed of thatch instead of stone; giraffes, zebras, and other wildlife roam just outside the windows of the resort, designed to resemble an African *kraal* (animal enclosure). **Pros:** extraordinary wildlife and cultural experiences on-site; excellent restaurants; breakfast buffet in Boma is a bargain. **Cons:** shuttle to parks other than Animal Kingdom can take more than an hour; concierge-level rooms have $100-plus surcharge; long corridors. *Rooms from: $436* *2901 Osceola Pkwy., Animal Kingdom Resort Area* *407/938–3000* *www.disneyworld.disney.go.com/resorts* *1,404 rooms* *No meals.*

Disney's Coronado Springs Resort
$$$ | RESORT | FAMILY | Popular with convention-goers and families who appreciate its casual Southwestern architecture, this colorful property has a lively, Mexican-style food court, an elaborate swimming pool, and a moderate price for a Disney resort. **Pros:** great pool with a play-area arcade for kids and a bar for adults; lots of outdoor activities; wide range of dining choices. **Cons:** some accommodations are a long trek from the restaurants; standard rooms are on the small side; the lake is not for swimming. *Rooms from: $289* *1000 W. Buena Vista Dr., Animal Kingdom Resort Area* *407/939–1000* *www.disneyworld.disney.go.com/resorts* *Access to Disney courses* *2,384 rooms* *No meals.*

Chapter 7

DISNEY SPRINGS AND RESORT AREA

WITH TYPHOON LAGOON

7

Updated by
Gary McKechnie

Sights	Restaurants	Hotels	Shopping	Nightlife
★★☆☆☆	★★★★★	★★★★★	★★★★★	★★★★☆

PARK SNAPSHOT

TOP EXPERIENCES

■ **Being There:** Perhaps the most enjoyable aspect of Disney Springs is not a single store, club, or restaurant. It's soaking in the Springs' overall vibe (especially when it comes alive each evening).

■ **Cirque du Soleil:** The newest Cirque show, Drawn to Life, premiered in 2020 and promises to draw guests to its surreal elegance for years to come.

■ **Dinner, then Launch:** Take a 25-minute waterfront tour in an Amphicar, a vehicle that drives on land and floats on water, which launches from beside the BOATHOUSE restaurant.

■ **Splitsville:** This retro bowling alley puts a new spin on knocking down pins. It's cool, hip, and hours of fun.

■ **Treat Yourself:** Disney Springs presents the resort's greatest concentration of upscale dining experiences. So set aside the fast food and quick-grab kiosks, and treat yourself to a memorable evening meal.

■ **World of Disney:** There will never be a shortage of Disney souvenirs, and this sprawling store (the world's largest purveyor of all things Disney) proves how many ways they can market their magic.

PLANNING YOUR TIME

Disney Springs offers two distinct experiences. During the day, you can breeze through the four districts at a leisurely pace in about three hours; roughly an hour for dining and two for shopping. In the evening, those same three hours might limit your range since you'll be working through throngs of other guests, stopping to watch street performers and waiting for an available table at a restaurant. But if you don't mind dealing with the people, Disney Springs really lights up after dark. The shows of Cirque du Soleil, concerts at the House of Blues, street performers, strolling musicians, and interactive open-air stage shows all add a level of energy that makes this a truly magical entertainment complex and uniquely Disney experience.

GETTING HERE

■ You'll see Disney Springs from I–4. Arriving traffic is a constant and reaches its peaks as darkness descends. Disney resort guests should take a free shuttle bus from their hotel. There are three big garages, as well as surface lots. Self-parking is free, though one lot near the NBA Experience charges $10; valet parking costs $20.

QUICK BITES

■ **Earl of Sandwich.** The popular and affordable eatery anchors the east end of the Marketplace and offers freshly prepared sandwiches accented with creative toppings and spreads. ✉ *The Marketplace, Disney Springs.*

■ **Food Trucks.** A changing parade of Disney food trucks pulls up near Starbucks and then serves up some of the favorite Disney dishes you'd find in the theme parks and resort hotels. ✉ *West Side, Disney Springs.*

■ **Morimoto Street Food.** An add-on to the full-service restaurant, this quick-service window offers a wide assortment of items including sushi, rice bowls, sticky ribs, egg rolls, bao tacos, and beverages. ✉ *Morimoto Asia, The Landing, Disney Springs.*

East of EPCOT and close to Interstate 4 along a large lake is a vast shopping, dining, and entertainment complex built to serve both locals and Disney guests.

Rather than attractions, the main draw of Disney Springs is its vast array of shops and restaurants, although there are a few other things to do besides eat and shop. In Spring 2020, Cirque du Soleil premiered Drawn to Life, which replaced its long-running show, La Nouba. Nearby, an elaborate arcade gives way to the NBA Experience, which immerses you in a variety of challenges, drills, and basketball trivia. There's also a multiplex cinema, a retro-hip bowling alley, live concerts, virtual reality activities, and a level of energy unlike anywhere else at Disney.

Disney Springs

Disney Springs is comprised of four areas: the Marketplace, West Side, The Landing, and Town Center. To anchor the development, Disney Imagineers created a beautiful network of clear, turquoise waterways that replicate the look of Florida's natural springs. Thousands gather here each evening for people-watching, a leisurely stroll, shopping, dining, or simply to be part of the action. Several multistory garages offer free parking, which makes it easy to access, and added conveniences include locker, stroller, and wheelchair rentals as well as two Guest Relations (aka Guest Services) centers.

Marketplace

In the Marketplace, the easternmost Disney Springs area, you can meander along winding sidewalks and explore hidden alcoves. Children love to splash in fountains that spring from the pavement and ride the miniature train and old-time carousel. Toy stores entice with creation-stations and too many treasures to comprehend. There are plenty of spots to grab a bite, sip a cappuccino, or enjoy an ice cream along the lakefront (Ghirardelli's) while watching the volcano atop the Rainforest Café erupt—or head over to visit dinos at the T-Rex restaurant. Most Marketplace shops, boutiques, and eateries begin opening at 9:30 am and stay open through 11 pm or midnight.

Coffee and Quick Bites

The Marketplace has two table-service restaurants (**T-Rex Café** and the **Rainforest Café**), and there are several walk-up kiosks and counter-service options for on the go and casual meal sandwiches, snacks, and drinks. These include **AristoCrepes** (crepes with various fillings), **B.B. Wolf's Sausage Co.** (European-style sausages and sauces), **Dockside Margaritas** (plus brews), **Earl of Sandwich** (specialty sandwiches, soups, and salads), **Downtown Snow Company** (shave ice and cold drinks), **Ghiradelli's Soda Fountain and Chocolate Shop** (sundaes, floats, malts, shakes, and... chocolate), **Joffrey's** (tropical smoothies), **Starbucks** (you know), **Wetzel's Pretzels** (flavored pretzels, hot dogs), and **Wolfgang Puck Express** (quick-service breakfasts, pizza, salads, soups, sandwiches, chicken).

 Nightlife

Although the Marketplace offers little in the line of typical nightlife, there's hardly a more enjoyable place for families to spend a leisurely evening strolling to shop (or window-shop) for unique items in Disney stores of all types or to enjoy ice cream at a courtyard café. It's here that you can arrange for a princess-style makeover at the Bibbidi Bobbidi Boutique and peruse a dozen theme showrooms in the largest Disney store of all: The World of Disney.

 Shopping

Barcelona has Las Ramblas, Orlando has The Marketplace, a lakefront outdoor mall with meandering sidewalks, hidden alcoves, fountains for kids to splash around in, and absolutely fabulous toy stores. The Marketplace is a great place to spend a relaxing afternoon or active evening—especially if you're looking for a way to give the kids a break from standing in line. There are plenty of spots to grab a bite, rest your feet, or enjoy a cup of coffee while taking in the pleasant water views and the hustle and bustle of excited tourists. Things are generally open from 9:30 am to 11 pm, so you'll have plenty of time to explore. And if you happen to run out of cash while you're shopping, you can apply for instant Disney credit at any register. How convenient.

Drumroll, please ... 

Of more than 300 retail outlets at the Walt Disney World Resort, perhaps the best of all is the truly huge World of Disney store in the Marketplace section of Disney Springs. You could actually skip many of the stores in the theme parks, since you'll find just about everything you want right here. And although it might be a cliché, there really *is* something for everyone, whether you're looking for something small and inexpensive like a $3 princess pen or a pricier Disney collectible like an elegant Mickey timepiece or figurine.

The Art of Disney
ART GALLERIES | For nearly a century, Disney has created distinct and iconic characters, theme parks, and films that have become fan favorites as well as the subjects of collectible works of art. In this intriguing gallery you'll find a dazzling array of Disney images captured in a variety of media, including sculptures, limited-edition Sericels, lithographs, framed prints, original paintings, and figurines. For beginners, it's nice to find that it doesn't cost a fortune to become a collector of Disneyana—you can even start with a collectible postcard. Check the calendar: Disney artists often come here to meet guests and sign their works. ✉ *The Marketplace, Disney Springs* 🌐 *www.disneysprings.com/shopping/the-art-of-disney.*

Disney's Pin Traders
GIFTS/SOUVENIRS | Many cast members and guests share (and wear) a common interest: pins that reflect favorite characters, special events, and all things Disney. Often affixed to lanyards, these Disney pins are a curiously treasured part of the company's subculture, with owners buying and swapping pins the way kids used to trade baseball cards. This Marketplace shop is one of Disney's premier pin-trading destinations—and where you can also buy Mickey ears and MagicBands. ✉ *Marketplace, Disney Springs* 🌐 *www.disneyworld.disney.go.com/shops/disney-springs/disneys-pin-traders.*

The LEGO Store

TOYS | When you spy a LEGO sea serpent in the lagoon, you know you're in the right place for a LEGO shopping spree. An impressive collection of large, elaborate sculptures and piles of colorful LEGO bricks welcome children, who head straight to hands-on play tables and begin work on toy castles, cars, and pirate ships. Check out the Pick-A-Brick Wall, where kids can create anything from a *Star Wars* spaceship to a miniature Sydney Opera House, and snap a photo with oversize character models like Woody and Buzz Lightyear. The discounted merchandise section is worth a look. ✉ *Marketplace, Disney Springs* 🌐 *www.disneyworld.disney.go.com/shops/disney-springs/the-lego-store.*

Once Upon A Toy

TOYS | Classic board games and activity stations will keep you entertained in this well-stocked store. Theme toy rooms feature princess and fairy items or *Star Wars* stations where you can create your own light saber. There are lots of classic games redesigned with Disney themes, like a Haunted Mansion version of the Game of Life. You can test-drive many of the toys, and at the Mr. Potato Head Creation Station, you can fill a box with assorted eyes, lips, noses (and even Mickey ears) and make your own potato sculpture ✉ *Marketplace, Disney Springs* 🌐 *www.disneyworld.disney.go.com/shops/disney-springs/once-upon-a-toy.*

Tren-D

CLOTHING | This Marketplace boutique has "hip" and "eclectic" written all over it (hence the name), with ever-changing merchandise that gives (primarily teenage) shoppers a chance to wear clothing imprinted with 1980s and '90s cartoon characters, fashions from the Disney Parks Forever Collection, and chic sundresses with subtle Mickey-ear designs that are perfect for an evening at the shops and clubs of Disney Springs. Designer items are from Billabong, Dooney & Bourke, Harveys (The Original Seatbeltbags), and Roxy, with many featuring fairies and princesses. ✉ *Marketplace, Disney Springs* 🌐 *www.disneyworld.disney.go.com/shops/disney-springs/trend.*

World of Disney

TOYS | Beware of sensory overload at *the* world's largest Disney superstore—where approximately half a million items are featured in a dozen rooms that cover 50,000 square feet. Theme shopping areas like the princess room (hello, Cinderella dress or Ariel costume) help steer you to just the right toys, clothing, collectibles, candy, housewares, photo frames, books, dresses, cookware, and collectible Disney pins. The Bibbidi Bobbidi Boutique, similar to the one at the Magic Kingdom, finds skilled stylists applying make-up, costumes, glitter, and magic to transform normal little girls into sparkling princesses. ✉ *Marketplace, Disney Springs* 🌐 *www.disneyworld.disney.go.com/shops/disney-springs/world-of-disney.*

The Landing

Situated on a small island, this family-oriented dining and entertainment district is the part of Disney Springs that features nearly a dozen eateries, some run by celebrity chefs such as Masaharu Morimoto, Art Smith, and Rick Bayless. The restaurants all offer indoor and patio dining, and some, such as Raglan Road, also offer entertainment, in this case music and traditional Irish step-dance performances every night and during weekend brunch. A massive entertainment complex, The Edison, offers daytime dining and nighttime cabaret (and acrobats), while the adjoining Maria & Enzo's serves high-end Italian cuisine. The BOATHOUSE features attractive waterfront dining, with views of the water taxis delivering folks across the lake, and the tiny, colorful boat-cars tootling up and

Disney Springs
Disney's Saratoga Springs Resort & Spa
Broadway
Union Avenue
Broadway
0
500 ft
0
100 m
Lake Buena Vista
DISNEY SPRINGS
West Side Dock
The Landing Dock
West Side
The Landing
Cirque du Soleil: Drawn to Life
Town Center
East Buena Vista Drive
East Buena Vista Drive
Interstate 4 South Bound Ramp
A
B
C
D
E
F
1
2
3
4
5
6
7
8
9

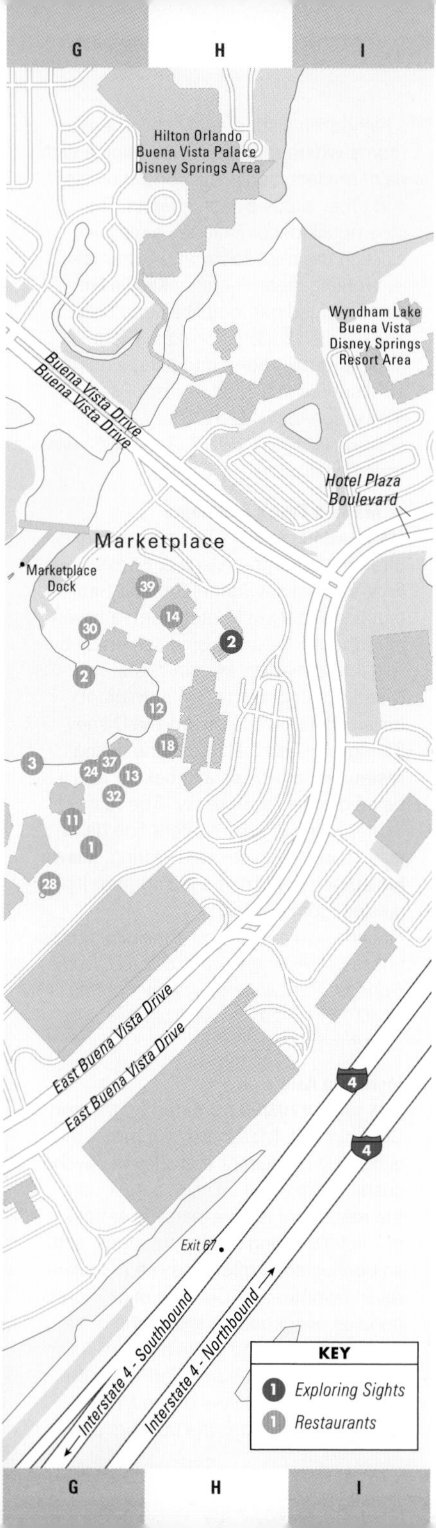
G
H
I
Hilton Orlando
Buena Vista Palace
Disney Springs Area
Wyndham Lake
Buena Vista
Disney Springs
Resort Area
Buena Vista Drive
Buena Vista Drive
Hotel Plaza
Boulevard
Marketplace
Marketplace
Dock
East Buena Vista Drive
East Buena Vista Drive
4
4
Exit 67
Interstate 4 - Southbound
Interstate 4 - Northbound
KEY
Exploring Sights
Restaurants
G
H
I

Sights

1 NBA Experience at Disney Springs **C6**

2 Star Wars™: Secrets of the Empire by ILMxLAB and The VOID **H4**

Restaurants

1 Amorette's Patisserie **G6**

2 AristoCrêpes **G4**

3 B.B. Wolf's Sausage Co. **G5**

4 The Basket at Wine Bar George **F5**

5 Blaze Pizza **E6**

6 The BOATHOUSE **E5**

7 Chef Art Smith's Homecomin' **E6**

8 Chicken Guy! **E6**

9 City Works Eatery and Pour House **C6**

10 D-Luxe Burger **F6**

11 The Daily Poutine **G5**

12 Dockside Margaritas ... **H5**

13 Downtown Snow Company **G5**

14 Earl of Sandwich **H4**

15 The Edison **E6**

16 Erin McKenna Bakery NYC **F5**

17 Frontera Cucina **F6**

18 Ghirardelli's Soda Fountain and Chocolate Shop **H5**

19 House of Blues **C5**

20 Häagen-Dazs® Ice Cream Shop **E6**

21 Jaleo by José Andrés **C6**

22 Jock Lindsey's Hangar Bar **E5**

23 Joffrey's Coffee **F5**

24 Joffrey's Smoothies **G5**

25 Maria & Enzo's Ristorante **E6**

26 Morimoto Asia **E5**

27 Paddlefish **F5**

28 The Polite Pig **G6**

29 Raglan Road Irish Pub **F5**

30 Rainforest Café **G4**

31 Sprinkles Disney Springs **F5**

32 Starbucks **G5**

33 Stargazers Bar **E6**

34 T-Rex Café **F5**

35 Terralina Crafted Italian **F5**

36 Vivoli Il Gelato **F5**

37 Wetzel's Pretzels **G5**

38 Wolfgang Puck Bar & Grill **E7**

39 Wolfgang Puck Express **G4**

40 YeSake Kiosk **E6**

down the ramp. Paddlefish, a three-story eatery inspired by a Mississippi paddle steamer, serves seafood, and the view from the top-floor lounge includes the erupting volcano at Rainforest Cafe across the water.

Restaurants

The BOATHOUSE

$$$$ | SEAFOOD | Who knows why the contemporary and upscale BOATHOUSE on the Disney Springs waterfront uses all CAPITALS in its name, but it does. Maybe it's just to draw attention to itself and its fresh seafood, raw bar, and premium steaks and chops. **Known for:** fresh seafood; lobster bake for two with whole Maine lobster and clams; "Amphicars" for rent. *Average main: $35* *The Landing, Disney Springs* *407/939–2628* *disneyworld.disney.go.com/dining.*

Chef Art Smith's Homecomin'

$$$ | AMERICAN | FAMILY | Superstar chef Art Smith, recognized by foodies for having worked for Oprah and cooked for heads of state, incorporates locally sourced ingredients from nearby farms, ranches, and fisheries in this tribute to downhome Southern cooking. Having been a part of Disney's College program (he started his career with a culinary internship here), his past has brought him back to present dishes like his famous fried chicken, deviled eggs, shrimp and grits, pork chops, fried green tomatoes, mashed potatoes, and Southern slaw. **Known for:** celebrity chef Art Smith's comfort food; fried chicken; signature cocktails and hummingbird cake. *Average main: $28* *The Landing, Disney Springs* *407/560–0100* *www.homecominkitchen.com.*

The Edison

$$$ | ITALIAN | A massive brick structure that, according to Disney lore, was the original power plant for the town of Disney Springs, now houses The Edison, an entertainment arena of more than a half-dozen distinct and richly themed rooms where food and drink mingle with palm readers, aerialists, contortionists, and other circus sideshow acts. The steampunk decor includes a massive clock in the main lobby and a dramatic, working steam engine. **Known for:** sophisticated bar food like lamb balls and candied bacon; speakeasy late-night entertainment; intriguing industrial atmosphere in a "power plant" setting. *Average main: $25* *The Landing, Disney Springs* *407/939–6244* *www.theedisonfla.com.*

★ **Maria & Enzo's Ristorante**

$$$ | ITALIAN | FAMILY | This complex of three restaurants—Maria & Enzo's, Enzo's Hideaway Tunnel Bar and Restaurant, and Pizza Ponte—form a haven of authentic Italian cuisine served up by two internationally known chefs. The Disney "story" tells of an immigrant Italian couple who convert the Disney Springs Air Terminal into a fine dining restaurant, a pizzeria and bakery, and a belowground "speakeasy." The reality is that Maria & Enzo's offers fine Italian cuisine in a sophisticated setting. **Known for:** authentic Roman and southern Italian cuisine; some of the best steaks in Orlando; whimsical and detail-rich atmospheres. *Average main: $25* *Disney Springs, The Landing, Disney Springs* *407/560–8466* *www.patinagroup.com/maria-enzos.*

Morimoto Asia

$$$$ | ASIAN FUSION | Created by the Iron Chef himself, Masaharu Morimoto, this is his first restaurant that moves beyond sushi. While you'll still find a sushi bar, the restaurant is an expansive setting of multiple dining spaces, lounges, and an open kitchen offering a menu of pan-Asian favorites like Chinese duck, Korean noodles, Singaporean laksa, and more. **Known for:** high-end sushi and Pan-Asian cuisine; late-night hours until 1 am on weekends; best views of the Disney Springs lagoon from the upstairs patio.

$ Average main: $35 ✉ The Landing, Disney Springs ☎ 407/939–6686 🌐 www.patinagroup.com/morimoto-asia.

Paddlefish

$$$$ | **SEAFOOD** | Housed in a paddleboat on Lake Buena Vista, Paddlefish (the once popular Fulton Crab House) is a sophisticated seafood destination with multiple outdoor dining areas. Same-day fresh-catch selections are presented in any number of ways, from raw bar delicacies to traditional Gulf-shore jambalaya or the Build-Your-Own Seafood Boil. **Known for:** freshest possible seafood from around the world; casual, late-night vibe from the rooftop lounge bar; raw bar and impeccably cooked dishes. $ *Average main: $34* ✉ *The Landing, Disney Springs* ☎ *407/939–2268* 🌐 *disneyworld.disney.go.com/dining.*

★ **Raglan Road Irish Pub**

$$$ | **IRISH** | **FAMILY** | If an authentic Irish pub—actually transported from the Old Country plank by plank—is your thing, Raglan Road is the place to go, for superb traditional and inventive dishes. In addition to excellent fish-and-chips and shepherd's pie, the chefs twist Irish cuisine to include Gulf shrimp and risotto with buffalo mozzarella and fresh peas. **Known for:** first-rate dining and special chef-driven events; extensive beer and ale selections, including exclusive brews; nightly, sometimes hourly, entertainment. $ *Average main: $25* ✉ *The Landing, Disney Springs* ☎ *407/938–0300* 🌐 *www.raglanroadirishpub.com.*

Terralina Crafted Italian

$$$ | **ITALIAN** | Under the guidance of James Beard Award winner and *Top Chef* master Tony Mantuano, Terralina brings back sophistication and southern Italian cuisine to Disney Springs. Meticulously planned to look like a resort in Italy's Lake District, Terralina's open design and wood-fired grills provide a stylish atmosphere and some of the best recipes Mantuano can create, including wood-fired, hand-tossed pizzas along with salads and sandwiches. **Known for:** antipasti tower starter; wood-fired pizzas, steaks, and seafood; stylish, Italian country atmosphere. $ *Average main: $30* ✉ *The Landing, Disney Springs* ☎ *407/939–6244* 🌐 *www.terralinacrafteditalian.com.*

Coffee and Quick Bites

When on-the-go in The Landing, look for some along-the-way places like **The Basket at Wine Bar George** (more than 100 wines as well as small plate meals), **Erin McKenna Bakery NYC** (gluten-free and vegan options), **Jock Lindsey's Hangar Bar** (beers, cocktails, small plates), **Joffrey's** (coffees), and **Vivoli Il Gelato** (gelato, paninis, and espresso).

Shopping

Largely populated by nautical-theme restaurants, The Landing has its share of cleverly appointed shops.

The Art of Shaving

SPECIALTY STORES | Sure, shaving is a daily task for many men, but there's something wonderfully indulgent about really doing it right. For that, the staff will remind you that you need high-end shaving creams, brushes, gels, aftershaves, moisturizers, and razors, which just happen to be sold in this intriguing shop. For added indulgence, drop by the Barber Spa for a hot towel shave, haircut, facial, scalp therapy, or any assortment of special treatments that "make handsome happen." ✉ *The Landing, Disney Springs* 🌐 *www.disneyworld.disney.go.com/shops/disney-springs/art-of-shaving.*

Chapel Hats

CLOTHING | Bride-and-groom ears are among the most recognizable fashion statements you'll see here, but they represent just a fraction of the inventory. Shelves are stacked with every shape and style: broad-brimmed sun hats, jaunty Panama hats, 1960s-style porkpie hats, brightly colored fascinators, Indiana

Jones–inspired fedoras, and a few dozen others to top off your trip. ✉ *The Landing, Disney Springs* 🌐 *www.disneyworld.disney.go.com/shops/disney-springs/chapel-hats.*

West Side

Disney's West Side was fairly quiet following the closure of Cirque du Soleil's long-running show, La Nouba. In 2020, though, the troupe premiered its new Drawn to Life show, which has re-energized the district. To be fair, the West Side's buzz had been increasing steadily with the earlier arrival of Splitsville Luxury Lanes, a modern take on the American classic bowling alley, with 30 lanes on two floors, weekend DJs, and upscale eats like filet sliders and sushi at indoor and outdoor tables. The district also got a swoosh from the NBA Experience, a basketball-focused attraction where you can find out what it's like in the pros as you dribble, shoot, and compete in trivia and arcade games.

Elsewhere in this entertainment-rich district, you can still enjoy concerts or the Sunday morning Gospel Brunch at the House of Blues, and you can marvel at aerial park views on a tethered flight aboard the classic Aéro30 helium balloon. Add shopping in an assortment of boutiques, dining in such restaurants as Jaleo by José Andres or City Works Eatery & Pour House, and taking a water taxi across the lagoon to the Marketplace, and you've got yourself a splendid evening. Shops open at 9:30 or 10:30 am, and closing time is between 11 pm and 2 am.

Sights

NBA Experience at Disney Springs

SPORTS—SIGHT | **FAMILY** | In a building inspired by the soaring architecture of NBA arenas around the country, this state-of-the-art attraction includes interactive games and competitions, immersive experiences, a retail store, and a theme restaurant. You have full access to a range of activities, including shooting baskets in a timed competition, trying to sink shots by launching basketballs from a slingshot, getting tips on dribbling, being tested on basketball trivia, testing your skills as a ref, being challenged on arcade games, and experiencing the sensation of being selected in the NBA draft. ✉ *West Side, Disney Springs* 🌐 *www.disneysprings.com/entertainment/nba-experience* 🎟 *$34.*

Star Wars™: Secrets of the Empire by ILMxLAB and The VOID

ARTS VENUE | This multisensory, untethered, hyper-reality adventure places you inside the drama and action of films, the most popular being *Star Wars: Secrets of the Empire.* Wearing special headgear that meshes the real world with the virtual one through 3-D imagery and sound, members of your group appear as stormtroopers transported to the molten planet of Mustafar, where you'll blast away at giant lava monsters and work to recover Imperial intelligence to help save the rebel alliance. Simple right? New challenges based on films such as Wreck-It Ralph and Marvel characters are often introduced to give you a chance to enter entirely new virtual environments. Guests under 16 must have a parent or guardian present. ✉ *West Side, Disney Springs* 🌐 *www.disneysprings.com/attractions/the-void* 🎟 *$40.*

Restaurants

City Works Eatery and Pour House

$$ | **AMERICAN** | Nearly 100 beers as well as eight wines on tap provide reasons enough for Disney guests and a fair share of Disney cast members to frequent what's called the "ultimate sports bar." Paired with a global collection of rare, limited, and special brews are meals large enough to share; burgers big enough for one; and bar bites like flatbreads, nachos, and wings to whet your appetite. The omnipresent sight of 17 high-def televisions makes watching live sporting events a natural in this active joint. **Known for:** extensive selection of beers on tap; over-the-top sports bar atmosphere; discounted drinks and food during extended happy hours. *Average main: $16 Disney Springs West Side, Lake Buena Vista 407/801–3730 www.disneysprings.com/dining/city-works.*

House of Blues

$$ | AMERICAN | FAMILY | Be prepared for a soundtrack of high-decibel music as you dine on an eclectic menu that offers everything from ribs to shrimp and grits to a tasty chicken Caesar salad. Consider trying the Juicy Lucy, a bacon cheeseburger with jalapeño and chipotle mayo; the pulled-pork sandwiches and the cornbread are also delicious. **Known for:** high-end burgers and New Orleans fare; Sunday gospel brunch; loud background music at all times. *Average main: $21 West Side, Disney Springs 407/934–2583 www.houseofblues.com.*

Jaleo by José Andrés

$$ | SPANISH | Jaleo (pronounced huh- *lay*-oh) means "revelry," and in this contemporary and spacious setting that opened in 2020 diners celebrate with authentic paellas cooked over a wood fire, as well as chef José Andrés's signature dishes such as *gambas al ajillo* (shrimp sautéed with garlic and chili) and *croquetas de pollo* (classic Spanish chicken fritters). An extensive selection of tapas are perfect when you'd just like to taste-drive a variety of items. **Known for:** authentic Spanish entrees and tapas; fire-pit prepared paellas and steaks; contemporary, multilevel design. *Average main: $18 Disney Springs West Side, Walt Disney World 321/348–3211 www.disneysprings.com/dining/jaleo-by-jose-andres.*

Coffee and Quick Bites

In this active area of nightclubs and extravaganzas, a few simple dining and drinking options stand out: **Chicken Guy!** created by celebrity chef Guy Fieri and restaurateur Robert Earl (chicken sandwiches and chicken tenders with 20 types of sauces), **Häagen Dazs** (ice cream, shakes, and malts), **Stargazers Bar** (cocktails and mixed drinks), and **YeSake Kiosk** (a mix of Asian and Mexican counter service meals).

Nightlife

West Side nightlife is anchored by the House of Blues. A short walk away, you'll also find retro-cool bowling at Splitsville and trendy films shown at the Disney Springs 24. West Side is worth a visit for its waterside location, wide promenade, and diverse shopping and dining. Opening time is 11 am, closing time around 2 am; crowds vary with the season, but weeknights tend to be less busy. For entertainment times and more information, call *407/824–4500* or *407/824–2222.*

House of Blues

BARS/PUBS | The restaurant serves up live blues performances and rib-sticking Mississippi Delta cooking all week long, and there's often a jam session on the front porch. The attached concert hall has showcased name performers such as David Byrne, Los Lobos, Steve Miller, and Willie Nelson, but check the calendar in advance since large acts like these are rare these days. Come hungry (and with an admission ticket) for the popular Sunday Gospel Brunch, where there's always a show and all-you-can-eat Southern food. *West Side, Disney Springs 407/934–2583 www.disneyworld.disney.go.com/entertainment/disney-springs/house-of-blues-shows.*

Performing Arts

Cirque du Soleil - Drawn to Life

CIRCUSES | **FAMILY** | This entirely new Cirque du Soleil experience replaced long-running La Nouba. The show—the first collaboration between Cirque and Disney Animation—is designed to wow both young and old by bringing timeless Disney stories to life in fresh, unforgettable ways. The show follows Julie, a courageous and determined girl who discovers an unexpected gift left by her late father: an unfinished animation piece. Guided by a surprising pencil, she embarks on an inspiring quest sprinkled with her Disney childhood memories. During her journey, she learns to imagine new possibilities and animate the story of her future. The closure of the Walt Disney Resort meant that the show did not premier as expected in spring 2020. ✉ *West Side, Disney Springs* ☎ *855/473–7783 Tickets* 🌐 *www.cirquedusoleil.com/drawn-to-life* 🎫 *From $79.*

Shopping

The West Side is a wide promenade with an intriguing mix of shops, clubs, and restaurants. You'll also find a multiplex movie theater, a bowling alley, and the House of Blues, which has its own gift shop.

NBA Experience Store

SPORTING GOODS | Basketball apparel and other items have been specifically designed for this emporium by Disney, so this isn't exactly like other NBA stores you might have visited. It's where you'll find phone cases, logo- and cartoon-emblazoned basketballs, specialty MagicBands, and the popular Mickey-ear backpack created with a basketball surface-material. As a nod to the NBA's five-man teams, Disney's Fab Five—Mickey, Minnie Mouse, Goofy, Donald, and Pluto—are prominently featured across a range of products, including an array of jerseys that fit normal-sized people. ✉ *Disney Springs West Side, Walt Disney World* 🌐 *www.disneysprings.com/shopping/nba-store.*

Pelé Soccer

SPORTING GOODS | Soccer (or football, as the rest of the world knows it) has slowly but surely gained ground in the United States—especially during the World Cup. Here, teams from around the world are represented in a colorful array of club jerseys, including those of superstar Pelé, from both his time in Brazil and his time with the New York Cosmos. If you don't find a jersey you like, create your own by choosing a design and adding your favorite player's name and number. Also featured are soccer gear and apparel for all ages and Pelé's own World Cup trophy (which makes for a wonderful photo op). ✉ *West Side, Disney Springs* 🌐 *www.disneyworld.disney.go.com/shops/disney-springs/pele-soccer.*

Town Center

The Town Center is the shopping mecca of Disney Springs, with dozens of upscale shops and chain stores such as Zara, Uniqlo, Superdry, and Sephora selling everything from clothing to jewelry to perfume. In between sprees, have a bite at The Polite Pig, a locally owned eatery that serves fast-casual farm-to-table fare. Or, if a Mexican snack is what you want, try Rick Bayless's Frontera Cocina to-go window.

Restaurants

Frontera Cucina

$$ | **MEXICAN** | **FAMILY** | Under the watchful eye of celebrity chef Rick Bayless, Frontera brings a sophisticated yet casual approach to classic Mexican food. Look for genuine dishes from Oaxaca and Mexico City like house-made guacamole and short-rib tacos, as well as exquisite pan-roasted Florida shrimp. **Known for:** hand-crafted tortillas and guacamole; vegetarian options like zucchini enchiladas and mushroom tortas; fun and flavorful kids' meals. 💲 *Average main: $20* ✉ *Disney Springs, Town Center, Disney Springs* ☎ *407/560–0100* 🌐 *www.fronteracocina.com.*

The Polite Pig

$$ | **AMERICAN** | **FAMILY** | The James Beard Award–nominated chef-owners of the Ravenous Pig gastropub in nearby Winter Park opened this sit-down restaurant to give Disney visitors a taste of Orlando's finest. They do it by sourcing as many ingredients as possible from local farmers and purveyors; house-smoking the ribs, brisket, and chicken; and offering special Southern sides like tomato-and-watermelon salad and smoked corn with lime butter. **Known for:** locally sourced ingredients; meats smoked on premises; locally owned and operated by critcally acclaimed chefs. Ⓢ *Average main: $18* ✉ *Town Center, Disney Springs* ☎ *407/938–7444* 🌐 *politepig.com.*

Wolfgang Puck Bar & Grill

$$$$ | **AMERICAN** | **FAMILY** | Celebrity chef Wolfgang Puck's California-crafted eatery serves a mixture of dishes, from Mediterranean-influenced entrées and signature pizzas to seared Florida red snapper with mango and corn salsa to whole grilled fish, mesquite-girilled pork chops, flat-iron steaks, and filet mignon. Gooey desserts, crafted cocktails, and a gelato bar complete the cosmopolitan scene. **Known for:** name-brand dining in familiar surroundings; a California ranch-style atmosphere; world-famous pizza. Ⓢ *Average main: $35* ✉ *Disney Springs Town Center, Disney Springs* ☎ *407/938–9653* 🌐 *www.wolfgangpuckcafeorlando.com.*

Coffee and Quick Bites

Although Town Center is the smallest of Disney Springs' four districts, you'll never go hungry. Aside from table service restaurants, there's **Amorette's Patisserie** (high-end pastries), **Blaze Pizza** (build-your-own pizza in just three minutes), **D-Luxe Burger** (classic, barbecue, veggie, and more), **The Daily Poutine** (Canadian snack of thick-cut fries smothered in cheese curds and gravy), **Sprinkles Disney Springs** (cookies, slow-churned ice cream, and handcrafted cupcakes).

Shopping

The greatest concentration of shops at Disney Springs is in this area, where several blocks of retailers showcase Anthropologie, Sephora, Kate Spade, Pandora, ZARA, Tommy Bahama, Vera Bradley, and Central Florida's legendary Ron Jon Surf Shop.

L'Occitane en Provence

SPA/BEAUTY | Filled with fragrant beauty products, this French-inspired apothecary has everything you need to pamper yourself, from all-natural lotions, gels, creams, and oils to toners and serums to cleansers, moisturizers, and exfoliating scrubs. Shaving and grooming items for men are also well represented. Stop by and you can sample products, mix your own essential oils, and even get a complimentary minifacial or hand massage. ✉ *Town Center, Disney Springs* 🌐 *www.disneyworld.disney.go.com/shops/disney-springs/loccitane-en-provence.*

Orlando Harley-Davidson

CLOTHING | America's largest motorcycle manufacturer has been going strong since 1903, and the apparel has been popular for nearly as long. Harley enthusiasts of all ages can buy biker jackets, vests, T-shirts, patches, and other gear. Climb aboard an iconic hog for a photo op. ✉ *Town Center, Disney Springs* 🌐 *www.disneyworld.disney.go.com/shops/disney-springs/orlando-harley-davidson.*

Disney Springs Resort Area

Nearly half a century ago, as Walt Disney World was welcoming its first guests, this area was simply the Lake Buena Vista shopping village, with just a handful of stores. As Disney World expanded, so did this district. Initially, there were only two hotels and a campground close to

Disney's sprawling Port Orleans Resort has two sections: the French Quarter and the more family-friendly Riverside, pictured here.

the Magic Kingdom, which was then Disney's only theme park. Over time, Lake Buena Vista saw the addition of hotel after hotel; today, there are more than dozen in or near the area now known as Disney Springs. And that original handful of shops? Well, it's now a robust selection of stores, restaurants, and nightclubs—not to mention a golf course right around the corner.

The proximity to Walt Disney World naturally means that Disney Springs lodgings—a mix of hotels that are both Disney owned and not—tend to have higher room rates. If you can swing a stay here, though, you'll be in a good location, and, since the district's non-Disney hotels are on Disney property, they have some (but not all) of the privileges of official Walt Disney World Resort hotels.

Restaurants

Boatwright's Dining Hall

$$$ | CAJUN | FAMILY | Located riverside at Disney's Port Orleans Resort, this very impressive, handcrafted dining hall looks like the internal workings of a wooden sailing ship, complete with an inverted hull on the ceiling and weathered shipbuilding tools. True to the N'awlins theme is a menu of tasty bayou dishes ranging from Louisiana étouffée to crawfish bisque to andouille-stuffed catfish. **Known for:** out of the way resort offering fine Louisiana cuisine; Cajun bayou catfish and jambalaya; Charleston-style seafood grits. *Average main: $30* ✉ *Disney's Port Orleans Resort–Riverside, Disney Springs Resort Area* ☎ *407/939–5277* 🌐 *disneyworld.disney.go.com/dining* 🕓 *No lunch.*

Hotels

In addition to the Walt Disney World hotels, eight hotels on Hotel Plaza Boulevard, which carry a Lake Buena Vista address but are still on Disney property, are designated as "official" Walt Disney World hotels and are within walking distance of Disney Springs. These include the B Resort & Spa Disney Springs Resort Area, Best Western Lake Buena Vista Resort, DoubleTree Suites by Hilton Orlando Disney Springs Area, Hilton Orlando Buena Vista Palace Disney Springs Area, Hilton Orlando Lake Buena Vista, Holiday Inn Orlando–Disney Springs Area, Wyndham Lake Buena Vista Disney Springs Resort Area, and Wyndham Garden Lake Buena Vista. What this means is that the guests of these hotels get some of the perks of Disney resort guests, including free park shuttles, Extra Magic Hours, and Fastpass+ access; they do not get free MagicBands, free parking at the theme parks, or charging privileges. *For reviews of these hotels, see Kissimmee, Lake Buena Vista, and Celebration.*

Disney's Old Key West Resort
$$$$ | **RESORT** | **FAMILY** | Disney is nothing if not a master of theming, and this collection of home-style villas and studio units reflective of vintage Key West homes is a shining (and pricey) example. **Pros:** quiet and romantic; full kitchens in villas; laundry facilities. **Cons:** long walks between rooms and restaurants, recreation facilities, bus stops; bus service to parks can be frustrating; no elevators. *Rooms from: $550 1510 N. Cove Rd., Disney Springs Resort Area 407/827–7700 www.disneyworld.disney.go.com/resorts 761 units No meals.*

Disney's Port Orleans Resort–French Quarter
$$$ | **HOTEL** | In this theme lodge, cobblestone streets, gas lamps, wrought-iron balconies and fragrant magnolia blossoms create a Disneyfied (ie: clean) version of the French Quarter. **Pros:** authentic—or as authentic as Disney can make it—fun, New Orleans style; moderate price; lots of recreation options, including elaborate pool, boat rentals, and carriage rides. **Cons:** even though there are fewer kids here, public areas can still be quite noisy; shuttle service is slow; food court is the only on-site dining option. *Rooms from: $282 2201 Orleans Dr., Disney Springs Resort Area 407/934–5000 www.disneyworld.disney.go.com/resorts 1,008 rooms No meals.*

Disney's Port Orleans Resort–Riverside
$$$ | **RESORT** | **FAMILY** | Considered a more family-friendly choice than its neighbor (the French Quarter resort), this lodging on the man-made Sassagoula River immerses you in a Creole setting—from the white-column mansions of Magnolia Bend to Alligator Bayou's backwoods cottages. **Pros:** carriage rides through picturesque settings; river transportation to Disney Springs; lots of recreation options for kids. **Cons:** shuttle to parks can be slow; no shortage of noisy youngsters; the Old South vibe might not be everyone's cup of tea. *Rooms from: $282 1251 Riverside Dr., Disney Springs Resort Area 407/934–6000 www.disneyworld.disney.go.com/resorts 2,048 rooms No meals.*

Disney's Saratoga Springs Resort & Spa
$$$$ | **RESORT** | **FAMILY** | This sprawling property takes its inspiration from 19th-century Gilded Age spa resorts in upstate New York, where hot springs and lakes ruled the landscape. **Pros:** water taxis whisk you to Disney Springs; kitchens can shave down the food bill; abundance of rooms with whirlpool baths. **Cons:** it's a fair hike from some accommodations to the restaurant and other facilities; one bar-and-grill restaurant; bus transportation can be slow and crowded. *Rooms from: $483 1960 Broadway, Disney Springs Resort Area 407/934–7639 www.disneyworld.disney.go.com/resorts 1,260 units No meals.*

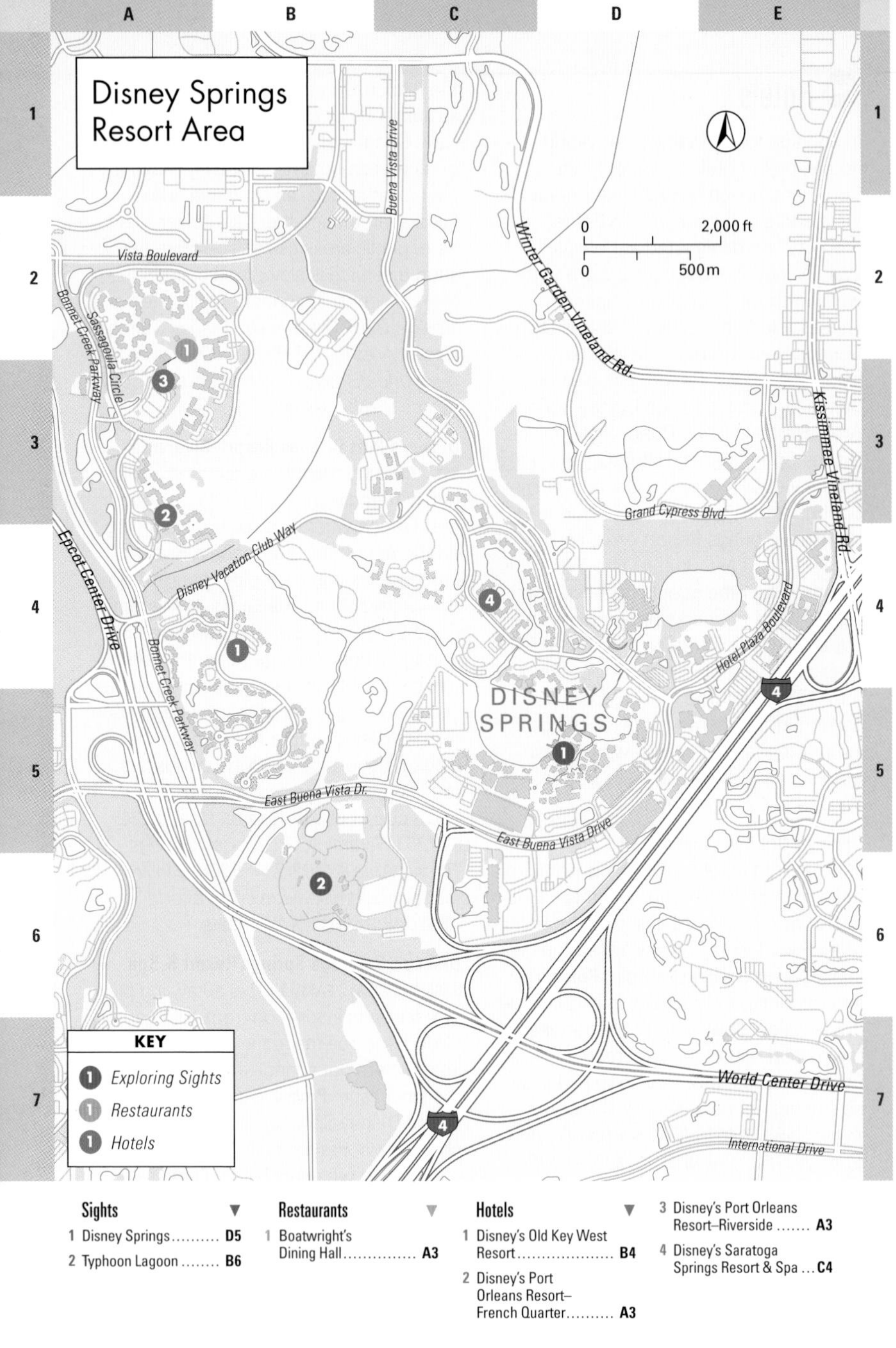

Sights

1 Disney Springs **D5**

2 Typhoon Lagoon **B6**

Restaurants

1 Boatwright's Dining Hall **A3**

Hotels

1 Disney's Old Key West Resort **B4**

2 Disney's Port Orleans Resort– French Quarter **A3**

3 Disney's Port Orleans Resort–Riverside **A3**

4 Disney's Saratoga Springs Resort & Spa ... **C4**

Top Spas

If you hit the ground running after arriving in Orlando, at some point you might need to shift your pace from "fast forward" to "pause." If so, head directly to one of Orlando's resort spas. The area has enough standout pampering palaces to indulge every theme-park–weary parent, aching golfer, parched sunbather, and Disney princess.

Each ospa is known for something special, whether it's the Balinese four-hand massage at the Mandara at Portofino Bay or customized therapies at the Waldorf. Several spas draw on Florida's citrus-producing region to offer refreshing orange, grapefruit, and lime therapies. And you can go global with massage techniques from Japan, Thailand, Polynesia, and Sweden.

Families who want to stay together can even spa together at treatment centers specializing in youth facials, massages, and manicure/pedicure (aka: mani-pedi) packages. The Ritz-Carlton Orlando treats kids like royalty with manicures, pedicures, and facials. Disney's Senses Spas at Saratoga Springs and the Grand Floridian offer Magical Manicures and Princess Pedicures.

Make your spa excursion special by planning enough time to use complimentary whirlpools, saunas, and steam rooms. Most spas offer free access to impressively equipped fitness centers and relaxation rooms stocked with herbal teas, fresh fruits, and other goodies. Book treatments early, and ask about gratuities—often 18% to 20%—which might or might not be included in your treatment or package.

Top Spas

Blue Harmony, Wyndham Grand Orlando Resort Bonnet Creek, Disney Springs Resort Area

Eforea Spa at Hilton Orlando, Destination Drive, Orlando

Portofino Bay Mandara Spa, Portofino Bay Resort, Universal Orlando

Ritz-Carlton Spa, Grande Lakes Orlando, South Orlando

Senses Spa, Disney's Saratoga Springs Resort, Disney Springs Resort Area

Senses Spa, Grand Floridian Resort, Magic Kingdom Resort Area

Activities

SPAS

Blue Harmony

FITNESS/HEALTH CLUBS | Infused with the colors of ocean and sky, this spa lives up to its name. Its signature treatment combines exfoliation with marine salt and oil, polishing with marine salt and lavender, and a massage based on Thai techniques. Body treatments use oil-infused seawater gels to add natural minerals to the skin and end with a cozy wrap and massage. Two of the eight treatment rooms are outdoors, and daily specials can include from Marvelous Monday (20% off on all services) to the Tuesday Two-fer, which combines massages and facials at a reduced rate. The serene relaxation lounge offers beverages and tea while you wait for your treatment. Bring the family, as the spa offers treatments for teens as well. ✉ *Wyndham Grand Orlando Resort Bonnet Creek, 14651 Chelonia Pkwy., Disney Springs*

Resort Area ☎ *407/390–2442* 🌐 *www.blueharmonyorlando.com.*

Senses Spa at Disney's Saratoga Springs Resort

FITNESS/HEALTH CLUBS | The spa may share its name with the Grand Floridian's, but the atmosphere is quite different at this two-story, stone-and-wood spa, inspired by the legendary lodges at the mineral springs of the Adirondacks. Fruit-infused elixirs and the scent of frankincense soothe you as you enter either the separate men's or women's waiting room. Signature treatments include the hydrotherapy package that combines water and stone to exfoliate, soak, wrap, and relax that stressed-out body, and the Bamboo Fusion massage that combines warm stones and an ancient technique using heated bamboo segments. There are two wet relaxation rooms, with steam bath, pool, and heated, glass-tile-covered lounge chairs. You can even bring the family—there's a couples' treatment room and a mani-pedi for kids ages 4–12. Swimsuits are required in wet rooms. ✉ *Disney's Saratoga Springs Resort, 1960 Broadway, Disney Springs Resort Area* ☎ *407/939–7727* 🌐 *www.disneyworld.disney.go.com/spas/saratoga-springs-resort-and-spa/senses-spa-saratoga.*

Typhoon Lagoon

The beauty of Disney's water parks is that you can make the experience fit your mood. Like crowds? Head for the lounge chairs along the Surf Pool at Typhoon Lagoon or Melt-Away Bay at Blizzard Beach. Prefer peace? Walk past lush foliage along each park's circular path until you spot a secluded lean-to or tree-shaded patch of sand.

According to Disney legend, Typhoon Lagoon was created when the lush Placid Palms Resort was struck by a cataclysmic storm. It left a different world in its wake: surfboard-sundered trees, once-upright palms imitating the Leaning Tower of Pisa, and a lagoon cut off from the sea, trapping thousands of tropical fish. Nothing, however, topped the fate of *Miss Tilly,* a shrimp boat from "Safen Sound, Florida," which was hurled high in the air and became impaled on Mount Mayday, a magical volcano that periodically tries to dislodge *Miss Tilly* with huge geysers.

Ordinary folks, the legend continues, would have been crushed by such devastation. But the resourceful residents of Placid Palms were made of heartier stuff—and from the wreckage they created 56-acre Typhoon Lagoon, the self-proclaimed "world's ultimate water park."

GETTING ORIENTED

The layout is so simple. The wave and swimming lagoon is at the park's center. (Note that the waves are born in the Mount Mayday side and break on the beaches closest to the entrance.) Any attraction requiring a gravitational plunge starts around the summit of Mount Mayday. The cleverly named Miss Adventure Falls and Ketchakiddee Creek flank the lagoon, to Mount Mayday's right and left, respectively, as you enter. The Crush 'n' Gusher water coaster is due right of Singapore Sal's.

You can take Disney bus transportation or drive to Typhoon Lagoon. There's no parking charge. Once inside, your options are to walk, swim, slide, or sleep.

WDW Information

Disney water parks often close during off season for maintenance. Call WDW Information or check 🌐 *www.disneyworld.com*'s park calendars for days of operation. ✉ *1534 Blizzard Beach Dr., Blizzard Beach* ☎ *407/824–4321.*

WHAT TO EXPECT

You can speed down waterslides with names like Crush 'n' Gusher and Humunga Kowabunga, bump through rapids and falls at Mount Mayday, or join a treasure hunt at Miss Adventure Falls. You can also bob along in 5-foot waves in a surf pool the size of two football fields or, for a mellow break, float in inner tubes along the 2,100-foot Castaway Creek. Rubberneck as fellow human cannonballs are ejected from the Storm Slides, or hunker down in a hammock or lounge chair and read a book. Ketchakiddee Creek, for young children, replicates adult rides on a smaller scale. It's Disney's version of a day at the beach—complete with friendly lifeguards. Most people agree that kids under 7 and older adults prefer Typhoon Lagoon. Bigger kids and teens like Blizzard Beach.

During the off-season between October and April, Typhoon Lagoon closes for several weeks for routine maintenance and refurbishment.

PARKS AMENITIES

Dining: Picnicking is permitted, but coolers too large for one person to carry are forbidden, as are glass containers, and alcoholic beverages not bought in the park. There are tables at Getaway Glen, Typhoon Tilly's, and at pavilions across the park. You can always fork out $40 to $60 a day, depending on the season, for a reserved umbrella from Getaway Glen, which includes two loungers, two beach chairs, a drink table, and towels. Arrive early, though, and you can stake out a great spot for free. Park eateries and food stands have salads, burgers, pizza, and other treats, with a sweet emphasis on ice cream.

Dressing Rooms and Lockers: There are thatched-roof dressing rooms and lockers to the right on your way into the park. It costs $10 a day to rent a small locker and $15 for a large one; there's also a $5 deposit. There are restrooms in every nook and cranny. Most have showers and are much less crowded than the dressing rooms. If you forgot your towel, rent ($2) or buy one at Singapore Sal's.

First Aid: The small first-aid stand, run by a registered nurse, is on your left as you enter the park.

Guest Services: The staff at Typhoon Lagoon's Guest Services window outside the entrance turnstiles, to your left, can answer many questions. **TIP→ A chalkboard inside gives water temperature and surfing information.**

Lost People and Things: Ask about your misplaced people and things at the Guest Services window near the entrance turnstiles. Lost children are taken to an area by the Tip Board near the front of the park, where Disney cast members entertain them with games.

Private Patios: The park has a dozen premium, roped-off Beachcomber Shacks (patios, really) that groups of as many as six can rent. They generally offer shade and sun as well as plush loungers and other chairs, a table with an umbrella, and an ice chest with two bottles of water per guest (up to six). Each guest also gets two beach towels and a refillable soft-drink mug. The whole group gets a locker to share and an attendant to take and deliver food orders (cost of meals not included). The patios cost about $325 during peak season (usually March through late August) and between $160 and $240 the rest of the year. Reserve (☎ *407/939–8687*) well in advance or arrive very early to book one at High 'N Dry. In summer, any patio that isn't prebooked sells out within a half hour of the park opening.

Services for People with Disabilities: The paths connecting the different areas are wheelchair accessible, but most of the waterslides are not. There is, however, an elevator that takes you to the loading zone of the Crush 'n' Gusher water coaster. If you transfer from your chair to a raft or inner tube, you can float in Typhoon Lagoon Surf Pool or Castaway Creek.

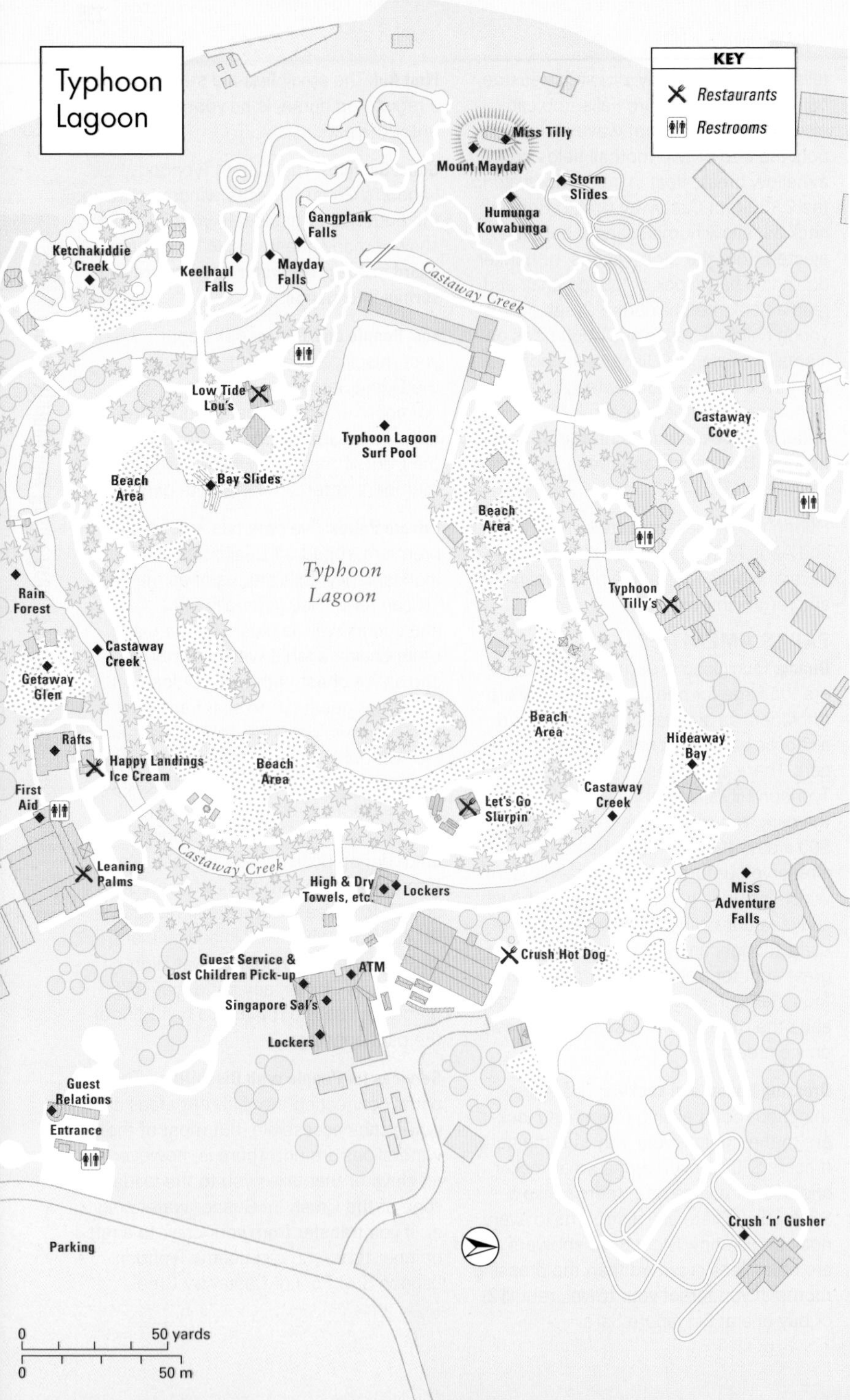
Typhoon Lagoon
KEY
Restaurants
Restrooms
Miss Tilly
Mount Mayday
Storm Slides
Humunga Kowabunga
Gangplank Falls
Ketchakiddie Creek
Keelhaul Falls
Mayday Falls
Castaway Creek
Low Tide Lou's
Typhoon Lagoon Surf Pool
Castaway Cove
Beach Area
Bay Slides
Beach Area
Typhoon Lagoon
Rain Forest
Typhoon Tilly's
Castaway Creek
Getaway Glen
Beach Area
Hideaway Bay
Rafts
Happy Landings Ice Cream
Beach Area
First Aid
Castaway Creek
Let's Go Slurpin'
Leaning Palms
Castaway Creek
High & Dry Towels, etc.
Lockers
Miss Adventure Falls
Guest Service & Lost Children Pick-up
ATM
Crush Hot Dog
Singapore Sal's
Lockers
Guest Relations
Entrance
Crush 'n' Gusher
Parking
0
50 yards
0
50 m

Wheelchairs are available at the entrance turnstile area and are free with ID. You can trade a land-based wheelchair for chairs that go into the water by asking a lifeguard.

Supplies: You can get inner tubes at Castaway Creek and inner tubes, rafts, or slide mats at the rides. Borrow life vests at **High 'N Dry**. Near the main entrance is **Singapore Sal's,** where you can pick up free life jackets, buy sundries, and rent (or buy) towels and lockers.

VISITING TIPS

In summer, come first thing in the morning (early birds can ride several times before the lines get long), late in the afternoon when park hours run later, or when the weather clears after a thundershower (rainstorms drive away crowds). Afternoons are also good in cooler weather, as the water is a bit warmer. To make a whole day of it, avoid weekends, when locals and visitors pack in.

Women and girls should wear one-piece swimsuits unless they want to find their tops somewhere around their ears at the bottom of the waterslide.

Invest in sunscreen and water shoes. Plan to slather sunscreen on several times throughout the day. An inexpensive pair of water shoes will save tootsies from hot sand and walkways and from restroom floors.

Arrive 30 minutes before opening, so you can park, buy tickets, rent towels, and snag inner tubes before the crowds descend, and, trust us, it gets very crowded.

Bay Slides

AMUSEMENT PARK/WATER PARK | Kids scramble up several steps tucked between faux-rock formations, where a lifeguard sits to supervise their slide into Blustery Bay. The incline is small, but the thrill is great for young kids, who whoosh into the bay (sometimes into the arms of waiting parents). These two scaled-down versions of the Storm Slides are geared to kids shorter than 60 inches. **TIP→ Kids really burn up energy going up the steps and down the slides repeatedly. Parents should be prepared for their wanting to ride over and over again.** ✉ *Typhoon Lagoon* ☞ *Duration: Up to you. Crowds: Light to moderate. Audience: Small kids.*

Castaway Creek

AMUSEMENT PARK/WATER PARK | This circular, 15-foot-wide, 3-foot-deep, 2,000-foot-long waterway is supremely relaxing and satisfyingly soothing. Just snag an inner tube and float placidly along a clear creek that winds through the park and around the Surf Pool and beaches. You'll pass through a rain forest that showers you with spray, slide through caves and grottoes, float by overhanging trees and flowering bushes, and get drenched from the "broken pipes" at the Water Works. The current flows a gentle 2½ feet per second. Along the way there are five landing areas where you can hop in and out. **For people with disabilities:** Guests using wheelchairs must transfer to an inner tube. **TIP→ A full circuit takes about 20 minutes, longer if you stop at one of the five lifeguard-manned launches.** ✉ *Typhoon Lagoon* ☞ *Duration: Up to 20 mins. Crowds: Vary by season. Audience: All ages.*

★ Crush 'n' Gusher

AMUSEMENT PARK/WATER PARK | If flume rides, storm slides, and tube races aren't wild enough for your inner thrill-seeker, get ready to defy gravity on Disney's multipassenger water coaster. Designed to propel you uphill and down along a series of flumes, caverns, and spillways, this ride should satisfy the most enthusiastic daredevil. Keeping with park lore, Crush 'n' Gusher flows through what appears to be a rusted-out tropical fruit factory, weaving in and out of the wreckage and debris that once transported fruit through the plant's wash facilities. Three "fruit chutes" are aptly named Banana Blaster, Coconut Crusher, and Pineapple Plunger—one of which is designed for solo riders. Guests shouldn't ride if they are pregnant or have heart, back, or neck problems. **For people with disabilities:** An elevator takes guests using wheelchairs to the loading area; there's a short distance between this area and the ride. **TIP→ Ride first thing in the morning before lines get too long. And don't forget to say cheese for the cameras!** ✉ *Typhoon Lagoon ☞ Duration: 1 min. Crowds: Moderate to heavy. Audience: Not small kids. Height requirement: 48 inches.*

Gangplank Falls

AMUSEMENT PARK/WATER PARK | Families who scale Mount Mayday have to haul their raft to the peak before the adventure begins. Upon takeoff, a 6½-foot-long inflated raft plunges down the slide with impressive speed, getting bumpy at times along the 300-foot river. A pleasant ride for families, it's not too scary for kids and not too dull for adults. Those who are pregnant or have heart, back, or neck problems should sit this one out. **TIP→ The inner tubes are heavy, so be sure to have at least two willing carriers. Also be prepared to ride with two to four riders (five if some are smaller kids).** ✉ *Typhoon Lagoon ☞ Duration: 1 min. Crowds: Vary by season. Audience: Not small kids.*

Humunga Kowabunga

AMUSEMENT PARK/WATER PARK | There's little time to scream, but you'll hear just such vociferous reactions as the survivors emerge from the catch pool. The basic questions are: want to get scared out of your wits in four seconds flat—and did you like it enough to go back for more? The three side-by-side Humunga Kowabunga speed slides deserve acclaim among thrill lovers, as they drop 214 feet downhill at a 60-degree angle in seconds. Oh yes, and then you go through a cave. In the dark. The average speed is 30 mph; however, you can really fly if you lie flat on your back, cross your ankles, wrap your arms around your chest, and arch your back. One caveat: the ride lasts only a few seconds—too short for us—and lines are often too long to requeue for another plunge. This ride isn't appropriate for guests who are pregnant or who have heart, back, or neck problems. **TIP→ Race against your friends or family; there are three slides at the top.** ✉ *Typhoon Lagoon ☞ Duration: 4 secs. Crowds: Heavy. Audience: Not small kids. Height requirement: 48 inches.*

Keelhaul Falls

AMUSEMENT PARK/WATER PARK | Do you need to chill out after the high-velocity Humunga Kowabunga? Then venture up to Keelhaul Falls, a laid-back trip down the left side of Mount Mayday. Just kick back and relax as your blue tube cruises down the 400-foot slide and splashes into the pool below. Keelhaul feels a little slow if you ride it right after Mayday Falls, so thrill seekers might be disappointed. Yet its winding path and scenic descent make for a satisfying ride for guests of all ages. This ride isn't appropriate for guests who are pregnant or who have heart, back, or neck problems. **TIP→ Ride before or after Mayday Falls.** ✉ *Typhoon Lagoon ☞ Duration: 1 min. Crowds: Vary by season. Audience: Not young kids.*

Ketchakiddee Creek

AMUSEMENT PARK/WATER PARK | Typhoon Lagoon's play area for young children has slides, mini rapids, faux sand castles, squirting whales and seals, bouncing barrels, waterfalls, sprinklers, and all the other ingredients of a splash fiesta. The bubbling sand ponds, where youngsters can sit in what seems like an enormous whirlpool bath, are special favorites. Little ones also love the tiny-scale tube ride. Small water cannons let kids engage in water-spray wars. Families can camp beneath lots of shady lean-tos when not in the water. **For people with disabilities:** Accessible for people using water-appropriate wheelchairs. **TIP→ Parents can**

Grab an inner tube, and head for Castaway Creek, Typhoon Lagoon's lazy river.

take turns watching the kiddies here and riding the thrill slides. ✉ *Typhoon Lagoon* ☞ *Duration: Up to you. Crowds: Light. Audience: Small kids. Height requirement: Adults must be accompanied by a child under 48 inches and vice versa.*

Mayday Falls

AMUSEMENT PARK/WATER PARK | This 460-foot slide in bright-yellow inner tubes is the longest and bumpiest of the three falls. It's a long trek up to Mayday Falls—even higher than Keelhaul—but the increased speed and longer descent are worth the climb since the watery route slips through caves, slides under bridges, and skims past thundering waterfalls before splashing down into a pool. This ride isn't appropriate for guests who are pregnant or who have heart, back, or neck problems. **TIP→ While you're in the neighborhood, ride Keelhaul Falls, too.** ✉ *Typhoon Lagoon* ☞ *Duration: 1 min. Crowds: Vary by season. Audience: Not young kids.*

Mount Mayday

AMUSEMENT PARK/WATER PARK | What goes down can also go up—and up and up. Climbing Mount Mayday "[is] like climbing Mount Everest," one teenager moaned about a climb that seems a lot steeper than an 85-foot peak should be. Nevertheless, after you've passed hibiscus flowers, traversed a rope bridge, and trod across stepping-stones set in plunging waters you'll be near the summit where the view encompasses the entire park. Lovers of white-water rafting should head over to Mayday Falls, Keelhaul Falls, and Gangplank Falls, which utilize oversize inner tubes as they take guests plunging down the mountain's slope, ✉ *Typhoon Lagoon.*

★ Storm Slides

AMUSEMENT PARK/WATER PARK | Each of these three body slides is about 300 feet long and snakes in and out of rock formations, through caves and tunnels, and under waterfalls, but each has a slightly different view and offers a twist. The one in the middle has the longest tunnel; the others feature secrets you'll have to discover for yourself. Brace for splashdown on all three slides! Maximum speed is about 20 mph, and the trip takes about 30 seconds. These slides are not appropriate for guests who are pregnant or who have heart, back, or neck problems. **TIP→ Try each of the three slides for different twists.** ✉ *Typhoon Lagoon* ☞ *Duration: 30 secs. Crowds: Moderate to heavy. Audience: Not young kids.*

★ Typhoon Lagoon Surf Pool
AMUSEMENT PARK/WATER PARK | This is the heart of the park, a swimming area that spreads out over 2½ acres and contains almost 3 million gallons of clear, chlorinated water. It's scalloped by coves, bays, and inlets, all edged with white-sand beaches—spread over a base of white concrete, as bodysurfers soon discover when they try to slide into shore. Ouch! The waves are the draw. Twelve huge water-collection chambers hidden in Mount Mayday dump their load into trapdoors with a resounding whoosh to create 6-foot waves large enough for Typhoon Lagoon to host amateur and professional surfing championships.

A piercing double hoot from *Miss Tilly* (the boat that legend says was deposited on Mount Mayday's highest peak during a storm) signals the start and finish of wave action, which will generate the bigger waves every 90 seconds in 90-minute sessions, followed by 30 minutes of more placid bobbing waves. Even during the big-wave periods, however, the waters in Blustery Bay and Whitecap Cove are protected. On certain days, skilled surfers and novices alike can enter the park before it opens for private sessions and training lessons. Instruction and a soft-sided surfboard are included in the $165 cost, and the surfing experience (ages 8 and older) lasts for 2½ hours. Reserve your waves by calling *407/939–7529.* **For people with disabilities:** Accessible for people using water-appropriate wheelchairs. **TIP→ See the chalkboard at beach's edge for the day's wave schedule if you want to time your bodysurfing.** ✉ *Typhoon Lagoon* ☞ *Duration: Up to you. Crowds: Heavy. Audience: All ages.*

Restaurants

To your left as you enter the park, **Leaning Palms** has burgers, pizzas, turkey sandwiches, salads, beer, and, of course, ice cream and frozen yogurt. **Typhoon Tilly's,** on the right just past Miss Adventure Falls, is a walk-up kiosk where you can grab fried shrimp, fish baskets, and chicken wraps. They also serve sandwiches, salads, and snacks of all kinds and pours of mostly sugary, nonalcoholic grog—though you can grab a Davy Jones "lager." **Let's Go Slurpin'** is a beach shack on the edge of Typhoon Lagoon that dispenses frozen margaritas as well as wine and beer.

Chapter 8

KISSIMMEE, LAKE BUENA VISTA, AND CELEBRATION

Updated by
Jennifer Greenhill-Taylor
and Joseph Hayes

Sights	Restaurants	Hotels	Shopping	Nightlife
★★★☆☆	★★★☆☆	★★★★☆	★★★★☆	★★★☆☆

NEIGHBORHOOD SNAPSHOT

TOP EXPERIENCES

■ **Celebration:** Celebration, formerly a spark in Walt Disney's imagination, has become a place for fine dining, casual bike excursions, and relaxing in small town comfort.

■ **Downtown Kissimmee:** downtown Kissimmee is historical and quaintly modern, with an air of Old Florida and a buzz of approaching modernity.

■ **Entertainment:** Route 192 across the lower boundary of Disney has unique entertainment possibilities, like dinner shows at Capone's, Medieval Times, and Pirates Dinner Adventure.

■ **Fishing:** Kissimmee is one of the fishing capitals of America, with record-breaking catches recorded every year in a variety of massive lakes.

■ **Old Florida Attractions:** southern Orlando lets you experience Florida's past, with Gatorland, swamp airboat rides and eco-tourism kayaking available.

■ **Proximity to Disney Springs:** the respite from Lake Buena Vista's hotel canyons, aside from Disney itself, is the shopping and dining extravaganza of Disney Springs.

GETTING HERE

Kissimmee is 18 miles south of Orlando, 10 miles southeast of Walt Disney World. Celebration is tucked along U.S. 192, the main east–west route to downtown Kissimmee. Lake Buena Vista is actually on the eastern edge of Disney property.

PLANNING YOUR TIME

The draw of these three communities, which abut Walt Disney World, are proximity without the high Disney prices. If you are looking for cheaper places to stay and eat but still want to be within easy reach of Disney's gates (and also the rest of Orlando), any of these areas can be good places to stay. And at night there are even entertainment and dining options to pull you away from the resorts.

QUICK BITES

■ **Disney Springs.** Lake Buena Vista is in the heart of Disney-access country and is the best place for a quick bite in one of dozens of Disney Springs choices that offer free self-parking. ✉ *1486 Buena Vista Dr., Lake Buena Vista* 🌐 *www.disneysprings.com.*

■ **Market Street Diner.** Order breakfast, lunch, dinner, or simply a cup of coffee, just like at any diner. ✉ *701 Front St., Celebration* 🌐 *marketstdiner.com.*

■ **Nadia's Cafe.** Quick Mediterranean bites like spinach pies and kebabs are offered from 11 am to 5 pm only. ✉ *127 Broadway, Kissimmee* 🌐 *nadiascafe.net.*

In an area of contrasts, you can vacation just outside Disney's doors in the still-pristine wilderness of Kissimmee, visit the new old small town community of Celebration, and stay in vast resorts and quirky boutique hotels in the manufactured neighborhood called Lake Buena Vista.

Kissimmee is a prime example of Old Florida retaining its charm; it's here where you can relax along clear lakes that yield prize-winning fish, visit cattle ranches and rodeos, and ride in airboats along waterways that have changed little since the days of the Florida cowboys. The relatively new SunRail commuter train has made downtown Kissimmee a renewed recreation location. As it's now just 30 minutes from downtown Orlando, more people take advantage of the lunchtime and early dinner treats of Kissimmee's main street and the Lake Tohopekaliga waterfront.

There's no shortage of places to stay in the boulevards surrounding the Disney theme parks proper that has long been called Lake Buena Vista (there really is such a lake, but it's not for recreation). Hotels that offer posh rooms and intimate dining compete with family- and pet-friendly resorts. Properties with names like Waldorf and Four Seasons are also home to some of the best restaurants in Orlando and some of the most extravagant spas anywhere in the country.

Celebration offers good dining, pleasant and bikeable surroundings, and a touch of small-town flair.

For entertainment, there's nothing like the unique dinner-and-a-show spots that line the east–west corridor that runs from Celebration to Kissimmee: shows that combine jousting (Medieval Times), gangsters (Capone's Dinner and Show), and magic (The Outta Control Magic Comedy Dinner Show) along with food.

Kissimmee

18 miles south of Orlando, 10 miles southeast of Walt Disney World (WDW).

Although Kissimmee is primarily known as the gateway to Disney (technically, the vast Disney property of theme parks and resorts lies in both Osceola and Orange counties), its non-WDW attractions just might tickle your fancy. They range from throwbacks to old-time Florida to dinner shows for you and 2,000 of your closest friends. Orlando used to be prime cattle country, and the best sampling of what life was like is here during the Silver Springs Rodeo in February and June.

With at least 100,000 acres of freshwater lakes, the Kissimmee area brings anglers and boaters to national fishing tournaments and speedboat races. A 50-mile-long series of lakes, the

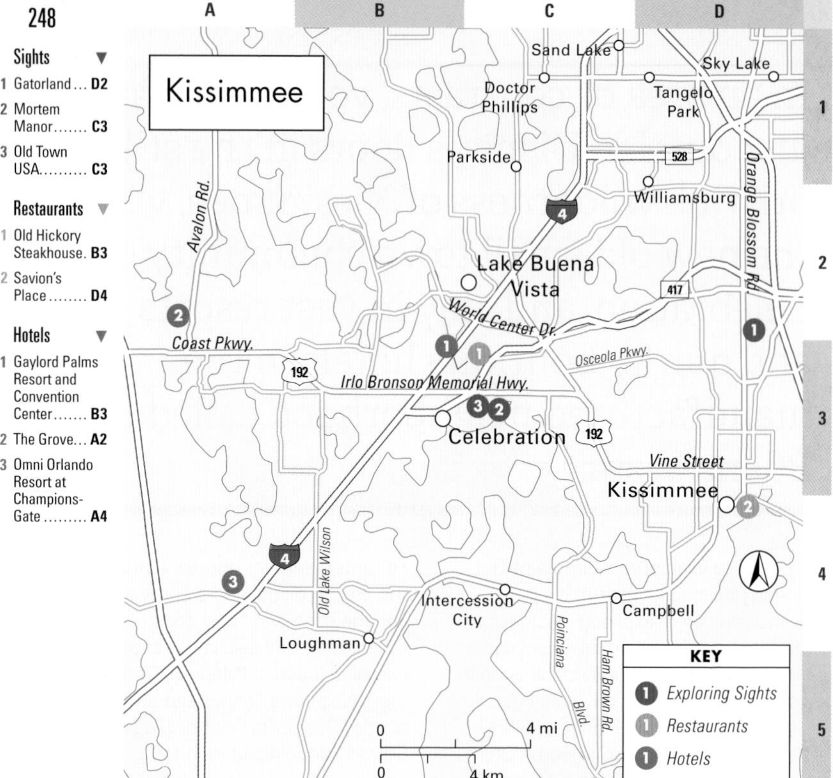

Kissimmee Waterway, connects Lake Tohopekaliga—a Native American name that means "Sleeping Tiger"—with huge Lake Okeechobee in South Florida, and from there, to both the Atlantic Ocean and the Gulf of Mexico.

From downtown Orlando it's easy to reach Kissimmee's main road, U.S. 192, from Interstate 4, Exit 64, just past the last Disney exit. Osceola Parkway (Toll Road 522) heads directly from Disney property, and Florida's turnpike runs north–south through Kissimmee.

TOURS

Historic Downtown Kissimmee

ORIENTATION | **FAMILY** | Established well over a century ago, Kissimmee has a story rooted in the founding of the state. It was an important air base during World War II (even a POW camp), and, with ranches and a railroad hub, it was vital in the development of the Orlando cattle and orange industries. With fresh access from downtown Orlando via the SunRail commuter train, Kissimmee is a renewed destination. The visitors bureau sponsors chili cook-offs and a Tuesday evening farmers' market. You can learn more on the self-guided audio tour or free map tour available at the Main Street Welcome Station or downloadable from the Experience Kissimmee website. ✉ *215 Celebration Pl., Kissimmee* ☎ *407/569–4800* 🌐 *www.experiencekissimmee.com/visitor-information.*

★ Kissimmee Swamp Tours

ECOTOURISM | **FAMILY** | The 60- or 90-minute cruises in high-powered airboats take you through the marshes and swamps of Lake Kissimmee—home to hundreds of species of birds and other critters. The 36,000-acre lake features a view of (very)

Old Florida. ✉ *4500 Joe Overstreet Rd., Lake Kissimmee, Kenansville* ☎ *407/436–1059* 🌐 *www.kissimmeeswamptours.com* 🎫 *From $49.*

VISITOR INFORMATION

CONTACTS Experience Kissimmee. ✉ *215 Celebration Pl., Suite 200, Kissimmee* ☎ *407/742–8200* 🌐 *www.experiencekissimmee.com.*

Sights

Gatorland

AMUSEMENT PARK/WATER PARK | FAMILY | This campy attraction near the Orlando–Kissimmee border on U.S. 441 has endured since 1949 without much change, despite competition from the major parks. Indeed, over the years, the theme park and registered conservancy have managed to retain a gator-rasslin' spirit. Kids get a kick out of this unmanufactured, old-timey thrill ride.

The Gator Gulley Splash Park is complete with giant "egrets" spilling water from their beaks, dueling water guns mounted atop giant gators, and other water-park splash areas. There's also a small petting zoo and an aviary. A free train ride is a high point, taking you through an alligator breeding marsh and a natural swamp setting where you can spot gators, birds, and turtles. A three-story observation tower overlooks the breeding marsh, swamped with gator grunts, especially come sundown during mating season.

For a glimpse of 37 giant, rare, and deadly crocodiles, check out the Jungle Crocs of the World exhibit. To see eager gators leaping out of the water to catch their food, come on cool days for the Gator Jumparoo Show (summer heat just puts them to sleep). The most thrilling is the first one in the morning, when the gators are hungriest. There's also a Gator Wrestlin' Show, and although there's no doubt who's going to win the match, it's still fun to see the handlers take on those tough guys with the beady eyes. In the educational Upclose Encounters show, the host handles a variety of snakes. Recent park additions include Panther Springs, featuring brother-and-sister endangered panthers, and the wheelchair-accessible Screamin' Gator and Gator Gauntlet ziplines (additional cost). The park's newest offering is the Stompin' Gator Off-Road Adventure, a cross between a pontoon boat and an off-road monster truck that tours untamed Florida. This is a genuine experience, and you leave knowing the difference between a gator and a croc. **TIP→ Discount coupons are available online.** ✉ *14501 S. Orange Blossom Trail, Kissimmee* ✣ *Between Orlando and Kissimmee* ☎ *407/855–5496, 800/393–5297* 🌐 *www.gatorland.com* 🎫 *$30; $10 off-road tours. Free parking.*

Mortem Manor

ARTS VENUE | FAMILY | This year-round haunted attraction turns the haunted house on its head. The two-floor, actor- and animatronic-filled house frankly scares the heck out of visitors, with dark tableaux and unexpected frights. For those with unshakable stamina, the Last Ride "burial simulator" reduces the experience down to several sound-filled minutes in an actual coffin; it might be of questionable taste, but visitors seem to enjoy it. ✉ *5770 W. Irlo Bronson Memorial Hwy., Kissimmee* ☎ *407/507–0051* 🌐 *www.mortemmanor.com* 🎫 *$15; $5 Last Ride Simulator* ⏲ *Closed Mon. and Tues.*

Old Town USA

AMUSEMENT PARK/WATER PARK | FAMILY | A collection of shops and theme restaurants, Old Town was literally the heart of tourist Kissimmee before Disney moved in. With a new owner and new carnival-type rides, the 1950s theme continues. Magic shows in the Great Magic Hall, a haunted funeral parlor attraction, video game and shooting arcades, a laser-tag hall, go-karts and bumper cars, and long-standing weekly classic

Did You Know?

Old Town in Kissimmee—just one of many Orlando-area sights outside the theme parks—has several dozen shops, nine restaurants, 18 rides and attractions, and three or so antique-car shows a week.

car shows. Shopping has become the realm of "As Seen on TV" stores and flea market staples, and dining takes the form of generic food courts and sports bars. ✉ *5770 W. Irlo Bronson Memorial Hwy., Kissimmee* ☎ *407/396–4888* 🌐 *www.myoldtownusa.com* 🎫 *Free.*

Restaurants

Kissimmee offers a huge number of dining choices, many of which are of the "burger barn" or dinner theater variety, but there are notable exceptions. Allow about 15 to 25 minutes to travel from WDW or about 35 minutes from International Drive.

Old Hickory Steakhouse

$$$$ | **STEAKHOUSE** | **FAMILY** | This upscale steak house in the Gaylord Palms resort is designed to look like rustic cabins in the Everglades. Beyond the playful facade is a polished restaurant with a classic menu of steaks and chops. Try the cowboy rib eye, porterhouse, or center-cut fillet, priced for the hotel's convention goers. The chef gets creative with a few appetizers like braised pork belly with black-eyed pea succotash, but most are standards such as onion soup, shrimp cocktail, and wedge salad. Artisanal cheese plates are on the menu, and desserts are interesting, such as fudge-dipped derby pie. **Known for:** particularly good steaks; free valet parking; consistently good service. $ *Average main: $47* ✉ *Gaylord Palms Resort, 6000 W. Osceola Pkwy., Kissimmee* ✣ *I–4 Exit 65* ☎ *407/586–1600* 🌐 *www.marriott.com* ⊙ *No lunch.*

★ **Savion's Place**

$ | **CARIBBEAN** | **FAMILY** | At this independently owned restaurant, the down-home American dishes are given island twists. Prince Edward Island mussels share space with lobster mac-and-cheese, and mushroom Marsala meat loaf can appear on the table with "Grandma's recipe" jambalaya. There's live music Thursday–Saturday evening, and kids eat free on Saturday. **Known for:** home cooking with a Haitian flair; seafood gumbo and jambalaya; kids eat free on Saturday. $ *Average main: $12* ✉ *16 E. Dakin Ave., Kissimmee* ☎ *407/572-8719* 🌐 *savionsplace.com.*

Hotels

Gaylord Palms Resort and Convention Center

$$$$ | **RESORT** | **FAMILY** | Built in the style of a grand turn-of-the-20th-century Florida resort, this huge building is meant to inspire awe, with an enormous glass-roofed atrium and re-creations of Florida destination icons such as the Everglades, Key West, and Old St. Augustine; there's also a water park and movie events. **Pros:** you could have a great vacation without ever leaving the grounds; free shuttle to Disney; excellent on-site dining. **Cons:** $30 daily resort and parking fee; distant from Universal or downtown Orlando; hotel is so big that you will get your exercise walking within the building. $ *Rooms from: $489* ✉ *6000 W. Osceola Pkwy., Kissimmee* ☎ *407/586–0000* 🌐 *www.marriott.com* *1,406 rooms* *No meals.*

The Grove

$$ | **RESORT** | **FAMILY** | A large, all-suites property near the back gate of Disney offers upscale, modern decor in the rooms and public areas, as well as a substantial water park area with a surf simulator and waterslides. **Pros:** all-suites accommodations suitable for families and groups; choice of on-site eateries and water park; rural location but five-minute drive to busy dining/shopping district on Highway 192. **Cons:** $35 resort fee; $18 parking; long walk from some suites to lobby and amenities; 25-minute drive to Magic Kingdom. $ *Rooms from: $189* ✉ *14501 Grove Resort Ave., Kissimmee* ☎ *407/545–7500, 844/203–0209* 🌐 *www.groveresortorlando.com* *1,040 units* *No meals.*

Go gator! After a visit to Kissimmee's authentic, rustic Gatorland, you'll truly know the difference between a gator and a croc (and you'll see both).

Omni Orlando Resort at ChampionsGate
$$$ | **RESORT** | **FAMILY** | This huge, Mediterranean-style, award-winning resort just 6 miles south of Disney and within a 45-minute drive of LEGOLAND, includes a 1,200-acre golf club with two courses, a David Leadbetter academy, and a multifield sports complex. **Pros:** excellent Mokara spa; huge water park with lazy river and wave pool; five restaurants ranging from a casual café to upscale dining. **Cons:** remote location; daily resort fee for Internet, Disney shuttles, and gym; separate daily fee for parking. $ *Rooms from: $259* ✉ *1500 Masters Blvd., South of Kissimmee, ChampionsGate* ☎ *407/390–6664, 800/843–6664* 🌐 *www.omnihotels.com* 🛏 *720 units* 🍽 *No meals.*

Nightlife

DINNER SHOWS

Capone's Dinner and Show
THEATER | **FAMILY** | This musical dramedy brings you back to gangland Chicago of the 1930s, when mobsters and their molls were the height of underworld society. You'll meet Al Capone and learn that you can become a member of the "family," but you've got to help take care of a rat in the organization. Flashy costumes and musical numbers are accompanied by an all-you-can-eat American and Italian buffet that includes beer and cocktails as well as non-alcoholic mixed drinks for kids. Check the website for a 50% off coupon. ✉ *4740 W. Irlo Bronson Memorial Hwy., Kissimmee* ☎ *407/397–2378, 800/220–8428* 🌐 *www.alcapones.com* 🎫 *$70; online discounts.*

Medieval Times
THEATER | **FAMILY** | In a huge, ersatz-medieval manor you'll marvel at a tournament of sword fights, jousting matches, and other exciting games. The two-hour tournament and four-course feast has more than a dozen charging horses and a cast of 75 knights, nobles, wizards, and maidens participate. Sound silly? It is. But it's also a true extravaganza. That the show takes precedence over the meat-and-potatoes fare is obvious: everyone sits

facing forward at long, narrow banquet tables stepped auditorium-style above the tournament area. Kids love eating without forks; adults are swept away by the tremendous horse-riding artistry. Check the website and area attractions booklets for discounts. ✉ *4510 W. Vine St., Kissimmee* ☎ *407/396–1518, 888/935–6878* 🌐 *www.medievaltimes.com* 🎟 *From $65.*

Activities

RODEOS

Silver Spurs Rodeo

RODEO | FAMILY | A throwback to the days when cattle and horses ruled Central Orlando, Silver Spurs claims to be the largest rodeo east of the Mississippi. Started in 1944, the twice-yearly show brings contestants from across the country to compete in bull riding, saddle bronc riding, and barrel racing for $100,000 in prize money. Rodeos fill Kissimmee with cowboys during the second and third weekend in February and first weekend in June (the summer rodeo is free). ✉ *1875 Silver Spur La., Kissimmee* ☎ *321/697–3495* 🌐 *www.silverspurs-rodeo.com* 🎟 *$20.*

SPAS

Mokara Spa at Omni Orlando Resort at Championsgate

FITNESS/HEALTH CLUBS | Golf courses surround this resort, which might explain why Mokara Spa offers special treatments to ease tension and soreness in stressed shoulders and backs. The Sports Massage incorporates muscle-warming oil and stretching to make sure you're ready for another round. There are plenty of choices for the nongolfer in the group—customized massages, deep tissue, aromatherapy, reflexology, hot stones, salt stones, and a full-service salon for hair and nail treatments. Separate locker rooms, steam rooms, and relaxation rooms ensure privacy while you wait. Packages include the Mokara Classic, a 2½-hour treatment that consists of an 80-minute signature massage followed by a 50-minute facial for $285. A 20% gratuity is added to the bill. Parking is validated if you're a day-spa visitor. ✉ *Omni Orlando Resort at Championsgate, 1500 Masters Blvd., ChampionsGate* ☎ *407/390–6603* 🌐 *www.omnihotels.com.*

Relâche Spa & Salon at Gaylord Palms Resort

FITNESS/HEALTH CLUBS | The 20,000-square-foot spa is in the Everglades Atrium of this giant, Florida-theme resort, and you might feel like an explorer in a tropical wilderness as you make the trek toward tranquillity. Soft pastels and generous chaise longues in the tearoom radiate serenity. Fresh fruit and beverages keep you hydrated while you wait, then it's on to serious relaxation. The Escape to Paradise treatment is almost good enough to eat, with a coconut milk bath for relaxation, a pineapple sugar scrub for exfoliation, and warm butter application for skin nourishment. Then you're wrapped into a cozy cocoon topped by hot stones (order a Fijian scalp massage for dessert). A 20% gratuity is added onto the bill. Day pass available for a fee. ✉ *Gaylord Palms Resort, 6000 W. Osceola Pkwy., Kissimmee* ☎ *407/586–4772* 🌐 *www.marriott.com.*

Lake Buena Vista

This small city southeast of Walt Disney World rings the Disney theme parks with additional lodging options, chain restaurants, and heavy traffic. On Hotel Plaza Boulevard, eight hotels—within walking distance of Disney Springs and actually on Disney property—are designated as "official" Walt Disney World Hotels. Guests at these properties get a few of the perks of staying at Disney, including free park transportation, Fastpass+ access, and Early Magic Hours, but that's about it. Similarly, two hotels in Bonnet Creek (the Hilton Orlando Bonnet Creek

Kissimmee's Lake Tohopekaliga (affectionately known as Lake Toho) is famous with fishers the world over. It's also great for wildlife spotting—an especially exhilarating experience when done from an airboat.

and Waldorf Astoria Orlando) are also designated as "official" hotels, receiving similar perks to the other official hotels although they're not on Disney property.

Restaurants

Lake Buena Vista, just to the east of Disney Springs, is essentially a collection of midscale hotels, convention hotels, and chain restaurants catering to off-site visitors to Disney World.

American Kitchen Bar & Grill

$$$ | AMERICAN | FAMILY | A focus on locally sourced ingredients from a network of Florida farmers makes this hotel restaurant particularly appetizing. The chef-driven menu includes American Wagyu beef, house-made pasta, and Florida seafood. Classic cocktails with a modern twist highlight the bar menu. **Known for:** locally sourced ingredients from family farmers; free-range chicken; local Wagyu beef. *Average main: $26 B Resort & Spa, 1905 Hotel Plaza Blvd., Lake Buena Vista 407/828–2828 bhotelsandresorts.com.*

Covington Mill

$$ | AMERICAN | FAMILY | A polished space offering hearty buffet and à la carte breakfasts plus light lunches, Covington Mill turns into a kidfest on Sunday morning. That's when Disney characters join the early risers, cheerfully signing autographs and posing for photographs. **Known for:** buffet breakfast free for hotel guests; Disney character Sunday; create your own omelet option. *Average main: $20 Hilton Orlando Lake Buena Vista, 1751 Hotel Plaza Blvd., Lake Buena Vista 407/827–4000 www.hiltonorlandolakebuenavistahotel.com No dinner.*

Hemingway's

$$$$ | SEAFOOD | FAMILY | Business travelers and vacationers put on their khakis and sundresses to dine in this quiet seafood house loosely themed around Ernest Hemingway's travels. The woodsy dining room provides views of the Hyatt Regency's manicured grounds, a treat in summer when the sun sets late. Choose the Hemingway's "Cayo Hueso" crab cake, served with corn salsa and sweet corn coconut grits, or a Seafood Plateau sampler of assorted cooked shellfish. Other options are the Duvall Street shrimp scampi, a tribute to the author's love of shrimp, here served with truffled pasta, or the paella, a nod to the time he spent in Spain. Since the Keys were another favorite spot, the key lime baked Alaska is a fitting meal ender. **Known for:** tropical Key West atmosphere; seafood with Caribbean accents; Duval Street shrimp scampi. *Average main: $36 Hyatt Regency Grand Cypress, 1 Grand Cypress Blvd., Lake Buena Vista 407/239–3854 www.grandcypress.hyatt.com No lunch.*

La Luce

$$$ | ITALIAN | La Luce brings Italian cuisine with a Napa Valley farm-fresh flair to this upscale Hilton at the edge of Walt Disney World. Pastas are made fresh, steaks are handled with Italian care, and the cocktail bar is second to none. Try the gnocchetti with wild porcini and sausage ragu, the grilled rib eye with gremolata butter, or a simple seared salmon fillet with a tomato-chive-butter sauce. **Known for:** upscale and authentic Italian cuisine; "silk handkerchief" pasta; craft cocktail bar. *Average main: $30 Hilton Orlando Bonnet Creek, 14100 Bonnet Creek Resort La., Bonnet Creek, Lake Buena Vista 407/597–3600 www.laluceorlando.com No lunch.*

Lakeview Restaurant

$$$ | AMERICAN | FAMILY | Lake views for breakfast and dinner keep this hotel restaurant bustling twice a day. Yet the spot is at its peak on Tuesday, Thursday, and Saturday morning when Disney characters come to visit. Two classic costumed friends visit with guests as the diners help themselves to morning specialties from the buffet, including custom omelets. The character breakfast is free for children under some lodging plans. Dinner entrées are American faves such as pan-seared salmon and New York strip steak. **Known for:** Disney character breakfast; lakefront view; almond-crusted chicken. *Average main: $24 Wyndham Lake Buena Vista Resort, 1850 Hotel Plaza Blvd., Lake Buena Vista 407/828–4444 www.wyndhamlakebuenavista.com No lunch.*

Letterpress Cafe

$ | AMERICAN | FAMILY | Southern-style cooking is the highlight of the breakfast, brunch, and dinner menus. High-end, Florida-sourced ingredients like Anson Mills grits, Angus beef, and locally baked bread elevate the Letterpress Cafe above the ordinary hotel restaurant. On Sunday morning, classic Disney characters join breakfasting guests as they eat their cinnamon-apple French toast and steak-and-egg burritos. **Known for:** kettle soups; Florida fish; Southern-style cooking. *Average main: $13 Buena Vista Palace Hotel & Spa, 1900 E. Buena Vista Dr., Lake Buena Vista 866/397–6516 www.buenavistapalace.com.*

The Venetian Chop House

$$$$ | EUROPEAN | This fine-dining restaurant inside one of Lake Buena Vista's many convention hotels might have been designed as a place for execs on expense accounts to seal deals, but it has also become a haven for nontrendy locals seeking an old-fashioned romantic retreat. The architecture alone—it looks like Renaissance Venice—is enough to lure you. The entry door is topped by a giant copper dome, and the dining room has dark wood furniture, crystal chandeliers, and carpets that could grace a European palace. Deep booths are surrounded on two sides by etched glass. The waiters wear tuxes. Begin with the signature lobster bisque, an ultrarich soup topped with flaky pastry. Follow that with a good filet mignon, Dover sole, or pan-roasted veal chop in porcini cream sauce. Grand Marnier soufflé is the signature dessert. **Known for:** lobster bisque; romantic Italian decor; black Angus beef.

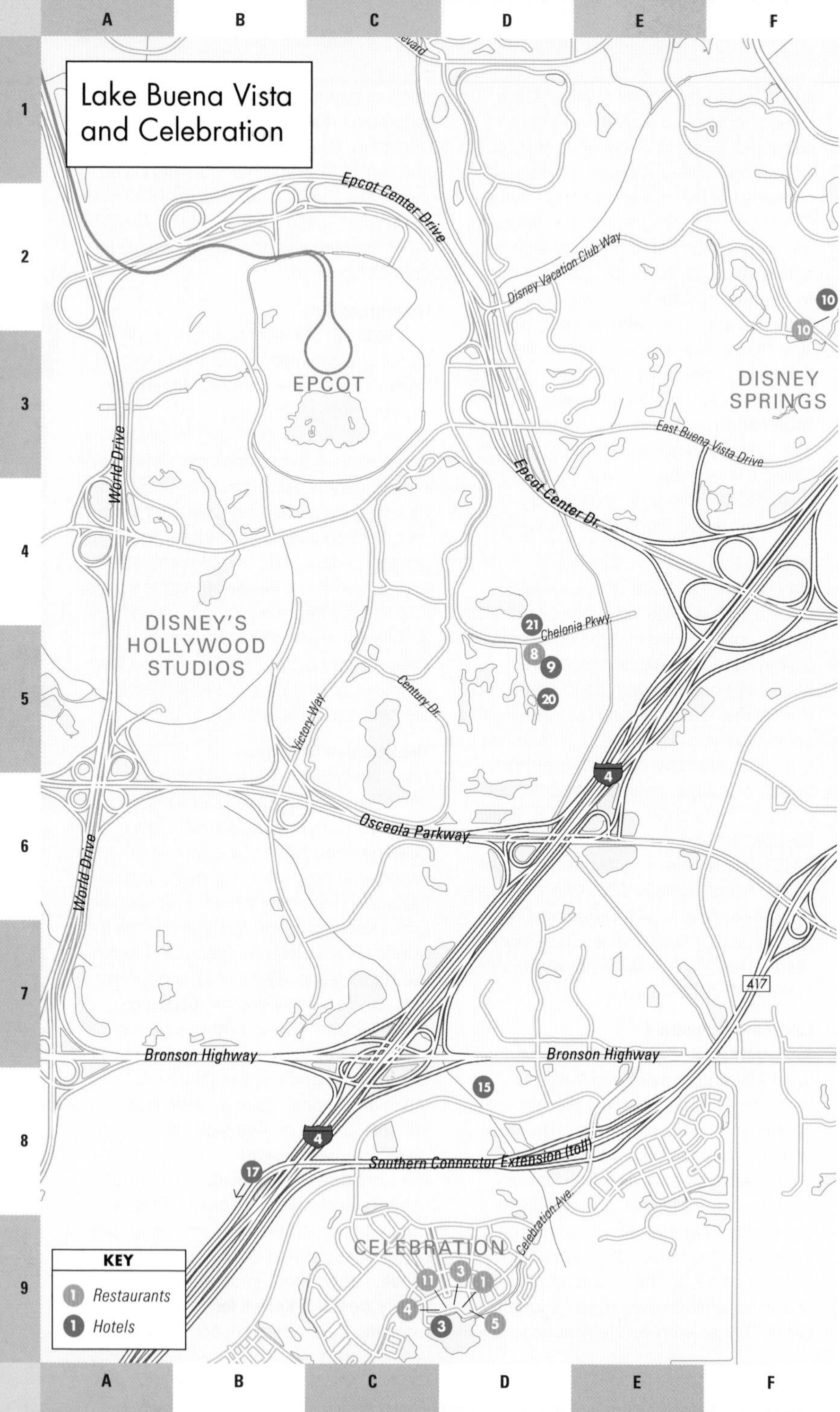

A
B
C
D
E
F
1
2
3
4
5
6
7
8
9
Lake Buena Vista and Celebration
Epcot Center Drive
Disney Vacation Club Way
EPCOT
DISNEY SPRINGS
World Drive
East Buena Vista Drive
Epcot Center Dr.
DISNEY'S HOLLYWOOD STUDIOS
Chelonia Pkwy.
Century Dr.
Victory Way
4
Osceola Parkway
World Drive
417
Bronson Highway
Bronson Highway
4
Southern Connector Extension (toll)
Celebration Ave.
CELEBRATION
KEY
Restaurants
Hotels

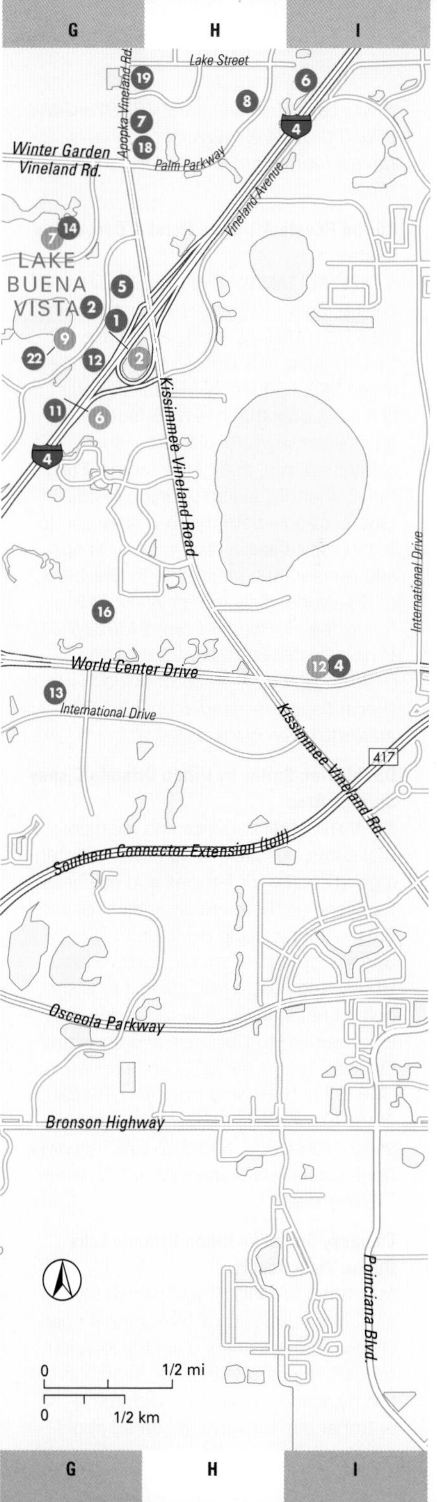

Restaurants ▼

1 Ari Celebration D9
2 American Kitchen Bar & Grill G2
3 Café d'Antonio D9
4 Celebration Town Tavern C9
5 Columbia Restaurant D9
6 Covington Mill G3
7 Hemingway's G2
8 La Luce D5
9 Lakeview Restaurant... G2
10 Letterpress Cafe F2
11 Market Street Diner D9
12 The Venetian Chop House I4

Hotels ▼

1 B Resort & Spa Disney Springs Resort Area G2
2 Best Western Lake Buena Vista Resort G2
3 Bohemian Hotel Celebration D9
4 Caribe Royale All-Suite Hotel & Convention Center I4
5 DoubleTree Suites by Hilton Orlando Disney Springs Area ... G2
6 Embassy Suites by Hilton Orlando Lake Buena Vista Resort I1
7 Fairfield Inn & Suites by Marriott Lake Buena Vista G1
8 Hawthorn Suites by Wyndham Lake Buena Vista Orlando H1
9 Hilton Orlando Bonnet Creek D5
10 Hilton Orlando Buena Vista Palace Disney Springs Area F2
11 Hilton Orlando Lake Buena Vista G3
12 Holiday Inn Orlando–Disney Springs Area ... G2
13 Holiday Inn Resorts Orlando Suites—Waterpark G5
14 Hyatt Regency Grand Cypress Resort G2
15 Meliá Orlando Suite Hotel at Celebration D8
16 Orlando World Center Marriott G4
17 Reunion Resort & Golf Club B8
18 Sheraton Lake Buena Vista Orlando Resort ... G1
19 Staybridge Suites Lake Buena Vista G1
20 Waldorf Astoria Orlando D5
21 Wyndham Grand Orlando Resort, Bonnet Creek D4
22 Wyndham Lake Buena Vista Disney Springs Resort Area G2

Average main: $40 Caribe Royale, 8101 World Center Dr., Lake Buena Vista 407/238–8060 www.cariberoyale.com No lunch. Closed Sun. Free parking with dinner reservation.

Hotels

The eight hotels on Hotel Plaza Boulevard within walking distance of Disney Springs are considered "official" hotels, so they have a few extra perks. Hotels just beyond the Disney Springs area tend to be less expensive than those right on Hotel Plaza Boulevard. If you're willing to take a 10-minute drive or shuttle ride, you might save as much as 35% off your room tab.

B Resort & Spa Disney Springs Resort Area
$$ | **RESORT** | **FAMILY** | Driving up Hotel Plaza Boulevard toward the Disney Springs complex, you'll come to this towering hotel whose chic and contemporary interior suggests it's designed solely for hip young couples, but families might be impressed by the offering as well. **Pros:** walk to Disney Springs; kids' activities; park shuttles, Extra Magic Hours, and Fastpass+ access. **Cons:** resort fee $30; parking fee $22–$28; need a car to get to Universal or downtown Orlando. *Rooms from: $175 1905 Hotel Plaza Blvd., Lake Buena Vista 407/828–2828 www.bhotelsandresorts.com/b-walt-disney-world 394 rooms No meals.*

★ **Best Western Lake Buena Vista Resort**
$ | **RESORT** | **FAMILY** | Commanding the skyline across from Disney Springs, this is a family-friendly choice with rooms that sleep six and where kids eat free (they love the Mickey waffles at breakfast). **Pros:** a quick walk to shopping and restaurants; free park shuttle, Extra Magic Hours, and Fastpass+; kids eat free. **Cons:** inconvenient to Universal and downtown Orlando; transportation to the parks can be slow and crowded; resort fee ($14) and parking fee ($8–$12). *Rooms from: $159 2000 Hotel Plaza Blvd., Lake Buena Vista 407/828–2424, 800/780–7234 www.lakebuenavistaresorthotel.com 325 rooms No meals.*

Caribe Royale All-Suite Hotel & Convention Center
$ | **RESORT** | **FAMILY** | This big, all-suites pink palace, on 53 tropical acres just 10 minutes from Disney, melds affordable prices with luxurious decor, business-traveler amenities, and family-friendly ingredients like a big pool that has a 65-foot slide, an interactive water-play area, cushy cabanas, a spa, and game rooms. **Pros:** family-friendly; award-winning restaurant; scheduled shuttle to Disney and to outlet mall. **Cons:** a hike to other shops and restaurants; no shuttle to Universal or SeaWorld; daily fee for Wi-Fi; $28 resort fee. *Rooms from: $140 8101 World Center Dr., Lake Buena Vista 407/238–8000, 800/823–8300 www.thecaribehotelsorlando.com 1,335 suites Free breakfast.*

DoubleTree Suites by Hilton Orlando Disney Springs Area
$$ | **HOTEL** | **FAMILY** | Price and location make this all-suites, Hilton-owned hotel a good choice for families and business travelers, as there are amenities for both. **Pros:** within walking distance to Disney Springs; free park shuttle, Extra Magic Hours, and Fastpass+; access to Disney golf courses. **Cons:** daily fee for Wi-Fi; inconvenient to Universal and downtown Orlando; resort fee ($20) and parking fee ($18–$22). *Rooms from: $175 2305 Hotel Plaza Blvd., Lake Buena Vista 407/934–1000, 800/222–8733 www.doubletreeguestsuites.com 229 units No meals.*

Embassy Suites by Hilton Orlando Lake Buena Vista Resort
$$$ | **HOTEL** | **FAMILY** | This Spanish-style all-suites hotel just off Interstate 4 near Disney Springs offers a central location for park hoppers with a car, in addition to roomy accommodations, with refrigerator and microwave, a heated pool

with cabanas, a tennis court, and kids activities. **Pros:** free shuttle to all Disney parks; free Wi-Fi; free manager's cocktail reception. **Cons:** $19.95 nightly resort fee and $14 self-parking fee; no shuttle to other parks; long walk to shops and restaurants. *Rooms from: $285 8100 Lake St., Lake Buena Vista 407/239–1144, 800/257–8483, 800/362–2779 www.embassysuites.com 334 suites Free breakfast.*

Fairfield Inn & Suites by Marriott Lake Buena Vista

$ | **HOTEL** | **FAMILY** | Less than a mile from Disney Springs and within walking distance of a variety of restaurants and shops, this hotel, renovated in 2017, has in-room amenities and an attractive budget price. **Pros:** refrigerators and microwaves in every room; free shuttle to Disney; free parking. **Cons:** no real on-site restaurant; small pool; no room service. *Rooms from: $114 12191 S. Apopka Vineland Rd., Lake Buena Vista 407/239–1115, 888/236–2427 www.marriott.com/mcofv 170 rooms Free breakfast.*

Hawthorn Suites by Wyndham Lake Buena Vista Orlando

$ | **RESORT** | **FAMILY** | A large, marble-columned lobby welcomes guests to this all-suites lodging less than a mile from Disney's door, and the amenities continue into the suites, most with a fully equipped kitchen, living room, and bedroom with multiple TVs. **Pros:** free hot breakfast, Wi-Fi, and parking; free shuttle to Disney and factory outlet mall; on public bus route. **Cons:** pool area can be noisy; no on-site restaurant; no free shuttle to Universal or SeaWorld. *Rooms from: $159 8303 Palm Pkwy., Lake Buena Vista 407/597–5000, 866/756–3778 www.hawthornlakebuenavista.com 112 suites Free breakfast.*

Hilton Orlando Bonnet Creek

$$ | **RESORT** | **FAMILY** | The Hilton more than lives up to its next-door neighbor the Waldorf Astoria Orlando, with plenty of amenities, including a 3-acre lagoon pool with a lazy river, rooms with deluxe bedding and flat-screen TVs, family-friendly activities, a golf course, and transportation to Disney parks. **Pros:** serene setting, just moments from Disney by shuttle; access to Waldorf Astoria Golf Club; next door to Waldorf and its amenities. **Cons:** nothing within walking distance, so car is helpful; $29 daily parking fee; $45 resort fee. *Rooms from: $232 14100 Bonnet Creek Resort La., Bonnet Creek, Lake Buena Vista 407/597–3600 www.hiltonbonnetcreek.com 1,009 rooms Free breakfast.*

Hilton Orlando Buena Vista Palace Disney Springs Area

$$ | **RESORT** | **FAMILY** | This towering hotel just a five-minute walk from Disney Springs caters to business and leisure guests and offers many on-site amenities and recreational options in addition to free shuttles to Disney parks, character breakfasts, and access to Disney golf courses. **Pros:** good restaurants and bars on-site; kids' activities and on-site water park; free park shuttle, Extra Magic Hours, and Fastpass+. **Cons:** inconvenient to Universal and downtown Orlando; steep daily resort fee ($35) for Wi-Fi and fitness center; parking fee ($18–$24). *Rooms from: $209 1900 E. Buena Vista Dr., Lake Buena Vista 407/827–2727 www.buenavistapalace.com 1,012 rooms No meals.*

Hilton Orlando Lake Buena Vista

$$$ | **HOTEL** | **FAMILY** | Disney character breakfasts and its Disney Springs location (a 10-minute walk away via a skybridge) make this a family-friendly resort, with relaxed and airy rooms with white duvet-style bedding, flat-screen TVs, great views, on-site eateries, and two heated pools. **Pros:** character breakfasts on-site; free park shuttle, Extra Magic Hours, and Fastpass+; access to advance tee times at Disney golf courses. **Cons:** pricey resort fee ($35); parking fee ($18–$24); need a car to get to Universal

and downtown Orlando. $ *Rooms from: $250* ✉ *1751 Hotel Plaza Blvd., Lake Buena Vista* ☎ *407/827–4000, 800/782–4414 reservations* 🌐 *www.hilton.com* ⇨ *814 rooms* 🍴 *No meals.*

Holiday Inn Orlando–Disney Springs Area
$ | HOTEL | FAMILY | Location is what sets this hotel apart, as it's only a 15-minute walk from Disney Springs. **Pros:** free parking; walking distance to Disney Springs; free park shuttle, Extra Magic Hours, Fastpass+. **Cons:** no free shuttle to Universal or SeaWorld; resort fee ($22); need a car to get to Orlando. $ *Rooms from: $149* ✉ *1805 Hotel Plaza Blvd., Lake Buena Vista* ☎ *407/828–8888, 888/465–4329* 🌐 *www.hiorlando.com* ⇨ *323 rooms* 🍴 *No meals.*

Holiday Inn Resorts Orlando Suites—Waterpark
$ | RESORT | FAMILY | The six-story resort, formerly the Nickelodeon Hotel, is built around a colorful water park with slides, splash bucket, and climbing zones. **Pros:** kids eat breakfast and dinner free; Disney shuttles included in resort fee; minigolf course and waterpark. **Cons:** daily resort fee of $30, parking $15; way too frenetic for folks without kids; poolside rooms can be noisy. $ *Rooms from: $130* ✉ *14500 Continental Gateway, Lake Buena Vista* ☎ *407/387–5437, 866/462–6425* 🌐 *www.ihg.com* ⇨ *777 rooms* 🍴 *Free breakfast.*

★ **Hyatt Regency Grand Cypress Resort**
$$ | RESORT | FAMILY | Sitting amid 1,500 palm-filled acres just outside Disney's gate, this huge luxury resort has a private lake with watercraft, four golf courses, and miles of trails. **Pros:** elaborate spa; lots of on-site recreation options, including huge pool, golf courses, equestrian center, and good restaurants; shuttles to Disney, Universal, and SeaWorld. **Cons:** need a car or taxi to get to downtown Orlando or Universal; $38 daily resort and $25 parking fees; lots of conventioneers. $ *Rooms from: $220* ✉ *1 Grand Cypress Blvd., Lake Buena Vista* ☎ *407/239–1234, 800/233–1234* 🌐 *www.hyatt.com* ⇨ *779 rooms* 🍴 *No meals.*

Orlando World Center Marriott
$$ | RESORT | This luxury golf resort is one of Orlando's largest, catering to conventions and families (because of its proximity to Disney). **Pros:** full-service spa; wide variety of on-site eateries; Hawk's Landing Golf Course. **Cons:** $24 daily fee for parking, $30 daily resort fee for park shuttles and Internet; on-site restaurants have expense-account-size prices; nothing within walking distance. $ *Rooms from: $249* ✉ *8701 World Center Dr., Lake Buena Vista* ☎ *407/239–4200, 800/621–0638* 🌐 *www.marriottworldcenter.com* ⇨ *2,010 rooms* 🍴 *No meals.*

Sheraton Lake Buena Vista Orlando Resort
$$ | RESORT | FAMILY | This hotel, conveniently situated near the Disney Springs entrance to WDW, is a pool-centered oasis of cool; some guest rooms transform into family suites with a separate bedroom and bunk beds. **Pros:** waterslides for kids; Disney shuttle; on-site restaurants. **Cons:** on a busy commercial strip; relatively close to Disney Springs but a tad too far to walk in the summer heat (about 1 mile); $20 resort fee, $16 parking fee. $ *Rooms from: $199* ✉ *12205 S. Apopka Vineland Rd., Lake Buena Vista* ☎ *407/239–0444, 800/423–3297* 🌐 *www.marriott.com* ⇨ *486 rooms* 🍴 *No meals.*

Staybridge Suites Lake Buena Vista
$ | HOTEL | FAMILY | Close to Disney, this pleasant all-suites hotel is the perfect home away from home for big families on small budgets; it's only a few miles along Palm Parkway from SeaWorld, Universal, and even the airport, so the frenzy of Interstate 4 can be avoided altogether. **Pros:** free scheduled shuttle service to WDW; free hot breakfast; free Wi-Fi and parking. **Cons:** no restaurant; no shuttles to Universal and SeaWorld; pool and dining areas can be crowded. $ *Rooms from: $172* ✉ *8751 Suiteside Dr., Lake*

Buena Vista ☎ *407/238–0777* 🌐 *www.ihg.com* 🛏 *150 rooms* 🍽 *Free breakfast.*

★ Waldorf Astoria Orlando

$$$$ | RESORT | Although it can't duplicate the famed original in New York City, this Waldorf echoes it with imagination and flair. **Pros:** lavish and luxurious hotel; free transportation to Disney parks; great spa and Rees Jones–designed golf course. **Cons:** pricey, but you knew that; if you can bear to leave your cabana, you'll need a car to see anything else in the area; $45 daily resort fee, $37 parking. $ *Rooms from: $578* ✉ *14200 Bonnet Creek Resort La., Bonnet Creek, Lake Buena Vista* ☎ *407/597–5500* 🌐 *www.waldorfastoriaorlando.com* 🛏 *328 rooms* 🍽 *Free breakfast.*

Wyndham Grand Orlando Resort, Bonnet Creek

$$$ | RESORT | FAMILY | Despite being surrounded by Disney property, the lakeside locale of this family-friendly resort can feel remote, but generous accommodations, transportation to Disney parks, a full spa, access to Waldorf golf, and several pools offer diversions for everyone. **Pros:** practically in Mickey's lap; free shuttles to Disney parks; pet friendly. **Cons:** not convenient to Universal or downtown Orlando; $35 daily resort fee; $22 parking fee. $ *Rooms from: $349* ✉ *14651 Chelonia Pkwy., Bonnet Creek, Lake Buena Vista* ☎ *407/390–2300* 🌐 *www.wyndhamgrandorlando.com* 🛏 *1,149 rooms* 🍽 *Free breakfast.*

Wyndham Lake Buena Vista Disney Springs Resort Area

$$ | RESORT | FAMILY | Any hotel within a skip and a hop of Disney Springs is a great draw, and one with a water-playground complex that can entice kids away from the Magic Kingdom during the midday heat is even better; deluxe bedding, large TVs, Disney fireworks views, and character breakfasts are the icing on the cake. **Pros:** good kids' programs; walk to Disney Springs; free shuttle to all Disney parks and attractions. **Cons:** daily resort fee ($25); no shuttle to Universal and downtown Orlando; daily parking fee ($20). $ *Rooms from: $224* ✉ *1850 Hotel Plaza Blvd., Lake Buena Vista* ☎ *407/828–4444* 🌐 *www.wyndhamlakebuenavista.com* 🛏 *623 rooms* 🍽 *No meals.*

Activities

SPAS

The Spa at Orlando World Center Marriott

FITNESS/HEALTH CLUBS | Finding the spa in this sprawling, multitower resort outside the entrance to Walt Disney World can be a challenge, but once you arrive, tranquility rules. Robes and slippers are provided in the locker rooms, but there are no private changing rooms. If you are modest, you must retreat to the bathroom or shower. The waiting room is co-ed. Steam rooms, a pool, and a fitness facility are available for use before or after a therapy in one of the 14 treatment rooms. The extensive Half-Day Escape includes massage, facial, and mani-pedi for $310. Gratuities are at your discretion. ✉ *Orlando World Center Marriott, 8701 World Center Dr., Lake Buena Vista* ☎ *407/239–4200* 🌐 *www.marriott.com.*

The Waldorf Astoria Spa

FITNESS/HEALTH CLUBS | In this spacious, 22-treatment-room spa, everything is designed for the hotel guest—not a coincidence, since they are the only ones privy to treatments. In your plush robe and slippers, you can flit from a eucalyptus steam room to an experiential shower (it surrounds you with water, sound, and light) and then to a tea lounge. Try the Golden Body Treatment, a decadent, over-the-top process that incorporates gold-enriched creams to scrub and strengthen the skin. The salon offers every service imaginable. A 20% service charge is added. ✉ *Waldorf Astoria Orlando, 14200 Bonnet Creek Resort La., Bonnet Creek, Lake Buena Vista* ☎ *407/597–5360* 🌐 *www.waldorfastoriaorlando.com* ☞ *Parking: valet only, complimentary with spa validation, but please tip.*

Celebration

Walt Disney's original residential concept for EPCOT has emerged farther south with designer homes, beautiful lakeside diversions, and a small-town-feeling center. If you are familiar with Seaside and some of the planned towns on the Panhandle, this area will look familiar. There's also a hotel and several restaurants, so some guests visiting Walt Disney World base themselves here.

This community, where every blade of grass in every lawn seems perfect, is as picturesque as a movie set—although, to some critics, it would be one used in *The Stepford Wives.* But Celebration is a model of good American architecture and urban planning as well as a delightful place to spend a morning or afternoon.

Things appear nearly as faux as on Main Street, U.S.A., but as they unfold, you see signs of reality—and a pleasant one it is. Celebration is a real town, with its own hospital and school system. Houses and apartments spread out from the compact, restaurant-filled downtown area, which wraps around the edge of a lake. Sidewalks are built for strolling, restaurants have outdoor seating with lake views, and inviting shops beckon. After a walk around the lake, take youngsters over to the huge interactive fountain and have fun getting soaked.

The town has a year-round roster of special events and a noteworthy Sunday Farmers' Market. Starting the last Saturday in November and continuing through New Year's Eve, honest-to-goodness snow sprinkles softly down over Main Street every night on the hour from 6 to 9.

Restaurants

The town's Market Street–area restaurants (predominately upscale) face a pastoral (though man-made) lake. To get here, take Interstate 4 to Exit 64 (192) and follow the "Celebration" signs.

Ari Celebration

$$$ | JAPANESE FUSION | FAMILY | This bright, modern restaurant serves fairly standard sushi rolls and an interesting range of hot dishes. Menu standouts include the beef bulgogi bowl (thin, marinated slices of beef or pork grilled on a barbecue) and kalbi (Korean barbecued short ribs). There is another location in Orlando. **Known for:** Japanese and Korean specialties; affordable lunch specials; Korean bento box combinations. *Average main: $22 ✉ 671 Front St., Celebration ☎ 407/566–1889 ⊕ arisushi.net.*

Café d'Antonio

$$ | ITALIAN | FAMILY | The wood-burning oven and grill are worked pretty hard here. The mountains of hardwood used in the open kitchen flavor the best of the menu—pizza, grilled fish and chicken, steaks and chops, and even the lasagna. A standout is the wood-fired veal chop stuffed with prosciutto, fontina, and spinach. For a less expensive meal, you can pick your own ingredients for a personal wood-oven pizza. The terrace overlooking the lake is enclosed and air-conditioned. **Known for:** fine Italian dining; wood-fired veal chop; mixed antipasto platter. *Average main: $21 ✉ 691 Front St., Celebration ☎ 407/566–2233 ⊕ cafedantonios.com.*

Celebration Town Tavern

$$$ | SEAFOOD | FAMILY | This New England–cuisine eatery, operated by a family with Boston roots, has a double personality. The interior is a brass, glass, and dark-wood-paneling kind of place, while the outside patio has table seating plus the Paddy O' Bar. The food ranges from landlubber treats like baby back ribs, prime rib, and half-pound burgers (from $8) to exquisite seafood including Ipswich clams, lobster rolls, Boston scrod, and two-pound lobsters (all flown in from Boston), plus, on occasion, a salute to the Sunshine State with Florida

Celebration has a picture-perfect main street, and no wonder since it's a planned community designed by Disney.

stone crabs in season. Although the place has a polished demeanor, there are plenty of menu choices right out of a working-class Boston bar—meatball hoagies, Philly cheesesteak sandwiches, and Buffalo-style chicken wings. For dessert there's great—what else?—Boston cream pie. **Known for:** 99-beer selection; fried Boston scrod; steak scampi. *$ Average main: $27 ✉ 721 Front St., Celebration ☎ 407/566–2526 🌐 www.thecelebrationtowntavern.com.*

★ Columbia Restaurant

$$$ | **LATIN AMERICAN** | **FAMILY** | Celebration's branch of this family-owned high-end chain might be better than the original in Tampa, which has been operating for a century. For your main course, zero in on the paella—either *à la Valenciana* (with meat and seafood) or *campesina* (a "farmer's" paella from Spain, with beef, pork, chorizo, and chicken). The best dessert, *brazo gitano cien anos* (sponge cake with strawberries that is soaked in syrup and Spanish sherry and flambéed table-side), was created for the restaurant chain's 100th anniversary in 2005, and is well worth its price just for the show. **Known for:** oldest continuous restaurant chain in Florida; upscale Cuban cuisine; paella à la Valenciana. *$ Average main: $29 ✉ 649 Front St., Celebration ☎ 407/566–1505 🌐 www.columbiarestaurant.com.*

Market Street Diner

$ | **AMERICAN** | The menu at this upscale diner ranges from breakfast classics like French toast and the house-special baked-potato omelet, to comfort classics like beef Stroganoff and homemade chicken potpie. In addition to a hearty version of the quintessential American hamburger (best enjoyed with a creamy milk shake), there are also salmon and portobello burgers for the cholesterol wary. An outdoor seating section in front of the restaurant makes for a pleasant dining destination. **Known for:** classic diner food; breakfast until 2 pm daily; homemade desserts. *$ Average main: $12 ✉ 701 Front St., Celebration ☎ 407/566–1144 🌐 marketstdiner.com.*

Celebration is immediately south of the Walt Disney World Resort, and while it's relatively close to the parks, the resorts in Lake Buena Vista, just west of Disney Springs, are closer to everything but Animal Kingdom.

Bohemian Hotel Celebration

$$$ | HOTEL | FAMILY | Like everything in the Disney-created town of Celebration, this pet-friendly boutique hotel in the middle of the charming village borrows from the best of the 19th, 20th, and 21st centuries. **Pros:** Lakeside Bar & Grill has great high-end dining; rental bikes and golf carts make touring the village a breeze; free shuttle to Celebration Golf and Fitness Center and free Wi-Fi. **Cons:** $16 fee for parking; need a car (or ride share) to get anywhere other than Celebration; it's a long way to Universal. *Rooms from: $314 ✉ 700 Bloom St., Celebration ☎ 407/566–6000, 888/249–4007 🌐 www.kesslercollection.com 115 rooms No meals.*

Meliá Orlando Suite Hotel at Celebration

$ | HOTEL | FAMILY | Much like a European boutique hotel, the Meliá Orlando is very human in scale and minimalist in decor; it;s also only minutes from Disney. **Pros:** shuttle to Celebration and Disney parks; spa privileges at Celebration Day Spa; dog-friendly. **Cons:** busy U.S. 192 is close by; $20 daily resort fee; need a car to visit Universal, SeaWorld, or downtown Orlando. *Rooms from: $132 ✉ 225 Celebration Pl., Celebration ☎ 407/964–7000, 888/956–3542 🌐 www.melia.com 240 rooms No meals.*

Reunion Resort & Golf Club

$$ | RESORT | FAMILY | Ten miles southwest of Disney and 45 minutes from LEGOLAND, this 2,300-acre resort with condo-style villas and estate-style houses contains three private golf courses—designed by Tom Watson, Arnold Palmer, and Jack Nicklaus—nine pools, a 5-acre water park complex, a spa, and tennis courts. **Pros:** concierge grocery delivery; 11 pools and water park; has one of the best restaurants in the area, Eleven. **Cons:** $35 daily resort fee, $20 parking; about a 10-mile drive to Disney parks; no theme-park shuttles, so you'll need a car. *Rooms from: $216 ✉ 7593 Gathering Dr., I–4 Exit 58, Reunion ☎ 407/396–3200, 866/880–8563 🌐 www.reunionresort.com 360 units No meals.*

Chapter 9

UNIVERSAL ORLANDO

UNIVERSAL STUDIOS, ISLANDS OF ADVENTURE, VOLCANO BAY, CITYWALK

Updated by
Gary Mckechnie

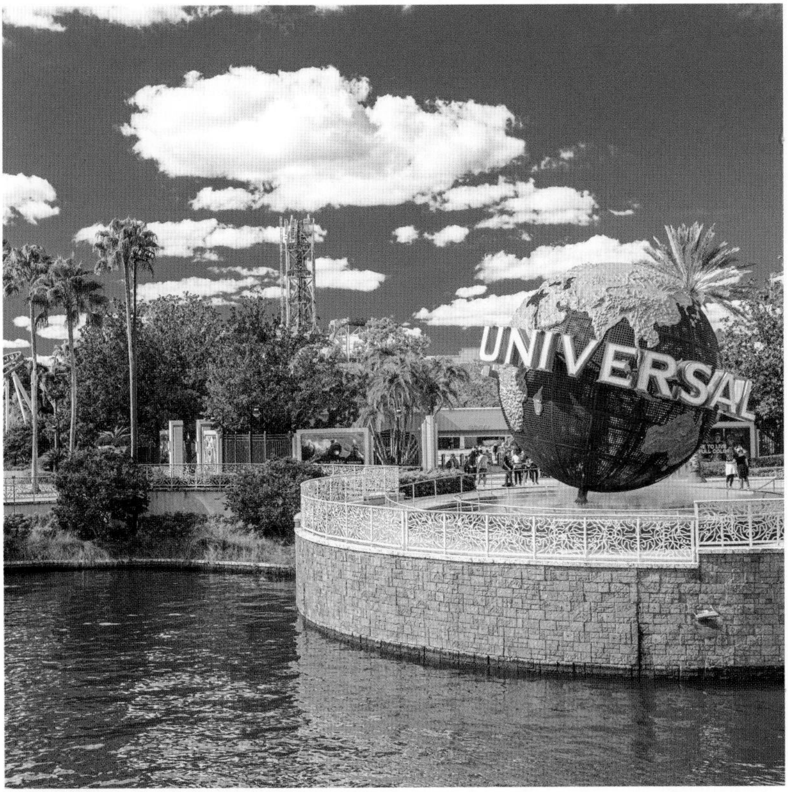

Sights ★★★★★ | Restaurants ★★★★★ | Hotels ★★★★★ | Shopping ★★★★★ | Nightlife ★★★★★

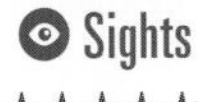

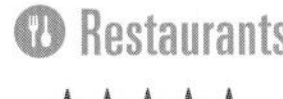

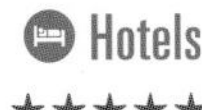

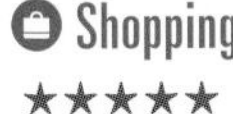

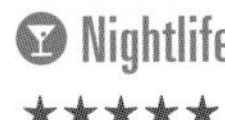

PARK SNAPSHOT

TOP EXPERIENCES

■ **CityWalk:** At the hub of both theme parks this collection of shops, restaurants, nightclubs, and concert venues is going day and night (especially night).

■ **Harry Potter:** Not just one, but two lands based on J.K. Rowling's fantastical books and the haracters she created have given Universal Orlando an enormous boost—and fans new worlds to explore.

■ **Horror Make-Up Show:** No Disney fantasies or princesses here—just slapstick comedy, quick one-liners, and gross gags that delight kids and tickle adults.

■ **Incredible Hulk Coaster:** While Universal loves to showcase its high-tech virtual-reality attractions, this super-fast and super-exciting roller coaster gets back to the basics.

■ **Volcano Bay:** Centered on a land of ingeniously designed water activities, this elaborate water theme park can be as exciting or as tranquil as you desire.

PLANNING YOUR TIME

Universal has two theme parks (plus Volcano Bay) to explore. The resort also includes hotels (and their restaurants and activities) as well as CityWalk and its nightclubs, stores, boutiques, restaurants, shows, and concert venues. On a first time visit, Universal Studios is likely to be your first choice. The original theme park is where you'll find both classic attractions (i.e., E.T.'s Adventure) and new additions like The Mummy, Fast & Furious: Supercharged and, Harry Potter's Diagon Alley. This single park can take a full day (or two), but if you're here for just one day (and if Harry Potter is your main draw) then a one-day, *two-park* ticket is likely what you need to access both sections of The Wizarding World of Harry Potter. The parks are less crowded in February, May, and early October. Another dip in attendance happens between Thanksgiving and the days before Christmas.

GETTING HERE

■ Universal Orlando is midway between downtown Orlando and Walt Disney World, off I–4. From the interstate as well as bordering Kirkman Road, International Drive, and Sand Lake Road, well-marked signs will point you toward two massive parking garages ($26) or, for an extra fee, valet parking. It's even easier if you catch a ride here via taxi, Lyft, Uber, or a shuttle bus from your hotel since they can drop you off closer to the park entrance. Staying at a Universal resort hotel also saves you the parking fee and provides free transportation to the parks as well as (at some hotels) expedited admission into the attractions with the use of Universal Express.

QUICK BITES

■ **Blondies.** Hot dogs, subs, and slices from a mammoth "Dagwood" sandwich are fast and filling. ✉ *Toon Lagoon, Islands of Adventure.*

■ **Classic Monsters Cafe.** The quick-service restaurant offers slices of pizza and hot dogs for a quick boost. ✉ *Production Central, Universal Studios.*

■ **Mel's Drive-In.** The 1950s flashback diner can get crowded, but service is pretty fast. ✉ *Hollywood, Universal Studios.*

Universal Orlando's personality is revealed the moment you arrive in the theme parks, where music, cartoonish architecture, abundant eye candy, subtle and overt sound effects, whirling and whizzing rides, plus a throng of fellow travelers will follow you nearly everywhere. For peace and quiet, seek sanctuary at one of the resort hotels.

At a breathless pace, there's a chance you *could* visit both Universal parks (Universal Studios and Islands of Adventure, aka IOA) in a single day, but to do that you'll have to invest in a Universal Express Pass. Without it, you'll spend a good portion of that day waiting in line at the premium attractions. So allow two days, or perhaps three; a day for each park plus a "pick-up" day to return to your favorite attractions—or skip them both in favor of a leisurely day at Volcano Bay. Which attractions are the main attractions? At Universal Studios, Revenge of the Mummy and The Simpsons are always popular; at IOA, the Incredible Hulk Coaster and the Amazing Adventures of Spider-Man are hits. At both parks, it's definitely the entire scope of shops and attractions at the Wizarding Worlds of Harry Potter.

Universal Studios appeals primarily to those who like loud, fast, high-energy attractions—generally teens and adults. Covering 444 acres, it's a rambling montage of sets, shops, and soundstages housing theme attractions, as well as reproductions of New York, San Francisco, London, and the fictional town of Springfield.

When IOA first opened in 1999, it took attractions to a new level. Each section—from Marvel Super Hero Island to Toon Lagoon to Seuss Landing and the Lost Continent—was impressive enough to suggest that Universal had out-Disneyed Disney. And when the 20-acre Wizarding World of Harry Potter–Hogsmeade opened in 2010, IOA received well-deserved worldwide attention. Universal Studios made another huge leap forward with the 2014 unveiling of a full-scale version of Diagon Alley, complete with Gringotts Bank and a magical train that departs for IOA from Platform 9¾. Knowing how Harry's cast a spell on generations of fans, Universal is always finding ways to expand the Potter magic with new angles, attractions, and shows. So stay tuned.

Planning

Getting Here and Around

East on Interstate 4 (from WDW and Tampa), exit at Universal Boulevard (75A); take a left into Universal Orlando, and follow the signs. Heading west on Interstate 4 (from downtown or Daytona), exit at Universal Boulevard (74B), turn right, and follow Hollywood Way.

Both Universal Studios and IOA require a lot of walking—a whole lot of serious walking. Start off by using the parking area's moving walkways as much as possible. Arrive early at either park, and you might be able to complete a single lap that will get you to the main attractions.

Operating Hours

Universal Studios and IOA are open 365 days a year, with opening/closing times typically from 9 am to 7 pm but changing throughout the year (and sometimes varying by the week). Check online for the most accurate hours of each park and CityWalk. Some Universal resort hotel guests receive early admission (see below).

Parking

Universal's two garages total 3.4 million square feet, so after you park, *note your parking space.* The cost is a super steep $26 for cars and motorcycles (although it's free after 6 pm as a nod to guests arriving for the nightlife of CityWalk), $32 for RVs and buses, and $40 for "prime" parking, which puts you on a lower level closer to the entrance. Although moving walkways get you partway, you could walk up to a half mile to reach the gates, which explains why some guests opt for valet parking ($26 for up to two hours, $55 for more than two hours), which literally puts them at the entrance to CityWalk and near the turnstiles of the parks.

Admission

The at-the-gate, per-person, per-day, single-park rate for either Universal Studios Florida or IOA changes throughout the year based on how busy the parks are. The least expensive one-day admission is $119 for an adult (i.e., anyone over 9 years old), with one-day, two-park tickets starting at $174. Less expensive are multiday passes that are available in an equally diverse range of prices and combinations. To save money (and avoid the painfully long lines at the ticket kiosks), order your tickets online at a slightly discounted rate.

Express Passes

Another ticket option that comes with a widely varied price range is the Universal Express Pass that takes you to the front of most lines and can save you a lot of time. Unlike Disney Fastpasses, you don't get these for free, even in limited quantities, and they are very expensive. The price ranges from around $80 off-season to around $140 for one park in peak and holiday seasons. Keep in mind, the pass is for one use only at each attraction, and only at attractions that accept the pass (a few new or unusually popular attractions don't accept the passes). A more expensive "unlimited" pass that takes you to the head of the line again and again and again ranges from around $90 to $170 for a single park. For a pass that works at both parks, add about $20 to $30 to the standard or unlimited option. **TIP→ If you're a guest at one of Universal's premium hotels (Royal Pacific, Hard Rock, Portofino Bay), this perk is free; your room key serves as an unlimited Express Pass from the day you check in to the day you check out.**

Universal Dining Plan

You can save up to 30% by paying in advance for a Quick Service meal, which includes one meal, one snack, and a nonalcoholic beverage ($26 adults, $18 kids). There are more than 100 locations where you can use the plan in the parks and at CityWalk, from full-service to quick-dining options. Some of the more popular choices are Mel's Drive-In, Louie's Italian, Beverly Hills Boulangerie, and the Classic Monsters Café at Universal Studios and the Comic Strip Café, Croissant Moon, the Burger Digs, and Café 4 at IOA.

For People with Disabilities

The *Studio Guide for Guests with Disabilities* (aka *Rider's Guide*) details attractions with special entrances and viewing areas, interpreters, Braille scripts, and assistance devices. In general, if you can transfer from your wheelchair unassisted or with the help of a friend, you can ride many attractions. Some rides have carts that accommodate manual wheelchairs, though not motorized wheelchairs or electronic convenience vehicles (ECVs).

Contacts

Universal Orlando Resort ☎ *407/363–8000* 🌐 *www.universalorlando.com*

Universal (Loews Resorts) Room Reservations ☎ *877/819–7884*

Universal Studios

Inspired by the California original and opened in Orlando in 1990 (when the city assumed it would become "Hollywood East"), Universal Studios was meant to celebrate the movies. Like the back-lot sets at a film studio, the park is a jumble of areas and attractions that can make navigating a challenge, but the payoff is the opportunity to immerse yourself in this highly creative take on motion picture magic.

The first area past the entrance is Production Central, where large soundstages house attractions based on TV programs and films like *Shrek, Despicable Me,* and *The Transformers.* Because it's right near the entrance, it can be the park's most crowded area.

Past Production Central is New York. Nearly every studio has its own Big Apple sets, and Universal is no exception. A cleverly constructed collection of sparkling public buildings, well-worn neighborhoods, and back alleys is the next-best thing to Manhattan itself (but not even NYC has Revenge of the Mummy or a Jimmy Fallon virtual reality ride).

Subtle changes in architecture and design tell you you're entering San Francisco, home of the new-in-2018 attraction Fast & Furious: Supercharged. A nice spot to pause for a bite, the area offers places for burgers, pastries, and candy, as well as table-service meals at the waterfront Lombard's Seafood Grille.

You'll next reach the land adored by wizards and muggles alike—the Wizarding World of Harry Potter: Diagon Alley. What the books describe and what filmmakers created, Universal has replicated in great detail, immersing you in this fantastic world.

Just ahead, World Expo features a single attraction—MEN IN BLACK: Alien Attack, a futuristic experience that's the polar opposite of neighboring Springfield: Home of the Simpsons, which is perhaps the park's most visually dynamic area. Its next door neighbor, Woody Woodpecker's KidZone, offers colorful attractions designed for toddlers and the under-10 crowd with diversions that include a junior-sized roller coaster, a mini–water park, and a chance to meet E.T. and Barney the dinosaur.

Although the quiet parks, theme restaurants, and facades of flashy Rodeo Drive are truly appealing, Hollywood also has a few standout attractions, including Universal Orlando's Horror Make Up Show. By the time you've circled the park, you really will feel that Universal has put you in the movies.

Save the planet from interstellar invaders in World Expo's interactive MEN IN BLACK: Alien Attack. Zap aliens in city streets and compete with other guests to score points.

GETTING ORIENTED

On a map, the park appears neatly divided into eight areas positioned around a huge lagoon. First, there's Production Central, which covers the entire left side of the Plaza of the Stars. This is followed by New York, with rides along with various street performances; San Francisco and the new-in-2018 Fast & Furious: Supercharged; the streets of London that lead to the Wizarding World of Harry Potter: Diagon Alley; the futuristic World Expo; Homer and Bart's hometown of Springfield; Woody Woodpecker's KidZone; and, finally, Hollywood.

What's tricky is that—because it's designed like a series of movie sets with side streets, city blocks, and alleyways—there's no straightforward way to tackle the park. You'll probably make some detours and do some backtracking.

TOURING TIPS

It's best to purchase your tickets online because it gives you plenty of time to consider your many options and includes a discount. If you're confused by the array of options, call Universal for advice. Entering Universal Studios can be overwhelming as you and thousands of others flood through the turnstiles at once. Pick up a map in the entryway to CityWalk or by the park turnstiles, and spend a few minutes reviewing it. Map out a route, find show schedules, and select restaurants. If a host is nearby, ask for insider advice on what to see first.

The "right" way. Upon entering, avoid the temptation to go straight toward the towering soundstages and loop the park clockwise. Instead, consider heading right—bypassing shops, restaurants, and some crowds to primary attractions like the Horror Make-Up Show, The Simpsons Ride, and MEN IN BLACK: Alien Attack.

Photo ops. Universal Studios posts signs that indicate photo spots and show how best to frame your shot.

Rendezvous. Good meeting spots include the Hello Kitty shop near the entrance; Mel's Drive-In, which is roughly in the center of the park at the top of the lagoon; or by the purple triple-decker Knight Bus in the Wizarding World of Harry Potter.

PARK AMENITIES

Baby Care: There are diaper-changing stations in many of the men's and women's restrooms, and a nursing station offers comfort and privacy at the park's first-aid station near the entrance. Baby supplies (diapers, food, wipes, and so on) are available at larger stores; ask for them at the counter, though, as they're not displayed on shelves.

Photos: Just inside the main entrance, On Location was primarily a camera and film shop before cameras and film were condensed into smartphones. Nowadays the shelves are stocked with gifts, sunglasses, hats, souvenirs, and drinks. Staffers here also assist guests with souvenir photos taken by Universal's squad of photographers.

First Aid: There are two first-aid centers: one just inside the turnstiles, to the right near the Studio Audience Center, and another around the corner from Louie's Italian Restaurant in New York.

Guest Services (aka Guest Relations): You can get strategic advice *before* visiting the park by calling Guest Services at ☎ *407/224–4233.*

Lockers: Daily rates for lockers near the park entrance are $10 for a small unit and $15 for a larger one. There are free lockers near the entrances of some high-speed attractions (such as MEN IN BLACK: Alien Attack and Revenge of the Mummy), where you can stash your stuff before your ride. Those lockers are available to you for up to 90 minutes.

Lost People and Things: If you plan to split up, be sure everyone knows where and when to reconnect. Staffers take lost children to Guest Services near the main entrance. This is also where you might find lost personal items.

Services for People with Disabilities: Universal has made it as easy as possible for guests with disabilities to enjoy the park. It starts when you arrive in the parking garage, where you can rent wheelchairs or ECVs before making the long trek to the park entrance (though there are also chair rentals at the entrance), and extends to guidebooks with icons indicating which shows feature sign-language interpreters.

Guest Services (near the entrance just outside and inside the park) is the place to pick up assisted-listening and other devices, such as clickers that trigger closed-captioning. Other services include special viewing areas for people in wheelchairs, automatic doors, well-equipped restrooms, and walking areas for service animals. Be sure to pick up the *Studio Guide for Guests with Disabilities* (aka *Rider's Guide*), which is full of details on equipment and other services.

Accessibility information is posted at each attraction. Note that although ride lines can accommodate standard wheelchairs, often you'll be ushered into a waiting area while the rest of your party goes through the line. Many shows have seating to accommodate manual wheelchairs, but, in general, you'll have to transfer from your chair to ride vehicles.

For hearing-impaired guests, captioning, assisted listening, and/or ASL interpreters are available at Despicable Me, Shrek, MEN IN BLACK: Alien Attack, Transformers: The Ride 3-D, Animal Actors, and A Day in the Park with Barney.

Stroller Rentals: Just inside the main entrance, there are strollers for $18 (single) and $28 (double) a day. You can also rent small kiddie cars ($18) or large ones ($28) by the day.

Wheelchair Rentals: You can rent manual wheelchairs ($15 per day) at the parking garages and inside the main entrance. Because there are limited quantities of ECVs (available in the park for $55), reserve one in advance. A photo ID and a $50 deposit on a credit card are required for wheelchairs. ECVs with a sunshade canopy are $75 per day.

Where to Snack: Surpassing the number of rides are the number of restaurants—some of which are on the cost-saving Universal Dining Plan (check online or when purchasing the plan). You can satisfy your appetite at **Mel's Drive-In,** a *Happy Days*–era soda shop–burger joint; **Louie's Italian Restaurant** (pizza, spaghetti, salads); and the **Classic Monsters Café** (pizzas, hot dogs, pasta, salads, rotisserie chicken). **Beverly Hills Boulangerie** has breakfast croissants and pastrie. Full-service restaurants include **Finnegan's Bar and Grill** (Irish pub) and **Lombard's Seafood Grille** (seafood).

Among the self-serve restaurants are **Richter's Burger Co.** for burgers and salads; **Schwab's Pharmacy** for ice cream; and the **Kid Zone Pizza Company** for pizza, chicken tenders, and other kid-geared dishes. At Diagon Alley, the **Leaky Cauldron** serves British pub fare, including cottage pie, bangers and mash, fish-and-chips, and cool, smooth mugs of butterbeer. Near The Simpsons Ride, a strip called Fast Food Boulevard includes several Springfield-inspired eateries, including **Krusty Burger** (hamburgers, hot dogs), **Cletus' Chicken Shack** (chicken sandwiches, platters), the **Frying Dutchman** (fried seafood), **Luigi's Pizza, Lard Lad Donuts** (pastries, sweets), **Bumblebee Man's Taco Truck** (Mexican), and **Lisa's Teahouse of Terror** (salads, wraps, sandwiches). Want a cold one? Drop by **Moe's Tavern** for a Duff's beer or a Flaming Moe.

SHOPPING

Massive soundstages, busy streets, and music flowing from every corner might be overwhelming when you first arrive, but you'll soon find shops, kiosks, and department stores sprinkled throughout the park. The largest concentration is near the park entrance, around **Production Central,** as well as in **Hollywood.** The Universal Studios Store—at the nexus of the two—offers one-stop shopping with items from the studio (and even some merchandise from IOA's most popular attractions). By far the most active retail center is in the monstrously popular Wizarding World of Harry Potter: Diagon Alley.

TOURS

VIP Tours

GUIDED TOURS | FAMILY | Universal has several VIP tours that are worthwhile if you're in a hurry, if crowds are heavy, if you're with a large group—and if you have the money to burn. The tours include extras like front-of-the-line access (that is, the right to jump to the head of the line), plus breakfast and lunch. You can also arrange for extras like priority restaurant seating, bilingual guides, gift bags, refreshments at check-in, wheelchairs, strollers, and valet parking. You'll need to arrange the tour at least 48 hours in advance by calling ahead or setting it up online. Prices cited here do not include sales tax or, more important, park admission; and tour prices vary by season, so consider these just estimated costs.

Nonexclusive one-day tours (i.e., you'll tour with other park guests) cost $189 per person for one park (five hours) and visit a minimum of eight major attractions. The cost goes up to $199 per person for a two-park, seven-hour tour. Then there are exclusive tours for your group only. If you're traveling with up to 10 people, consider splitting the cost of an eight-hour customized tour, which includes a sit-down breakfast, lunch, and dinner at the park of your choice. The private VIP tour starts at $3,099 plus tax for a group of five, with an extra $350 for each additional person. ✉ *Orlando* ☎ *866/346–9350* 🌐 *www.universalorlando.com.*

Hollywood

The quintessential tribute to the Golden Age of the Silver Screen, this area to the right of the park entrance celebrates icons like the Brown Derby, Schwab's Pharmacy, and Art Deco Hollywood.

Sights

★ Universal Orlando's Horror Make-Up Show

AMUSEMENT PARK/WATER PARK | This funny, highly entertaining show begins in an intriguingly creepy preshow area where masks, props, and rubber skeletons from classic and contemporary horror films and tributes to great makeup artists like Lon Chaney, Rick Baker, and Jack Pierce make a great backdrop for a horrifying family photo. Inside the theater, your host brings out a special-effects expert who describes and shares some secrets about what goes into (and oozes out of) creepy movie effects (e.g., corn syrup and food coloring make for a dandy blood substitute). Despite the potentially frightening topic, most of the audience gets a kick out of the whole show, because the subject is handled with an extraordinary amount of dead-on humor. Older children, in particular, eat up the blood-and-guts stories. One-liners delivered with comedy-club timing, audience participation, knives, guns, loose limbs—all this goes into creating a flat-out fantastic show that entertains everyone. **For people with disabilities:** The theater is wheelchair accessible. Good scripts and good shtick mean that those with visual impairments can enjoy the show. **TIP→ If busy, use Express Pass, or come in the afternoon or evening. Arrive about 15 minutes before showtime (doors close immediately after show starts).** ✉ *Hollywood, Universal Studios* 🌐 *www.universalorlando.com* ☞ *Duration: 25 mins. Crowds: Light. Audience: Not small kids.*

Restaurants

Mel's Drive-In

$ | AMERICAN | FAMILY | At the corner of Hollywood and Vine is a flashy 1950s-style eatery with a pink-and-white 1956 Ford Crown Victoria parked out in front. For burgers and fries, this is one of the best choices in the park, and it comes complete with a roving doo-wop group during peak seasons. **Known for:** drive-in styling; live entertainment; frosty milk shakes and grilled burgers. $ *Average main: $13* ✉ *Hollywood, Universal Studios* ☎ *407/363–8766* 🌐 *www.universalorlando.com.*

Coffee and Quick Bites

If you arrive in the park and need breakfast, stop by the **Today Show Cafe** for great coffee, pastries, and breakfast sandwiches. In the heart of Hollywood, **Schwab's Pharmacy** is a re-creation of the legendary drugstore where—studio publicists claim—Lana Turner was discovered. What you'll discover is a quick stop where you can order soda-fountain treats as well as hand-carved turkey and ham sandwiches. The catch? Hours are limited, and it might be closed off-season.

Shopping

Betty Boop Store—Hello Kitty

GIFTS/SOUVENIRS | These side-by-side stores at the corner of Hollywood and Production Central are packed with souvenirs celebrating two of the most marketable icons in the merchandising world. Representing Old Hollywood is cartoonish flapper Betty Boop, whose image is affixed to mugs, apparel, gifts, jewelry, and other collectibles. Walk through the rainbow archway connecting the stores, and you'll find similar souvenirs celebrating internationally popular (and super-cute) Hello Kitty. There's no shortage of choices, with specialty sections like the Hello Kitty Lounge (robes, slippers, toys

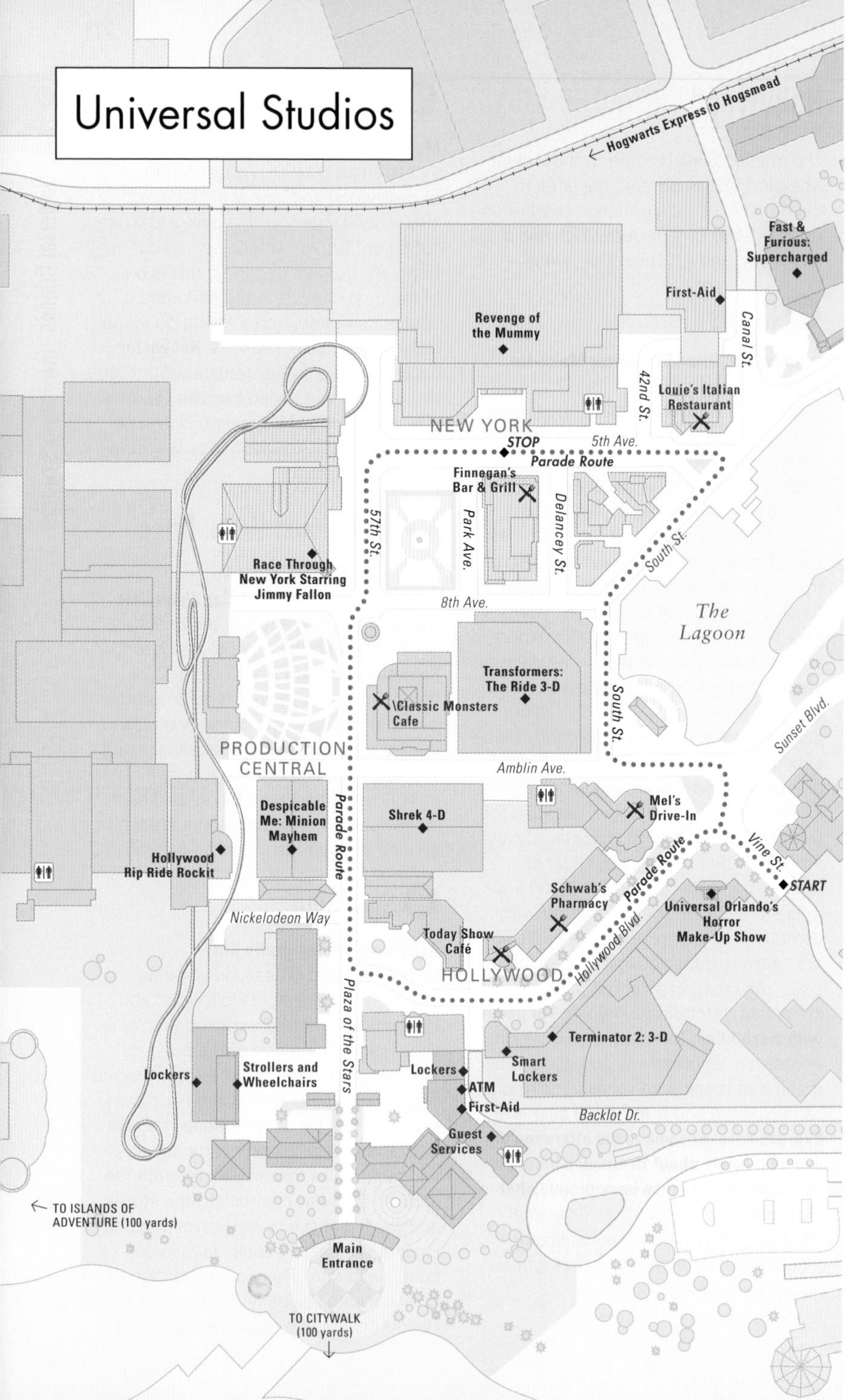
Universal Studios
Hogwarts Express to Hogsmead
Fast & Furious: Supercharged
First-Aid
Revenge of the Mummy
Canal St.
42nd St.
Louie's Italian Restaurant
NEW YORK
STOP
5th Ave.
Parade Route
Finnegan's Bar & Grill
57th St.
Park Ave.
Delancey St.
South St.
Race Through New York Starring Jimmy Fallon
8th Ave.
The Lagoon
Transformers: The Ride 3-D
Classic Monsters Cafe
South St.
Sunset Blvd.
PRODUCTION CENTRAL
Amblin Ave.
Despicable Me: Minion Mayhem
Shrek 4-D
Mel's Drive-In
Parade Route
Hollywood Rip Ride Rockit
Vine St.
START
Schwab's Pharmacy
Parade Route
Universal Orlando's Horror Make-Up Show
Nickelodeon Way
Today Show Café
Hollywood Blvd.
HOLLYWOOD
Terminator 2: 3-D
Smart Lockers
Plaza of the Stars
Lockers
Strollers and Wheelchairs
Lockers
ATM
First-Aid
Backlot Dr.
Guest Services
TO ISLANDS OF ADVENTURE (100 yards)
Main Entrance
TO CITYWALK (100 yards)

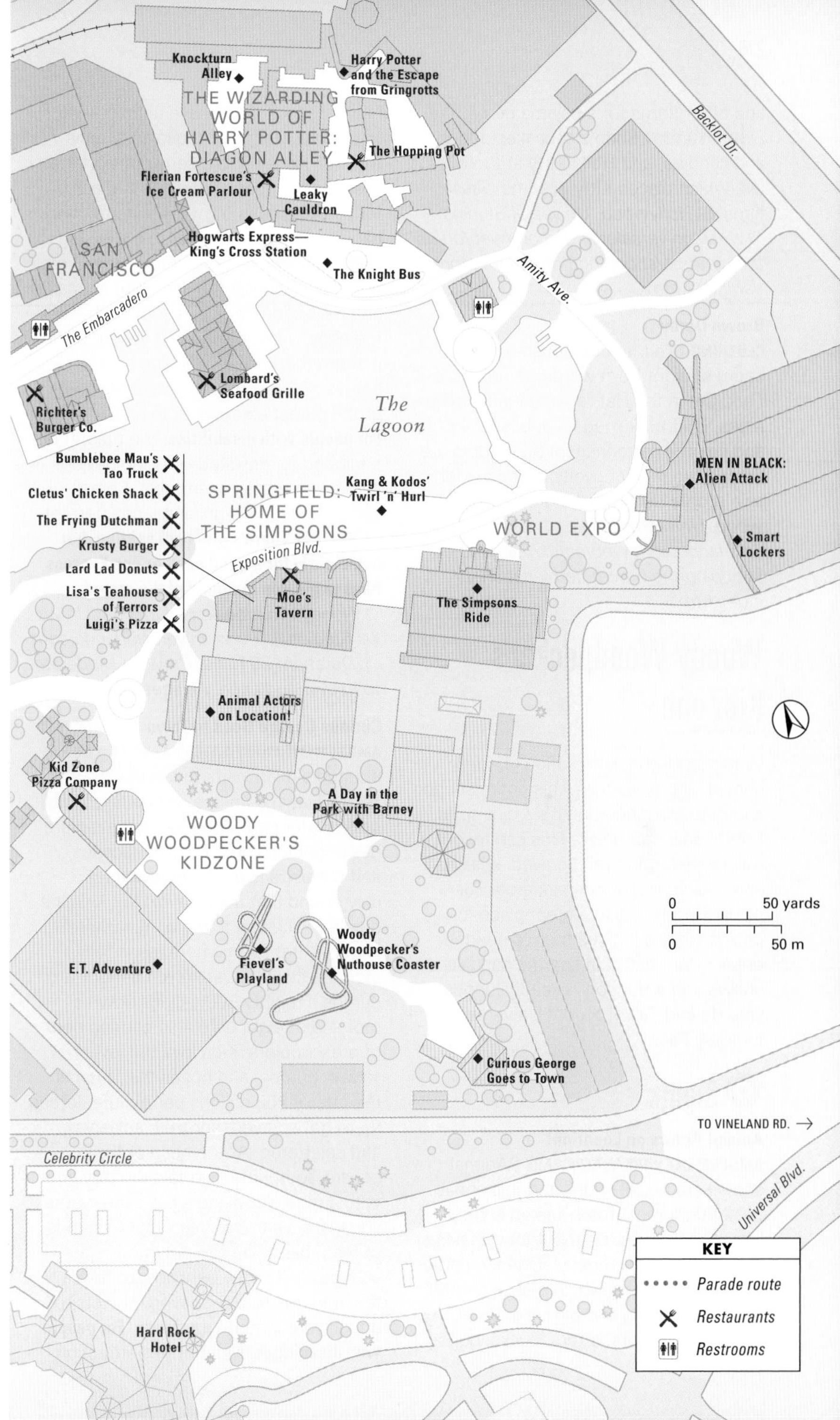
Knockturn Alley
Harry Potter and the Escape from Gringrotts
THE WIZARDING WORLD OF HARRY POTTER: DIAGON ALLEY
The Hopping Pot
Florian Fortescue's Ice Cream Parlour
Leaky Cauldron
Hogwarts Express—King's Cross Station
The Knight Bus
Backlot Dr.
Amity Ave.
SAN FRANCISCO
The Embarcadero
Lombard's Seafood Grille
Richter's Burger Co.
The Lagoon
Bumblebee Man's Taco Truck
Cletus' Chicken Shack
The Frying Dutchman
Krusty Burger
Lard Lad Donuts
Lisa's Teahouse of Terrors
Luigi's Pizza
SPRINGFIELD: HOME OF THE SIMPSONS
Kang & Kodos' Twirl 'n' Hurl
Exposition Blvd.
Moe's Tavern
The Simpsons Ride
WORLD EXPO
MEN IN BLACK: Alien Attack
Smart Lockers
Animal Actors on Location!
Kid Zone Pizza Company
A Day in the Park with Barney
WOODY WOODPECKER'S KIDZONE
0
50 yards
0
50 m
E.T. Adventure
Fievel's Playland
Woody Woodpecker's Nuthouse Coaster
Curious George Goes to Town
TO VINELAND RD. →
Celebrity Circle
Universal Blvd.
Hard Rock Hotel
KEY
Parade route
Restaurants
Restrooms

and other items for a pajama party), the Sweet Yummy Shop's cupcakes, fudge, and candies, and Hello Kitty at the Movies, which places Kitty in some classic films. ✉ *Hollywood, Universal Studios* 🌐 *www.universalorlando.com/web/en/us/things-to-do/shopping/betty-boop-store-usf/index.html.*

Brown Derby

CLOTHING | Felt fedoras, bush hats that seem straight from wardrobe for *Jurassic Park,* Cat in the Hat red-and-white stovepipes, Duff beer mug hats, baseball caps, and colorful cartoon-inspired toppers are among the many novelty chapeaux for sale at this Hollywood store. ✉ *Hollywood, Universal Studios* 🌐 *www.universalorlando.com/web/en/us/things-to-do/shopping/the-brown-derby-hat-shop/index.html.*

Woody Woodpecker's KidZone

With its colorful compilation of rides, shows, and play areas, this entire section caters to preschoolers. It's a pint-sized Promised Land, where kids can try out a roller coaster and get sprayed, splashed, and soaked in a water-park area. Surprisingly, this is also a great place for parents, since it gives them a needed break after nearly circling the park. All shows and attractions except Curious George and Fievel accept Universal Express Pass.

Sights

Animal Actors on Location!

AMUSEMENT PARK/WATER PARK | Animal shows are usually fun—and this one is better than most thanks to an arkful of live animal stars. The tricks (or *behaviors*) they perform are mostly audience-participation segments, which makes it entertaining for young and old alike. Birds, cats, pigs, parrots, otters, ducks, dogs, hawks, and a skunk have been trained to portray a range of thespian actions that are woven into a series of vignettes, from a clever parrot that has a knack for plucking cash from the outstretched hand of an audience member to a dog that is a convincing actor in a staged melodrama. Although the line-up of animals and the scenes they perform might vary, the show's fast pacing and variety make it seem that you're watching several shows in one. Enjoy it! These are some of the cutest actors ever to hit the stage. **For people with disabilities:** The theater is equipped for assisted-listening devices and is wheelchair accessible. Some shows include a sign language interpreter. **TIP→ There's plenty of seating, but come early for a good seat, or use Express Pass to get you in ahead of the crowd.** ✉ *Woody Woodpecker's KidZone, Universal Studios* 🌐 *www.universalorlando.com* ☞ *Duration: 20 mins. Crowds: Moderate to heavy. Audience: All ages.*

Curious George Goes to Town

AMUSEMENT PARK/WATER PARK | The celebrated simian visits the Man with the Yellow Hat in a no-line, no-waiting, small-scale water park. The main town square has brightly colored building facades, and the plaza is an interactive aqua playground that adults avoid but kids are drawn to like fish to water. Yes, there's water, water everywhere, especially atop the clock tower, which periodically dumps a mighty 500 gallons down a roof and straight onto a screaming herd of preschoolers. Kids love the levers, valves, pumps, and hoses that gush at the rate of 200 gallons per minute, letting them get sprayed, spritzed, splashed, and splattered. At the head of the square, footprints lead to a dry play area, with a rope climb and a ball cage where youngsters can frolic among thousands of foam balls. You can get into the act, sit it out on nearby benches, or take a few minutes to buy souvenir towels to dry off your waterlogged kids. **For people with disabilities:** Most of this attraction is barrier-free. ■ TIP➔ **Crowds are heavy mid-morning: come in late afternoon or early evening—especially in the summertime. Kids will get drenched; so stash a bathing suit or change of clothing in a nearby locker.** ✉ *Woody Woodpecker's KidZone, Universal Studios* 🌐 *www.universalorlando.com* ☞ *Duration: Up to you. Crowds: Moderate to heavy. Audience: Small kids.*

A Day in the Park with Barney

AMUSEMENT PARK/WATER PARK | If your kids can't get enough of the big purple dinosaur, here he is again! A fairly long preshow features a goofy, kid-friendly emcee before you and your preschoolers enter a pleasant theater-in-the-round filled with brilliantly colored trees, clouds, and stars. Within minutes, the kids will cheer like baby boomers at a McCartney concert as their beloved TV playmate and Baby Bop dance and sing though clap-along, singalong monster classics including "Mr. Knickerbocker," "If You're Happy and You Know It," and (of course) "I Love You." Following the very pleasing and thoughtful show and a chance to meet Barney up close, you exit to an elaborate play area with hands-on activities—a water harp, wood-pipe xylophone, and musical rocks—that propel the already excited kids to even greater heights. **For people with disabilities:** The theater is equipped for assisted-listening devices and is wheelchair accessible. ■ TIP➔ **Arrive 10–15 minutes early for a good seat—up close and in the center. Express Passes may be used here.** ✉ *Woody Woodpecker's KidZone, Universal Studios* 🌐 *www.universalorlando.com* ☞ *Duration: 20 mins. Crowds: Light. Audience: Small kids.*

E.T. Adventure

AMUSEMENT PARK/WATER PARK | This well-meaning, circa 1990, ride is looking (and even smelling) a little tired, although you might still get a kick out of the take on Steven Spielberg's *E.T.* Once Spielberg himself advises you that it's your mission to help E.T. return to his planet, you board a bicycle mounted on a movable platform and fly 3 million light years from Earth, past a squadron of policemen and FBI agents, to reach E.T.'s home. Here colorful characters climb on vines, play xylophones, and swing on branches in what looks like an alien Burning Man festival. Listen very closely for the payoff: having given your name to a host at the start of the ride, E.T. is supposed to bid you a personalized good-bye. This ride isn't suitable for guests with heart, back, neck, or motion-sickness problems. **For people with disabilities:** Guests with mobility issues must be in a standard-sized wheelchair or transfer to a ride vehicle. Service animals aren't permitted. There's some sudden tilting and accelerating, but those for whom these movements are a concern can ride in E.T.'s orbs (spaceships) instead of the flying bicycles. ■ TIP➔ **Use Universal Express Pass, or come early.** ✉ *Woody Woodpecker's KidZone, Universal Studios* 🌐 *www.universalorlando.com* ☞ *Duration: 5 mins. Crowds: Moderate to heavy. Audience: All ages. Height requirement: 34 inches.*

Fievel's Playland

AMUSEMENT PARK/WATER PARK | Based on the Spielberg animated film *An American Tail,* this playground features larger-than-life props and sets designed to make everyone feel mouse-size. An ingenious collection of massive boots, cans, and other ordinary objects disguise tunnel slides; water play areas; ball crawls; and a gigantic net-climb equipped with tubes, ladders, and rope bridges. A harmonica slide plays music when you slide along the openings, and a 200-foot waterslide gives kids (and a parent if so desired) a chance to swoop down in Fievel's signature sardine can. It should keep the kids entertained for hours. The downside? You might have to build one of these for your backyard when you get home. **For people with disabilities:** Unfortunately, this ride isn't fully accessible to people using wheelchairs, although an elevator can transport wheelchairs to the top of the

Universal Studios Grown-Up Tour 

The genius here is in the details, so take your time, and notice the secondhand items in the windows of New York shops, for instance, or the cable-car tracks running through San Francisco.

South Side

Upon entering, don't head straight into Production Central; instead, turn right—onto Rodeo Drive. In a few steps, you're in the heart of Hollywood where the first attraction you'll pass is the new-in-2020 **Bourne Stuntacular,** a live-action stunt show. If you're tempted to stop for a soda at Schwab's or a burger at Mel's, try to schedule your meal in time to catch **Universal Orlando's Horror Make-Up Show** just down the street. As you continue past the lovely Garden of Allah bungalows (that look as if they were actually moved from Tinseltown), you'll see the entrance to Woody Woodpecker's KidZone, which most adults will be happy to skip.

After this, it's Springfield: Home of the Simpsons. Although **The Simpsons Ride** is a thrill, so is the amazing pop art that sets the stage for it. The facade is decorated like a carnival, with games of chance bordering the towering face of Krusty the Clown. Watch for the kiosk that sells Squishees ("America's favorite icy goo"), and take your time along Fast Food Boulevard where you'll have plenty of food ops—and photo ops—including Lard Lad (of donut fame), Moe's Tavern, and Bumblebee Man's taco truck. Really.

North Side

The facade of this Wizarding World looks like a fashionable London district, but be sure to look for the broken brick wall that masks the entrance to **Diagon Alley,** a complete re-creation of Harry Potter's world.

Cobblestone streets, redbrick buildings, and a waterfront inspired by Fisherman's Wharf create San Francisco, which is home to the full-throttled attraction, **Fast & Furious: Supercharged.**

With narrow alleys, fire escapes, a Chinese laundry, pawnshops, secondhand stores, offices, Italian restaurants, and an Irish pub, New York captures the character of nearly every borough. Round a corner, and you'll even see the Guggenheim Museum. It's an amazing assemblage of styles, with clever signage, props, effects and attractions like **Revenge of the Mummy** and **Race Through New York Starring Jimmy Fallon.**

Completing the circle, you'll arrive in Production Central, where several blocks of soundstages present attractions that bring movies and television to life.

waterslide. **TIP→ On hot days, come after supper to avoid waits for the waterslide. Kids will get drenched; stash a bathing suit or change of clothing in a nearby locker.** ✉ *Woody Woodpecker's KidZone, Universal Studios* 🌐 *www.universalorlando.com* ☞ *Duration: Up to you. Crowds: Light to moderate. Audience: Small kids.*

Woody Woodpecker's Nuthouse Coaster
AMUSEMENT PARK/WATER PARK | Unlike the maniacal coasters that put you through zero-g rolls and inversions, this is a low-speed, mild-thrill version (top speed 22 mph) that makes it a safe bet for younger kids (who must be at least 36 inches tall) and action-phobic adults. It races (a

relative term) through a structure that looks like a gadget-filled factory; the cars are shipping crates—some labeled "mixed nuts," others "salted nuts," and some tagged "certifiably nuts." Children generally love this low-level introduction to thrill rides (which is duplicated at Flight of the Hippogriff at the Wizarding World of Harry Potter). **For people with disabilities:** Guests using wheelchairs must transfer to a ride vehicle. **TIP→ Use Express Pass and/or come at park closing, when most little ones have gone home.** ✉ *Woody Woodpecker's KidZone, Universal Studios* 🌐 *www.universalorlando.com* ☞ *Duration: 1½ mins. Crowds: Moderate to heavy. Audience: Small kids.*

Shopping

SpongeBob StorePants
TOYS | With its cartoonish nautical theme (pink jellyfish overhead, a pineapple home in the middle of the store), this silly shop will have you stocking up on weird, fascinating SpongeBob merchandise from mugs to shorts to swimwear. ✉ *Woody Woodpecker's KidZone, Universal Studios* 🌐 *www.universalorlando.com/web/en/us/things-to-do/shopping/spongebob-storepants/index.html.*

Springfield: Home of the Simpsons

One of television's longest-running shows inspired one of the park's most enjoyable lands; a strangely surreal yet familiar small town filled with landmarks you'd recognize, from Moe's Tavern to the towering Lard Lad of doughnut fame. The two primary attractions—The Simpsons Ride and Kang & Kodos' Twirl 'n' Hurl—offer fast admission with Universal Express Pass.

Sights

Kang & Kodos' Twirl 'n' Hurl
AMUSEMENT PARK/WATER PARK | Inspired by the intergalactic creatures that make an occasional appearance in Springfield, here's a new spin on an old favorite. About a dozen flying saucers encircle a towering statue of Kang (or Kodos), the one-eyed, fang-toothed, octopus-tentacled alien. As at Seuss Landing's One Fish, Two Fish, Red Fish, Blue Fish, once you've climbed into your saucer, the spinning ride takes flight and whirls you and your co-pilot around Kang (or Kodos). Kids who love the opportunity to take the controls raise and lower the craft in hopes of avoiding the jets of water shot from surrounding poles. It's a pleasing, fun, low-thrill attraction that kids enjoy. ✉ *Springfield: Home of the Simpsons, Universal Studios* 🌐 *www.universalorlando.com* ☞ *Duration: 3 mins. Crowds: Light to medium. Audience: Small kids and up.*

★ **The Simpsons Ride**
AMUSEMENT PARK/WATER PARK | As you enter this ride through Krusty the Clown's gaping mouth, and then receive a video greeting by citizens of Springfield, police chief Clancy Wiggum reminds you that if you must get sick, do it in your hat—and thus the tone is set for your arrival in one of television's most popular animated communities. The preshow explains that Krusty has expanded his empire to include a theme park, which his disgruntled former sidekick, Sideshow Bob, plans to sabotage. After a fairly tame start, your virtual car soars through virtual Springfield, plunging toward familiar businesses and buildings and narrowly escaping disaster as Sideshow Bob tears up the tracks and sends you racing through wild scenes in a variety of locations such as Disney, SeaWorld—and hell. Several times you're saved by the split-second timing of an unexpected hero. If you have even a scintilla of motion sickness, this one

One of the most popular areas of Universal Studios (after The Wizarding World of Harry Potter) is Springfield: Home of the Simpsons.

will throw you for a colorful, cartoonish loop. Guests who are pregnant or who have heart, back, or neck problems shouldn't ride. **For people with disabilities:** Guests in wheelchairs must transfer to a ride vehicle. **TIP→ Use Express Pass.** ✉ *Springfield: Home of the Simpsons, Universal Studios* 🌐 *www.universalorlando.com* ☞ *Duration: 6 mins. Crowds: Heavy. Audience: Not small kids. Height requirement: 40 inches minimum; under 48 inches must ride with an adult.*

Shopping

Kwik-E-Mart

GIFTS/SOUVENIRS | This re-creation of the animated convenience store from *The Simpsons* is one of the park's most popular shopping stops. You'll find Kwik-E-Mart (Apu Nahasapeemapetilon, proprietor) caps and smocks, Duff Beer mugs, Lard Lad donuts, Marge-style blue bouffant wigs, and Homer T-shirts packaged in Duff Beer cans. In 2013, an assortment of Springfield-inspired locales appeared, making the shop and its surroundings one of the park's best photo ops. ✉ *Springfield: Home of the Simpsons, Universal Studios* 🌐 *www.universalorlando.com/web/en/us/things-to-do/shopping/kwik-e-mart/index.html.*

World Expo

At the far end of the park is a futuristic set of buildings containing one of Universal Studios' most popular attractions, MEN IN BLACK: Alien Attack.

Sights

MEN IN BLACK: Alien Attack

AMUSEMENT PARK/WATER PARK | The pre-show of "the world's first ride-through video game" provides the storyline: To earn membership in MIB you must round up aliens that escaped when their shuttle crashed on Earth. On board your vehicle with a few others, you enter the backstreets of a city where aliens pop out from windows, trash cans, and doorways. Fire at them with that laser gun mounted to your futuristic car, and since there's no limit to the number of shots you can take, blast away. Even though the gun's red laser dot is just a pinpoint, an onboard scoreboard helps you keep track of what you've hit. Aliens fire back at you, and if they score a hit, it'll cause your car to spin out of control. Depending on the collective score, your ride will wrap up with one of 35 endings, ranging from a hero's welcome to a loser's farewell. All in all, it's pretty exciting. The spinning nature of the cars might cause dizziness, so use caution if you're prone to motion sickness. Don't ride if you have heart, back, or neck problems. **For people with disabilities:** Equipped for assisted-listening devices. Guests using wheelchairs must transfer to a ride vehicle. **TIP→ In summer, waits can be up to an hour. Come first thing, or save time by using Express Pass.** ✉ *World Expo, Universal Studios* 🌐 *www.universalorlando.com* ☞ *Duration: 4½ mins. Crowds: Heavy. Audience: Not small kids. Height requirement: 42 inches to ride without an adult.*

The Wizarding World of Harry Potter: Diagon Alley

Don't think the facade of London row homes is all there is to see here. On the contrary, as in the *Harry Potter* movies, the good stuff remains hidden to mere mortals. When you spy an opening through a broken brick wall and step into Diagon Alley, the world changes as you see what an incredible blueprint J.K. Rowling created through her words. You can literally spend hours in this one district looking at the complete range of Potter-centric places: Universal Studios' version of Ollivanders wand shop; Weasleys' Wizard Wheezes (magical jokes and novelty items); the Magical Menagerie (all creatures furry, feathered, or scaly); Madam Malkin's Robes for All Occasions (wizard wear); Wiseacre's Wizarding Equipment; and Quality Quidditch Supplies. Practitioners of the Dark Arts should venture down Knockturn Alley and step inside Borgin and Burkes. For an appetizing break, stop at the Leaky Cauldron, the land's signature restaurant, or cool off at Florean Fortescue's Ice-Cream Parlour.

And when you're ready to head to the village of Hogsmeade (conveniently located at the neighboring IOA), make sure you have a park-to-park pass before stepping aboard the wonderful, magical Hogwarts Express—now departing to IOA from Platform 9¾.

★ Harry Potter and the Escape from Gringotts

AMUSEMENT PARK/WATER PARK | How do you know you've reached Gringotts Bank? Aside from a massive dragon perched on top of the building is the statue of a Gringotts goblin standing atop a towering stack of gold coins. Those two features alone will tell you that what lies ahead will be highly themed—and highly entertaining. The queue to the ride is an essential part of the attraction itself: you'll walk through the bank where a multitude of goblins are each working at their desks, diligently and wordlessly ... eerie. Soon you're in a ride vehicle, and, after it departs the station, it's only a matter of moments before Bellatrix Lestrange notices your presence and then does everything in her supernatural power to prevent you from traveling any farther. So, from here on out, your vehicle will come face to 3-D face with a towering security detail that destroys the tracks and sends you deeper into the bank's recesses. Be warned that your first encounter with the one who shall not be named (aka Lord Voldemort) isn't your last. After he presents you with a fiery souvenir, he and Bellatrix return again—but they're no match for the scaly superhero who comes to your rescue. If you've ridden Universal's Spider-Man or

A fire-breathing dragon is the centerpiece of The Wizarding World of Harry Potter: Diagon Alley.

The Transformers, you'll recognize the technology that blends virtual reality, 3-D effects, 4-D sensations, and gargantuan movie screens featuring scenes synchronized with the motion of your vehicle. Thankfully, this attraction tones down much of the volume and excess motion that pushes the envelope on the others, so it's enjoyable for everyone. **For people with disabilities:** Guests using wheelchairs must transfer to a ride vehicle. **TIP→ Lines can still be quite long, so use an Express Pass.** ✉ *The Wizarding World of Harry Potter, Diagon Alley, Universal Studios* 🌐 *www.universalorlando.com* ☞ *Duration: 5 mins. (ride) Crowds: Yes! Audience: Everyone but small kids. Height requirement: 42 inches minimum.*

Hogwart's Express—King's Cross Station
AMUSEMENT PARK/WATER PARK | When Universal announced the Studios' Diagon Alley would connect to IOA's Hogsmeade via a train ride, many fans assumed an open-air train ride through the park's backstage area. But many people aren't nearly as creative as the geniuses at Universal. To reach Hogsmeade, you walk through an exact re-creation of a London rail station where a magical effect takes you to Platform 9¾. Even as the train pulls in, you're already being transported into another world. Settle into the compartment with other guests, and soon the ride is an attraction in itself. Outside your window as you chuff away from of the station, an owl follows you out of London, music plays, and you get the sense you're traveling hundreds of miles across the English countryside. Adding to the magic, silhouettes of Harry, Ron, and Hermione appear in the corridor outside your window, with their narration adding to the drama of the trio's attempt to banish Dementors (and to corral a loose box of chocolate frogs). By the time Hagrid appears and you arrive in Hogsmeade, you really feel as if ... *you've arrived in Hogsmeade.* **TIP→ Express Pass is accepted here, but it might not save you a lot of time except near park closing, when the lines can be very long.** ✉ *Universal Studios* 🌐 *www.universalorlando.com.*

Restaurants

Leaky Cauldron
$ | **BRITISH** | **FAMILY** | British pub staples are fitting fare for Diagon Alley's restaurant. The drinks menu complements those hearty meals with kooky-sounding beverages from the Harry Potter books like Tongue-Tying Lemon Squash, Otter's Fizzy Orange Juice, and Fishy Green Ale (it's minty, with blueberry-flavored boba). **Known for:** quick-service, Potter-inspired meals; plowman's lunch of meats, cheeses, and salad; butterbeer, of course. *Average main: $14* ✉ *The Wizarding World of Harry Potter: Diagon Alley, Universal Studios* ☎ *407/224–9716* 🌐 *www.universalorlando.com.*

Coffee and Quick Bites

Although the lines can be quite long, the ice cream at **Florian Fortescue's Ice-Cream Parlour** is worth the wait. In addition to the famous butterbeer flavor, there's Earl Grey and Lavendar and Peanut Butter and Strawberry, as well as many flavors of soft serve. You can also get butterbeer ice cream at **The Hopping Pot,** which also serves regular and frozen butterbeer (or, in colder weather, hot butterbeer).

Shopping

J.K. Rowling's pages comes to life in this magical village, where a fire-breathing dragon atop Gringott's Bank towers over cobblestone streets lined with Harry Potter–themed shops. And more shops. Spend a few hours getting lost in Madame Malkin's Robes for All Occasions for cloaks, Ollivander's for a wand, Weasley's Wizard Wheezes for jokes and gags, Borgin and Burkes for dark-arts objects and oddities, and Quality Quidditch Supplies for a broom or an elusive Golden Snitch.

Borgin and Burkes
GIFTS/SOUVENIRS | The somewhat macabre items that fill this gloomy shop include Death Eater masks, skulls, pendants, rats (fake), snakes (same), wanted-poster replicas and picture frames, costume replicas, apparel, jewelry, collectibles, a wide variety of T-shirts (with a wide assortment of characters and graphics), and the famed Vanishing Cabinet. ✉ *Wizarding World of Harry Potter: Diagon Alley, Universal Studios* 🌐 *www.universalorlando.com/web/en/us/things-to-do/shopping/borgin-and-burkes.*

Madam Malkin's Robes for All Occasions
CLOTHING | In this shop "Where Well-Dressed Witches and Wizards Buy Their Wares" the couture is dazzling. For those who love to play dress-up, the choices include replicas of Hermione's Yule Ball gown, along with a full line of Hogwarts apparel, so it's not just robes but also house scarves and sweaters, as well as anything else you can think of. ✉ *Wizarding World of Harry Potter: Diagon Alley, Universal Studios* 🌐 *www.universalorlando.com/web/en/us/things-to-do/shopping/madam-malkins-robes-for-all-occasions.*

Ollivander's Wand Shop
GIFTS/SOUVENIRS | As you explore Diagon Alley, you might feel empty-handed when you notice other guests are carrying wands—some with the ability to cast spells throughout the streets. Inside this cramped shop are thousands of wands waiting to choose their wizards—which they do with a little help from the wand keeper himself. ✉ *Wizarding World of Harry Potter: Diagon Alley, Universal Studios* 🌐 *www.universalorlando.com/web/en/us/things-to-do/shopping/ollivanders-diagon-alley.*

Quality Quidditch Supplies
GIFTS/SOUVENIRS | Like Star Trek fans learning to speak Klingon, Harry Potter fans have learned to appreciate Quidditch, and this richly themed shop is one of the world's leading suppliers of this fantasy

sport's equipment. Look around, and you'll be amazed at the range of Quidditch sweaters, brooms, hats, pennants, Golden Snitches, Bludgers, Bludger bats, Quaffles, and more. ✉ *Wizarding World of Harry Potter: Diagon Alley.*

Weasley's Wizard Wheezes

GIFTS/SOUVENIRS | Practical jokes and novelties are a never-ending source of amusement—at least for the person who owns them. This is where you can stock up on cheap gags that'll keep you entertained (and others annoyed) for weeks. Highlights included Pygmy Puffs, U-No-Poo pills, Skiving Snackboxes, Puking Pastilles, Sneakoscopes, Bombtastic Bombs, Peruvian Instant Darkness Powder, Decoy Detonators, Extendable Ears, chattering teeth, and whoopee cushions. It's everything a kid (and some juvenile adults) could ever want. ✉ *Wizarding World of Harry Potter: Diagon Alley, Universal Studios* 🌐 *www.universalorlando.com/web/en/us/things-to-do/shopping/weasleys-wizard-wheezes.*

San Francisco

Although this neighborhood is adjacent to and blends in with New York, changes in architecture and design indicated when you've crossed the continent to the wharves and warehouses of San Francisco's Embarcadero and Fisherman's Wharf districts.

Sights

Fast & Furious: Supercharged

AMUSEMENT PARK/WATER PARK | For fans of the film franchise, the chance to join the crew on a wild and hair-raising car chase is the appeal of this virtual reality attraction. Two preshows lead to a ride vehicle that's racing down the highway in a bumper-to-bumper, side-by-side combination race and gunfight (which includes helicopter gunships) and incorporates the same style of rocking and rolling technology that you'll find at Universal's other adrenaline-inducing attractions like Spider-Man, Harry Potter, Transformers, and Jimmy Fallon. Knowing guests will have time to kill while waiting: more than a dozen cars from the film are displayed in the queue area, and the Universal Orlando app includes a game that allows you to test your Fast & Furious knowledge in trivia matches, receive messages from the crew, and take a quiz to reveal what kind of ride suits your personality. **■ TIP→ Universal Express Pass is accepted.** ✉ *San Francisco, Universal Studios* 🌐 *www.universalorlando.com* ☞ *Crowds: Moderate. Audience: Not younger kids. Height requirement: 40 inches minimum; under 48 inches must ride with an adult.*

Restaurants

Lombard's Seafood Grille

$$ | **SEAFOOD** | **FAMILY** | Designed to resemble a Fisherman's Wharf warehouse from 19th-century San Francisco, Universal Studios' flagship restaurant serves fresh fried fish, fried shrimp, and assorted other takes on seafood. At this popular full-service restaurant, you can also get a Boursin steak sandwich with fried onion strips, hamburgers, chicken sandwiches, and big salads. **Known for:** Fisherman's Wharf decor; fresh-catch fish basket; Lombard's lobster roll. $ *Average main: $19* ✉ *San Francisco, Universal Studios* ☎ *407/224–6400* 🌐 *www.universalorlando.com.*

Coffee and Quick Bites

Richter's Burger Co. (across from Fast & Furious: Supercharged) lets you drop in and dress up your own burger or grilled-chicken sandwich. It's pretty quick, pretty convenient, and there are seats inside and out.

New York

Universal has gone all out to re-create New York's skyscrapers, commercial districts, ethnic neighborhoods, and back alleys—right down to the cracked concrete. Hidden within these structures are restaurants, arcades, gift shops, and key attractions. And although they're from Chicago, the Blues Brothers drive from the Second City to New York City in their Bluesmobile for free performances at 70 Delancey. Here you can use Universal Express Pass at Revenge of the Mummy and Race Through New York Starring Jimmy Fallon.

Sights

★ Race Through New York Starring Jimmy Fallon

AMUSEMENT PARK/WATER PARK | Walking through the queue area is like walking through the history of *The Tonight Show,* with showcases featuring memorabilia that pays tribute to more than a half century of hosts who have put their stamp on the most famous program in late night: Steve Allen, Jack Paar, Johnny Carson, Jay Leno, Conan O'Brien, and now Jimmy Fallon. Fond memories of the past pave the way to a rocketing road trip that begins only after a serenade by the Ragtime Gals, a visit by Hashtag the Panda, and a preshow area where, for the first time anywhere (more than likely) safety instructions are offered in a freestyle rap performed by Tariq "Black Thought" Trotter of The Roots. After the doors open, you'll find a seat before a towering screen that really comes to life when you fasten your seat belt, put on your 3-D glasses, and find yourself on the set of the show getting ready to race Jimmy through the halls of 30 Rock, down Broadway, through the streets of New York—and beyond. You follow in your own "car" beside Jimmy as you whip past taxis, pedestrians, and local landmarks, before heading into space to land on the moon. **For people with disabilities:** Guests using wheelchairs must transfer to a ride vehicle. **TIP→ Cut down on wait times by using Express Pass, or come early or late. Free lockers are available for loose items. Use them.** ✉ *New York, Universal Studios* 🌐 *www.universalorlando.com* ☞ *Duration: 7 mins. Crowds: Heavy. Audience: Not young kids (under 7). Height requirement: 40 inches minimum.*

Revenge of the Mummy

AMUSEMENT PARK/WATER PARK | Action, adventure, and horror are in abundance in this $40-million, spine-tingling thrill ride that combines roller-coaster technology, pyrotechnics, and some super-scary skeletal warriors. The entrance is set up like the tomb of a pharaoh, which means you'll walk through winding catacombs in the near-dark, passing Egyptian artifacts and archaeological scenes before reaching your vehicle. After boarding the multipassenger coaster car and zipping into the heart of a haunted labyrinth, "dead" ahead, you're given the chance to sell your soul for safety and riches. Whether you take the deal or not, a guardian mummy thinks it's high time to send you hurtling through underground passageways and Egyptian burial chambers, where you must escape a beetle-infested burial chamber, zip backward through fog, and then race full-tilt into the mummified mouth of Imhotep. Take note: you feel the 1.5 g-forces when flying uphill, and much of the ride takes place in the dark, which adds to its unforgettable intensity. Needless to say, this isn't a good choice for expectant mothers or anyone with neck, back, or heart problems. **For people with disabilities:** Guests using wheelchairs must transfer to a ride vehicle. **TIP→ Cut down on wait times by using Express Pass, or come early or late. By all means, use the available free lockers to stash loose items.** ✉ *New York, Universal Studios* 🌐 *www.universalorlando.com* ☞ *Duration: 3 mins. Crowds: Heavy. Audience: Not small kids. Height requirement: 48 inches minimum.*

Restaurants

Finnegan's Bar & Grill

$$ | IRISH | This Irish pub would look just right in lower Manhattan during the Ellis Island era. The menu offers classic Irish comfort food like shepherd's pie, corned beef and cabbage, bangers and mash, and fish-and-chips, plus Guinness on tap and a five-beer sampler. **Known for:** live music; classic Irish comfort food like shepherd's pie and beef stew; good place for a quick, filling sandwich. [$] *Average main: $18* ⊠ *New York, Universal Studios* ☎ *407/363–8757* 🌐 *www.universalorlando.com.*

Production Central

Expect plenty of loud, flashy, rollicking rides that appeal to tweens, teens, and adults. Clear the turnstiles, and go straight. You can use the Universal Express Pass at all attractions.

Sights

Despicable Me: Minion Mayhem

AMUSEMENT PARK/WATER PARK | Even if you've never seen the hit animated film, it doesn't take long to fall for Gru, the Scourge of Humanity, in this wild virtual-reality chase through the movie. Two extremely funny (and cute) preshow rooms—Gru's living room and laboratory—set the stage for the 3-D ride. With help from his adopted daughters Margo, Edith, and Agnes (and ever-so-anxious minions), Gru reviews everyone to make sure they're ready to become minions. Next, sporting your "minion goggles" (aka 3-D glasses) you are transformed into minions for the rollicking ride, which is filled with close calls and colorful characters as you pursue the ever-elusive prize: the girls' gift for their dad on the one-year anniversary of their adoption. To celebrate, the ride exits into a minion disco (of course). The 3-D experience, with preshows, lasts about 20 minutes. This is not recommended for expectant mothers or anyone with motion sickness or back, neck, or heart problems. **For people with disabilities:** Closed-captioned devices are available; wheelchair guests may remain in their chairs. **TIP→ Go for the stationary seats if you think you'll suffer from motion sickness.** ⊠ *Production Central, Universal Studios* 🌐 *www.universalorlando.com* ☞ *Duration: 5 mins. Crowds: Heavy. Audience: All ages. Height requirement: 40 inches minimum.*

★ **Hollywood Rip Ride Rockit**

AMUSEMENT PARK/WATER PARK | Looking like an endless strand of spaghetti, this half-mile-plus coaster loops, twists, dives, and winds above and through Production Central. After you're locked into your seat, you'll select your personal soundtrack (choose from heavy metal, techno, country, rap, and pop) to accompany the video (starring you) that's shot as you scream your way along. And you will scream! It all starts as you're hauled nearly *17 stories straight up* and then dropped nearly *17 stories straight down* before being lifted again into a towering loop and released into what seems like a never-ending series of twists, curves, sideways slings, and snap rolls at speeds up to 65 mph. By the time you return to the station, you might be woozy and a little spent—but you might spend a little more: the video with the soundtrack you selected is available for purchase. Off-season, the line never seems too bad. In season, consider using a Universal Express Pass. The ride isn't suitable for expectant mothers; anyone with neck, back, or heart problems; or people with a fear of heights. **For people with disabilities:** This does include closed-captioning, and guests using wheelchairs must transfer to a ride vehicle. **TIP→ Come early or late, and be sure to stow loose items in the available lockers.** ⊠ *Production Central, Universal Studios* 🌐 *www.universalorlando.com* ☞ *Duration: 2*

Did You Know?

On Production Central's Hollywood Rip Ride Rockit, you choose coaster-ride soundtrack from several genres of music. After the whole experience, you can buy a video of your ride with the music you selected.

What's New at Universal Orlando Reso 

Bigfire (CityWalk): Joining the crowd at CityWalk, this restaurant with the look and feel of a lakeside summer house centers on steaks and freshwater meals cooked over an open flame.

Bourne Stuntacular (Universal Studios, Hollywood): Through live action and film, you'll follow action hero Jason Bourne across three continents as he tries to stay ahead of a cast of sinister characters.

Hagrids Magical Creatures Motorbike Adventure (IOA, Hogsmeade): This wonderfully thrilling roller coaster ride quickly became a guest favorite following its 2019 premiere.

Today Cafe (Universal Studios, Hollywood): Food segments are an integral part of happy talk morning shows, and that sets the stage for this unique café—modeled after the *Today* show's familiar Studio 1-A—across from the Universal Studios Store. Step into the set, and grab a quick meal of baked goods, freshly prepared salads, healthy sandwiches, specialty coffees, beer, and wine.

Universal's Endless Summer Resort, Surfside Inn and Suites (Universal Orlando Resort): A twin pairing of resorts—the Surfside Inn and Suites and Dockside Inn and Suites—are new additions to the Value Line lodging.

mins. Crowds: You Bet! Audience: Not small kids. Height requirement: 51 inches minimum; 79 inches maximum.

Shrek 4-D

AMUSEMENT PARK/WATER PARK | It's been years since the hit film premiered, but *Shrek* fans still line up at this animated 3-D saga. Mike Myers, Eddie Murphy, Cameron Diaz, and John Lithgow reprise their vocal roles as the swamp-dwelling ogre, Shrek; his faithful chatterbox companion, Donkey; Shrek's bride, Princess Fiona; and the vengeful Lord Farquaad (or rather his ghost). The preshow stars the Gingerbread Man, Magic Mirror, and the Three Little Pigs; and although this intro is slightly entertaining, at about 15 minutes long, it's longer than the main attraction. Afterward, you're given Ogre-Vision (aka 3-D) glasses through which to view Shrek as he attempts to rescue Fiona from Lord Farquaad. The adventure includes a battle between fire-breathing dragons and a pretty scary plunge down a virtual 1,000-foot waterfall—all made more intense by special theater seats and surprising sensory effects (mainly blasts of air and sprinkles of water) that create the "4-D" part. The ride can be unsettling for those with motion sickness—but fun as all get-out for everyone else. **For people with disabilities:** Equipped for assisted-listening devices. Those using wheelchairs don't need to transfer to a ride seat. There are, however, eight seats that allow guests with disabilities to fully experience the sensory effects. **TIP→ Despite a capacity for 300, you might wait up to an hour to reach the preshow. Come early or late in the day. Accepts Express Pass.** ✉ *Production Central, Universal Studios* ☞ *Duration: 12 mins. Crowds: Heavy. Audience: All ages.*

Transformers: The Ride 3-D

AMUSEMENT PARK/WATER PARK | Based on the toy-turned-film franchise that's generated billions of dollars, this high-intensity attraction has the ability to generate a lot of thrills and screams. Inside the stark industrial building that's the headquarters of NEST (Nonbiological Extraterrestrial Species Treaty), the attraction is the Universal Studios equivalent of IOA's groundbreaking Spider-Man (and that's a good thing). Board your transport, and, in a flash, you're in an illusory world where 60-foot screens, fast-paced action, and plenty of 3-D effects ratchet up the excitement in a battle to save the planet as the heroic Autobots (including Optimus Prime and Bumblebee) try to keep the Allspark from falling into the hands of the evil Decepticons (Confused? Ask your kids). Since you're wearing 3-D glasses, you ride through the attraction getting spun, twirled, splashed, dropped, and faced with some tremendously realistic intergalactic encounters that rock and roll you through the Transformers' world. Very loud and very wild. The height minimum is 40 inches, and this ride isn't suitable for expectant mothers; anyone with neck, back, or heart problems; or people with a fear of heights. **For people with disabilities:** Guests using wheelchairs must transfer to a ride vehicle. **TIP→ Come early or late or use Universal Express.** ✉ *Production Central, Universal Studios* 🌐 *www.universalorlando.com* ☞ *Duration: 5 mins. Crowds: You bet! Audience: Not small kids.*

Coffee and Quick Bites

In the heart of Production Central, the self-serve **Classic Monsters Cafe** resembles a mad scientist's lab. It offers wood-fired-oven pizzas, pastas, chef salads, four-cheese ravioli, and rotisserie chicken. Inside the restaurant, actual props and costumes from vintage Universal horror films provide great photo ops.

Shopping

Super Silly Stuff

TOYS | Talk about truth in advertising. This colorful gift shop tied to Despicable Me: Minion Mayhem is filled with what seems to be millions of cute minions (both one-eyed and two-eyed) on T-shirts, mugs, and stuffed dolls. Gru fans can also sport a black-and-gray scarf like the one worn by the supervillain—sold separately or silk-screened onto a T-shirt. ✉ *Production Central, Universal Studios* 🌐 *www.universalorlando.com/web/en/us/things-to-do/shopping/super-silly-stuff/index.html.*

Universal Studios Store

GIFTS/SOUVENIRS | Like the Magic Kingdom's Emporium, this sizable store is the last retail outlet guests see before exiting the park. Although it doesn't have all the merchandise sold in individual park gift shops, as the park's central shopping destination it does have most of it—and some of the best, including T-shirts, stuffed animals, hats, backpacks, gifts, mugs, and limited-edition Universal trading pins. A big plus is that even if you don't visit IOA, you'll find popular merchandise sold primarily at the neighboring park. ✉ *Production Central, Universal Studios* 🌐 *www.universalorlando.com/web/en/us/things-to-do/shopping/universal-studios-store-usf/index.html.*

Islands of Adventure

More so than just about any other theme park, IOA has gone all out to create settings and attractions that transport you from reality into the surreal. What's more, no one island here has much in common with any other, so in a way, a visit here is almost like a visit to half a dozen different parks.

IOA's unique nature is first revealed when you arrive at the Port of Entry and are greeted by a kaleidoscope of sights and a cacophony of sounds. It's all designed to put you in the frame of mind for adventure.

When you reach the central lagoon, your clockwise journey commences with Marvel Super Hero Island and its tightly packed concentration of roller coasters and thrill rides. Of special note is the astonishingly high-tech and dazzling Amazing Adventures of Spider-Man. Although you'll get your recommended daily allowance of thrills on this one island alone, you've only just begun.

Stepping into Toon Lagoon is like stepping into the pages of a comic book; which is the exact opposite feeling you'll get at neighboring Skull Island, where you'll find the high-intensity attraction Skull Island: Reign of Kong. The prehistoric battles here set the tone for several attractions in the upcoming island, Jurassic Park, where you'll come face-to-face with dozens of dinosaurs.

You move from the world of science fiction into the world of magic when you segue into the Wizarding World of Harry Potter: Hogsmeade. For the first time anywhere, you—and not just a few fortunate actors—can wander through the magnificently fictional, yet now very realistic, realm of the young wizard and his Hogwarts classmates and tutors. Beyond belief.

But that's not the end of it. In the Lost Continent, the mood is that of a Renaissance fair, where crafters work inside colorful tents. It's as pronounced an atmosphere as that of the final island, Seuss Landing, which presents the incredible, topsy-turvy world of Dr. Seuss. The riot of colors and shapes and fantastic wildlife pays tribute to the good doctor's vivid imagination.

GETTING ORIENTED

Getting your bearings at IOA is far easier than at its sister park, Universal Studios. Brochures in a multitude of languages are in a rack a few steps beyond the turnstiles; a quick look inside and a foldout map will acquaint you with the park's simple layout (it's a circle). Ahead by the lagoon, boards are posted with up-to-the-minute ride and show information—including the length of lines at the major attractions.

After you pass through the turnstiles, you enter the Port of Entry plaza, a bazaar that brings together bits and pieces of architecture, landscaping, music, and wares from many lands—Dutch windmills, Indonesian pedicabs, African masks, restrooms marked "Loo's Landing," and Egyptian figurines that adorn a massive archway inscribed with the notice "The Adventure Begins." From here, theme islands—arranged around a large lagoon—are connected by walkways that make navigation easy. When you've done the full circuit, you'll recall the fantastic range of sights, sounds, and experiences and realize there can be truth in advertising. This park really *is* an adventure.

TOURING TIPS

Hosts. Just about any employee is a host, whether they're at a kiosk or attraction or turnstile. Ask them about their favorite experiences—and for suggestions for saving time.

Photo Ops. IOA posts signs that indicate picture spots and show how best to frame your shot.

Retreat. Explore little-used sidewalks and quiet alcoves, and you'll find sanctuaries to counter IOA's manic energy.

Split the difference. If the park's open late, consider splitting the day in half. See part of it in the morning, head off-site to a restaurant for lunch (your parking ticket is good all day), and then head to your hotel for a swim or a nap (or both). Return in the cooler, less crowded evening.

PARK AMENITIES

Baby Care: There are diaper-changing stations in many of the men's and women's restrooms at IOA, as well as a nursing station for comfort and privacy at the first-aid station near the entrance. Baby supplies (diapers, food, wipes, and so on) are available at larger stores; ask for those items at the counter, though, as they aren't out on the shelves.

Cameras: Just inside the park, on your right after the turnstiles, is DeFoto's, which, like its counterpart at Universal Studios, was primarily a camera and film shop before cameras and film were condensed into smartphones. Nowadays the shelves are stocked with gifts, souvenirs, and drinks, and the staff helps guests with souvenir photos taken by Universal's squad of photographers.

First Aid: There are two health-services/first-aid centers: one at the front entrance inside Guest Services and another near Sindbad's Village in the Lost Continent. Just look for the Red Cross symbol on the building across from Oasis Coolers (or ask a park host).

Lockers: There are $10-a-day lockers across from Guest Services at the entrance; for $15 a day you can rent a family-size model. You have unlimited access to both types throughout the day—although it's a hike back to retrieve things. Scattered strategically throughout the park—notably at the Incredible Hulk Coaster and Forbidden Journey—are so-called Smart Lockers that are free while you ride (usually up to 75 minutes). Fee lockers, which are available near other attractions like Jurassic Park River Adventure, cost a few dollars per hour and are a useful place to stash backpacks and cameras while you're being drenched on a watery ride or going through the spin cycle on a twisty one.

Lost People and Things: If you've misplaced something, head to Guest Services in the Port of Entry. This is also where park staffers take lost children.

Services for People with Disabilities: IOA has made an all-out effort to ensure that the premises are accessible for people with disabilities. Most attractions and all restaurants are wheelchair accessible, and all employees attend workshops on how to meet the needs of guests with disabilities. You might occasionally spot staffers using wheelchairs, and many employees have had basic sign-language training. There's also a counter in Guest Services where you can pick up assisted-listening and other devices.

You can rent manual wheelchairs ($15 per day) and ECVs ($55 per day, $75 for a model with a sun canopy) at the Port of Entry to the left after you enter the turnstiles. A photo ID and a $50 deposit on a credit card are required. Because it's a long way between the parking garages and the park entrance, you might want to rent a push wheelchair at the garages and then upgrade to an ECV when you reach the entrance. Quantities of the latter are limited, so reserve in advance.

Even when the crowds are heavy, the park's avenues are wide enough to maneuver a wheelchair. Hosts and hostesses will direct you to a special attraction entrance or a special show seating area. Icons on the guide maps indicate which of the shows include an interpreter.

Assisted-listening devices are available for Cat in the Hat, Sindbad, Spider-Man, Incredible Hulk, Doctor Doom, Jurassic Park, and Poseidon's Fury.

Stroller Rentals: You can rent strollers ($18 per day for singles, $28 for doubles) at the Port of Entry to your left after the turnstiles.

Where to Snack: If you decide to pay in advance, you can save a bit of money with Quick Service meals that include, for adults, one meal, two snacks, and a nonalcoholic beverage ($26). The kids' version ($18) includes one kids meal, one snack, and a nonalcoholic beverage. There are many options at IOA, including the **Comic Strip Café** (Asian, Italian, American, and fish), **Burger Digs** (hamburgers, chicken sandwiches, chicken fingers, milk shakes), **Café 4** (pizzas, subs, salads), and **Croissant Moon** (deli sandwiches, panini, and pastries).

In the Wizarding World of Harry Potter, the signature dining experience is **Three Broomsticks,** where you can order the "Feast for Four" that includes a combination of rotisserie smoked chicken, spareribs, corn on the cob, and roasted potatoes. Other popular options include **Circus McGurkus Cafe Stoo-pendous** (chicken, pasta, pizza, burgers, salads) in Seuss Landing, and, in Toon Lagoon, **Blondie's** (jumbo deli sandwiches). **Pizza Predattoria** and **Thunder Falls Terrace** (rotisserie chicken and ribs) are in Jurassic Park, and near the Port of Entry is the comparably more upscale **Confisco Grille,** with its steaks, salads, sandwiches, soups, pasta, and neat little pub. At IOA, the ultimate dining experience is the Lost Continent's **Mythos Restaurant.** Although its Continental dishes change seasonally, the warm, gooey, chocolate-banana cake is a constant.

Shopping

At IOA, the merchandise varies in each section of the park. If you simply must have a Spider-Man T-shirt or Incredible Hulk coffee mug, for example, head to Marvel Super Hero Island. The largest concentration of stores is near the gates at the **Port of Entry.** And, as at Universal Studios, a central emporium—the Trading Company—carries nearly every coveted collectible from nearly every park shop. Keep in mind that **Hogsmeade Village** in the Wizarding World of Harry Potter is the place for Potter-related memorabilia and wizard supplies, along with the train-connected Diagon Alley at Universal Studios (two-park ticket required).

Marvel Super Hero Island

The facades on Stanley Boulevard (named for Marvel's famed editor and co-creator Stan Lee) put you smack in the middle of an alternatively pleasant and apocalyptic comic-book world—complete with heroes, villains, and cartoony colors and flourishes. Although the spiky, horrific towers of Doctor Doom's Fearfall and the vivid green of the Hulk's coaster are focal points, the Amazing Adventures of Spider-Man is the must-see attraction. At various times, Doctor Doom, Spider-Man, and the Incredible Hulk are available for photos, and sidewalk artists are on hand to paint your face like your favorite hero (or villain). All rides here accept Universal Express Pass.

Amazing Adventures of Spider-Man
AMUSEMENT PARK/WATER PARK | One of Universal's most popular attractions, the experience combines moving vehicles, 3-D film with the highest-definition resolution available, simulator technology, and special effects. What does that mean? It means that after donning 3-D glasses, you drive through the streets of New York in a special car that will pitch and roll as you get swept into a weird, all-encompassing cartoon battle. How weird? When Spider-Man lands on your car, you feel the bump; when Electro runs overhead, you hear his steps. You feel the sizzle of electricity, the frigid spray of water from Hydro Man, and the heat from a flaming pumpkin tossed by the Hobgoblin. No matter how many times you visit, you cringe when Doc Ock breaks through a brick wall, raises your car to the top of a skyscraper, and then releases it for a 400-foot free fall. The bizarre angles and perspectives really do make you feel as if you're swinging from a web. *Do not miss this one.* Youngsters accustomed to action TV shows should be fine, but timid kids won't. Also skip this ride if you're pregnant or have heart, back, or neck problems. **For people with disabilities:** Equipped for assisted-listening devices. Guests using wheelchairs must transfer to a ride vehicle. **TIP→ Come early or at dusk to save on your wait time. Be sure to check out the wanted posters of Spider-Man villains on the walls.** ✉ *Marvel Super Hero Island, Islands of Adventure* 🌐 *www.universalorlando.com* ☞ *Duration: 4½ mins. Crowds: Absolutely. Audience: All but small kids. Height requirement: 40 inches minimum; under 48 inches must ride with an adult.*

Doctor Doom's Fearfall

AMUSEMENT PARK/WATER PARK | Although the 200-foot-tall towers look really scary, the ride itself is just *kind* of scary (but still pretty cool). Several sets of four chairs wrap around the tower, and you and three fellow guests are seated and strapped in just out of the sight of other riders before the disembodied voice of Dr. Doom tells you the contraption is designed to extract fear he'll collect to use and rule the world. Without warning, all the chairs are rocketed to the peak, which jump-starts a surge of adrenaline as it rises, falls, rises, and falls again in a very brief, but quite thrilling, experience. Often it's easy enough to have a second go, as you can actually step off and get right back into line again. Guests who are pregnant or have heart, back, neck, or motion-sickness problems should sit this one out. **For people with disabilities:** Guests using wheelchairs must transfer to a ride vehicle. **TIP→ Line moves fairly fast, though it's crowded early in the day; come late or use Express Pass.** ✉ *Marvel Super Hero Island, Islands of Adventure* ☞ *Duration: 1 min. Crowds: Light to moderate. Audience: All but small kids. Height requirement: 52 inches minimum.*

Incredible Hulk Coaster

AMUSEMENT PARK/WATER PARK | Just seeing this attraction from the sidewalk is a thrill: its cars shoot out from a 150-foot catapult that propels them from 0 to 40 mph in less than *two seconds.* If this piques your interest, get in line where the wait for the prized front-row seats is the longest; however, every seat lets you experience flesh-pressing g-forces that match those of an F-16 fighter. When you're launched into the ride (and we mean launched), you're whipped into an upside-down, zero-g position more than 10 stories up before being zipped into a dive at some 60 mph. You then race along the track before spinning through seven rollovers and making a plunge into two deep, foggy subterranean enclosures. Just when you think it's over—it's not. This coaster seems to keep rolling along well after you've exhausted your supply of screams and shrieks. Powerful. The smooth track creates a smooth ride for the neon-trimmed train cars; this also makes the ride itself quieter—an aspect that seems to amplify the sound effects and screams. Pregnant women and people with neck, back, heart problems, or motion-sickness issues shouldn't ride. **For people with disabilities:** Guests using wheelchairs must transfer to a ride vehicle. **TIP→ Come here first (effects are best in the morning and up front). Use Express Pass. Loose articles are not permitted, so stow things in a convenient locker.** ✉ *Marvel Super Hero Island, Islands of Adventure* ☞ *Duration: 2¼ mins. Crowds: Yes! Audience: All but small kids. Height requirement: 54 inches minimum.*

Storm Force Accelatron

AMUSEMENT PARK/WATER PARK | On this whirling ride, X-Men character Storm harnesses the weather to battle Magneto by having people like you board Power Orbs. Yes, the story line is that the containers convert human energy into electrical forces through the power of "cyclospin." Strip away the veneer, however, and what you've got seems like a faster version of Disney World's twirling teacups. Still, it's a high-adrenaline ride that's not for anyone who suffers from motion sickness. It's also not suitable for guests who are pregnant or who have heart, back, or neck problems. **For people with disabilities:** Guests using wheelchairs must transfer to a ride vehicle. **TIP→ Ride whenever—except right after eating. Use Express Pass when needed.** ✉ *Marvel Super Hero Island, Islands of Adventure* ☞ *Duration: 2 mins. Crowds: Light. Audience: All but small kids.*

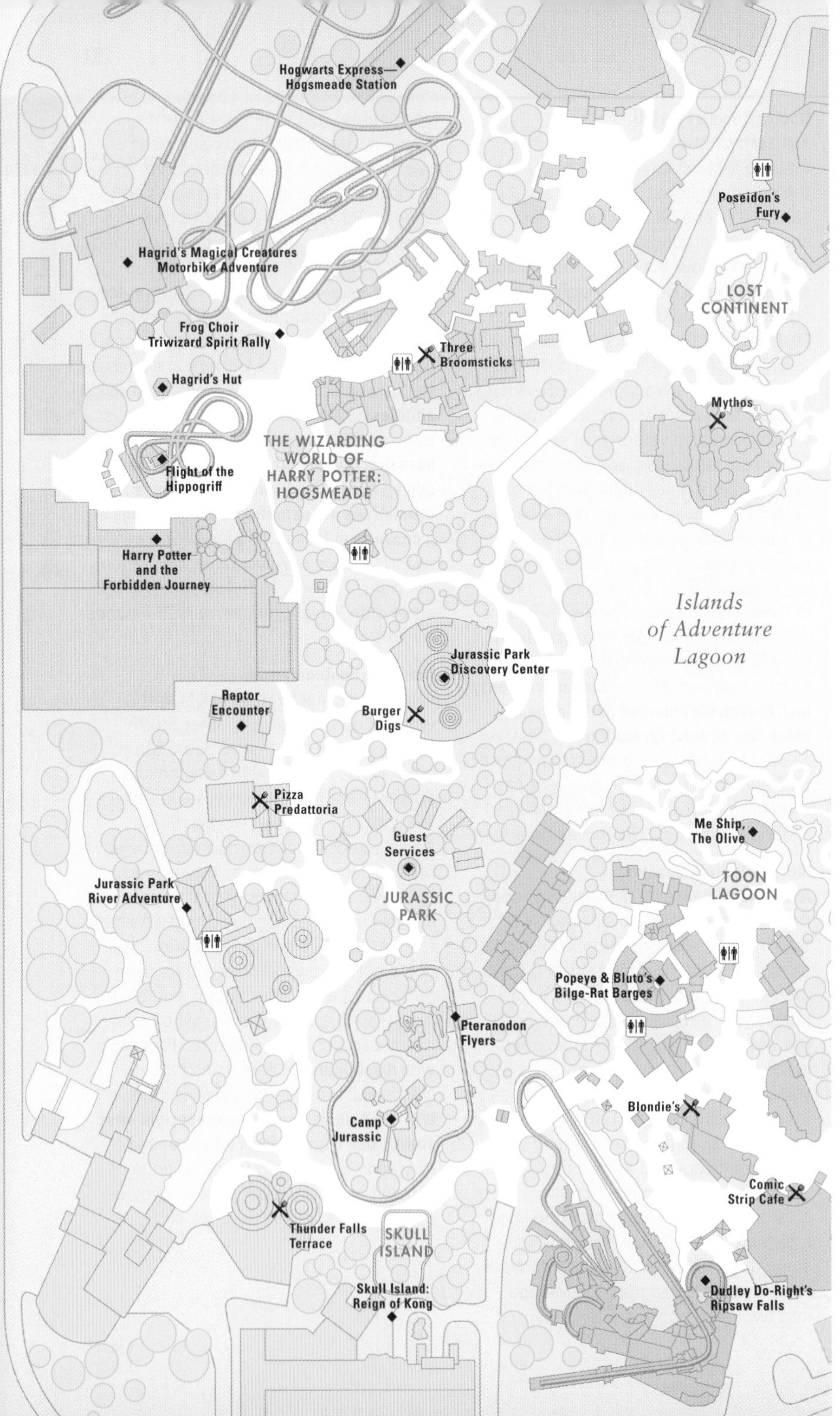

Hogwarts Express—
Hogsmeade Station
Poseidon's
Fury
LOST
CONTINENT
Hagrid's Magical Creatures
Motorbike Adventure
Frog Choir
Triwizard Spirit Rally
Three
Broomsticks
Hagrid's Hut
Mythos
THE WIZARDING
WORLD OF
HARRY POTTER:
HOGSMEADE
Flight of the
Hippogriff
Harry Potter
and the
Forbidden Journey
Islands
of Adventure
Lagoon
Jurassic Park
Discovery Center
Raptor
Encounter
Burger
Digs
Pizza
Predattoria
Me Ship,
The Olive
Guest
Services
Jurassic Park
River Adventure
TOON
LAGOON
JURASSIC
PARK
Popeye & Bluto's
Bilge-Rat Barges
Pteranodon
Flyers
Blondie's
Camp
Jurassic
Comic
Strip Cafe
Thunder Falls
Terrace
SKULL
ISLAND
Skull Island:
Reign of Kong
Dudley Do-Right's
Ripsaw Falls

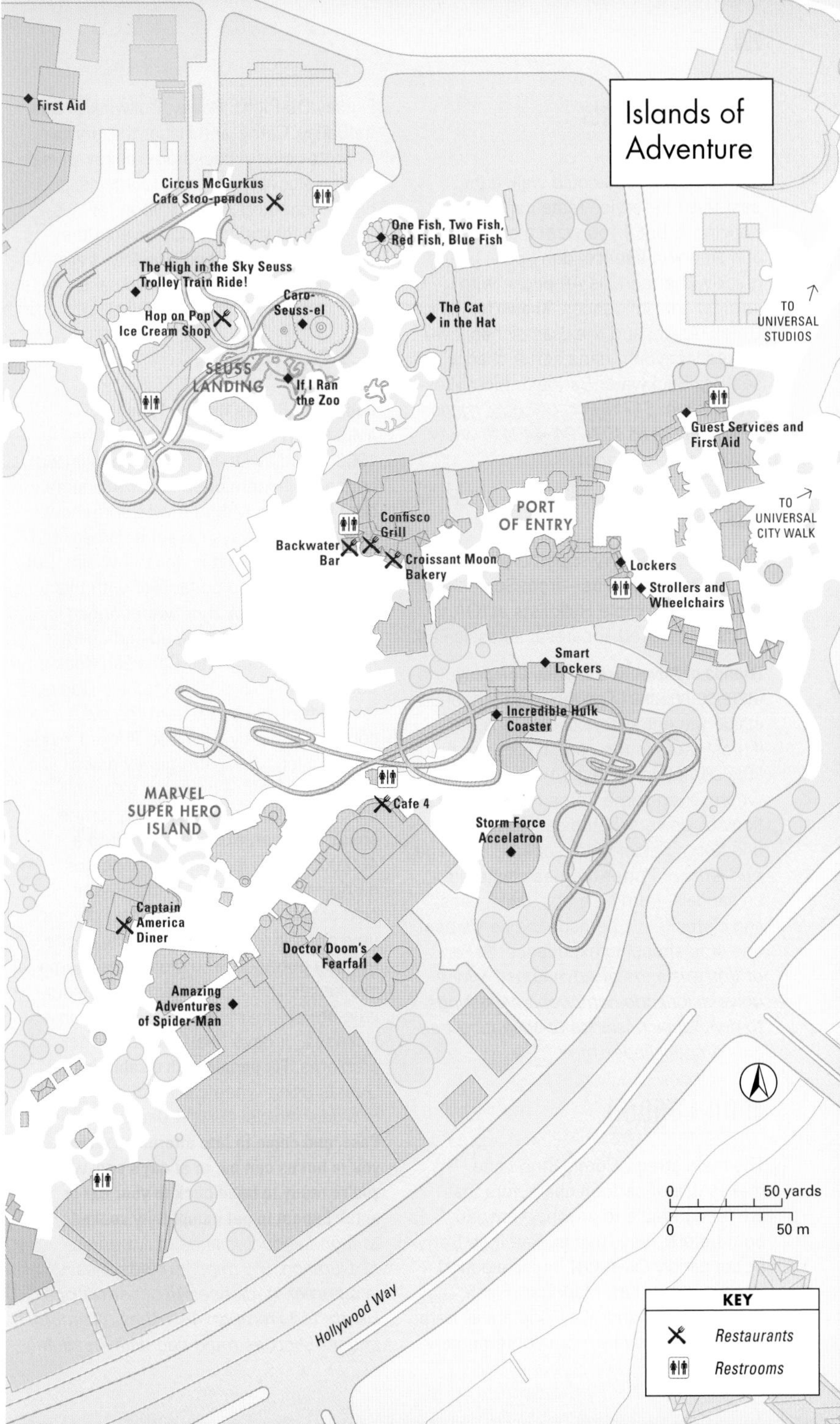

Islands of Adventure
First Aid
Circus McGurkus
Cafe Stoo-pendous
One Fish, Two Fish,
Red Fish, Blue Fish
The High in the Sky Seuss
Trolley Train Ride!
Caro-
Seuss-el
Hop on Pop
Ice Cream Shop
The Cat
in the Hat
TO
UNIVERSAL
STUDIOS
SEUSS
LANDING
If I Ran
the Zoo
Guest Services and
First Aid
PORT
OF ENTRY
TO
UNIVERSAL
CITY WALK
Confisco
Grill
Backwater
Bar
Croissant Moon
Bakery
Lockers
Strollers and
Wheelchairs
Smart
Lockers
Incredible Hulk
Coaster
MARVEL
SUPER HERO
ISLAND
Cafe 4
Storm Force
Accelatron
Captain
America
Diner
Doctor Doom's
Fearfall
Amazing
Adventures
of Spider-Man
0
50 yards
0
50 m
KEY
Restaurants
Restrooms
Hollywood Way

Restaurants

Confisco Grille

$$ | **AMERICAN** | You could walk right past this full-service restaurant without noticing it, but if you want a good meal and sit-down service, don't pass by too quickly. The menu is American with international influences. **Known for:** Italian, Greek, Asian, and Mexican dishes; overlooked location means better chance of seating; Backwater Bar next door. 💲 *Average main: $17* ✉ *Port of Entry, Islands of Adventure* ☎ *407/224–4404* 🌐 *www.universalorlando.com.*

Shopping

Several stores carry superhero and film-theme souvenirs—from Spider-Man gear and Incredible Hulk fists at IOA to dinosaur-inspired apparel at Jurassic Park.

Islands of Adventure Trading Company

GIFTS/SOUVENIRS | The rambling emporium inside the entrance/exit of IOA is the largest store in the park. It'sfilled with a little something of everything from everywhere, even some items from the attractions of Universal Studios. Here you'll find Kong, Spider-Man, superheroes, and *puh-lenty* of Potter themes plastered on sandals, frames, mugs, cups, caps, and clothing. It's perhaps the park's best one-stop shopping experience. ✉ *Port of Entry, Islands of Adventure* 🌐 *www.universalorlando.com/web/en/us/things-to-do/shopping/islands-of-adventure-trading-company/index.html.*

Toon Lagoon

The main street, Comic Strip Lane, makes use of cartoon characters that are recognizable to anyone—anyone born before 1940, that is. Pert little Betty Boop, gangly Olive Oyl, muscle-bound Popeye, Krazy Kat, Mark Trail, Flash Gordon, Pogo, and Alley Oop are all here, as are the relatively more contemporary Dudley Do-Right, Rocky, Bullwinkle, Beetle Bailey, Cathy, and Hagar the Horrible. With its colorful backdrops, chirpy music, hidden alcoves, squirting fountains, and highly animated scenery, Toon Town is a natural for younger kids (even if they don't know who these characters are). All attractions here accept Universal Express Pass except Me Ship, The Olive.

Sights

Dudley Do-Right's Ripsaw Falls

AMUSEMENT PARK/WATER PARK | In the 1960s, Dudley Do-Right was recognized as the well-intentioned (but considerably dim) Canadian Mountie who somehow managed to always save the damsel and "get his man" (that is, foil the villain). But you don't need to be familiar with this character to enjoy this "waterlogged" attraction. The twisting, up-and-down flume ride through the Canadian Rockies begins with your mission to help Dudley rescue Nell, his belle, from the evil, conniving Snidely Whiplash. Tucked inside a hollow log, you'll drift gently down the stream before dropping through the rooftop of a ramshackle dynamite shack. After an explosive dive into a 400,000-gallon lagoon, you're not just damp—you're soaked. If the weather is cold or you absolutely must stay dry, pick up a poncho at Gasoline Alley, opposite the ride entrance, and store other items in a locker. This isn't suitable for guests who are pregnant, experience motion sickness, or have heart, back, or neck problems. **For people with disabilities:** Guests using wheelchairs must transfer to a ride vehicle. **TIP→ Use Express Pass, and come in late afternoon, when you're hot as can be, or at day's end, when you're ready to head back to your car or hotel. Expect to get completely soaked.** ✉ *Toon Lagoon, Islands of Adventure* ☞ *Duration: 5½ mins. Crowds: Heavy in summer. Audience: All but small kids. Height requirement: 44 inches minimum; under 48 inches must ride with an adult.*

Me Ship, The Olive

AMUSEMENT PARK/WATER PARK | Disguised as a teetering-tottering ship, this is actually a fantastic three-story playground. From bow to stern, there are dozens of participatory activities to keep kids busy as they climb around this jungle gym moored on the edge of Toon Lagoon. Toddlers enjoy crawling in Swee' Pea's Playpen, and with high-powered squirt guns, older children and their parents can take aim at unsuspecting riders twisting through the rapids over at Popeye & Bluto's Bilge-Rat Barges ride. The most excited participants are small kids, who can't get enough of the whistles, bells, tunnels, and ladders. Check out the view of the park from the top of the ship. **For people with disabilities:** The playground area is wheelchair accessible. **TIP→ Come in the morning or around dinnertime.** ✉ *Toon Lagoon, Islands of Adventure* ☞ *Duration: Up to you. Crowds: Heavy. Audience: Small kids.*

Popeye & Bluto's Bilge-Rat Barges

AMUSEMENT PARK/WATER PARK | As with every ride at IOA, there's a story line here, but the real attraction is boarding the wide circular raft with 11 other passengers and then getting soaked, splashed, sprayed, or deluged as the watercraft bounces and bobs down and around the twisting stream. The degree of wetness varies, since the direction your raft spins might or might not place you beneath torrents of water flooding from a shoreline water tower or streaming from water guns fired with enthusiasm by guests at an adjacent play area. Pregnant women and guests with heart, back, neck, or motion-sickness problems should skip this one. **For people with disabilities:** Guests using wheelchairs must transfer to a ride vehicle. **TIP→ Come first thing in the morning or an hour before closing. Use Express Pass, and stow your items in a locker if needed, since you will likely get completely soaked.** ✉ *Toon Lagoon, Islands of Adventure* ☞ *Duration: 5 mins. Crowds: Heavy. Audience: All but small kids. Height requirement: 42 inches minimum; under 48 inches must ride with an adult.*

Coffee and Quick Bites

Blondie's is home of the Dagwood—the jumbo club sandwich that's sold in sections as it's much too large for any one person to tackle. The eatery also sells cookies and Nathan's hot dogs (Chicago, chili, Reuben, slaw), as well as turkey, roast beef, and tuna sandwiches.

Skull Island

If you've seen the 1933 classic *King Kong*, you might recall that, for its time (and ours), it was an intensely thrilling presentation of special effects and incredible characters. The same is true of this present-day incarnation, which re-creates the mood and settings found in the original. Tucked in an area between Toon Lagoon and Jurassic Park, Skull Island presents a singular attraction—and what an attraction it is: an ongoing battle between King Kong and a host of oversize adversaries. Parents should note that this is the only attraction where there's a warning that the *preshow* area might be too intense for kids.

Sights

Skull Island: Reign of Kong

AMUSEMENT PARK/WATER PARK | As you follow a winding path that leads into the heart of a towering mountain, the mood grows more ominous. Navigating darkened corridors that are inhabited by "scare actors" (hence the warning that kids might find the preshow too intense), you pass a proliferation of skulls and then meet an old crone, who hints that something unsettling lies ahead—and you'll find that out when you and your fellow travelers enter a primeval world where things get very scary, very quickly. To the eerie chants of "Kong!

Kong! Kong!" your guided tram drives through a towering set of doors where the skeletal remains of a great ape greet you. Put on your 3-D glasses, and soon other amazing sights will appear—namely Peg, a steely nerved scientist whose exploits are the centerpiece of the attraction. Swarms of bats are followed by swarms of pteranodons that lift her up and away, and now it's up to you to come to her rescue. Although Peg works to save herself, she lands in the middle of swamp infested with scorpions and slimy snakelike creatures. As she blasts them with a machine gun, you feel the splash of their guts before the tram speeds to the next scene, where velociraptors try taking a bite out of your tram. Those agile, snapping dinosaurs are soon overshadowed by a Tyrannosaurus rex, who is soon overshadowed by your hero: King Kong. With the action taking place on both sides of the tram, you're in the middle of a high-energy, over-the-top battle royale that's thrilling from start to finish. Hint: After riding it once, go back again and wait for a seat on the opposite side to catch scenes you may have missed (they're just as exciting). This ride might be too intense for preteens. Pregnant women and guests with heart, back, neck, or motion-sickness problems should also skip this one. **For people with disabilities:** Guests using wheelchairs must transfer to a ride vehicle. **TIP→ The preshow is part of the fun, so go even if the line is long. But not too long. Otherwise, use the Express Pass.** ✉ *Skull Island, Islands of Adventure* 🌐 *universalorlando.com* ☞ *Duration: 5 mins. Crowds: Often heavy. Audience: All but small kids. Height requirement: 36 inches minimum.*

Jurassic Park

Pass through the towering gates of Jurassic Park, and the music becomes slightly ominous, the vegetation tropical and junglelike. All of this, plus the high-tension wires and warning signs, does a great job of re-creating the Jurassic Park of Steven Spielberg's blockbuster movie (and its sequels). The half-fun, half-frightening Jurassic Park River Adventure (the only attraction here that uses U niversal Express Pass) is the standout, bringing to life key segments of the movie's climax. As of this writing, rumors that the Velocicoaster, a high-speed thrill ride, is scheduled to open in 2020, though the unexpected closure of the park due to Covid-19 may cause delays.

Camp Jurassic

AMUSEMENT PARK/WATER PARK | Remember when you were content with just a swing set and monkey bars? Well, such toys have been replaced by theme play areas like this. Though the prehistoric camp is primarily for kids, some adults join in, racing along footpaths through the forests, slithering down slides, clambering over swinging bridges and across streams, scrambling up net climbs and rock formations, and exploring mysterious caves full of faux lava. Watch for the dinosaur footprints; when you jump on them, a dinosaur roars somewhere (different footprints are associated with different roars). Also look out for the watery crossfire nearby—or join in the shooting yourself. **For people with disabilities:** Much of this attraction is wheelchair accessible (its upper levels probably aren't). **TIP→ Great anytime.** ✉ *Jurassic Park, Islands of Adventure* ☞ *Duration: Up to you. Crowds: Light to moderate. Audience: All ages.*

Jurassic Park Discovery Center

AMUSEMENT PARK/WATER PARK | Since it sits to the side of the walkway and doesn't reveal much from the outside, this attraction is often overlooked but may be worth a visit if you have kids who have a passion for dinosaurs. There are demonstration areas where a realistic

In the Jurassic Park Discovery Center, your kids might just learn something about dinosaurs that they didn't already know.

raptor is being hatched, and where you can see what you'd look like (or sound like) if you were a dino. In the Beasaur area ("Be-a-Saur"), you get a dinosaur's view of the world. There are numerous hands-on exhibits and a dinosaur trivia game, although the museumlike feel seems a little off-kilter at an amusement park. Burger Digs, the casual restaurant upstairs, is a nice place to take an air-conditioned break, and tables on the balcony overlook the lagoon. Step outside and a wide promenade affords a lovely perspective of the entire park. **For people with disabilities:** The attraction is fully wheelchair accessible. ✉ *Jurassic Park, Islands of Adventure* 🌐 *www.universalorlando.com* ☞ *Duration: Up to you. Crowds: Light. Audience: All but small kids.*

Jurassic Park River Adventure

AMUSEMENT PARK/WATER PARK | Your excursion begins as a peaceful raft cruise on a mysterious river past friendly, vegetarian dinosaurs. Naturally, something has to go awry, and a wrong turn is all that it takes to float you into the Raptor Containment Area. Drifting into a research lab, you'll see that it's been overrun by spitting dinosaurs and razor-clawed raptors—and this is when things get plenty scary: straight ahead is a towering, roaring T. rex, ready to use his sharp claws and teeth the size of hams to guard the getaway route. Just when you think you're about to become a Cretaceous period entrée, your raft slips down a tremendously steep, 85-foot plunge that will start you screaming. Smile! This is when the souvenir photos are shot. Thanks to high-capacity rafts, the line moves fairly quickly. Not suitable for guests who are pregnant or who have heart, back, or neck problems. **For people with disabilities:** Guests using wheelchairs must transfer to a ride vehicle; assisted-listening devices are available. **■TIP→ Come early in the morning and/or use Express Pass.** ✉ *Jurassic Park, Islands of Adventure* ☞ *Duration: 6 mins. Crowds: Heavy. Audience: All but small kids. Height requirement: 42 inches minimum.*

Pteranodon Flyers

AMUSEMENT PARK/WATER PARK | These prehistoric bird–style gondolas are eye-catching and might tempt you to stand in line for a lift. The catch is that this is a very slow, very low-capacity ride that can eat up a lot of your park time. Do it only if (1) your child asks, (2) you want a prehistoric-bird's-eye view of the Jurassic Park compound, or (3) you've been to the park a dozen times and this is the last ride to conquer. **For people with disabilities:** Guests using wheelchairs must transfer to a ride vehicle. **TIP→ Crowds are usually perpetual, and since the ride loads slowly, waits can be quite a while. Skip this on your first visit.** ✉ *Jurassic Park, Islands of Adventure* 🌐 *www.universalorlando.com* ☞ *Duration: 2 mins. Crowds: Heavy. Audience: All ages. Height requirement: Between 36 and 56 inches tall; taller adults must ride with a child who meets these height requirements.*

Raptor Encounter

AMUSEMENT PARK/WATER PARK | What ultimately amounts to a photo op (albeit a very intense one) begins with a guide offering the members of your group safety instructions prior to entering the paddock, where a life-size velociraptor resides. Once inside the paddock, the guide coaxes Lucy (the dinosaur) into view, which sets the stage for souvenir photos. But with your back turned and a row of razor-sharp teeth directly behind you, the snapshots are usually framed with a look of fear. It can be a very interesting, and very intense, experience that easily frightens kids—and usually scares adults. If you can handle it, the souvenir picture might be worth the brief flash of fear. ✉ *Jurassic Park, Islands of Adventure* 🌐 *www.universalorlando.com/web/en/us/things-to-do/character-encounters/raptor-encounter.*

Coffee and Quick Bites

Thunder Falls Terrace is open for lunch and dinner. Beneath towering ceilings in a spacious setting, one side is entirely glass, which makes it a great place to view the plunge at the adjacent Jurassic Park River Adventure. On a nice day, consider sitting outdoors next to the thundering waterfall and dine on barbecue ribs, wraps, chicken, turkey legs, soup, and salads. If Thunder Falls is too crowded, a short distance away are **Burger Digs** and **Pizza Predattoria.**

Shopping

Dinostore

GIFTS/SOUVENIRS | Above a juvenile chorus of "I want this!" are adults counseling their kids on what they actually *need.* That can be a monumental task in this large store, which is packed with dino hats, shorts, necklaces, cards, mugs, squirt guns, figurines, and the clever T-rex T-shirt emblazoned with the helpful suggestion "Bite Me." Rest assured there are educational dino toys, too. ✉ *Jurassic Park, Islands of Adventure* 🌐 *www.universalorlando.com/web/en/us/things-to-do/shopping/Dinostore/index.html.*

The Wizarding World of Harry Potter: Hogsmeade

In mid-2010, IOA fulfilled the fantasy of Harry Potter devotees when it unveiled the biggest theme-park addition since the arrival of Disney's Animal Kingdom in 1998. At the highly publicized premiere, even the actors from the *Potter* film franchise were amazed. Having performed their roles largely before a green screen, they had never seen anything like this. Neither have you. It's fantastic and unbelievable. The movie-magic-perfect re-creations of mythical locales such as Hogwarts and Hogsmeade Village are here, while playing supporting roles are a handful of candy shops, souvenir stores, and restaurants expertly and exquisitely themed to make you believe you've actually arrived in the incredible fantasy world of J.K. Rowling. Wands, candy, novelties, and more are unique to this magical land. Expect to be impressed—and to wait in line unless you can use your Universal Express Pass. And if you have a two-park pass, you can board the Hogwarts Express for a delightful train journey to Diagon Alley at Universal Studios.

Hogsmeade is the village that's the home of Hogwarts, the alma mater of Harry, Ron, and Hermione. You might also find it's a perfect representation of the imaginary land you visualize when engrossed in the pages of your favorite *Harry Potter* books. In the village, you can run errands, pick up sundries, and pretend you're really in Harry's world. Send a postcard or letter stamped with a novelty (and very real cancellation mark) at Owl Post before selecting (or being selected by) a magic wand at Ollivanders. If you can't get into Ollivanders due to the line, kiosks and small shops sell an impressive variety of wands—some that are even interactive and come with a chart informing young wizards how to move the wand to trigger flowing water, turn on lights, start a sign swinging, and so on at areas throughout Hogsmeade. Pick up some practical jokes (shrunken heads, extendable ears, screaming yo-yos) at Zonko's, and sample strange sweets at Honeydukes. But the best place to shop for Potterabilia is Dervish and Banges, where there are Hogwarts school uniforms, robes, scarves, T-shirts, and broomsticks—including the legendary Nimbus 2000. Highly recommended is savoring your time here, stopping at the signature restaurant, Three Broomsticks, which serves traditional British fare as well as an assortment of kids' meals, and the Hog's Head Pub, where you can down a pint of butterbeer (tastes like cream soda, butterscotch, and shortbread cookies) or pumpkin juice (pumpkin, apple cider, and spices).

To explore even more of Harry's favorite haunts, board the train to Universal Studios' Diagon Alley. Much more than a train ride, it's an exciting prequel to an equally enjoyable Potter-themed experience.

Sights

Flight of the Hippogriff

AMUSEMENT PARK/WATER PARK | This kid-friendly coaster is a simple way to introduce your children to the pleasures of g-forces and vertigo. The queue takes you past Hagrid's hut and then on board for a "training flight" above the grounds of Hogwarts Castle. On the brief journey, there are some nice little twists and dips that'll give them a pint-sized dose of adrenaline—just enough to please parents as well as the kids themselves. That said, this ride isn't appropriate for people with heart, back, or neck problems or who are prone to motion sickness. **For people with disabilities:** Guests using wheelchairs must transfer to a ride vehicle. **TIP→ Use Express Pass if the line is too long, but it often isn't.** ✉ *The Wizarding World of Harry Potter, Islands of Adventure* 🌐 *www.universalorlando.com* ☞ *Duration: 1 min. Crowds: Moderate. Audience: Small kids. Height requirement: 36 inches minimum.*

★ Hagrid's Magical Creatures Motorbike Adventure

AMUSEMENT PARK/WATER PARK | A roller coaster with a twist (and plenty of turns), this new-in-2019 attraction mixes in a magical blend of speed with an interesting collection from Hagrid's unusual menagerie on a ride that surpasses expectations, even if you have had to wait for 90 or more minutes. With a grip on the handlebars, you're shot from the starting line—amid Hagrid's commentary and the sound of a motorcycle revving—and you rocket into a series of low angle turns that snap around corners and into tight curves. You'll slow long enough to meet one of Hagrid's friends (one with an unusual defense mechanism),

Did You Know?

The level of detail in Hogsmeade is amazing, right up to the snow on the roofs. If you buy one of the “interactive” wands, you’ll be able to stand on a special medallion in the pavement and “cast” a spell.

and then it's back to the track with more speedy curves and more surreal creatures before you enter a fog bank... and begin the experience backward! One more turnaround, and you're blazing it full-speed to the exhilarating end. **■ TIP→ Lines can be incredibly long, so be sure to check the wait time before lining up. Parents can also take advantage of the child-swap option where one parent waits until the other has finished and then steps right up to ride. Universal Express might be offered in the future.** ✉ *Wizarding World of Harry Potter: Hogsmeade, Islands of Adventure* 🌐 *www.universalorlando.com/web/en/us/things-to-do/rides-attractions/hagrids-magical-creatures-motorbike-adventure* ☞ *Crowds: Huge. Audience: Everyone but young kids. Height Requirement: 48 inches minimum.*

★ **Harry Potter and the Forbidden Journey**
AMUSEMENT PARK/WATER PARK | Of all of Universal's rides, this is the one that *really* puts you in the movies. In the queue, you enter the hallowed halls of Hogwarts, where you are introduced to the founders of the school and the story of the journey. Inside the academy, you'll see the sights you know from the books and films: Headmaster Dumbledore's office, Defence Against the Dark Arts classroom, Gryffindor common room, Room of Requirement, and the greenhouse. You'll also encounter the Sorting Hat, the One-Eyed Witch statue, as well as several talking portraits. Keep in mind, so far all of this has just been the pre-show. Before you reach the actual ride, heroes Harry, Ron, and Hermione arrive and try to persuade you to skip a lecture and follow them on a soaring journey—and so you go. Thanks to a combination of live-action, robotic technology and innovative filmmaking, your broomstick flight brings you face-to-face with a flying dragon and the Whomping Willow before being propelled into the heart of a Quidditch match. You also zip through a dozen scenes and encounter supporting characters Albus Dumbledore, Rubeus Hagrid, Draco Malfoy, and members of the Weasley family. All in all, a fantastic attraction—especially for fans of the series who might feel like they've been written into the script of a *Harry Potter* blockbuster. Also, this ride isn't suitable for those with neck, back, or heart problems, as well as those who are pregnant or suffer from motion sickness. **For people with disabilities:** Guests using wheelchairs must transfer to a ride vehicle. **■ TIP→ Use Express Pass if the line is long, or simply relax and enjoy your tour of the school before boarding the ride; this is one time when the pre-show is a large part of the fun.** ✉ *The Wizarding World of Harry Potter, Islands of Adventure* 🌐 *www.universalorlando.com* ☞ *Duration: 50–60 mins. Crowds: Yes! Audience: All but small kids. Height requirement: 48 inches minimum; 75 inches maximum. Weight requirement: less than 250 pounds.*

Hogwart's Express—Hogsmeade Station
AMUSEMENT PARK/WATER PARK | If you're traveling on the Hogwarts Express for the first time, the trip will keep you under a magical spell so that when you arrive at King's Cross Station at Universal Studios (at Platform 9¾ no less), you're still in a wizarding state of mind. After you've settled into the compartment, you can look out your window and see the village of Hogsmeade and towering Hogwarts Castle. But it's when the train leaves the station that the visual effects really kick in. Hagrid waves good-bye, centaurs gallop beside you, and the Weasley brothers fly by on their broomsticks. The journey lasts about four minutes, as Hogwarts gradually disappears in the distance, and you travel briskly across the rainy British countryside, truly believing you're actually leaving a land known only to wizards. But wait. When you roll past the streets of London, you discover that the fantasy continues. When the train stops, you're only steps away from the magic of Diagon Alley. ✉ *Wizarding World of Harry Potter, Islands of Adventure* 🌐 *www.universalorlando.com.*

Islands of Adventure Family Tour

As you go through IOA, try to pretend that you are not so much a park guest as you are a fledgling explorer and amateur sociologist (sometimes just watching people having fun *is* the fun). Imagine that you're taking in an entirely new world, rather than merely visiting a theme park.

In **Marvel Super Hero Island**, most guests race into the Hulk roller coaster and Spider-Man attractions. Instead, spend some time on the bridge or along the waterfront, where you can watch the frequent launching of the Hulk coaster and perhaps meet some of Marvel's superheroes.

In **Jurassic Park**'s Camp Jurassic, paths loop through a prehistoric playground. Why not get lost for a while? Take time to explore the hallowed halls of Hogwarts and surrounding Hogsmeade village at the **Wizarding World of Harry Potter.** The **Lost Continent**, with its tents and crafters and colorful bangles, is yet another place to stop and take things in.

Toon Lagoon, the less intense alternative to Super Hero Island, provides plenty of places to explore, including a marked path that lets you follow the trail of Billy (of *Family Circus* comic fame), who's wandered off on his own. At **Seuss Landing**, find a quiet place to sit and spend some time just watching children (and adults). The closest thing here to a fountain of youth is spinning on a carousel, riding on a Seussian trolley, and meeting the fabled Cat in the Hat.

Restaurants

Three Broomsticks

$ | BRITISH | FAMILY | *Harry Potter* fans flock here to taste pumpkin juice (with hints of honey and vanilla) and butterbeer (sort of like bubbly butterscotch cream soda, or maybe shortbread cookies). They're on the menu along with barbecue and traditional British foods at this Hogsmeade restaurant. **Known for:** quirky Harry Potter atmosphere; quick and courteous service; full English breakfast daily. $ *Average main: $12* ✉ *The Wizarding World of Harry Potter: Hogsmeade, Islands of Adventure* ☎ *407/224–4233* 🌐 *www.universalorlando.com.*

Shopping

Both the Harry Potter parks conjure the spirit of the movies with atmospheric shops. You'll find the original **Ollivander's** here, though it's smaller than the branch at The Wizarding World of Harry Potter: Diagon Alley. For magical supplies, check out Dervish & Bangs. Zonko's, which shares space with Honeyduke's, sells magical tricks and jokes.

Filch's Emporium of Confiscated Goods

GIFTS/SOUVENIRS | The most wide-ranging logo and souvenir shop in Hogsmeade is this one, supposedly stocked by Argus Filch himself. ✉ *The Wizarding World of Harry Potter: Hogsmeade, Islands of Adventure* 🌐 *www.universalorlando.com/web/en/us/things-to-do/shopping/filchs-emporium-of-confiscated-goods.*

Honeyduke's

FOOD/CANDY | Come here for your chocolate frogs or every-flavor jelly beans and anything else you might want to buy from the movies. ✉ *The Wizarding World of Harry Potter: Hogsmeade, Islands of Adventure.*

Lost Continent

Just beyond a wooden bridge, huge mythical birds guard the entrance to a land where trees are hung with weathered metal lanterns, and booming thunder mixes with chimes and vaguely Celtic melodies. Farther along the path, the scene looks similar to a Renaissance fair. Seers and fortune-tellers practice their trade in tents, and the land's lone ride—Poseidon's Fury—lets you bypass lines using Universal Express Pass.

Sights

Poseidon's Fury

AMUSEMENT PARK/WATER PARK | This walk-through attraction begins only after a long walk through cool ruins guarded by the Colossus of Rhodes before a young archaeologist arrives to take you on a trek to find Poseidon's trident. Each chamber you enter looks interesting, and there's a story told in each one, but actually very little happens in most of them. Most of the time your group is simply walking through the ruins until the attraction attempts to ratchet up the entertainment for the final scene. That comes after you've walked through a water vortex and entered the final hall where, on a 180-degree movie screen, actors playing Poseidon and his archenemy appear. As they shout at each other, a memorable fire- and waterworks extravaganza erupts all around you and massive waves crash and scorching fireballs fly. This finale is loud, powerful, and hyperactive. Is it worth the investment of time? Meh. Give it a whirl if you've done everything else. **For people with disabilities:** The theater is equipped for assisted-listening devices and is wheelchair accessible. **TIP→ Stay left against the wall as you enter, and position yourself opposite the central podium. In each succeeding section of the presentation, get into the very first row, particularly if you aren't tall. Express Pass is accepted here but might not save you any time if you arrive just as a show is starting.** ✉ *Lost Continent, Islands of Adventure* ☞ *Duration: 20 mins. Crowds: Moderate. Audience: All but small kids.*

Restaurants

★ Mythos

$$$ | ECLECTIC | FAMILY | Built into a rock cliff, this enchanting eatery has a menu that includes such mainstays as pad Thai, pan-seared salmon with lemon-basil butter, seared lamb chops, and brick oven–roasted chicken. The building itself—which looks like a giant rock formation from the outside and a huge cave (albeit one with plush upholstered seating) from within—is enough to grab your attention, but so does the waterfront view of the big lagoon in the center of the theme park. **Known for:** spectacular decor; one of the best theme-park restaurants; lamb burgers, crab cake sandwiches. $ *Average main: $25* ✉ *The Lost Continent, Islands of Adventure* ☎ *407/224–4533* 🌐 *www.universalorlando.com* ⏲ *No dinner.*

Seuss Landing

This 10-acre tribute to Dr. Seuss puts you in the midst of his classic children's books. This means spending quality time with the Cat, Things 1 and 2, Horton, the Lorax, and the Grinch. From topiary sculptures to lurching lampposts to curvy fences (there was never a straight line in any of the books) to buildings that glow in lavenders, pinks, peaches, and oranges, everything seems surreal. It's a wonderful place to wrap up a day. Even the Cat would approve. All rides here except If I Ran the Zoo accept Universal Express Pass.

At Seuss Landing, Thing 1 and Thing 2 T-shirts are always a hit with couples and siblings. Or how about a couple of red-and-white-striped Cat in the Hat mugs?

The Cat in the Hat, Circus McGurkus, and fish both red and blue are among the attractions geared to the under-7 set at Seuss Landing.

Sights

Caro-Seuss-el

AMUSEMENT PARK/WATER PARK | Ordinary horse-centric merry-go-rounds seem so passé compared with the menagerie on this one: the cowfish from *McElligot's Pool,* the elephant birds from *Horton Hatches the Egg,* and the Birthday Katroo from *Happy Birthday to You!* It's an entire ark of imaginary and interactive animals—indeed, the animals' eyes blink, and their tails wag. It might be a cliché, but there's a good chance you'll feel like a kid again when you hop aboard one of these fantastic creatures. You'll love it. **For people with disabilities:** Modified mounts let guests using wheelchairs ride without having to transfer to a ride vehicle. **TIP→ Use Express Pass, and/or make this a special end to your day. Lines move pretty well, so don't be intimidated.** ⊠ *Seuss Landing, Islands of Adventure* ⊕ *www.visitorlando.com* ☞ *Duration: 2 mins. Crowds: Moderate. Audience: All ages. Height requirement: Under 48 inches must ride with an adult.*

The Cat in the Hat

AMUSEMENT PARK/WATER PARK | Enter the pages of this classic book, and you'll encounter a crazy cat ready to wreak havoc while your mom is out. As you sit on a couch that spins, whirls, and rocks its way through the house, you'll roll past 18 scenes, 30 characters, and 130 effects that will keep you on the edge of your seat. You're never alone. The mischievous cat appears balanced on a ball; hoists china on his umbrella; introduces Thing 1 and his wild sibling, Thing 2; and flies kites in the house while the voice of reason, the fish in the teapot, sounds the warning about the impending return of the family matriarch. As the tension builds, so does the fun—and kids love pointing out scenes from the book. This isn't the right ride for anyone who's pregnant; prone to motion sickness; or suffers from heart, neck, or back problems. **For people with disabilities:** The ride accommodates guests using wheelchairs and is equipped for assisted-listening devices. **TIP→ Use Express Pass and/or come early or late.** ⊠ *Seuss Landing, Islands of*

Adventure 🌐 *www.universalorlando.com* ☞ *Duration: 4½ mins. Crowds: Heavy. Audience: All ages. Height requirement: Under 48 inches must be accompanied by an adult.*

The High in the Sky Seuss Trolley Train Ride!

AMUSEMENT PARK/WATER PARK | Colorful and quirky miniature Seussian trains on separate tracks embark on a slow and pleasing tour that provides an aerial view of the area, with Seusslike narration along the way. You'll roll right through the Circus McGurkus Café Stoo-pendous and along the shores of the lagoon, where you can see the Sneetches as they enjoy the beaches. Kids love trains, and with its cartoonish design, they'll love this train even more. A treat for kids (and grown-ups, too!). **For people with disabilities:** Guests using wheelchairs must transfer to a ride vehicle. **■TIP→ Kids love trains, so plan to get in line, especially if you have young ones. Express Pass is available here.** ✉ *Seuss Landing, Islands of Adventure* 🌐 *www.universalorlando.com* ☞ *Duration: 3 mins. Crowds: Heavy. Audience: Small kids. Height requirement: 34 to 48 inches must ride with an adult.*

If I Ran the Zoo

AMUSEMENT PARK/WATER PARK | In this interactive Seussian maze, kids can leave the adults behind and have fun at their level. As they explore the playground, they'll come face-to-face with several of Dr. Seuss's fantasy creatures as they climb, jump, and crawl around them and then push buttons to animate strange and wonderful animals. Park designers have learned that kids' basic needs include eating, sleeping, and getting splashed, so they've thoughtfully added some interactive fountains as well. **For people with disabilities:** The area is wheelchair accessible. **■TIP→ If you can talk your kids into waiting, come at the end of your visit.** ✉ *Seuss Landing, Islands of Adventure* 🌐 *www.universalorlando.com* ☞ *Duration: Up to you. Crowds: Moderate. Audience: Small kids.*

One Fish, Two Fish, Red Fish, Blue Fish

AMUSEMENT PARK/WATER PARK | Dr. Seuss put elephants in trees and green eggs and ham on trains, so it doesn't seem far-fetched that his fish can circle "squirting posts" to a Jamaican beat. After a rather lengthy wait for what will seem like a very short experience, you climb into your fish, and as it spins around a center pole, you (or your child) control its up-and-down motion. The key is to follow the lyrics of the special song—if you go down when the song tells you to go up, you might be drenched courtesy of the aforementioned squirting post. Then again, if the guests ahead of you miss their cue, the water's still spraying—and will likely splash you, too. Mighty silly, mighty fun. **For people with disabilities:** Modified mounts let guests using wheelchairs ride without having to transfer to a ride vehicle. **■TIP→ Use Express Pass, and/or come early or late. Consider skipping it on your first visit.** ✉ *Seuss Landing, Islands of Adventure* 🌐 *www.universalorlando.com* ☞ *Duration: 2+ mins. Crowds: Heavy. Audience: Small kids. Height requirement: Under 48 inches must ride with an adult.*

Volcano Bay

It might come as a surprise that when you're at Volcano Bay, you're not at a water park. You're at a 25-acre *water theme park*. The distinction is clear when you arrive at the entrance and see detailed South Pacific theming woven into every attraction, every cabana, every locker, every restaurant, and every white-sand beach. It doesn't take much imagination to feel as if you really are on a South Seas island, miles from civilization but somehow surrounded by more than 30 unique experiences. Some guests drop by for a few hours after visiting Universal Studios or IOA, but with

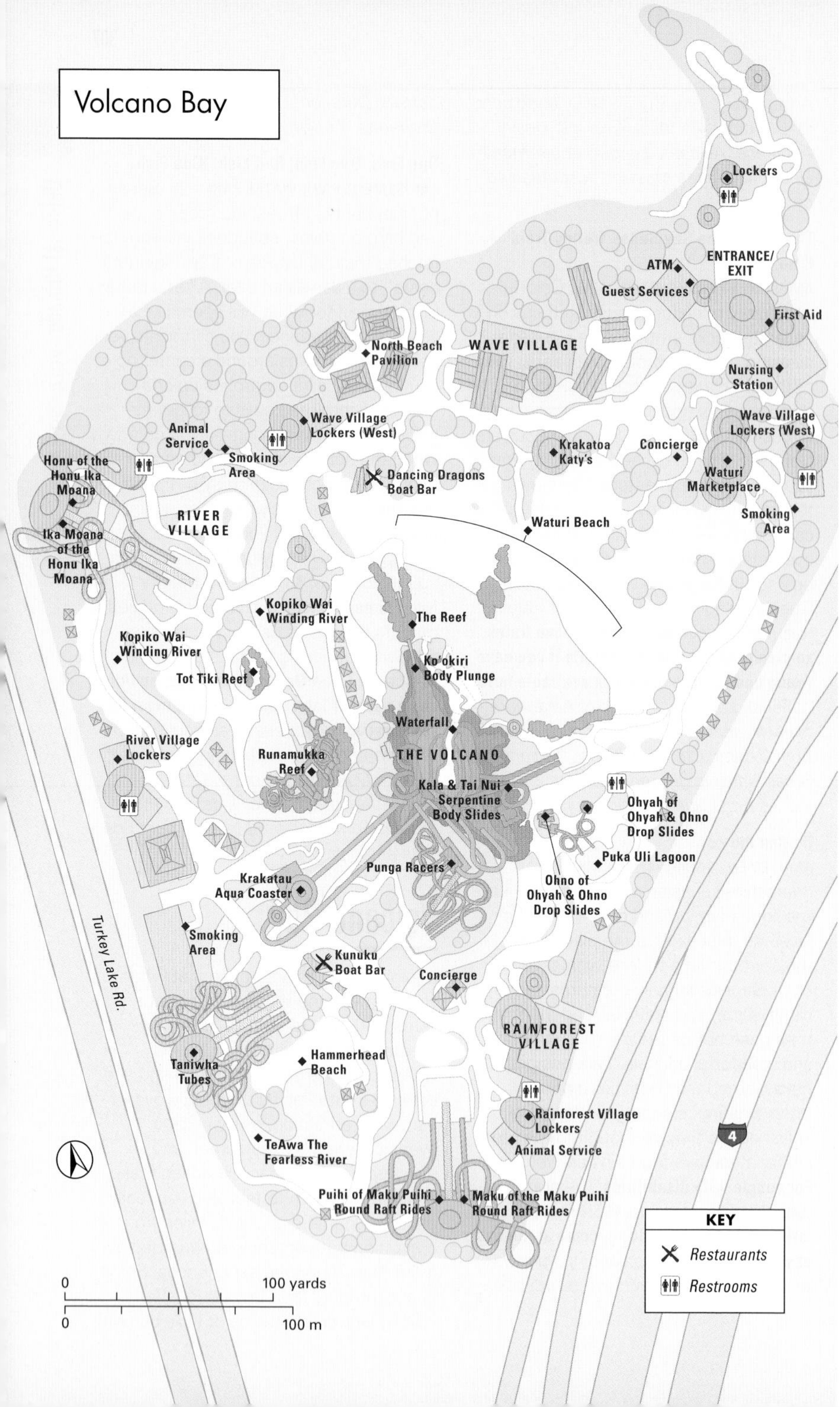

Volcano Bay

Lockers
ENTRANCE/ EXIT
ATM
Guest Services
First Aid
North Beach Pavilion
WAVE VILLAGE
Nursing Station
Wave Village Lockers (West)
Wave Village Lockers (West)
Animal Service
Smoking Area
Honu of the Honu Ika Moana
Krakatoa Katy's
Concierge
Waturi Marketplace
Dancing Dragons Boat Bar
RIVER VILLAGE
Ika Moana of the Honu Ika Moana
Waturi Beach
Smoking Area
Kopiko Wai Winding River
The Reef
Kopiko Wai Winding River
Ko'okiri Body Plunge
Tot Tiki Reef
Waterfall
River Village Lockers
THE VOLCANO
Runamukka Reef
Kala & Tai Nui Serpentine Body Slides
Ohyah of Ohyah & Ohno Drop Slides
Puka Uli Lagoon
Punga Racers
Krakatau Aqua Coaster
Ohno of Ohyah & Ohno Drop Slides
Turkey Lake Rd.
Smoking Area
Kunuku Boat Bar
Concierge
RAINFOREST VILLAGE
Taniwha Tubes
Hammerhead Beach
Rainforest Village Lockers
TeAwa The Fearless River
Animal Service
4
Puihi of Maku Puihi Round Raft Rides
Maku of the Maku Puihi Round Raft Rides

KEY
Restaurants
Restrooms

0 100 yards
0 100 m

Top Attractions

Ages 7 and Up

Kala & Tai Nui Serpentine Body Slides. Packed with a lot of twists, these twin drops inside the volcano send you through winding, serpentine tubes before you make a splashdown.

Ko'okiri Body Plunge. When a trapdoor is sprung, so begins a 12-story plunge from the top of the volcano into the pool below.

Ohyah and Ohno Drop Slides. Riding either of these sloshing tubes is a thrill that reaches its peak when you come to the end of the line. From here, it's a 4 (or 6)-foot fall into a deep pool.

TeAwa the Fearless River. More lively than your old run-of-the-mill streams, this not-so-lazy river's swift current and circuitous course takes you past attractions and through the volcano, making it worth some tube time.

Ages 6 and Under

Runamukka Reef and Tot Tiki Reef. The side-by-side play areas are filled with activities and water toys specifically designed for children under 48 inches.

the park's multidirectional wave pool, sandy beaches, winding river, multirider raft rides, body slides, and other aquatic attractions, you can definitely make a full day of it if you have the extra time to spend.

GETTING ORIENTED

Building on the foundation created by Wet 'n Wild, America's first full-scale water park and, until late 2016, one of Universal's satellite parks, Volcano Bay has given some of the "wettest and wildest" attractions a new twist, adding several other innovative designs and presenting them here in an incredibly well-detailed South Seas setting. But it's not just the attractions that are colorful, lively, and exciting—it's the entire park. You might experience moments of sensory overload from the visuals alone: the towering volcano—and the light and water shows within it—the multicolor slides and chutes, the torrents of whitewater, and the endless parade of people. But don't be overwhelmed. Just take your time, find a spot to settle down, and explore the park at your own pace.

Before you begin, you might detect one noticeable drawback: No parking. Getting to Volcano Bay requires waiting for a shuttle bus to take you to the entrance—but you'll still have to pay $26 to park at the main Universal garages if you aren't a resort guest. That plus the fact you might be carrying a beach bag filled with stuff and sitting on a bus in your bathing suit (and perhaps returning wearing a wet bathing suit and carrying a beach bag filled with stuff) can be a glitch. But, once you arrive and pass the turnstiles, all the inconvenience is forgotten, as you turn your attention to the park and the best way to see it.

One way you'll see the park is with a wristband. If you anticipated a day when you can lose track of technology, this is not that day. Every guest is given a waterproof "TapuTapu" wristband that can be paired with an account they create online, so meals and merchandise can be charged with a wave of their hand. Even if they opt out of tying it into a personal account, the wristband is still needed to reserve a place in a "virtual line" on most rides. You go to the attraction, pass the wristband by a scanner, and you're shown the estimated waiting time, with the wristband buzzing when it's time for you to return. So although you might be tied into technology, you'll avoid long waits in line.

Once you get settled in and find yourself lazing in a beach chair or reading a book in the shade of your private cabana, the day is yours. Make it as relaxing or exhilarating as you desire.

TOURING TIPS

Tap In. Volcano Bay prides itself on the technology tied to its TapuTapu wearable, waterproof wristband, a device that can assist in multiple ways including the aforementioned ability to save your place in a virtual line. In addition, its TapTu Play feature lets you try experiences throughout the park, such as shooting jets of water at guests floating down the Kopiko Wai Winding River, illuminating images in the volcano's hidden caves, or making whales spurt water at the Tot Tiki Reef. If you're comfortable with the thought of syncing your device to a credit card, use TapTu Pay to purchase meals and merchandise throughout the entire park. Link your whole party to your account—unlinking when you leave the park—and everyone can use the feature on their own wristbands.

Wanna Cabana? On the sands of Waturi Beach, there are hundreds of free beach chairs along with dozens of "premium seats"—a pair of padded loungers with an adjustable shade canopy, a built-in storage lockbox, and the services of an area attendant, who'll see to your food and drink orders (those start at $30 per day). The most luxurious offerings are private one- and two-story cabanas for between six and 16 guests. Each features padded lounge chairs, bottled water stored in a small refrigerator, complimentary fruit and snack baskets, towels and lockers, and concierge service that brings meals right to your door. There are cabanas throughout the park, with prices varying by season, from around $160 to $300 a day.

Stick Close. If you're a guest at the neighboring Cabana Bay Beach Resort, you can avoid the shuttle bus and extra parking fee by taking a walkway from the hotel to the Volcano Bay entrance. Next to Cabana Bay, the Sapphire Falls resort is also within walking distance; you just need to walk to Cabana Bay to reach the walkway (about 15 to 20 minutes). If you're staying at a premium resort (Hard Rock, Royal Pacific, Portofino Bay), shuttle buses depart directly from the hotels to Volcano Bay.

Tickets to Ride. Like you, every other guest is anxious to get inside, claim their spot, and start their day. So, as at the other theme parks, it's recommended you purchase your tickets in advance (online, at your Universal hotel, or when buying tickets for other Universal parks or activities) so you can start your day as soon as possible.

Early to Rise. By arriving early, you'll have a better choice of the better beach locations and get a lead on reaching the most popular rides and attractions. But if you're a little late, just head to the back of the park, where there's plenty more room. In fact, there are waterslides, lockers, restaurants, and refreshment kiosks in every part of the park.

Leisure Time. After you've reserved your place in a virtual line, how do you spend that wait time? Volcano Bay suggests several ways, including drifting along the Kopiko Wai Winding River, hanging out on Waturi Beach, taking time to grab a bite, or simply hanging out on your beach chair or in your cabana. You can also visit other attractions and watch for "Ride Now" signs, jumping into those attractions without losing your place in the virtual line.

Food for Thought. Peak dining times are between noon and 2 pm. Arrive an hour earlier or later, and chances are you'll avoid the long lunch lines.

Universal Orlando's new water park, Volcano Bay, has a giant water volcano as its centerpiece.

Liquid Sunshine. In the summer season especially, thunderstorms roll in from the coast—but usually don't last too long. While others pack up their things and go, duck out of the rain and into a gift shop or restaurant until the sun comes out.

Rendezvous. The park is surrounded by winding walkways that branch off toward attractions. Before you get lost, agree on a meet-up point like the visually memorable Dancing Dragons or Kunuku Boat Bars or, even simpler, Guest Services near the park entrance.

PARK AMENITIES

Baby Care: A nursing station is available near the entrance, by First Aid.

Photo ops. Volcano Bay is nothing if not a visual wonder, which is one reason there are interactive photo kiosks throughout the park. Take souvenir pictures through your TapTu Snap/My Universal Photo Access feature, and those pictures, which automatically link to your account, can be viewed, shared, and purchased later at the Waturi Marketplace.

First Aid: If you require care, tell a host or lifeguard. For more serious issues, you'll find First Aid near the entrance.

Lockers: Three different sizes of lockers are available throughout the park and can be linked up to four TapuTapu wristbands so the entire family has access. Your wristband will also unlock the locker. Without the link, lockers can be paid through cash or credit card.

Lost People and Things: Missing someone? Missing something? The first place to look is Guest Services near the entrance.

Services for People with Disabilities: There are no specific services for guests with disabilities.

Stroller Rentals: There are no stroller rentals in the park, but you're welcome to bring your own.

Wheelchair Rentals: Due to the nature of the park, there are no wheelchair rentals here.

Where to Snack: The range of dining options is impressive, with kiosks and sit-down restaurants flavored with South Pacific–inspired dishes, from mahimahi sandwiches to tropical salads to chocolate pineapple upside-down cake.

Sights

Hammerhead Beach

AMUSEMENT PARK/WATER PARK | If you arrive too late to find a prime spot on Waturi Beach, this smaller, secluded beach near the back of the park is the perfect alternative. Less crowded, it's between the entrance to TeAwa the Fearless River and the Maku and Puihi Round Raft Rides. ✉ *Volcano Bay* 🌐 *www.universalorlando.com.*

Honu of the Honu Ika Moana

AMUSEMENT PARK/WATER PARK | This attraction comes stamped with the postscript "Turtle and Whale," which simply means that when you reach the top you'll find two tubes (the other being the "Ika Moana" of Honu Ika Moana). It's similar to other rides where you slip into an inner tube and then ride through a slick channel, but the difference here is that you join three others in a four-person raft. Although the speed isn't as fast as single-rider attractions, the sensations are just as enjoyable as the raft sloshes and sweeps around huge walls and rounded corners, into tubes and then out again to flop into the final pool. ✉ *Volcano Bay* 🌐 *www.universalorlando.com* ☞ *Height requirement: 48 inches minimum.*

Ika Moana of the Honu Ika Moana

AMUSEMENT PARK/WATER PARK | The counterpart to the Honu four-passenger raft is a few feet away in this five-passenger raft. The ride is slow, sloshy, and easy to handle, even when the raft glides around turns and passes over geysers that erupt like whale spouts. Accepts Universal Express Pass. Wheelchair guests must transfer to raft. ✉ *Volcano Bay* 🌐 *www.universalorlando.com* ☞ *Minimum Height requirement: 42 inches minimu; under 48 inches must ride with an adult.*

Kala & Tai Nui Serpentine Body Slides

AMUSEMENT PARK/WATER PARK | A sign stating that this is a "freefall slide that starts when a trap door is removed" could be a warning to some, an invitation to others. If you're among the latter, then step into the volcano that's the centerpiece of the park, and begin your ascent. Scaling what seems like endless stairwells, you'll be sprinkled with water dripping from intertwined blue and green tubes twisting overhead. These are Kala and Tai Nui, which are soon to be your ride home. As you climb higher and higher, occasionally you'll catch a wonderful aerial view of the park (as well as neighboring I–4), a vista that reveals just how far you've come—and just how far you'll fall. When you enter your tube, cross your arms, cross your feet, and then just wait for gravity to do its stuff. When the door drops, so do you, shooting down the slick, splashing tube as it sends you into high, banking corners and spinning around for nearly 25 seconds in a thrilling race (with the person in the opposite tube) to a splashdown finish. ✉ *Volcano Bay* 🌐 *www.universalorlando.com* ☞ *Height requirement: 48 inches minimum.*

Ko'okiri Body Plunge

AMUSEMENT PARK/WATER PARK | The towering, steaming volcano commands attention from every part of the park. What commands the most attention from within the volcano itself is this simple, yet extraordinarily effective, experience. It's based on the concept that a body remains at rest until acted upon by another force. You step onto a seemingly solid floor that supports your body weight; the "other force" is when the door disappears. That's when the reaction is your body falling through the void and into a 12-story drop that has you flying on a dizzying descent that rockets you right into the splashdown pool. Rinse and repeat. ✉ *Universal Orlando Resort* 🌐 *www.universalorlando.com* ☞ *Height requirement: 48 inches minimum.*

Kopiko Wai Winding River

AMUSEMENT PARK/WATER PARK | Encircling a substantial portion of the park and winding through the lush foliage, this lazy river lets you go with the flow. As you drift on an inner tube past tropical surroundings, you're occasionally sprayed by streams of water triggered by guests along the banks. When you enter Stargazer's Cavern inside the volcano, the scenery changes again—this time to a brilliant night sky. There are several entrance and exit points along the way (some entrances are wheelchair accessible) as well as lifeguards keeping an eye on things. ✉ *Volcano Bay* 🌐 *www.universalorlando.com* ☞ *Height requirement: Under 48 inches must wear a life vest.*

Krakatau Aqua Coaster

AMUSEMENT PARK/WATER PARK | A sign that reads "Greater than any man-made thrill" greets you at this attraction. But is it really greater? You'll find out after you slip into a four-person canoe that speeds down a toboggan-style run, whips around corners, shoots you through dark, enclosed tubes, and then drops you down steep falls again and again and over and over until you're alternately screaming and laughing. A quick 60 seconds later, you plunge toward the finish through a shimmering waterfall. So, yeah, it's pretty great. Accepts Universal Express Pass. Wheelchair guests must transfer to "canoe."✉ *Volcano Bay* 🌐 *www.universalorlando.com* ☞ *Minimum Height requirement: 42 inches minimum; under 48 inches must ride with an adult.*

Maku of the Maku Puihi Round Raft Rides

AMUSEMENT PARK/WATER PARK | It will take several flights of stairs to reach the starting point of this ride, one that pairs you up with as many as five others on a rafting adventure. After settling in, a little push is all it takes to have gravity take over and water wash you into a humongous enclosed tube for a short stretch before you are spat out into the daylight and into a massive basin where your forward motion sends you up toward the rim (but not over it). From here, you wash back down again and slide into another tube before the cycle repeats, taking you through another tube followed by a circular tour of another basin before finally flowing into a calm pool. Universal Express Pass accepted. ✉ *Volcano Bay* 🌐 *www.universalorlando.com* ☞ *Height requirement: 42 inches minimum; under 48 inches must ride with an adult.*

Ohno of Ohyah & Ohno Drop Slides

AMUSEMENT PARK/WATER PARK | At some point, you'll realize that the most thrilling rides at Volcano Bay are ones that involve climbing several flights of stairs. Height is what makes thossuch attractions work, and this is one of them. On your way to the top, you cross a deep chasm and walk across rope bridges before finding yourself at the entrance to the Ohno tube (Ohyah is right over there). Like its counterpart, you'll slip and slide through a serpentine run until the tube runs out and you're flying out on a 6-foot drop into the waters at the base of Krakatau. Universal Express Pass accepted. ✉ *Volcano Bay* 🌐 *www.universalorlando.com* ☞ *Height requirement: 48 inches minimum.*

Ohyah of Ohyah & Ohno Drop Slides

AMUSEMENT PARK/WATER PARK | You don't need a mat; you don't need a raft; you just need *you* to enjoy the first of two side-by-side body slides that snake around corners and shoot into straightaways on a fast-paced slide to the finish. On this side of the ride, the finish comes with a 4-foot drop into a swirling pool. Oh yeah! Universal Express Pass accepted. ✉ *Volcano Bay* 🌐 *www.universalorlando.com* ☞ *Height requirement: 48 inches minimum.*

Puihi of Maku Puihi Round Raft Rides
AMUSEMENT PARK/WATER PARK | This multi-person rafting ride follows a journey similar to that of its neighbor, Maku. But this one includes a few different twists and turns—primarily one with a moment of zero-gravity hang time as you spring out of an immense funnel. The twists keep coming as you cling to the raft handles and rock and roll to a spectacular splash finish. Universal Express Pass accepted. ✉ *Volcano Bay* 🌐 *www.universalorlando.com* ☞ *Height requirement: 42 inches minimum; under 48 inches must ride with an adult.*

Puka Uli Lagoon
AMUSEMENT PARK/WATER PARK | A relaxing place for families, this small leisure pool is relatively secluded from the park's most active areas (albeit beside the splashdown pool of the Ohyah and Ohno slides) and includes elements that kids will appreciate—namely jets of water they can spray and tropical bongo drums they can beat. Wheelchair guests can transfer into pool. ✉ *Volcano Bay* 🌐 *www.universalorlando.com* ☞ *Height requirement: Under 48 inches must wear a life vest.*

Punga Racers
AMUSEMENT PARK/WATER PARK | For some friendly family competition, grab a mat and pick a lane. There are four tracks on this attraction, and once you have your mat, you'll launch yourself into a tube that twists and turns and then changes to an open-air slide just to keep things interesting. The first person to cross the finish line of this race receives a celebratory spray of water. Universal Express Pass accepted. ✉ *Volcano Bay* 🌐 *www.universalorlando.com* ☞ *Height requirement: 42 inches minimum; under 48 inches must ride with an adult.*

The Reef
AMUSEMENT PARK/WATER PARK | This intimate leisure pool has one of the best views in the park, at the base of Krakatau and beside the clear acrylic tube that carries those who've braved the Ko'okiri Body Plunge. You'll often see people lined up along the tube, watching as guests drop out of sight at the top of the mountain and reappear seconds later as they flash past on their way to a splashy finish. With its own waterfall, this is a nice spot to find a little peace and quiet that's still close to many of the park's main attractions. Guests can transfer from wheelchair. ✉ *Volcano Bay* 🌐 *www.universalorlando.com* ☞ *Height requirement: Under 48 inches must wear a life vest.*

Runamukka Reef
AMUSEMENT PARK/WATER PARK | This colorful, creative aquatic playground gives kids plenty to discover through a wide range of toys and activities that'll keep them busy and entertained. There are shallow wading areas, low-pitched slides (that probably seem stupendously huge from their perspective), spray guns, bubbling geysers, and dump cups. Wheelchair guests can transfer into water. ✉ *Volcano Bay* 🌐 *www.universalorlando.com* ☞ *Height requirement: Under 48 inches must wear a life vest.*

Taniwha Tubes
AMUSEMENT PARK/WATER PARK | Two slides are better than one, but this attraction doubles that with four slides that mimic the snaking trunks and twisting roots of puka trees. The tubes alternate in color (green and blue), and they alternate in experiences from channels that are completely enclosed for the entire run to tracks that are enclosed until they suddenly reveal the open air and use your speed to send you up on a high-banked turn. So take it for a spin. Or two. Or four. Universal Express Pass accepted. ✉ *Volcano Bay* 🌐 *www.universalorlando.com* ☞ *Height requirement: 42 inches minimum; under 48 inches must ride with an adult.*

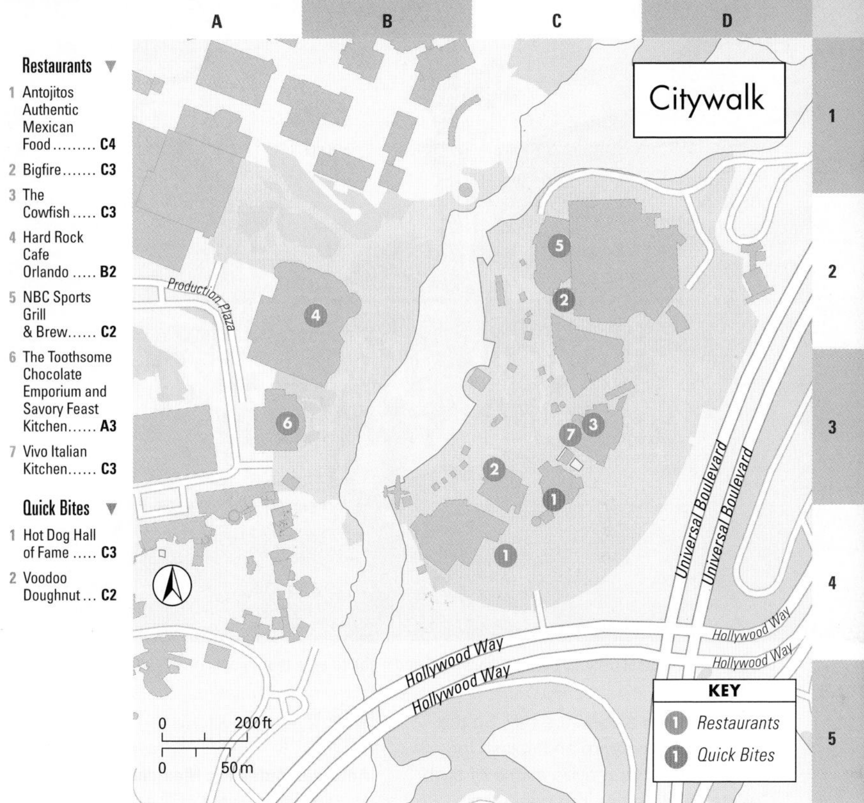

TeAwa the Fearless River

AMUSEMENT PARK/WATER PARK | This is definitely not your typical gentle river. The water's fairly shallow in this waterway, but since it flows at a pretty good clip the strong current means life vests are required (and that's on top of the inner tube you're on top of). There are several things to like about this ride, and one of those is its duration. Unlike other rides that are as short as 10 seconds, it takes a good six minutes to completely experience this river ride. In addition, the river flows past various areas of the park, passing beneath bridges and rides and by restaurants from Hammerhead Beach through the volcano and into the Rainforest Village, all of which reveal a new perspective on the village of Volcano Bay. Wheelchair guests can transfer into water. ✉ *Volcano Bay* 🌐 *www.universalorlando.com* ☞ *Height requirement: 42 inches minimum; under 48 inches must ride with an adult.*

Tot Tiki Reef

AMUSEMENT PARK/WATER PARK | Directly across from Runamukka Reef is this shallow-water play area with kid-sized slides, spraying fountains, singing whales, and a miniature water volcano. Guests can transfer from wheelchairs. ✉ *Volcano Bay* 🌐 *www.universalorlando.com.*

Waturi Beach

AMUSEMENT PARK/WATER PARK | In the shadow of Krakatau, the volcano that looms over the park, is this wide beach with chairs by the hundreds. Arrive early to claim the best spot, or upgrade by renting a premium seat that includes a sun canopy. Depending on your mood, you can park yourself in a chair and do absolutely nothing, or venture into the water where every so often a set of

CityWalk is Universal Orlando's dining, shopping, and nightlife area that's popular with both visitors and locals.

waves washes across the bay. So the choice is yours: swim and splash, or rest and relax. Or maybe a little of both. Guests can transfer into water from wheelchair. ✉ *Volcano Bay* 🌐 *www.universalorlando.com* ☞ *Height requirement: Under 48 inches must wear a life vest.*

CityWalk

Restaurants, bars, clubs, shops, live entertainment, and movie theaters make Universal CityWalk an attraction on its own. The upbeat expanse serves as the entrance to both Universal Orlando theme parks—you can't reach the parks from the parking lot without walking through—and is an after-dark destination for tourists and locals alike.

Restaurants

Antojitos Authentic Mexican Food

$$ | **MEXICAN** | **FAMILY** | The massive and very noisy Antojitos brings the specialties of Mexican cantinas and food carts to CityWalk. The outside looks like it's been spray-painted with shocking pastels. **Known for:** noisy atmosphere; table-side guacamole; beer-braised goat stew. 💲 *Average main: $17* ✉ *Universal CityWalk, 6000 Universal Blvd., CityWalk* ☎ *407/224–2807* 🌐 *www.universalorlando.com* 🕓 *No lunch.*

Bigfire

$$$ | **AMERICAN** | A flashback inspired by camping trips and cooking over an open flame, this new-in-2020 restaurant features a menu that also brings back memories. Among the entrées are buttermilk fried chicken, beer-glazed scallops, pork chops, lamb chops, skillet-roasted half-chicken, and the Heathstone Seafood Bake, which includes wood oven-baked northern whitefish, shrimp, cold water mussels, andouille sausage, fresh corn, red potatoes, and lemon butter. **Known for:** open-fire cooking; casual, nostalgic atmosphere; extensive menu. *$ Average main: $25 ✉ Universal Orlando CityWalk, 6000 Universal Blvd., CityWalk ☎ 407/224–2074 🌐 www.universalorlando.com/web/en/us/things-to-do/dining/bigfire.*

The Cowfish

$$ | **BURGER** | **FAMILY** | Burgers, sushi, and a combo the founders call "burgushi" bring Universal goers to this contemporary second-story restaurant. The setting is flashy, with colorful booths and playful decor touches complementing an array of video screens showing schools of fish swimming by, aquarium-style. **Known for:** unusual combinations of beef and fish sushi; signature "fusion" rolls; large burger menu. *$ Average main: $15 ✉ Universal CityWalk, 6000 Universal Blvd., CityWalk ☎ 407/224–9255 🌐 www.thecowfish.com ⊗ No lunch.*

Hard Rock Cafe Orlando

$$$ | **AMERICAN** | **FAMILY** | Built to resemble Rome's Colosseum yet surprisingly sophisticated inside, this 1,000-seat restaurant is huge, yet getting a seat at lunch or dinner can still require a long wait. The music is always loud, and the walls are filled with rock memorabilia. **Known for:** largest Hard Rock in the world; on-site smoked barbecue; cowboy rib-eye steak. *$ Average main: $23 ✉ Universal CityWalk, 6050 Universal Blvd., CityWalk ☎ 407/351–7625 🌐 www.hardrockcafe.com.*

NBC Sports Grill & Brew

$ | **AMERICAN** | **FAMILY** | Though it's not a working brewery (sorry to say, the giant beer tanks are just for show), the more than 100 beers in bottles and on tap should provide something for everyone. If not, they can be distracted by the more than 100 giant TV screens, which are everywhere. **Known for:** massive burgers; giant TV screens at every turn; more than 100 beers on tap and bottled. *$ Average main: $14 ✉ Universal CityWalk, CityWalk ☎ 407/224–3663 🌐 universalorlando.com.*

The Toothsome Chocolate Emporium and Savory Feast Kitchen

$$$ | **AMERICAN** | A steampunk atmosphere of gizmos, gears, pulleys, belts, and smokestacks is the backdrop for this very popular restaurant, where chocolate and sweets rule. Desserts—ranging from artisanal milk shakes and sumptuous sundaes to chocolate brownie bark, bacon brittle, and salted caramel flan—and are big draws. **Known for:** super-duper stupendous milk shakes; creative confections; lots of savory entrées in case dessert isn't enough. *$ Average main: $25 ✉ Universal Orlando CityWalk, 6000 Universal Blvd., CityWalk ☎ 407/224–3663 🌐 www.universalorlando.com/web/en/us/things-to-do/dining/toothsome-chocolate-emporium-and-savory-feast-kitchen.*

Vivo Italian Kitchen

$$$ | **ITALIAN** | House-made pasta and inventive cocktails are highlights at the ultrahip Vivo, which is styled after a trendy Roman nightclub. The waiters are attentive, the food—mussels marinara, lamb ragu, squid ink seafood—is quietly impressive, and the blazing wood-fired oven makes almost instantaneous pizzas. **Known for:** wood-fired pizza; fresh-made pasta; Tuscan chicken and beef specialties. *$ Average main: $22 ✉ Universal CityWalk, 6000 Universal Blvd., CityWalk ☎ 407/224–2691 🌐 www.universalorlando.com.*

Coffee and Quick Bites

Voodoo Doughnut has developed a cult following, which explains why you'll spy guests carrying to-go boxes packed with some of the more than 50 types of doughnuts they make each day. Selections like the Dirt Doughnut, Memphis Mafia, and Bacon Maple Bar are fuel for a day in the parks. For a less sugary snack,

CityWalk's Hard Rock Café is not only the largest in the world, but its Hard Rock Live concert hall draws big-name acts to Orlando year-round.

the **Hot Dog Hall of Fame** has a menu of specialty hot dogs from stadiums across America: Boston, New York, Washington, Chicago, Kansas City, and points farther west.

Nightlife

Bob Marley—A Tribute to Freedom

BARS/PUBS | Modeled after the King of Reggae's home in Kingston, Jamaica (even down to the air-conditioning window units), in a way this nightclub is also part museum, with more than 100 photographs and paintings showing pivotal moments in Marley's life. Though the place does serve Jamaican-influenced meals, most patrons are at the cozy bar or by the patio, where they can be jammin' to a (loud) live band that plays nightly. For a nice souvenir, pose by the wonderful Marley statue outside the club. Sunday is ladies' night from 10 pm to 2 am. ✉ *CityWalk* ☎ *407/224–2692* 🌐 *www.universalorlando.com/web/en/us/things-to-do/dining/bob-marley-a-tribute-to-freedom/index.html.*

CityWalk's Rising Star

BARS/PUBS | Here you and other hopeful (and hopeless) singers can really let loose in front of a live audience. You'll croon to recorded tracks on Sunday and Monday, but between Tuesday and Saturday, you'll be accompanied by a live band complete with backup singers. A full bar is always on tap. Friday and Saturday are reserved for an over-21 crowd. ✉ *6000 Universal Blvd., CityWalk* ☎ *407/224–2961* 🌐 *www.universalorlando.com/web/en/us/things-to-do/entertainment/rising-star-karaoke/index.html* 🎫 *$7 cover charge.*

the groove

BARS/PUBS | In this cavernous, multilevel hall, images flicker rapidly on several screens, with the lights, music, and mayhem appealing to a mostly under-30 crowd. Prepare for lots of fog, swirling lights, and sweaty bodies. The '70s-style Green Room is filled with beanbag chairs and everything you threw out when Duran Duran hit the charts. The Blue Room is sci-fi Jetson-y, and the Red Room is hot and romantic in a bordello sort of way. The music is equally diverse: Top 40, hip-hop, R&B, techno, and the occasional live band. When you need a break, step out to the balcony for some fresh air and a look over the action of CityWalk. **TIP→ There's a $7 cover charge after 10 pm.** ✉ *6000 Universal Blvd., CityWalk* ☎ *407/224–2692* 🌐 *www.universalorlando.com/web/en/us/things-to-do/entertainment/the-groove/index.html.*

Hard Rock Cafe

MUSIC CLUBS | The Hard Rock Cafe here is the largest on Earth, which means you can see plenty of memorabilia, including such Beatles rarities as John Lennon's famous New York City T-shirt, Paul's original lyrics for "Let It Be," and the doors from London's Abbey Road studios plus hundreds of other fascinating collectibles. And the food's great, too. Next door, the Hard Rock Live concert hall (The Coliseum of Rock) hosts comedians, solo acts, and internationally recognized bands that make it one of the most popular venues at Universal. A few drawbacks: the seating's not the greatest, and if you arrive at the door carrying a large purse or bags, it won't be time to rock, it'll be time to walk—about a quarter-mile back to the parking garage to stow your stuff. For showtimes, call 407/351–5483. ✉ *CityWalk* 🌐 *www.hardrocklive.com.*

Jimmy Buffett's Margaritaville

BARS/PUBS | Buffett tunes fill the air at the restaurant here and at the Volcano, Land Shark, and 12 Volt bars. Inside there's a miniature Pan Am Clipper suspended from the ceiling, music videos projected onto sails, limbo and hula-hoop contests, a huge margarita blender that erupts "when the volcano blows," and live music nightly—everything that Parrotheads need to roost. Across the promenade, another full-size seaplane (emblazoned with "Jimmy Buffett, Captain") is the setting for the Lone Palm Airport, a pleasing and surprisingly popular outdoor waterfront bar. ✉ *6000 Universal Studios Plaza, Suite 704, CityWalk* ☎ *407/224–2155* 🌐 *www.universalorlando.com/web/en/us/things-to-do/dining/jimmy-buffetts-margaritaville/index.html.*

Pat O'Brien's

BARS/PUBS | An exact reproduction of the legendary New Orleans original, this comes complete with flaming fountain and dueling pianists who are playing for highly entertained regulars and visitors—even on weekday afternoons. Outside, the cozy and welcoming Patio Bar has a wealth of tables and chairs, allowing you to do nothing but enjoy the outdoors and your potent, rum-based Hurricanes in Orlando's version of the Big Easy. ✉ *6000 Universal Blvd., CityWalk* ☎ *407/224–2692* 🌐 *www.universalorlando.com/web/en/us/things-to-do/dining/pat-o-briens/index.html.*

Red Coconut Club

BARS/PUBS | Paying tribute to kitsch design of the 1950s, the interior here is part Vegas lounge, part Cuban club, and part Polynesian tiki bar. It's "where tropical meets trendy." There are three full bars on two levels, signature martinis, an extensive wine list, and VIP bottle service. Hang out in the lounge, on the balcony, or at the bar. On a budget? Take advantage of the daily happy hours and gourmet appetizer menu. Latin music takes over from 8 pm to midnight, then a DJ from midnight until 2 am. Thursday is ladies' night. **TIP→ There's a $7 cover charge after 10 pm.** ✉ *6000 Universal Blvd., CityWalk* ☎ *407/224–2425* 🌐 *www.universalorlando.com/web/en/us/things-to-do/entertainment/red-coconut-club/index.html.*

Performing Arts

FILM

AMC Universal Cineplex 20 with IMAX

FILM | Why spend your time watching a movie when you're on vacation? Who cares? It's your vacation. At the AMC Universal Cineplex, there are 20 screens and 5,000 seats in a bi-level theater that provides an escape from the crowds, and, in summer, the Florida heat. In addition to "meal deals" that include admission to a show, there are nightly midnight movies. Extra fees apply for IMAX and 3-D showings. ✉ *CityWalk* ☎ *407/354–3374 box office* 🌐 *www.universalorlando.com/web/en/us/things-to-do/entertainment/amc-universal-cineplex/index.html.*

THEATER

Blue Man Group

THEATER | FAMILY | At their own venue, the ever-innovative Blue Man Group continues to pound out new music, sketches, and audience interaction. Attempting to understand the apps on a GiPad (a gigantic iPad), they might appear clueless and perplexed about cutting-edge technology (which for them can be as basic as a can of paint), but they're always excited when they can drum out rhythms on lengths of PVC pipes and throw a rave party finale for all in attendance. The show is a surreal comic masterpiece. Three levels of admission (Poncho, Tier 1, and Tier 2) hint at how messy things can get when the Blue Men cut loose. ✉ *CityWalk* ☎ *407/258–3626* 🌐 *www.universalorlando.com* 🎫 *From $60.*

Shopping

This 30-acre entertainment and retail complex is at the hub of promenades leading to Universal Studios and IOA. Shops here sell fine jewelry, cool beachwear, fashionable clothing, and stylish accessories. The best stores are near the entrance/exit of the complex.

Fresh Produce

CLOTHING | Featuring fashions that look right at home in sunny Florida, this boutique showcases comfortable and colorful swimwear, blouses, Capri slacks, dresses, footwear, beach gear, and accessories designed for coastal comfort. ✉ *CityWalk* ☎ *407/363–9363* 🌐 *www.universalorlando.com/web/en/us/things-to-do/shopping/fresh-produce/index.html.*

Quiet Flight

CLOTHING | Granted the closest beach is about 60 miles east, but you can still get outfitted like a surfer at this shop, which sports an inventory featuring brand names such as Billabong, Quicksilver, Hurley, and Oakley. In addition to shorts and shirts, Quiet Flight also sells sandals, watches, sunglasses (Ray-Ban, Prada, and D&G among the featured names)—and surfboards! ✉ *CityWalk* ☎ *407/224–2125* 🌐 *www.universalorlando.com/web/en/us/things-to-do/shopping/quiet-flight-surf-shop/index.html.*

Universal Orlando Resort Area

Universal Orlando's three original on-site hotels were built in a little luxury enclave that has everything you need so you never have to leave Universal property. In minutes, you can walk from any hotel to CityWalk, or take a ferry to the parks. Cabana Bay Beach Resort and Lowes Sapphire Falls are farther afield but are adjacent to the new Volcano Bay.

In 2020, at the site of Universal's former waterpark, Wet n' Wild, the second of two hotels opened at the Endless Summer Resort: the Dockside Inn and Suites joined the Surfside Inn and Suites as a "Value" option—the least expensive of four tiers of pricing (the others are Prime Value, Preferred, and Premier.

A burgeoning hotel district across Kirkman Road and down to Sand Lake Road offers convenient accommodations and some even less expensive rates. Although these off-property hotels don't have the perks of the on-site places, you'll probably be smiling when you see your hotel bill.

Restaurants

BiCE Ristorante Orlando

$$$$ | ITALIAN | Trendy, pricey Bice is the Orlando unit of an international upscale chain of Italian restaurants. Bice (pronounced "*BEACH*-ay") is an Italian nickname for Beatrice, as in Beatrice Ruggeri, who founded the original Milan location of this family restaurant in 1926. **Known for:** upscale Italian cuisine; house-made pasta; braised veal osso buco. *Average main: $34 ✉ Loews Portofino Bay Hotel, 5601 Universal Blvd., Universal Orlando Resort ☎ 407/503–1415 🌐 www.orlando.bicegroup.com ⏲ No lunch.*

Islands Dining Room

$$$ | ASIAN FUSION | FAMILY | An airy room with a tropical decor and menu items inspired by the Pacific Rim, Islands not only serves breakfast and dinner, it also has a play area that keeps tots entertained. On Monday, Wednesday, and Thursday night, diners are treated to visits from assorted characters such as Scooby Doo and Shaggy—at no extra cost. **Known for:** character dining; breakfast buffet; extensive kids' menus. *Average main: $22 ✉ Loews Royal Pacific Resort, 6300 Hollywood Way, Universal Orlando Resort ☎ 407/503–3463 🌐 www.loewshotels.com ⏲ No lunch.*

Jake's American Bar & Grill

$$$ | AMERICAN | FAMILY | From noon through the evening, Jake's is more of a gastropub with an air-flight theme. Menus range from flatbreads and burgers to kale salad, lasagna, salmon, and lobster mac n' cheese. **Known for:** character breakfast; beer festival events; crawfish chowder. *Average main: $27 ✉ Loews Royal Pacific Resort, 6300 Hollywood Way, Universal Orlando Resort ☎ 407/503–3463 🌐 www.universalorlando.com.*

The Kitchen

$$$$ | MODERN AMERICAN | FAMILY | Contemporary yet comfy, this hotel restaurant tends to straddle various worlds. Its menu has comfort food with creative upscale twists. **Known for:** burgers and rotisserie chicken; special Kids' Crib area; visiting rock stars. *Average main: $31 ✉ Hard Rock Hotel, 5800 Universal Blvd., Universal Orlando Resort ☎ 407/503–3463 🌐 www.hardrockhotelorlando.com.*

Mama Della's Ristorante

$$$ | ITALIAN | Like stepping into Mama Della's dining room, this playfully themed Italian restaurant happens to have excellent food. The premise is that you're eating at a home-turned-restaurant—there's an actual "Mama Della" who appears nightly—and that warmth enhances the experience (as does the serenade by an accordionist, guitar player, and vocalist). **Known for:** intimate New York/Neapolitan environment; better-than-usual Italian cuisine; homemade gnocchi. *Average main: $30 ✉ Loews Portofino Bay Hotel, 5601 Universal Blvd., Universal Orlando Resort ☎ 407/503–3463 🌐 www.loewshotels.com ⏲ No lunch.*

The Palm Orlando

$$$$ | STEAKHOUSE | With its dark-wood interior and hundreds of framed celebrity caricatures, this pricey restaurant resembles its famed New York City namesake. For most diners, the steaks steal the show. **Known for:** steak, steak, and steak; surprisingly superb seafood starters; Italian dishes from old family recipes. *Average main: $42 ✉ Hard Rock Hotel, 5800 Universal Blvd., Universal Orlando Resort ☎ 407/503–7256 🌐 www.thepalm.com ⏲ No lunch.*

★ **Strong Water Tavern**

$$ | CARIBBEAN | Billed as a "hotel lounge," Strong Water breaks all the rules for hotel dining. The surroundings are comfortable, and the attentive staff serves some of the most memorable food in Orlando. **Known for:** Caribbean food and drink; surprisingly popular curried goat; extensive rum menu. *Average main: $20 ✉ Loews Sapphire Falls Resort at Universal Orlando, 6601 Adventure Way,*

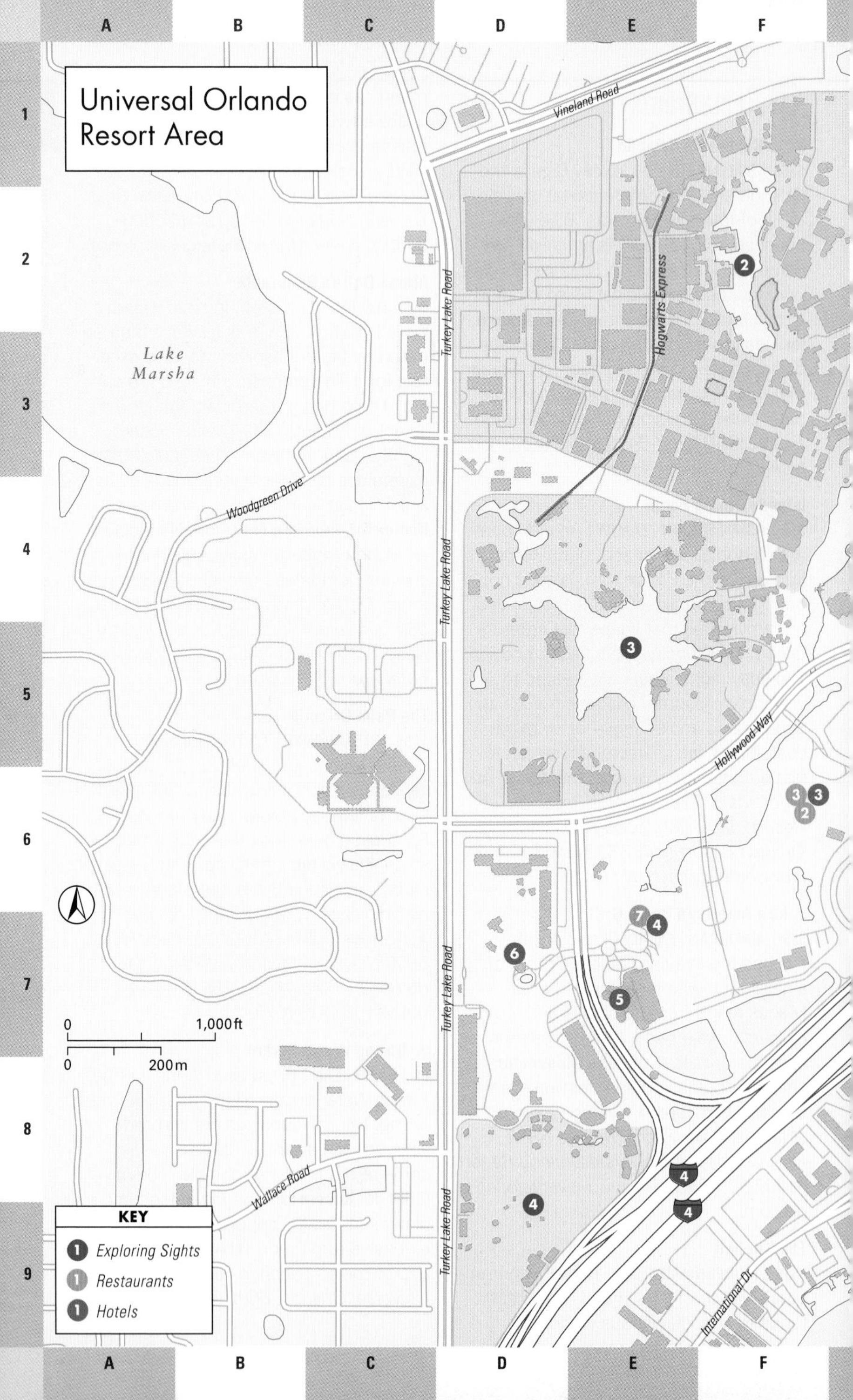

Universal Orlando Resort Area
Vineland Road
Hogwarts Express
Turkey Lake Road
Lake Marsha
Woodgreen Drive
Hollywood Way
Wallace Road
International Dr.
0
1,000 ft
0
200 m
KEY
Exploring Sights
Restaurants
Hotels

Sights

1 Universal CityWalk Orlando **G4**
2 Universal Studios Florida **F2**
3 Universal's Islands of Adventure **E5**
4 Universal's Volcano Bay **D9**

Restaurants

1 BiCE Ristorante Orlando **H1**
2 Islands Dining Room **F6**
3 Jake's American Bar & Grill....... **F6**
4 The Kitchen......................... **G3**
5 Mama Della's Ristorante........... **I1**
6 The Palm Orlando.................. **G3**
7 Strong Water Tavern **E7**
8 Trattoria Del Porto **I1**

Hotels

1 Hard Rock Hotel at Universal Orlando Resort......... **G2**
2 Loews Portofino Bay at Universal Orlando Resort...... **H1**
3 Loews Royal Pacific Resort at Universal Orlando Resort....... **F6**
4 Loews Sapphire Falls Resort at Universal Orlando Resort....... **E7**
5 Universal's Aventura Hotel **E7**
6 Universal's Cabana Bay Beach Resort....................... **D7**
7 Universal's Endless Summer Resort - Dockside Inn and Suites **H9**
8 Universal's Endless Summer Resort - Surfside Inn and Suites **G9**

Loews Portofino Bay Hotel at Universal Orlando

West Orlando ☎ 407/503–5000 ⊕ loews-hotels.com/sapphire-falls-resort/dining/lounges.

Trattoria del Porto

$$$ | **ITALIAN** | **FAMILY** | Overlooking a tranquil harbor, this is a family-friendly option with a dash of Italiano. Whether dining indoors or out, you can begin with a breakfast buffet of hot dishes, omelets, baked goods, and fruit; dinner features starters, sandwiches, and chef specialties (Thai chili swordfish, ocean bass, flat-iron steaks), as well as the Pasta Cucina option, where you can be your own chef, stirring up a variety of pastas, sauces, and fresh ingredients cooked to your specifications. **Known for:** family meals; in-house pastry chef; children's play area with cribs and high chairs. [$] *Average main: $26 ✉ Loews Portofino Bay Hotel, 5601 Universal Blvd., Universal Orlando Resort ☎ 407/503–3463 ⊕ www.loewshotels.com/portofino-bay-hotel.*

Hotels

Hard Rock Hotel at Universal Orlando Resort

$$$$ | **HOTEL** | Music rules in this mission-style building, from public areas decorated with rock memorabilia—Elvis's pajamas, Lady Gaga's latex gown, and Elton John's boots—to stylishly modern rooms, with deluxe bed linens, an entertainment center with a flat-panel TV, and lots of accessible media-device plugs. **Pros:** shuttle, water taxi, or short walk to Universal Parks and CityWalk; Universal Express Unlimited pass included; charge privileges extend to the other on-property Universal hotels. **Cons:** rooms and meals are pricey; fee for parking; loud rock music in public areas, even the pool. [$] *Rooms from: $390 ✉ 5800 Universal Blvd., CityWalk ☎ 407/503–7625, 800/232–7827 ⊕ www.hardrockhotelorlando.com 650 rooms No meals.*

★ Loews Portofino Bay at Universal Orlando Resort
$$$$ | **HOTEL** | The charm and romance of Portofino, Italy, are conjured up at this lovely luxury resort, where part of the fun is exploring the waterfront Italian "village" from end to end; the other part is relaxing in the well-appointed rooms (decorated in aqua and cream, with deluxe beds and flat-screen TVs) and by one of the three pools that offer aquatic fun or peaceful sunning. **Pros:** large spa; short walk or ferry ride to CityWalk, Universal; Universal Express Unlimited pass included. **Cons:** rooms and meals are pricey; daily fee for parking; not convenient to Disney parks. *Rooms from: $414 ✉ 5601 Universal Blvd., Universal Orlando Resort ☎ 407/503–1000, 800/232–7827 🌐 www.loewshotels.com/portofino-bay-hotel 795 rooms No meals.*

Loews Royal Pacific Resort at Universal Orlando Resort
$$$ | **RESORT** | **FAMILY** | This Pacific Rim–themed hotel lies amid 53 serene acres of lush shrubs, soaring bamboo, orchids, and palms and features lots of amenities, including a weekly Polynesian-style luau, daily character breakfasts, a 12,000-square-foot lagoon-style pool, an interactive water-play area, and kid-friendly activities. **Pros:** Universal Express Unlimited pass included; character dining; shuttle to CityWalk and parks. **Cons:** rooms can feel smallish; steep parking fee; can be busy with conventioneers. *Rooms from: $339 ✉ 6300 Hollywood Way, Universal Orlando Resort ☎ 407/503–3000, 800/232–7827 🌐 www.loewshotels.com/royal-pacific-resort 1,000 rooms No meals.*

Loews Sapphire Falls Resort at Universal Orlando Resort
$$ | **RESORT** | **FAMILY** | The romantic and sophisticated Sapphire Falls is connected by walkway and water taxi to Universal and CityWalk, the entertainment complex of shops, restaurants, and nightlife. **Pros:** all the perks of staying at a Universal property except Express Pass; boat takes you to Universal and CityWalk; outstanding on-property bar/restaurant. **Cons:** few activities for kids; water taxis and shuttles can be crowded; it's a long way to Disney. *Rooms from: $234 ✉ 6601 Adventure Way, Orlando ☎ 888/430–4999 🌐 www.loewshotels.com/sapphire-falls-resort 1,000 rooms No meals.*

Universal's Aventura Hotel
$$ | **HOTEL** | **FAMILY** | Within walking distance of Volcano Bay and within view of the three theme parks (best seen from the rooftop bar), this Miami Beach–style resort hotel has a casually elegant look with rooms that are simple and modern. **Pros:** new in 2019; access to amenities at other Loewe's hotels; free transportation to Universal theme parks. **Cons:** no Express Pass; limited storage space for families with a lot of luggage; high-tech tablets for room controls can be confusing. *Rooms from: $184 ✉ 6725 Adventure Way, Universal Orlando Resort ☎ 407/503–6000 🌐 www.loewshotels.com/universals-aventura-hotel 611 rooms No meals.*

★ Universal's Cabana Bay Beach Resort
$ | **RESORT** | **FAMILY** | Universal's nostalgic, mid-century-themed beach resort takes guests back in time to a 1950s Florida beach town with a modern twist; it also offers families a less-expensive but still benefit-rich alternative to on-site Universal properties. **Pros:** early access to Universal; bowling alley; two swimming pools. **Cons:** very expensive parking fee; Disney is not close by; some rooms open onto outdoor passageways. *Rooms from: $173 ✉ 6550 Adventure Way, Universal Orlando Resort ☎ 407/503–4000 🌐 www.loewshotels.com/cabana-bay 1,800 rooms No meals.*

Universal's Endless Summer Resort - Dockside Inn and Suites
$$ | **HOTEL** | **FAMILY** | The far larger half of a dual-resort created atop what was once the Wet n' Wild water park, this resort is massive even by Orlando standards, and about half the rooms are two-bedroom suites, making it a smart choice for families who need a little more space. **Pros:** an affordable option close to Universal and International Drive; early admission to the parks and free transportation; well-suited for families. **Cons:** some might find the massive size off-putting; add $15 per night for parking; not within walking distance to Universal theme parks. *Rooms from: $184* *7125 Universal Blvd., Universal Orlando Resort* *888/273–3111* *www.universalorlando.com/web/en/us/places-to-stay/universals-endless-summer-resort-dockside-inn-and-suites* *2,050 rooms* *No meals.*

Universal's Endless Summer Resort - Surfside Inn and Suites
$ | **RESORT** | **FAMILY** | Opened nearly in tandem with its larger sister property, the Dockside Inn and Suites, the family-friendly sun-andsurf-themes Surfside Inn and Suites is considered a value property thanks to its reasonable rates. **Pros:** one of Universal's least expensive properties; new in 2019; includes early admission to theme parks and free transportation. **Cons:** not directly on Universal Orlando property; it'll cost $15 per day to park; check-in is an hour later than usual, at 4 pm. *Rooms from: $139* *7000 Universal Blvd., Universal Orlando Resort* *407/503–7000* *www.loewshotels.com/surfside-inn-and-suites* *750 rooms* *No meals.*

Activities

SPAS

Mandara Spa at Loews Portofino Bay Hotel
FITNESS/HEALTH CLUBS | The doors to this 13,000-square-foot, Asian-themed sanctuary open to a tranquil world with bamboo screens, exotic statuary, and silk hangings. Warm blankets comfort you while you wait in the relaxation lounge for one of the 14 treatment rooms. Try the Ritual of the Hands and Feet, an indulgence that scrubs, exfoliates, and massages your extremities, finishing with a mani-pedi. The lounge and hydropool are co-ed, with separate men's and women's steam rooms and saunas. Portofino's serene sand-bottomed pool is next door, as is the fitness center. Facials and peels are available, as are full makeup, hair, and other salon services. *Loew's Portofino Bay Resort, 5601 Universal Blvd., Universal Orlando Resort* *407/503–1244* *www.mandaraspa.com/spa/orlando-loews-portofino-bay-hotel-at-universal-orlando.aspx.*

Chapter 10

ORLANDO

Updated by
Jennifer Greenhill-Taylor
and Joseph Hayes

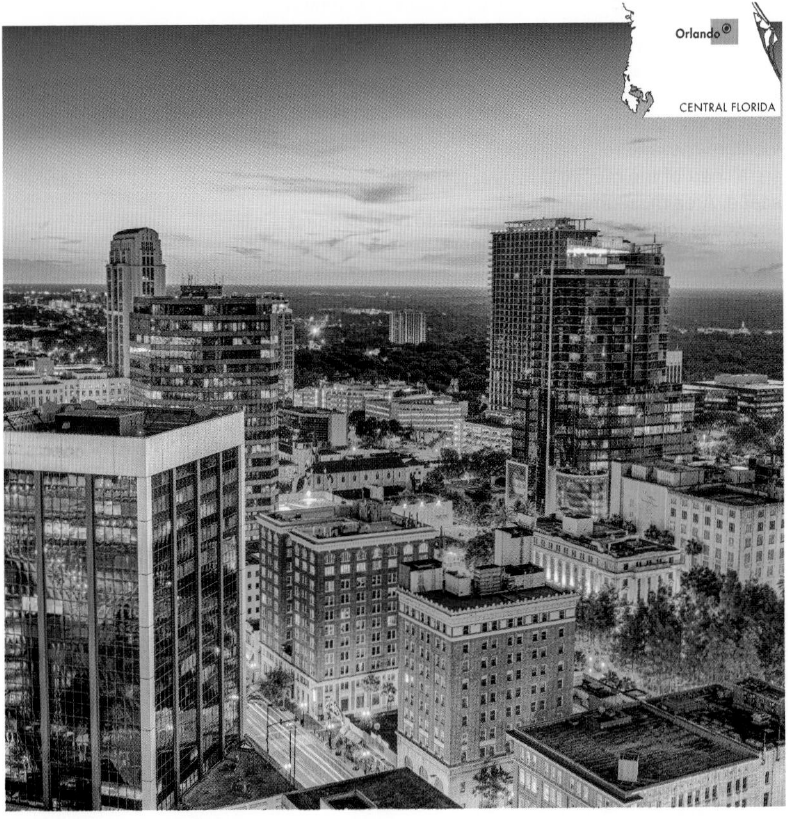

Sights	Restaurants	Hotels	Shopping	Nightlife
★★★☆☆	★★★★☆	★★★★★	★★★★☆	★★★☆☆

WELCOME TO ORLANDO

TOP REASONS TO GO

★ **Cultivated Spaces:** The Harry P. Leu Gardens are known for their historical blooms, camellias, and striking Floral Clock. Lake Eola Park has a landscaped waterfront stroll and azaleas, roses, and swans.

★ **Liberal Arts:** Orlando's theaters host symphony orchestras, Broadway road shows, and local thespians of all types. Jazz, blues, world music, and rock are all part of the music scene. Area museums showcase folk art, Tiffany glass, and 14th- through 20th-century European and American paintings.

★ **The Sciences:** The revamped Orlando Science Center has many worthwhile exhibits and hosts traveling exhibitions from around the world. At WonderWorks, simulators let you survive an earthquake or pilot a jet.

★ **Sports:** Orlando is home to the Orlando Magic, an NBA team housed at the Amway Center, in addition to Orlando City, a Major League Soccer team, which plays at Exploria Stadium.

1 Central Orlando. Orlando has a thriving downtown and bustling residential areas.

2 International Drive. Called "I-Drive," this conduit is lined with hotels, chain restaurants, and attractions.

3 South Orlando. South Orlando is the dynamic home of Lake Nona, one of the fastest-growing communities in Florida.

4 Sand Lake Road. The eastern side bisects I-Drive; the western end has been dubbed "Restaurant Row."

5 Orlando International Airport. Chain hotels and chain restaurants offer convenience for early-morning or late-night flights.

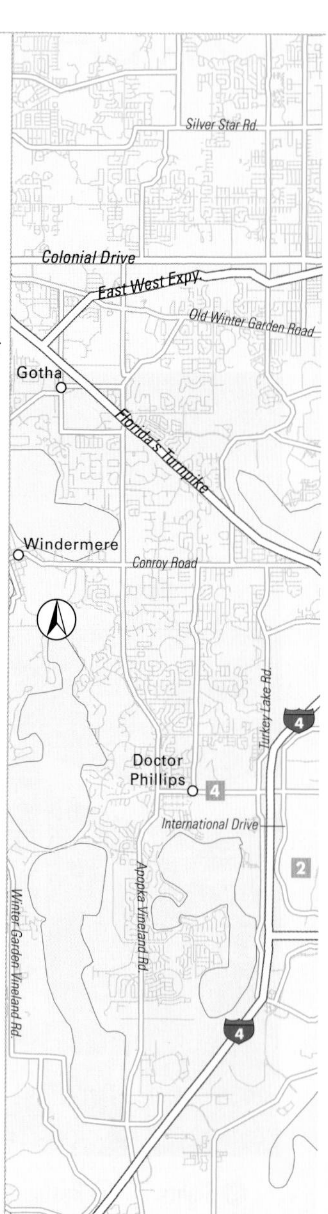

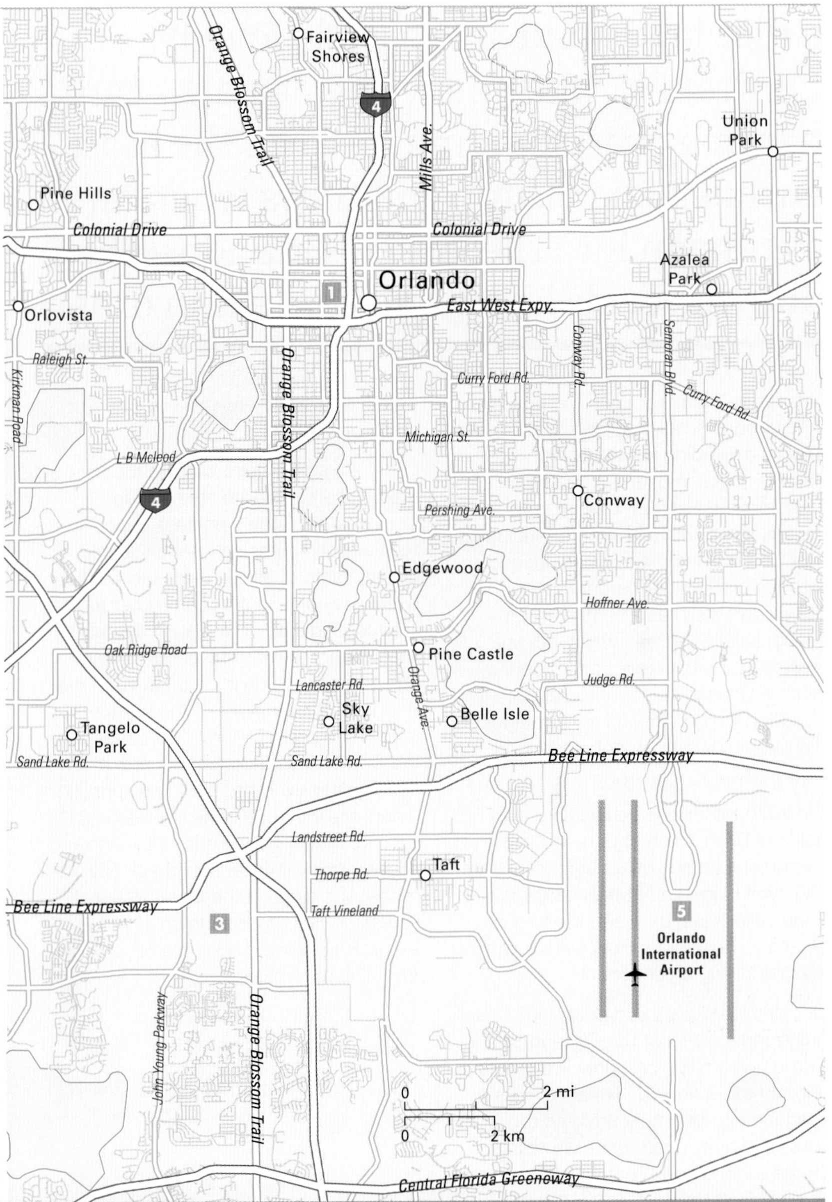
Fairview
Shores
Orange Blossom Trail
Mills Ave.
Union
Park
Pine Hills
Colonial Drive
Colonial Drive
Azalea
Park
Orlando
East West Expy.
Orlovista
Raleigh St.
Kirkman Road
Conway Rd.
Semoran Blvd.
Curry Ford Rd.
Curry Ford Rd.
Michigan St.
L B Mcleod
Conway
Pershing Ave.
Edgewood
Hoffner Ave.
Oak Ridge Road
Pine Castle
Judge Rd.
Lancaster Rd.
Orange Ave.
Sky
Lake
Belle Isle
Tangelo
Park
Sand Lake Rd.
Sand Lake Rd.
Bee Line Expressway
Landstreet Rd.
Taft
Thorpe Rd.
Bee Line Expressway
Taft Vineland
Orlando
International
Airport
John Young Parkway
Orange Blossom Trail
0
2 mi
0
2 km
Central Florida Greeneway

Most Orlando locals look at the theme parks as they would unruly neighbors: they're big and loud, but they keep a nice lawn (and are secretly loved). Central Florida's many theme parks can become overpowering for even the most enthusiastic visitor, and that's when an excursion into the "other" Orlando—the one the locals know and love—is in order.

Orlando is a diverse town. The downtown area, though small, is dynamic, thanks to an ever-expanding skyline of high-rises, sports venues, museums, restaurants, nightspots, a history museum, and several annual cultural events—including film festivals and the popular Orlando International Fringe Theater Festival. Downtown also has a central green space, Lake Eola Park, which offers a respite from otherwise frantic touring. Central Orlando neighborhoods such as Thornton Park, Baldwin Park (great for dining), and hipster Audubon Park are fun to wander.

Closer to the theme-park action, International Drive, the hub of resort and conference hotels, offers big restaurants and even bigger outlet-mall bargains. Sand Lake Road, between the two, is Orlando's Restaurant Row, with plenty of exciting dining prospects.

Got kids to educate and entertain? Check out WonderWorks or the Orlando Science Center, where you can view live gators and turtles, or visit ICON Park and its seaquarium, wax museum, and towering viewing wheel. Even more live gators (some as long as 14 feet) can be viewed or fed (or even eaten) at Gatorland, just south of Orlando.

There are ample opportunities for day trips in the immediate area. Mount Dora offers antiquers endless opportunities and surprisingly sophisticated dining; Sanford, easily reachable via the (weekday only) SunRail commuter train, is becoming a hip dining area; and LEGOLAND, an hour southwest of Orlando, offers a "we can do it" alternative to the Big Three theme parks. If the outdoors is your thing, you can swim or canoe at Wekiwa Springs State Park or one of the area's many other sparkling springs, where the water remains a refreshing 72°F no matter how hot the day. Alternatively, you can hike, horseback ride, canoe, and camp in the Ocala National Forest. ☞ *For information on all these excursions, see the separate "Excursions from Orlando" chapter.*

Planning

Getting Here and Around

Orlando is spread out and filled with lakes, making straight-line surface travel almost impossible. During rush hour, car traffic crawls along the often-crowded Interstate 4 (particularly now that the multibillion-dollar upgrade, expected to end in 2022, is underway, relocating and closing key exits and entrances), which runs to both coasts. If you're heading east, you can also take Route 528 (aka the Beachline), a toll road that heads directly for Cape Canaveral and points along the Space Coast. The Central Florida GreeneWay avoids major highway traffic between Sanford and Lake Mary to the north and Celebration to the south and is a pleasant, albeit expensive, way to approach Disney. Another toll road, Route 429, offers an easy journey from Disney to the north via the west side of Orlando.

Orlando International Airport is only 9 miles south of downtown, but it will take about 30 minutes via a circuitous network of highways (Interstate 4 west to Florida's Turnpike south to Route 528 east).

The SunRail commuter trains run weekdays and offer a traffic-free option on a south–north route from Kissimmee to Deltona, with stops that include downtown Orlando, downtown Winter Park, and Sanford along the way.

LYNX Bus service takes visitors from the main downtown depot to theme parks, outlet shopping, and even the airport for a fraction of taxi fare. And like most urban areas, Uber and Lyft are ubiquitous (and much cheaper than regular taxis), even within the theme parks..

CONTACTS LYNX Bus. ✉ *455 N. Garland Ave., Downtown Orlando* ☎ *407/841–5969* 🌐 *www.golynx.com.*

Visitor Information

CONTACTS Orlando Visitors Bureau. ✉ *8102 International Dr., Orlando* ☎ *407/363–5872* 🌐 *www.visitorlando.com.*

Central Orlando

Take Exit 83B off I-4 westbound, Exit 84 off I-4 eastbound.

Central Orlando is a thriving metropolis of brick-streeted neighborhoods, urban sprawl, quiet lakeside parks and, oh yes, the biggest theme parks in the world and lots of them.

Sights

CityArts Orlando
ART GALLERIES—ARTS | Housed in one of the oldest buildings in downtown, this charming, small gallery features mostly local and regional artists. ✉ *39 S. Magnolia Ave., Downtown Orlando* ☎ *407/648–7060* 🌐 *www.facebook.com/CityArtsFactory/.*

Crayola Experience Orlando
AMUSEMENT PARK/WATER PARK | **FAMILY** | One of the company's five "experiences" in the country, Crayola offers a 70,000-square-foot haven of color at the Florida Mall. An overwhelming 26 interactive stations extend throughout the two-floor center, including painting and modeling stations, where tykes can create animals out of clay and melted crayons. Don't miss the younger set's favorite: You Design, a virtual studio for coloring and digitally accessorizing a car or fashioning wardrobe and then seeing the design projected on a large screen. Also be sure to make it a priority to check out the Crayon Factory, where live demonstrations show the crayon creation process from wax to wrapper. ✉ *The Florida Mall, 8001 Orange Blossom*

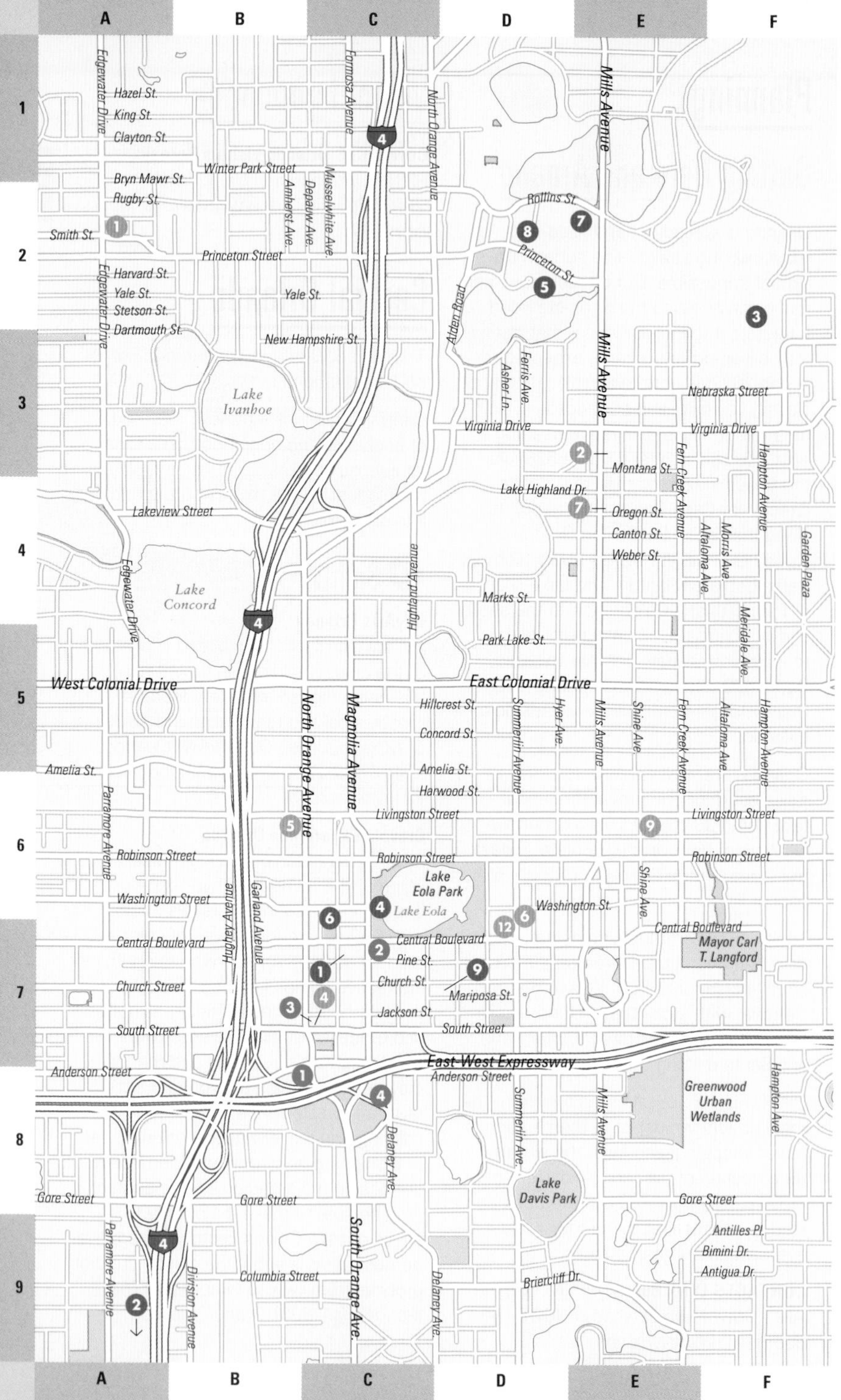
A
B
C
D
E
F
1
2
3
4
5
6
7
8
9
Edgewater Drive
Hazel St.
King St.
Clayton St.
Bryn Mawr St.
Rugby St.
Smith St.
Winter Park Street
Formosa Avenue
North Orange Avenue
Musselwhite Ave.
Depauw Ave.
Amherst Ave.
Princeton Street
Harvard St.
Yale St.
Stetson St.
Dartmouth St.
New Hampshire St.
Mills Avenue
Rollins St.
Princeton St.
Alden Road
Asher Ln.
Ferris Ave.
Lake Ivanhoe
Nebraska Street
Virginia Drive
Montana St.
Lake Highland Dr.
Oregon St.
Canton St.
Weber St.
Fern Creek Avenue
Altaloma Ave.
Morris Ave.
Hampton Avenue
Garden Plaza
Lakeview Street
Lake Concord
Highland Avenue
Marks St.
Park Lake St.
Meridale Ave.
West Colonial Drive
East Colonial Drive
Magnolia Avenue
Hillcrest St.
Concord St.
Amelia St.
Harwood St.
Summerlin Avenue
Hyer Ave.
Shine Ave.
Parramore Avenue
Livingston Street
Robinson Street
Washington Street
Hughey Avenue
Garland Avenue
Lake Eola Park
Lake Eola
Washington St.
Central Boulevard
Pine St.
Church Street
Church St.
Mariposa St.
Jackson St.
South Street
Mayor Carl T. Langford
Anderson Street
East-West Expressway
Greenwood Urban Wetlands
Hampton Ave.
Summerlin Ave.
Delaney Ave.
Lake Davis Park
Gore Street
South Orange Ave.
Antilles Pl.
Bimini Dr.
Antigua Dr.
Columbia Street
Division Avenue
Briercliff Dr.
4

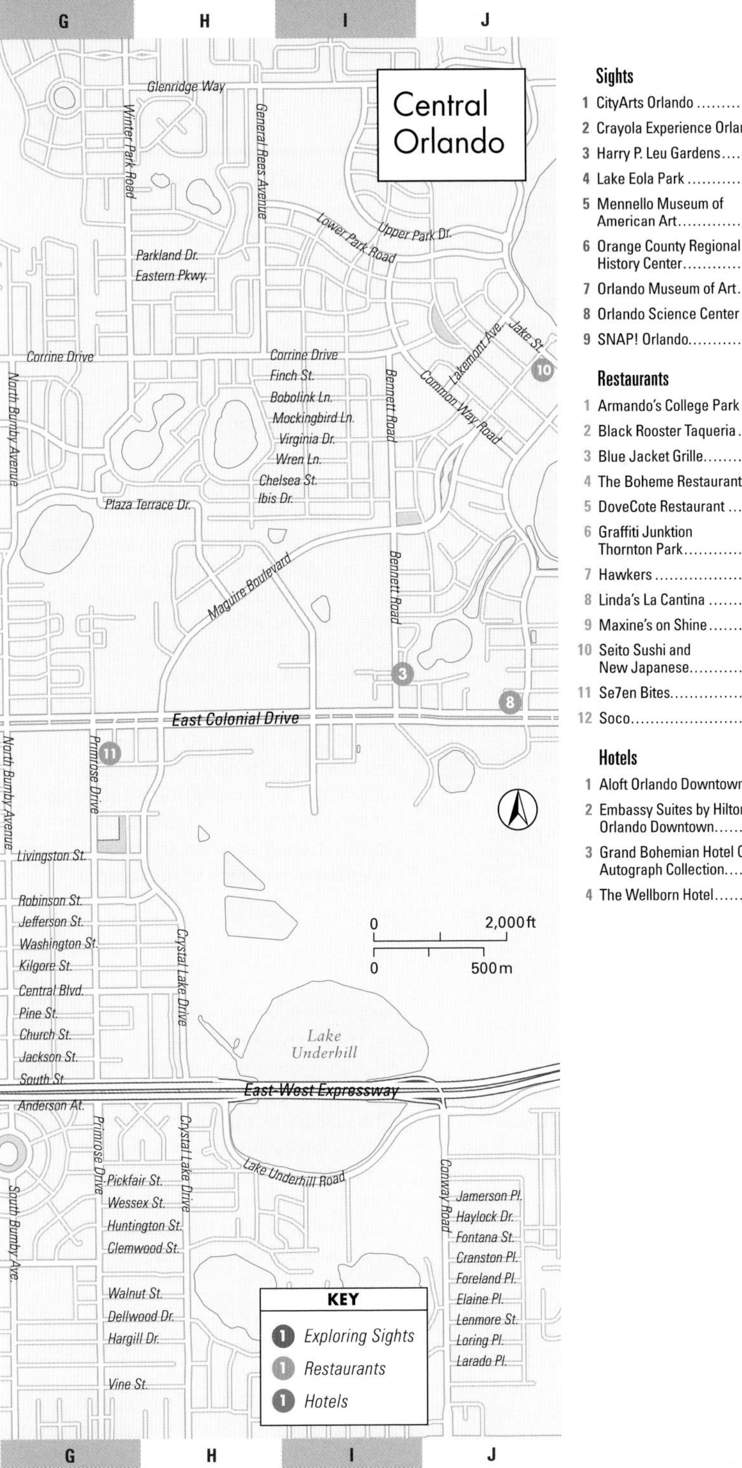

Sights

1 CityArts Orlando C7
2 Crayola Experience Orlando A9
3 Harry P. Leu Gardens............... F2
4 Lake Eola Park C6
5 Mennello Museum of American Art....................... D2
6 Orange County Regional History Center....................... C7
7 Orlando Museum of Art............ E2
8 Orlando Science Center D2
9 SNAP! Orlando..................... D7

Restaurants

1 Armando's College Park A2
2 Black Rooster Taqueria............ E3
3 Blue Jacket Grille.................. I5
4 The Boheme Restaurant........... C7
5 DoveCote Restaurant B6
6 Graffiti Junktion Thornton Park...................... D6
7 Hawkers E4
8 Linda's La Cantina J5
9 Maxine's on Shine.................. E6
10 Seito Sushi and New Japanese...................... J3
11 Se7en Bites......................... G5
12 Soco................................ D7

Hotels

1 Aloft Orlando Downtown C8
2 Embassy Suites by Hilton Orlando Downtown................ C7
3 Grand Bohemian Hotel Orlando, Autograph Collection............... C7
4 The Wellborn Hotel................ C8

Central Florida Art

Central Florida has a number of world-class art museums, including those that feature sublime stained-glass, American art. and folk art.

CityArts Orlando, Orlando. Housed in one of the oldest buildings in downtown, this small gallery features mostly local and regional artists.

Charles Hosmer Morse Museum of American Art, Winter Park. Known as the "Tiffany museum," the expanded galleries contain the largest and most comprehensive collection of art by Louis Comfort Tiffany, including stained-glass windows and lamps, blown-glass vases, and gem-studded jewelry.☞ *For more information, see Winter Park in "Excursions from Orlando."*

Mennello Museum of American Folk Art, Central Orlando. The Mennello holds the nation's most extensive permanent collection of Earl Cunningham paintings, as well as pieces by many other "outsider" artists. Works by Wyeth, Cassatt, Eastman, and others have made their Central Florida debuts here.

Modernism Museum, Mount Dora. A refined and dazzling private collection of American and international works from modernist artists features the work of George Nakashima and Wendell Castle, as well as that of the more radical group Memphis, including pieces collected by musician David Bowie.☞ *For more information, see Mount Dora in "Excursions from Orlando."*

Orlando Museum of Art, Orlando. Here you'll find contemporary, mid-18th- and 19th-century American art and one of the largest collections of ancient artifacts of the Americas in the South. In addition, the museum's collection of Chihuly glass is among the finest in the country.

Snap! Orlando. Artistic, thoughtful, and at times challenging, the two galleries operated by local photographer Patrick Kahn highlight the value of the still frame, with exhibits from internationally known artists and talented newcomers to the camera.

Trail, Central Orlando ☎ *407/757–1700* 🌐 *www.crayolaexperience.com* 🎟 *$25.*

★ Harry P. Leu Gardens

GARDEN | A few miles outside downtown—on the former lakefront estate of a citrus entrepreneur—is this 50-acre garden. Among the highlights are a collection of historical blooms (many varieties of which were established before 1900), ancient oaks, a 50-foot floral clock, and one of the largest camellia collections in eastern North America (in bloom November–March). Mary Jane's Rose Garden, named after Leu's wife, is filled with more than 1,000 bushes; it's the largest formal rose garden south of Atlanta. The simple 19th-century Leu House Museum, once the Leu family home, preserves the furnishings and appointments of a well-to-do, turn-of-the-20th-century Florida family. Admission is free on the first Monday of the month from January through September. ✉ *1920 N. Forest Ave., Audubon Park* ☎ *407/246–2620* 🌐 *www.leugardens.org* 🎟 *$10.*

Lake Eola Park

CITY PARK | **FAMILY** | This beautifully landscaped, 43-acre park is the verdant heart of downtown Orlando, its mile-long walking path a gathering place for families, health enthusiasts out for a run, and culture mavens exploring area offerings. The well-lighted playground is alive with children, and ducks, swans, and native Florida birds call the lake home. A popular and expanded farmers' market takes up residence on Sunday morning and afternoon. The lakeside Walt Disney Amphitheater is a dramatic site for concerts, ethnic festivals, and spectacular July 4 fireworks. Don't resist the park's biggest draw: a ride in a swan-shaped pedal boat. Up to five adults can fit comfortably in each. (Children under 16 must be accompanied by an adult.) The Relax Grill, by the swan-boat launch, is a great place for a snack. The park is surrounded by great downtown and Thornton Park restaurants and lounges. The ever-expanding skyline rings the lake with modern high-rises, making the peace of the park even more welcome. The landmark fountain features an LED-light-and-music show on summer evenings at 9:30. ✉ *195 N. Rosalind Ave., Downtown Orlando* ✢ *Center of Downtown Orlando* ☎ *407/246–4485 park, 407/246–4485* 🌐 *www.cityoforlando.net/parks/lake-eola-park* 🎫 *Swan boat rental $15 per ½ hr.*

★ Mennello Museum of American Art

MUSEUM | One of the few museums in the United States devoted to folk art has intimate galleries, some with lovely lakefront views. Look for the nation's most extensive permanent collection of Earl Cunningham paintings, as well as works by many other self-taught artists. There's a wonderful video about Cunningham and his "curio shop" in St. Augustine, Florida. Temporary exhibitions have included the works of Wyeth, Cassatt, and Michael Eastman. At the museum shop you can purchase folk-art books, toys, and unusual gifts. The Marilyn L. Mennello Sculpture Garden is always open to the public. Oversized outdoor sculptures include works by Alice Aycock and Barbara Sorensen, shown alongside the 350-year-old live oak tree called "The Mayor." The Mennello is the site of the free annual Orlando Indie-Folk Festival, held the second weekend of February. ✉ *900 E. Princeton St., Lake Ivanhoe* ☎ *407/246–4278* 🌐 *www.mennellomuseum.org* 🎫 *$5* 🕓 *Closed Mon.*

Orange County Regional History Center

MUSEUM | **FAMILY** | Exhibits take you on a journey back in time to discover how Florida's Paleo-Indians hunted and fished the land, what the Sunshine State was like when the Spaniards first arrived, and how life in Florida was different when citrus was king. Exhibitions cover the history of citrus-growing in Central Florida, samples of the work of the famed Highwaymen painters, and the advancement of the theme parks. Traveling exhibits bring modern technology and art to the museum. Free audio tours are available. ■ **TIP→ Ticket holders get two hours free parking**. ✉ *65 E. Central Blvd., Downtown Orlando* ☎ *407/836–8500, 800/965–2030* 🌐 *www.thehistorycenter.org* 🎫 *$8.*

Orlando Museum of Art

MUSEUM | **FAMILY** | Part of the City of Orlando's collection of arts venues, the Museum of Art sits in the Loch Haven Park complex. It exhibits contemporary, mid-18th- and 19th-century American art and an important collection of ancient artifacts of the Americas. In addition to American art created before 1945, and an extensive photography collection, exhibits of African textiles and graphic art from such artists as Andy Warhol and Jasper Johns add to the diversity of its displays. The museum's collection of Chihuly glass, obtained during an exclusive exhibition in 2004, is among the finest in the country. A live music and art social mixer, called 1st Thursdays, runs 6 to 9 pm. ✉ *2416 N. Mills Ave., Orlando* ☎ *407/896–4231* 🌐 *omart.org* 🎫 *$15* 🕓 *Closed Mon.*

★ Orlando Science Center

MUSEUM | **FAMILY** | The expanded, 11,000-square-foot Kids Town remains the center's most popular attraction.

The 300-seat Dr. Phillips CineDome, a movie theater with an eight-story screen at the Orlando Science Center, offers large-format IMAX films.

With exhibits about the human body, mechanics, computers, math, nature, the solar system, and optics, the science center has something for every child's inner geek. Traveling shows include an astronaut experience, the science of human anatomy, and the annual interactive technology expo called Otronicon.

The four-story internal atrium is home to live gators and turtles and is a great spot for simply gazing at what Old Florida once looked like. The 300-seat Dr. Phillips CineDome, a movie theater with a giant eight-story screen, offers IMAX films and planetarium programs. The Crosby Observatory and Florida's largest publicly accessible refractor telescope are here, as are several smaller telescopes; late-evening weekend date nights make the observatory a fun draw for adults, who can enjoy events like the annual Science of Wine and the very popular monthly Science Night Live. ✉ *777 E. Princeton St., Lake Ivanhoe* ☎ *407/514–2000* 🌐 *www.osc.org* 🎟 *$21; parking $5* 🕑 *Closed Wed. (except for 1st Wed. evenings).*

SNAP! Orlando

MUSEUM | Founded by international photographer Patrick Kahn, SNAP! is the leading repository of contemporary images in Orlando. Between the two locations in downtown Orlando and hipster Colonialtown, the galleries have shown cutting-edge photos from artists such as Shawn Theodore, Roger Ballen, and musician Moby, along with world premiere exhibitions, emerging graffiti artists, and even jewelry makers. The other location is at 1013 East Colonial Drive, 407/286–2185 (closed Sun.–Wed.). ✉ *420 E. Church St., Downtown Orlando* ☎ *407/286–2185* 🌐 *snaporlando.com* 🕑 *Closed Sun.*

Restaurants

Central Orlando is quintessential urban Florida and offers much more than typical chain restaurants. Here you'll find a local, independent dining scene that's driven by award-winning and inventive chefs, creating a hot spot for creative cuisine.

Armando's College Park

$$ | **ITALIAN** | **FAMILY** | Armando Martorelli has opened many local restaurants in his career since coming from Italy to Florida, but his namesake eatery is the epitome of his craft. Like the Winter Park location, here you'll find a relaxed, molto-Italian atmosphere with a great neighborhood vibe that keeps people coming back for superb seafood and what is perhaps the area's best pizza in the Neapolitan style. **Known for:** Neapolitan specialties; wood-fired oven pizza; extensive wine and cocktail list with a very popular bar area. *Average main: $18* *2305 Edgewater Dr., College Park* *407/930–0333* *armandosorlando.com.*

★ **Black Rooster Taqueria**

$ | **MEXICAN FUSION** | **FAMILY** | Nestled in the funky neighborhood of Mills 50, this small, casual taco place has everything from corn tortillas to guacamole that are made to order with every dish. Get the pulled roasted chicken tinga for sophisticated tastes, and the crispy fish for an unusual alternative to the Rooster's seared beef carne asada. **Known for:** inventive and flavorful tacos; chocolate chip spicy flan; made to order guacamole. *Average main: $4* *1323 N. Mills Ave., Central Orlando* *407/601–0994* *www.blackroostertaqueria.com* *Closed Mon.*

Blue Jacket Grille

$$ | **AMERICAN** | A humble hideaway located near a strip mall, Blue Jacket draws the hipster crowd as well as the still-vibrant former navy population. This is a (gourmet) burger and (craft) beer spot, with 20 brews on tap and another 40 by the bottle. **Known for:** very casual taproom with 20 brews; happy hour specials and trivia nights; chicken wings, burgers, and flatbreads. *Average main: $15* *745 Bennett Rd., Downtown Orlando* *407/868–9006* *thebluejacketgrille.com* *Closed Mon.*

The Boheme Restaurant

$$$$ | **ECLECTIC** | The Grand Bohemian, a boutique, luxury hotel, is the setting for a sleek city-center restaurant. As a prelude to your main, try the calamari served with lobster and crab bisque or grilled Spanish octopus. **Known for:** upscale, chef-driven dining in a fashionable hotel; pre- and postdinner bar; elaborate Sunday jazz brunch. *Average main: $34* *Grand Bohemian Hotel Orlando, Autograph Collection, 325 S. Orange Ave., Downtown Orlando* *407/313–9000* *www.grandbohemianhotel.com.*

★ **DoveCote Restaurant**

$$$ | **BRASSERIE** | Chef Clay Miller brings big city sophistication to downtown Orlando with a French-American fusion menu and craft cocktails. Everything that can be made in-house, such as pickles, condiments, and bread, are. **Known for:** handcrafted charcuterie and cocktails; raw bar with Florida oysters; braised short ribs with trumpet mushrooms. *Average main: $24* *Bank of America Building, 390 N Orange Ave., Downtown Orlando* *407/930–1700* *dovecoteorlando.com* *No dinner Sun.*

Graffiti Junktion Thornton Park

$ | **BURGER** | **FAMILY** | Astoundingly popular, Graffiti Junktion holds the casual burger/wrap/sandwich crowd in thrall. Noisy and visually loud, picnic benches and commissioned graffiti are the decor. **Known for:** late hours and noisy sports bar atmosphere; fresh-formed burgers with inventive toppings; hand-cut french fries. *Average main: $12* *700 East Washington St., Thornton Park* *321/424–5800* *graffitijunktion.com.*

★ **Hawkers**

$$ | **ASIAN FUSION** | **FAMILY** | Hipsters, families, and business groups dine side by side at this popular restaurant, a laid-back spot that specializes in Asian street food and has quickly become a Southern institution with 11 locations in 6 states. Travel the continent with scratch-made family recipes from all around Southeast Asia.

Known for: typical dishes like roti canai, sesame noodles, and stir-fried udon; hip and casual atmosphere; extensive and exotic beer selections. *Average main: $16 ✉ 1103 N. Mills Ave., Mills 50 District ☎ 407/237–0606 🌐 eathawkers.com.*

Linda's La Cantina

$$$ | STEAKHOUSE | FAMILY | A favorite among locals since 1947, this down-home steak house serves good cuts of meat, cooked expertly and served at a reasonable price. Butchery is done on premises, and there are no TVs over the bar to distract from a pleasant conversation over a great steak. **Known for:** classic Orlando institution; hand-cut, house-aged steaks; seafood and pasta entrées. *Average main: $26 ✉ 4721 E. Colonial Dr., Downtown Orlando ✥ Near Orlando Executive Airport ☎ 407/894–4491 🌐 lindaslacantinasteakhouse.com ⏲ No lunch. Closed Sun. and Mon.*

Maxine's on Shine

$$ | AMERICAN | A holdover to when neighborhood restaurants were actually in a neighborhood, Maxine's is casual, hip, local, and friendly. The menu ranges from sophisticated seafood to brisket burgers and Black Angus filet mignon. **Known for:** lively, neighborhood atmosphere; outdoor dining; seafood dishes from a veteran local chef. *Average main: $16 ✉ 337 N. Shine, Downtown Orlando ☎ 407/674–6841 🌐 maxinesonshine.com ⏲ Closed Mon.*

★ Seito Sushi and New Japanese

$$ | JAPANESE FUSION | FAMILY | The epitome of modern Japanese cuisine, Seito offers crowd-pleasing traditional ramen bowls as well as unique, handcrafted sushi combinations and Japanese "kitchen food." The sophisticated and fun bar specializes in cask whiskey and multiple exclusive sake brands. **Known for:** hand-pulled ramen noodles; exclusively crafted sushi; boneless, fried whole snapper for two. *Average main: $18 ✉ 4898 New Broad St., Central Orlando ☎ 407/898–8801 🌐 seitosushi.com Ⓜ Baldwin Park.*

★ Se7en Bites

$$ | AMERICAN | FAMILY | Trina Gregory-Propst and her team of bakers and cooks make the biggest and most satisfying breakfasts, lunches, and sweet treats in town. Try a scratch chicken pot pie with the most glorious crust, a mile-high meat loaf sandwich, or the "7th Trimester" of buttermilk garlic biscuit, over-medium egg, and smoked bacon, smothered in five-cheese mac-and-cheese. **Known for:** over-the-top Southern breakfast specials; funky downtown location; featured on Diners, Drive-ins, and Dives. *Average main: $15 ✉ 617 Primrose Dr., Central Orlando ☎ 407/302–0727 🌐 www.se7enbites.com ⏲ No dinner; closed Mon.*

Soco

$$$ | SOUTHERN | Under the talented hands of executive chef Greg Richie, Southern staples get mighty fancy at Soco, as both the decor and the menu mesh classic and creative in a suave way. Vegetarians get one of the best meatless entrées in town with the chicken-fried cauliflower steak, a massive dish finished with a rich tomato gravy. **Known for:** funky daily specials like TV Dinner Thursday; sophisticated bar; vegetarian options. *Average main: $23 ✉ 629 E. Central Blvd., Thornton Park ☎ 407/849–1800 🌐 www.socothorntonpark.com ⏲ No lunch.*

Hotels

Central Orlando, north of Walt Disney World and the I-Drive area, is a thriving business district on weekdays and attracts a club and restaurant crowd on weekend nights.

Aloft Orlando Downtown

$$ | HOTEL | In the heart of Orlando, steps from the arts center, sports arena, and nightlife, this former utilities building has been transformed into a trendy urban hotel, with a busy bar, innovative rooms, and high-tech amenities. **Pros:** just steps to downtown nightlife, arts, and sporting events; easy access to highways; trendy urban vibe. **Cons:** if Disney is your destination, it's a 45-minute hike down Interstate 4 to get there; only parking choice is valet or street parking; an urban vibe can be noisy. *Rooms from: $249 ✉ 500 S. Orange Ave., Downtown Orlando ☎ 407/380–3500 www.aloftorlandodowntown.com 111 rooms No meals.*

Embassy Suites by Hilton Orlando Downtown

$$$ | HOTEL | FAMILY | A short walk from a half-dozen cafés and restaurants, the Orange County History Center, and the performing arts center and sports venue, this hotel has numerous suites with views of nearby Lake Eola and its centerpiece fountain, swan boats, and jogging path. **Pros:** near Lake Eola and downtown; free continental breakfast and afternoon cocktail hour (with snacks); free Wi-Fi. **Cons:** traffic can be heavy; on-street parking is hard to find, and there's a fee for on-site parking; Disney is at least 45 minutes away (an hour or more during rush hours). *Rooms from: $261 ✉ 191 E. Pine St., Downtown Orlando ☎ 407/841–1000, 800/609–3339 www.embassysuites.com 167 suites Free breakfast.*

Grand Bohemian Hotel Orlando, Autograph Collection

$$$$ | HOTEL | Located in the heart of Orlando, this European-style property is downtown's only Four Diamond luxury hotel; it's adjacent to the performing arts center, a block from the sports venue, and it showcases hundreds of pieces of art, along with a rare Imperial Grand Bösendorfer piano, played by jazz pianists in the popular Bösendorfer Lounge. **Pros:** art gallery and sophisticated entertainment; great restaurant; quiet, adult-friendly atmosphere. **Cons:** little to attract kids; meals are pricey; fees for parking and far from Disney and Universal. *Rooms from: $379 ✉ 325 S. Orange Ave., Downtown Orlando ☎ 407/313–9000 www.grandbohemianhotel.com 212 rooms No meals.*

The Wellborn Hotel

$ | B&B/INN | Built more than a half century before Disney arrived, these three beautifully restored Victorian houses were rescued and moved to this palm-lined courtyard that's within blocks of the city's arts and sports venues. **Pros:** great Victorian architecture; short walk to downtown restaurants, the Amway Center, and performing arts center; free parking and Wi-Fi. **Cons:** far from theme parks and I-Drive; walking in some parts of downtown at night can be a bit dicey; lots of weddings take place here, so noise could be an issue. *Rooms from: $140 ✉ 211 N. Lucerne Circle E, Downtown Orlando ☎ 407/648–5188 www.wellbornhotel.com 20 rooms Free breakfast.*

Nightlife

The heart of Orlando nightlife extends several blocks from the intersection of Orange Avenue and Church Street. Bars, cantinas, lounges, dance clubs, movie theaters, a sports arena, and the performing arts center are all within this core area, creating an energetic blend of bourgeoisie and bohemian.

BARS

AERO

BARS/PUBS | On a starry, starry night it's a treat to escape the crowded street-level clubs of downtown to this rooftop nightclub on top of The Social. Surrounded by some of Orlando's tallest buildings, it exudes hip, trendy vibes that are just right for those looking to dance to a DJ outdoors. Ladies' nights, theme events, and even yoga classes are offered, but it's closed Monday through Wednesday. *✉ 60 N. Orange Ave., Downtown Orlando ☎ 407/274–8452.*

Bull and Bush Pub

BARS/PUBS | Here since 1987, this pub just a few miles east of downtown has become a neighborhood institution. It's still one of the most atmospheric places in town, where you can get a hand-drawn pint, play a game of darts, and have a (still) smoky chat. The tap lineup covers 11 imported beers and ales and quadruples that number in bottled selections, while the kitchen prepares fish-and-chips, cottage pies, and Scotch eggs. Darts leagues and weekly pub quizzes make it feel like a piece of old London. ✉ *2408 E. Robinson St., Downtown Orlando* ☎ *407/896–7546* 🌐 *www.bullandbushorlando.com* ⏲ *Closed Sun.*

Wall Street Plaza

BARS/PUBS | Wall Street Plaza created seven distinct, themed venues in one location. Choose the Wall Street Cantina for Mexican fare, the Hen House ("The World's Smallest Bardello") for craft beers, Hooch for an outdoor bar, the Shine dance club for its "moonshine warehouse" look, the Monkey Bar martini lounge, the outdoor WaiTiki Bar, or Sideshow for a party scene. With a calendar packed with events, this is considered Party Central for many in the downtown crowd. ✉ *19 N. Orange Ave., Downtown Orlando* ☎ *407/420–1515* 🌐 *www.wallstplaza.net.*

Wally's

BARS/PUBS | One of the city's oldest bars (circa 1954) has been renovated and reopened in 2019 after being closed for nearly a year. The longtime local favorite is a hangout for a cross section of cultures and ages. Some would say it's a dive—even in its cleaned-up state—but that doesn't matter to the students, bikers, lawyers, and barflies who land here. Just grab a stool at the bar to take in the scene and down a cold one. ✉ *1001 N. Mills Ave., Downtown Orlando* ☎ *407/896–6975* 🌐 *www.wallysonmills.com* ⏲ *Closed Sun.*

MUSIC CLUBS

Bösendorfer Lounge

MUSIC CLUBS | One of only two Imperial Grand Bösendorfer pianos in the world takes center stage at what might be the classiest gathering spot in Orlando. The highly civilized (but not stuffy) lounge attracts a cross section of trendy Orlandoans, especially the after-work crowd, among whom conversation and camaraderie flow as smoothly as the champagne, beer, wine, and cocktails. And with its location across the street from the performing arts center, it's a draw pre- and postconcert. Call in advance for the schedule of jazz combos and solo pianists who perform in the lounge. Many are among the area's finest and most talented musicians. ✉ *Grand Bohemian Hotel Orlando, Autograph Collection, 325 S. Orange Ave., Downtown Orlando* ☎ *407/313–9000* 🌐 *www.grandbohemianhotel.com.*

★ **The Social**

MUSIC CLUBS | Beloved by locals, The Social is a great place to see touring and area musicians. Up to seven nights a week, you can sip trademark martinis while listening to anything from indie rock to rockabilly to music mixed by DJs. Fans love the venue because the stage is low, the bands are close, and the enthusiasm is high. Hours vary, and there is usually a cover. ✉ *54 N. Orange Ave., Downtown Orlando* ☎ *407/246–1419* 🌐 *www.thesocial.org.*

Tanqueray's

MUSIC CLUBS | Of all the entertainment possibilities in downtown Orlando, the most interesting one might be the hardest to find. Housed in a former bank vault, Tanqueray's is a belowground hideaway featuring live music nightly and a full bar, including craft beers and nightly drink specials. You can enjoy a variety of entertainment from one night to the next, including reggae, funk, and high-energy blues. No food is served here. ✉ *100 S. Orange*

Ave., Downtown Orlando ☎ *407/649–8540* 🌐 *tanquerraysbar.com.*

NIGHTCLUBS

Chillers-Cahoots-Latitude

BARS/PUBS | Known as Orlando's original party bar (it's been here since 1992), Chillers is a Key West–themed nightspot that features an entire wall of frozen daiquiri machines. Upstairs, Chillers' sister club, Cahoots, offers more than 100 craft beers and 40 bourbon whiskeys. Latitudes is a large rooftop bar with a tropical theme and Top 40 music. ✉ *33 W. Church St., Downtown Orlando* ☎ *407/649–4270* 🌐 *www.churchstreetbars.com.*

Parliament House Resort

DANCE CLUBS | For those enamored of gay, lesbian, and high-camp entertainment, Parliament House is legendary and welcoming to every kind of audience. The 250-seat art deco performance space, which has been open since 1975, hosts live theater, musical acts, karaoke, cabaret, dance, and bawdy and hilarious drag shows. Le Club Disco and Dance bar, along with four other bars, draws thousands of partiers weekly. Unfortunately, Orange Blossom Trail remains a sketchy area, so wandering around the neighborhood isn't advised. ✉ *410 N. Orange Blossom Trail, Downtown Orlando* ☎ *407/425–7571* 🌐 *www.parliamenthouse.com.*

Performing Arts

THEATER

Bob Carr Theater

CONCERTS | **FAMILY** | Now under the umbrella of the Dr. Phillips Center, the Bob Carr is still an impressive hall with wonderful acoustics. Nationally recognized musicians (rock, jazz, easy listening, classical), comedians, musicals, plays, and tribute acts appear here. ✉ *401 W. Livingston St., Downtown Orlando* ☎ *407/440–7900* 🌐 *www.drphillipscenter.org/explore/theaters-spaces/bob-carr-theater.*

★ **Dr. Phillips Center for the Performing Arts**

ARTS CENTERS | **FAMILY** | When this stunning, state-of-the-art venue opened in the heart of downtown, it elevated the arts for Orlando. Encompassing three unique stages, it's where major Broadway productions found a home; where musicians such as Bob Dylan, Brian Wilson, and Elvis Costello have performed; and where opera, symphonies, ballet, and comedy shows fill the calendar year-round. ✉ *445 S. Magnolia Ave., Downtown Orlando* ☎ *844/513–2014* 🌐 *www.drphillipscenter.org.*

Mad Cow Theatre

THEATER | **FAMILY** | Orlando's longest-standing professional theater company is where risks are taken. Regional premieres, new works, and thoughtful interpretations of classics make this a stage worth seeking. Local actors eager to show their talents line up to work here. ✉ *54 W. Church St., Downtown Orlando* ☎ *407/297–8788* 🌐 *www.madcowtheatre.com.*

★ **Orlando Shakespeare Theater**

CULTURAL FESTIVALS | **FAMILY** | "Orlando Shakes" has four stages, where a typical season includes 11 plays covering classics (including Shakespeare, of course), contemporary, musicals, comedies, and family shows. The theater also hosts the very popular Orlando International Fringe Festival, the oldest in America. The season runs June through April, with the Fringe Festival in May. PlayFest! The Harriett Lake Festival of New Plays offers world-premiere and staged-reading opportunities for new playwrights. The theater is in Loch Haven Cultural Park, just a few minutes north of downtown, where the Orlando Science Center and the Museum of Art also stand. ✉ *812 E. Rollins St., Lake Ivanhoe* ☎ *407/447–1700* 🌐 *www.orlandoshakes.org.*

International Drive

The sprawl of hotels, time-shares, restaurants, malls, entertainment complexes, and dozens of small attractions known as International Drive (I-Drive to locals) makes a central base for visits to Walt Disney World, Universal, and other Orlando attractions. Parallel to I-4, this four-lane boulevard stretches from Universal in the north to near Kissimmee in the south. Entertainment choices range from roller coasters, eye-popping swing rides, go-carts and minigolf to a waxworks, all overseen by a giant observation wheel with breathtaking views of the entire, glittering, neon-shiny area. The hotels, many attached to the convention center, range from high-end luxury to affordable family spots.

Sights

Andretti Indoor Karting and Games

SPORTS VENUE | FAMILY | The racing legend lent his name to this entertainment facility that offers boutique bowling on black-lit lanes, video game and pinball arcade, sky trail ropes course with curved ziplines, virtual reality, a shoot-em-up 7-D dark ride, and naturally, racing. Pro racing simulators add motion, vibrations, sound effects, and even add tension in the seatbelt so you feel as if you're on an actual racetrack. When you're ready to actually race, three indoor kart tracks let you whip around corners, change elevation, and zip into banked curves on small, high-torque karts. Add laser tag, a restaurant, and more than 100 screens tuned into the day's top sporting events, and you have a lot of entertainment packed into one exciting complex. ✉ *9299 Universal Blvd., International Drive* ☎ *407/374–0042* 🌐 *andrettikarting.com/orlando* 🎫 *Racing from $22; ropes course, laser tag, other games from $13.*

Aquatica

AMUSEMENT PARK/WATER PARK | FAMILY | SeaWorld's water park offers a variety of both single-rider and family raft rides, fast and slow rivers, the enclosed body slide Dolphin Plunge, two massive wave pools and an extensive kids area. With 84,000 square feet of beaches and lagoons, pools and river rafting rides on 59 acres, Aquatica measures up comparably to Disney's water parks and Universal's Volcano Bay water theme park. And with more than 40 waterslides, from the gentle Kata's Kookaburra Cove to the freefall experience of Ihu's Breakaway Falls, Aquatica holds its own in water thrills. Kids are attracted to Walkabout Waters, a 60-foot-tall water-soaking jungle gym, where they can climb, slide, and get soaked. The new Ray Rush family raft ride offers multiple high-speed paths through enclosed tubes and transparent spheres. Teens and adults flock to the Dolphin Plunge, where two side-by-side transparent tubes allow you to join a pod of black-and-white dolphins underwater. Various mascot animals entertain throughout the park. There are height requirements of at least 42 inches for some rides, and all visitors need to know how to swim. ✉ *5800 Water Play Way, International Drive* ☎ *407/545–5500* 🌐 *aquaticabyseaworld.com/en/orlando* 🎫 *$60* 🕑 *Closed some days Jan. and Feb.*

Discovery Cove

AMUSEMENT PARK/WATER PARK | FAMILY | The only theme park in Orlando that may be called "exclusive," Discovery Cove offers you an uncrowded, daylong experience of animal encounters with dolphins, otters, sharks, and rays, as well as opportunities for relaxing swims and resort-style amenities. Lockers, wet suits, parking, breakfast, lunch, drinks, and snacks are all included in entry. Right next door to SeaWorld, the park has tropical landscaping, white-sand beaches, waterfalls, and vast freshwater lagoons to tempt waterbabies. The Explorer's Aviary houses hundreds of tropical birds. People come for the Atlantic bottlenose dolphin swimming experiences (which are an add-on to the regular park admission, and have been criticized by some animal rights activists). Regular park admission includes snorkeling with tropical fish and rays at the Grand Reef, hand-feeding exotic birds, or just floating on the Wind Away lazy river. Add-on experiences, such as using a diving helmet in the Grand Reef, or swimming with sharks, are available for an additional cost, and they often sell out. Prices vary wildly depending on day and package options (there are many). Visitors to Discovery Cove get unlimited admission to Sea-World and Aquatica for 14 consecutive days around the reservation date. ✉ *6000 Discovery Cove Way, International Drive* ☎ *407/513–4600* 🌐 *discoverycove.com* 🎟 *From $230; package options can add up to another $185.*

Fun Spot America

AMUSEMENT PARK/WATER PARK | FAMILY | You can see the neon-lit rides here from miles away as you approach International Drive. Four go-kart tracks offer a variety of driving experiences. Though drivers must be at least 10 years old and meet height requirements, parents can drive younger children in two-seater cars on several of the tracks, including the Conquest Track. Nineteen rides range from the dizzying Enterprise to an old-fashioned Ferris wheel to the twirling toddler Teacups. Fun Spot features Central Florida's only wooden roller coaster as well as the Freedom Flyer steel suspension family coaster, a kiddie coaster, and SkyCoaster—part skydive, part hang-glide. There's also an arcade. The park's newest addition is the Gator Spot, in partnership with the iconic Gatorland and starring several live alligators and other Florida wildlife; it's a throwback to the old days of Orlando roadside attractions. ✉ *5700 Fun Spot Way, International Drive* ✣ *From Exit 75A, turn south onto Grand National Dr., then east on Fun Spot Way* ☎ *407/363–3867* 🌐 *www.fun-spot.com* 🎟 *$46 for all rides (online discounts available); some rides extra; admission for nonriders free.*

Madame Tussauds Orlando

MUSEUM | FAMILY | Featuring wax copies of real and fictional characters, Madame Tussaud's allows visitors to grab a selfie with the faux superheroes, including Wonder Woman, Superman, Batman, and Aquaman, and with celebrities (both living and dead) from Taylor Swift to Pink, Pitbull, and Michael Jackson, along with the rich and famous from politics and sports. **TIP→ Tickets are cheaper when purchased in advance online (discount coupons are also widely available).** ✉ *8387 International Dr., International Drive* ☎ *321/209–9651* 🌐 *www.madametussauds.com/orlando* 🎟 *$30.*

Orlando Starflyer

AMUSEMENT PARK/WATER PARK | FAMILY | Guests can travel at 45 mph on a 450-foot-tall swing, said to be the tallest in the world, which also rotates 360 degrees. It's as terrifying as it sounds, so this ride is not for either the faint of heart or small children. **TIP→ You can buy tickets online at a discount (coupons are also widely available).** ✉ *ICON Park, 8265 International Dr., International Drive* ☎ *407/640–7009* 🌐 *starflyer.com* 🎟 *$13.*

Ripley's Orlando

MUSEUM | FAMILY | A 10-foot-square section of the Berlin Wall, a pain and torture chamber, two African fertility statues that women swear have helped them conceive—these and almost 200 other oddities (shrunken heads included) speak for themselves in this museum-cum-attraction in the heart of tourist territory on International Drive. The building itself is designed to appear as if it's sliding into one of Florida's notorious sinkholes. Give yourself an hour or two to soak up the weirdness, but remember: this is a looking, not touching, experience; it might drive antsy youngsters—and their parents—crazy. **TIP→ Buy tickets online**

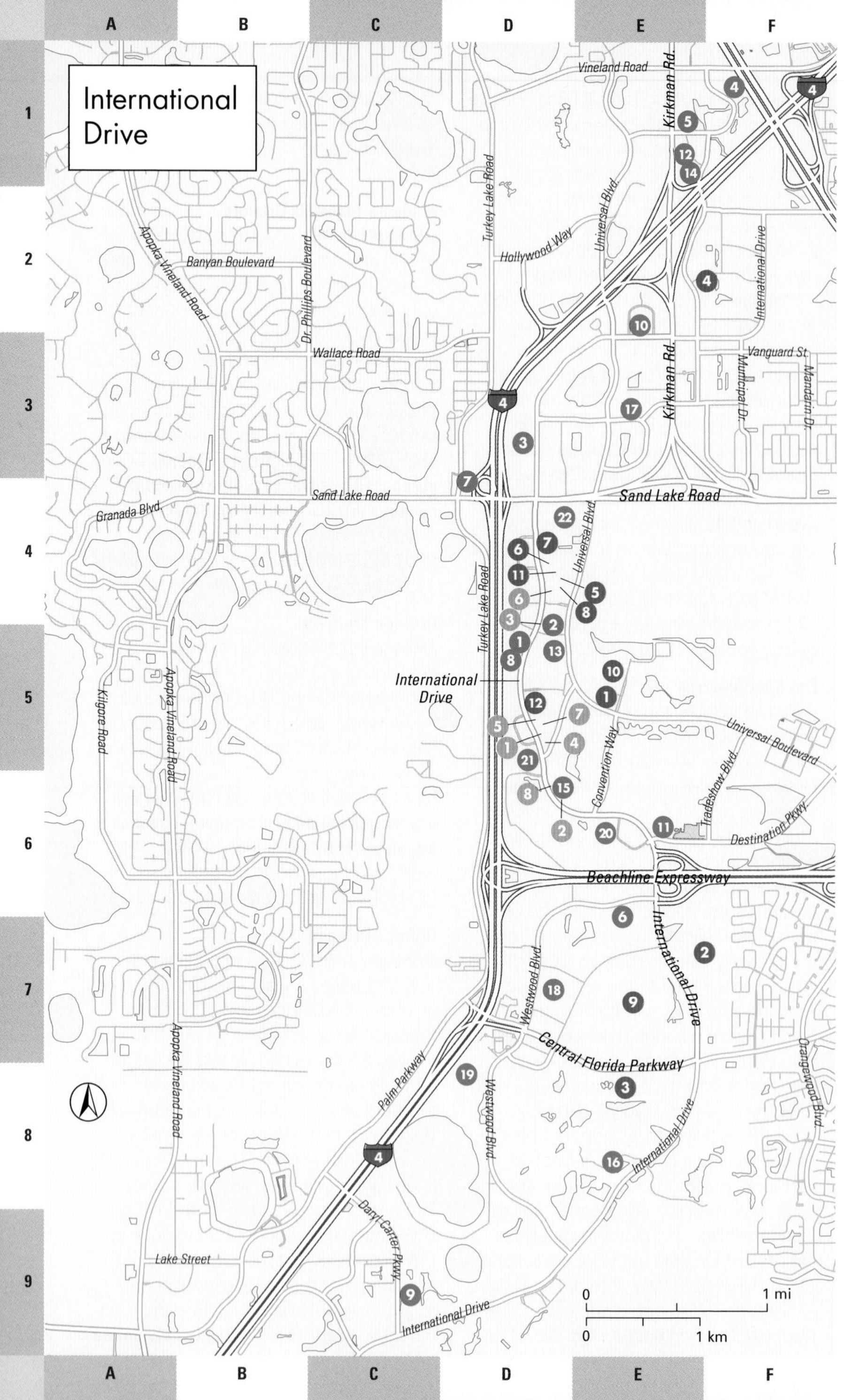

International Drive
A
B
C
D
E
F
1
2
3
4
5
6
7
8
9
Vineland Road
Kirkman Rd.
Turkey Lake Road
Universal Blvd.
Hollywood Way
International Drive
Apopka Vineland Road
Banyan Boulevard
Dr. Phillips Boulevard
Wallace Road
Vanguard St.
Municipal Dr.
Mandarin Dr.
Sand Lake Road
Granada Blvd.
Kilgore Road
International Drive
Convention Way
Universal Boulevard
Tradeshow Blvd.
Destination Pkwy.
Beachline Expressway
Westwood Blvd.
Central Florida Parkway
Palm Parkway
Orangewood Blvd.
Daryl Carter Pkwy.
Lake Street
0
1 mi
0
1 km

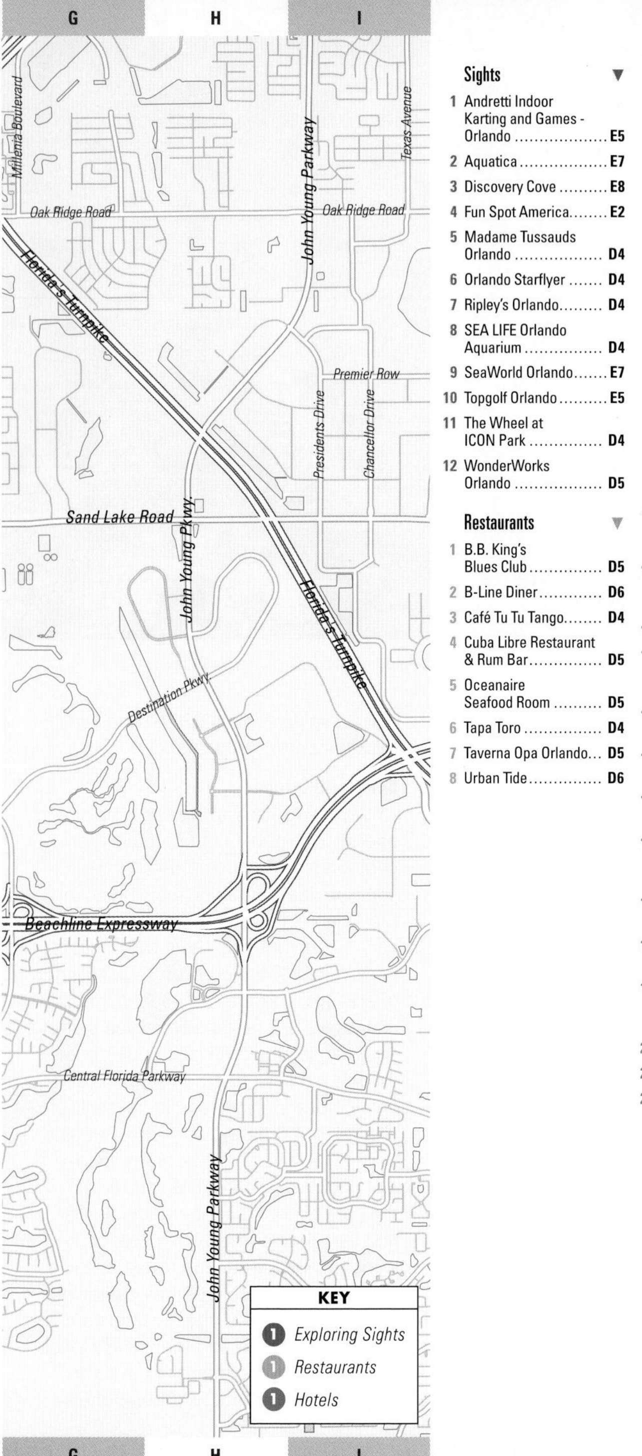

Sights

1 Andretti Indoor Karting and Games - Orlando **E5**

2 Aquatica **E7**

3 Discovery Cove **E8**

4 Fun Spot America........ **E2**

5 Madame Tussauds Orlando **D4**

6 Orlando Starflyer **D4**

7 Ripley's Orlando......... **D4**

8 SEA LIFE Orlando Aquarium **D4**

9 SeaWorld Orlando....... **E7**

10 Topgolf Orlando.......... **E5**

11 The Wheel at ICON Park **D4**

12 WonderWorks Orlando **D5**

Restaurants

1 B.B. King's Blues Club **D5**

2 B-Line Diner............. **D6**

3 Café Tu Tu Tango........ **D4**

4 Cuba Libre Restaurant & Rum Bar............... **D5**

5 Oceanaire Seafood Room **D5**

6 Tapa Toro **D4**

7 Taverna Opa Orlando... **D5**

8 Urban Tide............... **D6**

Hotels

1 Avanti Resort............ **D5**

2 Castle Hotel, Autograph Collection... **D4**

3 CoCo Key Hotel and Water Resort............ **D3**

4 Comfort Suites Near Universal Orlando Resort..................... **F1**

5 DoubleTree by Hilton at the Entrance to Universal Orlando **E1**

6 DoubleTree by Hilton Orlando at SeaWorld................. **E6**

7 Drury Inn and Suites near Universal Orlando Resort.......... **D4**

8 Embassy Suites by Hilton Orlando International Drive Convention Center...... **D5**

9 Floridays Resort Orlando **C9**

10 Four Points by Sheraton Orlando International Drive....... **E2**

11 Hilton Orlando............ **E6**

12 Holiday Inn Hotel and Suites Across From Universal Orlando **E1**

13 Hyatt Place Orlando/ Convention Center...... **D5**

14 Hyatt Place Orlando/ Universal.................. **E1**

15 Hyatt Regency Orlando **D6**

16 Parc Corniche Condominium Suite Hotel................ **E8**

17 The Point Hotel and Suites **E3**

18 Renaissance Orlando at SeaWorld............. **D7**

19 Residence Inn by Marriott Orlando at SeaWorld................ **D8**

20 Rosen Centre Hotel...... **E6**

21 Rosen Plaza Hotel **D5**

22 Wyndham Orlando Resort International Drive...... **D4**

The views from The Wheel at ICON Park can extend to more than 50 miles on a clear day.

ahead of time, and you can get discounts. ✉ *ICON Park, 8201 International Dr., International Drive* ☎ *407/351–5803* 🌐 *www.ripleys.com* 🎟 *$22; parking free; online discounts.*

★ SEA LIFE Orlando Aquarium

ZOO | FAMILY | In the shadow of a 400-foot observation wheel and within the ICON Park entertainment complex stands a kaleidoscope of underwater colors, where you can see some 5,000 sea creatures and explore various habitats. Plan to spend the better part of an afternoon exploring the attraction, as all ages delight at the close encounters with the aquarium's sharks, green sea turtles, and jellyfish. With an emphasis on education and conservation, exhibits are playful and informative, with fun features that include a 360-degree ocean tunnel and a children's soft play area. Combo tickets are available for SEA LIFE, The Wheel at ICON Park, and Madame Tussauds. ✉ *ICON Park, 8449 International Dr., International Drive* ☎ *321/ 209–9651* 🌐 *visitsealife.com* 🎟 *$29 (online and package ticket discounts).*

SeaWorld Orlando

AMUSEMENT PARK/WATER PARK | The oldest operating, biggest, and perhaps most controversial marine mammal park in the country, SeaWorld has been anchoring the Orlando Disney–alternative theme-park business since 1964. Much has been made of the company's handling of animals, and they've been in "rebuild and repair" mode for several years after attendance and stock prices plummeted. The park still features dolphins and orcas, but thrill rides and literal spills are the order of the day, with more swirling, looping, and very wet coasters than just about anywhere. The Icebreaker, the park's most recent attraction—its first launched coaster—features four launches, backward and forward, and a reverse launch into a 93-foot spike with 100-degree angle. Other coasters include Kraken Unleashed and the world's tallest river raft drop, the Infinity Falls River Rapids. The 400-foot Sky Tower offers a bird's-eye view of the park, while the Mako and Manta coasters skim tantalizingly close to the water; SeaWorld proclaims Mako as Orlando's tallest, fastest, and longest roller coaster. Kraken Unleashed soars to 150 feet while riders dangle their feet from the floorless track. The continuing animal attractions now focus more on education than performance, but dolphin and orca stadium shows are still a big draw. You can visit the ice-filled home of Puck the penguin in Antarctica: Empire of the Penguin, while Clyde and Seamore's Sea Lion High: The New Class brings out playful sea lions, walruses, and otters. Shark Encounter leads parkgoers through one of the world's largest underwater viewing tunnels to be surrounded by sharks, while the Stingray Lagoon offers encounters with stingrays and mantas. Much heralded by the park, marine animal rehab is the focus of the Manatee Rehabilitation Area, where visitors can see an up-close view of rescue operations; Pelican Preserve with bird rescue; and Pacific Point Preserve, which focuses on rehabilitating injured sea lions. ✉ *7007 SeaWorld Dr., International Drive* ☎ *407/545–5550* 🌐 *seaworld.com* 🎫 *$106, $25 parking, (online discounts).*

Topgolf Orlando

GOLF | **FAMILY** | A high-tech combination of bowling, golf simulators, and video games, Topgolf lets duffers hit electronic golf balls in climate-controlled, outdoor hitting bays surrounded by giant video screens. The mammoth complex offers kids golf lessons and something for nongolfers as well, with full bars featuring craft beer and cocktails, bar snacks, burgers, and desserts. ✉ *9295 Universal Blvd., International Drive* ☎ *407/218–7714* 🌐 *topgolf.com* 🎫 *From $30 per hr for up to 6 players.*

★ **The Wheel at ICON Park**

AMUSEMENT PARK/WATER PARK | **FAMILY** | Only 15 miles from Walt Disney World and near Universal Studios Orlando, ICON Park attractions include Madame Tussauds, SEA LIFE Orlando aquarium, and the 450-foot tall Starflyer swing ride. But the real star is the 400-foot-tall observation wheel known simply as The Wheel, which offers an almost unobstructed view of all the distant theme parks, lush green landscape, and the soaring buildings of the City Beautiful. The wheel's 30 high-tech capsules complete a rotation every 30 minutes. Apple iPad Air tablets on board help to locate points of interest throughout the trip, including the theme parks, scenic landscapes, and even the Atlantic coast. Visibility on clear days can be more than 50 miles, reaching all the way east to Cape Canaveral. Rent a private capsule for up to 15 people, with champagne, for a sky-high experience. ✉ *ICON Park, 8401 International Dr., International Drive* ☎ *407/270–8644* 🌐 *iconparkorlando.com* 🎫 *$28 (package prices available).*

WonderWorks Orlando

AMUSEMENT PARK/WATER PARK | **FAMILY** | The building seems to be sinking into the ground—at a precarious angle and upside down. Many people stop to take pictures in front of the topsy-turvy facade, complete with upended palm trees and broken sidewalks. Inside the upside-down theme continues only as far as the lobby. After that it's a playground of 100 interactive experiences—some incorporating virtual reality, others educational (similar to those at a science museum), and still others pure entertainment. You can experience an earthquake or a hurricane, land a space shuttle using simulator controls, make giant bubbles in the Bubble Lab, play laser tag in the enormous laser-tag arena and arcade, design and ride your own roller coaster, lie on a bed of real nails, and play baseball with a virtual Major League batter. An *Outta Control Magic Comedy Dinner Show* is held here nightly. ✉ *9067 International Dr., International Drive* ☎ *407/351–8800* 🌐 *www.wonderworksonline.com/orlando* 🎫 *$34; Outta Control Magic Comedy*

The clear tunnel at Shark Encounter in SeaWorld takes you underwater and underneath the sharks.

Dinner Show $32 (online discounts available); parking from $5.

Restaurants

A number of restaurants are scattered among the hotels that line International Drive. Many are branches of chains, from fast-food spots to themed coffee shops and up, but the food here can be quite good. To get to the area, take Interstate 4 Exit 72 or 74A. Count on it taking up to half an hour from the Kissimmee area or from a WDW property.

B.B. King's Blues Club

$$ | BARBECUE | FAMILY | This massive restaurant is dedicated to soul food, live blues, and the legacy of B.B. King. **Known for:** live bands and dancing; barbecued ribs, brisket, and shrimp and grits; messy and delicious burgers. *$ Average main: $18 ✉ Pointe Orlando, 9101 International Dr., International Drive ☎ 407/370–4550 🌐 bbkings.com/orlando.*

B-Line Diner

$$ | AMERICAN | FAMILY | Open 24 hours in the Hyatt Regency, this slick modern diner is not exactly cheap, but the salads, sandwiches, and griddle foods are tops. The classic combo—a thick, juicy burger with fries and a milk shake—is done beautifully. **Known for:** 1950s dinner theme; 24-hour service with late-night specials; large dessert menu. *$ Average main: $20 ✉ Hyatt Regency Orlando, 9801 International Dr., International Drive ☎ 407/284–1234 🌐 orlando.regency.hyatt.com.*

Café Tu Tu Tango

$$$ | ECLECTIC | FAMILY | The food here is served tapas-style—everything is appetizer-sized but plentiful and relatively inexpensive. The restaurant is designed to resemble an artist's loft; artists paint at easels while diners take a culinary trip around the world. **Known for:** small plates ideal for sharing; live entertainment and artists; "Wine Down Wednesday" drink specials. *$ Average main: $23 ✉ 8625 International Dr., International Drive*

☎ *407/248–2222* ⊕ *www.cafetututango.com.*

Cuba Libre Restaurant & Rum Bar
$$$ | **CUBAN** | **FAMILY** | The dining rooms at this Cuban restaurant feel as if they're movie sets of Old Havana, with dramatic touches upstairs and down. Start your meal with a meat-filled arepa rellena corn cake or a platter of two to four empanadas filled with savory ground beef and olives, chicken, cheese, or pork. **Known for:** menu via celeb chef Guillermo Pernot; extensive rum bar; seafood paella and Cuban sandwiches. $ *Average main: $28* ✉ *Pointe Orlando, 9101 International Dr., International Drive* ☎ *407/226–1600* ⊕ *www.cubalibrerestaurant.com* ⊗ *No lunch.*

Oceanaire Seafood Room
$$$$ | **SEAFOOD** | Don't let the 1930s-era ocean-liner interior fool you: as theme restaurants go, this place is a good one. The straightforward preparation—grilled or broiled, brushed with lemon butter—is welcome. **Known for:** exceptional seafood; large wine menu; "Grand Shellfish Tower" raw bar offering. $ *Average main: $46* ✉ *Pointe Orlando, 9101 International Dr., International Drive* ☎ *407/363–4801* ⊕ *www.theoceanaire.com* ⊗ *No lunch.*

Tapa Toro
$$$ | **SPANISH** | Diners can order authentic tapas and paella at this Spanish restaurant in the heart of the I-Drive 360 complex (look for the giant revolving observation wheel). Tapas dishes include a great gazpacho soup and fiery *patatas bravas* (home fries with a spicy tomato sauce), and the unique paella grills make short work of the national rice dish, which can be had with seafood, chicken, lamb, or vegetarian. **Known for:** family-style tapas and entrées; several varieties of paella; live entertainment. $ *Average main: $22* ✉ *8441 International Dr., International Drive* ☎ *407/226–2929* ⊕ *tapatoro.restaurant.*

Taverna Opa Orlando
$$$ | **GREEK** | **FAMILY** | This high-energy Greek restaurant offers a fun evening in a lively environment to supplement excellent Greek staples and a nice selection of *meze* (small plate) appetizers. Here the ouzo flows like a mountain stream, the Greek (and global) music almost reaches the level of a rock concert, and the roaming belly dancers actively encourage diners to join in. **Known for:** traditional Greek taverna food; live entertainment; large selection of meze, with vegetarian options. $ *Average main: $27* ✉ *Pointe Orlando, 9101 International Dr., International Drive* ☎ *407/351–8660* ⊕ *www.opaorlando.com.*

Urban Tide
$$$ | **AMERICAN** | A wide-ranging menu of high-end coastal Florida cuisine offers something for everyone, from extravagant steaks and seafood to a surprisingly complete vegetarian larder. The food at this chef-run spot is as appealing as the extensive wine list; it includes items like seafood charcuterie, lobster sausage, and salmon pastrami. **Known for:** house-made seafood charcuterie; locally sourced produce and meats; extensive wine list. $ *Average main: $30* ✉ *Hyatt Regency Orlando, 9801 International Dr., International Drive* ☎ *407/345–4570* ⊕ *orlando.regency.hyatt.com.*

Hotels

The sprawl of hotels, time-shares, motels, condos, and other rentals offers visitors a varied choice in a central area that makes a great base for visits to Walt Disney World, Universal, and other Orlando attractions.

The I-Ride Trolley travels the length of I-Drive from Florida's Turnpike to the outlet center on Vineland Avenue, stopping at Universal Orlando, and SeaWorld. I-Ride is a more worthy transportation tool than you might think. Lots of hotels don't offer shuttle service to Disney,

Manta is one of several thrilling roller coasters at SeaWorld Orlando.

even for a fee, but you can take I-Ride to hotels that do offer a fee-based Disney shuttle, which, depending on the size of the family or group, can be cheaper than a cab.

Avanti Resort

$ | RESORT | FAMILY | In the middle of all the activities on International Drive, and a short walk from ICON Park, this resort offers families a home away from home with plenty of amenities at a reasonable price; rooms and public areas are decorated in mid-century chic, and the large pool has a children's play area, a sandy beach with volleyball court, a shuffleboard court, and a bar and grill. **Pros:** scheduled shuttles to theme parks; complimentary cribs; laundry facilities. **Cons:** daily resort fee of $12 covers Wi-Fi, parking, shuttles; elevators can be slow for those on top floors; theme-park shuttles can be slow and crowded. *Rooms from: $115* *8738 International Dr., International Drive* *407/313–0100* *www.avantiresort.com* *652 rooms* *No meals.*

Castle Hotel, Autograph Collection

$$ | HOTEL | Amid International Drive's vibrant scene (you can almost reach out and touch The Wheel at ICON Park), the hotel offers a slightly kitschy sophistication, combining Alpine castle with Mardi Gras glitz. **Pros:** easy walk to I-Drive eateries and attractions; great views; sophisticated vibe. **Cons:** on a congested stretch of I-Drive; not close to Disney parks; self-parking fee. *Rooms from: $197* *8629 International Dr., International Drive* *407/345–1511, 800/952–2785* *www.castlehotelorlando.com* *214 rooms* *No meals.*

CoCo Key Hotel and Water Resort

$ | HOTEL | FAMILY | If swimming and sliding are among your family's top vacation desires, and your budget gets happy with value prices, this colorful resort with its on-property, 14-slide, three-pool water park could be the perfect destination. **Pros:** on-site water park; shuttle to Universal; value price. **Cons:** $32.95 daily resort fee for Wi-Fi, parking, and shuttle; some rooms overlook noisy

Popular Chain Restaurants

When all you want is a quick bite, consider these chain restaurants. They seem to crop up everywhere, and all have tables where you can sit for a few moments before heading back out to the shops and attractions.

Anthony's Coal-Fired Pizza: Thin-crust pizzas with generous toppings like arugula and pepperoni are baked—charred, really—in a coal-fired oven at these bustling spaces near Restaurant Row and in Altamonte Springs. The chicken wings are also popular. *www.anthonyscoal-firedpizza.com*

Bubbalou's Bodacious Bar-B-Que: A quintet of local smokers serves up mounds of Southern barbecue, from baby back ribs to pulled-pork sandwiches. The locations on Kirkman Road and Conroy-Windermere Road are minutes from Universal Orlando. *www.bubbalous.com*

Einstein Bros. Bagels: For a light breakfast or lunch, Einstein's satisfies with bagels, wraps, salads, and sandwiches. *www.einsteinbros.com*

First Watch: Breakfast classics like pancakes and waffles make First Watch a popular choice for locals, who line up on weekends for Key West "crepeggs" (a crepe filled with eggs that have been scrambled with turkey, avocado, bacon, tomatoes, and Monterey Jack cheese), and Floridian French toast with bananas, kiwi, and berries. *www.firstwatch.com*

Five Guys Burgers and Fries: This burger joint has a nearly cultlike following for its freshly ground beef. Fifteen toppings are available for no charge, and the fries are freshly cut. *www.fiveguys.com*

4 Rivers Smokehouse: The king of local barbecue slow-smokes Texas-style brisket, serves mountains of St. Louis ribs, and offers acres of towering desserts at 15 local and national locations. *www.4rsmokehouse.com*

Hawker's: This local Asian street food restaurant made good has expanded in recent years from one to 11 locations—and from here to Maryland. *www.eatathawkers.com*

Jimmy John's: Lunchtime lines are out the door at Orlando's many Jimmy John's, where the "world's greatest gourmet sandwiches" are essentially subs and clubs. *www.jimmyjohns.com*

Panera Bread: Fresh-baked pastries and bagels are the mainstays, although you can grab a hearty, inexpensive meal like smoked-turkey panino on three-cheese bread or a bowl of soup served in a hollowed-out sourdough loaf. *www.panerabread.com*

Pei Wei Asian Diner: Bold flavors from across Asia come together at these fast-casual restaurants, where a hearty noodle bowl, orange-peel beef, or sweet-and-sour tofu will come in at less than $10. *www.peiwei.com*

TooJay's Gourmet Deli: A New York deli it ain't, but the TooJay's chain offers a welcome pastrami fix for those with a yen for salty meat on crusty seeded rye. *www.toojays.com*

pools; water park closed some days in winter. $ *Rooms from: $129* ✉ *7400 International Dr., International Drive* ☎ *407/351–2626* 🌐 *www.cocokeyorlando.com* 🛏 *391 rooms* 🍽 *No meals.*

Comfort Suites Near Universal Orlando Resort

$ | **HOTEL** | **FAMILY** | If Universal's roller coasters and Harry Potter's Diagon Alley are your destinations, these homey accommodations just outside the park should fit the bill with budget-priced rooms that offer a kitchenette with microwave, refrigerator, and coffeemaker; some even have dining tables. **Pros:** free hot breakfast; free Wi-Fi and free parking; free shuttle to Universal and SeaWorld. **Cons:** a bit of a hike to shops, restaurants; long way to Disney parks; no on-site full-service restaurant or room service. $ *Rooms from: $129* ✉ *5617 Major Blvd., International Drive* ☎ *407/363–1967, 800/951–7829* 🌐 *www.choicehotels.com* 🛏 *150 suites* 🍽 *Free breakfast.*

DoubleTree by Hilton at the Entrance to Universal Orlando

$ | **HOTEL** | **FAMILY** | The name is a mouthful, but it's an accurate description for this value-priced hotel, which caters to business-trippers and pleasure seekers alike; it's so close to Universal that some of the tower rooms offer roller-coaster and Hogwarts views. **Pros:** three on-site restaurants; free Wi-Fi; free shuttle to Universal. **Cons:** fee for parking; on a fast-lane tourist strip; need a car to reach Disney and downtown Orlando. $ *Rooms from: $119* ✉ *5780 Major Blvd., International Drive* ☎ *407/351–1000* 🌐 *www.doubltreeorlando.com* 🛏 *742 rooms* 🍽 *No meals.*

DoubleTree by Hilton Orlando at SeaWorld

$ | **RESORT** | **FAMILY** | Combining low bungalow-style buildings and a 17-story tower, this Bali-inspired hotel creates a warm welcome and a comforting escape—lush linens, tranquil guest rooms, three pools, and tropical landscaping—from hectic I-Drive. **Pros:** on-site miniature golf; shuttles to Universal, SeaWorld, and Aquatica; carpet-free rooms available for those with allergies. **Cons:** $22.45 daily resort fee (includes Wi-Fi, shuttles, and parking); few shops and restaurants within walking distance; paid shuttle to Disney's Magic Kingdom. $ *Rooms from: $113* ✉ *10100 International Dr., International Drive* ☎ *407/352–1100* 🌐 *www.doubletreeorlandoseaworld.com* 🛏 *1,020 rooms* 🍽 *No meals.*

★ **Drury Inn and Suites near Universal Orlando Resort**

$ | **HOTEL** | **FAMILY** | This reasonably priced hotel, less than a mile from Universal, offers free Wi-Fi, free parking, free shuttle to Universal, free hot breakfast, free long-distance and local phone calls, and free hot food and cold beverages in the late afternoon. **Pros:** free everything; central location; reasonable price. **Cons:** if Disney is your destination, this might be a little far afield; next to two busy roadways; pool and gym are small. $ *Rooms from: $119* ✉ *7301 W. Sand Lake Rd., at I–4, International Drive* ☎ *407/354–1101* 🌐 *www.druryhotels.com* 🛏 *238 rooms* 🍽 *Free breakfast.*

Embassy Suites by Hilton Orlando International Drive Convention Center

$$ | **HOTEL** | **FAMILY** | An airy, eight-story atrium with palm trees and fountains lends an air of luxury to this moderately priced all-suites lodging, which offers free shuttles to all theme parks as well as free breakfast and late-afternoon drinks. **Pros:** easy walk to shopping, and dining; free shuttle to theme parks; free breakfast and afternoon cocktails. **Cons:** on congested stretch of I-Drive, a half mile from convention center; daily Wi-Fi charge in rooms; need a car to visit Disney. $ *Rooms from: $191* ✉ *8978 International Dr., International Drive* ☎ *407/352–1400, 800/433–7275* 🌐 *www.embassysuitesorlando.com* 🛏 *244 suites* 🍽 *Free breakfast.*

Floridays Resort Orlando

$$ | **RESORT** | **FAMILY** | This pleasant, two- and three-bedroom condo resort with full kitchens, halfway between Universal Orlando and Disney World, has six six-story buildings, two pools, a game room, gym, business center, and café with room service. **Pros:** great, self-contained environment for a family vacation; shuttles to all theme parks; on the I-Ride trolley route. **Cons:** a car would be helpful, as it's too far to walk to almost anything meaningful; daily resort fee for Wi-Fi, parking, shuttles; remote location. *Rooms from: $201 ✉ 12562 International Dr., International Drive ☎ 407/238–7700 🌐 www.floridaysresort.com 432 units No meals.*

Four Points by Sheraton Orlando International Drive

$ | **HOTEL** | **FAMILY** | With a hard-to-miss giant ball perched on top of its 20-story round tower, this hotel on the north end of International Drive is visible for blocks, and has a contemporary atmosphere, thanks to the clean, airy design of the lobby. **Pros:** convenient to Universal and SeaWorld; shuttle to Disney and Universal; free parking, Wi-Fi, and fitness center. **Cons:** located on a busy stretch of I-Drive; no on-site shop for essentials; restaurant is very basic. *Rooms from: $156 ✉ 5905 International Dr., International Drive ☎ 407/351–2100, 800/327–1366 🌐 www.fourpoints.com 301 rooms No meals.*

Hilton Orlando

$$$ | **HOTEL** | **FAMILY** | Families visiting this award-winning hotel get two pools, a palm-fringed lazy river to relax in, a kids' club, basketball court, tennis court, and a full-service spa; conventioneers appreciate the vast meeting space, direct connection to the convention center, substantial restaurants and bars, work desks with Herman Miller chairs, and an on-site steak house. **Pros:** multiple pools, including a lazy river; complimentary I-Ride Trolley to SeaWorld; direct walkway to convention center. **Cons:** about 80% of guests are conventioneers; no free shuttle to Disney World or Universal; $35 daily resort fee and $24 daily parking fee. *Rooms from: $290 ✉ 6001 Destination Pkwy., International Drive ☎ 407/313–4300 🌐 www.thehiltonorlando.com 1,417 rooms No meals.*

Holiday Inn Hotel and Suites Across from Universal Orlando

$ | **HOTEL** | **FAMILY** | Staying at this hotel directly across the street from Universal could be a savvy budget move: the value price joins the freebies on offer, from free theme-park shuttles and Wi-Fi to free kids meals and more. **Pros:** free Wi-Fi, parking, and kids meals; no resort fee; you can walk to Universal and area shops (although there's also a free shuttle). **Cons:** older hotel; need a car to get to Disney and downtown Orlando; busy traffic corridor. *Rooms from: $88 ✉ 5905 S. Kirkman Rd., International Drive ☎ 407/351–3333 🌐 www.hiuniversal.com 390 rooms No meals.*

Hyatt Place Orlando/Convention Center

$$ | **HOTEL** | Youngish, high-tech-consuming business travelers and vacationing families find value here because of the location and amenities, such as 42-inch flat-panel HDTVs, work areas with computer access panel, wet bar with mini-refrigerator, and heated pool. **Pros:** free parking, Wi-Fi; convenient to convention center, shopping, restaurants, and ICON Park; 24/7 fitness center. **Cons:** no kids' program or babysitting services; no theme-park shuttles; too far to walk to Convention Center. *Rooms from: $179 ✉ 8741 International Dr., International Drive ☎ 407/370–4720, 888/492–8847 🌐 www.hyatt.com 149 rooms Free breakfast.*

Hyatt Place Orlando/Universal

$$ | **HOTEL** | Hyatt Place supports tech-savvy guests in what Hyatt calls the 24/7 lifestyle, which means the hotel amenities available to guests at 3 in the afternoon are also on tap at 3 in the

morning, and rooms have work spaces and computer-ready, flat-screen TVs. **Pros:** walking distance to Universal as well as a free shuttle; free breakfast and parking; free high-speed Wi-Fi. **Cons:** no kids' programs or babysitting service; no shuttles to Disney; noise from nearby construction and highway. *Rooms from: $179 ✉ 5895 Caravan Ct., International Drive ☎ 407/351–0627 🌐 www.orlandouniversal.place.hyatt.com 151 rooms No meals.*

Hyatt Regency Orlando

$$ | **RESORT** | **FAMILY** | This deluxe high-rise conference hotel offers anything a resort customer could want, with richly appointed rooms, two pools with cabanas, a full-service spa and fitness center the size of your local Y, two large restaurants, and a 360-seat, glass-walled lounge overlooking the pool. **Pros:** good spa; walk to many shops and restaurants; on the I-Ride Trolley route. **Cons:** check-in can take a while if a convention is arriving; long walk from end to end; $30 daily resort and $27 daily parking fees. *Rooms from: $239 ✉ 9801 International Dr., International Drive ☎ 407/284–1234 🌐 www.orlando.regency.hyatt.com 1,641 rooms No meals.*

Parc Corniche Condominium Suite Hotel

$ | **HOTEL** | **FAMILY** | Set back from traffic on the south end of International Drive, this condo hotel offers a good deal for a family with suites that have separate bedrooms, flat-screen TVs, full kitchens with dishwasher, and bathrooms; the I-Ride Trolley passes the front door. **Pros:** free breakfast; well-equipped kitchens; free shuttle to Disney, Universal, and SeaWorld. **Cons:** not much within walking distance; $9.95 daily resort fee, $30 cleaning fee; heavy traffic on International Drive. *Rooms from: $156 ✉ 6300 Parc Corniche Dr., International Drive ☎ 407/239–7100, 800/446–2721 🌐 www.parccorniche.com 210 suites Free breakfast.*

The Point Hotel and Suites

$ | **HOTEL** | **FAMILY** | In the center of the entertainment triangle bounded by I-4, Florida's Turnpike, and the Beachline Expressway, this all-suites resort is close to Universal, outlet shopping malls, I-Drive attractions, and the convention center, making it a good option for family vacations, romantic getaways, and business travel. **Pros:** central to I-Drive entertainment; Wi-Fi throughout the resort; shuttle to Disney, SeaWorld, and Universal. **Cons:** shuttles can be slow and crowded; daily resort fee; no ergonomic chair for working. *Rooms from: $157 ✉ 7389 Universal Blvd., International Drive ☎ 407/956–2000 🌐 www.thepointorlando.com 244 suites No meals.*

Renaissance Orlando at SeaWorld

$$ | **HOTEL** | **FAMILY** | With a 10-story atrium full of ponds, palm trees, and, ironically, a sushi bar, this SeaWorld neighbor offers tiny black-and-white Shamus instead of rubber duckies in the bath; rooms feature a king or two queen beds, sectional couches, flat-screen TVs, lush bedding, and ergonomic work areas. **Pros:** across from SeaWorld; free shuttles to Universal, SeaWorld, Aquatica, and Disney; on-site water park for kids. **Cons:** can be a long walk to rooms; many conventioneers; $30 daily resort and $20 daily parking fees. *Rooms from: $239 ✉ 6677 Sea Harbor Dr., International Drive ☎ 407/351–5555, 800/468–3571 🌐 www.renaissanceseaworld.com 781 rooms No meals.*

★ Residence Inn by Marriott Orlando at SeaWorld

$$ | **HOTEL** | **FAMILY** | From the welcoming lobby to the well-appointed suites (including dishwasher, microwave, pots, pans, dishes) and the parklike atmosphere around the pool, this hotel is a great choice if SeaWorld, Aquatica, I-Drive shopping, Universal, or the convention center are on your to-do list; a huge laundry is a boon for families. **Pros:** free shuttles to all theme parks; well-equipped

kitchenettes; free breakfast, Wi-Fi, and parking. **Cons:** not much within walking distance; right next to busy Interstate 4; it's a hike to Disney. *Rooms from: $179 ✉ 11000 Westwood Blvd., International Drive ☎ 407/313–3600, 800/889–9728 🌐 www.marriott.com 350 suites Free breakfast.*

Rosen Centre Hotel

$$$ | RESORT | FAMILY | Connected by a covered sky-bridge to the Orange County Convention Center, this 24-story resort with five on-site restaurants attracts business customers but doesn't ignore families. **Pros:** free shuttles to Universal, SeaWorld, and Aquatica; preferred tee times at sister resort Rosen Shingle Creek Golf Club; high-speed Wi-Fi in rooms. **Cons:** no free shuttle to Disney; need a car to get anywhere off I-Drive; lots of convention guests. *Rooms from: $278 ✉ 9840 International Dr., International Drive ☎ 407/996–9840 🌐 www.rosencentre.com 1,334 rooms No meals.*

Rosen Plaza Hotel

$$$ | HOTEL | Close to the convention center, this 14-story hotel caters to its corporate clientele, but leisure travelers also like the prime location and long list of amenities, including a heated swimming pool, fitness center, babysitting services, and a vibrant nightclub that opens onto the pool. **Pros:** within walking distance of Pointe Orlando and other I-Drive restaurants and cinema; priority reservations at Shingle Creek Golf Course, the 18-hole golf course at nearby Rosen Shingle Creek; free shuttle to Universal. **Cons:** Convention Center traffic can be heavy; parking fee; not geared for families. *Rooms from: $253 ✉ 9700 International Dr., International Drive ☎ 407/996–9700, 800/366–9700 🌐 www.rosenplaza.com 800 rooms No meals.*

Wyndham Orlando Resort International Drive

$ | RESORT | FAMILY | Rebuilt and renovated in 2017 and located in the walkable neighborhood around Orlando's ICON Park entertainment complex, this resort offers a central location for family theme-park visits and also has high-tech amenities for the business traveler. **Pros:** guests get a discount at the adjacent ICON Park complex; within a safe walk of I-Drive restaurants and entertainment; shuttle to Universal and SeaWorld. **Cons:** no elevators; Disney (about 30 minutes away) shuttle is pricey; $30 one-time resort fee. *Rooms from: $159 ✉ 8001 International Dr., International Drive ☎ 407/351–2420, 800/996–3426 🌐 www.orlandowyndhamresort.com 613 rooms No meals.*

Nightlife

BARS

B.B. King's Blues Club

MUSIC CLUBS | The blues legend-turned-entrepreneur lent his name to a string of blues clubs across America, including this one in Orlando. Like the others, this club has music at its heart. There's a dance floor and stage for live performances by the B.B. King All-Star Band and touring musicians seven nights a week. The variety is impressive, with a wide range of tunes inspired by everyone from the King of Blues (B.B.) to the Queen of Motown (Aretha) to the Soul of Funk (take your pick). Since you can't really experience Delta blues without Delta dining, the club doubles as a restaurant with fried dill pickles, catfish bites, po' boys, ribs, and other comfort foods. Wash it all down with a drink from the full bar. *✉ Pointe Orlando, 9101 International Dr., International Drive ☎ 407/370–4550 🌐 www.bbkingclubs.com/orlando.*

DINNER SHOWS

The Outta Control Magic Comedy Dinner Show

THEATER | FAMILY | A preshow of sorts to the kid-friendly, hands-on science and activity center called Wonderworks, this dinner show is exactly as its name suggests: a magic show filled with jokes, gags, and tricks. The magicians' juvenile one-liners make this delightful for kids and pleasingly silly for adults, with audience participation playing a large role. A pizza/salad/soft drink buffet is open prior to the show. ✉ *Wonderworks, 9067 International Dr., International Drive* ☎ *407/351–8800* 🌐 *www.wonderworksonline.com/orlando/the-experience/the-outta-control-magic-comedy-dinner-show* 🎫 *$32; look for discounts online.*

NIGHTCLUBS

ICEBAR

BARS/PUBS | Thanks to the miracle of refrigeration, this is Orlando's coolest bar—literally and figuratively. Fifty tons of pure ice are kept at a constant 27°F and have been cut and sculpted by world-class carvers into a cozy (or as cozy as ice can be) sanctuary of tables, sofas, chairs, and a bar. The staff loans you a thermal cape and gloves (upgrade to a faux fur coat for an extra $10), and when you enter the frozen hall your drink is served in a glass made of crystal clear ice. There's no cover charge if you just want to hang out in the Fire Lounge or outdoor Polar Patio, but you will pay a cover to spend as much time as you can handle in the subfreezing ICEBAR. There's no beer or wine inside; it's simply too cold. **TIP→ For a nonfrozen evening, visit the attached Fire Lounge** ✉ *Pointe Orlando, 8967 International Dr., International Drive* ☎ *407/426–7555* 🌐 *www.icebarorlando.com* 🎫 *$20; upgrade packages available.*

Performing Arts

Dinner shows are an immensely popular form of nighttime entertainment around Orlando. For a single price, you get a theatrical production and a multicourse dinner. Performances run the gamut from jousting to jamboree tunes, and meals tend to be better than average; unlimited beer, wine, and soda are usually included, but mixed drinks (and often *any* drinks before dinner) cost extra. What the shows lack in substance and depth they make up for in grandeur and enthusiasm. The result is an evening of light entertainment, which youngsters in particular enjoy. Seatings are usually between 7 and 9:30, and there are usually one or two performances a night, with an extra show during peak periods. You might sit with strangers at tables for 10 or more, but that's part of the fun.

If you're in Orlando off-season, try to take in these dinner shows on a busy night—a show playing to a small audience can be uncomfortable. It's also good to make reservations, especially for weekend shows, and to verify show times in advance, as performance schedules can vary by season. Don't let the big prices fool you—there's a flood of coupons (sometimes half-off) offered online and in International Drive restaurants, hotels, and at the Orlando/Orange County Convention & Visitors Bureau. If you don't have a coupon when booking, ask about discounts *and* whether or not the cost includes a gratuity—servers anxious to pocket more cash might hit you up for an extra handout.

★ Sleuths Mystery Dinner Show

THEATER | FAMILY | If Sherlock Holmes has always intrigued you, head on over to this long-running show for a four-course meal served with a healthy dose of conspiracy. Sleuths is a hotbed of local acting talent, with 13 rotating whodunit performances staged throughout the year in three different theaters. The comedy-mystery show

Sleuths Mystery Dinner Show on International Drive near Universal Orlando Resort is one of several popular dinner theater performances in Orlando.

begins during your appetizer, and murder is the case by the time they clear your plates. You'll get to discuss clues and question still-living characters over dinner and solve the crime during dessert. Prizes go to top sleuths. Comedy and magic shows fill up the late-night lineup on weekends. ✉ *8267 International Dr., International Drive* ☎ *407/363–1985* 🌐 *www.sleuths.com* 🎫 *$66.*

Activities

SPAS

Eforea Spa at Hilton Orlando

FITNESS/HEALTH CLUBS | From the deeply cushioned chaise longues in the waiting room, where guests relax in fleecy robes and cozy blankets, to the complimentary infused water, juices, teas, and fruits, guests are made to feel cherished from the moment they enter this big (15 treatment rooms), tropical spa. Orange blossom is the source of the oil for the signature Neroli massage, and essences of rosemary, pine, and lavender soothe the senses during aromatherapy treatments. Guests are welcome to linger in the steam room, full-body showers, or full-service salon, or to arrange to have a treatment in a cabana by the pool. Every spa guest can enjoy complimentary use of the pool and 24-hour fitness center before or after any spa service, and special services are available for youngsters and teens in the salon. A20% service charge is added. Day passes are available, self-parking is free for nonhotel guests. ✉ *Hilton Orlando, 6001 Destination Pkwy., Orlando* ☎ *407/313–4300* 🌐 *www.thehiltonorlando.com/discover/spa-and-fitness.html.*

The Spa at Hyatt Regency Orlando

FITNESS/HEALTH CLUBS | Getting to this 22,000-square-foot, full-service contemporary retreat, set at the heart of a huge convention resort, can be quite a hike, so by the time guests arrive they're usually happy to shed their clothes and cares, don fluffy robes and slippers, and settle in for some serious rejuvenation. Guests have access to a co-ed relaxation lounge, while separate spa areas offer whirlpools,

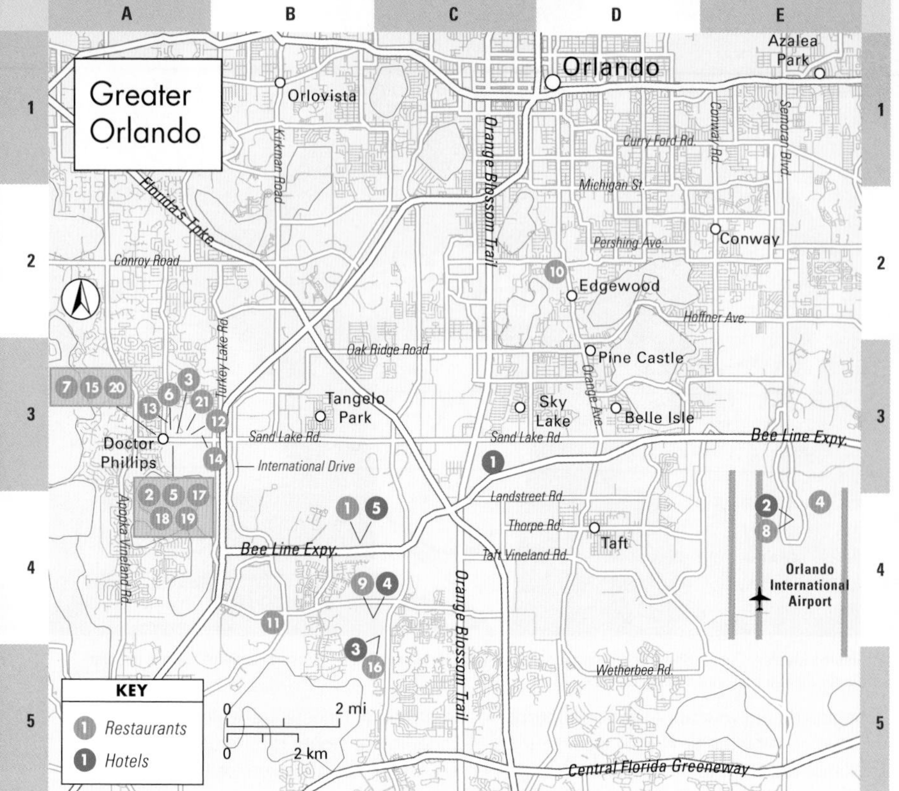

Restaurants

1 A Land Remembered ... **B4**

2 Bonefish Grill ... **A3**

3 Bosphorous Turkish Cuisine ... **A3**

4 Cask & Larder ... **E4**

5 Cedars Restaurant ... **A3**

6 Christini's Ristorante Italiano ... **A3**

7 Dragonfly Robata Grill & Sushi ... **A3**

8 Hemisphere ... **E4**

9 Highball & Harvest ... **B4**

10 Le Coq au Vin ... **D2**

11 Moe's Southwest Grill ... **B4**

12 MoonFish ... **A3**

13 Morton's The Steakhouse ... **A3**

14 Ocean Prime ... **A3**

15 Peperoncino ... **A3**

16 Primo ... **C4**

17 Rasa ... **A3**

18 Roy's Orlando ... **A3**

19 Seasons 52 ... **A3**

20 Urbain 40 ... **A3**

21 Vines Grille & Wine Bar ... **A3**

Hotels

1 The Florida Hotel & Conference Center ... **C3**

2 Hyatt Regency Orlando International Airport ... **E4**

3 JW Marriott Orlando Grande Lakes ... **C4**

4 Ritz-Carlton Orlando, Grande Lakes ... **C4**

5 Rosen Shingle Creek ... **B4**

steam room, and showers to enjoy before and after treatments. Massages, a variety of facials, and complete salon services are all available. A gratuity is added. ✉ *Hyatt Regency Orlando, 9801 International Dr., International Drive* ☎ *407/284–1234* 🌐 *www.hyatt.com/en-US/spas/The-Spa-Orlando/home.*

The Spa at Rosen Centre

FITNESS/HEALTH CLUBS | An intimate spa in a resort right across from the convention center caters to busy, stressed-out businesspeople as well as bridal parties, girlfriends' getaways, and spa parties. Once clothes and cares are exchanged for luxurious robes and comfy slippers in the separate locker rooms, guests move to the serene, candlelit, and aroma-enhanced separate relaxation rooms. If your muscles need a real workout, try a traditional Ashiatsu massage, where the masseuse, supported by a wooden frame, uses gravity and her bare feet to reach deep into knots. The Signature Lavish Milk and Honey Ritual is 90 minutes of indulgence, complete with skin firming milk and honey treatment, exfoliation, and warm honey butter body masque. Day passes are available for hotel guests and nonguests. Parking is validated for nonguests. ✉ *Rosen Centre Hotel, 9840 International Dr., International Drive* ☎ *407/996–1248* 🌐 *www.spaatrosencentre.com.*

South Orlando

South Orlando is home to expansive resort hotels, chain restaurants, the headwaters of the Everglades, and not much more.

Restaurants

A Land Remembered

$$$$ | **STEAKHOUSE** | The name of this award-winning steak house comes from the iconic novel about Florida by Patrick D. Smith. **Known for:** house-aged steaks; resort atmosphere; Cataplana broiled seafood sampler. $ *Average main: $58* ✉ *Rosen Shingle Creek, 9939 Universal Blvd., South Orlando* ☎ *407/996–9939* 🌐 *www.landrememberedrestaurant.com* 🕒 *No lunch.*

★ Highball & Harvest

$$$ | **SOUTHERN** | Modern spins on locally sourced Southern staples are the crux of this sprawling restaurant, where scratch cooking by Ritz chefs is the rule; produce is grown on the resort's own Whisper Creek private farm. Dinner entrées change regularly and might include fig-glazed ribs, a skirt steak marinated in Booker's bourbon, or the signature Pig-n-Potatoes, a hash of egg, potato, and pork cheek. **Known for:** hyperlocal produce from on-site farm; seasonal menus; handcrafted cocktails. $ *Average main: $25* ✉ *Ritz-Carlton Orlando Grande Lakes, 4012 Central Florida Pkwy., South Orlando* ☎ *407/393–4422* 🌐 *www.grandelakes.com.*

Le Coq au Vin

$$$$ | **FRENCH** | This traditional French restaurant, owned by Sandy and Reimund Pitz, is a hideaway located in a small nondescript house in South Orlando. In business since 1976, it seats 100 people in three quaint dining rooms. **Known for:** traditional high-style French cooking; steamed mussels and onion soup; exemplary service. $ *Average main: $32* ✉ *4800 S. Orange Ave., South Orlando* ☎ *407/851–6980* 🌐 *www.lecoqauvinrestaurant.com* 🕒 *No lunch. Closed Mon.*

★ Primo

$$$$ | **ITALIAN** | Chef Melissa Kelly cloned her Italian-organic Maine restaurant in an upscale Orlando hotel and brought her farm-to-table sensibilities with her. Here the daily dinner menu pays tribute to Italian cuisine utilizing produce grown in the hotel's organic garden. **Known for:** constantly changing menu using locally sourced ingredients; award-winning celebrity chef; homemade pastas. $ *Average main: $43*

⊠ *JW Marriott Orlando Grande Lakes, 4040 Central Florida Pkwy., South Orlando* ☎ *407/393–4444* 🌐 *www.primorestaurant.com* ⏱ *No lunch.*

Hotels

JW Marriott Orlando Grande Lakes
$$$ | RESORT | FAMILY | This lush resort, set in 500 acres of natural beauty, offers amenities galore, including a European-style spa, a Greg Norman–designed golf course, a lazy river–style pool complex, and kids' programs; rooms have ergonomic workstations and flat-screen TVs, and the restaurants are supplied from the property's organic farm. **Pros:** pool is great for kids and adults; shares amenities with the Ritz Carlton, including huge spa; free shuttle to SeaWorld and Universal. **Cons:** steep daily resort fee for parking and in-room Wi-Fi; the resort is huge and spread out; need a car to reach Disney or shopping. [$] *Rooms from: $289* ⊠ *4040 Central Florida Pkwy., South Orlando* ☎ *407/206–2300, 800/576–5750* 🌐 *www.grandelakes.com* *1000 rooms* *No meals.*

★ **Ritz-Carlton Orlando, Grande Lakes**
$$$$ | RESORT | FAMILY | Orlando's only Ritz-Carlton is a particularly extravagant link in the luxury chain: it shares a lush 500-acre campus with the JW Marriott, and offers exemplary service, excellent restaurants, children's programs, a golf course, and 40-room spa; suites have balconies, decadent white-marble baths, and deluxe bedding, and a Royal Suite satisfies even the most noble guest. **Pros:** truly luxurious; impeccable service; transportation to theme parks. **Cons:** remote from theme parks, attractions; lots of convention and meeting traffic; daily resort fee and parking fee. [$] *Rooms from: $729* ⊠ *4012 Central Florida Pkwy., South Orlando* ☎ *407/206–2400, 800/576–5760* 🌐 *www.ritzcarlton.com* *582 rooms* *No meals.*

★ **Rosen Shingle Creek**
$$$ | RESORT | FAMILY | Sitting amid 255 acres of subtropical landscape, including a cypress-fringed creek and a championship golf course, this award-winning luxury resort offers a golf academy; fishing; nature trails; four swimming pools; tennis, basketball, and volleyball courts; and a huge spa to soothe those aching muscles. **Pros:** many dining choices on property; huge spa and fitness center; free shuttle to Universal, SeaWorld, Aquatica. **Cons:** expansive grounds mean long walks between on-site amenities; no free shuttle to I-Drive or Disney; $18 daily parking fee. [$] *Rooms from: $296* ⊠ *9939 Universal Blvd., South Orlando* ☎ *407/996–9939, 866/996–6338 reservations* 🌐 *www.rosenshinglecreek.com* *1,501 rooms* *No meals.*

Activities

SPAS

Ritz-Carlton Spa Orlando, Grande Lakes
FITNESS/HEALTH CLUBS | Prepare to be wowed as you enter this lavish, grand spa, Orlando's largest with 40 treatment rooms, a fitness center, salon, private pool, and café—which means it can get busy. Get here in plenty of time to take a tour and get your bearings, shed your tourist togs, don a plush robe, and prepare to unwind. Unisex and co-ed waiting areas with couches and chairs are available, each on a different floor, with tea, water, fruits, and snacks. Treatments include massage, skin therapy, and deep-cleaning HydraFacials that gently extract impurities from the skin. A 20% service charge is added. ⊠ *Ritz-Carlton Orlando, 4024 Central Florida Pkwy., South Orlando* ☎ *407/393–4200* 🌐 *www.ritzcarlton.com/en/hotels/florida/orlando/spa* ☞ *Parking: valet parking discounted with spa validation.*

The Spa at Shingle Creek
FITNESS/HEALTH CLUBS | Most of the spa treatments feature Florida products such as citrus and cedar oils, aloe, and

Everglades sugar. The Everglades scrub and body wrap begins with a brown sugar body scrub and oils infused with sweet almond, apricot kernel, and wheat germ, followed by a wrap of nutrient-rich Everglades mud with hints of grapefruit, lime, jasmine, and lemongrass. Types of massage include Swedish, aromatherapy, warm stone, and Ashiatsu barefoot massage, in which the therapist uses gravity to reach deep into your muscle tissue. A variety of facials and salon treatments are available, and, for supreme relaxation, you can even add on a 25-minute siesta where you're wrapped in hot packs after your treatment and awakened by gentle bells. Gratuity is included in the cost. Parking, either self or valet, is validated for day guests. ✉ *Rosen Shingle Creek, 9939 Universal Blvd., South Orlando* ☎ *407/996–9939* 🌐 *www.spaatshinglecreek.com* ☞ *Parking: complimentary valet or self parking with spa validation.*

Sand Lake Road

The eastern side of Sand Lake bisects tourist-heavy International Drive at one of the busiest intersections in town; the west side has been dubbed "Restaurant Row" for its abundance of eateries.

Restaurants

This area, known as Restaurant Row, is the only place in town where locals dine beside convention goers and adventuresome theme-park visitors. From Interstate 4, take the Sand Lake Road exit, 74A.

Bonefish Grill

$$ | **SEAFOOD** | Fish dishes served in an upscale-casual setting distinguish Bonefish Grill from other area chains. Regulars rave about the Bang Bang Shrimp, a spicy appetizer of breaded and fried shrimp tossed in a tangy, spicy, mayonnaise-based sauce. **Known for:** seasonal fresh fish; happy hour and daily bar specials; pasta bowls and fish tacos. $ *Average main: $21* ✉ *Plaza Venezia, 7830 Sand Lake Rd., Sand Lake Rd. Area* ☎ *407/355–7707* 🌐 *www.bonefishgrill.com.*

Bosphorous Turkish Cuisine

$$$ | **TURKISH** | **FAMILY** | Exceptional Turkish cuisine served in a relaxing, indoor-outdoor setting is a welcome surprise among the big-budget chains on Sand Lake Road. Servers at this independently owned neighborhood favorite bring to the table piping-hot, oversize *lavas* (hollow bread) to dip in appetizers such as a hummus, *ezme* (a zesty, garlicky, chilled chopped salad), and baba ghanoush. **Known for:** Turkish appetizer plates; grilled sea bass; chicken and lamb shish kebab. $ *Average main: $26* ✉ *Marketplace at Dr. Phillips, 7600 Dr. Phillips Blvd., Suite 108, Sand Lake Rd. Area* ☎ *407/352–6766* 🌐 *www.bosphorousrestaurant.com.*

Cedars Restaurant

$$$ | **MIDDLE EASTERN** | This family-owned Lebanese eatery, set in a major upscale strip shopping center that's become part of Restaurant Row, serves Middle Eastern standards like shish kebab, baba ghanoush (an ultrasmoky variety that is the very best in town), and hummus as well as tasty daily specials. One of the most notable regular entrées is the *samak harra* (sautéed red snapper fillet topped with onions, tomatoes, and cilantro). **Known for:** authentic hummus and falafel; kafta kabab; rack of lamb. $ *Average main: $27* ✉ *Plaza Venezia, 7732 W. Sand Lake Rd., Sand Lake Rd. Area* ☎ *407/351–6000* 🌐 *www.orlandocedars.com.*

Christini's Ristorante Italiano

$$$$ | **ITALIAN** | Business travelers love to spend money at Christini's, one of the city's fanciest places for northern Italian cuisine. A throwback to elegant dining in the 1950s, the menu is filled with high-end versions of familiar dishes like chicken marsala and veal with lemon-wine sauce. **Known for:** Chris Christini,

the charming owner since 1984; upscale classic Italian cuisine; distinguished wine list. *$ Average main: $50 ✉ Marketplace at Dr. Phillips, 7600 Dr. Phillips Blvd., Sand Lake Rd. Area ☎ 407/345–8770 🌐 www.christinis.com ⏲ No lunch.*

Dragonfly Robata Grill & Sushi

$$ | **MODERN ASIAN** | Sleek and stylish, Dragonfly is a bit of everything the young and beautiful people want: a pretty space featuring sushi, colorful martinis, and modern, *izakaya*-style small plates. Groups of dressed-up twenty- and thirtysomethings gather indoors and out to share plates of *robata*-cooked meats and vegetables, along with tempura, rolls, noodle dishes, and salads, all beautifully presented. **Known for:** modern takes on traditional Japanese fare; robata charcoal-grilled specialties; daily happy hour specials. *$ Average main: $15 ✉ Dellagio, 7972 Via Dellagio Way, Sand Lake Rd. Area ☎ 407/370–3359 🌐 dragonflyrestaurants.com/orlando-florida ⏲ No lunch.*

Moe's Southwest Grill

$ | **SOUTHWESTERN** | At this great fast-food alternative, meals cost well south of $10—and come with free chips and assorted salsas. It is an immensely casual joint but by no means a dive, with a youthful vibrancy (music blares over the sound system) that makes it a great place for a quick meal. **Known for:** fast-casual service; massive burritos; inexpensive menu items. *$ Average main: $6 ✉ Dolphin Plaza, 11062 International Dr., International Drive ☎ 407/985–5808 🌐 www.moes.com.*

MoonFish

$$$$ | **SEAFOOD** | This splashy-looking restaurant caters to the convention crowd, with private rooms, polished service, and high prices—but the food is quite good. Ten to 15 fish varieties are flown in daily and prepared with a fusion of flavors from around the world. **Known for:** fresh fish; upscale atmosphere; Florida stone crab and lobster-encrusted trigger fish. *$ Average main: $35 ✉ The Fountains, 7525 W. Sand Lake Rd., Sand Lake Rd. Area ☎ 407/363–7262 🌐 www.talkofthetownrestaurants.com ⏲ No lunch.*

Morton's The Steakhouse

$$$$ | **STEAKHOUSE** | This fine choice among Orlando's many steak houses looks like a sophisticated private club, and youngsters with mouse caps are not common at the nationwide chain's local outpost. Center stage in the kitchen is a huge broiler, kept at 900°F to sear in the flavor of the porterhouses, sirloins, rib eyes, and other cuts of aged beef. **Known for:** house-aged steaks; seafood towers; mixed grill assortments with steak and lobster. *$ Average main: $46 ✉ Marketplace at Dr. Phillips, 7600 Dr. Phillips Blvd., Sand Lake Rd. Area ☎ 407/248–3485 🌐 www.mortons.com/orlando ⏲ No lunch.*

Ocean Prime

$$$$ | **SEAFOOD** | From the Berries & Bubbles martinis that start off the meal, to the ultrarich chocolate peanut butter dessert draped in bittersweet chocolate ganache, Ocean Prime wows at every turn. This local outpost of an upscale chain holds its own with consistently good food, if uneven service. **Known for:** great lakeside view; inventive seafood selections; gluten-free menu. *$ Average main: $34 ✉ Rialto, 7339 W. Sand Lake Rd., Sand Lake Rd. Area ☎ 407/781–4880 🌐 www.oceanprimeorlando.com ⏲ No lunch.*

★ **Peperoncino**

$$$ | **ITALIAN** | **FAMILY** | You'll be transported to Calabria at this comfortable Italian restaurant. Divided into trattoria and pizzeria, chef-owners Barbara Alfano and Danilo Martorano put out a fresh menu of Italian specialties every evening. **Known for:** southern Italian cuisine; duck breast and mushroom risotto; classic pizza. *$ Average main: $25 ✉ Dellagio, 7988 Via Dellagio Way, Suite 108, Sand Lake Rd. Area ☎ 407/440–2856 🌐 www.peperoncinocucina.com.*

★ **Rasa**

$$ | **SOUTH INDIAN** | **FAMILY** | From the owners of nearby Saffron, Rasa brings southern Indian and Indo-Chinese street food to the next level. This cozy, sophisticated restaurant is not your standard "gravy curry" place; instead, it features marvelously diverse bites that include rice crepe dosa, inventive haka noodles, and an Indian thali lunch special that is the best deal in town. **Known for:** southern Indian street food; authentic rice and noodle dishes; thali lunch special. *Average main: $18 ✉ Plaza Venezia, 7730 W. Sand Lake Rd., Sand Lake Rd. Area ☎ 407/370–0909 ⊕ www.eatatrasa.com.*

Roy's Orlando

$$$$ | **HAWAIIAN** | Chef Roy Yamaguchi has more or less perfected his own cuisine type, using European-style cooking techniques with Asian ingredients, primarily seafood, together with lots of imagination. The menu changes seasonally, but typical dishes include Hawaiian-style butterfish (black cod) with *furikake* rice, and hibachi-style grilled Atlantic salmon with Japanese citrus ponzu sauce. **Known for:** Hawaiian- and Philippine-inspired cuisine from celebrity chef Roy Yamaguchi; chef's tasting menu; hibachi salmon. *Average main: $34 ✉ Plaza Venezia, 7760 W. Sand Lake Rd., Sand Lake Rd. Area ☎ 407/352–4844 ⊕ www.roysrestaurant.com.*

Seasons 52

$$ | **AMERICAN** | **FAMILY** | Parts of the menu change every week at this innovative restaurant that serves different foods at different times of year, depending on what's in season. It's hard to believe that a chain restaurant can continue to offer healthful yet hearty and very flavorful food, yet it does. **Known for:** waits for tables, even when you have a reservation; $5 plates and wines during the daily happy hour; flatbread starters that are big enough to share. *Average main: $21 ✉ Plaza Venezia, 7700 Sand Lake Rd., Sand Lake Rd. Area ✣ I-4 Exit 75A ☎ 407/354–5212 ⊕ www.seasons52.com.*

Urbain 40

$$$ | **ECLECTIC** | This brasserie takes cues from classic French and Italian cuisine while adding a decidedly American spin. The simple elegant styling might recall a jazz club of the 1940s (hence the name) with live jazz piano during the evening, but people come for the food. **Known for:** inventive combinations of French, Italian, and Asian influences on American cuisine; perfectly prepared steak dishes; jazz lounge atmosphere during the evening. *Average main: $30 ✉ 8000 Via Dellagio Way, Sand Lake Rd. Area ☎ 407/872–2640 ⊕ urbain40.com.*

Vines Grille & Wine Bar

$$$$ | **STEAKHOUSE** | Live jazz and blues music fills the night at the bar section of this dramatically designed restaurant, but the food and drink in the snazzy main dining room are headliners in their own right. The kitchen bills itself as a steak house, but it really is far more than that. **Known for:** extensive wine selection and cocktails; prime steaks cooked on a wood-fired grill; live jazz performances. *Average main: $62 ✉ The Fountains, 7533 W. Sand Lake Rd., Sand Lake Rd. Area ☎ 407/351–1227 ⊕ www.seasons52.com ⏲ No lunch.*

Orlando International Airport

The area around the airport offers little to entice a traveler looking for a convenient base to explore the Orlando area unless it makes arrivals or departures more convenient. Fast food chains, hotel chains, car rental lots, long-term parking lots, and expensive gas stations make up the bulk of the businesses.

Restaurants

★ Cask & Larder

$$ | **SOUTHERN** | **FAMILY** | People have been known to check their bags at the airport and then go back through security and change terminals just to eat at C&L. The draws at this locally owned restaurant are the gastropub-inspired menu and the microbrews. **Known for:** farm-to-terminal dining; breakfast starts at 5 am; organic, locally sourced ingredients. *Average main: $15 Orlando International Airport, 9202 Jeff Fuqua Blvd., Southwest Terminal, Airport Area 407/204–3296 www.caskandlarder.com.*

Hemisphere

$$$$ | **AMERICAN** | The view competes with the food on the ninth floor of the Hyatt Regency Orlando International Airport hotel. Although Hemisphere overlooks major runways, you don't get any jet noise, just a nice air show. **Known for:** convenient airport location; sophisticated steak and seafood menu; relaxing lounge bar. *Average main: $32 Hyatt Regency Orlando International Airport, 9300 Jeff Fuqua Blvd., Airport Area 407/825–1234 hemisphereorlando.com Closed Sun. No lunch.*

Hotels

The area around the airport, especially the neighborhood just north of the Beachline Expressway, has a surfeit of hotels, mostly used by business travelers and airline staff. They're worth checking out if you have an early departure.

The Florida Hotel & Conference Center

$ | **HOTEL** | **FAMILY** | Five miles from the airport gates, this hotel is midway between Orlando International and I-Drive. **Pros:** in-room Wi-Fi; free parking; short drive to airport. **Cons:** neighborhood less than scenic; resort fee; Disney is 18 miles away, but there are no free shuttles. *Rooms from: $145 1500 Sand Lake Rd., Airport Area At S. Orange Blossom Trail 407/859–1500, 800/588–4656 www.thefloridahotelorlando.com 511 rooms No meals.*

Hyatt Regency Orlando International Airport

$$$ | **HOTEL** | **FAMILY** | If you have to catch an early-morning flight or have a long layover, this hotel inside the main terminal complex is a very convenient option; counting the time you spend waiting for the elevator, your room is a five-minute walk from the nearest ticket counter. **Pros:** despite being at the airport, rooms are quiet; people-watching from terminal-side balconies can be fun; terminal has 24-hour shopping and dining. **Cons:** nothing around but the airport; downtown Orlando and theme parks at least 30 minutes away; daily fee for parking. *Rooms from: $299 9300 Jeff Fuqua Blvd., Airport Area 407/825–1234, 800/233–1234 www.orlandoairport.hyatt.com 445 rooms No meals.*

Chapter 11

EXCURSIONS FROM ORLANDO

Updated by
Jennifer Greenhill-Taylor
and Joseph Reed Hayes

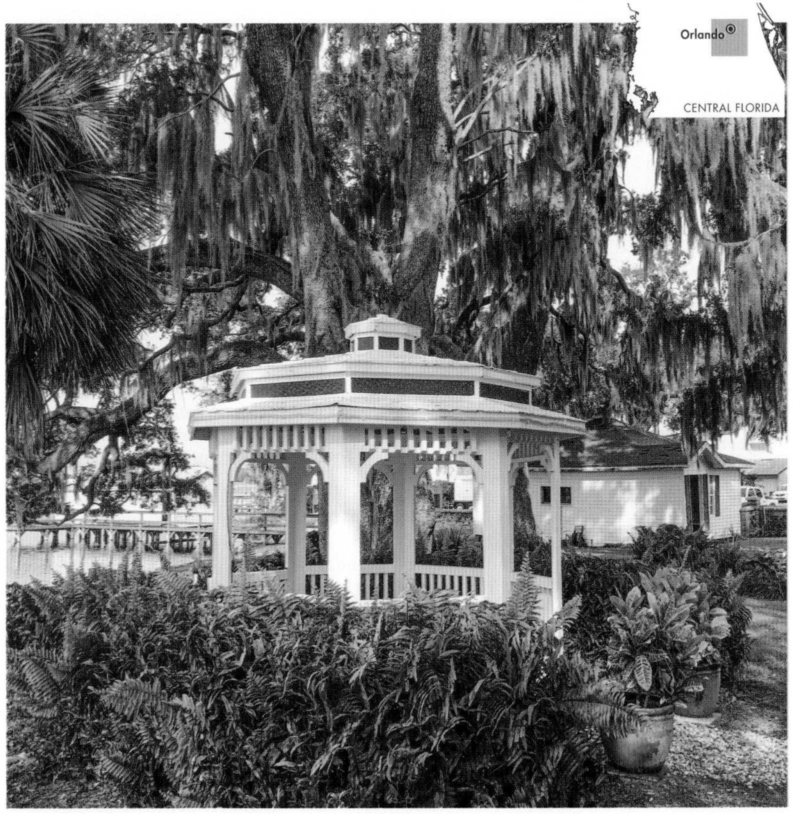

Sights ★★★★☆ | Restaurants ★★★★★ | Hotels ★★★★★ | Shopping ★★★★★ | Nightlife ★★★☆☆

WELCOME TO THE ORLANDO AREA

TOP REASONS TO GO

★ **Historic areas.** Sanford's main street is lined by low brick buildings that date from the mid-19th century. Maitland has three diminutive but fascinating history museums.

★ **LEGOLAND.** The biggest collection of plastic-brick constructions in the world offers fun that kids want to work at.

★ **Waterways.** Towns such as Sanford and Mount Dora have scenic lakefronts. Kayaks, canoes, and airboats are all available to cruise the region's waterways.

★ **Wild Florida.** Acres of untouched forests and crystal clear springs and rivers can be found only a few miles out of town. Maitland's Audubon Birds of Prey center houses and rehabilitates great raptors.

★ **Winter Park.** This charming town adjacent to Orlando offers brick-paved streets and a main thoroughfare that's perfect for strolling or sidewalk-café dining.

Most of these destinations are within minutes of Orlando and offer enough diversions to fill a day; some are a bit more distant. Combining a couple could make for a pleasant drive into the outlying countryside. Several of them are connected by the weekday SunRail commuter train line, a traffic-free alternative.

1 Winter Park. This upscale enclave just to the north of downtown Orlando features brick streets and a walkable downtown with a park and unique shops and eateries. For a taste of culture, the town also has two world-class art museums. A serene boat tour through lush landscapes affords glimpses of the lakefront homes built a century ago by escapees from the North who named the town.

2 Maitland. One of the oldest incorporated municipalities in the area, this town north of Winter Park features an Audubon sanctuary for birds of prey and several small museums, including one in nearby Eatonville dedicated to author Zora Neale Hurston.

3 Wekiwa Springs State Park. A crystal-clear fast-flowing spring is at the heart of this park, a half-hour drive from downtown Orlando. You can swim, canoe, and kayak along the river, enjoying Florida at its most natural.

4 Sanford. One of Central Florida's early towns, Sanford sits on the south shore of Lake Monroe. It retains a rustic, turn-of-the-century charm, with brick buildings housing restaurants, art galleries, and shops. In the 19th century, the town was a major entry port for adventurous Europeans arriving by steamboat on the St. Johns River.

5 Mount Dora. Another lakefront gem, this charming town 35 miles north of Orlando is known for its varied art galleries, its restaurants, and its antique boats.

6 LEGOLAND. Bricks of another sort line the streets of this theme park, where kids and adults can experience a whole world dedicated to colorful plastic LEGOs. Between driving little LEGO cars, hoisting themselves up tall LEGO poles, or floating in LEGO boats, kids leave happy and tired. With three hotels on-site, you don't have to make the nearly 90 mile round-trip from Orlando in one day.

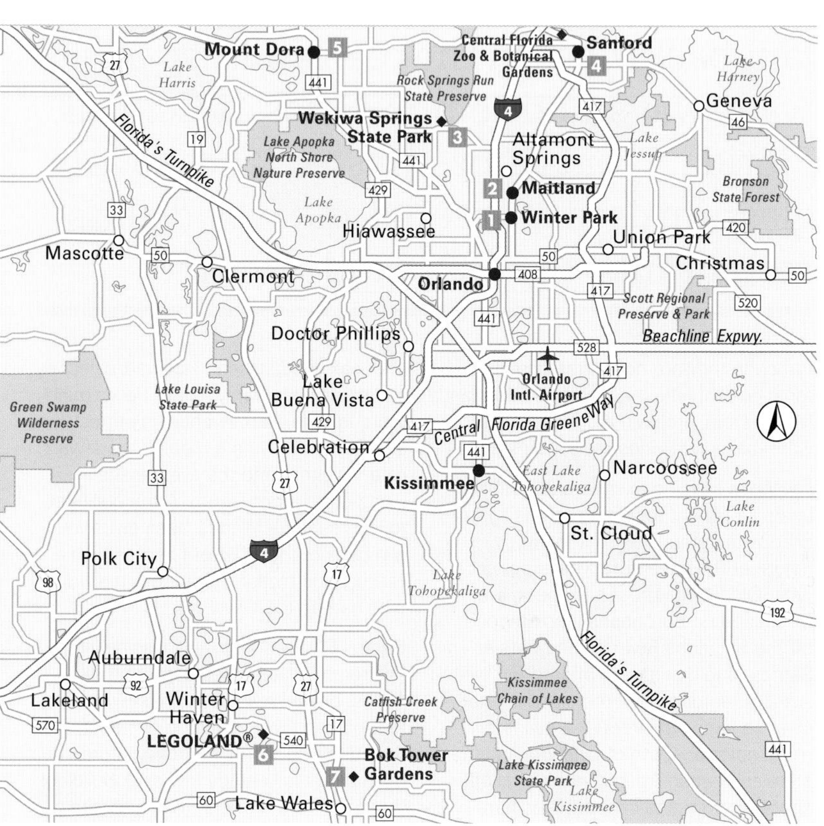

7 Bok Tower Gardens. One of Florida's oldest attractions, this contemplative garden designed by Frederick Law Olmstead, Jr.—whose father designed New York's Central Park—perches on one of the highest spots in the state, and its 205-foot-tall Singing Tower carillon has drawn millions of visitors since 1929.

Visitors to Orlando's theme parks looking to inject some reality into their vacations can experience thrills and chills or laid-back vibes in the real landscapes, waterways, and communities of Central Florida. From gator-infested lakes to art-glass-infused museums and world-class restaurants, the area exudes variety.

Although they are not on the ocean, most communities, including Sanford and Mount Dora, are built around lakes, so water-based activities are a mainstay.

For those seeking excitement, nothing beats an airboat rocketing across a lake filled with gators. Besides the edgy nature of the adventure, you experience what Old Florida must have been like for those first Europeans who stepped off the St. Johns River steamboats at Sanford and bravely set off into the wild. Acres of untouched forests and crystal clear springs and rivers sit a scant few miles north or south of Orlando, and the state and national parks in the area offer spots to swim and canoe. Hikes here let you explore some true wilderness filled with Florida's flora, as well as its fauna (some of which is dangerous). A silent journey along a river into the subtropical jungle, where turtles bask on logs and snakes and alligators—yes, alligators—snooze on the banks, is an unforgettable trip. At the end of any exploration on a blistering summer day, a leap into the refreshing 70-degree water of a turquoise spring cools the body and the mind.

For a more serene experience, several charming towns to the north of Orlando offer oak-lined streets, sidewalk cafés, and great restaurant. Winter Park's main thoroughfare, Park Avenue, is perfect for strolling or enjoying a meal at a sidewalk café. At either end the avenue sits a world-class art museum. A tranquil boat tour through lush landscapes gives you glimpses of the lakefront homes built a century ago by escapees from the North who named the town.

Central Florida's history is fascinating. The region was settled early, in the 1800s, because the St. Johns River formed a highway bringing pioneers into the state's daunting interior. Sanford's main street is lined by low brick buildings that date from that era. Maitland, site of a fort built during the Second Seminole War, has three diminutive but fascinating history museums.

For decades, Central Florida has been home to theme parks and other tourist attractions, some featuring the lush subtropical landscape. Today's visitors can still experience Bok Tower Gardens, a sanctuary of plants, flowers, trees, and wildlife surrounding the 200-foot Bok Tower carillon. Close by is Cypress Gardens, which is now part of LEGOLAND, so children and adults both have much to see and do in this theme park.

Winter Park

6 miles northeast of Orlando, 20 miles northeast of Walt Disney World.

This peaceful, upscale community might be just outside the hustle and bustle of Orlando, but it feels like a different country. The town's name reflects its early role as a warm-weather haven for those escaping the frigid blasts of Northeast winters. From the late 1880s until the early 1930s, wealthy industrialists and their families would travel to Florida by rail on vacation, and many stayed, establishing grand homes and cultural institutions. The lovely town retains its charm, with brick-paved streets, historic buildings, and well-maintained lakes and parkland. Even the town's bucolic nine-hole golf course (open to the public) is on the National Register of Historic Places.

On Park Avenue, you can spend a few hours sightseeing, shopping, or both. The street is lined with boutiques and fine restaurants and bookended by world-class museums: the Charles Hosmer Morse Museum of American Art, with the world's largest collection of artwork by Louis Comfort Tiffany, and the Cornell Fine Arts Museum, on the campus of Rollins College (the oldest college in Florida).

GETTING HERE AND AROUND

To reach Winter Park from downtown Orlando, take Interstate 4 (check construction updates first) for 4 miles to Exit 87, and head east on Fairbanks Avenue for 3 miles to Park Avenue. LYNX Buses 102 and 443 run from the main depot to Winter Park. The commuter train, SunRail, links downtown Orlando and Winter Park, running every half-hour on weekdays.

If you avoid rush-hour traffic (and keep an eye on construction updates for Interstate 4) traveling to points of interest shouldn't take too much time out of your vacation. Winter Park is no more than 20 minutes from downtown; International Drive and the theme parks are about 30 minutes away.

TOURS

Scenic Boat Tour

BOAT TOURS | FAMILY | Head east from Park Avenue to the end of Morse Boulevard, where you'll find the launching point for this tour, a Winter Park tradition since 1938. The one-hour cruise takes in 12 miles of waterways, including three lakes and narrow, oak- and cypress-shaded canals built in the 1800s as a transportation system for the logging industry. A well-schooled skipper shares stories about the moguls who built their mansions along the shore and points out wildlife and other remnants of natural Florida that still surround the expensive houses. Drinks (no alcohol) and snacks are allowed. Cash or check only is accepted. ✉ *312 E. Morse Blvd., Winter Park* ☎ *407/644–4056* 🌐 *www.scenicboattours.com* 🎟 *$14.*

VISITOR INFORMATION

CONTACTS City of Winter Park. ✉ *151 W. Lyman Ave., Winter Park* ☎ *407/644–8281* 🌐 *cityofwinterpark.org.*

Sights

Albin Polasek Museum and Sculpture Gardens

MUSEUM | Stroll along on a guided tour through gardens showcasing the graceful sculptures created by internationally known Czech sculptor Albin Polasek (1879–1965). The late artist's home, studio, galleries, and private chapel are centered on 3 acres of exquisitely tended lawns, colorful flower beds, and tropical foliage on the edge of Lake Osceola. Paths and walkways lead past classical life-size figurative sculptures and whimsical mythological pieces. Inside the museum are works by Hawthorne, Chase, and Mucha. The Capen House, a historic 1885 building, has been moved to the grounds to be used for public

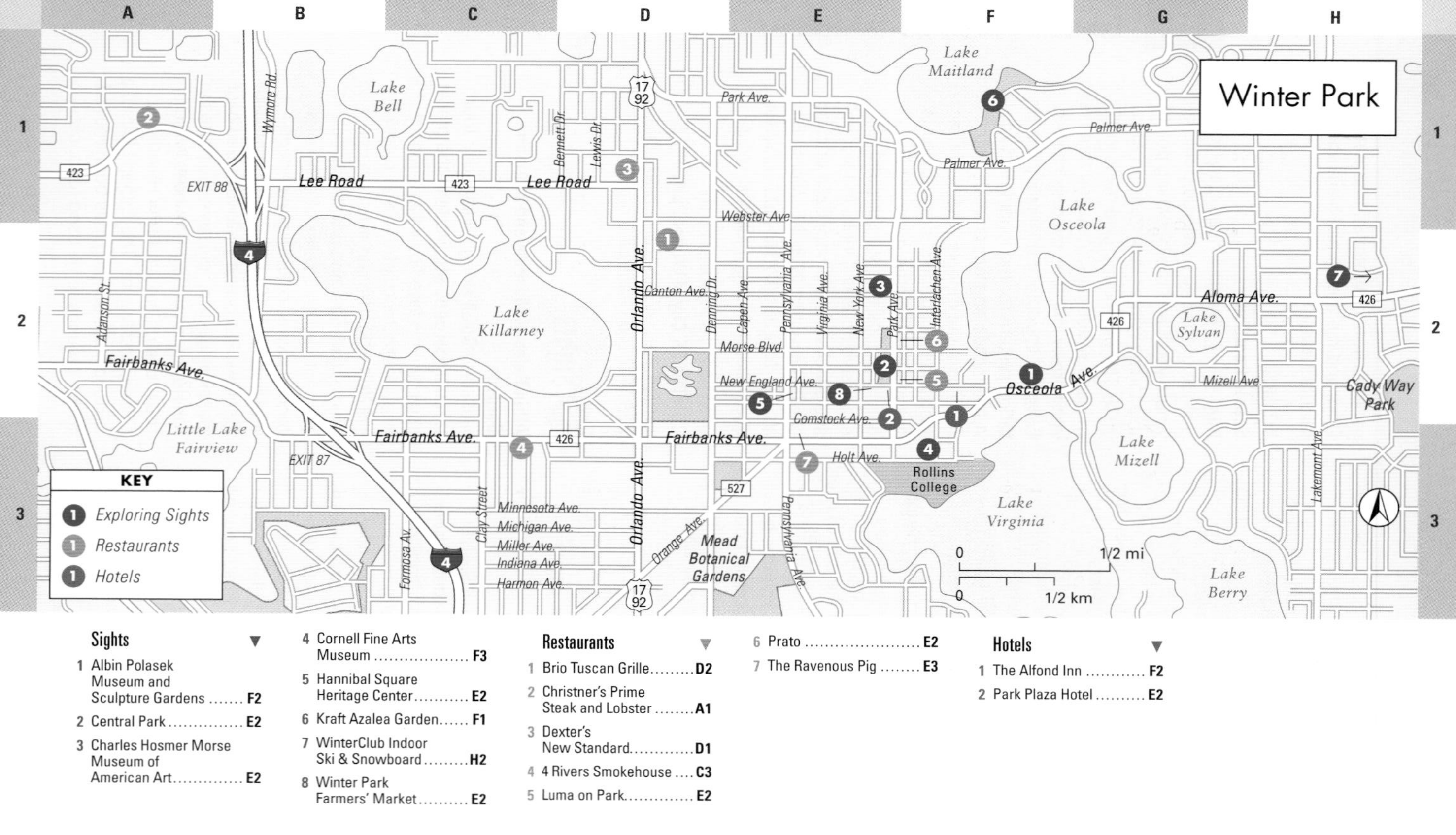

Sights

1 Albin Polasek Museum and Sculpture Gardens F2
2 Central Park E2
3 Charles Hosmer Morse Museum of American Art.............. E2
4 Cornell Fine Arts Museum F3
5 Hannibal Square Heritage Center........... E2
6 Kraft Azalea Garden...... F1
7 WinterClub Indoor Ski & Snowboard.........H2
8 Winter Park Farmers' Market.......... E2

Restaurants

1 Brio Tuscan Grille.........D2
2 Christner's Prime Steak and Lobster A1
3 Dexter's New Standard.............D1
4 4 Rivers Smokehouse C3
5 Luma on Park.............. E2
6 Prato E2
7 The Ravenous Pig E3

Hotels

1 The Alfond Inn F2
2 Park Plaza Hotel E2

events. ✉ *633 Osceola Ave., Winter Park* ☎ *407/647–6294* 🌐 *www.polasek.org* 🎫 *$10* ⏲ *Closed Mon.*

★ Central Park

GARDEN | FAMILY | Given to the City of Winter Park by the Genius family (benefactors of the Morse Museum), this 11-acre green spot has manicured lawns, specimen plantings, a beautiful rose garden available for private functions, a fountain, and a gazebo. If you take a seat and listen as the Amtrak passenger train rolls by, it's not hard to imagine how Winter Park looked and sounded in the late 19th century. The SunRail commuter train stops right within the park, giving great car-free access, particularly during the packed art festivals, to and from downtown Orlando, Kissimmee, and Sanford. The **Winter Park Farmers' Market** draws people to the southwest corner on Saturday morning. If you don't want to browse in the shops across the street, a walk through the park beneath the moss-covered trees is a delightful alternative. ✉ *251 Park Ave. S, Winter Park* 🌐 *cityofwinterpark.org.*

★ Charles Hosmer Morse Museum of American Art

MUSEUM | The world's most comprehensive and important collection of work by Louis Comfort Tiffany—including immense stained-glass windows, lamps, watercolors, and desk sets—is in this museum, which also contains American decorative art and paintings from the mid-19th to the early 20th century. Among the draws is the 1,082-square-foot Tiffany Chapel, originally built for the 1893 World's Fair in Chicago. It took craftsmen 2½ years to painstakingly reassemble the chapel here. Many of the works were rescued from Tiffany's Long Island estate, Laurelton Hall, after a 1957 fire destroyed much of the property. The 12,000-square-foot Laurelton Hall wing allows for much more of the estate's collection to be displayed at one time. Exhibits in the wing include architectural and decorative elements from Laurelton's dining room, living room, and Fountain Court reception hall. There's also a re-creation of the striking Daffodil Terrace, so named for the glass daffodils that serve as the capitals for the terrace's marble columns. Admission is free on Friday after 4 pm from November through April. ✉ *445 N. Park Ave., Winter Park* ☎ *407/645–5311* 🌐 *www.morsemuseum.org* 🎫 *$6* ⏲ *Closed Mon.*

Cornell Fine Arts Museum

MUSEUM | On the Rollins College campus, this museum houses Florida's oldest art collection (its first paintings acquired in 1896)—one with more than 5,000 works, from Italian Renaissance to 19th- and 20th-century American and European paintings. Special exhibitions feature everything from Native American artifacts to Soviet propaganda posters. Outside the museum, a small but charming garden overlooks Lake Virginia. Some of the museum's works grace the walls of the nearby, Rollins-owned, Alfond Inn. The museum is free to visit; free guided tours are offered on weekends at 1 pm. ✉ *Rollins College, 1000 Holt Ave., Winter Park* ☎ *407/646–2526* 🌐 *www.rollins.edu/cfam* 🎫 *Free* ⏲ *Closed Mon.*

Hannibal Square Heritage Center

MUSEUM | FAMILY | Almost crowded out by the glitz of new shops, restaurants, and art galleries is the original, once-thriving area of Hannibal Square, one of the oldest African-American communities in the country and home to Pullman porter families to this day. The Heritage Center has a permanent collection of photographs and oral histories of the significant West Winter Park area. It's a touching and important memorial to a neighborhood that influenced American history. ✉ *642 W. New England Ave., Winter Park* ☎ *407/539–2680* 🌐 *www.hannibalsquareheritagecenter.org* 🎫 *Free.*

The Charles Hosmer Morse Museum of American Art is also known as the Tiffany Museum because of its extensive collection of works by Louis Comfort Tiffany.

Kraft Azalea Garden

CITY PARK | **FAMILY** | Enormous cypress trees shade this 5-acre public park on the shores of Lake Maitland. It's hidden within an upscale neighborhood and comes alive with heady color from January through March. The thousands of blooming azaleas (hence the name) make a perfect backdrop for romantic strolls, and sunset weddings are common at the park's Exedra monument overlooking the lake. ✉ *1365 Alabama Dr., Winter Park* ☎ *407/599–3334* 🌐 *www.cityofwinterpark.org.*

WinterClub Indoor Ski & Snowboard

SPORTS VENUE | **FAMILY** | Snow enthusiasts can opt for the truly unique experience of skiing and snowboarding in shorts and a T-shirt at this indoor ski slope, proving that heading south doesn't necessarily cancel out winter sports. The region's first indoor ski center welcomes participants of all skill levels to practice and play on high-tech "endless slopes." WinterClub's interactive Ski Simulator fuses high-definition, large video wall ski runs with a unique chassis that allows skiers to experience the same g-force effects as they would in real life. ✉ *2950 Aloma Ave., Winter Park* ☎ *407/618–1123* 🌐 *www.winterclubski.com* 🎟 *From $49, packages available.*

Winter Park Farmers' Market

MARKET | **FAMILY** | It's worth getting up early on a Saturday morning and ambling through the local farmers' market (there are actually a couple of local farmers to make the name legit). A favorite for food, flowers, and fellowship since 1979, the market takes over a historical train station and its outside spaces every week. Upward of 85 vendors hawk everything from fresh vegetables to handmade croissants to local honey and dried fruit. Eggs from Lake Meadow Naturals share space with Luna moth and swallowtail chrysalises from the "Butterfly Man" and chopped pineapple at the Indian River fruit stand. A quick coffee and croissant are a good start to a day of Park Avenue shopping. You can park on nearby streets and the public lots on New York Avenue and Morse Boulevard and Lyman and New England avenues. To avoid traffic and parking hassles during the week, hop on the SunRail from Kissimmee, Orlando, or Sanford. ✉ *200 W. New England Ave., Winter Park* ☎ *407/599–3397* ⏲ *Closed Sun.–Fri.*

Restaurants

Winter Park has four restaurant hubs: Park Avenue, Orange Avenue, Hannibal Square, and Winter Park Village. To reach the area, follow Interstate 4 to Exit 87.

Brio Tuscan Grille

$$ | ITALIAN | FAMILY | Head to this trendy restaurant for wood-grilled meats and fish, Italian classics like chicken Milanese, and plenty of pasta. Try the strip steak topped with Gorgonzola or the mushroom ravioli with champagne brown butter sauce. **Known for:** casual dining atmosphere; fresh pasta like mushroom ravioli; Gorgonzola-crusted Angus beef. $ *Average main: $21* ✉ *480 N. Orlando Ave., Winter Park* ☎ *407/622–5611* 🌐 *www.brioitalian.com.*

★ Christner's Prime Steak and Lobster

$$$$ | STEAKHOUSE | Locals like this quiet, uncomplicated, family-run steak house, which delivers carefully prepared food and attentive service in a traditional setting of red leather and dark wood. When your steak arrives—still sizzling on a hot plate—the waiter asks you to cut into it and check that it was cooked as you ordered. **Known for:** simple, perfectly executed steaks; house-made desserts; extensive wine list. $ *Average main: $45* ✉ *729 Lee Rd., Winter Park* ☎ *407/645–4443* 🌐 *www.christnersprimesteakand-lobster.com* ⏲ *No lunch. Closed Sun.*

★ Dexter's New Standard

$$ | ECLECTIC | The name has changed, and the chain is smaller, but Dexter's has become a place for casual, chef-driven food, Florida oysters, local chicken and produce, and live music every day. It's really set a "new" standard for Winter Park dining. **Known for:** fresh Florida seafood; exceptional cocktails and wines; live music every night. $ *Average main: $16* ✉ *1035 N. Orlando Ave., Suite 101, Winter Park* ☎ *407/316–2278* 🌐 *www.newstandardwp.com.*

★ 4 Rivers Smokehouse

$ | BARBECUE | FAMILY | What started as a tiny business in a former tire repair shop has turned into a multistate dynasty. The popular 4 Rivers, now with 15 locations and more on the way, turns out slow-cooked barbecue standards like pulled pork and Texas-style brisket. **Known for:** slow-smoked ribs, brisket, and chicken; Sweet Shop bakeries; bacon-wrapped smoked jalapeños. $ *Average main: $13* ✉ *1600 W. Fairbanks Ave., Winter Park* ☎ *855/368–7748* 🌐 *4rsmokehouse.com* ⏲ *Closed Sun.*

★ Luma on Park

$$$ | MODERN AMERICAN | One of the Orlando area's best restaurants is run by award-winning chef Brandon McGlammery and is a popular spot for progressive American cuisine, which is served in a fashionable setting. Every ingredient is carefully sourced from local producers when possible, and scratch preparation—from pastas to sausages to pickled rhubarb—is the mantra. **Known for:** North Carolina flounder and Snake River flank steak; extensive wine list; attention to detail. $ *Average main: $30* ✉ *290 S. Park Ave., Winter Park* ☎ *407/599–4111* 🌐 *www.lumaonpark.com.*

★ Prato

$$$ | ITALIAN | Progressive Italian cuisine in a casual, bustling, wood-and-brick setting immediately made Prato a local favorite. Every item, from the pancetta to the amaretti, is crafted from scratch. **Known for:** young, hip clientele; outdoor curbside dining; Neapolitan pizzas and fresh pasta. $ *Average main: $23* ✉ *124 N. Park Ave., Winter Park* ☎ *407/262–0050* 🌐 *www.prato-wp.com* ⏲ *No lunch Mon. and Tues.*

★ The Ravenous Pig

$$$$ | MODERN AMERICAN | The first local restaurant to break into the "gastropub" category, the Pig is arguably Orlando's most popular foodie destination and has spawned several offshoots. Run by James and Julie Petrakis, a husband-and-wife chef team with multiple James Beard Award nominations, it dispenses delicacies like pork porterhouse or the pub burger. **Known for:** on-site Ravenous Pig Brewing Co. brewery; open until midnight Thursday–Saturday; house-made charcuterie. *$ Average main: $31 ⊠ 565 W. Fairbanks Ave., Winter Park ☎ 407/628–2333 ⊕ www.theravenous-pig.com.*

Hotels

Winter Park is a charming small town that's a 25- to 45-minute drive from the major attractions.

The Alfond Inn

$$ | HOTEL | This serenely sophisticated building in the heart of Winter Park, just steps from Park Avenue shops and restaurants and owned by neighboring Rollins College, combines an art gallery with an upscale hotel; rooms are decorated in cool grays, with touches of the iconic Winter Park peacock blue, and have work stations and flat-screen TVs. **Pros:** five-minute walk to Park Avenue for pleasant strolls and dining; restaurant on property; free Wi-Fi. **Cons:** at least an hour's drive to the theme parks; valet parking only ($10 daytime, $20 overnight); traffic passing on the brick streets can be a bit noisy at night. *$ Rooms from: $249 ⊠ 300 E. New England Ave., Winter Park ☎ 407/998–8090 ⊕ www.thealfondinn.com ⇜ 112 rooms ǁ○ǀ No meals.*

Park Plaza Hotel

$ | HOTEL | Small and intimate, this beautifully updated, 1922 establishment offers the charm of fern-bedecked wrought-iron balconies, along with free Wi-Fi and free breakfast in bed; the best accommodations are suites that open onto a flower-filled balcony over the street. **Pros:** valet parking; romantic atmosphere; view of Park Avenue shops and restaurants. **Cons:** railroad tracks are close, making for train noise at night; small rooms; a long way from theme parks. *$ Rooms from: $159 ⊠ 307 Park Ave. S, Winter Park ☎ 407/647–1072, 800/228–7220 ⊕ www.parkplazahotel.com ⇜ 28 rooms ǁ○ǀ Free breakfast.*

Shopping

Winter Park doesn't have just a few standout stores. It has dozens. By far the most alluring area is downtown's Park Avenue. Akin to Worth Avenue in Palm Beach, it's definitely a shopper's heaven. Carve out an afternoon (or evening) to meander the inviting brick street lined with chic boutiques, sidewalk cafés, and hidden alleyways that lead to peaceful nooks and crannies (with even more restaurants and shops). Chain stores are scarce; instead, indy shops offer merchandise that cannot be easily found elsewhere. Renowned Rollins College anchors one end of the avenue, a charming (and historic) nine-hole golf course the other. A few blocks away, you can take boat tours through a mansion-lined chain of lakes.Also neary by is Hannibal Square, another upscale dining and shopping district, at the intersection of New England and Pennsylvania avenues. Even if you don't buy a thing, the beauty of the avenue is priceless.

Farmers' Market

OUTDOOR/FLEA/GREEN MARKETS | If you schedule your visit to Winter Park for a Saturday morning, you can begin your day at the weekly farmers' market, which takes place from 7 am to 1 pm at the city's old train depot, just two blocks west of Park Avenue. It's a bustling, vibrant market with vendors selling farm-fresh produce, dazzling flowers, and prepared foods. Pick up locally harvested honey, locally made cheese, and freshly baked croissants. ✉ *200 W. New England Ave., Winter Park* ☎ *407/599–3397* 🌐 *www.cityofwinterpark.org/departments/parks-recreation/farmers-market.*

SPECIALTY SHOPS

Charles Hosmer Morse Museum Gift Shop

GIFTS/SOUVENIRS | The museum contains the world's most comprehensive collection of Tiffany stained glass, drawings, paintings, jewelry, pottery, and other objets d'art—so naturally shoppers come here for the representations of Tiffany glass, silk scarves with stained-glass motifs, and fine-art glass that Louis Comfort himself would have treasured. There are also many objects from world museum gift collections and a wide assortment of books about the Arts and Crafts movement. It's closed on Monday. ✉ *445 N. Park Ave., Winter Park* ☎ *407/645–5316* 🌐 *www.morsemuseum.org/museum-shop.*

Kathmandu

JEWELRY/ACCESSORIES | You'll think you're on a trek in the Himalayas instead of a stroll on Park Avenue when you spy this unique store, noticeable for its colorful, flag-festooned exterior. Items come from exotic locales like India, Indonesia, Nepal, and Turkey. Hats, turquoise and crystal jewelry, wooden necklaces, clothing, and brass figures of Indian gods are among the merchandise. Follow your nose to the smell of patchouli and sandalwood. ✉ *352 N. Park Ave., Winter Park* ☎ *407/647–7071* 🌐 *www.tribalasia.com.*

Shoooz on Park Avenue

CLOTHING | While strolling along Park Avenue, your feet might tell you that you need a new pair of shoes from this cozy shoe-only shop, which carries reliable designer brands including Mephisto, Naot, Arcopedicos, and BeautiFeel. ✉ *303 N. Park Ave., Winter Park* ☎ *407/647–0110.*

Ten Thousand Villages

GIFTS/SOUVENIRS | This fascinating little store sells fair-trade, artisan-crafted home decor, jewelry, paintings, and gifts of all kinds from the smaller corners of the world. ✉ *346 N. Park Ave., Winter Park* ☎ *407/644–8464* 🌐 *www.tenthousandvillages.com/winterpark.*

Maitland

10 miles northeast of Orlando, 25 miles northeast of Walt Disney World.

An Orlando suburb with an interesting mix, Maitland is home to the Florida Save the Manatee Society and one of Central Florida's larger office parks. A number of spectacular homes grace the shores of this town's various lakes, and there's a bird sanctuary and an art center.

GETTING HERE AND AROUND

Take Interstate 4 (check construction alerts first) Exit 90A, then Maitland Boulevard east, and turn right (south) on Maitland Avenue.

Sights

Art and History Museums Maitland

ARTS VENUE | FAMILY | This group of museums, divided into two campuses a block apart, includes the Maitland Art Center, the Maitland Historical Museum, the Carpentry Shop Museum, and the quirky Telephone Museum. Hidden down a tree-lined side street, the Maitland Art Center is a collection of 23 buildings in the Mayan Revival style—with Mesoamerican motifs—that contain an art gallery and artists' studios. Recognized by Florida as a historic site and on the National Register of Historic Places, the center was founded as an art colony in 1937 by American artist and architect André Smith (1880–1959), and it continues his tradition of art instruction and contains a major collection of his works. ✉ *231 W. Packwood Ave., Maitland* ☎ *407/539–2181* 🌐 *www.artandhistory.org* 🎟 *$9.*

Audubon Center for Birds of Prey

NATURE PRESERVE | **FAMILY** | More than 20 bird species, including hawks, eagles, owls, falcons, and vultures, make their home at this wildlife rehabilitation center on Lake Sybelia. You can take a self-guided conservation tour with interactive exhibits and walkways through the wetlands, or you can call ahead for a private tour ($100 for a group of up to 15), which includes an up-close look at different birds in the center. There's an earnestness to this working facility, which takes in more than 800 injured wild birds of prey each year. Fewer than half the birds can return to the wild; some permanently injured birds continue to live at the center and can be seen in the aviaries along the pathways and sitting on outdoor perches. From U.S. 17–92, turn west on Lake Avenue, then north on East Street. ✉ *1101 Audubon Way, Maitland* ☎ *407/644–0190* 🌐 *cbop.audubon.org* 🎟 *$8* ⏲ *Closed Mon.*

★ **Enzian Theatre**

ARTS VENUE | **FAMILY** | The nonprofit "club" called The Enzian is a cinematic treasure. First-run, quirky independent films are shown in this intimate theater, where locally sourced food is brought right to your table (yes, there are tables). Home to the acclaimed Florida Film Festival—as well as Jewish, South Asian, and Reel Short Teen film fests—the cinema also houses the very popular outdoor Eden Bar. ✉ *1300 S. Orlando Ave., Maitland* ☎ *407/629–0054* 🌐 *enzian.org* 🎟 *$12.*

Zora Neale Hurston National Museum of Fine Arts

MUSEUM | **FAMILY** | This museum, just a few minutes west of Maitland, is in Eatonville, the first African-American town to be incorporated after the Civil War. It showcases works by artists of African descent during five six-week-long exhibitions each year, with one reserved for up-and-comers. The museum is named after former resident Zora Neale Hurston (1891–1960), a writer, folklorist, and anthropologist best known for her novel *Their Eyes Were Watching God.* This is the home of Zora Fest, a street festival and cultural arts and music event celebrating Hurston's life, which is held each year in late January. ✉ *227 E. Kennedy Blvd., Eatonville* ☎ *407/647–3307* 🌐 *www.zoranealehurstonmuseum.com* 🎟 *Donations accepted.*

Restaurants

Kappy's Subs

$ | **AMERICAN** | **FAMILY** | Call it a sub shop, a hot dog stand, or a drive-in, Kappy's has been serving all-beef New York hot dogs for more than 50 years—and it looks the part. Behind the scenes, the cooking inside the vintage-Valentine stainless-steel diner car is surprisingly fulfilling, with a giant selection of grilled sandwiches, cheese steaks, and hot dogs, many made with local ingredients. **Known for:** vintage-diner atmosphere; hot dogs and Philly cheese steaks; outdoor and car seating. [$] *Average main: $8* ✉ *501 N. Orlando Ave., Maitland* ☎ *407/647–9099* 🌐 *www.kappyssubsfl.com.*

Wekiwa Springs State Park

13 miles northwest of Orlando, 28 miles north of Walt Disney World.

GETTING HERE AND AROUND

Take Interstate 4 (check construction alerts first) to Exit 94, west on State Road 434, then north on Wekiwa Springs Road.

Sights

★ **Wekiwa Springs State Park**

NATIONAL/STATE PARK | **FAMILY** | *Wekiva* is a Creek Indian word meaning "flowing water"; *wekiwa* means "spring of water." The different spellings appearing on signs are correct: each refers to either the river

Wildlife-rich Wekiwa Springs State Park is a great place to camp, hike, picnic, canoe, fish, swim, or snorkel.

or the springs. Regardless, the surrounding 6,400-acre Wekiwa Springs State Park is well suited to camping, hiking, picnicking, swimming, canoeing, and fishing. The area is also full of Florida wildlife: otters, raccoons, alligators, bobcats, deer, turtles, birds, and bears.

Canoes or kayaks may be rented at the park for $27 for two hours. Canoe trips can range from a simple paddle around the lagoon to observe a colony of water turtles to a full-day excursion through the less-congested parts of the river, which haven't changed much since the area was inhabited by the Timacuan Indians.

The park has 60 campsites: some are "canoe sites" that you can reach only via the river, and others are "trail sites," meaning you must hike a good bit of the park's 13½-mile trail to reach them. Most, however, are for the less hardy—you can drive right up to them. Sites have electric and water hookups. ✉ *1800 Wekiva Circle, Apopka* ✣ *Take I–4 Exit 94 (Longwood) and turn left on Rte. 434. Go 1¼ miles to Wekiwa Springs Rd.; turn right and go 4½ miles to entrance, on right* ☎ *407/884–4311* 🌐 *floridastateparks.org/parks-and-trails/wekiwa-springs-state-park* 🎟 *$2 per pedestrian or bicycle; $6 per vehicle* ⏲ *Closes at sundown.*

Sanford

30 miles northeast of Orlando, 45 miles northeast of Walt Disney World.

At one time, Sanford was the heart of Central Florida—a vital vacation spot and transportation hub on the St. Johns River. But that was long before vacationers focused on Orlando and Walt Disney World. In recent years, Sanford has been focusing on its downtown area, increasing the size of its airport (Orlando–Sanford International), and gaining new trendy restaurants.

GETTING HERE AND AROUND

From Orlando International Airport or downtown Orlando, Interstate 4 to Exit 104; follow U.S. 17–92 to West 1st

Street. The SunRail commuter has a regular shuttle that stops right in the heart of town. The Sanford stop on the SunRail commuter train has become popular with day-trippers.

Sights

Central Florida Zoo and Botanical Gardens

ZOO | **FAMILY** | Sanford has had a zoo since 1923, and although there's nothing here to rival San Diego or New York, there's a certain charm about the place. In addition to 400-plus animals, including giraffes (you can feed them), cheetahs, monkeys, and crocodiles, there's the Seminole Aerial Adventures, with rope bridges and a zipline through the treetops, and the Wharton-Smith Tropical Splash Ground, a mini water playground. The Florida black-bear habitat and Florida Trek are very popular. The steam-powered 1/5-scale train that puffs around the zoo is as fun for adults as it is for kids. ✉ *3755 N.W. U.S. 17–92, Sanford* ✣ *Take I–4 to Exit 104 and turn left on U.S. 17–92; zoo is on right* ☎ *407/323–4450* 🌐 *www.centralfloridazoo.org* 🎫 *$20; train extra charge.*

Restaurants

The Tennessee Truffle

$$$ | **SOUTHERN** | Using locally sourced ingredients, the chef at this small, independent redbrick eatery on Sanford's main drag loves to create Southern fusion dishes. His house-made biscuits and gravy are renowned, and the lunch menu includes a BLT with house-cured bacon and heirloom tomatoes. **Known for:** continuous service all day long; great Southern-inspired food; shrimp and grits. 💲 *Average main: $24* ✉ *125 W. 1st St., Sanford* ☎ *407/942–3977* 🌐 *www.thetennesseetruffle.com* ⏲ *Closed Sun., Mon., and Tues.*

Mount Dora

35 miles northwest of Orlando, 50 miles north of WDW.

The unspoiled Lake Harris chain surrounds remote Mount Dora, an artsy community with a slow-and-easy pace, a rich history, New England–style charm, and excellent antiquing. Although the town's population is only about 12,000, there's plenty of excitement here, especially in fall and winter. The first weekend in February sees the annual Mount Dora Art Festival, which opens Central Florida's spring art-fair season. Attracting more than 250,000 people over a three-day period, it's one of the region's major outdoor events.

The calendar here also includes the annual Storytelling Festival (January), Taste in Mount Dora event (March), a sailing regatta (March), a bicycle festival (October), a crafts fair (October), and many other happenings. In addition, Mount Dora draws large crowds during monthly antiques fairs (third weekend, except December) and thrice-yearly antiques "extravaganzas" (third weekends of January, February, and November) at popular Renninger's Twin Markets, an antiques center plus farmers' and flea markets. The revived Royal Palm Railroad Experience and Polar Express Christmas train runs between the cities of Mount Dora, Tavares, and Eustis.

GETTING HERE AND AROUND

Take U.S. 441 (Orange Blossom Trail in Orlando) north or take Interstate 4 to Exit 92, then Route 436 west to U.S. 441, and follow the signs. From the Disney area, take SR 429 north (a toll road) to Exit 34, then U.S. 441 north.

VISITOR INFORMATION

CONTACTS Mount Dora Chamber of Commerce. ✉ *341 Alexander St., at 3rd Ave., Mount Dora* ☎ *352/383–2165* 🌐 *www.mountdora.com.*

LEGOLAND Florida is a kid-friendly attraction a little more than an hour from Orlando.

Sights

Lakeside Inn

HOTEL—SIGHT | Listed on the National Register of Historic Places, this country inn, built in 1883, overlooks 4,500-acre Lake Dora and is Florida's oldest continuously operating hotel. A stroll around the grounds, where seaplane passengers board or disembark, makes you feel as if you've stepped into the pages of *The Great Gatsby.* You, too, can book a seaplane tour or a cruise; both leave from the inn's large dock. ✉ *100 N. Alexander St., Mount Dora* ☎ *352/383–4101* 🌐 *www.lakeside-inn.com.*

★ Modernism Museum

MUSEUM | **FAMILY** | A refined and dazzling private collection of American and international works from mid-20th-century modernist artists features the work of George Nakashima and Wendell Castle, as well as those of the more radical group Memphis; included as well are pieces collected by musician David Bowie. The museum shares resources and a gift shop with the 1921 restaurant across the street; special dining and exhibition events are held throughout the year. ✉ *145 E. 4th Ave., Mount Dora* ☎ *352/385–0034* 🌐 *www.modernismmuseum.org/* 🎫 *$8* 🕒 *Closed Mon.*

Mount Dora Center for the Arts

MUSEUM | **FAMILY** | Local and national artists are highlighted in this lovely art center, which grew out of the annual arts festival. The center is a focal point for the community, serving as headquarters of the arts festival, a gallery, a gift shop, and a place to take art lessons. ✉ *138 E. 5th Ave., Mount Dora* ☎ *352/383–0880* 🌐 *www.mountdoracenterforthearts.org.*

Restaurants

★ 1921 Mount Dora

$$$$ | **AMERICAN** | Founded by celebrity chef Norman Van Aken, 1921 now has a new team, but it retains its respect for Florida and Southern cuisine. Food that could easily be served in Miami, Chicago, or New York finds its way to tables in this converted tearoom that offers locally sourced ingredients and eye-rollingly good dinner and brunch. **Known for:** new interpretations of Florida cuisine; locally sourced seafood and chicken; in-house pastry chef. [$] *Average main: $32* ✉ *142 E. 4th Ave., Mount Dora* ☎ *352/385–1921* 🌐 *www.1921mountdora.com* ⏲ *Closed Mon.*

LEGOLAND

50 miles southwest of Orlando.

From 1936 to 2009, the sleepy town of Winter Haven was home to the Sunshine State's first theme park, Cypress Gardens. Today, the lush gardens are still there, in addition to the world's largest LEGOLAND, 150 acres of buildings built using nearly 56 million LEGOs.

GETTING HERE AND AROUND

About 54 miles and an hour from downtown Orlando, LEGOLAND is reached by Interstate 4 West to Exit 55 and U.S. 27 to SR 540/Cypress Gardens Boulevard. If this is an important destination, save yourself the commute time by spending a night or two here. Three hotels—the 152-room LEGOLAND Hotel, the seaside-themed Beach Retreat, and the just-opened Pirate Island Hotel—offer building-block accented accommodations right by the parks.

Sights

★ **LEGOLAND Florida**

AMUSEMENT PARK/WATER PARK | FAMILY | In addition to its 1:20-scale LEGO miniature reproductions of U.S. cities and sights, the park features more than 50 rides, shows, and attractions throughout 10 different zones, as well as the marvelous botanical gardens from the original park.

The Danish toy company's philosophy is to help children "play well." And play they do, as LEGOLAND attractions are very hands-on. Kids can hoist themselves to the top of a tower, power a fire truck, or navigate a LEGO robot. Sights include huge LEGO dragons, wizards, knights, pirates, castles, roller coasters, racetracks, villages, and cities.

The cityscapes in Miniland USA fascinate children and adults, who delight in discovering what's possible when you have enough bricks. Miniland opens with Kennedy Space Center, where a six-foot shuttle waits on the launch pad. Miami Beach features bikini-clad bathers and art deco hotels; St. Augustine and its historic fort play into LEGO's pirate theme; Key West's Mallory Square is accurate right down to the trained cats leaping through rings of fire. The rest of the country is not ignored: New York City, Las Vegas, San Francisco, and Washington, D.C., appear in intricate detail. Visitors spend hours looking for amusing details hidden in each city, like New York's purse snatcher.

Among other highlights are Ninjago, where kids battle computer-generated bad guys; LEGO Kingdoms, whose castle towers over a jousting area and a roller coaster where knights, damsels, dragons, and ogres are found; Land of Adventure, where you can explore hidden tombs and hunt for treasure; and the Imagination Zone, showcasing LEGO Mindstorms robots, where a giant head of Albert Einstein invites kids to explore and invent. Things get wild in LEGO Technic, the most active of the park's zones, where Test Track, Aquazone Wave Racers, and Technicycle let the family expend some energy. During the live Pirates' Cove show, seafaring sailors wearing LEGO suits defend a huge ship from attacking pirates on water skis. LEGO Movie World features rides and attractions from the blockbuster, including Splash Battle, Masters of Flight, where guests soar above the LEGO Movie universe aboard a triple decker flying couch,

Bok Tower rises 200 feet in a garden in Lake Wales that was designed in 1929 by Frederick Law Olmstead, Jr., the son of the builder of New York City's Central Park.

and Unikitty's Disco Drop, taking riders to the top of Cloud Cuckoo Land.

LEGOLAND Water Park features a wave pool; Build-a-Raft, where families construct a LEGO vessel and float down a lazy river; a 375-foot pair of intertwined waterslides that plunge riders into a pool; and a DUPLO toddler water play area. Not to be forgotten, Cypress Gardens, at the heart of the park, preserves one of Florida's treasures. Families can wander the lush, tropical foliage and gasp at one of the world's largest banyan trees. Three on-site hotels offer LEGO-theme accommodations and park packages. ✉ *1 LEGOLAND Way, Winter Haven* ☎ *855/753–8888* 🌐 *www.legoland.com* 🎟 *$99; parking $23; water park $25 additional* 🕒 *Closed Tues. and Wed. in Jan. and Feb.*

Bok Tower Gardens

57 miles southwest of Orlando, 42 miles southwest of Walt Disney World.

GETTING HERE AND AROUND

Interstate 4 West to Exit 55; U.S. 27 South to Burns Avenue in Lake Wales; follow Tower Boulevard to Gardens.

Sights

★ **Bok Tower Gardens**

GARDEN | FAMILY | You'll see citrus groves as you ride south along U.S. 27 to the small town of Lake Wales and the Bok Tower Gardens. This appealing sanctuary of plants, flowers, trees, and wildlife has been something of a local secret for years. Shady paths meander through pine forests with silvery moats, mockingbirds and swans, blooming thickets, and hidden sundials. The majestic, 200-foot Bok Tower is constructed of coquina—from seashells—and pink, white, and gray marble. The tower houses a carillon with 60 bronze bells that ring out each day at 1 and 3 pm during 30-minute recitals that might include early American folk songs, Appalachian tunes, Irish ballads, or Latin hymns. The bells are also featured in recordings every half hour after 10 am; sometimes there are even moonlight recitals.

The landscape was designed in 1928 by Frederick Law Olmsted Jr., son of the planner of New York's Central Park. The grounds include the 20-room, Mediterranean-style Pinewood Estate, built in 1930 and open for self-guided touring. From January through April, guides lead you on a 60-minute tour of the gardens (included in the admission price); tours of the inside of the tower are a benefit of membership. ✉ *1151 Tower Blvd., Lake Wales* ☎ *863/676–1408* 🌐 *boktowergardens.org* 🎟 *$15.*

Restaurants

Crazy Fish Bar and Grill

$ | **SEAFOOD** | **FAMILY** | You can enjoy outdoor patio dining at this popular seafood shack in Lake Wales, which was visited in 2016 by Emeril Lagasse for his show *Emeril's Florida*. Fresh shrimp, blue crab, and catfish in season are all on the menu. **Known for:** fresh Florida seafood; very casual atmosphere; appearance on Emeril's Florida TV show. [$] *Average main: $12* ✉ *802 Henry St., Lake Wales* ☎ *863/676–6361* 🌐 *www.crazyfishlakewales.com* 🕒 *Closed Sun. No lunch Mon.*

Chapter 12

ACTIVITIES

12

Updated by
Gary McKechnie

With the sun shining virtually every day and moderate temperatures throughout the year, nearly anytime is a good time to be outdoors and active in Orlando. Surfing, horseback riding, motorcycling, and skydiving just scratch the surface of what's available.

According to folks at the Orlando Convention and Visitors Bureau, there are more than 170 golf courses in the area (although another source, Golflink, pegs the number closer to 60-some), with about 20 golf academies offering lessons. Even the city's recreation department gets in on the act with country club–like golf courses accessible at bargain prices. Meanwhile, inside and outside the theme parks are hundreds of tennis courts (which are vastly outnumbered by thousands of lakes). Yes, in and around Orlando and Central Florida, you can navigate more than 2,000 lakes and waterways via canoe or kayak or airboat—or even on a fishing excursion, which is something to consider when visiting one of the bass-fishing capitals of the world. In addition, unique to Central and North Florida are natural springs where crystal clear waters flow at a constant (and cool) 72 degrees. Above it all, you can take to the air in a sailplane, hot-air balloon, or hang glider. If you prefer to stay firmly planted on the ground, you can explore forested hiking trails and modified rails-to-trails. Orlando's sports arena and its pro hockey and basketball teams bring in the crowds, and, as they've done for more than a century, professional baseball teams venture down from the frozen North to warm up during Spring Training at stadiums across Central Florida.

If your vacation is based at Walt Disney World, you'll find many of these outdoor activities right outside your door. Anglers get hooked on fishing charters, and runners and bikers get their adrenaline rush on trails across the property. Spectators can take themselves out to the ballgame, perhaps catching the Atlanta Braves take on the competition during Spring Training at the ESPN Wide World of Sports Complex. But it's not just baseball. Volleyball, cheerleading, softball, track, and weightlifting are just a few of the other events held here throughout the year in a wide world of competition. For Disney recreation information, call ☎ *407/939–7529*.

Auto Racing

Andretti Indoor Karting and Games
SPORTS VENUE | FAMILY | The racing legend lent his name to this entertainment facility that offers boutique bowling on blacklit lanes, video game and pinball arcade, sky trail ropes course with curved ziplines, virtual reality, a shoot-em-up 7-D dark ride, and naturally, racing. Pro racing simulators add motion, vibrations, sound effects, and even add tension in the seatbelt so you feel as if you're on an actual racetrack. When you're ready to actually

Top 5 Recreational Experiences

Airboat Tours. Long before theme parks were conceived, the attractions area was a desolate setting of prairies, lakes, and swamps. Outside the parks, you can still see the beauty and wildlife of those lakes and swamps on airboat tours that skim across the waters to take you straight into the heart of natural Florida.

Golf. Set aside a few hours for a round of golf, which (depending on your skill level) could be 18 holes at Arnold Palmer's Bay Hill, an easy 9 holes at the historic and charming Winter Park Country Club, a family round of minigolf at a theme park, or a high-tech practice session at the TopGolf driving range.

iFly Orlando. Totally safe skydiving? That's right. In this indoor chamber, a massive turbine allows you to fly like a bird without jumping out of an airplane (or even getting that far off the ground).

Seminole Lake Gliderport. There's hardly any experience simultaneously more thrilling and peaceful than being hauled to 2,000 feet in a sailplane, and then releasing the cord that secures you to the towplane in front of you. After that, it's a silent soaring adventure in the clear skies of Central Florida.

Wekiwa Springs State Park. About 40 minutes east of the theme parks, this state park is centered on a crystalline natural spring that flows into the Wekiwa River. The canoe and kayak concession here offers you a chance to go with the river's flow and immerse yourself in the beauty of natural Florida.

race, three indoor kart tracks let you whip around corners, change elevation, and zip into banked curves on small, high-torque karts. Add laser tag, a restaurant, and more than 100 screens tuned into the day's top sporting events, and you have a lot of entertainment packed into one exciting complex. ✉ *9299 Universal Blvd., International Drive* ☎ *407/374–0042* 🌐 *andrettikarting.com/orlando* 🎟 *Racing from $22; ropes course, laser tag, other games from $13.*

Ballooning

Central Florida's temperate weather is ideal for ballooning excursions, and it's not uncommon to rise early and see a colorful, puffy balloon—or even an entire flotilla of them—drifting slowly above the rural countryside. Prices and flight durations are roughly the same among the tight-knit community of balloonists in the Orlando area, as is the ceremonial toast at the conclusion of your flight. Often the gondola may be more tightly packed than you'd prefer, but the experience, along with the views, is unforgettable.

★ Bob's Balloons

BALLOONING | FAMILY | Flying since 1980, Bob will meet you in the predawn hours at the ChampionsGate golf resort before heading to one of several popular launch sites where you'll watch your balloon being prepared to go up, up, and away. From here, you'll float between the treetop level and as high as 1,000 feet for about an hour, with views of farms and forest land, along with horses, deer, wild boar, cattle, and birds flying *below* you. In the distance, you'll likely see Disney landmarks like the Animal Kingdom's Expedition Everest and Epcot's Spaceship Earth. Several balloons often launch at roughly the same time from nearby destinations, which provides an unparalleled sightline of these colorful sky ornaments. The memories will last forever, and perhaps even longer when Bob presents a flash drive of images from your flight. ✉ *Orlando* ☎ *407/466–6380, 877/824–4606* 🌐 *www.bobsballoons.com* 🎫 *From $195 per person.*

Orlando Balloon Adventures

BALLOONING | Like other ballooning services, this one is ready to go seven days a week (weather permitting) although the exact launch site is dependent on the direction of the breeze. Knowing what tourists love, pilots prefer to take to the skies near Walt Disney World, so you can take in an aerial view of the four theme parks. But wherever you travel—by Walt Disney World, above fragrant orange groves, or over the as-yet undeveloped Green Swamp area—each flight is unique and memorable. If you're staying near the attractions area (Kissimmee, Celebration, International Drive, etc.), the company can pick you up and return you to your hotel for an additional fee. ✉ *Orlando* ☎ *407/786–7473* 🌐 *www.orlandoballoonadventures.com* 🎫 *From $195.*

Painted Horizons Balloons

BALLOONING | Like its local counterparts, Painted Horizons is ready to fly every day of the year that the weather allows, and, like others, it offers specialties like private flights (at a premium, of course) and even proposal flights (for which you are accompanied by a plane towing a "Will You Marry Me" banner). Whichever you choose, once the balloon is ready to go, you might not even notice when it lifts slowly into the air since the rise is imperceptible. After flying wherever the wind decides to carry you, the flight concludes with a toast of sparkling wine or cider and snacks of pastries, cheese, and crackers. ✉ *Orlando* ☎ *407/578–3031* 🌐 *www.paintedhorizons.com* 🎫 *From $185.*

Basketball

Orlando Magic

BASKETBALL | Since it became the city's NBA team in 1989, the popularity of the Orlando Magic has waxed and waned, perhaps reaching its peak in the early 1990s, when Shaquille O'Neal became the team's most recognized player and helped it become the second-fastest team to advance to the NBA Finals. Its venue is now downtown's multimillion-dollar, state-of-the art Amway Center. The season runs October–June, and ticket prices vary greatly depending on where you sit and how well the season is going. Seats go for as little as $18, though courtside seats creep up toward $1,000 when the Magic is playing against a top team. ✉ *Amway Center, 400 W. Church St., Downtown Orlando* ☎ *407/896–2442* 🌐 *www.nba.com/magic* 🎫 *Tickets from $10; parking from $10; VIP parking from $50.*

Biking

Walt Disney World

Disney covers an area roughly the size of San Francisco, and within its boundaries are miles of paved trails that take you past forests, lakes, wooded campgrounds, and resort villas. If you're 18 or older, you can rent bikes at multiple locations, but you must ride them in the area where you rent them. Rental locations include several Disney resort hotels including Port Orleans, Old Key West, Caribbean Beach, Saratoga Springs, and at the Fort Wilderness Campground. If renting a bike is important to you, ask about their availability when booking your reservation.

Most locations have children's bikes with training wheels and bikes with toddler seats. Surrey bikes, which look like old-fashioned carriages and are a great way to take your family on a sightseeing tour, are another option. since the covered tops provide a rare commodity at Disney: shade. Rates start at $9 an hour for regular bikes ($20 for a full day) and go up to $20 to $25 per half hour for surrey bikes (depending on whether they have two, four, or six seats). Wear a helmet. Not only is it smart, it's free with each rental.

Orlando Area

Thanks to the Orlando community's commitment to the nationwide Rails to Trails program, the city now has several biking, running, and in-line skating trails—converted from former railroad lines—in both rural and urban surroundings.

City of Orlando Trails
BICYCLING | Weaving around busy Orlando and stretching into rural outposts throughout Orange County are miles of trails modified from old railroad tracks, and there are always more recreational trails in the works. A few miles from downtown, Winter Park's Cady Way Trail passes some picturesque lakes and connects restaurants and retail centers along the way. The Lake Underhill Path connects to six city parks, while 20 miles east of downtown, the 13-mile Orlando Southeast Trail is popular due to its distinctly rural landscapes and a generous 12-foot width. The 3-mile Orlando Urban Trail near downtown is considered the backbone of Orlando's trail network and connects several of the city's cultural highlights such as Lake Highland, Loch Haven Park, Mead Gardens, Orlando Cultural Park, and the Gaston Edwards Trail. The Shingle Creek Trail will eventually run through the city of Orlando and into the city of Kissimmee. For a comprehensive list of trails and where they lead, check the city's biking website. ✉ *Orlando* ☎ *407/246–2821* 🌐 *www.orlando.gov/Parking-Transportation/Bike-Trails-and-Paths.*

West Orange Trail
BICYCLING | With about 150,000 pedestrians, bicyclists, joggers, roller skaters, and skateboarders traveling some, or all, of its 22 miles every month, this is easily the most popular trail in the area thanks in large part to its pleasingly rural setting and a route that takes it through the charming community of Winter Garden. Spanning the Orange and Lake county lines, the 14-foot-wide path rolls through the towns of Killarney and Oakland, and across U.S. 441 through downtown Apopka with highlights including views of Lake Apopka and the butterfly garden at the Tildenville outpost. Among the trail's most popular access points is Chapin Station (✉ *501 Crown Point Cross Rd., Winter Garden*), since it's located just a few blocks from what is clearly the most popular place to rest and eat: Downtown Winter Garden. With sidewalk cafés, bicycle shops, gift shops, boutiques, candy stores, a community theater, history museum, and several other interesting sights, it's the perfect place to put down the kickstand and stay awhile. ✉ *501 Crown Point Cross Rd., Winter Garden* 🌐 *www.traillink.com/trail/west-orange-trail/.*

West Orange Trail Bikes & Blades
BICYCLING | Bicycles—comfort style, hybrids, road bikes, kids' bikes, tandems—and in-line skates can be rented from a log cabin on the West Orange Trail at Chapin Station, just a few blocks east of downtown. The facility is perfectly placed right beside the trail and offers parking, changing areas, bike racks, and assistance getting the bike fitted for the ride. This center's sister shop is the Winter Garden Wheel Works, a full-service store a few blocks away in the heart of the shopping village. ✉ *17914 State Rd. 438, Winter Garden* ☎ *407/877–0600* 🌐 *www.orlandobikerental.com* 🎫 *From $8 per hr.*

Boating

It's hard to believe, but Walt Disney World has one of the nation's largest fleets of rental pleasure craft. There are marinas at the Caribbean Beach Resort, Contemporary Resort,Disney Springs, Fort Wilderness Resort, Grand Floridian Resort, Old Key West Resort, Polynesian Resort, Port Orleans French Quarter and Riverside resorts, and the Wilderness Lodge. You can rent 12-foot sailboats, catamarans, motor-powered pontoon boats, pedal boats, kayaks, canoes, and tiny two-passenger Sea Raycers—a hit with children—for use on Bay Lake and the adjoining Seven Seas Lagoon, at Crescent Lake by the Epcot resorts, at Lake Buena Vista, or at the Buena Vista Lagoon. You can also sail and water ski on Bay Lake and the Seven Seas Lagoon. You'll find sailboats at the Fort Wilderness, Contemporary, Polynesian, and Grand Floridian marinas. Call ☎ *407/939–7529* for more information.

But Disney certainly isn't the only place where you can take to the waters. Head to the outskirts of Orlando, and you can see Florida's lakes and backwaters via speedboats, motorboats, airboats, and even houseboats.

★ Boggy Creek Airboat Ride

BOATING | Just outside the attractions area are creeks and lakes and swamps that comprise the headwaters of the Florida Everglades. On an airboat tour, you'll explore these still wild ecosystems where wetlands are populated with exotic birds, turtles, and alligators. Boggy Creek, the best Orlando-based airboat tour company, offers four different adventures, each of which will take you into the real Florida. When you're done, you can visit a recreation of a Native American village of the Jororo Tribe that lived along these same waterways hundreds of years ago. ✉ *2001 E. Southport Rd., Kissimmee* ☎ *407/344–9550* 🌐 *bcairboats.com* 🎫 *From $27.*

Marsh Landing Airboat Ride

BOATING | The thrill of an airboat really is something else. At this location, about 25 miles southeast of Disney, a fleet of 6-, 10-, and 14-passenger stadium-seating boats gives every passenger an unobstructed view of the water speeding past. With the airboat drawing just a few inches of draft, you'll skim through the reeds and near the shore to see alligators, cattle, egrets, anhingas, osprey, eagles, and deer, to name a few. Tours range in duration, distance, and cost, with the longest tour being a half-day venture into the marshlands of Osceola County. ✉ *2830A Neptune Rd., Kissimmee* ☎ *407/624–0973* 🌐 *orlandoairboattours.com* 🎫 *From $50.*

Fishing

Central Florida freshwater lakes and rivers teem with all kinds of fish, especially largemouth black bass but also perch, catfish, sunfish, and pike, which makes this area a popular spot for fishing tournaments.

To fish in most Florida waters, anglers over 16 need a **fishing license,** which is available at bait-and-tackle shops, fishing camps, most sporting goods stores, and in the sporting goods section of Walmarts and Bass Pro Shops. Some of these locations might not sell saltwater licenses, or they might serve non-Florida residents only; so call ahead to be on the safe side. For nonresidents of Florida, freshwater or saltwater licenses cost $17 for three consecutive days, $30 for seven consecutive days, and $47 for one year. For Florida residents under age 65, a freshwater or saltwater license is $17 per year for each or $32.50 for both. A five-year fishing license costs Florida residents $79 for both. Fishing on a private lake with the owner's permission—which is what anglers do at Disney World—does not require a Florida fishing license. For more information on proper licensing, contact

Florida Fish and Wildlife (☎ *850/488–4676* 🌐 *www.fwc.com/recreation*).

Walt Disney World

Disney Fishing Excursions

FISHING | Natural Bay Lake and the man-made Seven Seas Lagoon (whose excavation helped create the foundation of the Magic Kingdom) are connected by a channel, and each is heavily populated with fish. Two- and four-hour catch-and-release excursions—with additional hours upon request—depart in 21-foot, five-passenger Sun Tracker pontoon boats from the marinas at Fort Wilderness, Wilderness Lodge, Contemporary, Grand Floridian, and Polynesian resorts Other waterfront resorts, including the Yacht and Beach Club, Saratoga Springs, Caribbean Beach, Port Orleans, and Old Key West, also have excursions from their marinas, with the trips including a boat, equipment, live bait, and a guide for up to five anglers. Your guide is there to get you to the best fishing spots, bait your hook, unhook your catches, and even snap pictures of you with your fish during these catch-and-release excursions. Prices vary by time and number of guests, but generally two-hour guided excursions cost $270 (for up to five people) and depart daily at 7, 10, and 1. Since these are private lakes on Disney property, a fishing license is not required. ✉ *Magic Kingdom Resort Area* ☎ *407/939–2277 fishing reservations* 🎟 *From $235 per group.*

Ol' Man Island Fishin' Hole

FISHING | An inexpensive alternative to a fishing charter is casting a line from a dock at Port Orleans–Riverside. At Ol' Man Island Fishin' Hole, cane poles and bait are $15 per half hour for a family of up to six. You must rent equipment here to use the dock, and you're required to release any fish that you catch. ✉ *Disney's Port Orleans, 1251 Riverside Dr., Disney Springs Resort Area* 🌐 *www.disneyworld.com* 🎟 *From $15.*

Orlando Area

Although some once-great fishing spots have been affected by pollution, most have largely retained their freshwater status and remain among the area's best fishing lakes. A popular favorite is Lake Kissimmee, as well as the Butler and Conway chains of lakes, and Kissimmee's massive Lake Tohopekaliga (aka: Lake Toho), a Native American name meaning "Sleeping Tiger." (The name was given to the generally placid lake as its waters become incredibly rough during thunderstorms and have sent more than a few fishermen to a watery grave. Be careful in summer when you see storm clouds.) Lake Toho is held in high regard by the Bass Anglers Sportsman Society, since it is the source of the all-time record Tournament Catch. Your best chance for trophy fish is between November and April on Toho or Kissimmee.

For good creels, the Butler area is your best bet and has the additional advantage of its scenery: lots of live oaks and cypresses, plus the occasional osprey or bald eagle. Toho and Kissimmee are also good for largemouth bass and crappie. The Butler chain yields largemouth, some pickerel, and the occasional huge catfish. Services range from equipment and boat rental to full-day trips with guides and guarantees. Like virtually all lakes in Florida, the big Orlando-area lakes are teeming with alligators, which you'll find totally harmless unless you engage in the unwise practice of swimming at night. Small pets are more vulnerable than humans and should never be allowed to swim in Florida lakes or rivers. The key differences between the public lakes and the Disney lakes is that you have the option of keeping the fish you catch on the public lakes, while Disney has a catch-and-release policy. You'll also need a license when fishing on public lakes, but not on Disney's privately owned lakes.

That said, if you'd like a glimpse of Old Florida (what locals recall as what Orlando was like before Disney) just head to a fish camp, which you'll find around Lake Toho and other nearby natural waterways. With their weatherbeaten docks and rustic campgrounds, most retain an authentic look and feel that is distinctly different from the artificial visages of the theme parks and attractions. Most have general stores where you'll find a bait and tackle shop, boat rentals, snacks, beer, ice, and everything you need for a day on the water. There's never been a four-star fish camp, so lodging often consists of cabins or trailers with standard amenities and, occasionally, kitchenettes that are convenient for long-term stays. The primary appeal of a fish camp is the opportunity to see what Orlando looks like in its natural state—with picturesque lakes, quiet forests, colorful sunsets, and wildlife including deer, grazing cattle, osprey, raccoons, and bald eagles,

Guides operate out of the area's fishing camps, and you can usually make arrangements to hire them through the camp office. Rates vary, but for two people, a good price is around $300 for a half-day and $450 for a full day. Many area guides are part-timers, who fish on weekends or take a day off from their full-time job.

Bass Challenger Guide Service

FISHING | With Captain Eddie at the helm, BCG takes you wherever the fishing is best that day. It might be Lake Toho or the St. Johns River—Florida's longest and one of the few that runs north—which is a prime bass site. Indeed, bass is the only quarry. BCG also sells bait, arranges for transportation to and from your hotel, organizes multiday trips, and books area accommodations. Check in advance for advice on practical fishing apparel and accessories as well as license requirements. ✉ *Sanford* ☎ *321/377–2013* 🌐 *www.basschallenger.com* 🎟 *Half-day trips from $300.*

Boggy Creek Resort & RV Park

FISHING | You can see what kept tourists entertained in pre-Disney days at this camp, which has a restaurant and country store, sells live bait and propane, rents boats, and offers airboat rides.It's hard to believe this much of Old Florida is just a few minutes (but several decades) away from Walt Disney World, but it is, and that's why you're here. The camp has 286 RV sites and simple, rustic cabins. During peak winter and spring months, plan to reserve one of their 24 cabins at least two weeks in advance. ✉ *3705 Big Bass Rd., Kissimmee* ☎ *407/348–2040* 🌐 *www.boggycreekresortandrvpark.com* 🎟 *Cabins from $79 per night.*

Lake Charters

FISHING | This outfitter conducts trips from November to May on Lake Toho (January through April is high season, so reserve accordingly). Rods and reels are included in the cost, transportation is available, and you can also buy your licenses here. An informative website will fill you in on details regarding rates and what you'll catch (which might be a 14-pound bass). ✉ *1550 Scottys Rd., Kissimmee* ☎ *407/891–2275, 877/326–3575* 🌐 *www.lakecharter.com* 🎟 *Half-day trips from $275.*

Richardson's Fish Camp

FISHING | Rustic and remote, this camp on western Lake Toho is a place where time began standing still in the 1950s. Relaxing by the water, setting up a cookout, watching the wildlife (deer, osprey, eagles, and company), or catching a glorious Florida sunset are just a few of the activities you'll enjoy in a place where the most pressing issue is whether to fish or not (you'll probably fish). The camp has 7 cabins with kitchenettes, 16 RV sites, and 6 tent sites, as well as boat slips and a bait shop. The camp is peaceful, quiet, and pet-friendly. ✉ *1550 Scottys Rd., Kissimmee* ☎ *407/846–6540* 🎟 *Cabins from $44.*

Golf

With dozens and dozens of golf courses and golf academies in and around Orlando, it's no wonder the International Association of Golf Tour Operators has recognized Orlando as a top golf destination. Sunny weather almost year-round doesn't hurt, and though most of Florida is extremely flat, many of the courses feature hills that make them more challenging.

Resort hotels often let nonguests use their golf facilities. Some country clubs are affiliated with particular hotels, and their guests can play at preferred rates.

In general, even public courses have dress codes, so call ahead for specifics and be sure to reserve tee times. Greens fees usually vary by season, and virtually all include mandatory cart rental, except for the few 9-hole walking courses.

TIP→ **Twilight discounts often apply after 2 pm in busy seasons and after 3 pm the rest of the year; the discount is usually half off the normal rate.** Because golf is so incredibly popular, courses regularly raise rates.

GOLFPAC Travel

GOLF | GOLFPAC Travel packages golf vacations and arranges tee times at nearly all Orlando courses. Rates vary based on hotel and course, and 60 to 90 days' advance notice is recommended to set up a vacation. Their website has convenient searchable, clickable options that let you pick the time and place for a golf outing, adding them to a cart for checkout. ✉ *483 Montgomery Pl., Altamonte Springs* ☎ *407/260–2288, 888/848–8941* 🌐 *www.golfpactravel.com.*

Walt Disney World

Disney has three championship courses, plus a 9-hole walking course. Any guest at a WDW hotel who checks in specifically to play golf gets free transportation to the course.

Greens Fees. Rates change frequently, so the best source for up-to-date rates is Disney itself. Disney resort guests get a price break, and you should ask about twilight discount rates. If you plan to play only once, leave the gear at home—you can rent shoes, range balls, and clubs at any location.

Tee Times and Reservations. Tee times are available daily from dawn until dusk. You can book them up to 90 days in advance if you're staying at a WDW-owned hotel, 60 days ahead if you're staying elsewhere. You must cancel at least 24 hours out. For tee times and private lessons, call Disney's central World Golf reservations line ☎ *407/939–4653*. And be sure to bookmark Disney's golf website (🌐 *www.golfwdw.com*), which contains in-depth information on the courses, layout, rates, and tee times.

GREENS FEES

Disney's prime courses are operated by Arnold Palmer Golf Management, which provides an online chart showing rates that vary by time of day as well as time of year (🌐 *www.golfwdw.com/courses/golf-rates*). Rates at all 18-hole courses are generally the same in peak spring season: about $129 before 11 am and around $115 after. That said, the moment you know when you're ready to play, make your reservation (☎ *407/939–4653* 🌐 *www.golfwdw.com*). All fees include an electric cart, although the 9-hole Oak Trail is a walking course, and a pull cart for your bag is $6. If you've got the stamina and desire to play the same course twice in the same day, you can do so for half price the second time around, but you can't reserve that option in advance. This Re-Play Option, as Disney calls it, is subject to availability. Golf shoes rent for $10 a pair, and range balls are available between $7 to $11 a bucket. If you'd rather not pay a baggage fee to haul your clubs onto your plane, you can rent the latest TaylorMade woods, irons, and a putter for $45. If, for some reason, you have to cancel your tee time, they'll try to fill your spot, but if not, you'll be charged.

GOLF INSTRUCTION

One-on-one instruction from PGA-accredited professionals is available at any Disney course. Prices for private lessons vary: 45-minute lessons cost $75 for adults and $50 for youngsters 17 and under.

COURSES

Disney's Lake Buena Vista Golf Course

GOLF | A favorite among golfers, the Lake Buena Vista course has hosted the PGA Tour, LPGA Tour, and USGA events. As you play, you'll find the course winds among Disney Springs–area town houses and villas. Greens are narrow, and hitting straight is important because errant balls risk ending up in someone's bedroom. Be prepared for the famous island green on the 7th. This is a pleasant location surrounded by wonderful scenery. ✉ *1960 Broadway, Disney Springs* 🎫 *From $49* 🏌 *18 holes, 6,745 yards, par 72.*

The Magnolia

GOLF | One of the originals when the park opened in 1971, The Magnolia has been lavished with four stars by *Golf Digest* and was certified by Audubon International as a Cooperative Wildlife Sanctuary. The long but forgiving classic course features extra-wide fairways, and its name stems from the more than 1,500 magnolia trees that lineit. While you're working to avoid the woods, try avoiding the water hazards at 11 of the 18 holes. But that's not all. There are 97 bunkers spread throughout the fairway. Play here, and you're playing the course that welcomed Nicklaus, Palmer, Player, and other legends. ✉ *Shades of Green, 1950 W. Magnolia–Palm Dr., Magic Kingdom Resort Area* ☎ *407/939–4653* 🌐 *www.golfwdw.com* 🎫 *From $39* 🏌 *18 holes, 7,516 yards, par 72.*

Oak Trail

GOLF | Located across from the Grand Floridian at the Shades of Green Resort (a resort used primarily by military families), the Oak Trail was designed by Ron Garl to be fun for the entire family. It's noted for its small, undulating greens and particularly affordable fees. ✉ *Shades of Green, 1950 W. Magnolia–Palm Dr., Magic Kingdom Resort Area* 🌐 *disneyworld.disney.go.com/recreation/oak-trail-golf-course* 🎫 *From $39* 🏌 *9 holes, 2,913 yards, par 36.*

The Palm

GOLF | Although it's not as long as the Magnolia, nor as wide, The Palm has been confounding the pros for years. The course, located across the Grand Floridian Resort, has 9 water holes and 94 bunkers—including one in the iconic shape of Mickey Mouse's head. ✉ *Shades of Green, 1950 W. Magnolia–Palm Dr., Magic Kingdom Resort Area* ☎ *407/939–4653* 🌐 *www.golfwdw.com* 🎫 *From $45* 🏌 *18 holes, 7,011 yards, par 72.*

★ Tranquilo Golf Club at Four Seasons Resort

GOLF | Once known as Disney's Osprey Ridge, this Tom Fazio–designed course is on Disney property but part of the Four Seasons Resort Orlando. Sculpted from some of the still-forested portions of the huge WDW acreage, some of the tees and greens sit as much as 20 feet above the fairways keep competitive players from getting too comfortable. Amenities include luxury golf carts with GPS, a Cuban-American clubhouse restaurant, driving range, and putting green. Greens fees drop significantly for "twilight" play starting at 2 pm. Have time for only 7 holes? There's a special for that, too. ✉ *10100 Dream Tree Blvd., Lake Buena Vista* 🌐 *www.fourseasons.com/orlando/golf* 🎫 *From $175* 🏌 *18 holes, 6,968 yards, par 71.*

Orlando Area

Golf has no better hometown than Orlando. The longtime residence of the late Arnold Palmer, with dozens and dozens of public and private courses along with a moderate climate and predictable weather, the city has enticed scores of PGA professionals to make this their home as well. Palmer's landmark Bay Hill Invitational is held here each March, and the Daytona-based LPGA hosts several tournaments in Orlando every year. Appearing with great frequency (every single day) are the programs and tournaments aired on the Golf Channel, which broadcasts from Orlando. Note that the greens fees listed reveal a wide range of prices, which can change by season and time of day. Call the pro shop, or check the website ahead of time for the current rates.

Arnold Palmer's Bay Hill Club & Lodge

GOLF | It was golf legend Arnold Palmer who helped put Orlando at the forefront of the sport, and this course was his pride and joy. Each March, at the Arnold Palmer Invitational, pros and visiting amateurs anticipate the 18th hole here, which is considered one of the toughest on the PGA tour. Courses are open only to those who have been invited by a member or who book lodging at the club's 70-room lodge. But with double-occupancy rates for rooms overlooking the course running as low as $130 in summer, many consider staying at the club worthwhile. Keep in mind this rate does not include your greens fees, which are necessary since staying here in essence buys you a day of "membership" at the club. ✉ *9000 Bay Hill Blvd.* ☎ *407/876–2429, 407/422–9445* 🌐 *www.bayhill.com* 🎫 *Varies by season, from $75* ⛳ *18 holes, 7,207 yards, par 72; 9 holes, 3,409 yards, par 36.*

Celebration Golf Club

GOLF | Talk about a great pedigree—the Celebration course was designed by Robert Trent Jones Jr. and Sr. Located just 10 minutes from Walt Disney World, the course is paired with the master-planned Disney community, just one mile off the U.S. 192 strip. Lovely and serene, the fairways are framed by natural woods and wetlands to create what the Joneses envisioned: "Every hole a hard par and an easy bogey." Rates drop after 1 pm and again around dusk. ✉ *701 Golf Park Dr., Celebration* ☎ *407/566–4653* 🌐 *www.celebrationgolf.com* 🎫 *From $79* ⛳ *18 holes, 6,783 yards, par 72.*

ChampionsGate Golf Club

GOLF | Just about 10 minutes west of Disney, from the vantage point of I–4 you can see that there's some serious golfing inside the gates of ChampionsGate. The two courses here were designed by Australia's Greg Norman, and there's an on-site David Leadbetter Golf Academy. The 7,363-yard International has the "Down Under" style of Australia's coastal links, whereas the 7,128-yard National course is designed in the style of the better domestic courses, with a number of par-3 holes with unusual bunkers. The golf shop is ranked among the Top 100, and the Pipers Grille sports lounge is a great 19th hole. At sunset, step onto the veranda and watch a piper play as he walks the greens. Can't get enough? There's a four-star Omni hotel here. ✉ *1400 Masters Blvd., ChampionsGate* ☎ *407/787–4653 ChampionsGate, 407/787–3330 Leadbetter Academy, 888/633–5323 Leadbetter Academy* 🌐 *www.championsgategolf.com* 🎫 *From $45* ⛳ *International: 18 holes, 7,363 yards, par 72. National: 18 holes, 7,128 yards, par 72.*

Falcon's Fire Golf Club

GOLF | Designed by Rees Jones, Falcon's Fire has strategically placed fairway bunkers that demand accuracy off the tee. This club is just off Kissimmee's Irlo Bronson Memorial Highway and is convenient to the hotels in the so-called Maingate area. A round here includes complimentary valet parking, club cleaning, and golf carts equipped with GPS navigation. ✉ *3200 Seralago Blvd., Kissimmee* ☎ *407/239–5445* 🌐 *www.falconsfire.com* 💵 *From $49* 🏌 *18 holes, 7,015 yards, par 72.*

Grand Cypress Golf Resort

GOLF | When it opened, Grand Cypress elevated Orlando golfing with elegant courses that spread across what once had been pasture and prairie. The four courses include the three 9's (the North, South, and East courses) and the 18-hole New Course, fashioned after a Scottish glen. In addition, the Grand Cypress Academy of Golf, a 21-acre facility, has lessons and clinics. The North and South courses have fairways constructed on different levels, giving them added definition. The New Course, designed by Jack Nicklaus, was inspired by the Old Course at St. Andrews and has deep bunkers, double greens, a snaking burn, and even an old stone bridge. **TIP→ The greens fees are subject to what they call "dynamic pricing," which means that rates will adjust daily based on demand.** ✉ *1 N. Jacaranda* ☎ *407/239–1909, 407/239–1909* 🌐 *www.grandcypress.com* 💵 *From $125* 🏌 *North: 9 holes, 3,521 yards, par 36. South: 9 holes, 3,472 yards, par 36. East: 9 holes, 3,434 yards, par 36. New: 18 holes, 6,773 yards, par 72.*

Hawk's Landing Golf Club at the Orlando World Center Marriott

GOLF | Located near the entrance to Walt Disney World at the monumental World Center Marriott (the world's largest Marriott), the 220-acre Hawk's Landing course includes 15 water holes, lots of sand, and exotic landscaping. As you play, you'll see they've maintained the natural surroundings and enhanced the same with vibrantly colored azaleas. This is a good choice if you're here on business and want to get in a round. No need to pack your clubs—Callaway rental equipment is available. Need some help? Instruction is offered at the Jack Nicklaus Academy. ✉ *Orlando World Center Marriott, 8701 World Center Dr.* ☎ *407/238–8660, 800/567–2623* 🌐 *www.golfhawkslanding.com* 💵 *From $69* 🏌 *18 holes, 6,602 yards, par 71.*

Marriott Golf Academy

GOLF | The Marriott Golf Academy is an extensive-curriculum golf school and 9-hole golf course on the grounds of the corporation's biggest time-share complex, Marriott's Grande Vista. Here you can do anything from taking a one-hour lesson with a certified instructor to immersing yourself in a three-day extravaganza in which you learn more about golf technique than most nonfanatics would care to know. The Swing Studio offers high-tech teaching methods. The course, designed by Ron Garl, is geared to make you use every club in your bag—and perhaps a few you might elect to buy in the pro shop. ✉ *Marriott Grande Vista, 12001 Ave. Verde* ☎ *407/238–7677, 855/642–2369* 🌐 *www.marriottgolfacademy.com* 💵 *Lessons from $99; 3-day courses from $949* 🏌 *9 holes, 2,400 yards, par 32.*

Orange Lake Resort

GOLF | About five minutes from Walt Disney World's main entrance, Orange Lake has two 18-hole courses (the Legends and the Reserve), two 9-hole courses (Crane's Bend, Legends Walk), and pro instruction at the McCord Golf Academy (rates start at $65). The Legends is a signature Arnold Palmer–designed championship course; the Reserve was designed by Mike Dasher and has unique land and water challenges. Crane's Bend is family-friendly. Legend's Walk is an executive walker's course open until 9 pm nightly, where children 15 and younger play free with complimentary clubs. The signature hole for the entire group of courses is the Island Oak, No. 13, a 432-yard, par-4 hole in the Pines section (the back 9) of the Legends Course. ✉ *8505 W. Irlo Bronson Memorial Hwy., Kissimmee* ☎ *407/239–1050, 888/640–6522* 🌐 *www.golforangelake.com* 🎫 *From $35 for resort guests; from $60 for nonguests* 🏌 *The Legends: 18 holes, 7,072 yards, par 72. The Reserve: 18 holes, 6,670 yards, par 71. Crane's Bend: 9 holes, 1,901 yards, par 30. Legend's Walk: 9 holes, 1,581 yards, par 30.*

Rosen's Shingle Creek Golf Club

GOLF | Rosen's Shingle Creek Golf Club, designed by David Harman, lies alongside a lovely creek that is headwaters of the Everglades. The course is challenging yet playable, with dense stands of oak and pine trees and interconnected waterways. The golf carts even have GPS yardage systems. Since Universal Studios and the Orange County Convention Center are within a few minutes' drive, this is a favorite for conventioneers, ✉ *9939 Universal Blvd.* ☎ *407/996–9933, 866/996–9933* 🌐 *www.shinglecreekgolf.com* 🎫 *From $85* 🏌 *18 holes, 7,069 yards, par 72.*

TopGolf

GOLF | Way back when, bowlers would mark their own scores on a strip of paper. Then modern computers came along to track the ball's path, and scores would be tallied and automatically displayed on colorful screens. Now picture that level of technology at a driving range. At this fantastic complex near the Orange County Convention Center, golf balls are embedded with a tracking chip so you and your friends can enter your names on a computer, choose from a few dozen clubs, wait for a ball to drop out by a tee, and start swinging. Within seconds of hitting the shot, the height, distance, and course of the ball will be shown on a screen. Play for points by hitting the microchipped ball close to one of 11 targets that are spread out from 20 to 240 yards away. Multiple levels accommodate multiple golfers, and the pub and club atmosphere makes this a popular meeting place for friends—even if they've never swung a club. ✉ *9925 International Dr., International Drive* ☎ *407/218–7714* 🌐 *topgolf.com/us/orlando* 🎫 *From $30 per hr, per group.*

Waldorf Astoria Golf Club

GOLF | The Rees Jones–designed course has maintained some of the natural elements of the original landscape even while enhancing the land's existing contours. Majestic stands of pine and cypress line the fairways, which wind through a scenic wetland preserve and are sprinkled with bunkers reminiscent of century-old hazards. It has a five-tee system for all playing levels. ✉ *14224 Bonnet Creek Resort La.* ☎ *407/597–5500, 888/924–6531* 🌐 *www.waldorfastoriagolfclub.com* 🎫 *From $65* 🏌 *18 holes, 7,113 yards, par 72.*

Winter Park Country Club

GOLF | Located in Winter Park, an upscale suburb of Orlando, this charmingly simple course frames the north end of Park Avenue, Central Florida's version of Worth Avenue in Palm Beach or Rodeo Drive in Beverly Hills. A point of pride for residents, this historic country club offers nonresidents access to its immaculate golf course. Opened in 1914, the 9-hole walking course was modeled after authentic Scottish links. Notably, residents were once given a choice to sell the golf course to developers or raise their own taxes to preserve it for the city. They chose to tax themselves to keep the course, which remains one of the most affordable and authentic recreational experiences in Central Florida. ✉ *761 Old England Ave., Winter Park* ☎ *407/599–3339* 🌐 *www.winterparkcountryclub.com* 🎫 *From $16* 🏌 *9 holes, 2480 yards, par 36.*

Orlando's Solar Bears professional hockey team plays in downtown Orlando's Amway Arena.

Hockey

Orlando Solar Bears

HOCKEY | Taking the ice at downtown's Amway Center, the Orlando Solar Bears play in the South Division of the Eastern Conference Hockey League. One of three ECHL teams in the state, their season runs from October to April. ✉ *Amway Center, 400 East Church St., Downtown Orlando* ☎ *407/951–8200* 🌐 *orlandosolarbearshockey.com* 🎟 *From $12.*

Horseback Riding

Walt Disney World

Fort Wilderness Resort

HORSEBACK RIDING | A popular activity since the earliest days of Disney World, the backwoods horseback trail rides depart from the Tri-Circle-D Ranch at 8:30 am and continue through mid- to late afternoon. Children must be at least 9 years old and 48 inches tall to ride, and adults must weigh less than 250 pounds. Trail rides start at 45 minutes; hours vary by season. You must check in 30 minutes prior to your ride, and reservations must be made at least one day ahead. Both horseback riding and the campground are open to nonresort guests. Also available are wagon rides, carriage rides, and, for the kids, pony rides. ✉ *Tri-Circle D Ranch, 4510 Fort Wilderness Trail, Magic Kingdom Resort Area* ☎ *407/824–2832* 🎟 *From $55.*

Ice Skating

The Ice Factory

ICE SKATING | Ice-skating in Florida? Yup! This Olympic-class facility has two rinks and several theme evenings each week. Teens are drawn to Friday's DJ Night, there are family-night rates on Saturday, and you can arrange birthday parties as well. Skate rentals are included with admission, and an upgraded pair (which costs a little extra) include extra padding (wearing thick socks is an option). Hours vary, and often the rink is being used for training, so be sure to visit their website before you go for an updated schedule on public skating. New to the ice? No worries: you can also get private ice-skating and hockey lessons. And dress in layers—on the rink the temperature averages between 50 to 65 degrees year-round. Long pants and a sweater are usually fine since you're moving around. ✉ *2221 Partin Settlement Rd., Kissimmee* ☎ *407/933–4259* 🌐 *www.icefactory.com* 🎫 *From $5; skate rental $3.*

Miniature Golf

If minigolf is your game, Disney has two courses, but there are several others in Orlando.

Congo River

GOLF | FAMILY | In this clever creation, it's miniputt meets theme park as multilevel courses wander amid waterfalls, rocky summits, caves, and rain forests. Popular with families and, believe it or not, couples, kids are the prime audience. They love the live alligators (not loose on the course), the arcade room, and the treasure hunt. Congo River also has locations in Kissimmee and East Orlando. ✉ *5901 International Dr., International Drive* ☎ *407/248–9181* 🌐 *www.congoriver.com* 🎫 *From $13.*

Fantasia Gardens Miniature Golf

MINIATURE GOLF | Nearly every miniature golf course uses cartoon characters of some sort, but only Disney can use classic characters you'd recognize from Walt's bold experiment, *Fantasia.* Along the course are tutu-clad hippos, marching broomsticks, and pirouetting ostriches. Making things even more challenging are all the elements of a traditional golf course: sand traps, bunkers, water hazards, and sloping greens. ✉ *1205 Epcot Resorts Blvd., EPCOT Resort Area* ☎ *407/824–4500* 🌐 *disneyworld.disney.go.com/recreation/fantasia-gardens-fairways-miniature-golf* 🎫 *From $12.*

★ **Hollywood Drive-In Golf at Universal CityWalk**

MINIATURE GOLF | FAMILY | With a science-fiction alien invasion course paired with a 1950s horror movie monster course, there's something for kids and fun-loving adults alike. Spectacular lighting and sound effects mean that the play is different day and night. A 36-hole Double Feature package is available, and the course is open until 2 am for after theme-park romping. ✉ *6000 Universal Blvd., CityWalk* ☎ *407/802–4848* 🌐 *hollywooddriveingolf.com* 🎫 *From $17.*

Pirate's Cove Adventure Golf

MINIATURE GOLF | FAMILY | Two 18-hole miniature golf courses with a buccaneer theme wind around artificial mountains, through caves, beside waterfalls, and into lush foliage. The beginner's course is called Captain Kidd's Adventure; the more advanced course is Blackbeard's Challenge. In addition to this location at Lake Buena Vista (near Disney), there's a second Pirate's Cove on International Drive. ✉ *Crossroads Shopping Center, 12545 State Rd. 535, Lake Buena Vista* ☎ *407/827–1242* 🌐 *www.piratescove.net* 🎫 *From $12.*

Winter Summerland Miniature Golf

MINIATURE GOLF | Not content to build just one themed miniature golf course, Disney built two very different courses beside the Blizzard Beach water park: one themed for the Florida summer sun, the other covered with snow that remains a perpetual winter wonderland. The Summer course mixes things up with surfboards, sand castles, peppermint-striped inner tubes, and palm trees decorated with Christmas ornaments. As you play your way toward the North Hole on the Winter Course, obstacles include giant peppermints, hockey sticks, and the drawbridge of a melting castle. ✉ *Blizzard Beach, Blizzard Beach* ☎ *407/824–4500* 🌐 *disneyworld.disney.*

go.com/recreation/winter-summerland-miniature-golf 🎫 *From $14.*

Multisport Outfitters

Fort Wilderness Resort

FISHING | One of the original Disney resorts (the Polynesian and Contemporary were the others), Fort Wilderness offers a number of sporting and outdoors activities. For 90 minutes, you can get in some target shooting with an archery guide who oversees novice and expert marksmen (ages 6 and up). Nonresort guests are welcome to join campers, and the fee includes use of the compound bow and arrows, plus instruction. You can book up to 180 days in advance. But this isn't the only outdoor activity you can enjoy here.

A two-hour Wilderness Back Trail Adventure Segway tour is done on an off-road version of the vehicle, and begins with a training session to get you acquainted with its operation. Call ahead for reservations. You must be at least 16 and carry a photo ID. If you'd prefer to rent a bicycle, stop by the Bicycle Barn, where they rent for the hour or day. You can also rent fishing rods and tackle for fishing in the canals around Fort Wilderness Resort, but you must be 18 or older to rent. If you'd like to go fishing with a guide, that's possible, too.

✉ *4510 N. Fort Wilderness Trail, Magic Kingdom* ☎ *407/939–8687 Bike Barn* 🎫 *Archery from $48; Segway tour from $85; bike rentals from $12; fishing tackle rentals from $11; guided fishing trips from $270.*

Rodeos

Silver Spurs Rodeo

HORSEBACK RIDING | Many natives recall the era known as Old Florida, and that's the time before 1971 and the arrival of the theme parks. You can still find Old Florida on Disney's doorstep, right there in neighboring Kissimmee at the Silver Spurs Rodeo, which is pure Florida goodness. Launched here by ranching families in 1944, the largest rodeo east of the Mississippi is where you'll see bull riders and cowboys competing in a variety of high-energy, high-adrenaline competitions including bull and bronco riding, steer wrestling, and barrel racing. If you'd like to hang out with some of the original ranchers whose families pre-date Disney by a century, this is the place to do it. The main rodeo show is held each February with the National Barrel Horse Association competition held in June. From Interstate 4 Exit 77, take Florida's Turnpike south to Exit 244 (Kissimmee–St. Cloud). ✉ *1875 Silver Spur La., Kissimmee* ☎ *321/697–3495* 🌐 *www.silverspursrodeo.com* 🎫 *From $15.*

Running

Walt Disney World

The World has several scenic running trails from the Grand Floridian, Polynesian, and Contemporary in the Magic Kingdom area. At the Epcot resorts, you can get your heart rate up along the promenade that circles Crescent Lake past the BoardWalk and Yacht and Beach Club resorts. If you're staying at Port Orleans, you can work up a sweat on nearby trails; Coronado Springs guests run along the resort's one-mile esplanade.

The roads that snake through Disney Springs resorts are pleasant, and early in the morning traffic isn't too bad. At the Caribbean Beach Resort, there's a 1½-mile running promenade around Barefoot Bay. Fort Wilderness Campground has a woodsy 2-mile course with numerous exercise stations along the way.

Walt Disney World sponsors many running events throughout the course of the year, highlighted by its popular January marathon (🌐 *www.rundisney.com*).

Skydiving and Parasailing

★ iFLY Orlando

FLYING/SKYDIVING/SOARING | Okay, so technically you aren't really skydiving, but you come pretty close as you float atop a cushion of air in this 12-foot-high, 1,000-horsepower wind tunnel. Letting you experience everything skydivers do but closer to the ground, the two-hour, two-flight experience starts with instruction, warm-up, and stretching. You then suit up, and, with a certified instructor, you hit the wind tunnel, where you soar like a bird (or try to) atop a cushion of air. It's all so realistic that skydiving clubs come to hone their skills. Even when you're not flying, it's pretty surreal to look through the window and see people suspended in midair. The attraction is safe for anyone under 250 pounds and older than age 3. You can purchase a video of your "jump" at the end. ✉ *8969 International Dr., International Drive* ☎ *407/337–4359* 🌐 *www.iflyworld.com/orlando* 🎫 *From $50.*

Seminole Lake Gliderport

FLYING/SKYDIVING/SOARING | From settling into the sleek sailplane to closing the clear bubbletop canopy to being able to take the controls, flying without an engine is the rare peaceful adventure. With a pilot in the seat behind you, the adventure begins as a towplane takes off and carries you aloft where, at around 3,000 feet, you'll detach from the plane. The absence of engine noise will instantly be replaced by the sound of your pounding heart. Once you're accustomed to the sensation of flying without an engine, it's as pleasing as sailing a boat on a lake. The glideport is just outside Orlando in the countryside of Clermont Prices start at $140 for a 20-minute flight, and there's a weight limit of 240 pounds. ✉ *4024 Soaring La., Clermont* ⇔ *Clermont is 25 miles west of Orlando, 22 miles northwest of Walt Disney World* ☎ *352/394–5450* 🌐 *www.soarfl.com.*

Wilotree Park-Paradise Airsports

FLYING/SKYDIVING/SOARING | This grassy airfield has everything you need for assorted aerial adventures. For a hang gliding thrill, you and an instructor are towed as high as 5,000 feet before releasing the line from the towplane ahead of you. After that, you're free to experience what is best described as a motorcycle ride in the sky. The instructors will let you maneuver the glider so you can turn, bank, rise, and dip as you soak in incredible views of the Orlando countryside. Note that the higher you soar, the more you pay; from $179 at 2,000 feet to $279 at 5,000 feet. I ✉ *6548 Groveland Airport Rd., Groveland* ⇔ *Groveland is 30 miles west of Orlando, 31 miles northwest of Walt Disney World* ☎ *352/429–0210* 🌐 *www.wilotreepark.com.*

Surfing

Surfing? Here, in landlocked Central Florida? You bet. Early in the morning, before Typhoon Lagoon opens to water-park visitors, you can hit some man-made waves with 11 other novices and a professional instructor. Run by local surf pros, the three-hour session begins with a half-hour beachside lesson on surfing moves and basics. Each session comes packed with up to 100 waves, broken into sets of 25, so the chance of learning how to master the board is pretty good. Before you know it, you're in the heated wave pool and headed for your first ride. You must be at least 8 years old, and lessons cost $190 per person. Soft-sided boards are provided. You must have transportation to Typhoon Lagoon; even if you're staying at Disney, buses don't run before the class begins at 6:45 am. The program doesn't have a regular schedule, so call ☎ *407/939–7529* in advance for one of the 12 slots.

Tennis

Walt Disney World

You can play tennis at several Disney hotels: Bay Lake Tower at Disney's Contemporary Resort (two hard courts), BoardWalk (two hard courts), Old Key West Resort (two hard courts), Saratoga Springs Resort & Spa (two Hydrogrid clay courts), and Yacht Club Resort (one hard court). Courts are available without charge on a first-come-first-served basis for resort and nonresort guests. All have lights, and most have lockers and racquets available to rent or borrow. At the Walt Disney World Swan and Dolphin hotels, you can get an hour-long private lesson on one of four courts for $90 from 7 am to 9 pm. Call ☎ *407/621–1991*.

Orlando Area

Tennis is one of the most popular sports in Orlando, with hundreds of well-tended public tennis courts and resort hotels that offer a court or two (or more) for their guests. The city of Orlando operates more than 50 courts, some free and others reasonably priced.

Cesar Villaroel Tennis Academy
TENNIS | Based at the Mission Inn Resort, 6th Sense is run by Davis Cup player, Cesar Villaroel. It offers two-hour lessons all the way up to 5-day intensive programs for adults and seasonal tennis camps for kids in both winter and summer. The resort is approximately 40 miles west of Orlando. ✉ *10400 County Rd. 48, Howie In The Hills* ☎ *352/455–6815* 🌐 *www.thecvta.com.*

Fort Gatlin Tennis Complex
TENNIS | Close to downtown Orlando, Fort Gatlin has the finest city-run courts open to the public. Ten hard courts equipped for day or night play, a pro shop that's open daily, and lessons are among this beautiful facility's offerings. ✉ *2009 Lake Margaret Dr., Downtown Orlando* ☎ *407/254–9878* 🌐 *www.fortgatlin.com* 🎟 *From $4 per hr.*

Orlando Tennis Center
TENNIS | Run by the City of Orlando and located near downtown, this fine facility offers adult tennis clinics (18 and up), private lessons, and youth tennis programs (six and up). The center features five hard courts, 11 clay courts, two racquet ball courts, and three hitting walls. ✉ *363 N. Parramore Ave., Downtown Orlando* ☎ *407/246–4469* 🌐 *www.cityoforlando.net/recreation/orlando-tennis-centre* 🎟 *From $4 per hr.*

Index

A

B

C

D

N

O

P

V

W

Y

Z

Index

Front Cover: Matt Stroshane, DISNEY/HANDOUT [Description:Newest, most spectacular fireworks show in the history of Magic Kingdom Park with "Happily Ever After." Walt Disney World]. **Back cover, from left to right:** Disney, chensiyuan/wikimedia commons, Douglas Nesbitt. **Spine:** Jennifer Lynn/Flickr, [CC BY 2.0]. **Interior, from left to right:** Carrie Parkers (1). Viavaltours/Dreamstime (2). Kmiragaya/ Dreamstime (5). **Chapter 1: Experience Orlando and the Parks:** Greg Balfour Evans / Alamy (6-7). Tribune Content Agency LLC / Alamy (8). Rain0975/Flickr, [CC BY-ND 2.0] (9). Peanutroaster/Dreamstime (9). Theme Park Tourist/Flickr, [CC BY 2.0] (10). Theme Park Tourist/ Flickr, [CC BY 2.0] (10). Howie Muzika/Flickr, [CC BY-NC-ND 2.0] (11). Ingus Kruklitis / Shutterstock (12). Universal Orlando Resort. All rights reserved. (12). ALLAN HUGHES / Alamy (12). Donfink/Dreamstime (12). Larryfmscotland/Dreamstime (13). Quackersnaps/Dreamstime (13). L. Sloan/Flickr, [CC BY-NC-ND 2.0] (13). Theme Park Tourist/Flickr, [CC BY 2.0] (13). Brian Hubbard/Flickr, [CC BY-NC 2.0] (14). Andrew Barker / Alamy (14). Peter E. Lee/Flickr, [CC BY-NC 2.0] (14). msivyi/Dreamstime (14). Szilkov/Dreamstime (15). Blaine Harrington III / Alamy (15). Universal Orlando. All rights reserved. (16). Kphotos6411/Dreamstime(16). Rich Kane Photography / Alamy (16). ecadphoto/Dreamstime (16). Blackghost600/Dreamstime (17). M. Timothy O'Keefe / Alamy (22). Solarisys/Shutterstock (22). Visit Orlando (22). World Travel Collection / Alamy (23). aphotostory/Shutterstock (23). Universal Orlando Resort. All rights reserved. (24). Universal Orlando Resort. All rights reserved. (24). Courtesy of SeaWorld Orlando (24). Carrie Parker (24). Richard Green / Alamy (25). The Ravenous Pig (26). Yellow Dog Eats (27). Courtesy of Walt Disney World Resort (28). Courtesy of Rosen Shingle Creek (28). Hilton (28). Courtesy of Walt Disney World Resort (29). Courtesy of Walt Disney World Resort (29). Universal Orlando Resort (30). Debi Harbin/Disney (30). Disney (30). Disney (30). James Kilby/Disney (31). MontenegroStock/Shutterstock (31). Universal Orlando Resort (31). Disney (31). Courtesy Walt Disney World Resort (32). Courtesy Walt Disney World Resort (33). Photos 12 / Alamy (38). Dashu Dashu Pagla/Flickr, [CC BY 2.0] (38). Courtesy of Everett Collection (39). Courtesy of Everett Collection (40). Photo by: Mary Evans (40). Courtesy Everett Collection (40). Dashu Dashu Pagla/Flickr, [CC BY 2.0] (40). Walt Disney Co./courtesy Everett / Everett Collection (41). Courtesy of Everett Collection (41). Courtesy of Everett Collection (41). daryl_mitchell/Flickr, [CC BY 2.0] (41). Bob B. Brown/Flickr, [CC BY 2.0] (42). Buena Vista Pictures/Courtesy Everett Collection (42). Disneyland Paris by David Jafra/ Flickr, [CC BY 2.0] (42). Seanosh/Flickr, [CC BY 2.0] (42). Walt Disney Co./Courtesy Everett Collection (43). Prosthetic Lips/Flickr, [CC BY 2.0] (43). Walt Disney Co./Courtesy Everett Collection (43). Jeffrey Holcombe/Dreamstime (44). **Chapter 2: Travel Smart:** Richard Cummins / age fotostock (76). SeaWorld Parks & Entertainment (77). liangjinjian/Flickr (78). 2009 SeaWorld. All Rights Reserved. (78). Sleuths Mystery Dinner Shows (79). 2007 Universal Orlando Resort. All rights reserved. (79). Danp68/Dreamstime (80). Kmiragaya/Dreamstime (80). **Chapter 3: The Magic Kingdom and Resort Area:** Massimo Gherardi/Dreamstime (81). Jennifer Lynn/Flickr, [CC BY 2.0] (91). ckramer/Flickr, [CC BY 2.0] (94). Bob B. Brown/Flickr, [CC BY 2.0] (96). JoshMcConnell/Flickr, [CC BY 2.0] (98). SteamFan/WIkimedia Commons (101). Orlando CVB (103). Sam Howzit/Flickr, [CC BY 2.0] (105). ckramer/Flickr (110). Scott R. Smith/Flickr (119). **Chapter 4: EPCOT and Resort Area:** Jeff Whyte/Dreamstime (121). Matt Stroshane, Disney (122). ckramer/Flickr, [CC BY 2.0] (123). Meshmar2/Flickr, [CC BY 2.0] (123). Disney (136). yeowatzup/Flickr, [CC BY 2.0] (138). ckramer/Flickr (145). Theme Park Tourist/Flickr, [CC BY 2.0] (152). yeowatzup/Flickr, [CC BY 2.0] (154). wbeem/Flickr, [CC BY 2.0] (157). Craig Russell/Dreamstime (161). Tony Bosse/Dreamstime (162). **Chapter 5: Disney's Hollywood Studios with Blizzard Beach:** Lori Barbely / Alamy \ (165). Disney (166). Karen L/Flickr, [CC BY 2.0] (167). Karen L/Flickr, [CC BY 2.0] (167). daryl_mitchell/Flickr, [CC BY 2.0] (179). Hemis / Alamy (189). **Chapter 6: Disney's Animal Kingdom and Resort Area:** Tangibleday/ Dreamstime (195). flickr.com (201). Jason Pratt/Flickr, [CC BY 2.0] (204). tom.arthur/Flickr, [CC BY 2.0] (207). Brewie79/Dreamstime (208). Disney Animal Kingdom (211). Loren Javier/Flickr, [CC BY 2.0] (214). Courtesy Walt Disney World Resort (217). coconut wireless/Flickr, [CC BY 2.0] (219). **Chapter 7: Disney Springs and Resort Area:** VIAVAL/Shutterstock (221). mVkkarri/Dreamstime (234). Disney Magic / Alamy (243). **Chapter 8: Kissimmee, Lake Buena Vista, and Celebration:** MontenegroStock/Shutterstock (245). Orlando CVB (250). Orlando CVB (252). Kissimmee - The Heart of Florida/Flickr (254). Jerome LABOUYRIE/Shutterstock (263). **Chapter 9: Universal Orlando; Universal Studios, Islands of Adventure, Volcano Bay, CityWalk:** Mia2you/Shutterstock (265). 2007 Universal Orlando Resort. All rights reserved. (270). 2012 Universal Orlando Resort. All rights reserved. (280). Russell102/Dreamstime (282). 2009 Universal Orlando. All rights reserved. (287). Jessica Walsh (299). 2012 Universal Orlando Resort. All rights reserved. HARRY POTTER, characters, names and related indicia are trademarks of and © Warner Bros. Entertainment Inc. Harry Potter Publishing Rights © JKR. (s12) (302). PCL / Alamy (306). 2007 Universal Orlando Resort. All rights reserved. (311). Solarisys13/Dreamstime (316). Solarisys13/Dreamstime (318). 2007 Universal Orlando Resort. All rights reserved. (324). **Chapter 10: Orlando:** Sean Pavone/Shutterstock.com (327). Orlando CVB (336). elisfkc/Flickr, [CC BY-SA 2.0] (346). 2009 SeaWorld. All Rights Reserved. (348). 2009 SeaWorld. All Rights Reserved. (350). Experience Kissimmee/Flickr , [CC BY 2.0] (357). **Chapter 11: Excursions from Orlando:** Roberto Pascual Gomez/Shutterstock (365). Courtesy of The Charles Hosmer Morse Museum of American Art (372). spakattacks/Flickr (377). Ciolca/Dreamstime (379). Sean Pavone/Shutterstock (381). **Chapter 12: Activities:** Disney (383). Sharife/wikimedia (396). **About Our Writers:** All photos are courtesy of the writers.

**Every effort has been made to trace the copyright holders, and we apologize in advance for any accidental errors. We would be happy to apply the corrections in the following edition of this publication.*

Notes

Notes

Notes

Notes

Notes